Navigating the labyrinth of African christological narratives that present Christ inter-alia as revealer, mediator, emancipator and finally judge, the writers, with consummate hermeneutical dexterity provide a biblical African narrative of who Christ is – a narrative that is not revealed by "flesh or blood." Consequently, this book connects the experiential narratives of Christ to his wholistic divine description as "Christ, the Son of the Living God." The added portion relating to Mbiti's life, times and work provides a succinct model of African scholarship for emerging African theologians and for the many who want to remain and live as authentic Christian Africans. This is a clear approach to the muddy waters of African Christology and a must-read for all who care about the Christian African faith.

John Jusu, PhD
Regional Director for Anglophone Africa,
Overseas Council International

Africa Society of Evangelical Theology Series

We often hear these days that the center of Christianity is moving toward the Global South and Africa is a key player in that movement. This makes the study of African Christianity and African realities important – even more so when it is being done by Africans themselves and in their own context. The Africa Society of Evangelical Theology (ASET) was created to encourage research and sustained theological reflection on key issues facing Africa by and for African Christians and those working within African contexts. The volumes in this series constitute the best papers presented at the annual conferences of ASET and together they seek to fill this important gap in the literature of Christianity.

TITLES IN THIS SERIES

Christianity and Suffering: African Perspectives
2017 | 9781783683604

African Contextual Realities
2018 | 9781783684731

Governance and Christian Higher Education in the African Context
2019 | 9781783685455

God and Creation
2019 | 9781783687565

Forgiveness, Peacemaking, and Reconciliation
2020 | 9781839730535

ASET Series

Who Do You Say That I Am?

GLOBAL LIBRARY

Who Do You Say That I Am?

Christology in Africa

General Editors

**Rodney L. Reed
and
David K. Ngaruiya**

© 2021 Africa Society of Evangelical Theology (ASET)

Published 2021 by Langham Global Library
An imprint of Langham Publishing
www.langhampublishing.org

Langham Publishing and its imprints are a ministry of Langham Partnership

Langham Partnership
PO Box 296, Carlisle, Cumbria, CA3 9WZ, UK
www.langham.org

ISBNs:
978-1-83973-532-5 Print
978-1-83973-612-4 ePub
978-1-83973-613-1 Mobi
978-1-83973-614-8 PDF

Rodney L. Reed and David K. Ngariuya hereby assert their moral right to be identified as the Author of the General Editor's part in the Work in accordance with sections 77 and 78 of the Copyright, Designs and Patents Act 1988.

All rights reserved. No part of this publication may be reproduced, stored in a retrieval system or transmitted, in any form or by any means, electronic, mechanical, photocopying, recording or otherwise, without the prior written permission of the publisher or the Copyright Licensing Agency.

Requests to reuse content from Langham Publishing are processed through PLSclear. Please visit www.plsclear.com to complete your request.

All Scripture quotations, unless otherwise indicated, are taken from the Holy Bible, New International Version®, NIV®. Copyright ©1973, 1978, 1984, 2011 by Biblica, Inc.™ Used by permission of Zondervan.

Scripture quotations marked (ESV) are from The Holy Bible, English Standard Version® (ESV®), copyright © 2001 by Crossway, a publishing ministry of Good News Publishers. Used by permission. All rights reserved.

Scripture quotations marked (NASB) are taken from the New American Standard Bible®, Copyright © 1960, 1962, 1963, 1968, 1971, 1972, 1973, 1975, 1977, 1995 by The Lockman Foundation. Used by permission.

Scripture quotations marked (NRSV) are from the New Revised Standard Version Bible, copyright © 1989 National Council of the Churches of Christ in the United States of America. Used by permission. All rights reserved.

British Library Cataloguing-in-Publication Data
A catalogue record for this book is available from the British Library

ISBN: 978-1-83973-532-5

Cover & Book Design: projectluz.com

Langham Partnership actively supports theological dialogue and an author's right to publish but does not necessarily endorse the views and opinions set forth here or in works referenced within this publication, nor can we guarantee technical and grammatical correctness. Langham Partnership does not accept any responsibility or liability to persons or property as a consequence of the reading, use or interpretation of its published content.

Contents

Preface xiii

Acknowledgments xv

Part One: Christ in the Bible

1 Marital Infidelity through an African Women's Christological Hermeneutic 3
    A Dramatized Rereading of the Narrative of the Woman Caught in Adultery (John 7:53 – 8:11)
    Telesia K. Musili

2 An East African Perspective on Jesus as Revealer of the Father through His Use of the Friend at Midnight Parable as a Means for Teaching Powerful Prayer (Luke 11:1–13) 25
    Timothy J. Monger

3 Embracing Hybridity in Imaging Christ for Egalitarian Church Leadership through a Rereading of John 4:1–42 43
    Lydia Chemei

4 Exploring the Multidimensional Nature of Christology in Galatians through the Lens of an African Hermeneutic 57
    Elizabeth W. Mburu

5 The Crucified and Cursed Christ as the Ultimate Curse-Remover in Galatians 3:1–14 and Its Implications 77
    Elkanah Kiprop Cheboi

6 The Benefaction of the Messiah as the Supreme King in the Context of the Greco-Roman Ethic of Reciprocity 95
    An Exegetical Analysis of Romans 5:6–8
    Enoch O. Okode

7 Paul's Use of Μιμηταί and Its Relationship to His Christology 117
    Gift Mtukwa

8 A Christological Reading of Ephesians 5:21–33 137
    Christ as a Model for Married Men in Africa
    Moses Iliya Ogidis

Part Two: Christ in Theology and Church History

9 Christology in Africa En Route 155
   Encounter between Biblical and Indigenous African Concepts
   Daniel Mwailu

10 Jewish Messianism of the Intertestamental Period and
   Christological Confessions of the Early Church and Their
   Implications for African Christology. 181
   Juliana Nzuki and Elkanah Kiprop Cheboi

11 The Unitive Understanding of the Person of Christ in Cyril of
   Alexandria's Christology and Its Relevance for Contemporary
   African Christianity 197
   Henry Marcus Garba

12 Who Are You for Us, *Yesu Kristo*? Christological Confessions of
   the Early Church in Contemporary Africa...................... 221
   A Methodological Question
   John Michael Kiboi

13 Jesus Christ as *Ker* 239
   Toward an African High Priest Christology
   E. Okelloh Ogera

14 The Forgiven and Forgiving Body of Christ 257
   Musekura's Communal Perspective on Forgiveness in Dialogue with
   African Wisdom
   Stephanie A. Lowery

15 African Images of Christ 275
   "Jesus as Healer": Narratives and Treatable but as Yet Incurable Illness
   Thandi Soko-de Jong

Part Three: Christ in Praxis

16 Who Do You See and Say That I Am? 291
   Responses of Thirty-Seven St. Paul's University Staff and Students after
   Viewing Drawings of Jesus from *African Posters to Teach the Bible* and
   Vie de Jésus Mafa
   Rowland D. Van Es Jr.

17 "Missionaries Did Not Bring Christ to Africa – Christ Brought Them" (Bediako/Mbiti) 319
    Christ's Lordship in Mission in African Theology
    Alistair I. Wilson

18 Jesus in Islam.. 339
    A Theological Argument with a Missional Response
    Lawrence Oseje

19 Jesus in Islam.. 359
    Meaning and Theological Implications for Christian–Muslim Engagement
    Billy Chilongo Sichone

Part Four: Tributes to the Late Professor John S. Mbiti

20 John Mbiti's Perspective on Theological and Missiological Issues with Respect to Christianity and African Traditional Religion 393
    David K. Ngaruiya

21 Reflection on John S. Mbiti............................... 417
    Esther Mombo

22 The Life and Legacy of the Late John S. Mbiti 427
    A Tribute
    James Nkansah-Obrempong

23 A Tribute to John S. Mbiti................................ 437
    Jesse N. K. Mugambi

24 A Tribute to John S. Mbiti................................ 441
    Samuel Ngewa

List of Contributors 443

Subject Index.. 449

Scripture Index 455

Preface

Arguably the most important question in all of human history is the question Jesus asked Peter and his disciples, "Who do you say I am?" (Matt 16:15). It is the question that every individual who has ever encountered the gospel of Jesus Christ must answer. And from a Christian perspective *everything* hangs on the answer. The answer one gives to this question will determine much in one's life, religiously, culturally, socially. In some contexts, it will identify you as part of the majority culture with all the social and economic benefits that brings. In other contexts, it could mean that you are viewed as still hanging on to an antiquated and superstitious worldview that is slowly passing away in an evermore secular and pluralistic world. In still other contexts it could mean social and economic discrimination, persecution or even martyrdom. And assuming that what the Christian faith says about Jesus is true, it could mean the difference between heaven and hell. Indeed, much is at stake in how one responds to this simple question.

What makes this question even more intriguing is the diversity of answers given to it. Even within the Bible itself, there are many titles and names of Jesus: Christ, Messiah, Lion of Judah, Lamb of God, Son of Man, Son of David, Son of God, the Word, Savior, Emmanuel, Redeemer, Prophet, Priest and King, to name just a few. Inspired by the Holy Spirit, the biblical writers created or appropriated these titles because they believed the titles had explanatory power and value in describing to the people to whom they were writing who Jesus was and what he came to do.

But the story of Jesus doesn't end with the New Testament. In fact, the range of answers to Jesus's question grows even wider as one surveys the history of Christianity up to the present. One only needs to do a quick survey of Christian art down through the centuries to notice how various are the answers that have been given to Jesus's question – most of them with a very white European appearance! One would almost suspect that Jesus (or the biblical writers) intended that every generation in every cultural context should respond to his question afresh. Indeed, appropriately contextualizing the response to Jesus's question has been and still is one of the key goals of Christian theology through the centuries and around the world, for it is the absolutely indispensable prerequisite for evangelism, mission and discipleship.

However, there is a danger in this business of contextualization. That danger is that we will make Jesus in our image, instead of us being made in his image. In our efforts to find a Jesus who speaks to us, we run the risk of pouring into our image of him all of our prejudices, biases and cultural practices that may be at odds with the true nature of God. Albert Schweitzer, the great New Testament scholar of the turn of the twentieth century, in his seminal study *The Quest of the Historical Jesus*, was among the first to note the tendency of New Testament scholars to describe Jesus in ways that looked remarkably similar to themselves. So, in answering Jesus's question, there is a balance to find – the balance between describing Jesus in thought forms that are meaningful to oneself and one's audience on the one hand, and, on the other, ensuring that our images of Jesus are theologically consistent with the biblical teaching about Jesus.

African Christians are well within their rights to take their turn at answering the question "Who do you say I am?" and to identify a Jesus who speaks their language and speaks into their contexts. For a long time, Western missionaries brought to Africa a view of Jesus that was much too Western. Some have claimed that this is the reason for the shallowness of Christianity across much of Africa. This volume seeks to contribute to this discussion. Fortunately, much has already been written by African Christian scholars on this topic, but the debate is still ongoing and still more needs to be said.

There are four parts to this volume. Part 1, entitled "Christ in the Bible," groups together eight chapters that specifically address what various passages of Scripture have to say about Jesus. The meaning of those passages is then brought to bear on African realities. The seven chapters of part 2, "Christ in Theology and Church History," focus more specifically on issues of constructive theology regarding the doctrine of Christ and the development of that theology in the history of the Christian church. Of critical importance in this part is the relevance to the African context. Part 3, with four chapters, is entitled "Christ in Praxis" and gives deeper attention to the implications of an "African Christology" for the practice of ministry in such disciplines as discipleship, missions and interreligious dialogue. Finally, since these chapters were first presented as papers at the 2020 Africa Society of Evangelical Theology, it is important to note that at this conference, tribute was paid to the late Prof. John S. Mbiti, who passed away during the course of the preceding year. His influence upon this society and upon African Christian theology has been immense; hence, part 4 of the volume consists of a collection of five papers or tributes to Prof. Mbiti. While these may be largely unrelated to the theme of the book, they are still of significant value to those who seek to advance African Christian theology.

Rodney L. Reed, PhD

Acknowledgments

Saint Augustine said, "The world is a book, and those who do not travel read only one page." The diversity of the essays in this volume is a reflection of "traveling" in Africa seeking to understand Christology from that context. Thus, the pages that follow are a plethora of images of various scholars on Christology. The chapters in this volume feature the best of the papers presented at the tenth annual conference of the Africa Society of Evangelical Theology (ASET) which was held at Africa International University in Nairobi, Kenya, on 6–7 March 2020.

The Editorial Committee of ASET is grateful to a community that has made it possible to publish this sixth volume of the ASET series. That community comprises presenters at the 2020 annual conference, reviewers of papers, all committees of ASET and the conference host.

ASET is very grateful to the Tyndale House Foundation. The Foundation has provided support for the ASET series.

We also wish to thank a discussion panel that featured Prof. Jesse Mugambi, Prof. Samuel Ngewa, Prof. Esther Mombo, Prof. James Nkansah and Dr. Hermen Kroesbergen. I am personally very grateful for having had the privilege to facilitate the panel discussion on John Mbiti's Christology.

Much appreciation goes to Africa International University and their staff members for their hospitality in hosting this conference. We also greatly appreciate Langham Publishing for all their labour in getting this volume published. Much gratitude goes to Vivian Doub and her team at Langham, and also to Rodney Reed, with whom I have shared the joy of editing this volume.

David Ngaruiya, PhD
Co-Editor
Associate Professor,
International Leadership University, Nairobi, Kenya

Part One

Christ in the Bible

1

Marital Infidelity through an African Women's Christological Hermeneutic

A Dramatized Rereading of the Narrative of the Woman Caught in Adultery (John 7:53 – 8:11)

Telesia K. Musili

Lecturer, Department of Philosophy and Religious Studies, University of Nairobi, Kenya

Abstract

Marital infidelity is a complex challenge for church mission and the institution of marriage in Africa today. Marital infidelity challenges the norm of monogamous marital fidelity as the church's foundational teaching on marriage and its endeavor to uphold the reality of Christ's indwelling of his people. This chapter provides an exposition of the narrative of the unnamed woman caught in adultery found in John 7:53 – 8:11. It argues for a christological perspective in countering marital infidelity in the contemporary church. In reading this pericope, most scholars employ a feminist hermeneutic, since a woman is accused by men. However, this chapter will employ a reconstructive African women's christological hermeneutic to point out the primacy of personal/subjective morality in decision-making with regard to one's sexual activity, which, more often than not, is a hidden spiritual sin. The current situation of HIV/AIDS, where heterosexual transmission is the leading cause of new HIV infections, with women bearing the most blame, is adopted to give the narrative a contemporary context and perspective. Jesus invites all to a place of self-evaluation where judgment and condemnation are shunned. The chapter concludes with an affirmation of a merciful Jesus inviting all to repentance through a progressive Christology that is open to lived contexts and experiences. Thus, for the church to be successful in its mission of supporting marriage, it should uphold the virtue of mercy, a concrete action of love which by forgiving liberates, transforms, restores and changes lives.

Key words: marital infidelity, reconstructive African women christological hermeneutic, self-evaluation, liberative transformation

Introduction

The word "adultery" is derived from the Latin word *adulterium* and is defined as "voluntary sexual intercourse between a married person and someone other than that person's current spouse or partner."[1] It is judged biblically, socially, morally and legally to be a sin, with a corresponding prohibition on adulterers entering the promised kingdom of God.[2] With regard to the godly institution of marriage, adultery breaks trust between spouses and can easily lead to divorce, which is detestable in God's eyes. Yet, despite the universal disapproval of adultery by both religious and lay members of society, it is still prevalent. Globally, adultery is the leading cause of divorce.[3]

The forbidden sexual relationship has, however, been understood by scholars to house multilayered connotations, owing to circumstantial life situations. Blow and Hartnett point to the nuances of the meaning of "infidelity."[4] Several terms, such as unfaithfulness, extramarital, concurrent, extradyadic, and multiple sexual relations, are commonly used to denote sexual relations that do not embrace the expected exclusiveness of a marital relationship. Although each term has a particular nuance in connotation or by including certain behaviors, they all attempt to assess the same underlying construct, which we refer to as infidelity/unfaithfulness or adultery.

---

1. *Concise Oxford English Dictionary*.
2. See 1 Cor 6:9–10.
3. Ringrose, *Marriage and Divorce Laws*.
4. Blow and Hartnett, "Infidelity in Committed Relationships I," 183–216.

As noted above, the high rate of adultery/infidelity leads among the many causes of rampant divorce,[5] and has also resulted in the multiplication of new HIV infections in Kenya.[6] The National AIDS and STI Control Programme (NASCOP) released an assessment document on the "Kenya Population-Based HIV Impact," noting remarkable differences in HIV prevalence between men and women: the prevalence was higher among women, at 6.6 percent, than men, at 3.1 percent.[7] The Mode of Transmission study (MOT)[8] attributed the majority of new infections to multiple heterosexual partnerships within regular partnerships and casual heterosexual sex outside marriage by married individuals, which was reported to be at 44.1 percent.[9] Because of the high prevalence of HIV/AIDS among women compared to men as a result of concurrent sexual relationships, the blame is heaped squarely on women. Such contemporary indicators point to women as the culprits with regard to the disease, and as those challenging the established views of acceptable behavior. The breakup of families also poses a challenge to the church's mission of demonstrating God's message of love in the holy institution of marriage that represents God's relation to the church.[10]

It is against this backdrop that this paper seeks to invoke lenient perceptions of African women in contrast to the demeaning view that accuses them of driving the prevalence of HIV to alarming percentages in spite of their biological susceptibility. This work attempts to achieve the said objective through a literal and in-depth rereading of the "Pericope Adulterae," John 7:53 – 8:11, the pericope of the unnamed woman caught in adultery. In Africa, cultural/patriarchal repressions of adultery/infidelity create a male bias by condoning adultery on the part of men and branding it an "anathema" for women, just as was practiced in the Judaic culture. Such perceptions hurt the innermost selves of African women as well as the institution of marriage by fomenting gender inequities.

These androcentric tendencies of the Judaic era found their way into the church/religious institutions as well as marriage relationships. Male

---

5. Lagat, "Christian Ethics on Divorce," 1–15.

6. Kimanga, Ogola, Umuro et al., "Prevalence and Incidence of HIV Infection," 13–26.

7. National AIDS and STI Control Programme (NASCOP), "Kenya Population-Based HIV Impact Assessment (KENPHIA)," 11.

8. Gelmon, *Kenya HIV Prevention Response*, iv.

9. There are varying modes of HIV transmission, which include adultery/concurrent and casual heterosexual relations, sharing of contaminated needles among drug-injecting users, mother to child transmissions, as well as transfusion of infected blood.

10. Lagat, "Christian Ethics on Divorce," 11.

domination of women within a patriarchal setting plays vividly in the pericope of the woman caught in adultery. Far from it being a sexist story, as it is often understood, an African women's reconstructive christological understanding discovers that it portrays a criticism of the patriarchal relationship.

Worth noting is the fact that, even though Jesus is carrying out his mission within a patriarchal culture and society, the androcentric editors of the canonical literature, especially of the New Testament, have not in any instance portrayed Jesus in a sexist manner.[11] As James Borland notes,

> If we wish to understand biblical texts, we have not only to ask whether a tradition of androcentric interpretation has veiled their original intention but also to question whether the original narrator or author in an androcentric way has told history that was not androcentric at all.[12]

With regard to the presentation of Jesus in a nonsexist manner, the narrator holds on to the androcentric tendencies by which the power of men – Pharisees and scribes – objectifies the woman, bringing her into public shame.[13] It is the nonsexist standing of Jesus in this pericope that calls for the rereading and subsequent reconstruction of African women's Christology which is the main focus of this paper. The African theology of the celebration of life[14] forms the bedrock of reconstruction as we endeavor to remain true to the Scriptures as the authoritative word of God in our contemporary setting.

The author acknowledges the historical controversy surrounding the placement of the text as well as its interpretations by exegetes, New Testament scholars, feminist scholars and ministers. This paper supports the relevance of the text, owing to its moral standing regarding sex and marriage. A literal, dramatized rereading of the text follows, highlighting the significant areas of concern objectively. An endeavor toward a reconstruction of an African women's christological hermeneutic is pursued, which will be employed to guide the interpretation of the text. This particular lens aims at proclaiming a grace-filled and life-giving Christ who liberates, brings equality, transforms, restores and changes lives, not only for women but for all.

---

11. Borland, "Women in the Life and Teachings of Jesus," 115.
12. Borland, 31.
13. Mburu, *African Hermeneutics*, 69.
14. Van Eck, "The Word Is Life," 679–701.

Situating the Pericope Adulterae (PA) of John 7:53 – 8:11

Historically, the authenticity and placement of the text of the Pericope Adulterae (PA) has been disputed over the years, with no agreement in sight. Renowned New Testament scholars and exegetes have tried to address the controversy surrounding the passage, positing both external and internal evidence concerning its historicity, its authenticity with regard to John's style of writing, its placement, and its subsequent exclusion from or inclusion in the fourth gospel.[15]

Though these scholarly arguments concerning the authenticity, historicity and placement of the text are insightful, they are not worth duplicating in this work. This article is instead interested in the arguments concerning the text's supposed exclusion from or inclusion in the canon of the New Testament on moral grounds. Zane Hodges argues that the PA was part of the original gospel, but the copyists deleted it from the exemplar manuscript prior to 200 AD.[16] The plausibility of Hodges's claim is backed up by insights from various church fathers, including Ambrose, St. Augustine and Jerome.[17]

Bishop Ambrose of Milan (ca. 374), in his sermon on David's sin, made the following remark that demonstrated knowledge of the story of the woman caught in adultery:

> in the same way also the gospel lesson which has been read, may have caused no small offense to the unskilled, in which you have noticed that an adulteress was brought to Christ and dismissed without condemnation . . . Did Christ err that He did not judge righteously? It is not right that such a thought should come to our minds.[18]

The concern of the bishop of Milan was not centered on the woman taken in adultery, but on whether Christ judged righteously, regarding which he warns his hearers not to fault Christ. It is, however, clear that he knew the story of the woman caught in adultery.

St. Augustine, the bishop of Hippo (ca. 400), pointed to the omission of the text from the exemplar manuscript and the New Testament for moralistic

---

15. Bultmann, *Gospel of John*; Brown, *Gospel according to John*; Beutler, *Commentary on the Gospel of John*; Schnackenburg, *Gospel according to St. John*; Toensing, "Divine Interpretation or Divine Intrusion?," 259–72.

16. Hodges, "Problem Passages," 318–32.

17. Hodges, 320.

18. Ambrose, Corpus Scriptorum Ecclesiasticorum Latinorum, vol. 32, 359–360, quoted in Hills, *The King James Version Defended*, 123.

reasons. St. Augustine noted, "Certain persons of little faith, fearing, I suppose, lest their wives should be given immunity in sinning, removed from their manuscript the Lord's act of forgiveness towards the adulteress as if He who had said 'sin no more' had granted permission to sin."[19] St. Augustine's text alludes to an androcentric society of men who faulted Jesus for rendering forgiveness to the adulteress, fearing that the same pardon would be accorded to their women if the text remained documented. Thus, the men of power removed the text from the gospel. In this assertion, both the woman caught in adultery and Jesus are viewed with suspicion by the "persons of little faith."[20]

The Greek manuscript B (*Codex Vaticanus*)[21] and the old Latin codices b (*Codex Veronensis*)[22] and e (*Codex Laudianus*)[23] are documented to have contained the pericope later in the fifth century, as confirmed by Jerome (ca. 415). He noted that "in the gospel according to John in many manuscripts, both Greek and Latin, is found the story of the adulterous woman who was accused before the Lord."[24] Further, the *Didascalia*, that is, the teaching of the apostles of the third century and apostolic constitution of the fourth century, provides another evidence of its availability in early Greek manuscripts of John. A caption states that it would be wrong not

> to do as He also did with her that had sinned, whom the elders set before Him and leaving the judgment in his hands departed. But He, the searcher of hearts, asked her and said to her, "Have the elders condemned thee my daughter?" She saith to Him, "Nay Lord." He said unto her, "Go thy way. Neither do I condemn thee."[25]

Even before Ambrose of Milan vividly referred to the pericope of the adulterous woman, Eusebius (ca. 324), in his *Ecclesiastical History*, points to a similar story that was purported to circulate orally. Eusebius refers to an old

---

19. Augustine, Corpus Scriptorum Ecclesiasticorum Latinorum, vol. 41, 387, quoted in Hills, *The King James Version Defended*, 123–124.

20. *Augustinus*, quoted in Willker, *Textual Commentary on the Greek Gospels*, https://web.archive.org/web/20110409164438/http://www-user.uni-bremen.de/~wie/TCG/TC-John-PA.pdf.

21. Willker.

22. See "The Four Gospels from the Codex Veronensis," https://babel.hathitrust.org/cgi/pt?id=yale.39002013394987&view=1up&seq=8.

23. See "Codex Laudianus," http://www.thetextofthegospels.com/2017/10/codex-laudianus-ga-46-ga-46-ga-57-and.html.

24. Jerome, Migne, Patrologiae Cursus Completus, Series Latina, vol.23, col. 579, quoted in Edward F. Hills, *The King James Version Defended*, 124.

25. Connolly, *Didascalia Apostolorum*, 76.

treatise known to have been written by Bishop Papias of Hierapolis (d. 150). In reference to "interpretations of the oracles of the Lord," Eusebius writes of Papias, "The same writer used quotations from the Epistle of John, and likewise also from that of Peter." There he expounded another story "about a woman who was accused before the Lord of many sins, which the story according to the Hebrews contains."[26] Such references are clear indication that the story existed in oral tradition during the time of the apostles and was struggling to find its way into the canon despite androcentric fears. It is evident that prejudice hovered over the story in the early church, causing its rejection, which in turn aroused concerns from the church fathers, resulting in its later inclusion.

This later inclusion was because the above arguments grounded convincing claims in the interactions of Jesus and a woman in a patriarchal sociocultural environment. Schussler Fiorenza agrees:

> Although the story about the woman caught in adultery is a later addition to the Gospels' text, the interpolator nevertheless had a fine sense for the dynamics of the narrative, which places women as crucial points of development and confrontation, namely the prominence of women in the Johannine community.[27]

Even though the main focus of the story is, according to the narrator, to test Jesus (8:6), the triumph on the part of Jesus leaves the focus on the woman caught in adultery, who is exonerated. In contextualizing the story's sociocultural components of seeking to test and arrest Jesus, his triumph is not foreign or unexpected for either the immediate community or the contemporary reader. All the Johannine narratives in which Jesus interacts with women portray a (de)construction and (re)definition of patriarchy and hierarchy. For instance, at the wedding at Cana (John 2), the mother of Jesus directs him to supplement the wine which has run out, and he obeys. The Samaritan woman (John 4) finds herself speaking with the life-giver himself, to a point where he almost reveals his messiahship.

According to Daniel Harrington, we must not forget that the society within which Jesus was born and grew up was patriarchal and hierarchical.[28] Men were held in high regard and were not supposed to greet women in a public

---

26. "Church History of Eusebius," in *Eusebius: Church History, Life of Constantine the Great, and Oration in Praise of Constantine*, Vol. 1 of *A Select Library of the Nicene and Post-Nicene Fathers of the Christian Church*, Second Series, ed. Philip Schaff and Henry Wace, trans. Arthur Cushman McGiffert (New York: Christian Literature Co., 1890), 173.

27. Schüssler Fiorenza, *In Memory of Her*, 326.

28. Harrington, *Jesus: A Historical Portrait*, 53.

place. Women were regarded as property owned by their husbands, such that any conversation between a woman and a man who was not her husband was shunned. While still respecting his Jewishness, Jesus nevertheless had several conversations with women. In all his interactions with women in the Gospel of John, the conversations are short but liberating.[29] Thus Judith Plaskow notes that we "must seek to understand Jesus in relationship with his tradition and articulate his significance in such a way that does not negate the influence Judaism had on his liberative practices."[30]

Even though the woman caught in adultery is forgiven, the repression depicted in the drama elicits sympathy from the readers, who feel that Jesus, being the Jew he was humanly raised to be, would struggle to handle the poorly presented case. It therefore follows that whether the text was a later inclusion or not, it attracted a lot of interest and attention among scholars, who, as we shall later see, focused on rethinking patriarchy, masculinity, repressed women and/or sex, which is still a controversial subject.

A Dramatized Rereading of the Pericope Adulterae (PA) (John 7:53 – 8:11)

A dramaturgical rereading of a story and hence analysis, according to Robert Benford and Paul Hare, "illuminates how people derive shared understanding and collaboratively construct reality in everyday cultural, organizational, and institutional life."[31] The social roles performed in every dramatized story can be read and understood in line with the sociohistorical setting of the time vis-à-vis the contemporary replay of similar scenarios. The dramatized story of Jesus and the woman caught in adultery opens with people retreating to their homes and Jesus going to the Mount of Olives, as was his routine. Then early the next morning, at the temple of Jerusalem, crowds of people are flocking either to listen to the teachings of Jesus or, as Zane Hodges notes, because the Passover feast was approaching.[32] Jesus, in the temple setting, starts teaching. The sobriety of the setting is, however, interrupted by scribes and Pharisees,[33] who enter the holy space with an unnamed woman.

---

29. See Duehren, *Anti Judaism in Christian Feminist Theology*, 23.
30. Plaskow, "Anti-Judaism in Feminist Christian Interpretation," 91.
31. Benford and Hare, "Dramaturgical Analysis," 646, explains the concept of dramaturgy.
32. Hodges, "Problem Passages," 42–44.
33. O'Sullivan, "Reading John 7:53 – 8:11," 1–8.

In the imagined deafening silence, the scribes and the Pharisees, trying to maintain the status quo of their understanding of the law, call Jesus "Teacher," which could be a sincere address signifying that he knows the law better than they. With the case now with the right person, a woman with no name is brought – probably dragged – before Jesus, and is placed at the center of the crowd and the scribes and the Pharisees, in order to be stoned to death! "This woman was caught in the act of committing adultery," they accuse her. In order to ground their claim, they continue, "In the Law Moses commanded us to stone such women. Now what do you say?" It is recorded that they did this to test Jesus, so that they might have some charge to bring against him.

The deafening silence and the shame that must have engulfed this moment is unimaginable. First, Jesus, being all-knowing, understands the scheme of the scribes and the Pharisees. He already knows it is a trap. Second, according to the law of Moses, the case is poorly presented, and the scribes and the Pharisees know it. Exercising their mischievous religious authority, they are blinded and silenced by their expectation of Jesus's error. Even more, their knowledge of the law of Moses silences them as they fail to present a witness, which is a flaw or a "sin." There is no witness, despite the presentation of her being "caught in the act." One wonders where the man is who partnered in the act, or the husband who had been offended. According to Leviticus 20:10, the law of Moses that is quoted in John 8:5, the adulterous man as well as the woman was to be put to death.

Further, accusers biasedly refer to the Levitical law in framing their accusation as though it expected women to be faithful to their husbands, as if to imply that men could "socially" engage in extramarital relations. Given the deafening silence from the crowd, adultery as presented in this case appears to be considered by the populace to have been "solely a crime committed against the husband,"[34] who blinded themselves to the error before the Lord.

Third is the evident objectification of the woman in several ways. The narrator clarifies that she was just a pawn; the scribes and the Pharisees' interest was to trap Jesus. Further, owing to the sociocultural ordering of the Mediterranean world, women were not allowed to speak in public places.[35] The shame of finding herself accused publicly of sexual sin, something private and humiliating, would not allow her to speak. The fear of death was so apparent in her that she would have kept her face downwards, concealing her shame and

---

34. Swidler, "Status of Women," 8–14.
35. Kiambi, "Divining John 7:53 – 8:11," 1–15.

guilt in silence. Being "caught in the act" and dragged to Jesus also suggests that the woman was probably either naked or half dressed.

In the words of Noel Tshilumba, "Jesus is [so] profoundly displeased with them that he initially distances himself from them by his silence, posture and action."[36] Amid the silence, Jesus bends down and writes with his finger on the ground. Nothing is readable because the scribes and the Pharisees pester him to respond verbally to their claims. Jesus, upon straightening up, challenges them, "Let any one of you who is without sin be the first to throw a stone at her." Then Jesus bends down again and continues writing on the ground.

Astonishingly, the scribes and the Pharisees go away one by one, beginning with the elders. The judgment from Jesus they had pestered him for has been rendered. It is a conditional judgment: "if you are without sin." Jesus does not dispute the law of Moses; he indirectly affirms the stoning through a self-reflective meditation that is deeper and more personal. The departure of the scribes and the Pharisees, beginning with the older ones, demonstrates that they too, just like the unnamed woman, cannot claim righteousness as easily as they had imagined. They are actually at fault by having failed to present a witness and the man, as expected from the Levitical dictates.

The tense moment turns into an engaging conversation. The unnamed woman is given a voice and is no longer invisible. Jesus straightens up and asks about the whereabouts of the scribes and the Pharisees and whether anyone has condemned her. One can only imagine the relief that runs through her as she responds, "No one, Lord" (RSV). She acknowledges the Lordship of Jesus! One can even claim that she has come to believe, fulfilling the objective of the Johannine writer. Jesus responds, "Then neither do I condemn you . . . Go now and leave your life of sin." This is a very powerful extension of God's saving grace: an inviting opportunity for self-examination coated with words of counsel – "sin no more."

The exciting ending of this dramatic story captivates every woman, causing her to rethink the person of Jesus away from the exhorted super-masculine sonship that runs in the gospels. It was the endeavor to experience a relational Christ which prompted a reconstructive hermeneutic of rereading the PA from an African women's perspective.

Understanding a text written in the past and appropriating it to guide and speak to our contemporary lives requires interpretive modes that unearth relatable meaning. The Johannine evangelist portrays a Jesus who, according to Julius Gathogo, acts as "the ideal reconstructionist, the one who broke the

---

36. Tshilumba, "Exegetical Paper on John 8:1–11," 10.

cultural codes of his time in order to reconstruct the society."[37] Such a model of reconstruction "is the relevant model to our contemporary world."[38] Further, Volker Küster opined that a christological discourse as a hermeneutical event needs a hermeneutical circle to interpret reality and Jesus Christ as presented in the Scriptures.[39] This is a circle that accommodates identity, historicity and context, and is in congruence with the gospel.

In societies where male gender biases and repression are the norm, women will almost always be unappreciated. The androcentric climate and patriarchal spirit cuts across the gospel narratives, where women are often left without names, and are usually portrayed as sinners, defenseless and/or unclean. For the contemporary woman to own the Bible as Christ speaking abundant life into her world, African women theologians have endeavored to appropriate Jesus for their contexts and experiences. African cultures are known to repress and discriminate against women on several fronts. For instance, a woman is not allowed to own land, to question her husband's erroneous behavior, or even to eat some parts of animals and birds that are taken for food by men.

Noting these imbalances, Mercy Amba Oduyoye, the mother of African women's theology and the founder of the Circle of Concerned African Women Theologians, presents a relational African Christology.[40] Oduyoye, in her attempts to challenge the oppression of women through sexism, racism, colonialism, neocolonialism and androcentric tendencies, presents Jesus as a friend, a healer, an advocate, a liberator, a source of transformation, and a mother who nurtures life and cares for the weak; a mother who "suffers with the poor and oppressed . . . [who] empathizes by incarnating into the experiences of those who suffer."[41] Her theological reflections on Christ as a woman affirm the equality of both men and women, an impetus that pushed her to fight for women's liberation. Oduyoye presents a Christology that perceives women as fully human and hence does not need the presence and thoughts of men to engage with Christ.[42]

The mother of African women's Christology inspired other women to cling to the relational, experiential and liberating traits of Jesus. Anne Nasimiyu-Wasike affirmed,

---

37. Gathogo, "Reconstructive Hermeneutics," 1.
38. Gathogo, 1.
39. Küster, *Many Faces of Jesus Christ*, 58.
40. Gathogo, "Mercy Oduyoye," 1–10.
41. Oduyoye, "Christ for African Women," 32.
42. Oduyoye, "Search for a Two-Winged Theology," 31–56.

> The African woman's experiences call for a Christology that is based on a holistic view of life. She needs the Christ who affects the whole of her life, whose presence is felt in every corner of the village and who participates in everything and everybody's life. This God, the Christ, is the one who takes on the conditions of the African woman – the conditions of weakness, misery, injustice, and oppression.[43]

The relational-experiential concepts of African women's Christology were advanced by African women theologians incorporating contextualized liberating tendencies built on hope and transformation.

Analyzed from a transforming perspective, Jesus, though male, does not represent the patriarchal and androcentric attitudes advanced by African cultures, but he transcends them to represent humanity's totality.[44] African women theologians ought to appreciate the Jewish background and relationality of Jesus to experience his identity fully. Jesus, being a Jew, practiced Jewish norms and met cultural expectations, though he firmly held to his transcendence. Regarding the transcendence of Jesus's maleness in upholding liberating humanity, Rosemary Ruether is worth quoting:

> Theologically speaking then, we might say that the maleness of Jesus has no ultimate significance. It has social symbolic significance in the framework of societies of patriarchal privilege. In this sense, Jesus as the Christ, the representative of liberated humanity, and the liberating word of God, manifests the kenosis of patriarchy, the announcement of the new humanity through a lifestyle that discards hierarchical caste privilege and speaks on behalf of the lowly.[45]

The representation of liberating humanity translates to equality between men and women, both created in God's image and likeness. Jesus, being God incarnate, dismantles cultural and androcentric repressions that look down upon women. Detaching him from cultural expectations, though he was firmly grounded in his culture as a man, is a bold step to constructing a Christology that does not focus on the patriarchal titles of Jesus as the Messiah, Son of God, judge, prophet and king, among others. As Teresa Okure notes, "Christology

---

43. Nasimiyu-Wasike, "Christology and an African Woman's Experience," 130.
44. Nasimiyu-Wasike, 124.
45. Ruether, *Sexism and God-Talk*, 137.

did not fall from heaven, but it is constructed from experiences."[46] Therefore, there is "a need for a Christology that resonates with the experiences of African women."[47]

The reconstructive christological hermeneutic of African women builds on the ideologies of liberating relationality that Jesus represents in living out their contextual experiences. This hermeneutic springs from the implied freedom of expression and internalized sense of equality in daily expressions while interacting with both genders. It is a hermeneutic that breaks shaming silences and opens forbidden spaces. Inclusiveness and intersectionality become pillars dismantling the tendencies to push people to the margins and the periphery. Julius Kithinji Kiambi, using a postcolonial hermeneutic in reading the PA, warns against othering and profiling people "in societies that celebrate difference."[48] He concentrates on the negative profiling of the Pharisees in the text,[49] and also captures the outstanding othering of the unnamed adulteress profiled by the Pharisees.[50] Nonetheless, redeeming characters in a dramatized analysis narratively forces the reader to employ experiential biases, as affirmed by Zorodzai Dube. Dube notes that "a true theology should affirm life and connect with real experiences of African Women";[51] this starts "with people's experiences and not with textual criticism."[52] It is a call to a Christology that responds to a need for openness to the new Christian experiences and understandings of Christ that emanate from contemporary contexts of repression and emancipation, irrespective of gender, age or marital status.

It is against this backdrop that the story of the woman caught in adultery is interpreted by a woman in a contemporary setting. Biblical interpretations speaking to the vice of adultery require a hermeneutic that equates both genders if the church is to carry out its pastoral mission effectively in the contemporary setting.

---

46. Okure, "First Was Life Not the Book," 194.
47. Okure, 194.
48. Kiambi, "Decolonizing the Treatment of the Pharisees," 25458–25463.
49. Kiambi.
50. See Kiambi, "Divining John 7:53 – 8:11," 1–15.
51. Dube, "African Women Theologians' Contribution," 1.
52. Dube, "Salvation through God's Son," 91.

Context of Interpretation: Marital Infidelity and New Infidelities

Recent statistics indicate that many married people are engaging in concurrent extramarital relations, leading to high rates of new HIV infections. In Kenya and Tanzania, for instance, 44 percent of new HIV infections were attributed to extramarital affairs.[53] Men and women were said to engage in extramarital relations/adultery in equal measure. Secularism and advancements in technology coupled with the empowerment of women have challenged the once widely held cultural expectation that only men would engage in extramarital sex. The involvement of married women in adultery is now more of an amplified concern than married men involved in the same.

Male violence against women is still rampant in the contemporary setting, which is characterized by advocacy and lobbying for equal rights for all. Androcentric and patriarchal tendencies continue to fuel violence against women, especially along sexual lines. In Kenya, barely a week goes by without the reporting of deaths over sexual advances. For instance, the deaths of married and unmarried female university students such as Dorcas,[54] Sharon[55] and Ivy[56] indicate that a woman's body is still a contested space.

With the advent of secularism, advancements in technology and the passage of time, adultery/infidelity now goes beyond engaging in a sexual act with a person who is not your spouse. It includes an emotional attachment to other partners whether through kissing, sexting, watching pornographic clips, online/physical flirting, fondling, Internet relationships or engaging in oral sex. All these activities have been classified as emotional infidelity that is rarely noticed by one's spouse. These infidelities survive under the adage "What you do not know does not hurt you." While that may sound true, acting in secret attests not only to the inner guilt that comes with these secret emotional

---

53. Kimanga, Ogola, Umuro et al., "Prevalence and Incidence of HIV Infection," 13–26; Mtenga, Pfeiffer, Tanner et al., "Linking Gender, Extramarital Affairs, and HIV," 1–17.

54. Dorcas, a university student from South Eastern Kenya University (SEKU), was killed by her husband over marital disagreements regarding extramarital affairs. See C. Muthama, "Husband Kills Himself and 22 Year Old Wife," 15 June 2018, https://mauvoo.com/love-gone-sour-as-husband-kills-himself-and-22-year-old-wife-a-final-year-student-at-seku/.

55. Sharon, a Rongo University student, was murdered when she was seven months pregnant, pointing to extramarital relations with a high-profile man, who is said to have planned her killing. See Hillary Orinde, "Sharon Otieno Murder and the 2018 Governor Ogado Would Rather Forget," *The Standard*, 1 January 2019, https://www.standardmedia.co.ke/article/2001307934/sharon-otieno-murder-revisited.

56. Ivy, a Moi University medical student, was hacked to death because of what was purported to be a love triangle. See Meera Pattni, "Ivy Killed by Stalker, Spurned Lover – Classmate," *The Star*, 10 April 2019, https://www.the-star.co.ke/news/2019-04-10-ivy-killed-by-stalker-spurned-lover-classmate/.

engagements, but also to the fact that the actors value the expected norm of exclusivity in marital relations. The positive value attributed to this norm speaks to their conviction regarding societal and biblical expectations. Infidelity negatively impacts one's psychological health, creates room for divorce, and increases the chances of contracting sexually transmitted infections such as chlamydia, syphilis, gonorrhea and HIV/AIDS.[57]

The widening understanding of infidelity to include nonpenetrative sexual advances allows for new forms of infidelity that are psychologically oriented. Brenda Cossman, in her work "New Politics of Adultery," points out that "adultery is now framed as a violation of the promise of emotional and sexual exclusivity."[58] It is worth discerning the departure from an understanding of adultery as exclusively heterosexual penetrative sex with a person who is not your legal spouse to include emotional infidelities. Shirley Glass notes that "the greatest betrayals happen without touching."[59] These new infidelities occur between people who "unwittingly form deep passionate connections before realizing that they have crossed the line from platonic friendship into romantic love."[60] They are, however, aware of the betrayal that they are causing their spouses, hence the secrecy. This inner embeddedness of secretive affairs correlates with religiosity, which is usually integrated into a sense of self. The inbuilt conscience in every person is the judge of all actions in our immediate awareness, hence the inner sense of guilt and shame, regardless of gender. In addressing this vice, the church in its mission ought to transcend cultural bias and embrace a sense of equality in addressing infidelity.

In the African setting, men, owing to their patriarchal and androcentric power fueled by the cultural embrace of polygamy, involve themselves in extramarital affairs more often than women.[61] Sections 2, 3 and 6 of Kenya's Marriage Act No. 4 of 2014 legalizes polygamy, without limiting the number of women a man can keep.[62] The trend is, however, changing, with women who have strived to empower themselves through education and are in the working space now often reported to engage in infidelity.[63] The power imbalance between men and women persists in most cultures. Women, in spite of their struggle

---

57. Finer, Darroch and Singh, "Sexual Partnership Patterns," 228–36.
58. Cossman, "New Politics of Adultery," 275.
59. Glass, "Shattered Vows," 34.
60. Glass, 35.
61. Baloyi, "Critical Reflections on Polygamy," 164–81.
62. Marriage Act, Laws of Kenya, 2014, no. 4.
63. Tagler and Jeffers, "Sex Differences in Attitudes," 821–32.

for freedom and empowerment, still find themselves entangled in repressive spaces, from which even churches have not been exempt. Barren women, for instance, may still face sexual advances and even rape and/or psychological manipulation to engage sexually with male pastors, in the name of deliverance.

To survive in such repressive circumstances, women have strived relentlessly for their freedom. They have responded by reinterpreting biblical Scriptures and reconstructing Jesus Christ as acting in their favor. In the case we have examined (John 7:53 – 8:11), Jesus accords mercy to and acquits the woman caught in adultery, a story that is often read and referred to by contemporary women. In this text, Jesus not only shows mercy to the unnamed woman, but he also acquits her – not because she had not sinned, but because the case was maliciously staged. The guilty man was not produced and hence not punished!

According to the reconstructed African women's Christology, the story divides into three sections. First is the setting of the plot in a holy and sober space for Jesus to commence his teaching (John 7:53 – 8:2). Here, Jesus is set apart as the authority and the teacher who is the source and custodian of wisdom and knowledge. The second covers John 8:3–9, which presents the scribes and Pharisees, Jesus and the woman accused of adultery in their midst. The scene presents the classification of people into cultural castes, where Jesus is the authority, teacher and judge, the Pharisees and scribes are the accusers, and the woman is the accused person, lowly and ashamed. The man who was supposed to have been presented together with her is apparently missing! Following their malicious accusations, Jesus stoops down to write, possibly disappointed or in humility, figuratively and symbolically equating the woman and her accusers by their posture of standing. In Matthew 5:27, Jesus reminded them of the oral Judaic law: "You have heard that it was said, 'You shall not commit adultery.' But I tell you that anyone who looks at a woman lustfully has already committed adultery with her in his heart." He sets himself apart as lowly – not as the exalted judge, but as a sound teacher of the law. He also shifts the power balance. In stooping, he should have been less powerful, yet his action spotlights the patriarchal problem of the accusers in response to the woman who might have been cowering.

The stooping down and rising of Jesus posits a position of authority to judge, but in his wisdom, mercy and humility he invites the scribes and the Pharisees to examine their inner selves with a sober and straightforward statement: "Let any one of you who is without sin be the first to throw a stone at her." Following a deafening silence, they depart one at a time. Their departure affirms their hidden sins that only they know, embedded deep within their hearts. If we could argue in terms of sexual sin which they used to shatter the image of the unnamed woman, we might imaginatively accuse them of new infidelities that convicted them of inner guilt. The woman is not the only immoral actor, after all. Women may perpetrate immoral actions, as in our HIV/AIDS case, but it is men who, in an African setting, entertain concurrent sexual relationships without reproach.

Third, in John 8:10–11, Jesus is left with the woman and engages her in a conversation. Jesus is conversing with a sinner! Jesus, however, in his grace creates a liberating interdependence for the woman based not only on his mercy but also on an acquittal premised on social justice structures. This is because those who were allowed by the law to punish her acquit her indirectly based on the same systems they used to shame her. Leaving her unpunished in the presence of Jesus creates a space for breaking the silence and experientially relating her with Christ. Jesus's invitation to self-evaluation is subtle and yet very deep. In his wisdom, Jesus extricates himself from the trap of misappropriating the Mosaic law and invites the woman to receive forgiveness. She affirms his lordship and is dismissed with the gracious counsel not to sin anymore.

At the point of deep-seated weakness in their hearts, the Pharisees and the scribes, as well as the woman, meet with the Holy of holies, who reminds them of their equality in his presence. Cultural masculinity and androcentric traits are deconstructed indirectly by Jesus without condoning sin. The immorality of the woman, the scribes and the Pharisees is laid bare. Adultery is a sin not just committed by women against men, but a spiritual sin that all ought to shun.

The PA is a perfect foretelling drama giving a glimpse into understanding the mission and vision of Jesus's crucifixion. He who is without fault will be trapped (the scribes and the Pharisees wanted to trap him), judged falsely (they manufacture a false charge of treason), crucified, and will die for the forgiveness of our sins. Exercising his divinity, he succeeds in exonerating himself and creates a space for transformation. All that will happen to Jesus will be for our forgiveness. The woman is forgiven and invited to embrace grace visibly. Her name and hence her story call out for a change, from "the woman caught in adultery" to "the forgiven one" or even "Grace." Forgiveness and the grace of Jesus, the divine, stand out in this text.

In carrying out the mission of the church, ministers ought to learn from the "teacher," without leaning on culture and the patriarchy that excuses extramarital relations for men but not for women. The dynamics of power imbalance need a mutual critic if the institution of marriage is to hold in the contemporary setting, which is characterized by technology and secularism, components that fuel marital cheating. The glorification of Jesus in this drama, first by the woman and then by Jesus's extricating himself from the trap, paradoxically becomes a sign that deconstructs gender imbalances. A redeeming sense of grace points to a reconstruction of equality shared by all humanity, which is unearthed and revealed narratively.

Conclusion

This chapter has endeavored to undertake a rereading of the Pericope Adulterae with the aim of reconstructing an African women's christological hermeneutic that will create an avenue for interacting with biblical texts in contemporary contexts. The work began by affirming the view of the patristic fathers that the text was omitted and later included on moral grounds. The contemporary context in Africa is characterized by high rates of marital infidelity that challenge the mission of the church, especially with regard to the institution of marriage. Patriarchal tendencies uphold infidelity among men but condemn it among women. A change of this order in today's world has resulted in heightened violence against women, often with fatal consequences. Women have been accused of spreading HIV/AIDS owing to androcentric thinking in which it is men who can engage in extramarital relations unnoticed. With this in mind, the reconstructed African women's christological hermeneutic argues for a liberating equal relationality among humanity in living out their contextual experiences. The reconstructive hermeneutic narratively breaks shaming silences and opens forbidden spaces. This hermeneutic also speaks to African church ministers about how to address issues around HIV in the African church. Using the hermeneutic, inclusiveness and intersectionality become pillars for dismantling the tendencies that push people to the margins. The Christology presented by the African women's hermeneutic is reflexive and open to changing contexts and lived experiences. It brings about a realization that authentic humanity calls for authentic subjectivity that springs from within the self once an all-embracing Christ renders a humbling and yet loving invitation. This invitation brings out transformation, not only for the woman but also for all men and demeaning social structures. The reconstructive hermeneutic alludes to an incorporation of the text in John under the heading "the forgiven woman" or "grace unmerited." In interacting with biblical texts, we need to understand that they are dynamic mediums of interaction with Christ, the author and perfector of our faith, where the congruence of mercy, gentle rebuke and unmerited grace governs our Christian living, hence dismantling androcentric-fueled violence against women in contemporary contexts.

Bibliography

Baloyi, Elijah M. "Critical Reflections on Polygamy in the African Christian Context." *Missionalia* 41, no. 2 (2013): 164–81.

Benford, Robert D., and A. Paul Hare. "Dramaturgical Analysis." In *International Encyclopedia of the Social & Behavioral Sciences*, edited by James D. Wright, 645–49. 2nd ed. Amsterdam: Elsevier, 2015.

Beutler, Johannes. *A Commentary on the Gospel of John*. Grand Rapids, MI: Eerdmans, 2017.

Blow, Adrian J., and Kelley Hartnett. "Infidelity in Committed Relationships 1: A Methodological Review." *Journal of Marital and Family Therapy* 31, no. 2 (2005): 183–216. https://doi.org/10.1111/j.1752-0606.2005.tb01555.x.

Borland, James. "Women in the Life and Teachings of Jesus." In *Recovering Biblical Manhood and Womanhood: A Response to Evangelical Feminism*, edited by J. Piper and W. Grudem, 105–116. Wheaton: Crossway, 1991.

Brown, Raymond E. *The Gospel according to John: Chapters 13–21*. Vol. 2. Garden City: Doubleday, 1970.

Bultmann, Rudolf. *The Gospel of John*. Philadelphia: Westminster Press, 1971.

Concise Oxford English Dictionary. Edited by C. Soanes and A. Stevenson. New York: Oxford University Press, 2009.

Connolly, Richard Hugh, ed. *Didascalia Apostolorum*. Oxford: Clarendon Press, 1929.

Corpus Scriptorum Ecclesiasticorum Latinorum. *Academia Litteerarum Vindoboriensis*, Vol. 32, 359–60.

Cossman, Brenda. "New Politics of Adultery." *Columbia Journal of Gender and Law* 15, no. 1 (2006): 274–94.

Dube, Zorodzai. "The African Women Theologians' Contribution towards the Discussion about Alternative Masculinities." *Verbum et Ecclesia* 37, no. 2 (2016): 1–6.

———. "Salvation through God's Son: Gendering the Salvation Motif." *Journal of Gender and Religion in Africa* 19, no. 2 (2016): 91–108.

Duehren, Caitlyn. *Anti-Judaism in Christian Feminist Theology: Recovering the Roots of Liberation*. Boston: Boston College Centre for Christian Jewish Learning, 2011.

Finer, Lawrence B., Jacqueline E. Darroch and Susheela Singh. "Sexual Partnership Patterns as a Behavioral Risk Factor for Sexually Transmitted Diseases." *Family Planning Perspectives* 31, no. 5 (1999): 228–36.

Gathogo, Julius. "Mercy Oduyoye as the Mother of African Women's Theology." *Journal of Theology and Religion in Africa* 34, no. 1 (2010): 1–10.

———. "Reconstructive Hermeneutics in African Christology." *Theological Studies* 71, no. 3 (2015): 1–8.

Gelmon, Lawrence. *Kenya HIV Prevention Response and Modes of Transmission Analysis*. National AIDS Control Council, 2009.

Glass, Shirley. "Shattered Vows: Getting beyond Betrayal." *Psychology Today* (1998): 32–42.

Harrington, Daniel J. *Jesus: A Historical Portrait*. Cincinnati: St. Anthony Messenger Press, 2007.

Hills, Edward F. *The King James Version Defended*. Christian Research Press, 1984.

Hodges, Zane C. "Problem Passages in the Gospel of John, Part 8: The Woman Taken in Adultery (John 7:53–8:11): The Text." *Bibliotheca Sacra* 136 (1979): 318–332.

———. "Problem Passages in the Gospel of John, Part 9: The Woman Taken in Adultery (John 7:53–8:11): Exposition." *Bibliotheca Sacra* 137 no. 545 (1980): 41–53.

Kiambi, Julius Kithinji. "Decolonizing the Treatment of the Pharisees in John 7:53–8:11." *International Journal of Development Research* 9, no. 1 (2019): 25458–63. https://www.journalijdr.com/decolonizing-treatment-pharisees-john-753-811.

———. "Divining John 7:53–8:11 for Textual Gender-Motivated Violence: A Postcolonial Approach – Biblical Hermeneutics." *Women and Gender* (2012): 1–15. https://papers.ssrn.com/sol3/papers.cfm?abstract_id=2017643.

Kimanga, Davies O., Samuel Ogola, Mamo Umuro et al. "Prevalence and Incidence of HIV Infection, Trends, and Risk Factors among Persons Aged 15–64 Years in Kenya: Results from a Nationally Representative Study." *Journal of Acquired Immune Deficiency Syndromes* 66, Suppl no. 1 (1 May 2014): 13–26.

Küster, Volker. *The Many Faces of Jesus Christ: Intercultural Christology*. London: SCM, 2001.

Lagat, Daniel. "Christian Ethics on Divorce." *Jumuga Journal of Education, Oral Studies, and Human Sciences (JJEOSHS)* 1, no. 1 (2018): 1–15.

Mburu, Elizabeth. *African Hermeneutics*. Carlisle: Hippo, 2019.

Mtenga, Sally M., Constanze Pfeiffer, Marcel Tanner, Eveline Geubbels and Sonja Merten. "Linking Gender, Extramarital Affairs, and HIV: A Mixed Methods Study on Contextual Determinants of Extramarital Affairs in Rural Tanzania." *AIDS Research and Therapy* 15, no. 1 (2018): 1–17.

Nasimiyu-Wasike, Anne. "Christology and an African Woman's Experience." In *Jesus in African Christianity: Experimentation and Diversity in African Christology*, edited by Jesse Mugambi and Laurenti Magesa, 123–35. Nairobi: Initiatives, 1989.

National AIDS and STI Control Programme (NASCOP). "Kenya Population-Based HIV Impact Assessment (KENPHIA)." Ministry of Health Kenya, 2018.

Oduyoye, Mercy Amba. "The Christ for African Women." In *With Passion and Compassion: Third World Woman Doing Theology – Reflections from Women's Commission of the Ecumenical Association of Third World Theologians*, edited by V. Fabella and M. A. Oduyoye, 35–46. Maryknoll: Orbis, 1988.

———. "The Search for a Two-Winged Theology: Women's Participation in the Development of Theology in Africa." In *"Talitha Qumi": Proceedings of the Convocation of African Women Theologians 1989*, edited by Mercy Amba Oduyoye and Musimbi Kanyoro, 31–56. Accra: Sam-Woode Press, 1990.

Okure, Teresa. "First Was Life Not the Book." In *To Cast Fire upon the Earth: Bible and Mission Collaborating in Today's Multicultural Global Context*, edited by Teresa Okure, 194–214. Natal: Cluster Publications, 2000.

O'Sullivan, Michael F. "Reading John 7:53–8:11 as a Narrative against Male Violence against Women." *HTS Teologiese Studies/Theological Studies* 71, no. 1 (2015): 1–8. DOI: 10.4102/hts.v71i1.2939.

Plaskow, Judith. "Anti-Judaism in Feminist Christian Interpretation." In *Judith Plaskow: Feminism, Theology, and Justice*, edited by Hava Tirosh-Samuelson and Aaron W. Hughes, 83–95. Leiden: Brill, 2014.

Ringrose, Hyacinthe, ed. *Marriage and Divorce Laws of the World*. [No place]: Good Press, 2018.

Ruether, Rosemary Radford. *Sexism and God-Talk: Toward a Feminist Theology; With a New Introduction*. Boston: Beacon, 1993.

Schaff, Philip, and Henry Wace, eds. *Eusebius: Church History, Life of Constantine the Great, and Oration in Praise of Constantine*. Vol. 1 of A Select Library of the Nicene and Post-Nicene Fathers of the Christian Church, Second Series. Trans. Arthur Cushman McGiffert. New York: Christian Literature Co., 1890.

Schnackenburg, Rudolf. *The Gospel according to St. John*. New York: Herder & Herder, 1968.

Schüssler Fiorenza, Elizabeth. *In Memory of Her: Feminist Theological Reconstruction of Christian Origins*. London: SCM, 1983.

Swidler, Leonard. "The Status of Women in Formative Judaism." *Women in Judaism* 8 (2012): 8–14.

Tagler, Michael J., and Heather M. Jeffers. "Sex Differences in Attitudes toward Partner Infidelity." *Evolutionary Psychology* 11, no. 4 (2013): 821–32.

Toensing, Holly. "Divine Interpretation or Divine Intrusion? Jesus and the Adulteress in John's Gospel." In *A Feminist Companion to John*, Vol. 1, edited by Amy-Jill Levine and Marianne Blickenstaff, 259–72. New York: Sheffield Academic, 2003.

Tshilumba, Noel K. "An Exegetical Paper on John 8:1–11: The Woman Caught in Adultery." Unpublished Thesis, University of South Africa: Pretoria, 2012.

Van Eck, Ernest. "The Word Is Life: African Theology as Biblical and Contextual Theology." *HTS: Theological Studies* 62, no. 2 (2006): 679–701.

Willker, Wieland. *Textual Commentary on the Greek Gospels*. Vol. 4b, *The Pericope de Adultera: John 7:53 – 8:11 (Jesus and the Adulteress)*. Bremen 8th edition, 2011. https://web.archive.org/web/20110409164438/http://www-user.uni-bremen.de/~wie/TCG/TC-John-PA.pdf.

2

An East African Perspective on Jesus as Revealer of the Father through His Use of the Friend at Midnight Parable as a Means for Teaching Powerful Prayer (Luke 11:1–13)

Timothy J. Monger
Emmanuel International Tanzania Country Director
Lecturer, St. Paul College, Mwanza, Tanzania

Abstract

Jesus's telling of the parable of the friend at midnight comes in the context of his teaching on prayer (Luke 11:1–13). In telling this parable, Jesus assumes the cultural norms of hospitality whereby to offer hospitality to guests is both an expectation and an honor, rather than being considered a burden or an inconvenience. In this regard, agreeing to the request of a friend to be hospitable would have been a natural outcome. A key interpretive issue in determining the intended meaning of this parable and of the whole passage is the meaning of the word *anaideia* in verse 8, commonly translated as "persistence" or "importunity." This unfortunately includes the widely used Swahili translations today, but it leads to a misunderstanding of the parable and a denial of its potency. This chapter examines this parable within its historical and literary setting, paying attention to the background on hospitality, considering carefully within this Lukan context the meaning of *anaideia* (better taken as "avoiding shame"), and interpreting the parable from the point of view of an African village setting, which even today has similar perspectives on the importance of hospitality, whereby a person is a guest not only of the individual but of the whole village. Thus, to refuse to help a friend to be hospitable would bring shame not only on the individual but also on the whole village. In this light, Jesus's intent in verses 1–13 is seen. As Son, he reveals to his followers the true nature of the Father, who, like the sleeper in the parable, will grant their requests, acting to preserve his name. In this way, appreciating the Christology in this prayer and from an East African village perspective can transform prayer.

Key words: Christology, prayer, fatherhood, hospitality, *anaideia*, avoiding shame, honor, African perspective

Introduction

Prayer is not often considered to be an important topic in connection with Christology.[1] This is surprising since Luke's gospel is well known for its emphasis on prayer and paticularly prayer in the ministry of Jesus, with Luke 11:1–13 being Jesus's main teaching to the disciples on the subject. Yet this passage is fraught with interpretive and cultural difficulties, such that it is easy to miss Jesus's thrust. This is not least because Jesus employs a parable in the middle of the passage, and its meaning and connection to the whole passage are seldom grasped. Indeed, it is the position of this paper that interpretations are often deficient, for the following reasons:

1. They frequently fail to connect this passage sufficiently to *the identity of Jesus* and the immediate and wider literary context.

2. The cultural background of hospitality is often not well understood in seeking to appreciate what Jesus is saying.

3. Coupled to point 2, the meaning of *anaideia* in 11:8 in Jesus's explanation of the parable is not always examined sufficiently but is commonly assumed to mean "persistence," a meaning which this paper will seek to show is both unlikely and misleading.

---

1. E.g. see Bird, *Evangelical Theology*; and Kunhiyop, *African Christian Theology*.

4. Western commentators, without realizing that modern Western culture is far removed from the Palestinian setting of the passage, have not only misunderstood the intended meaning of the passage but sadly unduly influenced, for example, Swahili translations of it and African Bible commentaries on it. Had those responsible for these African translations and commentaries paid more attention to African contexts, they might have produced more accurate and valuable treatments of this passage.

What this means is that Jesus's teaching on prayer here has frequently not had the intended power in an East African setting. This is not to say that efforts have not been attempted in addressing these four points. Kenneth Bailey and others have produced good studies of the Palestinian settings of the parable and sought to apply them to Jesus's teaching.[2] Joel Green has produced an excellent commentary concerning a narrative approach to this gospel.[3] An Asian reading of the parable has also been proposed.[4] In this chapter, I seek to address all four issues above, using these and earlier studies. But I have also engaged with Christians from Kenya, Tanzania and Uganda to gain their cultural perspectives and biblical reflections on the passage, to lead to a fresh reading.

The purpose of this paper, therefore, is to propose an East African reading of Luke 11:1–13, which shows Jesus as Revealer of the Father as he uses the friend at midnight parable as a means for teaching powerful prayer.

To this end, the culture of hospitality that informs the passage is outlined, and alongside this, African hospitality is described first. A key question considered is "How can an understanding of African hospitality aid us to appreciate the hospitality implied in this passage?" It is believed that if we prioritize an African reading, this will also lead to a more helpful reading, even for Westerners. Second, the literary context of the passage is outlined, paying careful attention to how *Jesus's identity*, *prayer* and *hospitality* lead up to the passage. With these two foundations laid, the passage is, third, examined in detail, with a particular eye to how Jesus's identity plays out, all the while bringing to bear contributions from an East African context. And fourth, some final applications to the African church are offered.

---

2. Bailey, *Poet and Peasant*; and Johnson, "Assurance for Man," 123–31.
3. Green, *Gospel of Luke*.
4. Nguyen, "Asian View of Biblical Hospitality," 25–39.

Hospitality in the Bible and East Africa
Hospitality in the Bible and Luke

Jesus's parable has a New Testament Palestinian village setting, and he assumes the practice of hospitality, which underpins this passage. In biblical times, hospitality operated within the general ancient Near East (ANE) context, particularly with it being an obligation,[5] whereby the host would respond generously by providing for the needs of the guest. But it was also set within the framework of God's hospitality. God, as host, provided a good world for humanity (Gen 1–2) and for Israel's needs in the wilderness, and later for them as his guests in a good land (e.g. Exod 17:1–7; 23:20–23; Lev 25:23; Num 14:21–24; Deut 1:34–35; 26:9).[6] He is seen as the exemplary host (Ps 23:5–6), who will also provide a lavish eschatological feast for all peoples as part of his cosmic renewal (Isa 25:6–8). In light of God's generous hospitality, God's people are expected to share their possessions with others, especially with the outsider and the alien in their midst (cf. Exod 23:9; Deut 24:17–22).

In New Testament times, with various political groups operating in Palestine and few inns existing, hospitality practices became standardized to ensure the safety of all and provision for strangers.[7] But as Ryken points out, "The failure of a community to approach the strangers and issue an invitation before nightfall to dine and lodge in an established household was a serious breach of honor, signifying an insult toward the strangers and an indication of the locals' bad character."[8]

Jesus himself, as the one who extended God's hospitality, frequently received such hospitality, but once in place, would often assume the role of host to reveal God's invitation to all as a means of reordering hospitality in a kingdom framework.[9] He would eat and drink "with tax collectors and sinners" so as to extend the kingdom welcome to them. The motif of hospitality in Luke's gospel has been well explored,[10] being seen in Luke 2:7; 5:27–32; 7:36–50; 9:10–17; 10:25–42; 13:22–30; 14:1–24; 15:11–32; 19:1–10; 22:14–20; 24:28–35.[11] In particular, "For Luke, failure in hospitality leads to a fractured community and, if left unattended, hinders kingdom exploits. From the gospels, Christians are

---

5. Ryken, *Dictionary of Biblical Imagery*, 402.
6. Cf. Janzen, "Biblical Theology of Hospitality," 10.
7. See Vogels, "Hospitality in Biblical Perspective," 164–69.
8. Ryken, *Dictionary of Biblical Imagery*, 403.
9. Janzen, "Biblical Theology of Hospitality," 13.
10. E.g. Bryne, *Hospitality of God*; and Mittelstadt, "Eat, Drink, and Be Merry."
11. Luke 14:15–24 picks up Isa 25:6–8 and looks forward to Rev 19:9.

called to the practice of hospitality for the sake of themselves, their neighbors, and the kingdom."[12]

Hospitality continues to be addressed in the rest of the New Testament as a means of both looking after the Christian family and mission (Rom 12:13; Heb 13:1–2; 1 Pet 4:9).

Hospitality in East Africa

It is instructive to consider African hospitality here and the extent to which it coheres with New Testament hospitality. Gathogo defines African hospitality as "that extension of generosity, giving freely without strings attached."[13] The Swahili word *ukarimu* means both "hospitality" and "generosity," which shows that in much of East Africa, you cannot have the first without the second! Healey and Sybertz point out, "Hospitality is a very important cultural and social value in African society . . . The host will drop everything for the visitor and provide for their needs to ensure their visit is as pleasant as possible."[14] Guests are always joyfully received, being seen as a blessing, as shown by the oft-quoted Swahili proverb, "Guest come, so that the host recovers."[15] The interpretation of this proverb is multifaceted, including (1) receiving the gifts the guest may bring, (2) hearing the heartwarming news of the guest, (3) enjoying with the guest the chance to eat a more lavish meal than normal, and (4) putting aside differences with family members or neighbors to receive the guest together. In this way, the unexpected guest is never an inconvenience but is always warmly received, not just by the individual but also by the community. Among Christians, hospitality is also viewed as an aid to mission, as it shows kindness and provides the opportunity for dialogue.[16]

In preparing this paper, a survey was undertaken among East African people to understand the practice of hospitality in East Africa, both in traditional categories and as a changing concept, and to appreciate how this hospitality interfaces with Luke 11:5–8. Answers from the respondents revealed the following trends:[17]

- the joy of receiving visitors;

---

12. Mittelstadt, "Eat, Drink, and Be Merry," 131.
13. Gathogo, "African Hospitality," 23.
14. Healey and Sybertz, *Towards an African Narrative Theology*, 168–70.
15. *Mgeni njoo, mwenyegi apone* is the proverb in Swahili.
16. Healey and Sybertz, *Towards an African Narrative Theology*, 191–93.
17. The first four points agree closely with biblical hospitality.

- the importance of generosity to guests at the hosts' expense;
- the communal nature of hospitality;
- the shame or loss of standing in the community if they fail to host properly or to assist neighbors or family members who are hosting guests;
- that these values of hospitality are beginning to be lost in the twenty-first century, particularly through the influence of Western culture and capitalism.

Several respondents noted explicitly how African village culture opens the door to understanding this parable. One said, "My culture helps me understand the passage clearly. Jesus gave an African example to teach hospitality." Another commented, "This passage is well understood by any East African because it really depicts how people lived, and are living, on this side of the world. The common culture is 'sharing' since the days of primitive communalism, and it has been passed on to generation after generation."

It is therefore apparent that the cultural practices of hospitality in the New Testament and traditionally in Africa are extremely similar, and differ from Western approaches to hospitality.[18] It is now time to approach Luke 11 with biblical and African eyes.

Luke 11:1–13: Jesus as Revealer of the Father as Lavish Host
Literary Context of Luke 11:1–13

It is helpful to set our passage, 11:1–13, in the context of Jesus's unfolding ministry and the story Luke is seeking to tell. Luke opens his gospel by revealing that he is writing an orderly "account of the things that have been fulfilled among us" (cf. 1:1–4), namely, the good news of salvation which has come through the life, death and resurrection of Jesus. He begins his story by setting the context to Jesus's birth, leading into Jesus's birth itself and childhood (1:5 – 2:52). Jesus's identity comes to the fore, and though he is given several titles ("Lord," "Davidic Messiah," "Savior of all"), it is his designation as "God's Son" or "Son of the Most High" that is most significant and draws the other titles together under it. Indeed, Luke is interested in displaying through his story Jesus as God's Son and what this means for us, especially in his reign on David's throne over an enduring kingdom (1:31–37). At Jesus's birth, set within an imperial framework, Luke reveals that God has broken through; it is good news

---

18. See Gathogo, "African Hospitality," 23–53; Huffard, "Parable of the Friend at Midnight."

for all: a new era is coming (2:1–32). Next, he shows Jesus's progress as a boy in the temple, where Jesus reveals who his true Father is (2:41–52).

Luke moves on to describe the preparation for Jesus's ministry (3:1 – 4:13). He narrates Jesus's baptism by John (3:21–22) and then Jesus's testing in the wilderness by Satan (4:1–13). Both of these accounts develop the theme of Jesus as God's Son. First, a voice comes from heaven: "You are my Son, whom I love; with you I am well pleased" (3:22). As the Son, he is uniquely placed to carry out the Father's desire – but before embarking on it Jesus is praying (3:21).[19] And second, like Israel after coming through the Red Sea, so Jesus, after his baptism in the River Jordan, is also led into the desert. There he is tempted by the devil, who tries to incite him to exploit his being God's Son. Here Jesus is reliving Israel's story; but unlike Israel ("God's Son," Exod 4:22) when they were tested in the desert, Jesus does not give in to the devil's tests.

The author then describes Jesus's Galilean ministry (4:14 – 9:50). This begins with Jesus, having defeated the devil and emerging as the true and tested Son of God, returning to Galilee in the power of the Spirit. The stage is set, and the question is now, "As Son of God, what will Jesus do?"[20] Immediately this is answered as Jesus launches his kingdom manifesto, with a New Exodus, promising good news to the poor and oppressed, to liberate them and set a new order in place (4:14–30; cf. Isa 61:1–2). The astonished response is, "Isn't this Joseph's son?" (4:22b). But no, that is not who he is (4:41), and his ministry will go beyond the borders of Israel. Jesus then begins his Father's kingdom ministry in word and deed, often checking in to pray to the Father (5:16; 6:12; 9:18, 28–29; 10:21–24; 11:1; 22:32, 41–44; 23:34, 46), showing that Sonship for him means close partnership with his Father in carrying out the Father's mission. It is a ministry showing Jesus's profound relationship with the Father by virtue of his powerful authority over creation (8:22–25), sickness (5:17–26; 8:26–48) and death (7:11–17; 8:49–56), as well as his compassion (7:36–50) and hospitality in miraculous feeding (9:10–17). Within this section, Jesus begins to refer to himself as "the Son of Man" (e.g. 5:24; 6:5; 7:34; 9:22) in a way which Luke never interprets. While scholars debate the meaning of this phrase, it likely is drawn from Daniel 7:13–14.[21] And this, for our purposes, particularly emphasizes Jesus's humanity, in which he is represented as the New

---

19. This is followed by Jesus's genealogy, where Luke reveals, "He was the son, *so it was thought*, of Joseph" (3:23) and the representative of all humanity as "the son of Adam, the son of God" (3:38).

20. Green, *Gospel of Luke*, 207.

21. In Daniel 7, "one like a son of man" is given authority to inflict total defeat on evil, will be vindicated, and will thus receive an everlasting kingdom.

Adam (cf. 3:38) and shows his solidarity with people, including suffering for them.[22] Naturally, in view of his great deeds, the issue of his identity surfaces, and Jesus asks, "Who do the crowds say I am?" Even as Peter gives his answer, "God's Messiah," Jesus refines the disciples' understanding of messiahship as including suffering and death (9:18–27). As Jesus is transfigured in the midst of prayer, a voice comes from the cloud, disclosing, "This is my Son, whom I have chosen; listen to him" (9:35), affirming Jesus's identity and unique ability to speak God's authoritative word.

To complete his ministry for all people, Jesus must go to Jerusalem, and Luke recounts this journey in 9:51 – 19:27. In the midst of growing opposition (11:14–54; 13:10–35), Jesus reveals the nature of his messiahship and forthcoming suffering, and teaches what it means to be his disciples and follow him (9:57 – 11:13; 12:1 – 13:9). Jesus sends out the disciples for mission (10:1–16) and emphasizes that the ethics of the kingdom are essentially being in right relationship with God and one's neighbor, which includes the hospitality of helping those in need (10:25–37). The hospitality theme continues with Jesus at the home of Martha and Mary (10:38–42). Mary gives the hospitality Jesus is looking for by attending to him fully, as she sits at his feet, listening to and learning from him (cf. 9:35), which the disciples will do in the next scene on prayer (11:1–13).

Exegesis of Luke 11:1–13

This passage is sometimes not treated as a unit, possibly in part because sections are found in different locations in Matthew's gospel.[23] But it seems clear Luke has shaped this material into a unified whole. First, there is no break between verse 4 and verse 5, and verses 1–4 and 5–8 are also linked by "bread" (vv. 3 and 5). Second, verse 9 begins, "So I say to you," as Jesus applies the parable (vv. 5–8) to his hearers (vv. 9–10). Third, the two stories of verses 5–8 and 11–12 both begin similarly with "Suppose you . . ." and "Which of you . . ." (vv. 5 and 11). And fourth, verse 13, as the final application, begins with, "If you *then*." Thus, the structure of the passage is as follows:

    11:1–4: Jesus teaches the Disciples' Prayer

---

22. Cf. Hallig, "Eating Motif and Luke's Characterization," 203–18.

23. Vv. 1–4 are found in Matt 6:9–13 and vv. 9–13 in Matt 7:7–11. Matthew's setting is within a sermon, whereas Luke's is within Jesus's journey to Jerusalem. Luke's form is slightly different and shorter.

11:5–8: Jesus's first story about how the one who is asked will give to preserve his honor

11:9–10: Jesus applies the first story to how the Father will give to those who ask

11:11–12: Jesus's second story about how fathers give what their sons ask for

11:13: Jesus applies the second story to how much more the Father will give the Holy Spirit to those who ask

Jesus Opens His Extraordinary Relationship with the Father to His Disciples (11:1–4)

And it was while he was praying in a certain place, as he stopped, one of his disciples said to him, "Lord, teach us to pray, as also John taught his disciples." And he said to them, "When(ever) you pray, say, 'Father, let your name be honored as holy, let your kingdom come, give us each day our daily bread, and forgive us our sins, for we also forgive everyone indebted to us, and do not lead us into temptation.'"[24]

The passage opens with Jesus praying – his regular practice (cf. 5:16; 9:18). Prayer was central to the Jews. And the disciples have been around prayer their whole lives, but as they watch Jesus pray, they are stunned! "No one prays the way he does. It's as if we don't even know how to pray." They have seen that, as Son, he alone enjoys intimacy in prayer with the Father and has the ability to reveal the Father to them (10:22).

And so their request is, "Lord, teach us to pray!" Jesus responds by giving them a distinctive prayer as John the Baptist may have given his disciples.[25] He begins, "When[ever] you [plural] pray, say" – meaning that this prayer should be their custom, practice and pattern, corporately as well as personally. Jesus, as Son, simply opens with "Father!"[26] The profundity of this should not be missed! No prayer in the Old Testament starts this way.[27] Jesus opens up to us

---

24. Own translation.

25. But as Green, *Gospel of Luke*, 446, says, "[Luke] is not so much concerned with the technology of prayer as he is with the shaping of prayer in relation to an accurate recognition of the one to whom prayer is offered."

26. This is even more direct than Matthew's "Our Father in heaven" (Matt 6:9).

27. The notion of the Lord as Israel's Father is, however, appreciated in the OT (e.g. Isa 63:16).

his relationship with God *as Father*.[28] There is no need to jump through hoops or clear the ground in prayer – the way is open for us to the Father, access surpassing that offered through the temple. As Son, Jesus is completely one with the Father, fully submitting to the will of his Father, and fully revealing the Father to humanity. In that culture, although a father has authority, he also "is bound by love and loyalty to his family."[29] In Jesus's great revelation of God *as Father*, there is also the further revelation that those who pray this prayer *are sons*. So, in addressing God as Father, the disciples are positioning themselves as sons, as obedient sons, ready to do the Father's will. The stanzas that follow implicitly involve them, calling them to align themselves to the Father and his work, as Wright sets out:

> It is a prayer for people who are following Jesus on the kingdom-journey. Jesus was on the way to Jerusalem, to act on behalf of God's name, which has been dragged in the mud as his people had turned away from him in rebellion. He was on the way to accomplish the "Exodus" in which the long-awaited kingdom of God would become a reality. He had provided bread for the journey, and "the breaking of bread" was to become a sign of his presence in the church, and the bond between his followers. He was already offering forgiveness, and would accomplish it completely in his death – and he was already demanding from his followers that they imitate the graciousness of their God in forgiving their enemies, let alone each other . . . [and] he was waging war against the powers of evil, a war that would reach its decisive battle on Calvary. This is a prayer that grows out of the mission of Jesus himself.[30]

Indeed, the whole prayer is a prayer for the implementation of Jesus's complete kingdom agenda (1:32–33; 4:18–19). Luke, writing to Gentiles, wants them to see the eschatological framework of the kingdom. After addressing God as "Father," the disciples are now instructed to pray for God's name to be honored and his kingdom to come – two requests that are intrinsically connected. It is possible with the first request that Ezekiel 36 stands in the background, where God, whose name had been profaned by

---

28. "Father" is the very word Jesus himself used to address his prayer to God in 10:21–22 (cf. also 22:42; 23:34, 46). What the Father is like will be unfolded in this passage.
29. Tannehill, *Luke*, 188.
30. Wright, *Luke for Everyone*, 133.

Israel's disobedience (vv. 22–23), promises to bring a great reversal for Israel and make the land fertile like the garden of Eden (vv. 24–36), thus restoring his honor. The second clause, "your kingdom come," completes that thought, urging God to reign for his people in the world, while also looking ahead to the consummation of that reign.

Having begun by setting the attention of his disciples firmly on God, his honor and his kingdom, Jesus now instructs his disciples to ask the Father to meet their needs, so as to be able to live out his kingdom mission as good sons.[31] He starts with "Give[32] us each day our daily[33] bread." Bread was a staple food in that culture, much like ugali in East Africa today. The Swahili translations, in place of "bread," use the word *riziki*, meaning "daily needs," which captures the heart of Jesus's intention. "Bread"[34] also picks up God's provision for Israel in the wilderness through "bread from heaven" (Exod 16:4), a provision which Jesus has already demonstrated is still available in his feeding of the five thousand (Luke 9:10–17). Jesus announced in Nazareth in Luke 4 that liberation was to be a significant theme of his ministry, and now he urges his followers to ask God to extend it in their lives by the forgiveness of sins, as they themselves extend that liberation to others by releasing them from the debts they have.

The last petition is for the Father not to "lead us into temptation" (v. 4), possibly meaning "not to allow us to succumb to temptation." Israel faced many temptations and tests in the wilderness, which they failed, causing them as a whole to miss out on the promised land. And Jesus, as he journeys to Jerusalem, is experiencing much opposition, an opposition which is designed to throw him off course and miss the Father's will. But as the Son, he has been praying and submitting to this will (4:18–19), and will do so again in Gethsemane. And so Jesus, knowing his followers will also face a tough journey ahead, instructs them to pray that the Father might cause them to avoid such testing.

But having prayed this prayer, how do we know if the Father will answer us? To answer this, we need to turn to the parable of the friend at midnight.

---

31. Jesus has been modeling this dependency on God, and now he describes this to the disciples.

32. In comparing Luke's version of the Disciples' Prayer with Matthew's, the words used are generally identical (except for Matthew's extra words). However, in this petition, Luke has *didou* ("give," present tense) instead of Matthew's *dos* ("give," aorist tense), so as to foreground the asking for basic needs which is carried through in vv. 5–8 and 9–13.

33. There is some doubt over the meaning of *epiousios*. Does it mean "bread for today," "bread for the coming day," or "bread for subsistence" (see Tannehill, *Luke*, 188)? Whichever is selected, the meaning is essentially the same – our request for God to supply us with what we need, which is basic for life, either physical or spiritual bread.

34. *Artos* can mean "bread" or "food."

The Friend at Midnight Parable (11:5–8)

> And he said to them, "Which one of you has a friend and goes to him at midnight and should say to him, 'Friend, lend me three loaves of bread, because a friend of mine has arrived from a journey to me and I have nothing to set before him.' And that one inside answering should say, 'Do not give me trouble, the door has already been locked and my children are with me in bed. I am not able to get up to give you [anything].' I say to you, even if he will not get up and give to him because he is his friend, yet because of his *anaideia* he will get up and give him as much as he needs."[35]

Jesus tells this parable in which a person experiences the surprise visit of a friend[36] at midnight and has no food to set before him, so goes to a friendly neighbor to solicit help in the form of three loaves of bread. Vital for understanding this story is the ancient Near Eastern village context where the family is already locked inside their most likely one-room house sharing a mat together on the floor, something which is still common in African villages today. So, for the father to get up would be a major upheaval for the whole family, who would likely be woken up. Therefore, the one inside the house refuses his friend. But Jesus has begun the story with, "Which one of you has a friend" who will refuse to help? The hearers would all cry, "None of us!" Everyone knows the parable is preposterous. No friend, especially in that culture, would fail in such a duty (see the hospitality survey above). Jesus knows that as he gives his interpretation (v. 8): "*even if* he will not get up and give to him because he is his friend" – most likely friendship will be sufficient, but if it is not – "because of his *anaideia* he will get up and give him as much as he needs."

The key question is, what is the meaning of *anaideia* (v. 8)? Is it "persistence" (NASB, NRSV, NLT, Swahili Union and Neno Versions), "boldness"[37] (KJV, ESV, NIV) or "avoidance of shame"[38] (NIV margin, NLT margin, NASB margin)? It is complicated in that *anaideia* appears only here in the New Testament. Bailey and Johnson examined its usage in ancient Greek literature

---

35. Own translation.

36. "Friend" is mentioned four times in vv. 5–8, highlighting relational connections between the characters which would be expected to yield the desired result.

37. There are nuances to this, such as "importunity" and "audacity." Some translations even try to bring the second and third meanings together with "shameless persistence."

38. This is translated variously as "yet to preserve his good name," "to avoid shame" or "so his reputation will not be damaged," but the meanings are similar.

and found that nowhere does it mean "persistence" but instead it always means "shamelessness."[39] Before considering how this meaning works out in our passage, there is a further issue to consider. Does the pronoun (in "*his* shamelessness") refer to the sleeper inside the house or the petitioner outside? Bailey, in his analysis, shows the verse can be set out as follows:[40]

> even if he will give to him
> > having got up
> > > because of being his friend,
> > > yet because of his *anaideia*
> > getting up
> he will give him as much as he needs.

In this way, "his *anaideia*" parallels "his friend," and in both cases the pronoun most likely refers to the sleeper inside.[41] So what does "his shamelessness" actually signify in the passage? Bailey, Green and Johnson all argue persuasively that the householder will not be judged as shameless but will act "to avoid shame,"[42] and to preserve his good name, by granting his friend's request. And he will not simply give the three loaves requested; rather, he will give *as much as he needs*, which in the village context heightens the generosity.

This fits with the cultures of hospitality surveyed above. If the householder were to refuse, it would be all over this closely knit peasant village by morning, and his name would be shamed, and not just his reputation but the reputation of the whole village would be damaged. Respondents noted that this connects well with East African village culture, with one asserting, "Shame is a big thing in this culture. People are more scared of shame than sin. You would rather avoid shame than say 'No' to the neighbor. You would prefer to keep a good name than have people speak ill of you." Another respondent said, "The first one expects his neighbor to cover his shame of having nothing to give the guest," and if he refuses, he will be shamed by the community and considered

---

39. Bailey, *Poet and Peasant*, 119–41; and Johnson, "Assurance for Man," 123–31.

40. Bailey, 128; Johnson, 129.

41. So also Johnson, 129. But see Snodgrass, "*Anaideia* and the Friend at Midnight," 505–13, for the alternative view.

42. See Bailey, *Poet and Peasant*, 131–32; Johnson, "Assurance for Man," 130–31; and Green, *Gospel of Luke*, 446–48. Walter Bauer lists the option as meaning the sleeper "does not wish to lose face by shameless disregard of conventions concerning hospitality" (Arndt, Danker and Bauer, *Greek-English Lexicon*). The "boldness" option arises only if "shamelessness" is applied to the host.

cruel. Thus, taking lexical, literary and cultural concerns together, "avoiding shame" is the most likely reason for the sleeper to help.

Jesus's purpose is to apply this to the Father[43] to reveal his nature: he will always act to preserve the honor of his name (cf. "hallowed," 11:2). Of course, the Father is not like the grumpy sleeper, but even if he were, he would still act. He does not want it known that one of his children came to him at midnight and he refused to help! This connects with African notions of fathers as providers, *and* transcends them with God displayed as the unique Father.

Jesus Shows That Knowing the Father Enables Powerful Prayer (11:9–13)

> So I say to you, ask, and it will be given to you, seek, and you will find, knock, and it will be opened to you. For everyone who asks receives, and the one who seeks finds, and to the one who knocks it will be opened.
>
> And which one of you fathers [if your] son asks for a fish, instead of a fish will give him a snake? And if he asks for an egg, will give him a scorpion?
>
> If then you, although being evil, know how to give good gifts to your children, how much more will the Father in heaven give the Holy Spirit to those who ask him![44]

Jesus turns to apply the parable to his disciples (vv. 9–13) with his "So I say to you: Ask and it will be given to you . . ." He works from the lesser to the greater: what is true of human beings (vv. 5–8) will be ever truer of God (vv. 9–10). The Father will not just lend us three loaves of bread; he will give us as much as we need. So Jesus implores that we ask, we seek and we knock (v. 9), for he says God will answer us, he will cause us to find and he will open the door to us. We can have complete confidence in God and be *liberated* to ask!

Many commentators emphasize the present tense of these verbs, "ask," "seek," "knock," as urging ongoing action, as in "keep on asking."[45] But the present tense in Greek does not necessitate continuous action. Rather, it is the context that determines whether continuous action is in view or not. It seems it is not. Quite the opposite: the Father does not need to be nagged in order to

---

43. Green, *Gospel of Luke*, 449, notes that "'father' is a synonym for 'lord of the house,'" showing the close association between the Father and the householder in the parable.

44. Own translation.

45. The parable of the persistent widow (Luke 18:1–8) does urge ongoing prayer, but Jesus's point there should not be simply assumed to be his point here. And even there, Jesus says, "Will [God] keep putting them off? I tell you, he will see that they get justice, and quickly."

answer! The emphasis falls on the simplicity of prayer, as in "Ask and it will be given to you." This, Jesus reveals, is the nature of the Father. The whole passage accents the nature of the Father, rather than the effort of the disciples in prayer. And to insist on continuous action would seem to undercut the whole purpose of the parable (vv. 5–8) where avoidance of shame, rather than persistence, was the cause of the sleeper's assistance.

To bring to his hearers greater assurance of the Father's willingness to answer, Jesus uses another illustration (vv. 11–12) of how earthly fathers respond to their children. "Which of you fathers, if your son asks for a fish, will give him a snake instead? Or if he asks for an egg, will give him a scorpion?" All his hearers would exclaim, "None!" No earthly father would refuse his son's request for something wholesome and give him something harmful instead! Jesus again moves from the lesser (human fathers) to the greater (God), whose goodness and ability to give gifts far exceeds theirs, by his saying "how much more will your Father in heaven give the Holy Spirit to those who ask him!" Jesus springs a surprise by identifying the Father's good gift with the Holy Spirit. The gift of the Holy Spirit is a key emphasis in Luke–Acts and the cause of the disciples' ability to carry out their mission in the world. And in "both Luke–Acts and Paul's letters, the experience of a new, closer relationship to God through the Spirit lies behind this connection between the Spirit and God as Father."[46]

Encapsulating Jesus's Revelation in Luke 11:1–13

Taken as a whole, this passage shows Jesus revealing God as the *hospitable, good, dependable* and *willing* Father. He absolutely will grant what his children ask from him and will therefore maintain his name. As one respondent to the survey said, "The passage shows to Africans that Jesus is the *perfect bridge* to the Father." Is this not the *Son of God* and *Son of Man* in unison? Pray-ers can be assured that Jesus is bringing them into his relationship with such a God and Father. The three sections of the passage are all intrinsically linked by the requests for basic needs – "bread" (11:3), "bread" (11:5), and "fish," "egg" and "the Holy Spirit" (11:11–13). Therefore, Jesus's emphasis here, and in light of his kingdom mission, is for the disciples to know the Father so as to ask him to give them what they need to be hospitable to a hurting world (cf. "You give them something to eat," 9:13). Jesus is on the way to Jerusalem to establish God's kingdom through his death, to act on behalf of God's name. He calls us to join him on this difficult journey, knowing the Father will provide what we

---

46. Tannehill, *Luke*, 191. Cf. also Rom 8:15–16; Gal 4:6.

need. All we need do is ask! And most of all, he will provide the Holy Spirit, God's very own empowering presence.

The Rest of Luke after This Exposition on Prayer

After this passage, Jesus continues his journey to Jerusalem, fulfilling his mission by working out this prayer (11:1–4) in healing people along the way (e.g. 11:14; 14:1–6; 17:11–19; 18:35–43), but also amid opposition and challenging the crowd (e.g. 11:14–54) while continuing to prepare his disciples, especially to trust in God and truly be his disciples in light of persecution and the future (12:1–48). Finally, Luke describes Jesus reaching Jerusalem and teaching in the temple, which is supposed to be "a house of prayer for all nations" (19:28 – 21:38). This is followed by the events of Jesus's passion (22:1 – 23:56) – the ultimate hospitality – whereby the kingdom of God is established (cf. 11:2) and the way to the Father is opened for all (23:45; cf. 10:22; 11:2). After Jesus's resurrection, the disciples are commissioned to preach repentance and forgiveness in Jesus's name to all nations, after waiting for the promise of the Holy Spirit (24:1–53; cf. 11:13).

Summing up Luke 11:1–13 in an East African Perspective

Jesus's revelation of the Father in this passage has great potential for Africans in prayer if it is understood in light of East African cultures. Like New Testament culture, East African cultures are based on honor–shame, and it is such a culture that underpins the ultimate reason why the sleeper in the parable will enable the person to be hospitable. The desire to avoid shame is prevalent and causes Africans to fix what needs to be fixed, even at extreme personal cost. God the Father, Jesus discloses, is like them, and this should inspire them to be bold in prayer.

Second, the revelation of God as Father has the power to transform prayer. As Mburu says, Africans often have a transactional attitude to God, in which they understand him to reward the good things they do.[47] This, of course, has allowed the prosperity gospel to flourish in Africa. But Jesus invites us into a Father–child relationship, where we can have assurance of God's goodness and readiness to help us as his children. As we understand God's nature as Father and ours as his children, this will change our praying.

Third, while Jesus urges us to ask God knowing that he will not refuse us, we must, as one respondent noted, appreciate that this comes within the context

---

47. Mburu, *African Hermeneutics*, 29.

of his kingdom agenda in Luke's gospel. Unfortunately, many people, including in Africa, frequently cut verses 9–13 loose from their context, believing with certainty that God will give them the selfish things they request. There can be no certainty in this case! But Jesus himself frames our requests by our first praying for God's name to be sanctified and his kingdom to come. By appreciating this, we will selflessly ask God boldly for what honors him and advances his kingdom. This is what we see Jesus modeling in prayer in Luke. As we follow Jesus the Son, we will grow in our relationship as sons and daughters with our Father, and our requests will be attuned to his will. God is a Father who loves to give his children what they ask for. How better can God's name be honored, and how better can his kingdom come, than when he can give us what we ask so others experience his blessing, or when he is able to forgive us or help us when we are in the midst of temptation?

Fourth, we must see *mission* and *hospitality* as running through this section on prayer. Indeed, this gospel shows that salvation is available to all people – Gentiles, women, prostitutes, sinners and tax collectors, the poor, the outcasts, the marginalized: "the disciples are called to be at the heart of the *missio Dei*, the mission of God. But how are we to live and participate effectively in God's mission? A major answer provided by Luke is through prayer."[48] Prayer changes our agenda, ability and desire to participate in God's mission. In particular, God's mission impacts our hospitality. It was noted above that African Christians have traditionally seen hospitality as an aid to mission. Hospitality has been a great strength of East Africans, and there is an opportunity to recover this for the mission of God and to enlarge our approach to this mission. So where do we need to be hospitable, to whom do we reach out, and what are we omitting to do? Let us ask our Father, who gives generously. He is hospitable, and we are to be like him.

And fifth, can Africans see the link between the gift of the Holy Spirit and the need to extend kindness to others? As we receive the Holy Spirit, we will be empowered to share in Jesus's mission of seeing his transforming love reach others. God will not send us out without supplying us with what we need, with the Spirit as our main resource. So let us be bold in our asking.

So, in response to "Who do you say I am?," Jesus, in this passage, implicitly answers this question as "I am the Revealer of the unique, generous and honorable Father who grants his children what they request so they can participate in the mission he has given me, a mission that experiences opposition but will go to every people group in Africa and in the world."

---

48. Bartholomew, *Revealing the Heart of Prayer*, Kindle loc. 320.

Bibliography

Arndt, William F., Frederick W. Danker and Walter Bauer, eds. *Greek–English Lexicon of the New Testament and Other Early Christian Literature*. 3rd ed. Chicago: University of Chicago Press, 2001; BibleWorks v.8.

Bailey, Kenneth. *Poet and Peasant: A Literary-Cultural Approach to the Parables in Luke*. Grand Rapids: Eerdmans, 1976.

Bartholomew, Craig G. *Revealing the Heart of Prayer: The Gospel of Luke*. Bellingham: Lexham, 2016.

Bird, Michael F. *Evangelical Theology: A Biblical and Systematic Introduction*. Grand Rapids: Zondervan Academic, 2013.

Bryne, Brendan. *The Hospitality of God: A Reading of Luke's Gospel*. Collegeville: Liturgical, 2000.

Gathogo, Julius Mutugi. "African Hospitality: Is It Compatible with the Ideal Christ's Hospitality?" *Swedish Missiological Themes* 94, no. 1 (2006): 23–53.

Green, Joel B. *The Gospel of Luke*. NICNT. Grand Rapids: Eerdmans, 1997.

Hallig, Jason Valeriano. "The Eating Motif and Luke's Characterization of Jesus as the Son of Man." *Bibliotheca Sacra* 173 (April–June 2016): 203–18.

Healey, Joseph, and Donald Sybertz. *Towards an African Narrative Theology*. Maryknoll: Orbis, 1996.

Huffard, Evertt W. "The Parable of the Friend at Midnight: God's Honor or Man's Persistence?" *Restoration Quarterly* 21 (1978): 154–60.

Janzen, Waldemar. "Biblical Theology of Hospitality." *Vision* (Spring 2002): 4–15.

Johnson, Alan F. "Assurance for Man: The Fallacy of Translating *Anaideia* by 'Persistence' in Luke 11:5–8." *Journal of the Evangelical Theological Society* 22, no. 2 (June 1979): 123–31.

Kunhiyop, Samuel Waje. *African Christian Theology*. Grand Rapids: Zondervan Academic, 2012.

Mburu, Elizabeth. *African Hermeneutics*. Carlisle: Hippo, 2019.

Mittelstadt, Martin William. "Eat, Drink, and Be Merry: A Theology of Hospitality in Luke–Acts." *Word & World* 34, no. 2 (Spring 2014): 131–39.

Nguyen, Van Thanh. "An Asian View of Biblical Hospitality (Luke 11:5–8)." *Biblical Research* 53 (2008): 25–39.

Ryken, Leland, ed. *Dictionary of Biblical Imagery*. Downers Grove: InterVarsity Press, 1998.

Snodgrass, Klyne. "*Anaideia* and the Friend at Midnight (Luke 11:8)." *Journal of Biblical Literature* 116, no. 3 (Fall 1997): 505–13.

Tannehill, Robert C. *Luke*. Abingdon New Testament Commentary. Nashville: Abingdon Press, 2011.

Vogels, Walter A. "Hospitality in Biblical Perspective." *Liturgical Ministry* 11 (Fall 2002): 161–73.

Wright, N. T. *Luke for Everyone*. London: SPCK, 2001.

3

Embracing Hybridity in Imaging Christ for Egalitarian Church Leadership through a Rereading of John 4:1–42

Lydia Chemei

PhD Student and Adjunct Lecturer at St. Paul's University, Kenya

Abstract

This paper makes use of the African women's hermeneutical framework to reread John 4:1–42 toward imaging Christ as the egalitarian leader. The dominant analyses of this text have rightly celebrated Jesus as a standard of inclusivity since he breaks down gender, cultural, ethnic, social and even religious barriers in his interaction with the nameless woman of Samaria. However, despite this posture exemplified by Jesus, there is not enough to celebrate in terms of practical replication of this inclusivity within church leadership in Africa. This could be attributed to a reliance on Eurocentric approaches in the analysis of the Christology of John's gospel. Such approaches are not only foreign but also fail to engage African realities in a way that is relevant and intelligible to Africans. In his lengthy discourse with the woman of Samaria, Jesus Christ emerges as the inclusive one, the nonjudgmental one, the teacher and the nurturer. Using the concept of hybridity, these qualities are mainstreamed in imaging Christ as the egalitarian leader to formulate an African Christology that addresses the need for egalitarian leaders who model authentic servanthood as Christ did. Consequently, Christ's egalitarian model of leadership is underscored as a yardstick for enhancing egalitarian church leadership that is rooted in servanthood in the African context.

Key words: Christology, Christ, John, African, hybridity, church, egalitarian, Eurocentric

Introduction

African Christians cherish their belief in Christ. For many African Christians, Christ is at the center of their daily endeavors, and their commitment to emulate his character and qualities is evident. But traditional Christology, which relies on Eurocentric approaches, presents Christ to Africans in foreign categories. As a result, traditional christological titles do not adequately resonate with Africans and the varied contextual issues they face, leading to a disparity in their actual emulation of Christ's qualities. This paper contributes to African Christology by offering a rereading of John 4:1–42 centered on Christ's egalitarian leadership qualities. The qualities of Christ which emerge in this ordinary incident at a well are mainstreamed into the Johannine christological discourse through the use of the category of hybridity to image Christ as the egalitarian leader. That the woman of Samaria encounters Christ in her ordinary endeavors reflects the case of African Christians. Their experiences of Christ are significantly shaped by how they experience him in their lived realities.

The paper first delineates the parameters of the African women's hermeneutic framework, which guides its analyses. A reflection on the portrait of Christ in the Gospel of John follows. This analysis is then used as a backdrop for rereading John 4:1–42 with the aim of fostering egalitarian church leadership in the African context. Jesus Christ, the perfect model for egalitarian leadership, is the inclusive one, the nonjudgmental one, the teacher and the nurturer. These qualities of Christ, which are relatable and comprehensible among African Christians, are highlighted as a yardstick for bridging the gap in actual emulation of Christ's leadership qualities and obediently following him.

The African Women's Hermeneutical Framework

The African women's hermeneutical framework is a reading posture instigated by African women in their biblical and theological reflections. Reading with this stance encompasses African methods and ways of theorizing in biblical and theological conversations. It endeavors to place Africa, Africans and

African realities within the interpretive framework. It aims to communicate the gospel to Africans in a manner that is intelligible and relatable. It intentionally focuses on engaging practical realities affecting African people in biblical and theological discourses. Teresa Okure elaborates on this framework's characteristics, which include the inclusivity of women and men and the use of interdisciplinary approaches in theological reflections. Okure points out that this reading posture is rooted in promoting life and embracing African cultures, particularly their communitarian and life-affirming aspects, as a basis for analyses.[1]

The dominant christological analyses of the Gospel of John, which make use of Eurocentric approaches, focus on traditional christological titles such as Word, Messiah, Son of God and Son. Eurocentric approaches are Western, and hence lead to a presentation of Christ in categories that are alien to Africans, thus creating tension in the actual emulation of Christ's qualities, and particularly in church leadership. But through the use of an analytical framework that arises from the African context and is shaped by Africans' lived realities, the potency of John 4:1–42 to contribute to christological discourses is considered through focusing on Christ's leadership qualities demonstrated in the narrative. John 4:1–42 has rightly been celebrated as a text of triumph in which Jesus breaks down various barriers in his extensive discourse with the woman of Samaria at the well. Alongside that, reading this text through an African women's hermeneutical optic demonstrates that a focus on the qualities of Jesus contributes to understanding who he is. This is achieved by using the category of hybridity to formulate a portrait of Christ that is relatable and consequential in praxis.

Various scholars have made use of this reading lens in analyzing John 4:1–42. For instance, Musa Dube has analyzed it through a decolonizing stance in which she calls attention to the effectiveness of the narrative in fostering liberating interdependence which recognizes and nurtures diversity.[2] In another rereading of the same narrative, Dube has used the storytelling method. She likens the story of the Samaritan woman to the precolonial, colonial and postcolonial story of southern African people and Africa at large. Dube uses her retelling both to show how breaking down barriers of oppression in search of liberation is an ongoing struggle, and to summon the church to responsible Christian practices that are liberating and bring dignity to all God's people.[3]

---

1. Okure, "Invitation to African Women's Hermeneutical Concerns," 48–53.
2. Dube, "Reading for Decolonization (John 4:1–42)," 51–75.
3. Dube, "John 4:1–42: The Five Husbands," 40–65.

For her part, Rose Teketi Abbey has also used the storytelling method to reread John 4:1–42.[4] Abbey places emphasis on the fact that Christ is a liberator who truly liberates the woman of Samaria by offering her living water. Consequently, she puts her in an apostolic role of going to her people and inviting them to meet Christ.[5] Teresa Okure, in her analyses of the same narrative, focuses on how Christ freed the woman of Samaria from the barriers and prejudices of culture, gender, social status and human traditions of worship.[6] Christ ultimately offered her God's free gift of salvation to all who believe, and the woman in response led her townspeople to similar freedom.[7]

The examples cited above illustrate the diversity of the African women's hermeneutic lens in biblical and theological reflections in view of the issues of concern in the African context. The nuance of this rereading will be a focus on Christ's qualities which emerge in the narrative which paint him as an egalitarian leader. The rereading is distinctively guided by recognizing the twofold nature of Jesus Christ as both divine and human. In what follows, the portrait of Christ in the Gospel of John will be gleaned as a backdrop for the rereading that will follow.

Christ in John's Gospel

A comprehensive analysis of the presentation of Jesus Christ in the gospels confirms that he is both divine and human. From the evangelists' narratives, various christological titles can be deduced. Whereas the Synoptic Gospels attest to Jesus's divinity in largely implicit language, the Gospel of John does so overtly. This is evident in the prologue of the gospel. John 1:1 starts with an introductory formula that is akin to Genesis 1:1. The reader is introduced to the "Word," who "was" in the beginning. The "Word" is further described as having been with God and as being God. The third verse gives an additional description of the Word as an agent of creation. Then in 1:14, it is related that the Word became flesh and dwelt among humanity. These descriptions highlight the divinity of Jesus Christ as the pre-existent Word, sharing the nature of God, and his real humanity, since the Word became flesh. Therefore, "Jesus, the incarnate God, is the Word and God in John's gospel."[8]

---

4. Abbey, "I Am the Woman," 23–24.
5. Abbey.
6. Okure, "Jesus and the Samaritan Woman," 401–18.
7. Okure.
8. Kithinji and Chemei, "Decolonizing and Reassembling," 89.

It is noteworthy that the christological title "the Word" is used by John only in the first chapter of his gospel. Nonetheless, it remains a significant title, as it sets the foundation for understanding the portrayal of Jesus Christ in the rest of the gospel. Donald Guthrie describes John's statements about the Word as a summary of his basic Christology, since the statements "combine the greatest possible exaltation with the humiliation of incarnation."[9] Therefore, in the rest of the gospel, where Jesus's distinctive nature is further illustrated, the initial ascription of the title "Word" is sustained. John relates seven signs that Jesus performs, and another seven "I am" statements that Jesus makes use of in reference to himself. The signs that Jesus performed were intended to spur belief that Jesus was the Christ, the Son of God (John 20:31). The "I am" statements point back to God's self-revelation to Moses in Exodus 3:14. Thus, the trajectory of Christ's portrait in the whole gospel has its basis in the initial "Word" title. In line with Christ's ultimate role of redeeming humanity, the "Word" is an all-inclusive term for his divine and human identity. It points the whole of humanity to the true foundation of its being.[10]

From a stance of holding to this understanding of Christ as both divine and human in line with the Christology of the entire Gospel of John, John 4:1–42 is reconsidered below to deduce an image of Christ that resonates with lived realities in the African context. A focus on Christ's qualities in John 4:1–42 offers a fresh perspective on the narrative. The passage is reread while considering the wider frame of John's gospel that underscores Christ's deity, informed by the Word motif.

Christ's Portrayal in John 4:1–42 through a Hybridized Optic

The concept of hybridity is used in rereading John 4:1–42, focusing on the qualities of Jesus Christ as a model for egalitarian leadership in the African context. "Hybridity" carries various meanings in scholarly usage. It is used here to refer to the option of expanding the language and titles used for Christ. In this regard, it enlarges the scope for imaging Christ beyond the customary and traditional christological titles. Hybridity creates room for naming and describing Christ in view of individuals' encounters with him, and subsequently mainstreaming such naming and descriptions in christological discourse. In this case, it incorporates a way of imaging Christ that resonates with African people and African realities in keeping with the aim of biblical

---

9. Guthrie, *New Testament Theology*, 328.
10. Nasimiyu-Wasike, "Christology and an African Woman's Experience," 129.

African Christology. Douglas W. Waruta explains that the pursuit of African Christology endeavors to "translate Jesus Christ to the tongue, style, genius, character, and cultures of African peoples."[11]

Emphasis on Jesus Christ as the pre-existent Word, which dominates analyses of the Christology of the Gospel of John, offers an ideal starting point in using the category of hybridity to image Christ. The "Word" is particularly the immanence of God. In endeavoring to make use of a hybridized space to name and image Christ as the egalitarian leader, the divinity and humanity of Christ are upheld as a necessary starting point. It is because Christ is not simply human but also divine that an encounter with him does not leave one the same. Jesus Christ is no ordinary being. He is the holy one who became flesh to accomplish redemption for all who believe in him.

In John 4:1–42, Jesus sets out on a journey from Judea to Galilee. John 4:4 says that Jesus "had to pass through Samaria" (ESV). Samuel M. Ngewa explains that two alternative routes could be used to travel from Judea to Galilee. The shorter route passed through Samaria, whereas the longer route avoided it, crossing the Jordan to bypass Samaria, then crossing back again into Galilee.[12] Jews often preferred the latter route to avoid mingling with Samaritans, whom they did not regard highly. This animosity is attested by John in his editorial comment in the second part of verse 9: "Jews have no dealings with Samaritans" (ESV). The fact that Jesus chose this route that was less popular among Jews is thus distinctive. J. Ramsey Michaels argues that Jesus's choice of the route that went through Samaria was theological. He states that Jesus's movements were dictated by his divine calling and not by circumstances. In this case, Samaria was a mission field ripe for harvest, and so Jesus had to go there and accomplish this task.[13]

Jesus Christ arrived at Sychar, a city of Samaria, about "the sixth hour." The sixth hour was equivalent to midday. Since he was weary from the journey, he sat by the well while his disciples were in the city buying food. Then a woman from Samaria came to draw water, and he initiated a conversation with her by asking her for a drink. This request was a gesture that superseded the cultural regulations that governed relations between Samaritans and Jews in the Greco-Roman setting. Nasimiyu-Wasike notes that the woman represented two suspect groups: Samaritans and women. She elaborates that these groups were suspect from a Jewish standpoint because Samaritans were enemies of the Jews

---

11. Waruta, "Who Is Jesus Christ for Africans Today?," 45.
12. Ngewa, *Gospel of John*, 65.
13. Michaels, *John*, 69.

and women were regarded as inferior and dangerous to men's chastity.[14] Jesus Christ thus surpassed popular expectations by having a public dialogue with this woman who was on the margins of society. Jesus ignored these norms and showed that his ministry was "above the boundaries set by human prejudice."[15]

By going against the norms, Jesus Christ showed that cultural and ethnic inclusivity was possible with and in him. Furthermore, by having a conversation with a woman in a public place, Jesus Christ demonstrated gender inclusivity. He was not deterred by the custom of the day, which forbade public conversation between a man and a woman, especially for him as a Jewish teacher. He therefore modeled cultural, ethnic and gender inclusivity that superseded context-specific barriers. As the inclusive one, Christ emerged as "a concrete and personal figure who engenders hope in the oppressed,"[16] particularly those subjugated by human-induced barriers and restrictions, as was the woman of Samaria.

As the conversation between Jesus Christ and the woman continued, he revealed to her the details of her life – that she had had five husbands, and presently had a sixth who was not hers – without a judgmental attitude. This revelation immediately made the woman of Samaria connect with the extraordinariness of Jesus Christ. He knew about her past and present life, yet he remained nonjudgmental. Jesus Christ overlooked who she *was* based on her lack of adequate knowledge of him, and saw her as she *would be* with adequate knowledge of him. The focus of Christ was on the potential of the woman encountering him, rather than on the details of her past and present life, which he knew well. It was Christ's inherent power that is released to human beings when they encounter him that immediately transformed the woman and made her start exploring who Jesus was.

Christ, the nonjudgmental one, modeled how a compassionate and accepting attitude opens the way for encountering him. His nonjudgmental attitude set the woman of Samaria at ease, and subsequently she was able to encounter Christ's transforming power. Instead of the woman being shunned because of her marital status and behavior, Jesus's compassion, love and kindness ushered her into God's saving grace. As a result, the woman left her water jar, and under the influence of Christ's forgiving, reassuring and life-giving power, went into the city and invited the people to "come and see" a

---

14. Nasimiyu-Wasike, "Christology and an African Woman's Experience," 128.
15. Ngewa, *Gospel of John*, 72.
16. Hinga, "Jesus Christ and the Liberation of Women," 191–92.

man who had told her all she had ever done. As she bore witness to Christ, many Samaritans of that city believed in him (John 4:39).

Christ also emerges as the ideal teacher. When he revealed to the woman of Samaria the details of her life, she first wondered whether he was a prophet since, according to popular belief, only a prophet could reveal such details without any prior familiarization. With her willingness to know more having been laid bare, Jesus taught her about the true worship of God, who is Spirit. Once again, based on her understanding, the woman attested to knowing of a coming messiah who would tell them everything. Jesus responded to her teachable demeanor and candor in sharing what she knew by asserting that he was the Messiah. By stating that she knew a messiah would come, the woman of Samaria used a Jewish term, yet Samaritans expected a *Taheb*. Beasley-Murray describes the woman of Samaria's declaration as "a faithful reflection of the Samaritan's messianic expectation of a *Taheb*, who as another Moses" was to have the responsibility of not only restoring true belief in and worship of God, but also revealing the truth.[17] In his affirmative response to the woman that he himself was the Messiah (John 4:26), Christ, the ideal teacher, proceeded to correct her misconceptions of the Messiah by teaching her through clarifying the necessary basics. In this gesture of teaching her, he committed to teaching one who would probably have been considered an unsuitable beneficiary of such teaching. Nonetheless, Christ considerately met her at her level and experience, and went ahead to teach her with tolerance.

Furthermore, Christ appeared as the ultimate nurturer. First, the silent yet overt discomfort of his disciples (John 4:27) did not deter him from nurturing the woman of Samaria, who undoubtedly was a receptive recipient of his transforming power. Christ, the perfect nurturer, entrusted the woman of Samaria with a leadership role right away: to go into the city and invite people to come and meet him. To Christ's disciples, who marveled that he was talking with the woman, he used the image of the harvest to remind them that his priority was to accomplish the mission for which he had been sent by his Father (John 4:34). After the woman of Samaria bore witness to the Samaritans and they came to him, the Samaritans implored him to stay with them, and he lingered for two days (John 4:40). Jesus's presence in Samaria for those extra days reflects a commitment to raise, nurture and grow those receptive to his saving grace. He opted to stay and be with these new converts for a little longer, rather than proceed with his journey.

---

17. Beasley-Murray, *John*, 62.

The aforementioned qualities of Christ, the egalitarian leader, demonstrate that he "meets people where they are; he respects, esteems, appreciates, understands and trusts them, and enlists their friendship."[18] The woman of Samaria was attending to the ordinary task of drawing water from the well and it was here that she encountered Jesus Christ. Her case is typical of the experience of many African Christians, who experience Christ in the common daily endeavors that characterize their lives. In fact, for them, "faith is not expressed through creedal formulations or theological statements but in a day-to-day encounter with the challenges of life. As a result, every experience is interpreted both in an earthly and spiritual way."[19] This hybridized portrait of Jesus with a focus on his qualities thus brings Christ close to Africans in comprehensible and relatable language. Also, the qualities emerging from the hybridized portrait speak directly to contemporary leadership concerns within the church in Africa. Zablon Nthamburi rightly argues that Christology in Africa is meaningful only when it is translated to the contextual situations that characterize the daily lives of Africans.[20] Therefore, Christ, the egalitarian leader, summons church leaders in Africa to reconsider the character of their leadership in view of what he models for them to emulate.

Christ, the egalitarian leader, is further relatable to African Christians since he demonstrates that all human beings are valuable, and their dignity must be upheld. In a continent where divisions based on ethnicity, social status, gender and age, among other factors, are still witnessed and practiced, Christ enlivens hope for equity based on his saving grace that he offers freely to all who believe in him. For the underprivileged and exploited, Christ, the egalitarian leader, offers hope by challenging the leadership to care for those they lead as Christ would. Equally, Christ liberates the led to hold their leaders accountable as they all ultimately look up to his perfect model of egalitarianism. Joseph Galgalo observes that when the oppressed and disempowered encounter Jesus, "they find a powerful ally who fills them with hope."[21] They find in Jesus a leader who ushers them into their authentic destiny of definitive victory and liberation.[22] Therefore, Christ, the egalitarian leader, is a close friend who is meaningfully intelligible to African Christians. Through his qualities, he sets an example

---

18. Nasimiyu-Wasike, "Imaging Jesus Christ," 110.
19. Waruta, "Who Is Jesus Christ for Africans Today?," 45.
20. Nthamburi, "Christ as Seen by an African," 57.
21. Galgalo, *African Christianity*, 79.
22. Galgalo.

that can be practically emulated in view of the various contextual issues of concern to African Christians.

Toward Egalitarian Church Leadership in Africa

The portrait of Christ above, crafted through hybridizing the approaches of imaging Christ by focusing on his qualities, offers new scope for Africans to emulate Christ in familiar categories toward egalitarian church leadership. The church in Africa needs leaders who will usher it into egalitarianism. Egalitarianism is rooted in the inclusivity of women and men, forgiveness and trust, and also a commitment to teach and mentor others to lead. The leader is Christ, the only authentic model of egalitarianism. In emulating Jesus Christ, the church in Africa is summoned to embrace Christ-driven transformation that ultimately will yield leadership akin to that modeled by him. An important foundational aspect of imitating Christ with regard to egalitarian leadership is the need for church leaders in Africa to exude servant leadership. This is the recognition that leadership is a call to serve God and God's people with humility and integrity, rather than being a license to dominate and control. Church leaders in Africa must exercise power "in a spirit of service, simplicity, humility and compassion."[23]

Christ, the egalitarian leader, used his power and influence as a leader to demonstrate inclusivity, to forgive and affirm, and also to teach and mentor, without discrimination. One challenge facing African leaders is the inclination to follow Western models of leadership that are not intentionally structured toward servant leadership. Douglas W. Waruta observes, "The western models of Christian leadership – whether bishops, priests or moderators in church leadership – have been grossly tainted by their authoritarianism, pomposity and lack of a servant spirit demonstrated by Jesus."[24] For this reason, embracing servant leadership, by understanding that leadership is a God-given responsibility that positions leaders to be accountable first and foremost to God, remains indispensable. Once church leaders possess a servant spirit in their leadership, they will then display the necessary predisposition that facilitates emulating Christ as the egalitarian leader.

Church leaders in Africa will consequently need to practice inclusivity as modeled by Jesus. This will entail eradicating all forms of discrimination by reconsidering the means used to decide who qualifies to be a leader and who

---

23. Kanyandago, "Biblical Reflection," 117.
24. Waruta, "Who Is Jesus Christ for Africans Today?," 52.

does not. It means growing leadership that is inclusive of all God's people without discrimination, as Jesus did. This will be a leadership that incorporates persons with disabilities, young people, women and men for the African context. Such inclusivity follows an acknowledgment that it is God who gifts leaders with the potential and capacity to lead. Such consideration will set the ground for emulating Christ by embracing leadership inclinations that recognize and affirm that God calls his children as he pleases and gives them the ability to lead.

In addition, it entails embracing leadership that is intentionally attuned to biblical gender equity, that is, consciousness of the fact that "women and men can serve side by side, utilizing the gifts God has given them in the fear of our Lord Jesus Christ."[25] Such consciousness is an affirmation of the value of every member of the body of Christ. Biblical gender equity is a subject that has attracted much attention in the church, with the core dilemma being whether women ought to be fully included in church leadership. Some churches in Africa have had a tradition of excluding women from church leadership based on a selective application of the so-called gender-biased Pauline texts. However, a careful study of Pauline texts reveals that Paul affirmed women's ministry by acknowledging several female colleagues with whom he served (Rom 16) and in his declaration in Galatians 3:28 that all humanity is one in Christ. The example of the Samaritan woman is another example affirming that women, too, are called to participate in leadership within Christian circles. For this reason, "the African churches ought to appropriate the theme of inclusivity and create a new social reality that replaces gender prejudice with gender equity."[26]

In addition, for church leaders in Africa to emulate Christ's egalitarian leadership model, they must revive their commitment to forgive and show love and compassion as they lead God's people. This is a call to see beyond an individual's past or present circumstances and perceive that person as he or she would be after encountering the transforming power of Christ. It is doing what Christ did; he trusted the Samaritan woman to play a leadership role in his mission to the Samaritans, despite her past and present life, and even though she was a woman from a marginalized ethnic group. Additionally, to adopt egalitarian leadership as modeled by Christ requires a commitment to teach, mentor and nurture other leaders. Leadership in Africa is sometimes characterized by selfishness, evident in using various means to prolong one's stay in power. Other times, it is shown in efforts to destroy healthy democracy

---

25. Semenye, "Women Leaders in the New Testament," 108.
26. Gatumu, "New Testament Evidence," 55.

in the process of electing leaders. Such church leaders fall into the trap of acting as though the efficient running of the church and its activities depended on them, whereas such effectiveness is made possible solely by Christ.

Therefore, egalitarian leadership, as modeled by Christ, demands that leaders widen the leadership space and pave the way for other people whom God has gifted to participate in leading too. One means of making this possible is for leaders to be intentional in mentoring younger people and giving them opportunities to participate in leadership as they learn from those who already have experience. There should be a commitment to support young people in accessing leadership positions in church and church-related institutions. This includes their participation in teaching and mentoring young people right from the time they pursue theological training. Since theological training is a significant prerequisite for church leadership, mentoring should start at the training level. Established leaders and teachers must desist from the folly and cowardice of feeling threatened by younger people who look up to them for mentoring and nurturing. Such inclinations are akin to the discomfort manifested by the disciples of Jesus when they found him conversing with the woman of Samaria. Leaders and teachers who have such tendencies ought to be awakened to the fact that the call to teach, mentor and nurture younger people is a call to emulate Christ, who has graciously privileged them with their positions of influence.

Ultimately, emulating Christ's egalitarian model of leadership is an invitation to church leaders in Africa to embrace the discomfort of vulnerability. Choosing to exude servant leadership and model egalitarian leadership may not always be popular. It necessitates a willingness to be vulnerable while obediently following the leading of Christ. Christ embraced vulnerability by risking his reputation to reach out to the woman of Samaria who, in turn, took a leadership role by advancing the kingdom of God through sharing her testimony. Similarly, Christian leaders ought to be willing to render themselves vulnerable in order to reach out to and minister to the diverse people whom God has entrusted to their care.

Conclusion

This rereading of John 4:1–42 through the optic of the African women's hermeneutic has expanded the ways of imaging Christ by offering a hybridized portrait of Christ as the egalitarian leader. Unlike the traditional titles of Jesus, this portrait, carved from the qualities exemplified by Jesus Christ, is easily comprehensible to African Christians. The portrait has the potential to bridge the current gap through celebrating how Jesus breaks down barriers in John 4:1–42. Yet there is hardly any evidence of replication of Christ's model among leaders in the churches in Africa today. Imaging Christ as the egalitarian leader fosters egalitarian leadership in the church and church-related institutions. It means participating in a leadership fashioned after Christ's inclusive model: a leadership that affirms, gives dignity to and cares for God's people, and intentionally commits to teach, mentor and nurture.

Bibliography

Abbey, Rose Teketi. "I Am the Woman." In *Other Ways of Reading: African Women and the Bible*, edited by M. W. Dube, 23–26. Geneva: WCC, 2001.

Beasley-Murray, G. R. *John*. Word Biblical Commentary 36. Waco: Word, 1987.

Dube, Musa. "John 4:1–42: The Five Husbands at the Well of Living Waters: The Samaritan Woman and African Women." In *Talitha Cum! Theologies of African Women*, edited by N. J. Njoroge and M. W. Dube, 40–65. Pietermaritzburg: Cluster, 2001.

———. "Reading for Decolonization (John 4:1–42)." In *John and Postcolonialism: Travel, Space and Power*, edited by M. W. Dube and J. F. Staley, 51–75. New York: Sheffield Academic, 2002.

Galgalo, Joseph. *African Christianity: The Stranger Within*. Limuru: Zapf Chancery Publishers Africa, 2012.

Guthrie, Donald. *New Testament Theology*. Downers Grove: InterVarsity Press, 1981.

Hinga, Teresa M. "Jesus Christ and the Liberation of Women in Africa." In *The Will to Arise: Women, Tradition and the Church in Africa*, edited by M. A. Oduyoye and M. R. A. Kanyoro, 183–94. New York: Orbis, 1992.

Hyun, KeumJu Jewel, Diphus Chosefu Chemorion and Joseph D. Galgalo. *The Quest for Gender Equity in Leadership: Biblical Teachings on Gender Equity and Illustrations of Transformation in Africa*. Eugene: Wipf & Stock, 2016.

Kanyandago, Peter. "A Biblical Reflection on the Exercise of Pastoral Authority in the African Churches." In Mugambi and Magesa, *Jesus in African Christianity*, 112–22. Nairobi: Acton Publishers, 2003.

Kithinji, Julius, and Lydia Chemei. "Decolonizing and Reassembling the Voice of John's Gospel in a Time of Ecological Crisis." *African Multidisciplinary Journal of Research* 3, no. 1 (2018): 74–91.

Michaels, J. Ramsey. *John*. New International Biblical Commentary Series. Peabody: Hendrickson, 1984.

Mugambi, J. N. Kanyua, and Laurenti Magesa, eds. *Jesus in African Christianity: Experimentation and Diversity in African Christology*. Nairobi: Acton, 2003.

Nasimiyu-Wasike, Anne. "Christology and an African Woman's Experience." In Mugambi and Magesa, *Jesus in African Christianity*, 123–35.

———. "Imaging Jesus Christ in the African Context at the Dawn of a New Millennium." In *Challenges and Prospects of the Church in Africa: Theological Reflections of the 21st Century*, edited by N. W. Ndung'u and P. N. Mwaura, 102–18. Nairobi: Paulines Publications, 2005.

Ngewa, Samuel M. *The Gospel of John: For Pastors and Teachers*. Nairobi: Evangel Publishing, 2003.

Nthamburi, Zablon. "Christ as Seen by an African: A Christological Quest." In Mugambi and Magesa, *Jesus in African Christianity*, 54–59.

Okure, Teresa. "Invitation to African Women's Hermeneutical Concerns." In *Interpreting the New Testament in Africa*, edited by N. Getui, T. Maluleke and J. Ukpong, 42–63. Nairobi: Acton, 2001.

———. "Jesus and the Samaritan Woman (John 4:1–42) in Africa." *Theological Studies* 70, no. 2 (2009): 401–18.

Semenye, Lois. "Women Leaders in the New Testament: Biblical Equity Reflected in the Ministries of Jesus and the Apostle Paul." In Hyun, Chemorion and Galgalo, *Quest for Gender Equity in Leadership*, 96–108.

Wa Gatumu, Kabiro. "New Testament Evidence of Biblical Equity Revealed in Creation and Redemption." In *The Quest for Gender Equity in Leadership: Biblical Teachings on Gender Equity and Illustrations of Transformation in Africa*, edited by KeumJu Jewel Hyun and Diphus C. Chemorion, 42–64. Eugene: Wipf & Stock, 2016.

Waruta, Douglas W. "Who Is Jesus Christ for Africans Today? Prophet, Priest, Potentate." In *Jesus in African Christianity*, edited by J. N. K. Mugambi and L. Magesa, 40–53. Nairobi: Acton Publishers, 2003.

4

Exploring the Multidimensional Nature of Christology in Galatians through the Lens of an African Hermeneutic

Elizabeth W. Mburu

Langham Literature Regional Coordinator, Africa
Adjunct Faculty, Pan Africa Christian University, Kenya
Extraordinary Researcher, NorthWest University, South Africa

Abstract

Western Christianity has, for centuries, presented Christology in a particular way. This paper proposes that such an understanding of Christology has stunted the growth of a robust Christianity in Africa. This trend is of grave concern, given that Africa is now responsible for shaping the global church of the future. Recent inroads in African theology and hermeneutics have exposed the multidimensionality of the Christian faith. These studies naturally have implications for prior conclusions arrived at regarding the person of Christ. This paper seeks to demonstrate, through an African hermeneutical analysis of Galatians, the multidimensional nature of the person of Christ. It begins with a brief overview of the christological approaches of the twentieth and twenty-first centuries and then provides an overview of African Christologies. It then uses a specific African intercultural hermeneutical approach to uncover aspects of Christology in Galatians. This method, the four-legged stool, is one that uses five steps – parallels with the African context, theological context, literary context, historical context, and application. This paper shows that facets of Christology not immediately evident to Western thought provide a more complete understanding of Christology for African believers.

Key words: multidimensional, Christology, African hermeneutics, intercultural, Galatians

Introduction

The Christian faith is multidimensional. By implication, therefore, Christian theology is multidimensional. What do I mean by the multidimensionality of the Christian faith? Multidimensionality recognizes that while theology is universal, given the universal nature of its source, it must also be specific to specific contexts. It is a dynamic, rather than a static, entity. In other words, multidimensionality captures "the global character of the Christian faith."[1] While we have, understandably, used Western categories to define our theology, other categories might speak better to our contexts. Additionally, even though affirmations such as the Nicene Creed originated in an African context, they may not be immediately viewed as relevant in twenty-first-century Africa. It must be remembered that such creeds were crafted to address contextual issues at a given time – for instance, heresies surrounding the nature of Christ, such as his deity (Ebionism and Arianism) and his humanity (Docetism and Apollinarianism). Pobee, who rightly argues that Christology lies at the heart of the interaction between Christianity and African culture, emphasizes the need for a cultural consideration in Christology in Africa. He affirms that it is "important who the African is, because homo Africanus is encountered by Christ as he or she is."[2] This means that both geographical and temporal considerations (and here we must consider the digital space) must be taken into account.

Unless the question "Who is Christ?" is answered from the perspective of the average African Christian, whose life is filled to overwhelming with the challenges of daily life, it is not a relevant Christology. The church in Africa will continue to experience severe systemic challenges that will threaten its

---

1. This is a dominant theme that characterized Lamin Sanneh's writings.
2. Cited in De Jongh, "Contemporary Trends," 15, https://www.academia.edu/6912417/Contemporary_Trends_in_Christology_in_Africa_Full_Thesis_.

healthy existence. We have only to look at Europe today to see that it is possible for the church to diminish, no matter how great its former glory.

This chapter will show that facets of Christology not immediately evident to Western thought provide a better understanding of Christology for African believers. It will begin with a brief overview of the christological approaches of the twentieth and twenty-first centuries, and then provide an overview of African Christologies. The paper will use the African intercultural hermeneutics to explore the various aspects of Christology found in Paul's letter to the Galatians. This letter has played a significant role in the theology of the church throughout church history. I will allow the categories to suggest themselves from the text through a dialogue between the biblical text and context and the Kenyan context. It is hoped that the findings will contribute to the already existing African Christologies and that they will demonstrate the importance of African hermeneutical approaches in theology.

Christological Approaches of the Twentieth and Twenty-First Centuries

According to Gathogo, there are six christological approaches of the twentieth century (and, of course, now the 21st).[3] The first christological trend commits itself to interpret and adapting Christology to the modern mentality and situation (here we find the cosmological perspective of Teilhard de Chardin and Karl Rahner, the anthropological, existential and personalistic perspective of Bultmann, the historical perspective of Pannenberg and Schillebeeckx, the secular perspective of Schoonenberg, and the political perspective of Boff and Boff and Sobrino. The second christological trend is geared exclusively to the historical Jesus (H. Küng, E. Käsemann and G. Bornkamm). The third christological trend conceives Christology as the upholding of Trinitarian theology (Karl Barth, H. U. von Balthasar). The fourth christological trend is Christology based on the proclaimed Christ and the historical Jesus (W. Kasper and Jürgen Moltmann). The fifth christological trend comprises the Asian Christologies of inculturation and liberation (Raimundo Panikkar). The final approach is African Christologies, which will be handled in the next section.

---

3. Gathogo, "Reconstructive Hermeneutics," 2–3.

Overview of African Christologies

While Western categories are useful, we also need a Christology that is deeply relevant to the lived experiences of the African people. It cannot be an abstract philosophical Christology that is difficult to grasp by the ordinary reader of the Bible. An African Christology simultaneously asks the questions "Who is Christ?" and "How does he affect my life?" To answer these questions, various African scholars have come up with categories that resonate with the church in Africa.

Scholars generally propose two categories of African Christology.[4] According to Wachege, Nyamiti and Stinton, African Christology is divided into Christologies of liberation and Christologies of inculturation. Most scholars lean toward this categorization. African Christologies of liberation have an affinity with those of Latin America (Boff, Gutiérrez and Sobrino). However, the major difference is that liberation Christologies in Africa are more inclined toward cultural and religious values and less prone to secular and Marxist ideologies. Christologies of inculturation are in two main categories: ancestral (B. Bujo, J. Mutiso-Mbinda, C. Nyamiti, John Pobee and E. Penoukou) and nonancestral (K. A. Kubi, A. T. Sanon, Harry Sawyerr, Canaan Banana, Anne Nasimiyu-Wasike, John Mbiti, Kwesi Dickson, Zablon Nthamburi and P. N. Wachege).

While useful, this twofold categorization of Christology is nevertheless limiting. Note the following comment by Gathogo:

> African Christology is dominated by inculturation, reconciliation, liberation, and reconstruction Christologies amongst others. Again, it is critical to appreciate that even though liberation and inculturation can be said to be some of the widely published paradigms in African Christianity, since the 1960s, there are other not-so-commonly published paradigms that African Christologies fall within. They include Symbolic and oral paradigms, Charismatic, Restorative, Market-theology, and Rural-ministry paradigms amongst others.

Of great importance to note is that reconstructive Christologies, in twenty-first-century Africa, have become the dominant motif.[5]

This idea is demonstrated in the work of Kä Mana, who views reconstruction as the overriding paradigm in twenty-first-century African theologies. He

---

4. The following summary is from Gathogo, 2–5.
5. Gathogo, 5.

integrates other motifs "of identity, inculturation, reconciliation, and liberation thereby reconstructing Africa as well as the world, in accord with humane requirements."[6] Jesse Mugambi, whose reconstructive Christology identifies "Christ as guest," also differs from this narrow categorization.[7]

Charles De Jongh introduces another paradigm. He also identifies two main trends, which he identifies as cultural and functional.[8] In the cultural trend (which overlaps with inculturation) are found scholars such as Kurewa, Waruta, Adeyemo, Bediako, Pobee, Hearne, Ntetem, Bujo and Nyamiti, to name just a few. A formidable representative of this approach is Bujo (Jesus as proto-ancestor). He argues, "I believe that a truly dynamic Christianity will only be possible in Africa when the foundation for the African's whole life is built on Jesus Christ, conceived in specifically African categories."[9] African culture must, therefore, be taken seriously. The essence of this trend is its desire to secure the Christian faith, interact with African culture, and communicate the gospel message in the most meaningful and relevant manner possible.

In the functional trend, which places more emphasis on Jesus's function or work than on his person or nature, De Jongh identifies scholars such as Buthelezi, Nthamburi, Mbiti, Dzobo and Moila. The essence of this trend is its desire to communicate that Christ is relevant (counteracting an over-spiritualized gospel), Christ is present (not in some super-spiritual realm) and Christ is current.[10]

Although not referring specifically to African Christologies, Erickson notes that such functional Christologies overlook some features of the biblical witness and distort others. His caution that "any Christology to be fully adequate must address and integrate ontological and functional matters"[11] is well taken. Nevertheless, the functional approach has value in that it resonates with the church in Africa because of its very practical and concrete approach. It has also exposed the gap in Western theologies which tend to de-emphasize the value of functionality in theology.

Some titles of Jesus Christ that have emerged from various African Christologies include Liberator (e.g. Takatso Mafokeng, Allan Boesak, Jean Marc Ela, Laurenti Magesa, T. Souga, L. Tappa, M.A. Oduyoye and E. Amoah),

---

6. Gathogo.
7. Mugambi, *From Liberation to Reconstruction*, 9.
8. De Jongh, "Contemporary Trends," 3.
9. Quoted in De Jongh.
10. De Jongh, 6.
11. Erickson, *Introducing Christian Doctrine*, 221.

Chief, Master of Initiation (championed originally by Anselme Titianma Sanon), Healer (Anne Nasimiyu-Wasike), Ancestor (Charles Nyamiti [brother-ancestor] and Benezet Bujo [proto-ancestor]) and Victor (John Mbiti).

Approach: An African Intercultural Hermeneutic

In the next few sections, I will show how an African intercultural approach provides us with other relevant categories of Christology. Some of these overlap with those already identified above but they are nevertheless included in order to be faithful to the text of Galatians. In terms of categorization, this method lies more in the cultural trend. However, as is the case with many African Christologies, the method used here does not make a clear distinction between ontology and functionality.

There is no neutral interpretation of a text, as many scholars have pointed out over the years. Our worldviews will always influence our understanding of Scripture, either positively or negatively. For instance, our prior understanding of God will influence how we understand passages that talk about God. Worldviews are shaped within specific cultural contexts.

This method is an intercultural approach that is based on the concept of moving from the known to the unknown.[12] It therefore moves directly from theories, methods and categories that are familiar in our world into the more unfamiliar world of the Bible, without taking a detour through any foreign methods. This is one way of avoiding the dichotomy that exists in African biblical interpretation. It recognizes that parallels between biblical and African cultures and worldviews can be used as bridges to promote understanding, internalization and application of the biblical text. This approach to unlocking the African understanding of biblical texts is not new. It is doing what Jesus did, for he too used elements of his culture to teach, moving from the known to the unknown, particularly in his parables. Paul was also an expert in this kind of intercultural dialogue (Acts 17). As African readers of the biblical text, we must discover our cultures and worldview and apply them in our hermeneutics. However, as we do so, we must be careful to interrogate our assumptions so as not to displace biblical revelation. Our conclusions must be in alignment with the biblical metanarrative.

---

12. Mburu, *African Hermeneutics*.

This method can be described using the metaphor of a four-legged stool.[13] A stool is a familiar object in Africa, both in the past and in the present. Just as a good stool is stable and supports our weight, so this hermeneutical stool is one we can put our weight on, confident that it provides a stable or accurate interpretation of the biblical text. This contextualized approach has four legs. The first leg of the stool, the place where we begin our search for understanding, involves identifying the theological and cultural contexts that are the primary contributors to our worldview, as well as any relevant features of our social, political and geographical contexts. We consciously identify our context and discover the points of contact between it and the biblical context. It is at this point that we begin to examine our assumptions. The second leg is the theological context, and it involves identifying the theological themes that arise from the text. It provides us with the parameters within which the meaning of the text should be sought. The third leg is the literary context. Here we identify the type of literature we are dealing with, including its genre, literary techniques, language used, and the progression of the text in relation to surrounding texts. The fourth leg is the historical and cultural context. This leg provides us with valuable information that validates the uncertain meaning and application arrived at in the previous steps. These legs support the seat, which represents the final stage of interpretation: the application. In application, we must determine the meaning of the text to its original readers before coming to a final determination of its significance for our present African context.

What this hermeneutic does is foster an intercultural dialogue that allows parallel issues between the biblical worldview, the African worldview, and culture to come forth. Because of this connection, it is thus possible to allow christological themes that relate to the African context to emerge from the text. In identifying the christological emphases of Galatians, all aspects of this stool will be analyzed, but only the aspects relevant to the scope of this chapter will be highlighted.

Background

Galatians is a letter to specific recipients, namely believers who belong to the churches in Galatia (1:2). The letter is occasional in its content. It uses the

---

13. Mburu, 65–89. Stools throughout African communities can have as few as one and as many as five legs. This particular model works with four.

literary style and conventions common in that period. In terms of subgenre, it is a rebuke-request letter. Such letters contained requests to set things right.[14]

Although Paul wrote the epistle for various reasons, the major issue was the understanding of the centrality of Christ in the Galatian church. The contents of the letter give us a clue about the specific historical context and purpose for Paul's communication. Various verses in the letter reveal that there was conflict and confusion in the Galatian church that centered around the accusation that Paul was preaching a defective or inadequate gospel. Some people in the church were teaching that certain practices of Judaism, such as circumcision, were essential for salvation. Scholars identify these troublemakers as Judaizers. Even in Paul's time, religion played a significant role in determining identity. Circumcision, observance of the Sabbath, and keeping the Mosaic law were markers of identity peculiar to the Jewish people.[15] Paul therefore writes to refute these Judaizers and to provide the Galatian believers with the proper foundation for a genuine Christian identity.[16] As he does so, he uncovers aspects of Christ's identity that lead to the inevitable conclusion that it is the teaching of the Judaizers that is defective.

Christological Emphases in Galatians
The Liberator

The first parallel to African culture and worldview in this letter is that of witchcraft, expressed in the language of bewitching. Paul makes it clear that the behavior of the Galatians was like that of those bewitched. The idea of witchcraft and of being bewitched is still evident in many communities of Africa. People live in fear of unseen powers. They try to do all they can to gain control over their world. They are oppressed and imprisoned. Consequently, witchcraft is still a reality in the African church. People must find a power that is greater than that which oppresses them. This is the law of power that underlies the worldview of dynamism.[17] Our worldview regarding external reality and dynamism means that people seek to gain power and control over their circumstances in any way possible. While this is familiar territory, what Paul was likely talking about is not identical to what we experience in Africa

---

14. Hansen, "Galatians," 329.

15. Hansen, 327.

16. See Mburu, "Galatians." In this work, I argue that Galatians is not primarily about legalism or the law. The underlying issue in this letter is that of identity.

17. Turaki, *Foundations of African Traditional Religion*, 34–35.

today. Nevertheless, our experience forms a valuable point of contact in that it uncovers a syncretistic approach to Christianity.

A theological theme that arises from Galatians is that of liberation. Paul makes several significant declarations with respect to Christ as the liberator of humankind. As the divine Lord and Son of God (1:3, 16; 2:20; 4:4, 6), Christ rescued humanity from the present evil age by giving himself for our sins (1:4). Paul immediately thinks of Christ in functional terms and interprets this phrase soteriologically.[18] The verb ἐξαιρέω (deliver) is used together with the purpose conjunction ὅπως, thus revealing that Christ gave himself for the purpose or goal of rescuing us from the present evil age. This looks back to the Old Testament and God's deliverance of the Israelites from Egyptian bondage.[19] In terms of literary analysis, this word is found in the same semantic domain as setting free or delivering. Paul reiterates this liberation motif in the letter when he states that Christ's action also accomplished the task of freeing the Galatians from slavery so that humankind would no longer be slaves, but live as God's children and heirs of salvation (4:28 – 5:1). Paul emphasizes this liberation motif because the Galatians were enslaving themselves again with their insistence on keeping the law (4:1, 9–10; 3:7). He affirms that Christ has set us free so that we might live in freedom and not allow ourselves to be enslaved again (5:1, 13). In identifying the law as a yoke rather than as an agent of liberation, Paul moves away from the standard Jewish view.[20]

Another significant area of terminology that Paul uses to emphasize the liberating work of Christ is that of redemption. Using two purpose clauses (ἵνα), Paul writes that Christ was born under the law *to* redeem humankind so that they might receive adoption as God's sons and the promise of the Spirit (3:13; 4:4–5). Circumcision, or any other aspect of the law that the Judaizers were promoting (cf. 4:10), was never intended to be *the* avenue to fulfill this promise. The verb ἐξαγοράζω (redeem; 1:4) can also mean to release or to set free in the New Testament. While it might literally mean "to release by means of paying a price" (which promoted the wrong view in the Middle Ages that God paid the price to the devil), Paul means this metaphorically. We are the beneficiaries and not God. As Büchsel affirms, "In this liberation from the curse of the Law, the essential point is that it confers both an actual and also a legally established freedom ensuring against any renewal of slavery."[21]

---

18. Longenecker, *Galatians*, 7–8.
19. Schreiner, *Galatians*, 77.
20. Schreiner, 307.
21. Büchsel, "ἐξαγοράζω," 126.

What does this mean for the Galatian readers? In their present circumstances, the Galatians had imprisoned themselves in their past religious heritage and diluted the power of Christ in their lives to liberate them from sin. Paul affirms that they have been delivered and redeemed through the sacrificial death of Christ and that a syncretistic approach to their faith is not tenable.

Given this truth, how does the understanding of Christ as liberator apply to an African believer? Unfortunately, because the understanding of Christ's identity as the liberator has not developed, there are those who, much like the Galatians, believe in a "Christ and . . ." philosophy. In other words, Christ on his own is not powerful enough to liberate them from their circumstances. The parallels identified above reflect this syncretistic tendency. This tendency minimizes both the person and the work of Christ in justification and sanctification. Speaking of Christ as a liberator, de Carvalho again affirms the present nature of Christ in the lives of people: "Jesus as our liberator is another experience of incarnation in the African situation. God reveals himself in Jesus Christ in order to destroy oppression once for all and to bring liberation. Liberation from sin and from all the consequences of sin."[22] The African worldview, in which many live in fear of demonic forces, witchcraft, evil spirits, curses, and so forth, has been confronted and overturned by Christ. We no longer need to perform protective rituals, consult witchdoctors, healers and spirits, buy "anointed" items at exorbitant prices or revert to those aspects of our culture that contradict Christianity.

This liberating aspect of Christ's identity should not be seen as limited to the spiritual realm. It also speaks to our physical realities. The phenomenon has been understood particularly by many in the African Instituted Churches that read those parts of the Bible that speak of Christ as liberator very literally. Because Christ is the liberator par excellence, he is also able to deliver us from physically oppressive political, social and economic situations. We must therefore become participants with Christ in the liberation of the oppressed and marginalized. Such a Christology challenges us to engage with the issues rather than stand aside as passive observers. We have a mandate to be a "prophetic voice" that spurs our institutional structures to become better.

The Unifier of the Church

A second parallel is that of ethnic differences, gender inequities, socioeconomic distinctions and political differences that characterize many African churches.

---

22. De Jongh, 8, from De Carvalho, "What do Africans say that Jesus Christ is?", 17.

Indeed, one has only to observe to see that even churches develop and grow along these lines. In the postelection violence of 2007/8, Kenyans were shocked to see fellow believers slaughtering one another because of different ethnic affiliations, a situation exacerbated by political rhetoric. Men and women who had worshiped together for years, who fellowshipped together, were overnight turned into mortal enemies. Ethnic identity, as so often happens in Africa, overshadowed Christian identity. This is because, while it is encouraged by our political systems, it also has historical roots. The same can be seen even in our oral literature. One ethnic group in Kenya has a proverb that reveals that people from other tribes were often viewed in a dehumanizing way: "Hit the head; this animal is not one of us – he comes from a strange place."[23] Negative ethnicity depicts the other as less than human.

Unity in diversity is another theological theme that is prominent in Galatians. In the Galatian church, superiority along socioeconomic, gender and ethnic lines was the norm. Jews hated Gentiles because they believed that their Jewishness made them ethnically and religiously superior. Socioeconomic divisions in the first century, particularly in the Roman world, had resulted in a class system that marginalized and disenfranchised the weak while promoting the rights of the powerful minority. Women had almost no rights in society and were oppressed in every area of life. The social situation of the time can be summarized as follows: "Some Greeks thanked the deity for not making them animals, women or non-Greeks; some Jewish teachers thanked God for not making them Gentiles, women or ignorant people [in some versions, slaves]."[24] All these ills were destroying the church at Galatia.

Paul shows how these distinctions collapse in the face of the unifying aspect of Christ's identity. What the law could not do, Christ accomplished. Paul emphasizes that Christ has broken down socioeconomic, gender and ethnic barriers. This kind of unity can be achieved only "in Christ." This is a favorite phrase with Paul, and it signifies the "personal, local, and dynamic relation of the believer to Christ."[25] Little wonder that Paul publicly rebuked Peter when he hypocritically broke away from temple fellowship with Gentiles (Gal 2:11–14)! Because such fellowship would have been taken as "an official stamp of approval on the union and equality of Jews and Gentiles in the church,"[26] Peter's action would have compromised this unity. Paul declares that Jewish–Gentile,

---

23. Mburu, *African Hermeneutics*, 136.
24. Keener, *IVP Bible Background Commentary*, 532.
25. Longenecker, *Galatians*, 152.
26. Hansen, "Galatians," 331.

master–slave and male–female distinctions are no longer valid (3:26–29). The thought was indeed a revolutionary one in the slave society of the Roman Empire, where language and customs separated different peoples, and where there was a pronounced difference between male and female. Nevertheless, in challenging the societal conventions of the day, Paul does not seek to eliminate diversity (see Rom 14).[27] He argues for "unity in diversity." The implication of these new relationships, forged as a result of Christ's work, is that love, not hate, becomes the status quo (5:14–15).

For the Galatian readers, this meant that it was only those who had faith in Christ who belonged to the family of Abraham.[28] Christ, who is the unifier, equalizes all people by this standard. Distinctions disappear because salvation is a gift offered to all regardless of their standing in society; this is the unifying key. Those who put their faith in Christ put on a new identity – that of children of God. How then can one oppress a fellow Christian who has received acceptance by Christ on an equal basis?

If, as Paul argues, Christ is our unifier, how does this apply to the church in Africa? While our ethnic identity is undeniable, our new identity as believers united by Christ must take precedence. The church must become "our new ethnic group." Negative ethnicity has no place in the church. In addition, this means that leadership and membership should incorporate members from different socioeconomic strata, gender, education, age, and so forth. Policies must be developed and enforced to ensure that the church demonstrates genuine unity in diversity.

The Victor

A third parallel with Galatians is the seeming inability of the church in Africa to live in line with the values espoused in Scripture. Systemic problems plague the church. These include misappropriation of funds, moral failure, social injustices, and syncretistic doctrines and practices. Galgalo observes that much of Kenyan Christianity is an apostate Christianity in which "the true sense of values is so corrupted that sin has become an ally of sorts – sanitized, cleansed, absolved," normalized, "and accommodated."[29] Galatians brings the message that this doesn't have to be our reality. Because Christ was victorious through

---

27. Keener, *Galatians*, 308–13.
28. Schreiner, *Galatians*, 257.
29. Galgalo, "Syncretism in African Christianity," 77.

the cross, he empowers us to be victors in our everyday circumstances. Through his Holy Spirit, Christ transforms us and enables us to live Spirit-led lives.

The transformation of the believer is a significant theological theme in Galatians. The Judaizers not only argued that obedience to the law was necessary for salvation, they also insisted that the law on its own was able to restrain sinful conduct. Meanwhile, others in the Galatian church said that it did not matter if believers sinned because they were saved by faith alone. Paul opposed both groups, teaching that personal righteousness was very important but could be attained only with the help of the Holy Spirit (5:5, 22–25).

Paul writes of his own experience: "I have been crucified with Christ and I no longer live, but Christ lives in me. The life I now live in the body, I live by faith in the Son of God" (2:20). For Paul, crucifixion with Christ "implies not only death to the jurisdiction of the Mosaic law (v. 19) but also death to the jurisdiction of one's own ego."[30] Paul recognized that both the law and the flesh are incapable of enabling one to gain righteousness. If indeed they could achieve this, then Christ's death was meaningless (2:21)! Christ's death opened the avenue for the Holy Spirit to reside in the Galatian believers. This new identity has ethical implications (5:1, 13, 24). Nevertheless, just as they began their spiritual journey by faith and not works, so their sanctification would be achieved in the same way (3:1; 5:22).

Paul's intention was for the Galatian readers to understand that the Christian life is one of victory because of the new life in them. No amount of effort on their part could help them attain personal righteousness. They needed to be completely dependent on Christ, who transforms and empowers.

The same also applies to the church in Africa. Christ has broken the power of sin on the cross. The result is that he enables believers to overcome the power of sin in everyday life. As Mbiti wrote years ago,

> The Christian message brings Jesus as the one who fought victoriously against the forces of the devil, spirits, sickness, hatred, fear, and death itself . . . He is the victor, the one hope, the one example, the one conqueror: and this makes sense to African peoples, it draws their attention, and it is pregnant with meaning. It gives to their myths a new dimension. The greatest need among African peoples is to see, to know, and to experience Jesus Christ

---

30. Longenecker, *Galatians*, 92.

as the victor over the powers and forces from which Africa knows no means of deliverance.[31]

How does this apply to the lived experiences of African believers? We must depend on the victory of Christ to rise above the ills in our societies. A victorious Christian life that reflects true biblical values cannot be achieved by the sheer force of one's will. It takes both individual and corporate prayer, fasting (in some instances), diligence to study the Bible, and accountability to the community of faith.

The Truth

The fourth parallel with Galatians relates to teachings that pervert and corrupt the gospel. The most prominent is the prosperity health and wealth gospel, which teaches that the blessings that come from faith in Christ are material and that if we are not receiving abundant material blessing, there is something wrong with our faith. Many syncretistic beliefs and practices confuse Christians about what is truly biblical faith and practice. While this is not all that Christianity is in Africa, it has been observed that African Christianity, in its openness to varied religious views, is incurably pluralistic.[32] In an environment where false "gospels" bombard us from every direction, fueled by modern technology and the digital age, the truth is often difficult to recognize. It doesn't help that many churches and denominations show no real concern for doctrinal correctness and teaching in their regular worship services.[33] Although the issues we face in Africa are not identical to the issues Paul addresses in this text, the idea that the gospel may be perverted is not strange to an African reader.

Another theological principle that emerges, then, is that of truth. Paul highlights the superiority of the gospel of grace in justification. He insists that faith in Christ is all that is needed. The Galatians are not saved by obedience to the Old Testament law. Rather, salvation is accomplished through Christ's substitutionary death. Paul was writing to people who were confused because they heard two different gospels. One was the true gospel, and the other was a corrupted version of it. The Judaizers, in preaching a different gospel, were displacing Christ by insisting that the law had equal status. While not outrightly rejecting Christianity, the Judaizers were preaching a perverted version of the gospel.

---

31. De Jongh, 6, from Mbiti, *Some African Concepts*, 55.
32. Galgalo, *African Christianity*, 27.
33. Galgalo, "Syncretism in African Christianity," 83.

This was shocking, and Paul expressed this sentiment with a letter that was strongly worded and full of rebuke. The Judaizers argued that keeping the law of Moses (and in particular the rite of circumcision) was essential for salvation. Circumcision was a key identity marker in the Jewish community and was essential for entry into the people of God. The teaching was not new. A similar group of Judaizers had also caused trouble in Antioch with the same message (Acts 15:1). The problem with this teaching was that it undermined the work and the person of Christ in salvation. For Paul, the fact that the Judaizers had convinced the Galatians to turn away from the true gospel was particularly incredible given the Galatians' own experience of Christ (3:1–6). Paul urges his readers to reject this false "gospel" and return to the one he had preached, the true gospel (2:5). It could be trusted because of its authoritative source (1:12). Most importantly, "the standard of the gospel was not derived from human tradition; it was given by 'the revelation of Jesus Christ' (Gal 1:11–12): Jesus Christ is both the source and the subject of the gospel."[34] This is why he is the Truth. Paul emphasizes the centrality of Christ and his salvific work on the cross in the Christian faith. What this means for the Galatian believers is that the message of the gospel negates works of the law and renders both circumcision and uncircumcision useless. The truth is to be found in Christ alone.

How does this apply to the church in Africa? While we do not face controversies about Old Testament law, we nevertheless encounter many situations in which some try to corrupt the gospel of truth. Like the Galatians, we need to understand the foundation of our faith and study the Bible so that we are not deceived into adopting doctrines and practices that are contrary to Christianity.

The Curse-Bearer

The fifth parallel in this letter is that of blessing and curse. In traditional Africa, curses were pronounced on members of the community who had offended the spiritual realm or the physical community. It was believed that these curses would have both spiritual and physical consequences. As demonstrated by the proverb from the Akamba of Kenya, "*Kiumo ti, 'Wookw'wa*" (A curse is not simply telling someone "May you die"), curses go deeper than a mere utterance.[35] At the same time, not all curses are effective.[36] The language of

---

34. Hansen, "Galatians," 330.
35. Joshua, "Christian Response to Curses," 148.
36. Joshua.

blessing and curse is still very evident, even in modern Africa. When a person experiences persistent negative circumstances, it is not unusual to hear that person wondering whether he or she has been cursed. Little wonder, then, that some Christians devote themselves to extended classes and deliverance sessions designed to remove ancestral and other curses. Paul's statement that anyone who perverts the gospel is cursed is familiar territory for an African reader.

A final theological truth that emerges is that of Christ as the curse-bearer. Several curses are documented in the Bible, both from God on human beings and between human beings. The idea of curses was also familiar in the ancient world, as can be seen in the many magical papyri. Curses were central to ancient magic for offensive or defensive reasons. Indeed, Jewish sources recognized that curses could be effective as well as dangerous.[37] Paul writes that Christ paid the penalty for sin by dying a cursed death on the cross so that sinners might be made right with God (1:4; 3:10–14). In other words, Galatians emphasizes the substitutionary nature of Christ's death. Paul argues that a reliance on obedience to the law to obtain a right standing with God can only lead to a curse. This teaching is because no one can obey every aspect of the law perfectly (as implied by the word "all" in 3:10). God's curse implies final destruction and condemnation, the eschatological punishment administered by God.[38] Paul uses the Jewish principle of linking Old Testament texts based on keywords, and here he cites Deuteronomy 27:26.[39] Although Paul is aware that, according to Jewish teaching, human obedience is always imperfect and God does not expect it, he reinterprets Deuteronomy 27:26 "for all that he can get from it – after all, God was in a position to demand perfection."[40] The curse is therefore applied to all who fail to perform the whole law (3:10).

In Paul's words, those who pervert the gospel are under a curse (1:7–9; 3:10) because only Christ justifies (2:16). If one insisted on living under the law, one therefore had to obey it perfectly. However, the law had become problematic because atonement was no longer possible through the Old Testament sacrificial system. What Paul is saying is that the law can never be enough because it "requires perfect obedience and human performance whereas faith looks to what God has done in Christ for salvation."[41] Paul

---

37. Keener, *Galatians*, 209.
38. Longenecker, *Galatians*, 17.
39. Keener, *IVP Bible Background Commentary*, 530.
40. Keener.
41. Schreiner, *Galatians*, 210.

explains that the law was a temporary custodian and guardian that was now obsolete with the coming of Christ (3:23–24).

What does this mean for the Galatian readers? Because the Mosaic sacrificial system had been abolished, all who insisted on living under it remained cursed. However, by dying a substitutionary death on the cross, Christ had abolished this system and taken the curse on himself.

This truth is important for African believers. Just as it was in Paul's day, it is difficult to understand how one who was cursed could achieve salvation for us. Cursed people are to be avoided, not embraced, lest the curse they bear somehow rub off on us. Nevertheless, because Christ died the death we were condemned to die, we can celebrate the fact that the curse has been lifted. This means that we need to let go of the cultural solutions we attempt to provide for ourselves and other believers who seem unable to live in the freedom won for us by Christ. Just as the law was inadequate in Paul's day, so too are any solutions outside of Christ and his work.

Implications

Several practical implications arise from this intercultural dialogue with the text and the uncovering of a multidimensional Christology. I will highlight only three.

The first implication has to do with our lived experiences. Such a Christology is relevant to the lived experiences of ordinary African believers. For one, the biblical text finds a home in the African heart because it speaks to the contextual realities that believers face daily. It is no longer an object that has been imposed on us, but rather a relevant text that allows us to engage in constructive dialogue and confronts us where it matters.

The second implication of this Christology has to do with our awareness of and response to the religious spaces we occupy. What defines insiders as opposed to outsiders? All too often, African Christians feel like outsiders within the fabric of world Christianity. It is because of this feeling that syncretism is so attractive. Syncretism reinforces a sense of identity and ownership of faith. Religious spaces in Africa are often very fluid or porous. When we allow religious spaces to blend indiscriminately, we will find ourselves drifting into syncretism. The digital space is crucial in this discussion because cultural and religious spaces are not as distinct as they were previously, and influence is frequently unconscious. Such a Christology as has been defined in this paper removes the insider–outsider dichotomy because it helps us realize that the contexts we share with the biblical world provide us with a common point of contact. This forms a bridge that enables an intercultural dialogue and validates our experience of Christ in the wider context of world Christianity.

The third implication has to do with our identity as African Christian believers. Our identity can only truly define itself in dialogue with that of Christ. Our identity markers are not to be imposed upon us by our past, be it African Traditional Religions, cultures, or even worldviews. Rather they are defined through this christological grid. Nevertheless, we should not shy away from expressing our identities as African Christians. So, for instance, a respect for the elderly, family values, hospitality, a sense of community, an appreciation of the arts, or nuanced spiritism, can all be useful in defining who we are. An understanding of the identity of Christ confronts us. It challenges us to reclaim our rightful identities by interrogating our cultures and asking what values and practices we can use with benefit. In this way, we will be in a position to incorporate the positives and let go of the negatives.

Conclusion

This chapter began with the premise that Christology is multidimensional. It argued that unless the question "Who is Christ?" is answered from the perspective of the average African Christian, it is not a relevant Christology. The church in Africa will continue to experience severe systemic challenges that will threaten its healthy existence. After a brief overview of the christological approaches of the twentieth and twenty-first centuries and an overview of African Christologies, the text of Galatians was analyzed to uncover various facets of Christology. The four-legged stool method facilitated a dialogue between the biblical text and context and the African context. The lived experiences of the African peoples, in particular worldviews and cultures, provided the foundational data. Categories that were identified as a result of this dialogue included Liberator, Victor, Unifier of the church, Truth and Curse-Bearer. While some of these categories overlapped with existing African Christologies, others were different. It is hoped that these findings will contribute to the already existing African Christologies and that they will demonstrate the importance of African hermeneutical approaches in theology.

Bibliography

Büchsel, Friedrich. "ἐξαγοράζω." In *Theological Dictionary of the New Testament*, Vol. 1, edited by Gerhard Kittel, 126. Grand Rapids: Eerdmans, 1964.

De Carvalho, E. J. M. "What do Africans say that Jesus Christ is?" *African Theological Journal* 10, no. 2 (1981): 17–25.

De Jongh, Charles. "Contemporary Trends in Christology in Africa." *South African Baptist Journal of Theology* (2008). https://www.academia.edu/6912417/Contemporary_Trends_in_Christology_in_Africa_ Full_Thesis.

Erickson, Millard. *Introducing Christian Doctrine*. 2nd ed. Grand Rapids, MI: Baker Academic, 2001.

Galgalo, Joseph D. *African Christianity: The Stranger Within*. Limuru: Zapf Chancery Publishers Africa, 2012.

———. "Syncretism in African Christianity: A Boon or a Bane?" In *African Contextual Realities*, edited by Rodney Reed, 75–96. ASET. Carlisle: Langham Global Library, 2018.

Gathogo, Julius. "Reconstructive Hermeneutics in African Christology." *HTS Teologiese Studies/Theological Studies* 71, no. 3 (2015): Art. #2660. https://doi.org/10.4102/hts.v71i3.2660.

Hansen, G. W. "Galatians, Letter to the." In *Dictionary of Paul and His Letters*, edited by Gerald F. Hawthorne and Ralph P. Martin, 323–34. Downers Grove: InterVarsity Press, 1993.

Joshua, Nathan Nzyoka. "A Christian Response to Curses in Africa." In *Christianity and Suffering: African Perspectives*, edited by Rodney Reed, 145–66. ASET. Carlisle: Langham Global Library, 2017.

Keener, Craig S. *Galatians: A Commentary*. Grand Rapids: Baker Academic, 2019.

———. *The IVP Bible Background Commentary*. 2nd ed. Downers Grove: IVP Academic, 2014.

Longenecker, Richard N. *Galatians*. Word Biblical Commentary. Nashville: Nelson Reference and Electronic, 1990.

Mbiti, J. S. "Some African Concepts of Christology." In *Christ and the Younger Churches*. Edited by G. F. Vicedom, 51–62. London: SPCK, 1972.

Mburu, Elizabeth. *African Hermeneutics*. Carlisle: HippoBooks, 2019.

———. "Galatians." In *Reading the N.T. – Majority World*. Grand Rapids: Baker Academic, forthcoming.

Mugambi, Jesse N. K. *From Liberation to Reconstruction: African Christian Theology after the Cold War*. Nairobi: East African Educational Publishers, 1995.

Pobee, J. S. "In Search of Christology in Africa." In *Exploring Afro-Christology*, edited by J. S. Pobee, 9–20. Frankfurt: Peter Lang, 1992 (Studies in the Intercultural History of Christianity: band 79).

Schreiner, Thomas R. *Galatians*. Zondervan Exegetical Commentary on the New Testament. Grand Rapids: Zondervan, 2010.

Turaki, Yusufu. *Foundations of African Traditional Religion and Worldview*. Nairobi: WordAlive, 2006.

5

The Crucified and Cursed Christ as the Ultimate Curse-Remover in Galatians 3:1–14 and Its Implications

Elkanah Kiprop Cheboi

Lecturer in Theology & Biblical Studies, Kabarak University, Kenya

Abstract

In the Pauline corpus, Jesus Christ is presented both as sin and as curse-remover. It is in Galatians 3:1–14 that the crucified and cursed Christ is presented as the one who removes the "curse of the law." Specifically, in Galatians 3:13, Paul remarks that Christ became "a curse for us," and within this context he applies the work of Christ on the cross to the human problem of curses. It has been argued that in antiquity, curses and the practice of cursing was a widespread phenomenon. The prevalence of curses was coupled with the fear of curses, since it was believed that curses brought about death or the cessation of blessings. The ancients avoided coming under the oppressive power of curses and binding spells. However, when this was unavoidable, there were several ways in which curses could be removed. Paul thus develops his Christology of the cursed and crucified Christ as the remover of curses against this backdrop of the ancient understanding and practice of curses. The first section of this paper examines Paul's thought in Galatians 3:1–14 to establish his argument of the crucified and cursed Christ. The second section looks at the prevalence of the practice of cursing in the ancient world in which curses and binding spells were prevented or reversed. The third section focuses on the uniqueness of Christ as a curse-remover over against the ancient alternatives. The fourth section looks at the implications of Paul's Christology regarding curses for African Christology.

Key words: curse, binding spells, crucified, cursed, law, Jesus Christ, Paul, Christology

Introduction

The theme of curses runs throughout the Bible, from the Old Testament to the New. The curses mentioned include, for instance, curses pronounced by God against his creation (humanity, earth, plants; Gen 3:14–19; Mark 11:20–21), and curses by human beings imploring God to act on their behalf (Josh 6:26; Acts 13:11; 1 Cor 16:22). Arguably, this mirrors a cultural practice that was prevalent in antiquity. In the Bible, curses are construed as a disastrous consequence of sin. In his letter to the Galatians, the apostle Paul develops a robust Christology that addresses the issue of curses. He presents the crucified and cursed Christ as the solution to the human problem of curses. While discussing justification by faith and the redemptive story, Paul in Galatians 3:13 distinctively presents the accursed Christ as the one who bore the curses of humanity so that the blessing given to Abraham might come to the Gentiles. He profoundly articulates his Christology using the Christ event of the cross. He demonstrates that the cross brought about the solution to the problem of sin and the curse.

Paul's letter to the Galatians highlights several themes, including the nature of the true gospel, the authenticity of Paul's apostleship, justification by faith instead of the observance of the law, and Christian freedom. In Galatians 1 and 2, Paul is saddened that the Galatians are quickly turning away from the One who called them (God the Father) by grace, to a different gospel (1:6). Due to the influence of false teachers, referred to as οἱ ταράσσοντες ("the troublemakers," Gal 1:7; 5:10) or οἱ ἀναστατοῦντες ("agitators," 5:12), the Galatians were now turning to a gospel that esteemed observance of the Mosaic law instead of justification by faith. The following section examines Paul's argument in Galatians 3:1–14 exegetically. However, we will not delve deeply into every exegetical detail in this portion of Scripture, due to limited space.

Paul's Argument in Galatians 3:1–14

The idea of the cursed and crucified Christ is developed within the pericope of Galatians 3:1–14. In verses 1–5, by using five rhetorical questions, Paul highlights the theological challenge faced by the church in Galatia. Further, from verse 6, Paul uses a series of Old Testament quotations and allusions, revealing his high view of Scripture. In verses 6–9, he illustrates his argument concerning justification by faith using the example of Abraham to show that salvation has all along been through justification by faith and not according to works. He proves from Scripture that the way the Galatians first came to salvation was in line with the experience of Abraham, the archetype of all believers, and that God's dealings with Abraham remain normative.[1] In verses 10–12, Paul looks at the limitation of the law, and the scope and intensity of curses. In verses 13–14, he presents Jesus Christ as the solution to the problem of curses, and the purpose of God's salvation.

The Theological Problem in Galatia (Gal 3:1–5)

Paul begins the chapter with a reprimanding tone in a rhetorical question: "Who has bewitched you?" Noting that the Galatians had strayed from the One who had called them (1:6), Paul uses strong language, referring to them as ἀνόητοι ("foolish"), perhaps to bring attention to the seriousness of their error. The Galatians were turning away from God and from the true gospel they had received. Here, Paul is not necessarily implying that the Galatians were under the influence of sorcery or magic; but he expresses his astonishment at the confusion they had got themselves into – a confusion reminiscent of people under the influence of some sort of evil power.[2]

Christology is the first theological aspect that Paul highlights in this context. Initially, the Galatians had been recipients of a gospel that highly esteemed Jesus Christ; but now they were quickly turning away to a gospel that was no gospel. Before the Judaizers distorted their focus, Jesus was "portrayed as crucified." It is clear from other Pauline passages that Paul's kerygma (preaching) highly esteemed Christ (1 Cor 2:2–4). Indeed, Christ was the object of Paul's preaching; the crucified Christ was the foundational message he wanted his audience to uphold. Therefore, by embracing the "Moses-gospel,"[3] or salvation based on observance of the law,[4] the Galatians were committing

---

1. Byrne, *Sons of God, Seed of Abraham*, 148.
2. We should also not underestimate Paul's statement as a casual comment because he makes it in a context where sorcery, witchcraft and magic were real. They were not necessarily literally "bewitched," but, in their confusion, they bore the characteristics of people under the power of a spell.
3. Garlington, *Exposition of Galatians*, 204.
4. Garlington, 149.

a serious christological error by having a cross-less Christianity. Emphatically, the true gospel esteems the person and work of Christ on the cross.

The second theological aspect that was in question, according to verses 2–4, was the Holy Spirit. Paul uses two rhetorical questions to highlight apparent problems among the Galatians in relation to the Third Person of the Trinity. He asks, "Did you receive the Spirit by the works of the law, or by believing what you heard?" Presumably, the Galatians had been misled to falsely attribute their reception of the Holy Spirit to their observance of the law. Nonetheless, the answer to this rhetorical question was already hinted at in Galatians 2:16: "Know that a person is not justified by the works of the law, but by faith in Jesus Christ." Through a rhetorical question, Paul leads his hearers to discover how they had become senseless by setting aside the basics of their salvation. If the Galatians were serious enough to ponder Paul's questions, they would certainly realize that their salvation was not founded on their observance of the law but on faith in Jesus Christ.

Further, Paul questions their wisdom: "Are you so foolish? After beginning by means of the Spirit, are you now trying to finish by means of the flesh?" Here, Paul notes that the Galatians had begun right, with the crucified Christ and a salvation message of justification by faith. With this, they were on the path of truth, life and freedom. However, along the way, they strayed and tried to attain their goal of perfection by human effort ("flesh"), a path that certainly leads to deception, death and slavery. Paul interprets their inconsistency as foolish; they were contradicting the apostolic teachings they had formerly received.[5] Again, their foolishness was evident when they sought their end goal (perfection) through human effort, a feat that is unattainable and therefore futile.[6] Initially, Christ was portrayed before them as crucified. They also knew that they had received the Spirit of God because their belief was in what they heard, not in the law. In verse 4, Paul regrets that the Galatians will stand to lose the value of their suffering should they persist in acting in a manner inconsistent with their foundational teachings.

The other theological concern in Galatia was about God the Father. The problem is expressed in Paul's last rhetorical statement: "Does God give you his Spirit and work miracles among you by the works of the law, or by your believing what you heard?" (v. 5). Paul's main concern was that the Galatians were falsely attributing these graces to their observance of the law instead of to

---

5. Betz, *Galatians*, 133.
6. Martyn, *Galatians*, 284.

God the Father. It was God the Father, the One whom they were deserting, who graciously gave them his Spirit and continued to perform miracles among them.

In summary, verses 1–5 deal with a problem in Galatia which concerned God (Father, Son and Holy Spirit). Hence, the problem was theological, but it manifested itself in practical ways in the believers' lives. The true gospel, as Paul preached it, portrayed Christ as both crucified and supreme. The true gospel is about the work that the Spirit of God has begun and will complete, and it is about God who freely gives his Spirit and continues to work miracles among his people. It is this gospel that brings salvation, life and blessings. To be restored to the path of truth, life, faith and blessing, the Galatians needed to rectify their understanding not only of God, but also of Scripture and salvation history, as we shall see in the next section.

Scriptural and Historical Considerations (Gal 3:6–9)

Paul advances his argument in verses 6–9 by proving that the message of justification by faith is a message that is consistent with God's salvific dealings with humankind in the past. To this end, Paul employs six Old Testament quotations and references to salvation history. Using Abraham, the man of faith, Paul demonstrates that the message he is preaching is consistent with God's dealings and promises to Abraham. Underlying Paul's quotation of Genesis 12 is Paul's emphatic claim that God's dealings in salvation matters have never changed. Salvation has all along, since the time of Abraham, been by faith and not by merit. Hays comments, "Abraham is understood by Paul not as an exemplar of faith in Christ but as a typological foreshadowing of Christ himself, a representative figure whose faithfulness secures blessing and salvation vicariously for others."[7] Those who have faith in Christ have a spiritual connection to Abraham, and this spiritual connection brings blessings to those who believe like Abraham.

The apostle Paul wanted his hearers to realize that the first gospel they heard was like the gospel Abraham accepted. Abraham "believed God, and it was credited to him as righteousness." Thus, those of faith (both Jews and Gentiles) are blessed with Abraham, the man of faith, and together they form a community of faith, where God's blessings flow.

It should be observed here that the covenant with Abraham in Genesis 12 responds to the human problem in Genesis 3. The promise of blessing (that brings life) in Genesis 12 is a remedy to the curse (that brings death) in Genesis

---

7. Hays, *Faith of Jesus Christ*, 166.

3 occasioned by the disobedience of humanity.[8] Abraham's call represents the inauguration of a grand salvation plan against the former backdrop of the fall of humanity, with its resultant sin, curse and separation from God (death). Through God's call to Abraham, a Gentile, God's salvation plan and heart for the nations was revealed.

The Scope of the Problem of the Curse (Gal 3:10–12)

In verses 6–9, Paul addressed those who belong to Abraham, the people who are blessed with Abraham. But what happens to those who are not spiritually associated with Abraham? Paul now contrasts blessing with the curse; in these verses, he develops the idea of the curse – its scope and intensity.

On the one hand, Paul argues that those who rely on the law (for salvation) are under a curse. Observance of the law is not necessarily evil (Rom 7:7–14) but it is deficient for salvation, especially in the new dispensation of Christ. According to Paul, relying on the law brings a curse and not blessings or justification (v. 10a).

On the other hand, he quotes Deuteronomy 27:26, a passage that seems to contradict his former thought. The Deuteronomy passage as quoted by Paul reads, "Cursed is everyone who does not continue to do everything written in the Book of the Law." The self-fulfilling curse in this quotation applies to the disobedient. The adjective πᾶς ("everyone") in the quotation emphasizes that the curse applies to "everyone" who does not continue to do everything written in the law.[9] This curse is thus inevitable because no one (Jew or Gentile) can perfectly fulfill the law's demands. The curse of the law (pronounced by the law) falls on both the observant and the nonobservant.[10] The Gentiles are also under this curse of the law; although they do not have the Mosaic law, what the law requires is innately written in their hearts.[11]

Thus, Paul strongly argues that all humanity is ὑπὸ κατάραν (literally, "under a curse"). It should be noted here that in antiquity, to be ὑπὸ κατάραν ("under a curse") was a serious matter. In the Old Testament world, people understood curses as having the power to "deprive covenant violators of

---

8. Wright, *Mission of God's People*, 60.

9. The Septuagint transforms the Masoretic text by introducing the adjective πᾶς ("everyone"), which emphasizes the scope of the curse. For more discussion, consult Cheboi, "Crucified and Cursed Christ," 94–97.

10. Martyn, *Galatians*, 311.

11. Bruce, *Epistle to the Galatians*, 167.

security, freedom, health, and blessings."[12] Having specified the helpless and powerless situation faced by the Galatians and humanity as a whole, Paul proceeds to provide solutions to the curse from outside the law.

The Cursed Christ as the Solution to the Problem of the Curse (Gal 3:13–14)

Again, having established that the curse is universal and affects both those who observe the law for justification and those who do not observe everything written in it, Paul then moves to point to the divine solution to the problem of the curse. Earlier, in verses 6–9, Paul referred to the example of Abraham, to demonstrate the truth about justification by faith and the revelation of God's heart to reach out to the nations with blessings. But now he introduces Christ, the antitype of Abraham.

Paul does not introduce Jesus Christ with a fanciful title; rather, he calls him the accursed Christ.[13] Emphatically, he writes, "Christ redeemed us from the curse of the law by becoming a curse for us" (v. 13). Here, the personal pronoun ἡμᾶς ("us") is understood to refer to both Jews and Gentiles since, throughout the letter to the Galatians, Paul consistently addresses his hearers without making a distinction.

The indicative aorist verb ἐξηγόρασεν ("redeemed") can be understood as a constative aorist showing the redemptive work of Christ as a historical event. Here, the use of the verb ἐξαγοράζω best refers to a release from bondage to the Torah and/or the curse of the law rather than the manumission of slaves. Christ is the means by which the curse (and death) is removed.[14]

The preposition ὑπὲρ ("for"/"on behalf of") in verse 13 can be taken as a genitive of substitution/exchange, or a genitive of advantage to show benefit. Cheboi writes concerning the quotation in verse 13, "Looking at the socio-rhetorical intertexture of this verse, Paul reconfigures a criminal hanged on a tree to a crucified Messiah who becomes accursed so that he can be an end to the curse suffered by humanity."[15]

---

12. Ryken, Wilhoit, Longman et al., *Dictionary of Biblical Imagery*, 187.

13. Likewise, the title of the "crucified Christ" as the center of human salvation was unattractive to some of Paul's audience (1 Cor 1:23).

14. Cheboi, "Crucified and Cursed Christ," 194–95. He observes that "I bind" is a key phrase that is common in ancient curse texts and binding spells (*defixiones*); he then suggests that the use of the verb ἐξαγοράζω (redemption) possibly shows that Christ paid the redemption price for the release from the bondage of curses and binding spells.

15. Cheboi, 114.

Further, in verse 14, Paul points out the benefits of Christ's redemption: it is so that the blessings of Abraham might come to the Gentiles, and so that we might receive the promise of the Spirit through faith. According to Paul, before Christ, there was law, curse and death; but now, in Christ, there is faith, blessing and life.[16]

The Practice of Cursing in the Ancient Near East and Greco-Roman Contexts

It has been widely observed that cursing and blessing practices were common both in the ancient Near East and in the Greco-Roman world. Anne Kitz has done extensive studies on ancient Near Eastern practices and notes that "every member of society used [curses], from slave to king, from young to old, from men and women to the deities themselves. They crossed cultural lines and required little or no explanation, for curses were the source of great evil."[17] Gager concurs regarding the widespread nature of this phenomenon, and quotes S. A. B. Mercer:

> The malediction in Babylonian and Assyrian times was a highly developed legal and religious ceremony, universally practiced and respected. It not only figured in ceremonies of great occasions but also penetrated the everyday life of the people. It seemed to have served almost the same purpose as Common Law does among modern people, for it acted as a restraint, corrective, and stimulant to better deeds.[18]

Likewise, in the Greco-Roman world, it is argued that nearly 99 percent of the population believed in the power of spells and curses.[19] Apart from believing in the presence of curses and binding spells, the ancients also feared curses; as Pliny the Elder remarked, "There is no one who is not afraid of curses and binding spells."[20]

---

16. Lührmann, *Galatians*, 62.
17. Kitz, *Cursed Are You!*, 3.
18. Quoted in Gager, *Curse Tablets and Binding Spells*, 27.
19. Gager, 244.
20. Quoted in Gager, 220.

The Functions of Curses and Binding Spells in the Ancient World

Curses and binding spells that were used in the ancient world can be put into two broad categories. The first category of curses and binding spells were used by people, in consultation with a professional curse-dispenser, against others, and primarily for personal gain. Such curses include, first, those used in sports and competitions. The main purpose of these curses was to hinder one's opponent from winning and to increase one's chances of gaining victory. Second, some curses and binding spells were used in relation to sex, love and marriage.[21] Gager estimates that one-quarter of all surviving curse tablets concern "matters of the heart." Specifically, these curses were used to win or lure lovers into a relationship or marriage. Third, curses and binding spells were used in business to manage competition and rivalry and to safeguard one's economic interests. Fourth, curses and binding spells were used in legal and political disputes to manipulate litigation processes for one's own benefit. As noted above, curses in this category were specifically used by people against each other for personal gain.[22]

However, there was a second distinctive category of curses, referred to as judicial curses (pleas for justice and revenge), which were pronounced out of a need for justice and punishment for an offense by known or unknown offenders. These curses were directed to a deity to execute justice or revenge on behalf of the victim.[23] Judicial curses were greatly feared since deities were implored to act on behalf of a victim of injustice.

A survey of the use of curses and binding spells in all these areas of ancient life is a testament to the fact that the practice of cursing and the fear of being cursed were real. Moreover, every event, both in private and in public life, was interpreted through the lenses of curse and blessing. In such a context, Paul's audience must have understood and appreciated Paul's Christology with greater insight.

Prevention and Removal of Curses in the Ancient World

Ancient people were not only conscious of the problem of curses in their world, but they were also aware of a variety of ways in which curses and binding spells could be prevented or canceled. Even before reading Galatians 3:13, a Galatian

---

21. Janowitz, *Magic in the Roman World*, 47.
22. Gager, *Curse Tablets and Binding Spells*, discusses these curses in detail. He translates extant curse tablets that were used in each of these categories.
23. Versnel, "Beyond Cursing," 68.

reading 3:10 must have understood the seriousness of humanity being under a curse. Still, the person would have thought through some contemporary ways in which a curse could be canceled.

Curses were generally prevented at all costs because of the potentially disastrous consequences they were believed to bring. However, if someone came under the oppressive powers of a curse, the ancient cultures offered ways in which the curse could be reversed.

Briefly, the ancients believed that curses could be prevented, and so they put in place some countermeasures, including the wearing of amulets and stones of Hermes. These amulets were worn close to some part of the body, usually the neck, an arm or a leg, and were believed to help ward off or neutralize curses and binding spells.[24] However, in cases where the curse had already been uttered, a remedial alternative was used to remove the curse. There were several ways of removing curses in the ancient world.

Ways of Removing Curses in Antiquity

Scapegoat Rituals

In the ancient Near East and Greco-Roman contexts, the scapegoat (apotropaeic) ritual was one way of curing curses and their disruption of social harmony. In these contexts, "the scapegoat ritual embodies that once sin had blighted the people, it would work itself out upon them unless a substitute could be provided upon whom it might be discharged."[25]

Like sin, curses are disastrous and bring death unless remedied. In Judaism, apotropaeic victims were exclusively animals; however, McLean notes that within the surrounding culture, the Bible records instances where apotropaeic rituals involved human beings. In 2 Samuel 21:1–10, during a famine crisis in Israel, the Gibeonites demanded that King David hand over to them human scapegoats to avenge the blood of murdered Gibeonites. Interestingly, when seven men were offered, the famine ceased. Further, the sailors who threw the prophet Jonah to the raging sea were offering Jonah as an apotropaeic ritual (Jonah 1:1–10). In the New Testament, Caiaphas, the high priest, received a revelation that it was better for one man to die than for the whole nation to perish (John 11:50).[26]

---

24. Gager, *Curse Tablets and Binding Spells*, 239.
25. McLean, *Cursed Christ*, 77.
26. McLean, 101–2.

This background possibly helped Paul's audience to understand the aspect of the transferability of curses and their remedy. In addition, this cultural resource may have helped them put into perspective the substitutionary death of Christ, the curse-bearer who dies for many.

Sacrifice Rituals

In any religious society, sacrifice is central. The ancient people sacrificed to the gods, but of great importance here is the fact that they used sacrifices to reverse curses and binding spells.[27] Old Testament Judaism forbade human sacrifice; that is why the sacrificial system involved only animals and, in some cases, birds (Lev 18:21). The Old Testament animal sacrifices were a type whose antitype was Christ. God permitted animal sacrifice in the meantime, in anticipation of the coming of the ultimate sacrifice, Jesus Christ. John the Baptist referred to Jesus as the Lamb of God who takes away the sin of the world (John 1:29). Thus, those among Paul's audience who interpreted the work of Christ using the sacrificial paradigm, might have appreciated the unblemished nature of Christ's sacrifice, the transference of sin to an unblemished sacrifice for the benefit of the worshipper, and the significance of the death of the sacrifice.

Herbal Antidotes

In antiquity, curses were also reversed with the help of a curse specialist, who would prescribe a herbal formula, from specific plants, to counter curses and binding spells. The procedure for removing a curse or a binding spell by means of a herbal antidote required following strict instructions and rituals.[28]

Cursing Curses and Exorcism

Another way the ancient people removed curses and binding spells was to consult a curse professional who would direct curses to existing curses. Kitz notes that in the new curses pronounced, "he [the curse specialist] loosened, removed, dismissed, and unbound imprecations. He cursed curses with curses. He also dealt with the surrounding of the victim. He traveled to private residences and directed the performance of rites for and by the sufferer."[29]

---

27. McLean, 52–64. Here, McLean discusses sacrifices in ancient religions.
28. Gager, *Curse Tablets and Binding Spells*, 237.
29. Kitz, *Cursed Are You!*, 3.

Confession

As mentioned above, the judicial curses emanated from a need to correct wrongdoing or revenge. Judicial curses uttered on an unknown offender could be reversed if the offender confessed his or her wrongdoing[30] – that is, if the cursed person acknowledged and repented of his or her sin that led to the curse.

In summary, Paul's audience was aware of various alternatives by which curses and binding spells could be removed. Like the scapegoat ritual, some alternatives, such as sacrifice rituals and confession, must have largely contributed to their understanding of Christ's substitutionary death in relation to the curse. It was believed that when these ways were followed, the curse was erased, and the victim regained blessings.

Ineffectiveness of the Ancient Ways of Removing Curses

Although Paul was aware of the prevailing means by which curses and binding spells could be removed, he still developed a Christology that addressed the issue. The pervasive and enduring fear of curses among ancient people is a clear testament to the fact that the issue of curses remained largely unsolved.

The ways of removing curses in the ancient world only managed the situation and did not offer the ultimate solution. For example, the Akkadian *māmīt pašāru* (curse-releasing) ritual had a limited dual role: "It principally bans active, extant evils. These malevolences are enticed to go elsewhere, down the river, up in the sky like smoke, down into the earth, or destroyed outright, and burned."[31] From this inscription we see that curses were not removed; rather, as the Akkadian ritual demonstrates, they were only "enticed to go elsewhere," and could perhaps return.

The Crucified and Cursed Christ as the Ultimate Remover of Curses

In Galatians 3:13, Paul presents Jesus Christ as the good remover of curses. Paul anchors his argument on the death of Christ on the cross. He presents the crucified Christ not only as a curse-bearer but also as the ultimate curse-breaker. In Jesus, the curse is not rebuked but remedied.[32] Although Jesus was tempted in every way, Hebrews 4:15 notes that he remained sinless; therefore,

---

30. Crawford, *Blessing and Curse*, 115.
31. Kitz, *Cursed Are You!*, 331.
32. Dunn, *Epistle to the Galatians*, 177.

he was not under the curse of the law. He voluntarily took upon himself the curse of lawbreakers, faced death, which is a consequence of the curse, but emerged victorious.

The crucified Christ offered himself to bring a solution not just to the problem of sin but also to the problem of the curse. Through his death, Jesus represented all those who are under the curse, and he destroyed the power of the curse. Christ's death obliterated other deaths that are occasioned by curses so that believers can have the life and blessings of God. Through their union with Christ (Gal 2:20), believers can benefit from the substitutionary work of Jesus on the cross.

It is worth noting that the solution Paul gives in Galatians 3:13 is unique; "Paul developed his solution of curses around a Person and not on herbal prescription, etc. The use of amulets, animal sacrifices, and rituals to break curses in the ancient world falls short of God's ordained way in which curses are broken."[33] Paul's approach takes the problem of curses as something serious and internal that needs a divine solution. The crucified and cursed Christ is the solution that Paul fronted before the Galatians and, by extension, to today's readers of Galatians.

Implications for African Christology

The problem of curses is a critical aspect of the African cosmology. From the past to the present, many African societies have believed in curses and cursing practice. Curses are prayers to the spiritual world intended to inflict harm on a target person. It is argued that

> in Africa, a curse is any attempt to use an invocation to cause harm to someone. An utterance whose cause is to do damage to the intended victim is a curse. It may be uttered by an individual with a particular religious or moral status. In such a situation, it is often considered necessary for the victim to invoke an ancestor, Spirit, or deity to respond.[34]

The invocation of the spiritual world to intervene in human affairs is what makes curses something to be dreaded.

Due to the dire consequences of curses for individuals, families and societies, people fear curses, whether real or imagined. Fear of curses and

---

33. Cheboi, "Crucified and Cursed Christ," 184.
34. Asante and Mazama, *Encyclopedia of African Religion*, 188.

belief in their efficacy is widespread in Africa.[35] Further, "from the earliest times in ancient Africa, curses were used to frighten enemies and explain certain conditions of harm that came to people."[36] Many Africans continue to use the lenses of blessing and curse to interpret severe circumstances or happenings in personal, family and communal life. For example, when there are successive deaths in a family for no apparent reason, this can easily be interpreted as the consequence of a curse. Likewise, other unexplained life-taking experiences are attributed to curses. Of course, the truthfulness of such a conclusion attracts divergent views. Still, we need to realize that based on such experiences to which people closely relate, the African worldview readily offered or offers solutions.

In societies where cursing is practiced, such curses are commissioned either by an individual or by the community. Just as in the world of the Bible, some curses in the African belief system are pronounced by individuals out of envy. However, a category of curses in Africa originated from wrongdoing, such as the violation of a taboo or an oath.[37] In some African communities, curses have been used as "a powerful instrument of justice"[38] – that is, to address injustice caused by known or unknown offenders. It is important to note here that the African cursing system acknowledges that a curse results from sin or from a violation of societal norms.

Ways of Removing Curses in the African Belief System

Traditionally, it is believed that "unless the power of the word is broken, a person who has been cursed will remain under the curse forever. Rituals are thus important as a means of removing curses or rendering them impotent."[39] One way a curse was removed in the African belief system was by a traditional specialist demanding that certain sacrifices be made. In this way, the required unblemished sacrifice died on behalf of the accursed person, in order for the curse to be removed and for blessings to be restored.[40] In some instances, the accursed person(s) paid a fee as compensation.[41] Second, a curse was annulled

---

35. Lugira, *African Traditional Religion*, 85.
36. Asante and Mazama, *Encyclopedia of African Religion*, 188.
37. Asante and Mazama, 188.
38. Kipkorir and Welbourn, *Marakwet of Kenya*, 9.
39. Kunhiyop, *African Christian Theology*, 109.
40. Cheboi, "Crucified and Cursed Christ," 212.
41. Asante and Mazama, *Encyclopedia of African Religion*, 189.

when the violator (the one cursed) confessed his or her wrong.[42] In this case, the curse was reversed, and the victim paid the penalty stipulated.

Third, the removal of curses in some communities such as the Marakwet tribe in Kenya was carried out by a team of respectable individuals called *Ōsis*. The community constituted a panel of individuals from a different community (but within the tribe) who had an outstanding reputation for being neutral, peace-loving, just and impartial.[43] Such people were accorded the responsibility of determining the cause of a curse and performing the necessary rituals that would free the accursed person(s).

Based on this brief survey of possible ways in which a curse could be removed in the African belief system, we can note some possible areas for applying Galatians 3 to the African context. First, the belief that some curses emanate not just from envy but from wrongdoing can provide a rich beginning point for engaging the biblical truth, which supports the fact that curses are a consequence of sin. Second, the African idea of the need for an unblemished sacrifice to remove a curse can be related to the perfect sacrifice of Jesus (Heb 4:15) and its substitutionary nature. The idea of confession of sin as a means of removing a curse is expounded below. It can be concluded here that, to those who believe in him, the innocent Lamb of God (John 1:29), through his death, ends deaths occasioned by curses. This single death of the Son of God restores life, peace and blessings to individuals, families and communities. The way Jesus took our curse upon himself is the same way we gain his blessings and righteousness.

It is worth noting that, although African people have many ways of removing curses, the fear of curses remains. The helplessness that comes with curses makes people succumb to fear; some Christians who do not have strong biblical foundations become unsure what to do when faced with situations that are thought to be occasioned by curses. The animal sacrifices for curse-removal needed to be conducted repeatedly; in each instance, there was a curse. This is an area that the supremacy and the once-for-all sacrifice of Jesus can significantly address and provide an answer. Further, African people know that "curses placed on human beings by human beings are inevitably removed by force that must be equal to or greater than the force of the curse."[44] Jesus Christ, as both God and human being in his nature, is that person (not force) who is greater and able to deal with the problem of curses effectively and completely.

---

42. Evans-Pritchard, *Nuer Religion*, 175.
43. Cheboi, "Crucified and Cursed Christ," 210.
44. Asante and Mazama, *Encyclopedia of African Religion*, 189.

A biblically based approach to this problem should lead African people to believe in the death of Jesus Christ as the ultimate sacrifice that removes both sin and the curse.

A Pastoral Response to the Problem of Curses

So how, practically, can African pastors respond to a situation that people interpret to be the consequence of a curse? This question is related to this study but goes beyond this study's scope, so a suggestion will suffice. Pastorally, to deal with curses there is, first, a need to discern truth from (false) allegations. Kunhiyop cautions that some fear of curses, even among Christians, might be based on deception by some preachers.[45] The role of prayer in this process is thus critical for determining whether the cause of a recurrent misfortune in a person's life or family is indeed the result of a curse.

Second, I suggest we develop a biblical solution based on one of the ancient and African ways of removing curses, which also has a biblical foundation, namely confession. This approach would lead us to rightly appropriate the work of Jesus on the cross on the matter, since confession is also a key part of Christianity. Interestingly, the ancients put value on confession as one of the ways of reversing curses. H. S. Versnel, who has examined some confessional inscriptions from the second and third centuries AD, notes that a curse was removed when a cursed person confessed that he or she had transgressed both people and the God(s).[46] Also, repentance could be occasioned by the severity of the punishments from the deities. Versnel further observes that when the accursed person confessed his or her guilt, appeased the gods, made reparation and fulfilled the ritualistic requirements, the deities cured that person.[47] It has also been noted above that confession is one way in which curses have been removed in African communities.

Thus, a biblical, theological and pastoral approach should be based on the work of Jesus (the cursed and crucified Christ) on the cross and confession of sin. It should also take into consideration issues such as forgiveness and compensation, but it should be devoid of ritualistic tendencies. Christians should be equipped through biblical teaching to overcome the fear of curses and be helped to understand that through the death of Christ, believers have the power to overcome death and be a blessing.

---

45. Kunhiyop, *African Christian Theology*, 114.
46. Versnel, "Beyond Cursing," 75.
47. Versnel, 76.

Conclusion

This paper looked at Paul's presentation of Jesus Christ in Galatia as both crucified and cursed. The true gospel esteems the person of Jesus Christ and the ongoing ministry of God the Father through his Holy Spirit. Paul argues that justification by faith brings salvation, life, freedom and blessing. This was the promise that was first delivered to Abraham, who became the beneficiary of the same gracious gift of salvation. The gospel pronounced to Abraham also revealed God's redemptive plan for the nations. However, for life, freedom and blessings to be realized, the problem of the curse has to be dealt with. Paul argues that all human beings are affected by the curse, whether they rely on observing the law or not. This forms the background against which Paul presents Jesus Christ as the solution to the problem of the curse. He presents Jesus as the cursed Christ who took upon himself the curse of the law so that those who are united to him become free from the curse, and so that the blessing given to Abraham might come to the nations.

This paper then established that the practice of cursing was widespread in the ancient Near East and the Greco-Roman world. Curses and binding spells were used in every area of life, from business, sports, love and marriage, to judicial matters. The ancients feared curses, and so they found means to prevent coming under the power of curses. However, if they became cursed, people in antiquity found ways of reversing curses. Paul's Christology, in relation to the issue of curses, was originally understood in light of prevailing cultural means of removing curses. The apostle Paul developed a solution that puts the person of Jesus and Jesus's work on the cross at the center.

Finally, the study briefly presented the practice of cursing in many African cultures. The study pointed out some areas where the biblical truth can be relevantly appropriated into the African belief system while maintaining the supremacy of Christ's role as the ultimate curse-remover.

Bibliography

Asante, Molefi Kete, and Ama Mazama, eds. *Encyclopedia of African Religion*. Thousand Oaks: SAGE, 2009.

Betz, Hans Dieter. *Galatians*. Hermeneia. Philadelphia: Fortress, 1979.

Bruce, F. F. *The Epistle to the Galatians: A Commentary on the Greek Text*. New International Greek Testament Commentary. Grand Rapids: Eerdmans, 2002.

Byrne, Brendan. *Sons of God, Seed of Abraham: A Study of the Idea of the Sonship of God of All Christians in Paul against the Jewish Background*. Analecta Biblica 83. Rome: Biblical Institute, 1979.

Cheboi, Elkanah Kiprop. "Crucified and Cursed Christ: A Socio-Rhetorical Analysis of Galatians 3:1–14 and Its Relevance to Marakwet Culture." PhD diss., Africa International University, 2019.

Crawford, Timothy G. *Blessing and Curse in Syro-Palestinian Inscriptions of the Iron Age*. American University Studies, Series 7, Theology and Religion, 120. New York: Peter Lang, 1992.

Dunn, James D. G. *The Epistle to the Galatians*. Black's New Testament Commentaries. Peabody: Hendrickson, 1993.

Evans-Pritchard, E. E. *Nuer Religion*. New York: Oxford University Press, 1956.

Gager, John G., ed. *Curse Tablets and Binding Spells from the Ancient World*. New York: Oxford University Press, 1992.

Garlington, Don B. *An Exposition of Galatians: A New Perspective/Reformational Reading*. 2nd ed. Eugene: Wipf & Stock, 2004.

Hays, Richard B. *The Faith of Jesus Christ: The Narrative Substructure of Galatians 3:1 – 4:11*. 2nd ed. The Biblical Resource Series. Grand Rapids: Eerdmans, 2002.

Janowitz, Naomi. *Magic in the Roman World: Pagans, Jews, and Christians*. Religion in the First Christian Centuries. London: Routledge, 2001.

Kipkorir, B. E., and Frederick Burkewood Welbourn. *The Marakwet of Kenya: A Preliminary Study*. New ed. Nairobi: East African Educational, 2008.

Kitz, Anne Marie. *Cursed Are You! The Phenomenology of Cursing in Cuneiform and Hebrew Texts*. Winona Lake: Eisenbrauns, 2014.

Kunhiyop, Samuel Waje. *African Christian Theology*. Carlisle: HippoBooks, 2012.

Lugira, Aloysius Muzzanganda. *African Traditional Religion*. 3rd ed. World Religions. New York: Chelsea House, 2009.

Lührmann, Dieter. *Galatians*. 1st Fortress Press ed. A Continental Commentary. Minneapolis: Fortress, 1992.

Martyn, J. Louis. *Galatians: A New Translation with Introduction and Commentary*. The Anchor Bible 33A. New York: Doubleday, 1997.

McLean, B. Hudson. *The Cursed Christ: Mediterranean Expulsion Rituals and Pauline Soteriology*. Journal for the Study of the New Testament Supplement Series 126. Sheffield: Sheffield Academic Press, 1996.

Ryken, Leland, Jim Wilhoit, Tremper Longman, Colin Duriez, Douglas Penney and Daniel G. Reid, eds. *Dictionary of Biblical Imagery*. Downers Grove: InterVarsity Press, 1998.

Versnel, H. S. "Beyond Cursing: The Appeal to Justice in Judicial Prayers." In *Magika Hiera: Ancient Greek Magic and Religion*, edited by Christopher A. Faraone and Dirk Obbink, 60–106. New York: Oxford University Press, 1991.

Wright, Christopher J. H. *The Mission of God's People: A Biblical Theology of the Church's Mission*. Grand Rapids, MI: Zondervan, 2010.

6

The Benefaction of the Messiah as the Supreme King in the Context of the Greco-Roman Ethic of Reciprocity

An Exegetical Analysis of Romans 5:6–8

Enoch O. Okode

Dean, School of Theology, Scott Christian University, Machakos, Kenya

Abstract

Romans 5:7 has presented an exegetical conundrum to the readers of Romans over the centuries. Many interpreters skip over this verse, or say little about it, claiming that the gist of Paul's argument is clear enough even without it. Some exegetes treat the verse as an unnecessary parenthetical comment or as a digression. Such approaches miss out on a key point of Paul's goal to depict the Messiah as the supreme royal benefactor. If we read Romans 5:7 within the framework of the Greco-Roman benefaction system and within the immediate context of 5:6–8, then we will see that Paul portrays Jesus as a king whose benefaction is superior and surprising because it overturns key aspects of the Greco-Roman ethic of reciprocity. Many Greco-Roman writers affirm that no sacrifice is too great to pay for the sake of "the good" (ἀγαθός).

The term ἀγαθός is often used to refer to the benefactor who wins great honor due to his generosity and concern for the welfare of others. In Romans 5:7, Paul alludes to the rare but not inconceivable practice whereby the beneficiary of a favor would be willing to die on behalf of his benefactor. The Messiah, however, lays down his life neither for a just person nor for "the good," but for the weak, ungodly and sinners, and in so doing, he offers an indiscriminate gift that subverts the Greco-Roman expectation of a heroic act of reciprocity. Christ's indiscriminate gift should, in turn, be the basis for how believers view one another within our respective contexts.

Key words: benefaction, the good, gift, reciprocity, Romans 5:7, sacrifice, substitutionary death, obligation

Introduction: A Survey of Romans 5:7 Scholarship

Romans 5:7 has presented an exegetical conundrum to the readers of Romans over the centuries. Paul writes: "For rarely would anyone die for a righteous person [δικαίου]; though perhaps for the sake of the good person [τοῦ ἀγαθοῦ] one would dare even to die" (AT).[1] Does Paul use δίκαιος and ἀγαθός interchangeably, or do they bear distinct connotations? Does Paul commit an exegetical frivolity? Could this verse be an unnecessary parenthetical comment or a digression? While many interpreters skip over this verse, or say little about it, claiming that the gist of Paul's argument is clear enough even without it, I contend in this paper that Paul's argument makes better sense when read within the framework of the Greco-Roman benefaction system and the ethic of reciprocity that sustains it.

There are at least three common approaches to Romans 5:7. The first approach, which is also the least helpful, is resorting to exegetical agnosticism. Werner G. Kümmel represents this approach when he asserts that there can never be certainty regarding the meaning of 5:7.[2] The second approach is to trivialize the details of Romans 5:7. C. K. Barrett suggests that the details of the verse "are insignificant," whereas Ernst Käsemann argues that the analogy of 5:7 "is of no help" since it "pushes Christ's death into the sphere of the heroic."[3] The third approach recognizes that Paul uses the analogy of substitutionary

---

1. Unless indicated otherwise, all translations are the author's (marked as AT).
2. Kümmel, *Exegetical Method*, 63.
3. Barrett, *Epistle to the Romans*, 99; Käsemann, *Commentary on Romans*, 99. Closely related is McFarland (*God and Grace in Philo and Paul*, 119), who states that in 5:7 "Paul digresses from 5.6 to set up an antithesis with 5.8."

death, but even those who fall into this category often inadequately address the relationship between a "righteous" person and "the good" person.[4]

All these interpretive approaches underscore the need to once again grapple with the exegetical puzzles of Romans 5:7. Paul's aims in Romans 5:1–11 depict the Messiah as the supreme royal benefactor who offers the ultimate indiscriminate gift to the unworthy.[5] If we read Romans 5:7 within the framework of the Greco-Roman benefaction system and within the immediate context of 5:6–8, then we will see that Paul portrays Jesus as a king whose benefaction is superior and surprising because it overturns important aspects of the ethic of reciprocity. I will build on Andrew Clarke's argument that "the good" denotes one's benefactor even as I maintain that Paul alludes to the rare but not inconceivable practice whereby beneficiaries of a favor would be willing to die on behalf of their benefactors.[6] The Messiah, however, lays down his life neither for a just person nor for "the good," but for the weak, ungodly and sinners, and in so doing, he subverts the Greco-Roman expectation of a heroic act of reciprocity. The Messiah's surprising and indiscriminate benefaction should, in turn, be foundational for how believers relate to one another within the body of Christ.

This work employs the methodology of a multidisciplinary comparative study involving both sociohistorical and theological analyses. Jonathan A. Linebaugh writes, "Texts look different when they are allowed to talk," as familiar passages become "strange and come alive."[7] One of the premises of contextual studies is that the text's meaning is inextricably embedded in how the text interacts with its sociohistorical context. Texts are cultural artifacts whose meaning may not be apparent to those who read them hundreds of years after composition. Because no text is composed in a historical vacuum, it is necessary to investigate how authors might be interacting with their contemporary values and worldviews. In this work, I am mainly interested in how understanding some aspects of the ancient royal benefaction system might illuminate our reading of Paul's portrait of Jesus as found in Romans 5:7. As

---

4. Andria, *Romans*, 95–96; Kasali, "Romans," 1385; Moo, *Epistle to the Romans*, 307–8. Also related is Dunn, *Romans 1–8*, 266. Dunn finds echoes of martyr theology in Rom 5:7. For a helpful summary of interpretations of Rom 5:7, especially regarding the relationship between δίκαιος and ἀγαθός, see Clarke, "The Good and the Just," 132–33.

5. "Benefactor" is the English rendition of the Greek technical term εὐεργέτης, which is also translated as "euergetism." Although Paul Veyne did not coin the term "euergetism," he popularized it in his book *Bread and Circuses*. For a brief history of the term, see Garnsey, "Generosity of Veyne," 164–68.

6. Clarke, "The Good and the Just."

7. Linebaugh, *God, Grace, and Righteousness*, 20.

Paul writes in the Greco-Roman social context, there is every likelihood that his readers, who inhabit the same social context, would recognize that he is employing benefaction language and that his christological discourse presents Jesus Christ as the supreme royal benefactor whose gift overturns key aspects of the ethic of reciprocity.

This essay has four main sections. The first section establishes an interpretive framework by providing an overview of the Greco-Roman benefaction system, with particular focus on the ideal ruler as a gift-giver, as well as the convention that benefactions are obligatory. The second section examines Paul's argument in Romans 5:7 by discussing how Paul subverts the ethic of reciprocity. The third section situates Romans 5:7 within the context of Romans 5:6–8. The final section considers how the Messiah's indiscriminate gift should inform how we relate to one another as believers.

An Overview of the Greco-Roman Benefaction System

My argument is that Paul depicts Christ as the supreme royal benefactor, whose superior gift overturns critical aspects of the Greco-Roman ethic of reciprocity. Greco-Roman benefaction may be defined as a system of calculated gift exchange that seeks to enhance social cohesion by the ethic of reciprocity.[8] The ideal king is a generous benefactor who is committed to the welfare of his subjects.[9] Dio Chrysostom writes that the good king receives his scepter from Zeus and finds great pleasure in using it for the welfare of his subjects (*1 Regn.* 12–13; cf. 84).[10] Such a king delights in bestowing benefits (*2 Regn.* 26). Pliny notes in *Panegyricus* for Trajan that the ideal emperor is a benefactor and paternal protector (e.g. 2, 21, 28–31, 50). Augustus's *Res Gestae* recounts his benefactions and services to the Roman people as the emperor portrays himself as a generous benefactor and an effective agent of the Pax Romana. Arrian

---

8. There is debate as to whether benefaction is identical to patronage. Broadly speaking, patronage may denote a long-term, inegalitarian social control system in which gifts and favors are exchanged between patrons and clients (Saller, *Personal Patronage*, 1). Many scholars use "benefaction" and "patronage" interchangeably while some argue for a clear distinction between the terms (a representative of the former is Moxnes, "Patron–Client Relations," 241–70; for the latter, see Joubert, *Paul as Benefactor*, 59). The goal of this study is not to resolve this debate. We will be using the term "benefaction" (as defined above) while acknowledging that at times we might use it where some would prefer "patronage."

9. See Bringmann, "King as Benefactor," 7–24; Erskine, "Romans as Common Benefactors," 70–87; Stevenson, "Ideal Benefactor," 421–36.

10. Unless otherwise noted, the editions and translations consulted for Greek and Roman sources are from the Loeb Classical Library, often with slight modification.

writes that Alexander sparingly used money "for his own pleasures, but [was] most liberal in employing it for the benefit of others" (*Anab.* 7.28.3). Seneca states that the good king ensures that his subjects lack nothing and adorns them by his kindness (*Ep.* 90.5). In brief, a good ruler is a generous benefactor.

In addition to generosity, the ideal ruler needs to distribute benefactions judiciously. Benefactions must be commensurate with the worthiness of the beneficiary (Aristotle, *Eth. nic.* 4.1.7–18; Cicero, *Off.* 1.15.46–49; 2.15.55; cf. 1.16.50; Dio, *3 Regn.* 110). To give gifts indiscriminately is to act foolishly and to destroy social cohesion. Indiscriminate benefaction destroys social cohesion because it fails to reward the virtuous and punish the impious. The impious ought to be punished by withholding gifts from them. Therefore, the benefactors are urged to apply the rule of censorship and strategically place their gifts (Seneca, *Ben.* 4.28.5–6).[11] A gift given to a person who is base is dishonorable (Seneca, *Ben.* 4.9.3). Benefits should be bestowed, not merely upon people, but *because of who they are* (Seneca, *Ben.* 6.18.2). Noncalculating gift-giving is "the thoughtless indulgence that masquerades as generosity" (Seneca, *Ben.* 1.4.3); it is like a farmer who sows seed in "worn-out and unproductive soil," and who inevitably suffers a loss (Seneca, *Ben.* 1.1.2).[12] One needs to place gifts like a skilled player pitching the ball to a skilled catcher (Seneca, *Ben.* 2.27.3–5). A gift needs to "go by a path, and not wander" (Seneca, *Ben.* 1.14.2). Instead of scattering gifts indiscriminately, they should give them selectively since "it is more important who receives a thing than what it is he receives" (Seneca, *Ep.* 19.11–12). Giving to the wrong people (namely the base, enemies and the ungrateful) is not a sign of generosity; rather, it indicates thoughtlessness and indifference to excellence and reputation.

In turn, benefactions are reciprocated by honoring the benefactor since, in Greco-Roman society, gifts come with inalienable ties of obligation.[13] Reciprocity is simply a conventional structure of exchange necessary for the maintenance of social cohesion as the beneficiaries discharge their obligation to the benefactor by rendering gratitude and loyalty. Reciprocity also consolidates

---

11. By the rule of censorship, I simply mean the act of identifying the impious and punishing them by withholding gifts from them. The benefactors should distribute gifts to the virtuous only.

12. Seneca writes: "Thoughtless benefaction is the most shameful sort of loss" (*Ben.* 4.10.3).

13. For further discussion on the obligations created by gifts, see Hands, *Charities and Social Aid*, 26–48; Bourdieu, *Le Sens pratique*, 167–231; Bourdieu, "Marginalia," 231–41; Irigaray, "Selections from the Logic of Practice," 190–230.

the relative status of the benefactor and the beneficiaries.[14] So at the heart of generosity is the benefactor's love of honor; therefore, the benefactor seeks to maintain his elevated status through publicized reciprocity and ongoing dependency of the subjects.[15] To underline the need for reciprocity, Sophocles states that "it is always one kindness (χάρις) that begets another, and if a man allows the memory of a kindness to slip away, he can no longer be accounted noble" (*Aj.* 522–24). Aristotle states that "in the interchange of services, justice in the form of reciprocity is the bond that maintains the association" (*Eth. nic.* 5.5.6). According to Lucian, "the king's most important reward is praise, universal fame, reverence for his benefactions, statues and temples and shrines bestowed on him by his subjects." He adds that such rewards "are payment for the thought and care which such men evidence in their continual watch over the common weal and its improvement" (*Merc. cond.* 13). Failure to give appropriate honor to a benefactor is disgraceful and might be viewed as a manifestation of impiety toward the gods, who are the ultimate benefactors.[16] Thus without reciprocity, benefaction would collapse, leading to social disintegration.[17] Honors and expressions of gratitude may be in the form of honorary inscriptions, public praise, social or political support, statues, crowns, seats of honor, and vicarious death.

It is evident from the initial overview of the Greco-Roman benefaction system that the ideal ruler is a benefactor appointed by the gods to promote the welfare of the people. He demonstrates his generosity and philanthropy by

---

14. Joubert ("One Form of Social Exchange or Two?," 24) rightly states, "The person in ancient Graeco-Roman society was a reciprocal being, *homo reciprocus*" (italics original). Also see Sahlins (*Stone Age Economics*, 191–96) who suggests that there were three forms of reciprocity in the ancient world: generalized reciprocity ("selfless"), balanced reciprocity ("commercial") and negative reciprocity ("self-interested").

15. According to Stegemann and Stegemann (*Urchristliche Sozialgeschichte*, 43), there were four primary forms of ancient reciprocity: (1) "*Familiäre Reziprozität*," which was operative at the household and clan level, with brotherly love as a social form of expression; (2) "*Ausgeglichene Reziprozität*" or egalitarian reciprocity, which was found between friends and neighbors, with hospitality, friendship and benefaction as social forms of expression; (3) "*Generelle Reziprozität*" or inegalitarian reciprocity, such as found between patrons and clients, or rich and poor, with almsgiving, patronage, religious service and discipleship as social forms of expression; and (4) "*Negative Reziprozität*," which existed between strangers and enemies, with hospitality and love as social forms of expression. Also see Sahlins (*Stone Age Economics*, 191–96), who suggests that there were three forms of reciprocity in the ancient world: generalized reciprocity ("selfless"), balanced reciprocity ("commercial") and negative reciprocity ("self-interested").

16. See Harland, *Associations, Synagogues, and Congregations*, 79; Hoklotubbe, *Civilized Piety*, 118–19; Blanton, *Spiritual Economy*, 3.

17. Mott ("Power of Giving and Receiving," 60) states that reciprocity is the dynamic factor in the "phenomenon of benefactor and beneficiary relationships" that ensures its social impact.

bestowing benefactions. Such benefactions might include overcoming enemies, maintaining peace, supplying grain, providing banquets and remitting taxes, among others. Yet gift-giving is also discriminatory as the benefactor must distribute gifts based on the worthiness of the beneficiaries. Additionally, because gifts are obligatory, the beneficiaries must be willing to reciprocate by honoring the benefactor. The goal of the section that follows is to demonstrate that Paul draws upon this ancient portrait of the ideal ruler as he presents Jesus as the supreme royal benefactor whose indiscriminate gift overturns the expectation of a vicarious death as a reciprocal act.

Paul's Subversion of the Ethic of Reciprocity in Romans 5:7

What exactly does Paul mean in Romans 5:7? It is unhelpful to skip over this verse or say little about it, claiming that the gist of Paul's argument is clear enough even without it. To treat this verse as an unnecessary parenthetical comment is to miss out on a key point of Paul's goal to depict the Messiah as the supreme royal benefactor.[18] Structurally, Romans 5:7 is an expansive comment on the main statement of 5:6 and highlights the extraordinary character of Christ's sacrifice.[19]

To substantiate our claim that this verse subverts critical aspects of the Greco-Roman ethic of reciprocity, we need to consider one central question: Why does Paul imply that there are greater obligations to the good than to a righteous person? The terms δίκαιος and ἀγαθός are distinct and yet related.[20] In Greco-Roman usage, a δίκαιος person "is one who upholds the customs and norms of behavior."[21] The righteous one is indeed a law-abiding citizen, but such a person does not necessarily care about the welfare of the city. But the one who is ἀγαθός meets "a high standard of worth and merit," mainly due to that person's "usefulness to humans and society in general."[22] A. W. H. Adkins comments that beginning with Homeric days, ἀγαθός was among the highly

---

18. In addition to the commentaries, some of the relevant resources here are Wisse, "Righteous Man and the Good Man," 91–93; Landau, "Martyrdom in Paul's Religious Ethics"; Clarke, "The Good and the Just"; Hammond Bammel, "Patristic Exegesis of Romans 5:7," 532–42; Martin, "The Good as God," 55–70.

19. Cranfield, *Romans I–VIII*, 264.

20. See, for example, Luke 23:50, where both terms are used about Joseph, who was from the Jewish town of Arimathea.

21. Danker et al. *Greek–English Lexicon*, 246.

22. Danker et al., 3.

valued words of praise in Greek society.²³ As Clarke notes, the term "described one who was valued because of considerable benefit to his immediate society."²⁴ Such people used their wealth to assist and offer protection to others. Therefore, the term was closely associated with the wealthy and ruling elite.²⁵ The good person's concern for the welfare of others explains why people would feel more obligated to that person. Adkins writes:

> To be *agathos* had always been more important than merely to be *dikaios*, and one's injustice did not traditionally . . . impair one's *arete*.[excellence or virtue] Again, to be *agathos* was to be a specimen of the human being at his best, making to society the contribution that society valued most; and the poorer citizens could not deny this, nor yet that they were not *agathoi* themselves.²⁶

As a technical description of the wealthy and elite, ἀγαθός is often employed in reference to benefactors. The good man bestows favors on the people, who, in turn, are expected to reciprocate. Dio castigates the people of Rhodes for their failure to honor their benefactors:

> It is regarding these matters, men of Rhodes, that I ask you to believe that the situation here among you is awful and unworthy of your state, your treatment, I mean, of your benefactors [τοὺς εὐεργέτας], and of the honors given to your good men [τῶν ἀγαθῶν ἀνδρῶν], although originally you did not handle the matter thus – most assuredly not! (*Or.* 31.8; cf. 31.14, 27, 65).

Concerning his father as a benefactor, Dio writes that "there is no need for me to tell whether he was a good [ἀγαθός] citizen, for you are always singing his praises, both collectively and individually, whenever you refer to him, as being no ordinary citizen" (*Or.* 46.2-3). Plutarch equates benefactors with good men who ought always to receive reward and gratitude from their beneficiaries (*Phil.* 21.6). The good man "cannot escape the thanks" of the beneficiaries (*Mor.* 1098E), for he is a benefactor to his friends (*Mor.* 218A). Aristotle states not only that "beneficence is a function of the good man and of virtue" (ἐστὶ τοῦ ἀγαθοῦ καὶ τῆς ἀρετῆς τὸ εὐεργετεῖν, *Eth. nic.* 9.9.2), but also that the king should be appointed based on benefaction, and that doing this "is a task for the good men" (ἐστὶν ἔργον τῶν ἀγαθῶν ἀνδρῶν, *Pol.* 3.10.11-12). Dio writes that

---

23. Adkins, *Merit and Responsibility*, 30–31.
24. Clarke, "The Good and the Just," 134.
25. Clarke, 135.
26. Adkins, *Moral Values and Political Behaviour*, 124.

nothing is nobler "than to show honor to our good men [τοὺς ἀγαθοὺς ἄνδρας] and to keep in remembrance those who have served us well" (*Rhod.* 31.7–8).

Sometimes honoring the good man calls for a heroic act, such as the willingness to die. It would be shameful for a beneficiary to refuse to suffer to the point of death on behalf of the good benefactor. Dio writes:

> For whereas in the cause of justice and virtue and ancestral rights and laws and for a good king, a noble soul, one that does not cling to life, will, if need be, suffer and even die. Yet, if a man hangs himself for the sake of his chorus-girl, a low-born outcast, not fit to live, what depths of disgrace does that betoken! (*Or.* 32.50)

Seneca shares similar sentiments concerning paying the ultimate price as a form of reciprocity to the good king: "In his [the king's] defense they [the subjects] are ready on the instant to throw themselves before the swords of assassins, and to lay their bodies beneath his feet if his path to safety must be paved with slaughtered men . . . against assailing dangers they make themselves a rampart" (*Clem.* 1.3.3). Seneca adds that when the subjects ransom a single life with many deaths, they publicize their love to the king (*Clem.* 1.3.4). No sacrifice is too great to pay for the sake of the good king.[27]

This background to the use of ἀγαθός within the Greco-Roman benefaction system sheds light on Paul's argument. Contrary to John Barclay, who maintains that "the labels appear to be general, and there is no good reason to take the second as a benefactor,"[28] there appears to be a distinction between the terms, with ἀγαθός denoting one's benefactor. Whereas δίκαιος simply refers to a law-abiding citizen who is not necessarily committed to the welfare of others, ἀγαθός refers to a benefactor whose concern for the well-being of others wins him great honor.[29] Rafael Rodríguez writes, "The social value of being *agathos* tapped into the cultural script of *benefaction*, in which the wealthy and élite members of a city provided goods and services to the city's population in exchange for public recognition, honor, and praise" (italics original).[30] We may, therefore, paraphrase the verse as follows: "For rarely would anyone

---

27. Valerius Maximus writes about L. Petronius, who showed loyalty to his benefactor by taking his own life and that of Caelius, thereby saving his benefactor from dying at his enemies' hands (*Memorable Doings and Sayings*, 4.7.5). For additional examples of vicarious deaths in Classical tradition, see Gathercole, *Defending Substitution*, 90–102. For more evidence of willingness to lay down one's life for one's friends or relatives, see Arrian, *Epict. diss.* 2.7.3; Philostratus, *Vit. Apoll.* 7.12. Also relevant here is Seeley, *Noble Death*, 83–112.

28. Barclay, *Paul and the Gift*, 477–78 n. 71.

29. For the possible use of ἀγαθός to refer to a benefactor in the LXX, see Pss 72:1; 117:1.

30. Rodríguez, *If You Call Yourself a Jew*, 103.

be willing to die on behalf of a law-abiding person, although[31] perhaps for the sake of[32] his benefactor one might even dare to die."[33] Paul knows that such a vicarious death for one's benefactor is rare, but it is not inconceivable, especially due to reciprocity. Yet what the Messiah does completely overturns this expectation. Jesus inverts the dominant transcript by giving his own life as a gift; the righteous one offers his gift indiscriminately to the entire sinful human race. Christ lays down his life, not as a heroic act of reciprocity to the good benefactor, but for the sake of the unworthy, to rescue them from sin and death. It is not the many who are ransoming the life of the one good benefactor (cf. Seneca, *Clem.* 1.3.3–4), but the one righteous and supreme benefactor ransoms the life of the many who are neither righteous nor good. The context of Romans 5:6–8 strengthens our argument that Christ's indiscriminate gift overturns the Greco-Roman expectation of a heroic act of reciprocity.

Romans 5:7 within the Context of 5:6–8

The Messiah, the supreme royal benefactor, offers his life *for us* as a gift. But who are we that the Messiah would die *for us*? As we have seen above, gift-giving in Greco-Roman society is deeply discriminatory as benefactors must judiciously identify worthy beneficiaries. Benefactors must apply the rule of censorship and of rating to place their gifts strategically. They must act as careful farmers, sowing their seed in productive soil, and as skilled players, pitching the ball to skilled catchers. Favors conferred on the wrong people do not yield returns; in fact, it is thoughtless and unacceptable to assist the base. Aristotle writes that whoever gives to the wrong people is not generous (*Eth. nic.* 4.1.14, 22–23). Cicero insists that a man should be favored to the extent that he exemplifies justice, self-control and temperance (*Off.* 1.15.46). Seneca asserts that to give to the base is dishonorable (*Ben.* 4.9.3). Gifts are bestowed on people *because of who they are* (6.18.2). Cicero urges that one's purse should not be "so loosely held as to be open to everybody" (*Off.* 2.15.55).

---

31. The Greek word here is γάρ, which would normally mean "for." But when the particle is repeated after a clause with a similar assertion, it might have a concessive force (cf. Danker et al., *Greek–English Lexicon*, 189).

32. The article has a possessive force here. Gathercole (*Defending Substitution*, 89), however, suggests that the article specifies "death on behalf of a particular *type* rather than necessarily seeing a specific individual in view."

33. Cranfield, *Romans I–VIII*, 265: "We understand Paul's meaning then to be that, whereas it is a rare thing for a man deliberately and in cold blood to lay down his life for the sake of an individual just man, and not very much less rare for a man to do so for the sake of an individual who is his benefactor, Christ died for the sake of the ungodly."

Does the Messiah's benefaction meet the ancient stipulation that favors ought to be conferred on the worthy? The answer to this question is found in how Paul describes those *for whom* the Messiah died and the *timing* of Christ's death. Paul uses three keywords to represent humanity. First, Romans 5:6 states that the Messiah died for the helpless (ἀσθενῶν). The adjective ἀσθενής means "weak" or "powerless." More specifically, it can denote "suffering from a debilitating illness" or "experiencing some incapacity or limitation."[34] Paul often uses the noun ἀσθένεια and the adjective ἀσθενής and related terms in a general sense "to characterize the human inability that is an inevitable part of life – even redeemed life – on this earth" (e.g. Rom 8:26; 1 Cor 15:43; 2 Cor 11:21 – 13:9).[35] But Paul does not seem to use this term here to describe human limitation in general. Contrary to James D. G. Dunn, who argues that "ἀσθενής does not have any particular theological overtones here" and that Paul uses it to characterize "the weakness of the creature over against the omnipotence of the Creator,"[36] the broader context of Romans 1–5 suggests that the term bears a negative theological connotation.

In Romans 1–3, Paul declares that humans are so enslaved to sin that they cannot rescue themselves. It is a situation marked by complete moral incapacitation. If Paul is simply describing humanity's limited power "over against the omnipotence of the Creator," then this term hardly contributes any point to his argument. Redemption does not aim to rescue humanity from its limitation and make it as powerful as God. The weakness that this term underlines is something from which society needs deliverance. Thus humanity is weak, not in the general sense of human finiteness, but in the negative sense of moral helplessness and inability to secure one's liberation.

The remaining two terms (ἀσεβῶν [5:6] and ἁμαρτωλῶν [5:8]), which Paul uses to describe those for whom the Messiah offered his life, are less problematic. The adjective ἀσεβής literally means "irreverent, impious, ungodly"; it pertains to "violating norms for a proper relationship to a deity."[37] Paul uses the same word in 4:5 when he declares that God makes the ungodly righteous. In 1:18, the cognate noun ἀσέβεια is used almost synonymously with ἀδικία ("unrighteousness"): "For the wrath of God is revealed from heaven

---

34. Danker, *Greek-English Lexicon*, 142.

35. Moo, *Epistle to the Romans*, 306 n. 63. Also see Dunn, *Romans 1–8*, 254. Sometimes Paul uses the adjective ἀσθενής along with its cognates to describe physical illness (1 Cor 11:30; Gal 4:13; Phil 2:26–27; cf. 1 Tim 5:23; 2 Tim 4:10), but that is certainly not how it functions in Rom 5:6.

36. Dunn, *Romans 1–8*, 254.

37. Danker, *Greek-English Lexicon*, 141.

against all ungodliness and unrighteousness of men." The adjective ἀσεβής thus designates a relational deficiency characterized by irreverence toward God. It is closely related to the third term, ἁμαρτωλός ("sinner"). Paul has already declared that the whole human race has sinned (3:9), and that those who sin, whether without the law or under the law, will perish (2:12). The godless and sinners deserve death rather than the gift of life.

Taken together, the terms "weak," "ungodly" and "sinners" underscore the complete unworthiness of humanity as recipients of the Messiah's gift.[38] Commenting on these terms, Barclay states, "The variety of terms, portraying the absence of value from multiple perspectives, seems designed to underline as emphatically as possible that the conditions for the gift were anything but positive."[39] Barclay adds that "no fitting features can be traced in the recipients of God's love, not even in their hidden potential."[40] Paul is depicting Christ's royal benefaction in conventional and yet surprising ways. What appears traditional is that a great gift has been given to the people. The one who offers his life as a gift is "Χριστός" (the Messiah, 5:6, 8). For the first time in Romans, Paul simply refers to Jesus by the title Χριστός by itself in 5:6 and repeats it in 5:8. In both cases, the main statement is Χριστὸς ἀπέθανεν ("the Messiah died"). Richard Longenecker comments that this double occurrence of Χριστός by itself "seem[s] somewhat strange in this passage."[41] Dunn suggests that the statement "Christ died" "may well reflect the summary assertion of earliest Christian apologetic that Jesus' crucifixion was no disproof of his messiahship: it was precisely as the crucified that he was the Messiah."[42] By employing the title Χριστός, Paul does not leave his political agenda in doubt; failure to recognize this is to miss the central pillar of Paul's Christology. Paul wants to be clear to his readers that the one who died vicariously is the Davidic king and Yahweh's anointed one who brings eschatological deliverance to the oppressed and establishes righteousness and peace.

When read against the backdrop of the Greco-Roman royal benefaction system, this point is conventional and yet surprising because the king is both the giver and the gift. It was not unusual for the Greco-Roman ruler to demonstrate kindness and steadfast care to his subjects by the sacrificial distribution of resources (cf. Seneca, *Ben.* 4.32.2). Aristotle writes that sometimes a virtuous

---

38. Also see 5:10, where Paul uses the term "enemies."
39. Barclay, *Paul and the Gift*, 477.
40. Barclay.
41. Longenecker, *Epistle to the Romans*, 563.
42. Dunn, *Romans 1–8*, 254.

person may even die for others (*Eth. nic.* 9.8.9). The Aristotelian virtuous man is willing to die for others because that is how he attains greater nobility for himself. The Athenians declared in their praise of Demetrios the Great (AD 336–283) that, in his bid to secure freedom for the Hellenes, he "endured danger and hardship."[43] The historian Dio Cassius writes that the Roman emperor Otho refused to continue to wage war against Vitellius, and instead opted to commit noble suicide for his supporters:

> Indeed it is far better and far more just that one should perish for all than many for one and that I should refuse on account of one man alone to embroil the Roman people in the civil war and cause so great a multitude of human beings to perish . . . I shall free myself [i.e. commit suicide], that all men may learn from the event that you chose for your emperor one who would not give you up to save himself, but rather himself to save you. (63.13.2–3)

According to Plutarch, Otho would not listen to the soldiers who "begged him not to abandon them, and not to betray them to their enemies, but to use their lives and persons in his service as long as they had breath" (*Oth.* 15.3). Rather than allowing the many to die for him, the emperor asked them not to rob him "of a greater blessedness – that of dying nobly on behalf of fellow-citizens so many and so good. If I was worthy to be Roman emperor, I ought to give my life freely for my country" (*Oth.* 15.4).[44] Although "the dominant transcript" is for the many to sacrifice their lives on behalf of the one, it is not entirely unheard of in the ancient world, whether hypothetically or in reality, for rulers to express the willingness to die for their subjects.[45] Thus, Paul depicts the Messiah as having offered the greatest gift that one could ever imagine in the ancient world. Yet this gift is very surprising, not just because it is contrary to the dominant transcript, but also because of *how* and *when* it is given!

The Messiah offers a noncalculating gift. The ideal ruler is indeed generous, yet to ensure reciprocity, he must judiciously identify worthy recipients of his good deeds. In contrast, Paul shows that the Messiah offers a noncalculating and indiscriminate benefaction to all people. Peter Leithart states that Jesus's act of giving gifts to those who could not repay is "revolutionary in the Greco-Roman world," where one gives gifts to those who are able to repay.[46] The

---

43. Danker, *Benefactor*, no. 30.
44. Also see Tacitus, *Ann.* 2.46; Martial, *Epigr.* 6.32; Suetonius, *Otho* 10.1–2.
45. Scott, *Domination and the Arts of Resistance*.
46. Leithart, *Gratitude*, 7.

Messiah does not strategically place his gifts to maximize the possibility of a return; he does not carefully pitch the ball to skilled catchers, and he does not choose the productive soil in which to sow his seeds. In fact, Christ would be termed an unwise and wasteful benefactor who sows his seed in "worn-out and unproductive soil" (Seneca, *Ben.* 1.1.2). His failure to apply the rule of censorship means that he confers his favor on the wrong people. Aristotle would tell the Messiah that he should never think that he was generous by giving to the unworthy. Seneca would accuse him of committing a dishonorable deed. Cicero would condemn him for acting foolishly by making his purse accessible to the morally base. Plutarch would excoriate the Messiah for acting disgracefully (*Mor.* 582F). Because of the indiscriminate nature of the Messiah's gift, one may justifiably characterize it as a "strange and nonsensical phenomenon" and *"the ultimate incongruous gift"* (italics original).[47]

According to the Greco-Roman benefaction system, the only way to ensure reciprocity is by benefiting the virtuous. Giving gifts to those who are morally wanting erodes social cohesion and weakens moral standards since it amounts to rewarding vice with favors. So what Paul says in this text is very radical. The Messiah is neither indifferent to humanity's moral standing nor lacks the discernment needed to identify worthy recipients. Instead, he understands more than anybody that "no one is righteous" (Rom 3:10) and that "all are under sin" (Rom 3:9). He knows that humanity's condition only merits wrath, yet he comes to their rescue by dying for them.

To emphasize further the Messiah's indiscriminate gift to the undeserving, Paul writes in 5:6 that the Messiah died "at that time" (κατὰ καιρόν).[48] The phrase κατὰ καιρόν has elicited various interpretations, most of which highlight God's ordained time. It has been taken as indicating "the eschatological time as that to which God's purpose has been moving and in which he has acted decisively,"[49] "the fitting character of the time when Jesus died for human sinfulness,"[50] or "the culminating, eschatological 'time' of God's intervention in Christ."[51] Syntactically, the phrase modifies what follows; namely, the Messiah

---

47. Barclay, *Paul and the Gift*, 478–79.
48. Danker, *Greek-English Lexicon*, 512. This is a less common expression in Paul. Whenever he uses the noun καιρός it is usually with the prepositions πρό ("before"; cf. 1 Cor 4:5), περί ("concerning"; cf. 1 Thess 5:1), πρός ("for"; cf. 1 Cor 7:5; 1 Thess 2:17) or ἐν ("in"; cf. Rom 3:26; 11:5; 2 Cor 8:14; 2 Thess 2:6). The only other occurrence of κατά with καιρός is in Rom 9:9.
49. Dunn, *Romans 1–8*, 255.
50. Fitzmyer, *Romans*, 399.
51. Moo, *Epistle to the Romans*, 307.

died for the ungodly. Considering the context, the temporal appropriateness of the Messiah's death is intricately linked to the identity of the beneficiaries as ungodly (as well as weak and sinners).

Aristotle gives three basic guidelines for bestowing benefits: (1) carefully identify worthy recipients of benefactions; (2) give the right amount; and (3) give *at the right time* (*Eth. nic.* 4.1.7, 12). To elaborate, Aristotle writes:

> He [the generous person] will not be careless with his property, since he wishes to employ it for the good of others. He will not give indiscriminately, so that he may be able to give to the right persons and *at the right time*, and where it is noble to do so [ἵνα ἔχῃ διδόναι οἷς δεῖ καὶ ὅτε καὶ οὗ καλόν]. (*Eth. nic.* 4.1.17–18)

Although Paul uses the prepositional phrase κατὰ καιρόν rather than the adverb ὅτε that we find in Aristotle, both share the same concept. Discriminatory gift-giving takes place *when* the beneficiary has demonstrated his worthiness. Otherwise, any gift given would be at the wrong time, hence unfit. Paul's assertion that the Messiah died *at that time* therefore implies that, having taken perfect cognizance of human unworthiness, the Messiah did not for a moment contemplate withholding his gift until such a time as would be more fitting. According to the norms of the ancient benefaction, the Messiah's gift was *untimely*, but according to God's plan, the Messiah's death was necessary to rescue the unworthy. So the Messiah's gift of his own life that brings peace with God breaks all three Aristotelian guidelines for calculated gift-giving: (1) the Messiah offers his life to the entire sinful human race; (2) the Messiah gives more than "the right amount"; he provides the unquantifiable gift of his own life; and (3) the Messiah's gift comes *at the right time*, not in the Greco-Roman sense of being offered selectively to virtuous people who can return a favor, but in the sense of being delivered to a people entirely lacking in merit and worthy of death. As Rodríguez states, "Paul moves *up to the top* of the social scale to find a person for whom someone might possibly give his life" but finds none (italics original).[52] The Messiah offers an *incommensurate gift*, not as a heroic act of reciprocity, but as a demonstration of God's surprising love.

What kinds of communities does Christ's gift form? The next section will address this question.

---

52. Rodríguez, *If You Call Yourself a Jew*, 103.

Communities Rooted in Christ's Indiscriminate Gift

Christ's subversive and indiscriminate gift of himself to us should transform how we view and welcome each other within the body of Christ. Reciprocity is ingrained in African societies. Familial reciprocity occurs when gifts are exchanged in kin relationships. Inegalitarian reciprocity is prevalent between patrons and clients, or rich and poor. Egalitarian reciprocity is common among friends and neighbors who belong to the same socioeconomic class. Discrimination is present in all these different types of reciprocity. One must be a family member to enjoy the mutual benefits of give-and-take within familial reciprocity. Clients must demonstrate worthiness and loyalty to enjoy their patrons' favors. Likewise, one must belong to a particular social class, gender or neighborhood in order to practice egalitarian reciprocity. The question is: Does Christ's indiscriminate gift subvert any aspects of African reciprocity? Given the limitations of this work, I will briefly discuss how practicing egalitarian reciprocity within the body of Christ might be detrimental to believers' identity as recipients of Christ's indiscriminate gift.

Jesus's incommensurate benefaction should provide the pattern for our socialization as believers. Discrimination is one of the leading causes of disunity and conflict. We discriminate by creating the criteria for inclusion and exclusion. In egalitarian reciprocity, discrimination might be based on race, gender, language, region, social class, politics, education, age, and so on. Exclusion, marginalization, oppression and "othering" others are vices that continue to plague the church in Africa. Lamenting the scourge of negative ethnicity, Rubin Pohor writes,

> The protection offered by a tribe is distorted when it is used as an excuse to show favoritism to those who belong to one's own family, tribe or ethnic group. It is also distorted when the protection of one's own group leads one to despise other groups, tell them "go home," and even resort to violence.[53]

For us to overcome the devastating effects of discrimination as seen in egalitarian reciprocity, we must recognize that Christ's indiscriminate gift demolishes all imaginable criteria for worth. Any church that is cliquey does not recognize how this radical movement called Christianity is formed. The church is not a club of the like-minded and the qualified. None of us can lay claim to Christ's gift based on some pre-existing moral, social, religious, ethnic, political or biological distinctive. The ground is level at the cross of Jesus, for

---

53. Pohor, "Tribalism, Ethnicity and Race," 316.

the entire human race is weak, ungodly and sinful, hence unworthy of God's grace. If we allow such external criteria for worth as race, education, politics, social class and gender to divide us, then our participation in Christ's mission is jeopardized. The ethic of Christ's kingdom is based on accepting the fact that we are all without hope apart from God's grace, and that the transforming love of God is accessible by faith to all people groups equally.

The gospel unifies Hispanics and Asians, Africans and Americans, Blacks and Whites, poor and rich, men and women, old and young, Jews and Gentiles. Faithful participation in Christ's redemptive mission demands a radical transformation of the stereotypical attitudes that we often have toward each other. The redemption story reveals that God is recreating for himself a diverse people from all the ends of the earth. We all become one family with a common identity in Christ. As Paul writes in Romans 15:7, we must welcome one another just as Christ has welcomed us. The incommensurate hospitality that we have experienced in Christ is the same incommensurate hospitality we have to give to each other and the world. It is Christ's incongruous gift alone that can eternally heal and reconcile warring communities. As Christ's followers, we must rise above ethnic and social prejudice so that we may be faithful and effective agents of the Messiah's gift. If we believe that Jesus has broken down the dividing wall, we should not erect other walls by creating boundaries and showing favoritism.

There is no place for a condescending attitude within Christ's body since no one occupies a position of moral superiority. The believer should not entertain an attitude that might suggest that God erred when he saved a certain person or group. We should not view others from a worldly perspective, whereby we judge each other based on our skin color, ethnicity, the clothes we wear, or any other external set of values. Instead of such a demeaning attitude that reflects a superficial understanding of the gospel, let us exemplify loyalty to King Jesus by exercising love, humility and compassion, even as we remember that without Jesus, all of us are doomed. Because the church is a gathering of the needy under a gracious king who enables us to be agents of grace to others, we must regard each other as members of a family overflowing with Christ's incommensurate grace.

Conclusion

Throughout this work, I have argued that in Romans 5:7 Paul draws upon the rare but not inconceivable Greco-Roman practice whereby the beneficiary of a gift would be willing to die on behalf of his benefactor. But Paul argues that the Messiah's supreme benefaction subverts the Greco-Roman ethic of reciprocity as the Messiah's death is not a heroic act of returning a favor. It is not unheard of in Greco-Roman society for a ruler to be willing to die for the sake of his people. However, the dominant script is for the people to willingly face danger as an expression of love and devotion to their ruler. No sacrifice is too great to pay for the sake of "the good" (ὁ ἀγαθός). The term ἀγαθός is often used to refer to the benefactor who wins great honor due to his generosity and concern for the welfare of others. Paul subverts this dominant script when he declares that our Lord Jesus the Messiah died neither for a just person nor for "the good," but for the unworthy to demonstrate God's love (5:8).

Similarly, Christ's benefaction is surprising because it is indiscriminate. There is a profound mismatch (or "unfittingness") between the Messiah's gift and humanity's unworthiness. Paul refers to humanity as "weak," "ungodly" and "sinners." According to the Greco-Roman benefaction system, the Messiah's indiscriminate benefaction, which abounds against the backdrop of an avalanche of sin, would be termed foolish, disgraceful, and a threat to social cohesion. But Paul declares that the Messiah's supreme benefaction is deliberately and wisely bestowed on a people who lack moral, social or ethnic standing. Its wisdom and intentionality are evident in the fact that it is bestowed "at that time" (5:6), by which Paul implies the temporal appropriateness of the Messiah's death for the ungodly. The Messiah offered his life with complete knowledge of human depravity. Christ's supreme benefaction should, in turn, transform the lives of his allegiant communities. The church must embody the ethic of impartiality and indiscrimination as exemplified by Jesus's nonselective and supreme benefaction.

Bibliography

Adkins, A. W. H. *Merit and Responsibility: A Study in Greek Values*. Chicago: University of Chicago Press, 1975.

———. *Moral Values and Political Behaviour in Ancient Greece: From Homer to the End of the Fifth Century*. London: Chatto & Windus, 1972.

Andria, Solomon. *Romans*. Africa Bible Commentary Series. Edited by Samuel Ngewa. Grand Rapids: HippoBooks, 2011.

Barclay, John M. G. *Paul and the Gift*. Grand Rapids: Eerdmans, 2015.

Barrett, C. K. *A Commentary on the Epistle to the Romans*. HNTC. San Francisco: Harper & Row, 1957.

———. *The Epistle to the Romans*. BNTC. Peabody: Hendrickson, 1991.

Blanton, Thomas R. *A Spiritual Economy: Gift Exchange in the Letters of Paul of Tarsus.* New Haven: Yale University Press, 2017.

Bourdieu, Pierre. "Marginalia: Some Additional Notes on the Gift." In *The Logic of the Gift: Toward an Ethic of Generosity*, edited by Alan D. Schrift, 231–41. New York: Routledge, 1997.

———. *Le Sens pratique.* Paris: Minuit, 1980.

Bringmann, Klaus. "The King as Benefactor: Some Remarks on Ideal Kingship in the Age of Hellenism." In *Images and Ideologies: Self-Definition in the Hellenistic World*, edited by A. W. Bulloch, E. S. Gruen, A. A. Long and A. Stewart, 7–24. Hellenistic Culture and Society 12. Berkeley: University of California Press, 1993.

Clarke, Andrew D. "The Good and the Just in Romans 5:7." *Tyndale Bulletin* 41 (1990): 128–42.

Cranfield, C. E. B. *A Critical and Exegetical Commentary on the Epistle to the Romans: Introduction and Commentary on Romans I–VIII.* ICC. Edinburgh: T&T Clark, 1975.

Danker, Frederick W. *Benefactor: Epigraphic Study of a Graeco-Roman and New Testament Semantic Field.* St. Louis: Clayton Publishing, 1982.

Danker, Frederick W., Walter Baur, William F. Arndt and F. Wilbur Gingrich. *Greek-English Lexicon of the New Testament and Other Early Christian Literature.* 3rd ed. Chicago: University of Chicago Press, 2000.

Dodd, C. H. *The Epistle of Paul to the Romans.* MNTC 6. Collins: Fontana, 1959.

Dunn, James D. G. *Romans 1–8.* WBC 38A. Nashville: Thomas Nelson, 1988.

Erskine, A. "The Romans as Common Benefactors." *Historia* 43 (1994): 70–87.

Fitzmyer, Joseph A. *Romans: A New Translation with Introduction and Commentary.* AB 33. New York: Doubleday, 1993.

Garnsey, Peter. "The Generosity of Veyne." *Journal of Roman Studies* 81 (1991): 164–68.

Garnsey, Peter, and Richard Saller. *The Roman Empire: Economy, Society and Culture.* Berkeley: University of California Press, 2015.

Gathercole, Simon J. *Defending Substitution: An Essay on Atonement in Paul.* ASBT. Grand Rapids: Baker Academic, 2015.

Gordon, Richard. "The Veil of Power: Emperors, Sacrificers and Benefactors." In *Pagan Priests: Religion and Power in the Ancient World*, edited by Mary Beard and John North, 201–31. Ithaca: Cornell University Press, 1990.

Griffin, Miriam T. "De Beneficiis and Roman Society." *Journal of Roman Studies* 93 (2003): 92–113.

Hammond Bammel, Caroline P. "Patristic Exegesis of Romans 5:7." *Journal of Theological Studies* 47 (1996): 532–42.

Hands, A. Robinson. *Charities and Social Aid in Greece and Rome.* Ithaca: Cornell University Press, 1968.

Harland, Philip A. *Associations, Synagogues, and Congregations: Claiming a Place in Ancient Mediterranean Society.* Minneapolis: Fortress, 2003.

Harrison, James R. *Paul's Language of Grace in Its Graeco-Roman Context*. WUNT 2.172. Tübingen: Mohr Siebeck, 2003.

Hoklotubbe, T. Christopher. *Civilized Piety: The Rhetoric of Pietas in the Pastoral Epistles and the Roman Empire*. Waco: Baylor University Press, 2017.

Irigaray, Luce. "Selections from the Logic of Practice." In *The Logic of the Gift: Toward an Ethic of Generosity*, edited by Alan D. Schrift, 190–230. New York: Routledge, 1997.

Jewett, Robert. *Romans: A Commentary*. Edited by Eldon J. Epp. Minneapolis: Fortress, 2007.

Jipp, Joshua W. *Christ Is King: Paul's Royal Ideology*. Minneapolis: Fortress, 2015.

Joubert, Stephan. "One Form of Social Exchange or Two? 'Euergetism,' Patronage, and Testament Studies." *Biblical Theology Bulletin* 31 (2001): 17–25.

———. "Patrocinium and Euergetism: Similar or Different Reciprocal Relationships? Eavesdropping on the Current Debate amongst Biblical Scholars." In *The New Testament in the Graeco-Roman World: Articles in Honour of Abe Malherbe*, edited by Marius Nel, Jan G. van der Watt and Fika J. van Rensburg, 171–95. Zurich: LIT, 2015.

———. *Paul as Benefactor: Reciprocity, Strategy and Theological Reflection in Paul's Collection*. WUNT 2.124. Tübingen: Mohr Siebeck, 2000.

Kasali, David M. "Romans." *Africa Bible Commentary*, edited by Tokunboh Adeyemo, 1375–1402. Grand Rapids: Zondervan, 2006.

Käsemann, Ernst. *Commentary on Romans*. Grand Rapids: Eerdmans, 1980.

Kümmel, Werner Georg. *Exegetical Method: A Student's Handbook*. New York: Seabury, 1981.

Landau, Y. "Martyrdom in Paul's Religious Ethics: An Exegetical Commentary on Romans 5:7." *Immanuel* 15 (1982): 24–38.

Leithart, Peter J. *Gratitude: An Intellectual History*. Waco: Baylor University Press, 2014.

Linebaugh, Jonathan A. *God, Grace, and Righteousness in Wisdom of Solomon and Paul's Letter to the Romans: Texts in Conversation*. WUNT 2.152. Boston: Brill, 2013.

Lomas, Kathryn, and Tim Cornell, eds. *Bread and Circuses: Euergetism and Municipal Patronage in Roman Italy*. London: Routledge, 2003.

Longenecker, Richard N. *The Epistle to the Romans: A Commentary on the Greek Text*. NIGTC. Grand Rapids: Eerdmans, 2016.

Martin, Troy W. "The Good as God (Romans 5.7)." *Journal for the Study of the New Testament* 25 (2002): 55–70.

McFarland, Orrey. *God and Grace in Philo and Paul*. Leiden: Brill, 2016.

Moo, Douglas J. *The Epistle to the Romans*. NICNT. Grand Rapids: Eerdmans, 1996.

Mott, Stephen C. "The Power of Giving and Receiving: Reciprocity in Hellenistic Benevolence." In *Current Issues in Biblical and Patristic Interpretation: Studies in Honor of Merrill C. Tenney*, edited by Gerald F. Hawthorne, 60–72. Grand Rapids: Eerdmans, 1975.

Moxnes, Halvor. "Patron–Client Relations and the New Community in Luke–Acts." In *Social World of Luke–Acts: Model for Interpretation*, edited by Jerome H. Neyrey, 241–70. Peabody: Hendrickson, 1991.
Neyrey, Jerome H. "God, Benefactor and Patron: The Major Cultural Model for Interpreting the Deity in Greco-Roman Antiquity." *Journal for the Study of the New Testament* 27 (2005): 465–92.
Pickett, Raymond. "The Death of Christ as Divine Patronage in Romans 5:1–11." *Society of Biblical Literature Seminar Papers* 32 (1993): 726–39.
Pohor, Rubin. "Tribalism, Ethnicity and Race." In *Africa Bible Commentary*, edited by Tokunboh Adeyemo, 316. Grand Rapids: Zondervan, 2006.
Rodríguez, Rafael. *If You Call Yourself a Jew: Reappraising Paul's Letter to the Romans*. Cambridge: James Clarke & Co., 2015.
Rodríguez, Rafael, and Matthew Thiessen, eds. *The So-Called Jew in Paul's Letter to the Romans*. Minneapolis: Fortress, 2016.
Sahlins, Marshall David. *Stone Age Economics*. New York: Aldine, 1972.
Saller, Richard P. "Patronage and Friendship in Early Imperial Rome: Drawing the Distinction." In *Patronage in Ancient Society*, edited by Andrew Wallace-Hadrill, 49–62. Leicester-Nottingham Studies in Ancient Society. London: Routledge, 1989.
———. *Personal Patronage under the Early Empire*. Cambridge: Cambridge University Press, 2002.
Schreiner, Thomas R. *Romans*. Grand Rapids: Baker, 1998.
Scott, James C. *Domination and the Arts of Resistance: Hidden Transcripts*. New Haven: Yale University Press, 1990.
Seeley, David. *The Noble Death: Graeco-Roman Martyrology and Paul's Concept of Salvation*. Sheffield: JSOT Press, 1990.
Smith, Julien. *Christ the Ideal King: Cultural Context, Rhetorical Strategy, and the Power of Divine Monarchy in Ephesians*. WUNT 2.313. Tübingen: Mohr Siebeck, 2011.
Stegemann, Ekkehard W., and Wolfgang Stegemann. *Urchristliche Sozialgeschichte: Die Anfänge im Judentum und die Christusgemeinden in der mediterranen Welt*. Stuttgart: W. Kohlhammer, 1995.
Stevenson, T. R. "The Ideal Benefactor and the Father Analogy in Greek and Roman Thought." *Church Quarterly* 42 (1992): 421–36.
Veyne, Paul. *Bread and Circuses: Historical Sociology and Political Pluralism*. Translated by B. Pearce. London: Penguin, 1990.
Wisse, Frederik. "Righteous Man and the Good Man in Romans 5:7." *New Testament Studies* 19 (1972): 91–93.
Wright, N. T. "The Letter to the Romans." In *The New Interpreter's Bible: General Articles and Introduction, Commentary, and Reflections for Each Book of the Bible, Including the Apocryphal/Deuterocanonical Books*, Vol. 10, edited by Leander E. Keck, 393–770. Nashville: Abingdon, 2002.

7

Paul's Use of Μιμηταί and Its Relationship to His Christology

Gift Mtukwa
Chair of Department and Lecturer, Department of Religion and Christian Ministry, Africa Nazarene University, Nairobi, Kenya

Abstract

The majority of the uses of μιμηταί [imitation] in the New Testament literature are found in the Pauline corpus. Μιμηταί is used ten times in the New Testament, eight of which are in the Pauline corpus (1 Cor 4:16; 11:1; Phil 3:17; 1 Thess 1:6; 2:14; 2 Thess 3:7, 9). This paper seeks to examine what exactly Paul expected his followers to imitate in Christ and his representatives (apostles). The paper argues that Paul's language of imitation has as much to say about the imitation of Christ as it does about the imitation of Paul. The paper looks at the use of μιμηταί in Jewish and Greco-Roman literature to provide background as to how Paul may have used the term. This is followed by an exegesis of Paul's use of μιμηταί. We will conclude by highlighting some implications for the church in Africa today.

Key words: christology, μιμηταί, imitation, Paul, Christ, *imitatio Christi*, *imitatio Pauli*

Introduction

The majority of the uses of μιμηταί in the New Testament literature are found in the Pauline corpus. Μιμηταί is used ten times in the New Testament, eight of which are in the Pauline corpus: in 1 Corinthians 4:16; 11:1; Philippians 3:17; 1 Thessalonians 1:6; 2:14; and 2 Thessalonians 3:7, 9. Most of Paul's uses of "imitation" have Christ as the object of the imitation, except Ephesians 5:1, which speaks of imitation in relation to God. Yet, even here, the way to imitate God is through imitating Christ.[1] The non-Pauline uses are found in Hebrews 6:12 and 3 John 11, where there is no connection to Christology. De Boer notes that "in these non-Pauline passages imitation has to do with bringing to expression in one's life something he has witnessed in another."[2] This paper examines what Paul expected his followers to imitate in Christ and his representatives (apostles). The paper argues that Paul's imitation language has Christ as its focus even in places where Paul calls for imitation of himself. We consider the use of μιμηταί in Jewish and Greco-Roman literature to provide background as to how Paul may have used it. The paper then follows with an exegesis of 1 Corinthians 11:1; Philippians 3:17; and 1 Thessalonians 1:6 to illustrate Paul's Christology in light of his use of μιμηταί. We will conclude by highlighting some implications for the African church today.

The word μιμηταί comes from μιμητής, which means "imitator." The act of imitation is captured by the term μιμέομαι, which means "to use as a model, imitate, emulate, follow."[3] The word has "the sense 'to imitate,' 'to mimic,' i.e., to do what is seen to be done by someone else."[4] According to Willis P. De Boer, "the essence of the idea is not so much in terms of sameness, complete likeness, exact reproduction, but rather in terms of bringing to expression, representation or portrayal."[5] This understanding helps to decontaminate the idea of imitation in today's world, where it is understood as copying someone without any input from the person imitating.

Some interpreters mistakenly distinguish imitating Paul from imitating Christ. They even say that statistically, Paul has more to say about imitating himself than about imitating Christ or other believers.[6] Taking the texts at face value, this may seem to be so, but upon further investigation, one realizes that the two are not mutually exclusive. Since "following Christ means giving up mimetic desire,"[7] Paul would not have had himself as the sole object of

---

1. De Boer, *Imitation of Paul*, 90.
2. De Boer, 14.
3. Danker et al., *Greek–English Lexicon*, 651.
4. Michaelis, "Μιμέομαι, Μιμητής, Συμμιμητής," 659.
5. De Boer, *Imitation of Paul*, 2.
6. De Boer, xi, 16.
7. Girard, *Things Hidden*, 431.

imitation. Willard M. Swartley has noted that "the mimesis enjoined by the NT canonical literature is grounded in the Jesus cross event, an event that exposes violence and, from Jesus's side, manifests the freedom and power of new creation."[8] De Boer even says, "To follow a Christian in Christianity was not essentially different from imitating Christ himself."[9]

"Imitation in Greek Understanding"

The idea of imitation is widespread in Greek literature. There are similarities as well as differences between the use of μιμέομαι in Greek thought and in the New Testament. In Plato, objects and the ideas behind those objects correspond with each other in terms of μιμέομαι; since the idea is the reality and the object the shadow, the object can only represent the idea partially. This usage of μιμέομαι is foreign to the New Testament.[10] Aristotle considered imitation to be natural to human beings; in fact, the difference between human beings and other creatures (animals) is that they learn by imitation. This is the reason human beings "delight in the works of imitation."[11] De Boer notes that Aristotle had a positive view of imitation in relation to fine arts. Whereas Plato thought of poets as mere imitators, Aristotle thought all should take "delight in the works of imitation."[12]

The idea of one person imitating another is most evident in Dio Chrysostom, who speaks of Socrates and how he was a zealous follower of Homer:

> For whoever follows anyone surely knows what that person was like, and by imitating his acts and words . . . he tries as best he can to make himself like him. But that is precisely, and it seems, what the pupil does – by imitating his teacher and paying heed to him, he tries to acquire his art.[13]

This usage of μιμέομαι is critical for our purposes in that it has the sense of becoming like the object of imitation by way of "reproducing their actions and feelings."[14] Isocrates's advice is that "if there are men whose reputations you

---

8. Swartley, *Covenant of Peace*, 357.
9. De Boer, *Imitation of Paul*, 91.
10. De Boer, 4.
11. Aristotle, "Works," 1448b.
12. De Boer, *Imitation of Paul*, 6.
13. Dio Chrysostom, *Discourse 55*, 384–85.
14. De Boer, *Imitation of Paul*, 6.

envy, imitate their deeds."[15] Elsewhere he says, "Be not satisfied with praising good men, but imitate them as well."[16] Seneca speaks of the importance of a teacher's example when he says:

> Of course . . . the living voice and the intimacy of ordinary life will help you more than the written word. First, you must go to the scene of action because men put more faith in their eyes than in their ears, and second because the way is long if one follows precepts, but short and helpful if one follows patterns. Cleanthes could not have been the express image of Zenon if he had merely heard his lectures; he shared in his life, saw into his hidden purposes, and watched him to see whether he lived according to his own rules. Plato, Aristotle, and the whole throng of sages who were destined to go each his different way, derived more benefit from the character than from the words of Socrates. It was not the class-room of Epicurus, but living together under the same roof, that made great men of Methodorus, Hermarchus, and Polyaenus.[17]

Seneca places value on living life together as a way for students to see a person living a normal life. The result of such imitation is that one becomes the image of the object of imitation. It is obvious, then, that one can learn something about the object of imitation by looking at the disciple.

One needed to imitate not only fellow human beings but the gods as well. Epictetus considered the imitation of the gods to be the purpose of human beings,[18] stating:

> The man who is going to please and obey them [the gods] must endeavor as best he can to resemble them. If the deity is faithful, he also must be faithful; if high-minded, he also must be high-minded, and so forth; therefore, in everything he says and does, he must act as an imitator of God.[19]

Even though there are different uses of the word μιμέομαι in Greek literature, the New Testament understanding of imitation is also found among Greek philosophers. As De Boer has noted, "the Greeks were keenly aware

---

15. Isocrates, *Cyprian Orations*, 38.60–63.
16. Isocrates, 61.112–13.
17. Seneca, *Epistles*, 26–29.
18. Epictetus, *Discourses*, 140–41.
19. Epictetus, 308–9.

of the power of both good and bad example over the behaviour and conduct of others. They recognized the important role which this kind of imitation played."[20] Aristotle's use of the word μιμέομαι is important as a background for the New Testament use, since the word was used of poets and what they did; one did not need to copy wholesale the object of imitation. Creativity was needed in how one went about imitation since one needed to bring a person to expression.[21] It is our contention that through the imitator, one can know something about the object of imitation. Let us now turn to consider the use of μιμέομαι in Jewish literature.

"Imitation" in Jewish Literature

The idea of μιμέομαι is absent from the Old Testament. The concept is, however, present in the Apocrypha and in pseudepigraphic literature. For instance, Wisdom of Solomon speaks about "childlessness with virtue," saying that "when [virtue] is present, people imitate it" (Wisdom 4:2 NRSV). What is to be imitated in this case is not a person or God but virtue, which, of course, is embodied; as such, people and God are, by implication, in view as the objects of imitation (Wisdom 4:1). The idea of imitation in Wisdom 15:9 is reminiscent of copying, and it is used of workers who compete with silversmiths and "imitate workers in copper" (NRSV) as they make counterfeit gods.

In 4 Maccabees 9:23 we find the phrase "μιμήσασθε με, ἀδελφοί," which is translated: "Imitate me, brothers" (NRSV). The context is of seven Jewish brothers who are martyred for refusing to repudiate the Torah, and this is the call of one of them to his brothers. In the same verse the speaker further says, "Do not leave your post in my struggle or renounce our courageous family ties." The brothers then respond in 4 Maccabees 13:9 as they encourage one another, "Brothers, let us die like brothers for the sake of the law; let us imitate the three youths in Assyria who despised the same ordeal in a furnace" (NRSV). It is clear that the object of their imitation is the three youths Shadrach, Meshach and Abednego and that this text is invoking their story and their courageous deeds. One can glimpse something of the people they were through what is to be imitated.

The idea of imitation of God is widespread in the pseudepigraphical literature. The *Testament of Asher* 4:3 says, "[The good man] followeth the Lord's example, in that he accepteth not the seeming good as the genuine

---

20. De Boer, *Imitation of Paul*, 7.
21. De Boer, 8.

good."²² Similarly, the *Letter of Aristeas* 188 states: "You would maintain it [the kingdom] best by imitating the constant gentleness of God." Here the object of imitation is God, and both texts reveal something of the nature of God which is to be imitated. In the *Testament of Asher* 4:3, God is portrayed as not accepting that which is not acceptable, and in *Aristeas* 188, it is the gentleness of God that is to be imitated. The command to imitate reveals something about that which is to be imitated. One can learn something about God's nature through the imitation language in Jewish literature.

The letter of *Aristeas* says, "As God is the benefactor of the whole world, so you, too, must imitate Him and be void of offence" (*Aris. Ex.* 210). Here the object of imitation is God as the benefactor of the world, and the recipients of the letter are urged to be like him to avoid causing offense. Elsewhere the word "imitation" is used with the king as the object of imitation. The king is revealed as one who hates evil, acts righteously, and constantly maintains a good reputation (*Aris. Ex.* 280). Even though the king is the object of imitation, he himself imitates God, whose actions toward men are good since he is their benefactor (*Aris. Ex.* 281). Imitating the beneficence of God is the only way to keep the kingdom unimpaired to the end, according to the king (*Aris. Ex.* 188).

Philo of Alexandria was heavily influenced by Plato in his understanding of imitation, particularly regarding the relationship between heaven and earth and how everything must correspond.²³ Nevertheless, Philo also speaks about imitating human examples. For instance, he says of Moses that his life was "a well-wrought picture, a piece of work beautiful and godlike, a model for those who are willing to copy it."²⁴ Even here in Philo, what Moses was like is revealed through what is to be imitated. Philo further speaks of imitation of God when he says, "Very properly therefore do his subject children, imitating the nature of their father, do all that is right without any delay, and with all diligence, their most excellent employment being the paying prompt and unremitting honour to God."²⁵ Philo reveals here that God does what is right promptly and with diligence.

Other uses of μιμέομαι in Philo simply reveal the fact of imitation but without necessarily giving details about the object of imitation. For instance, in *The Special Laws* 4 Philo says, "What greater good can there be than that

---

22. All citations of the Pseudepigrapha are from Charles, *Pseudepigrapha of the Old Testament*.
23. Michaelis, "Μιμέομαι, Μιμητής, Συμμιμητής," 663; De Boer, *Imitation of Paul*, 10.
24. Philo, *De vita Mosis* 1.158, in *Works*.
25. Philo, *On the Sacrifices of Abel and Cain* 68.103.

they [men] should imitate God."[26] When Philo speaks about Lot, he castigates him for not having imitated a better man (Abraham).[27] Not much is said about Abraham here, but only that he is a better man; we have to look elsewhere to learn how he was a better man.

In summary, certainly not every use of the word μιμέομαι reveals something about the object of imitation. However, we do have some instances where that is the case. Having considered the use of μιμέομαι in both Greek and Jewish literature, let us now consider Paul's use of this word to see what it reveals about the object of imitation – that is, Christ Jesus.

1 Corinthians 11:1

The context of 1 Corinthians 10 is eating food from the marketplace and having table fellowship with unbelievers without raising questions of conscience (1 Cor 10:27). The chapter division is not a natural one here.[28] This discussion of eating food occupies three chapters: 1 Corinthians 8; 10; and 11.[29] Mark Taylor asserts that "it is by eating and drinking that believers interact with each other (Lord's Supper) and in the same way should avoid all entanglements with idolatry. Eating and drinking in the ancient world was the locus of relational interaction where dominant worldviews collided."[30] In 1 Corinthians 8, Paul upholds two Christian principles – namely freedom and love – in relation to food. A believer is free to eat food that has been sacrificed to idols. Yet the way of Christian love stipulates that one should abstain from eating if such eating will cause others to stumble, particularly weaker believers.[31] In 1 Corinthians 10, the command to love is spelled out this way: "Let no man seek his own good, but each his neighbor's good" (1 Cor 10:24 ASV). The culmination of this command is found in 1 Corinthians 10:31, where Paul calls his Corinthian friends to do everything (including eating and drinking) for the glory of God and the advantage of many, as Paul himself has done.[32] As De Boer has noted, "where there is love and honor for God, people will be sensitive not only to the needs of weaker brethren, but to the needs of all their fellow men, whether

---

26. Philo, *The Special Laws* 4, 73.623.
27. Philo, *On the Migration of Abraham* 149.267.
28. Ciampa and Rosner, *First Letter to the Corinthians*, 498.
29. De Boer, *Imitation of Paul*, 155.
30. Taylor, *1 Corinthians*, 250.
31. De Boer, *Imitation of Paul*, 155.
32. De Boer, 155.

Jew, Greek, or fellow member of the church (10:32)."[33] The needs Paul has in mind are encompassed in the word "salvation": all he does is for the salvation of many. According to De Boer, "the salvation of others must take precedence over the pursuit of one's desires or the exercise of one's own rights."[34]

It is evident that all that Paul mentions about himself is just a footnote to the life of Jesus. He certainly did not seek his own good but lived his life for the sake of others, and all he did was for the glory of God and the many. Christ did more for the salvation of others than Paul could ever do. Nevertheless, "Paul knew Jesus Christ, the Son of man, who was minister to all and servant of all and who gave himself completely on behalf of men. This Christ Paul was bringing to expression in his imitation."[35] Surprisingly, however, some scholars do not see Paul calling the Corinthians to imitate Christ because Paul himself follows Christ.[36] Paul is the mediator between Christ and the Corinthians, and ultimately the Corinthians must be like Christ and like Paul to the extent that Paul is like Christ. Paul is but a vivid example of the life that Christ lived. As such, the focus should not be on Paul but on Christ himself, contra De Boer, who says, "It is rather a final stroke of the pen to accentuate the thought of the imitation of Paul."[37] To make Paul the final focus is to suggest that Paul preached himself. It must be clear that Paul preached Christ crucified and not Paul.

Ben Witherington notes that Paul "is alluding to Jesus's practice of eating with anyone, even notorious sinners, and to his ruling about no food being unclean."[38] The example of Christ as a servant who lived for others resulting in his death on the cross is also in view here.[39] The reference to Christ is important in that here, the imitation is not that of suffering, but in eating food. De Boer notes the aspects of imitation as "humility, self-denial, self-giving, self-sacrifice for the sake of Christ and the salvation of others."[40]

The image that then comes from this is that Jesus interacts with all people regardless of their status. The believers, then, are to imitate Christ, or rather

---

33. De Boer, 157.
34. De Boer, 158; see also Swartley, *Covenant of Peace*, 361.
35. De Boer, *Imitation of Paul*, 160.
36. See De Boer, 161.
37. De Boer, 161.
38. Witherington, *Conflict and Community*, 229.
39. Witherington, 229.
40. De Boer, *Imitation of Paul*, 207; cf. 154–69; See also Thiselton, *First Epistle to the Corinthians*, 796.

follow his example, in eating with people who are not like them. As Mark Taylor notes,

> All things boil down to the imitation of Paul who imitates Christ, and Paul imitates Christ by not seeking the things of himself but what is for the benefit of others that they might be saved (10:33–11:1; cf. 10:24). Ultimately the paradigm of "Christ crucified" (1:23; 2:2) is the guiding principle for Christian decision-making and behavior.[41]

In this regard, Karl Barth was right to recognize 1 Corinthians 10:31 as "the goal of this section."[42]

Andrew Clarke points out that ultimately it is not Paul who is to be followed, but Christ himself.[43] In a way, Paul is the physical embodiment of what it looks like to follow Christ. C. K. Barrett has noted that "Paul is wise enough to know that his own imitation of Christ was, if imperfect, a good deal more accessible than the historic life of Jesus."[44] In 1 Corinthians 9, Paul provides his example of how he applied the principles of freedom and love, which he has expounded in 1 Corinthians 8.[45] When Paul offers himself as an example in 1 Corinthians 9, among other things he has explicitly in mind his manual labor. His manual work was a way for him to refuse patronage which would result in a hierarchy in the community of Christ. Paul calls on the "strong to imitate him in his slavish behavior, which turns conventional roles and expectations upside down."[46] Even this is predicated on the fact that

> [Christ's] example of putting the needs of others before his own freedom or rights, and especially of doing whatever is necessary to secure their salvation (see again the preceding verse), was clearly the motivating force behind Paul's own approach to ministry as he has described it to the Corinthians and promoted it as a model for them to follow.[47]

---

41. Taylor, *1 Corinthians*, 250.
42. Barth, *Resurrection of the Dead*, 41.
43. Clarke, *Serve the Community of the Church*, 228.
44. Barrett, *First Epistle to the Corinthians*, 246.
45. De Boer, *Imitation of Paul*, 155–56.
46. Witherington, *Conflict and Community*, 229; Judge, "Cultural Conformity," 23.
47. Ciampa and Rosner, *First Letter to the Corinthians*, 498.

The implication is that "[Paul's] life provided the model of a Christ-like life for those who had no firsthand knowledge of Christ."[48]

In summary, when Paul calls the Corinthians to imitate him as he imitates Christ, it is evident that Paul's Christ is a Savior whose life was lived for others. All that Christ did was done for others and put the needs of others above his own. Christ did not exclude people, but he ate meals with sinners. Paul's example is predicated on Christ, the ultimate example, and this passage clarifies who Paul follows – his Savior Jesus Christ. The christological image that emerges from this is the humanity of Christ, not his divinity.

Philippians 3:17

Even though Paul does not use familial language here as he does elsewhere, the close relationship between him and the Philippians is evident.[49] This relationship becomes the basis upon which he calls on them to imitate him. In the Philippians text, Paul does not mention Christ as the object of imitation, but on closer scrutiny, one notices that he uses the word συμμιμητής to call the Philippians to be fellow imitators with him of Christ. Paul contrasts confidence in the flesh with righteousness based on the faith of Jesus Christ (Phil 3:9). In 3:10, Paul proceeds to declare that he wants to know the power of Jesus's resurrection and share in his sufferings, "becoming like him in his death." Swartley has stated, "Clearly, given the preceding context of sharing in the sufferings of Christ and the immediately following references to the cross of Christ, this use of *imitation* and *example* is oriented specifically to the cross and suffering."[50] Furthermore, it is possible to read the phrase "συμμιμηταί μου γίνεσθε" as either "become fellow imitators of me" or "become fellow imitators with me."[51] According to Gerald F. Hawthorne, "to draw in the 'example of the incarnate Lord' in the interpretation of 3:17 is a theological decision not required in the text."[52] However, the evidence points to the second of the two possible readings as the best understanding of the phrase; this usage is reflected in Plato (*Politicus* 274d) and it results in the paraphrase given by Peter O'Brien, "Be fellow imitators *with me* of someone else, that is, Christ."[53] This reading

---

48. Wanamaker, *Epistles to the Thessalonians*, 80.
49. De Boer, *Imitation of Paul*, 188.
50. Swartley, *Covenant of Peace*, 363.
51. Hawthorne, *Philippians*, 217.
52. Hawthorne, 217.
53. O'Brien, *Epistle to the Philippians*, 445.

of συμμιμητής is supported by Paul's call to the Philippians to have the same attitude that was in Christ Jesus (Phil 2:5–11).[54]

As such, this text is not about Paul trying to reinforce his authority and ensure there is sameness in the community, as suggested by Elizabeth Castelli.[55] The imitation to which Paul calls the Philippians requires practical reasoning, in order to discern appropriate ways of imitation. As such, "what one strives for is nonidentical repetition based on analogies one draws between the exemplar and the context in which one finds oneself."[56] Stephen E. Fowl has noted that "rather than a difference obliterating sameness, Paul's language of imitation in Philippians is designed to produce an ordered, harmonious diversity."[57] As Hans Conzelmann says, "His exemplariness consists in the fact that – in himself, objectively, on the basis of his calling – he is nothing. In all the passages on the *imitatio Pauli* the paradox of this exemplariness appears . . . The imitation of Christ takes its bearings . . . in the sense of Phil 2:6–11 – on his saving work."[58]

For Paul to imitate Christ is to be in him, as Michael J. Gorman asserts: "It is the result of being in Christ and of Christ being in him, it is a result of an influence, a power, that operates in and on Paul."[59] Christ then acts as more than just the object of imitation but as part of the subject, since he helps believers to imitate him.[60] According to Gorman, imitation is the same as cruciformity. Like cruciformity, imitation is not a result of human ingenuity.[61] Similarly, Dean Flemming asserts, "When Paul says, 'imitate me,' he is simply putting flesh on the invitation to embrace the cruciform pattern of Christ ([Phil] 2:5)."[62]

In summary, in Philippians 3:17 Paul calls the Philippians to become co-imitators of Christ with him. The Christ revealed in this passage is the one who suffered on the cross. Christ here is cruciform, and Paul is cruciform like the one he follows. Paul then calls on the Philippians to be co-imitators of the crucified one – Christ Jesus. Yet the crucified one helps those who imitate him to do so. Here we see Christ represented as both human and divine. He is not just an object of imitation; he offers divine help to those who imitate him.

---

54. O'Brien, 447.
55. Castelli, *Imitating Paul*, 21.
56. Fowl, *Philippians*, 168.
57. Fowl, 168.
58. Conzelmann, *1 Corinthians*, 179–80.
59. Gorman, *Cruciformity*, 48.
60. De Boer, *Imitation of Paul*, 212–23.
61. Gorman, *Cruciformity*, 48.
62. Flemming, *Philippians*, 197.

1 Thessalonians 1:6

The concern in 1 Thessalonians 1:6 is imitation amid suffering, which for Paul is a mark of true discipleship.[63] Suffering for Paul is not just present; the disciples are expected to participate in the suffering of the Messiah as they usher in the eschaton.[64] It is thought-provoking to note that when Paul mentions "the Lord" here, in view is the suffering earthly life of Jesus.[65] This is evidence that for Paul, there is no division between the earthly Jesus and the risen Lord. For Paul, the risen Lord is the earthly Jesus, and, in this case, he is the object of imitation. Even though Paul and his companions are great examples to be imitated, "the example of the Lord involved breadths and depths, and heights far beyond Paul's. It was the example of a man who not only faced suffering and death triumphantly, but who had also overcome death itself and had been crowned with everlasting life."[66] As such, "when Paul calls himself a μιμητής Χριστοῦ, or when he tells the Thessalonians they must show themselves to be μιμηταί τοῦ κυρίου, the point is that both he and they are followers of their heavenly Lord."[67]

Paul's addition of "the Lord" cannot be "self-correction of Paul after elevating himself as example to the Thessalonians," as suggested by Ernest Best.[68] For it is the same Lord who has made Paul what he is, and for Paul, it is not a problem to offer himself as an example. Our modern sense of humility does not allow us to do so, but for Paul, the natural way to teach people was by his example. If the gospel worked, it must have worked in his own life; as such, he offered himself and his Lord to his converts. As Best has noted, "The spirit of the Christian life is seen embodied better in a Christian life than in a code of instruction."[69]

The *thilipsis* ("persecution") mentioned in 1:6 was not just the mental or cognitive dissonance that the Thessalonians encountered when they received the gospel, as suggested by Malherbe.[70] The use of *thilipsis* in 1 Thessalonians 3:3 seems to signify external oppression as opposed to internal. Also, the fact that the Thessalonians became "an example to all the believers in Macedonia

---

63. Fee, *First and Second Letters to the Thessalonians*, 38; Paige, *1 & 2 Thessalonians*, 62.
64. Fee, *First and Second Letters to the Thessalonians*, 39.
65. De Boer, *Imitation of Paul*, 122.
66. De Boer, 123.
67. Michaelis, "Μιμέομαι, Μιμητής, Συμμιμητής," 672.
68. Best, *First and Second Epistles to the Thessalonians*, 78.
69. Best, 79.
70. Malherbe, *Paul and the Thessalonians*, 48.

and in Achaia" (1:7 NASB) suggests that Paul has in mind not just "distress and anguish of heart."[71] It is indeed true that we don't have evidence that either Jesus or Paul encountered such internal *thilipsis*.[72] Some scholars have suggested that their "receiving" the gospel must have come earlier than their "becoming imitators." This is a temporal reading of the adverbial participle δεξάμενοι τὸν λόγον.[73] However, according to Daniel B. Wallace, "when the aorist participle is related to an *aorist* main verb, the participle will often be contemporaneous (or simultaneous) to the action of the main verb."[74] The problem with making the participle and the main verb contemporaneous is that Jesus could not be a good example since he never received the gospel, so that the participle cannot be instrumental. An option that loosely relates the participle and the main verb seems to do better justice to the language of imitation; thus "and you received the message (attendant circumstance participle)" appears to be the best rendering.[75] Indeed what is in view here is not imitation in how they received the good news, as suggested by Wanamaker.[76] Contextually it makes sense if the imitation relates to a specific way of life after receiving the good news.[77] The passage can thus be paraphrased: "At the moment when you received the gospel, and in much affliction, you started out on a path of discipleship that entails imitating Jesus and his apostles."[78] Their imitation of Jesus was "spread over the whole range of human life, active and passive, attitudinal and bodily, inner and outer, personal, social, and political."[79]

The imitation of Paul and the missionary team and of the Lord had the result that "*their corporate life together, their ecclesial body as a whole*, in turn became a singular τύπος (*typos*, 'pattern, model') to all those who were exercising believing allegiance in Macedonia and Achaia (v. 7)."[80] As such, imitation becomes a cycle in which Paul imitates the Lord, and Paul's disciples imitate Paul and the Lord, and then other believers imitate Jesus, Paul and the Thessalonians. This imitation is communal and not individual,

---

71. Wanamaker, *Epistles to the Thessalonians*, 81.
72. Witherington, *1 and 2 Thessalonians*, 72.
73. Shogren, *1 and 2 Thessalonians*, 66.
74. Wallace, *Greek Grammar*, 624.
75. Shogren, *1 and 2 Thessalonians*, 66–67.
76. Wanamaker, *Epistles to the Thessalonians*, 80.
77. Johnson, *1 and 2 Thessalonians*, 47.
78. Shogren, *1 and 2 Thessalonians*, 67.
79. Harink, *Paul among the Postliberals*, 35.
80. Johnson, *1 and 2 Thessalonians*, 50; See also Malherbe, *Letters to the Thessalonians*, 115.

in that "the plural form, ὑμᾶς 'you,' and the singular form, τύπον 'an example,' means that the members of the church had, as a congregation, become a model church."[81] This "does not refer to the lives of certain outstanding individuals, but to the life of the whole Christian community which has influenced others."[82] This is very much at home in Africa, where most people operate within a communal worldview.

Yet even here, it is evident that Paul has more than suffering in mind. In 1 Thessalonians 1:9–10, Paul speaks about how the Thessalonians have turned from idols to serve the living God; it is evident that Paul has in mind the faithfulness of the Lord Jesus, who Paul elsewhere says

> took the form of a slave (*doulos*) in becoming human and then exhibited a loyalty to God that finally took him to his death on a cross. Hence, their assembly [the Thessalonians] *as a whole* exhibits a similar pattern of faithfulness as that of Jesus in his rectifying display of covenant faithfulness to the God of Israel.[83]

It should be clear, then, that this imitation means "exhibiting their own nonidentical repetition of the covenant faithfulness of Jesus expressed in fidelity (*pistis*) to God and the self-giving actions . . . toward others."[84] Here imitation is not commanded, but it is reported as something they have already done and continue to do. In a sense, it is evidence of their Christian faith and election.[85] Such imitation was "a bringing to expression in their own lives what they had seen and detected outside of themselves."[86]

The imitation language of 1 Thessalonians 1:6 reveals that for Paul, Christ is Lord. Christ experienced *thlipsis*, which Paul has experienced, and the Thessalonians have experienced as well. The sufferings of Christ are those he encountered on the cross. Through *thlipsis*, Jesus demonstrates covenant faithfulness to God. The Thessalonians have put this into practice as they "turned from idols to serve the living God" and "to wait for his Son" (1 Thess 1:9–10 NRSV). This text thus upholds both the humanity and the divinity of Christ.

---

81. Blight, *Exegetical Summary of 1 & 2 Thessalonians*, 25.
82. Ellingworth and Nida, *Paul's Letters to the Thessalonians*, 12.
83. Johnson, *1 and 2 Thessalonians*, 55.
84. Johnson, 57.
85. De Boer, *Imitation of Paul*, 123.
86. De Boer, 124.

Synthesis and Implications for the African Church

Having surveyed Paul's imitation texts, it is evident that even where Paul does not directly mention Christ, he still has Christ in mind in the background. Christ is the one Paul follows, and Paul is calling others to follow him as he follows Christ (1 Cor 11:1). As De Boer has stated, "In fact the way of life that Paul pictures is Christ's way. It is the way of Christ pictured in the gospels and presented as the way for his followers."[87] What emerges in these texts "is the accent of humility, self-denial, self-giving, self-sacrifice for the sake of Christ and the salvation of others. This is the way of life which Paul found himself representing, and it is the way of life which he expected to find appearing in his readers."[88]

Keeping Christ within the imitation texts is important because it helps with the problems noted by René Girard concerning the idea of imitation.[89] Christ is unique in that

> he was tempted with the acquisitive mimeses in all ways such as we are but did not yield to the mimetic pattern that generates rivalry and violence. Jesus as faithful Servant of the Lord has opened up for us a new world of hope and potential; we are saved by his transforming of our desire.[90]

It can be concluded from the texts we have surveyed that "Paul grounds his ethics in his Christology."[91] To the extent that his imitation language encompasses his ethics, for Paul, Christ is the paradigm for such ethics. Paul understood that the Christian truth could not be presented abstractly; these early Christians needed to see the life in Christ modeled by those who presented it.[92]

---

87. De Boer, 207.

88. De Boer, 207.

89. Girard says that "One always desires whatever belongs to that one, the neighbor." For Girard the neighbour plays a role in rendering what they possess desirable to another. As such if one imitates another then the end result is that they end up desiring what the one they follow desires resulting in what Girard calls "mimetic desires." This in turn creates what Girard calls "mimetic rivalry" which is a result of two people desiring the same thing. It is only the imitation of Christ which breaks the cycle of mimetic rivalry. He writes "If we do not imitate Jesus, our models become the living obstacles that we also become for them. We descend together on the infernal spiral that leads to generalized mimetic crisis and ultimately, to the mimetic state of all against one." Rene Girard, *I See Satan Fall Like Lightning*, trans. James G. Williams, First Edition (Maryknoll: Orbis, 2001), 9–40.

90. Swartley, *Covenant of Peace*, 376.

91. Hays, "Christology and Ethics in Galatians," 289.

92. Martin, *Philippians*, 163.

Contemporary Christianity, especially in Africa, is accustomed to seeking to reach huge crowds; however, "the influence of close personal relationships, of example and of imitation does not lend itself to these easy processes of multiplication."[93] De Boer suggests that "perhaps the church of Christ would be well served with more Christian leaders working at a slower pace, limiting their contacts and activities, and opening their personal Christian lives sufficiently to permit imitation – be it only by a few."[94] As the church in Africa does the work of discipleship, it needs to make clear that following Christ should result in imitation of Christ. Given that Christianity in Africa has been characterized as "a mile wide and an inch deep," the idea of imitating Christ can help the church become what Christ envisioned it to be.

As we have seen from Paul's imitation language, Christ suffered – he was cruciform, humbled himself, and acted on behalf of others. The church in Africa needs to be cruciform as Christ is cruciform. For example, the behavior of some religious practitioners (church leaders) in Africa of fleecing the flock is not aligned with Christ, who acts for others. Paul's example predicated on Christ, of working with his own hands so as not to be a burden to anyone, should be adopted by church leaders in Africa.

Conclusion

In summary, Paul's language of imitation reveals his Christology. For Paul, Christ is the suffering Son of God who lived a cruciform life for the sake of others; he is divine and human. For Paul, there is no difference between the earthly Christ and the risen Christ. For him, Christ is not just an object of study but an object of devotion; as such, Paul's Christology "forms part of what we may call his Christ-devotion, which in turn shaped his whole religious life."[95] Christ should not only be studied as a doctrine of Christian theology; he should become the object of devotion and imitation. The church in Africa should not only ask the question "Who is Christ to you?" but also "How should we imitate Christ?"

---

93. De Boer, *Imitation of Paul*, 216.
94. De Boer, 216.
95. Hurtado, "Paul's Christology," 185.

Bibliography

Aristotle. "The Works of Aristotle." In *De Poetica*, Vol. 11, edited by W. D. Ross, translated by I. Bywater, 1354–1462. Oxford: Clarendon Press, 1952.
Barrett, C. K. *The First Epistle to the Corinthians*. Black's New Testament Commentary. London: Continuum, 1994.
Barth, Karl. *The Resurrection of the Dead*. Eugene: Wipf & Stock, 2003.
Best, Ernest. *The First and Second Epistles to the Thessalonians*. Peabody: Hendrickson, 2003.
Blight, Richard C. *An Exegetical Summary of 1 & 2 Thessalonians*. Dallas: Summer Institute of Linguistics, 1989.
Castelli, Elizabeth A. *Imitating Paul: A Discourse of Power*. Literary Currents in Biblical Interpretation. 1st ed. Louisville: Westminster John Knox, 1991.
Charles, R. H. *Pseudepigrapha of the Old Testament*. Oxford: Clarendon Press, 1913.
Ciampa, Roy E., and Brian S. Rosner. *The First Letter to the Corinthians*. Pillar New Testament Commentary. Grand Rapids: Eerdmans, 2010.
Clarke, Andrew D. *Serve the Community of the Church: Christians as Leaders and Ministers*. Grand Rapids: Eerdmans, 2000.
Conzelmann, Hans. *1 Corinthians: A Commentary on the First Epistle to the Corinthians*. Translated by James W. Dunkly, James W. Leitch and George W. MacRae. Philadelphia: Fortress, 2008.
Danker, Frederick W., Walter Baur, William F. Arndt and F. Wilbur Gingrich. *Greek-English Lexicon of the New Testament and Other Early Christian Literature*. 3rd ed. Chicago: University of Chicago Press, 2000.
De Boer, Willis P. *The Imitation of Paul: An Exegetical Study*. Kampen: J. H. Kok, 1962.
Dio Chrysostom. *Discourse 55*. Translated by Henry Lamar Crosby. Vol. 4. Loeb Classical Library. Cambridge, MA: Harvard University Press, 2014.
Ellingworth, Paul, and Eugene Albert Nida. *A Handbook on Paul's Letters to the Thessalonians*. UBS Handbook Series. New York: United Bible Societies, 1976.
Epictetus. *Discourses*. Translated by W. A. Oldfather. Cambridge: Harvard University Press, 1925.
Fee, Gordon D. *The First and Second Letters to the Thessalonians*. Grand Rapids: Eerdmans, 2009.
Flemming, Dean E. *Philippians: A Commentary in the Wesleyan Tradition*. Kansas City: Beacon Hill, 2009.
Fowl, Stephen E. *Philippians*. Two Horizons New Testament Commentary. Grand Rapids: Eerdmans, 2005.
Girard, René. *Things Hidden since the Foundation of the World*. Translated by Jean-Michel Oughourlian and Guy Lefort. Stanford: Stanford University Press, 1987.
Gorman, Michael J. *Cruciformity: Paul's Narrative Spirituality of the Cross*. Grand Rapids, MI: Eerdmans, 2001.
Harink, Douglas. *Paul among the Postliberals*. Grand Rapids: Brazos, 2003.

Hawthorne, Gerald F. *Philippians*. Word Biblical Commentary 43. Dallas: Word, 2018.

Hays, Richard B. "Christology and Ethics in Galatians: The Law of Christ." *Catholic Biblical Quarterly* 49, no. 2 (1987): 268–90.

Hurtado, L. W. "Paul's Christology." In *The Cambridge Companion to St. Paul*, edited by James D. G. Dunn, 185–98. Cambridge Companions to Religion. Cambridge: Cambridge University Press, 2003.

Isocrates. *Cyprian Orations: Evagoras, ad Nicoclem, Nicocles aut Cyprii*. Translated by Edward S. Forster. New York: Arno Press, 1979.

Johnson, Andy. *1 and 2 Thessalonians*. Two Horizons New Testament Commentary. Grand Rapids, MI: Eerdmans, 2016.

Judge, E. A. "Cultural Conformity and Innovation in Paul: Some Clues from Contemporary Documents." *Tyndale Bulletin* 35 (1984): 3–24.

Malherbe, Abraham J. *The Letters to the Thessalonians: A New Translation with Introduction and Commentary*. New York: Doubleday, 2000.

———. *Paul and the Thessalonians: The Philosophic Tradition of Pastoral Care*. Philadelphia: Fortress, 1987.

Martin, Ralph. *Philippians*. Tyndale New Testament Commentary. Nottingham: Inter-Varsity Press, 2008.

Michaelis, Wilhelm. "Μιμέομαι, Μιμητής, Συμμιμητής." In *Theological Dictionary of the New Testament*, edited by Gerhard Kittel, Geoffrey W. Bromiley and Gerhard Friedrich, 659–74. Grand Rapids, MI: Eerdmans, 1994.

O'Brien, Peter T. *The Epistle to the Philippians: A Commentary on the Greek Text*. New International Greek Testament Commentary. Grand Rapids: Eerdmans, 1991.

Paige, Terence Peter. *1 & 2 Thessalonians: A Commentary in the Wesleyan Tradition*. Kansas City: Beacon Hill, 2017.

Philo of Alexandria. *The Works of Philo: Complete and Unabridged*. Translated by Charles Duke Yonge. Peabody: Hendrickson, 1995.

Seneca, Lucius Annaeus. *Epistles*. Translated by Richard M. Gummere. Loeb Classical Library 75. Cambridge: Harvard University Press, 1917.

Shogren, Gary S. *1 and 2 Thessalonians*. Zondervan Exegetical Commentary on the New Testament. 1st ed. Grand Rapids: Zondervan, 2013.

Swartley, Willard M. *Covenant of Peace: The Missing Peace in New Testament Theology and Ethics*. Grand Rapids: Eerdmans, 2006.

Taylor, Mark. *1 Corinthians: An Exegetical and Theological Exposition of Holy Scripture*. Nashville: Holman Reference, 2014.

Thiselton, Anthony C. *The First Epistle to the Corinthians: A Commentary on the Greek Text*. New International Greek Testament Commentary. Grand Rapids: Eerdmans, 2000.

Wallace, Daniel B. *Greek Grammar beyond the Basics: An Exegetical Syntax of the New Testament*. Grand Rapids: Zondervan, 2008.

Wanamaker, Charles A. *The Epistles to the Thessalonians: A Commentary on the Greek Text*. New International Greek Testament Commentary. Grand Rapids: Eerdmans, 1990.

Witherington, Ben, III. *Conflict and Community in Corinth: A Socio-Rhetorical Commentary on 1 and 2 Corinthians*. Grand Rapids: Eerdmans, 1995.

———. *1 and 2 Thessalonians: A Socio-Rhetorical Commentary*. Grand Rapids: Eerdmans, 2006.

8

A Christological Reading of Ephesians 5:21–33

Christ as a Model for Married Men in Africa

Moses Iliya Ogidis
*Serving with Evangelical Church Winning All (ECWA), Nigeria
Currently studying at St. Paul's University, Limuru, Kenya,
for PhD in Theology (New Testament)*

Abstract

This paper addresses the christological reading of Ephesians 5:21–33 to present Christ's attitude to women as a model for men in Africa. Most interpretations of the text focus on the patriarchal nature of the Greco-Roman culture in which the New Testament is located. Such interpretations focus on the hierarchical relationship between husbands and wives, which gives men power over women. Many men in Africa use such interpretations to exploit and suppress their wives, misusing the submission clause found in the passage. This leads to gender-based violence and abusive behaviors by some Christian men, and the use of culture to sustain such negative attitudes. This paper makes use of the historical-critical method, with the person of Christ within the text serving as the ideal model – being human and God – for husbands to emulate his sacrificial love. Jesus asked his disciples, "Who do you say I am?," and the characteristics of Christ found in this text serve as a model for African

Christian men to emulate for their wives. This paper holds to both the humanity and the divinity of Christ to serve as a model for the husband and wife. Christ is seen as the ideal man and husband, a friend, lover, provider, defender and protector of the weak.

Key words: Christology, household codes, model, marriage, sacrificial love, patriarchy, *paterfamilias*

Introduction

Toward the end of his letter to the Ephesian church, the apostle Paul, an unmarried man, prescribed with God-given creativity the household codes. These household codes formed the basis for family life in the Greco-Roman world, derived from the patriarchal nature of the Greco-Roman context within which the New Testament is socially located. Interpretations of Ephesians 5:21–33 viewed through a patriarchal lens motivate many Christian men.[1] In Africa, some men treat their wives as slaves. Such interpretations of the text lead to the oppression and subjugation of women. Indeed, Christian marriage itself is under threat, leading Amadi and Amadi to state that "the frightening spread of divorce and domestic violence by some Christian men makes one wonder if married life will survive the twenty-first-century and if it is still possible for a marriage to be a stable, nurturing environment for its members."[2] A substantial number of men do not emulate Christ's characteristics to their wives because they do not understand who Christ is and how to emulate his lifestyle. A christological reading of this text will help men to understand who Christ is so that he can serve as a model. This paper uses the historical-critical method in analyzing the christological teaching of Ephesians 5:21–33 with regard to how men should treat their wives following the example of Christ. A christological reading of Ephesians 5:21–33 can lead to a transformation in the way African men live with and treat their wives.

An Overview of Ephesians 5:21–33 in Its Greco-Roman Context

Mercy Oduyoye affirms that "the Bible is used for teaching, rebuking, correcting, and instructing for righteous living. Most Christian communities in Africa now

---

[1]. This paper focuses on African Christian men; wherever the paper talks of "African men" or "men," it refers to Christian men in Africa and not all African men.
[2]. Amadi and Amadi, "Marital Crisis," 134.

recognize the need for the church to guide believers through the Bible that speaks [to] and deals with human realities."[3] The same can be said for the household codes in Ephesians 5:21–33, which are used for teaching, rebuking, correcting and instructing Christian household members. The first part of the letter to the Ephesians contains profound theological truths that serve as the foundation for the practical application for believers that follows. The church is to be unified through the love of Christ and is to walk in love, light and wisdom. From Ephesians 5:21 through 6:9, the epistle makes an exciting transition to address Christian living in households. Ephesians 6:10–24 then deals with spiritual powers and how to use the armor of God. The letter ends with Paul's final greetings. Mazzalongo explains why the epistle was written:

> The 1st-century church was facing many problems as it sought to be established and grow in a pagan society. There were the immoral influences of pagan culture within the Roman Empire of that period and the open and active persecution of the church. There were also the dangers of false teachers creeping into the church with uninspired teachings. For example, many teachers of that time mixed Greek philosophical thought with Christianity, or mixed Jewish law-keeping and ceremonial law with the gospel of grace. Then there was the danger of syncretism with pagan religions that were common in that time and place.[4]

However, the household codes in Ephesians have received much attention from feminist scholars, such as Elizabeth Johnson, Schüssler Fiorenza and Shi-Min Lu, due to the gender construction found in the text and the Greco-Roman context. To better understand a biblical text, an interpreter needs to read or interpret it against the background of its historical context. This is not to suggest that in some way the text is inadequate to tell the truth. Any word or text removed from its historical, social and cultural context loses its ability to carry meaning, since the writers wrote within their particular context and understanding of their audiences. Therefore, to explore the full richness of the household codes in Ephesians, it is necessary to examine not only the literary context of household codes, but also the historical-cultural context.

Shi-Min Lu observes that the patriarchal and hierarchical nature of Roman society was evidenced in its familial structure. Since antiquity, the *paterfamilias*

---

3. Oduyoye, "Biblical Interpretation," 33–37.
4. Mazzalongo, *Ephesians for Beginners*, 24.

enjoyed unlimited power in his household,[5] not only over family possessions but also over all household members. Lu further states that "the family represent the larger society. The man acts as a priest over the cult of the ancestors. His role and responsibilities in the family are like that of the aristocracy, composed of the most important heads of families, in the political life of the state."[6] Men in the Roman Empire were given the great responsibility of leadership, with more power than women. Traditionally, Greco-Roman authors addressed three central household relationships, namely, those between husbands and wives, parents and children, and slaves and masters. Regarding these relationships, Aristotle says that "the investigation of everything should begin with its smallest parts, and the primary and smallest parts of the household are master and slave, husband and wife, father and children."[7]

According to Greco-Roman culture, the relationship between husband and wife should be one of subordination of women to men, due to the social, religious, political and cultural norms. Women were viewed as second-class citizens and without value or respect, whether married or unmarried. Plato affirms that "the better are the superiors of the worse, and the older in general of the younger; wherefore also parents are superior to their offspring, men to women and children, rulers to ruled."[8] Paul's injunction for wives to submit to their husbands (Eph 5:21–22) fits well within this general understanding of roles in the households of the empire. For instance, the husband's role as ruler of the household is affirmed by Aristotle: "It is a part of the household science to rule over wife and children."[9] Aristotle meant that women were to be led by men; the men were to rule over women in the household and even in public spheres. Aristotle believed that a healthy society depended on the orderly functioning and management of households. MacDonald therefore maintains that "the main issues that seem to be unresolved are the nature of Jewish and Graeco-Roman influences on the New Testament household codes, as well as the nature of the re-appropriation made by the New Testament authors concerning the ethical discourses of writers of the same period."[10]

For Greeks during antiquity, the husband was the provider, guardian, and overseer of public affairs, while the woman's place was in the home. For

---

5. Lu, "Woman's Role," 10.
6. Lu, 10.
7. Aristotle, *Politics*, 1.2.1, 1253b, in *Aristotle in 23 Volumes*.
8. Plato, *Laws*, 11.917a, in *Plato in Twelve Volumes*.
9. Aristotle, *Politics*, 1.5.1, 1259a.
10. MacDonald, "Beyond Identification," 66–70.

the Romans, the primary role of the wife was to manage the home and to be submissive to her husband; she was expected to understand domestic arrangements and the art of housekeeping.[11] Keener says that Paul understood the particular values of the ancient society of the Greco-Roman world well enough to know their impact. Those who thought morally during that time, based on their culture, called on wives to obey and husbands to govern their wives honorably.[12] Keener's point of departure is that the epistle to the Ephesians is focused on the cultural and social interaction during the time of Paul, and the situation faced by women during the first century. Since the first century, the emphasis for married women was on their having good qualities; according to Taiye, a good wife was to be

> chaste, domestic, a good house-keeper, a rearer of children, one to gladden you in health, to tend you in sickness, to be your partner in good fortune, to console you in misfortune; to restrain the mad passion of youth and temper the unreasonable harshness of old age.[13]

A substantial number of interpretations of the role of husband and wife in marriage have centered on women more than on men, especially in patriarchal societies. That is why most interpretations of Ephesians 5:21–33 focus on the submissiveness of the woman to the man, stated in verse 22, although the instruction to submit begins from verse 21 and is mutual. But MacDonald argues that the "household discourse is patriarchal discourse par excellence," and therefore the codes need to be read as "ideologies of masculinity,"[14] being intended to reinforce patriarchy, male control of household dependents, and male control of women's sexual experience. Mouton argues that the household codes were designed to structure the functioning of the different members of the household in terms of roles and duties that would enable them to be good, moral citizens.[15]

The Greco-Roman perspectives in the first-century Mediterranean world, as demonstrated by Botha, were rather negative with regard to the position and abilities of mothers, wives, sisters, female friends and daughters.[16] The men

---

11. Adamolekun, "Marriage and Divorce," 142.
12. Keener, *Paul, Women and Wives*, 157–60.
13. Adamolekun, "Marriage and Divorce," 143.
14. MacDonald, "Beyond Identification," 85–86.
15. Mouton, "Reimagining Ancient Household Ethos?," 167.
16. Botha, "Folklore, Social Values and Life," 2.

of antiquity regarded women as suited to be followers; as irrational, domestic beings, and not leaders, under their disposition. Keener affirms that "the vast majority of male writers viewed women as socially subordinate, often ignoring those women who violated the stereotype, or sometimes honouring them as exceptions to the rule."[17] Thus this patriarchal culture was strongly upheld in first-century household settings, with the aim of maintaining order and structure in society.

African Interpretations of Ephesians 5:21–33

The patriarchal interpretation of marriage from Ephesians 5:21–33 focuses on the husband as the one who has total authority within the marriage. Ogunkunle claims that the emphasis in the text reflects the patriarchal culture of the Greco-Roman world, and the kind of marriage that allows the husband to exercise power over his wife and her rights.[18] But through such an interpretation, men have oppressed and subordinated women, making them their slaves in the name of submission. Abbey-Mensah illustrates how the mention of submission in Ephesians 5:21–33 leads to the oppression and subordination of women in Ghana:

> There is a Christian couple in the house where she lived. On the early morning of a fine Saturday, the woman and the maidservant, as usual, got up to start the household chores. It came to a point when the maidservant had to go to town for an errand. A few seconds after the departure, the man of the house started shouting from the bedroom, calling the maid. My daughter, who was nearer the bedroom, informed the man of the girl's absence from the house. What happened? He called the woman of the house in a very furious . . . mood. It was a scene of laughter and pity. This woman, who, because of her size, finds it difficult to enter their room without first calculating the angle at which she should enter, has to run to attend to the call of "her boss." And what is it about? This man who feels so lazy to get up from bed, needed some drinking water from a jar, just some few yards from his bed. After attending to her master's call, this unfortunate woman missed a step and fell miserably on the cemented floor. Oh, what a touching

---

17. Keener, *Paul, Women and Wives*, 164.
18. Ogunkunle, "Biblical Injunction," 50.

scene! Yes, that is what we call respect, obedience, and submission of a Christian woman to a man, as alleged in Eph. 5:24.[19]

Such interpretations of Ephesians 5:24, "so also wives should submit to their husbands in everything," focus on the wives being submissive in *everything*, which leads to the abuse of authority by some men, as illustrated in the above story. The question that comes to mind from the story is: Is it wrong for the man to get out of bed and get himself the water to drink? Or must the wife be the one to fetch the water for him? Patriarchal interpretations contribute to the misuse of power, dominance, hierarchy and competition; to practices in which men dominate, oppress and exploit women. Abeda Sultana maintains that most interpretations of Ephesians 5:21–33 subordinate the experience of women in daily life; such subordination, "regardless of the class they might belong to, takes various forms; discrimination, disregard, insult, control, exploitation, oppression, violence (physical, emotional, verbal, spiritual) within the marriage, at the place of work, and in society."[20] Women are dehumanized and robbed of their personhood; they are mostly associated with a man, whether a father, husband or brother, and are not seen as individuals capable of deciding for their own lives.

The patriarchal interpretation and the hierarchical language found in the household codes of Ephesians 5:21–33, for example, continues to influence the functioning of gender roles within the family. The patriarchal interpretation seems to give men the license to abuse women, resulting in low self-esteem among women in Africa. Aina expresses that gender roles are a system of social stratification and differentiation based on sex, and this provides material advantages to men while simultaneously placing severe constraints on women's roles and activities. There are clearly defined gender roles, while various cultural taboos ensure conformity with specified gender roles within the religion and society.[21] Traditionally, in most African communities, men do not participate in domestic work, including child-rearing; such tasks are considered to be the exclusive domain of women. As observed by Aweda and Silberschmidt, men are classed as providers and protectors, having the following qualities: strength, vigor, virility/powerful courage, self-confidence, and the ability to meet the outside world.[22] The opposite qualities are attributed to women, who

---

19. Abbey-Mensah, "Violence against Women," 172.

20. Sultana, "Patriarchy and Women's Subordination," 7.

21. Aina, "Women, Culture and Society," 6.

22. Aweda, "Sex-Role Inequalities in the African Family," 188–97. Silberschimbt, *Women Forget That Men Are Masters*.

oversee the domestic chores, the raising of children, and seeing that the home is in order.

The majority of Christian women need and desire a good home where the husband is true to his word and reliable; a home where there is no blight of wrong; where there is peace, love, and where Christ is the one to be imitated. When marriages are peaceful, then the church and society will also be peaceful. If African society is to be peaceful and free of all forms of violence and corruption, the foundation must be laid in the home. The need and desire for a good home cannot be overemphasized. The leadership which a man gives to his wife and the love which he has for his family should result from his home training and the fear of God in him.

Most scholars that this author engaged with, in their contextual interpretations of Ephesian 5:21–33, gave a great deal of attention to the concept of submission in the text, but seemed to focus only on women submitting to their husbands, while some argued that the submission is mutual. But it seems that they did not consider the text's christological teaching, which serves as a model for Christian men.

A Christological Reading of Ephesians 5:25–30

Gordon Fee defines Pauline Christology as the study that "refers to the person of Christ, Paul's understanding of who Christ was/is, in distinction to the work of Christ; what Christ did for us as saviour and how we are to emulate the lifestyle of Christ."[23] Understanding the person and work of Christ is vitally important for understanding Christology as a whole, and for responding to the question Jesus asked his disciples: "Who do you say I am?" Omowole writes that a christological reading of Ephesians 5:21–33 articulates "how Christian husbands and wives are . . . to submit themselves to one another out of reverence for Christ."[24] A christological interpretation of the text will help husbands emulate Christ's analogy regarding the church – a good relationship which men need to model to sustain their families. Omowole further maintains that mutual submission should be the guiding principle within Christian households. Since Christian couples should not insist on their rights, there is a sense in which husbands are to submit to their wives. Indeed, they are to put the interests of their wives first.[25] The submission in the text is to be mutual:

---

23. Fee, *Pauline Christology*, 1.
24. Omowole, "Marriage and Divorce," 126.
25. Omowole, 127.

husbands loving their wives as Christ loved the church, that is, by giving his life for it. This mutual submission of men and women will reflect the forgiving spirit of Christ to the church: he is patient with the church and nurtures it, qualities which Christian men need to show their wives.

The household code in Ephesians 5:21–33 does not give husbands the license to exploit, oppress and subordinate their wives; instead, husbands are instructed to love their wives with the same self-sacrificial love that Christ has shown to the church. Christ, as a man, showed unconditional love, forgiving those who persecuted and even killed him. In the same way, Omowole observes that "the husband must put himself at the service of his wife."[26] Love for the wife should result in the husband cherishing and nourishing her. The words "nourish" and "cherish" (RSV) mean to keep her warm, to take care of her needs spiritually, physically, materially and emotionally. This speaks of caring for her needs and listening to her. In Ephesians 5:25–27, Paul urges the believing husband to show the same kind of love that Christ showed the church when he gave himself up for the church to make it holy. The type of love described here for husbands is not sensuous, possessive and self-seeking, but *agape* love, characterized by sacrifice. Amolo agrees that the husband's love should be self-giving, caring, providing and protecting. Just as the husband loves and cherishes his own body, so in the same way he should love his wife intimately.[27] With this kind of love the husband ought to "be committed" to his wife. This requires him to be there for her in all circumstances; this is vital in a marriage relationship, just as Christ is there for the church.

Further, Amolo states that "Paul demands that husbands should love their wives as Christ loved the church and gave himself selflessly and sacrificially for the church. The example of Christ, which lifts the marriage relationship above caprice or passion, is now the rule."[28] This speaks of the nature of the wife, how much she needs her husband's tender love, time, energy and care in all aspects of her life. This is what Peter means when he says, "Likewise you husbands, live considerately with your wives, bestowing honor on the woman as the weaker sex, since you are joint heirs of the grace of life, in order that your prayers may not be hindered" (1 Pet 3:7 RSV). Again, this means that a husband should create time to understand his wife's physical, spiritual, emotional, mental and material needs. This will make the husband considerate toward his wife when it comes to domestic chores, and will build her up and support her.

---

26. Omowole, 127.
27. Amolo, "Paul's Concept of Sexual Union," 170.
28. Amolo, 169.

Kato notes that most African husbands are better educated than their wives. Unfortunately, the gap continues to widen instead of narrowing after marriage.[29] It is in this regard that African women theologians such as Phiri argue that "African women who are in theological education are well aware that the reluctance on the part of some churches to send women for theological education or the reluctance of some seminaries to admit women as students is a theological one."[30] Even with empowerment programs for women in most African countries, there is a need for the husband to encourage and support his wife to further her education, and to be willing to sponsor her. She will do this better if she does not give birth to a baby every year. If she is not interested in furthering her education, the husband should assist her to start a business or seek employment.

Paul says that husbands should "love their wives as their own bodies. He who loves his wife loves himself" (Eph 5:28). It is the primary responsibility of the husband, as the head of the family, to provide for his wife and the children, as part of sacrificial love. Elsewhere, the apostle Paul has strong words of condemnation for husbands who do not fulfill these responsibilities: "If any one does not provide for his relatives, and especially for his own family, he has disowned the faith and is worse than an unbeliever" (1 Tim 5:8 RSV). This verse condemns any husband who selfishly neglects his family, especially his wife. A professing Christian husband who neglects his family is compared to a nonbeliever. The husband is required in Ephesians 5:24–33 to cherish his wife in the same way he cherishes himself. This kind of love seems to be difficult for most African Christian men. The men are to care and feed their wives, but the reverse is usually the case with most men: the woman is the one feeding the family, even when the man is earning and working. Husbands need to put their wives and children first after God.

Christ's Transformational Model for African Men

Many African men seem not to understand the christological teaching in the household codes, which serves as a model for them to emulate. Considering Christ's transformational model for African men, this paper draws on the way Jesus related to women during his earthly ministry and the model in Ephesians 5:21–33, as well as illustrations from African women theologians. One of the models for African men is the sacrificial love of Christ shown in the passage.

---

29. Kato, "Christian Leader and His Family," 5.
30. Phiri, "Major Challenges," 63.

As we have seen, through sacrificial love Christ gave himself up for the church, even though we are all sinners, to make the church holy. Mercy Amba Oduyoye and Elizabeth Amoah state a women's view of Christ: "the Christ whom African women worship, honour, and depend on is the victorious Christ, knowing that the subjugation, exploitation and oppression of women through culture and social norms is a reality."[31] This is not shying away from the reality of abuse of authority by some Christian men in Africa. There are still many men who abuse their wives. Similarly, Esther Mombo and Heleen Joziasse explain how the women of Kabuku and Nairobi in Kenya describe who Christ is to them. For most women, Jesus is their savior who saves them from their sins and from abusive treatment by men. The first part of the women's view of Christ is that they are saved from the traditional teaching that they should persevere in an abusive marriage, while nothing seems to be said to the men; the second part of their view is that Christ has fed the women and provided them with businesses or jobs.[32] From these women's experiences one can understand that they see Christ as the savior, as the protector from the oppression of misinterpretation of the Bible, intended to liberate people regardless of their gender.

A reading of Ephesians 5:25–27 begs the question, "How does Christ love the church?" Reading through the gospels, we see how Jesus, being both human and divine, related to women who were also among his disciples. For example, in John 4:9, the Samaritan woman asked Jesus: "You are a Jew and I am a Samaritan woman. How can you ask me for a drink?" In his interaction with this woman, Jesus broke the traditional cultural norm of Jewish men not speaking to Samaritan women, especially in public. We see something similar in his interaction with the woman who had suffered from bleeding (Matt 9:22; Mark 5:34; Luke 8:48) and with the woman caught in the act of adultery in John 7:53 – 8:11. Similarly, when anointed by a sinful woman in Luke 7:36–50, he refused to treat the woman as inferior or as a sinner. Given the negative cultural view of women in Jesus's time, each gospel writer testifies to Jesus's treating women with respect, frequently responding in ways that rejected the cultural, social and even religious norms of the time.

In contrast, Farida Dawkins notes that "African men are not the most expressive due to societal and cultural expectations. They can be quite elusive with their feelings, especially when it comes to being vulnerable and in love."[33] The Christian man should not be afraid to express his love to his wife, just as

---

31. Oduyoye and Amoah, "Christ for African Women," 43.
32. Mombo and Joziasse, "Jesus, a Man above All Other Men," 165.
33. Dawkins, "7 Unconventional Ways."

Christ expressed and showed love through his words and actions. Christ's love for the church, his people, was so real, sincere and dedicated, that he gave his own life for them, without setting conditions (John 3:16). That is, the blood of Christ, which he shed on the cross, paid the price for the sins of the world (John 1:29). The church is purchased through the blood of Christ Jesus. This was the sacrificial act of love: even when humans did not deserve it, Christ still died. And it is in this way that a husband is to love, care for and treat his wife. A husband should care for his wife, teach his wife, live a godly example, listen to his wife, and answer his wife's questions. Following the model of Jesus Christ, a Christian husband will be patient with his wife; he will be approachable, and will encourage his wife to do bigger and better things. He will pray for his wife, and instead of demanding his rights all the time, will meet his wife's needs. He will communicate openly with his wife about his plans and goals; he will care for his wife when she is feeling injured, hurt or rejected by others. This is what Christ did for the church while he was on earth, and this is what Paul is urging husbands to do for their wives.

Sacrificial love can also imply that Christ is a good friend, helper, redeemer, healer, lover, provider and personal Savior. Christ's model of being a friend to the church also applies to husbands with regard to their wives. Jesus said in John 15:13, "Greater love has no man than this, that a man lay down his life for his friends" (RSV). This means that Christ is always there for the church to comfort them, and to listen to the challenges the church is facing, even to the point of death. Likewise, a husband should be a friend who is ever willing to sacrifice what he has before the wife asks for it, whether it is his time, money or energy. A good friend is always there for someone; whether it is helping through the grief of losing a loved one or being by the side of individuals when they are sick, a good friend is present in good times and bad. Good friends are present, loyal and honest; and most African women want their husbands to be like this: someone they can count on in all situations. Similarly, Mombo and Joziasse describe the ideal husband:

> An ideal husband has one wife, children, and a home and takes care of his family. He is God-fearing, he protects, listens, and is respectful to his children and wife. He is open, social, and not hypocritical. He communicates with the family. An ideal husband is one who loves, who has loved and fulfills his promises. He does not listen to gossips and does not shout at his wife or children.[34]

---

34. Mombo and Joziasse, "Jesus, a Man above All Other Men," 167.

It is essential to give this christological teaching of Christ's role in relation to the church as a transformational model for African men. Love makes no headway when there is no room for sacrifice. Husbands should be willing to sacrifice their pride and any traditions and aspects of culture that do not glorify God. Such sacrifices include not being stingy with money, energy or time, even conjugal rights; doing domestic work; and creating time to cook for their wife. The concluding remark in the text (Eph 5:33) is that husbands should love their wives as Christ loved the church, because they are one with them: "However, each one of you also must love his wife as he loves himself, and the wife must respect her husband." How do husbands love themselves? It is in those ways that husbands are to love their wives. When husbands begin to love their wives as they love themselves, they fulfill Paul's teaching in Ephesians 5:31. A Christian man would act like a pagan if he did not take care of his wife, because she is "one flesh" with him. Some pagans even take better care of their wives, which should be a challenge to Christian men in Africa.

Conclusion

This paper has discussed the first section of the household code in Ephesians 5:21–33 from the point of view of christological teaching, which is to serve as a model for African men. It has been observed that the patriarchal nature of the Greco-Roman society influences interpretations of the portrayal of marriage in Ephesians 5:21–33, causing interpreters to focus on the hierarchy within the household without considering how the christological model can help men treat their wives according to Christ's example in relation to the church. Using the christological example and characteristics, it can be seen that there are various ways in which Christ can serve as an ideal man for husbands in Africa to emulate from Ephesians 5:21–33. The role of Christ in relation to the church is a model that African Christian men should imitate by treating their wives with respect and dignity. The household code deals specifically with the way in which Christ loved the church so much that he gave himself for it, so that in the future he could present the church to himself as a spotless bride, without spot or blemish. This becomes the model for husbands to love their wives just as Christ loves the church, feeding it and nurturing it. Christ is considered a lover, ideal husband, friend, helper, protector, provider, nourisher, and one who knows how to take care of the church. These are the qualities that, according to the text, a husband should possess in order to have a Christian home. When men possess these qualities, women will not be exploited, subordinated or treated as slaves by men.

Bibliography

Abbey-Mensah, Dinah B. "Violence against Women." In *Where God Reigns: Reflection on Women in God's World*, edited by Elizabeth Amoah, 171–81. Accra-North: Sam-Woode Ltd, for the Circle of Concerned African Women Theologians, 1997.

Adamolekun, Taiye. "Marriage and Divorce from Christian Perspective: An Examination of Pauline Corpus." In *Biblical View of Sex and Sexuality from African Perspective*, edited by S. O. Abogunrin and J. O. Akao, 138–50. Ibadan: Nigerian Association for Biblical Studies, 2006.

Aina, I. Olabisi. "Women, Culture and Society." In *Nigerian Women in Society and Development*, edited by Amadu Sesay and Adetanwa Odebiyi, 1–21. Ibadan: Dokun Publishing, 1998.

Amadi, Ugochukwu, and Felicia Amadi. "Marital Crisis in the Nigerian Society: Causes, Consequences and Management Strategies." *Mediterranean Journal of Social Sciences* 5, no. 26 (Nov. 2014): 133–43.

Amolo, Hope. "Paul's Concept of Sexual Union." *Biblical View of Sex and Sexuality from African Perspective*, edited by S. O. Abogunrin and J. O. Akao, 167–81. Ibadan: Nigerian Association for Biblical Studies, 2006.

Aristotle. *Aristotle in 23 Volumes*. Vol. 21. Translated by H. Rackham. Cambridge: Harvard University Press, 1944.

Aweda, A. David. "Sex-Role Inequalities in the African Family: Contemporary Implications." *Ife Social Sciences Review* 7, no. 1 & 2 (1984): 188–97.

Botha, P. J. J. "Folklore, Social Values and Life as a Woman in Early Christianity." *Southern African Journal for Folklore Studies* 3 (1992): 1–14.

Dawkins, Farida, "7 Unconventional Ways African Men Show Affection." Face2Face Africa. Accessed 21 March 2020. https://face2faceafrica.com/article/unconventional-ways-african-men-show-affection.

Fee, Gordon D. *Pauline Christology: An Exegetical-Theological Study*. Peabody: Hendrickson, 2007.

Kato, Byang H. "The Christian Leader and His Family." *Perception* 9 (June 1977): 1–9.

Keener, Craig S. *Paul, Women and Wives: Marriage and Women's Ministry in the Letters of Paul*. Peabody: Hendrickson, 1992.

Lu, Shi-Min. "Woman's Role in New Testament Household Codes: Transforming First-Century Roman Culture." *Priscilla Papers* 30, no. 1 (Winter 2016): 1–7.

MacDonald, Margaret Y. "Beyond Identification of the Topos of Household Management: Reading the Household Codes in Light of Recent Methodologies and Theological Perspectives in the Study of the New Testament." *New Testament Studies* 57, no. 1 (2010): 66–90.

Mazzalongo, Mike. *Ephesians for Beginners*. Choctaw: BibleTalk Books, 2015.

Mombo, Esther, and Heleen Joziasse. "Jesus, a Man above All Other Men." In *The Postcolonial Church: Bible, Theology, and Mission*, edited by R. S. Wafula, Esther Mombo and Joseph Wandera, 159–174. Alameda: Borderless Press, 2016.

Mouton, Elna. "Reimagining Ancient Household Ethos? On the Implied Rhetorical Effect of Ephesians 5:21–33." *Neotestamentica* 48, no. 1 (2014): 163–85. https://www.jstor.org/stable/43926977.
Oduyoye, Mercy Amba. "Biblical Interpretation and the Social Location of the Interpreter." In *Reading from This Place: Social Location in Global Perspective*, edited by Fernando E. Segovia and Mary Tolbert, 33–51. Minneapolis: Fortress, 1995.
Oduyoye, Mercy A., and Elizabeth Amoah. "The Christ for African Women." In *With Passion and Compassion: Third World Women Doing Theology*, edited by V. Fabella and M. A. Oduyoye, 37–45. Maryknoll: Orbis, 1990.
Ogunkunle, C. O. "Biblical Injunction on Marriage and Sexual Union in the Context of Christian Marriage in Nigeria." In *Biblical View of Sex and Sexuality from African Perspective*, edited by S. O. Abogunrin and J. O. Akao, 48–60. Ibadan: Nigerian Association for Biblical Studies, 2006.
Omowole, S. O. "Marriage and Divorce: The New Testament View." In *Biblical View of Sex and Sexuality from African Perspective*, edited by S. O. Abogunrin and J. O. Akao, 125–38. Ibadan: Nigerian Association for Biblical Studies, 2006.
Phiri, Isabel Apawo. "Major Challenges for African Women Theologians in Theological Education (1989–2008)." *Studia Historiae Ecclesiasticae* 34, no. 2 (2008): 63–81.
Plato. *Plato in Twelve Volumes*. Vols. 10 & 11. Translated by R. G. Bury. Cambridge, MA: Harvard University Press, 1967 & 1968.
Silberschmidt, Margrethe. *"Women Forget That Men Are the Masters": Gender Antagonism and Socio-Economic Change in Kisii District, Kenya*. Uppsala: Nordiska Afrikainstitutet, 1999.
Sultana, Abeda. "Patriarchy and Women's Subordination: A Theoretical Analysis." *The Arts Faculty Journal* (July 2010–June 2011). https://pdfs.semanticscholar.org/1b7e/4b01c57fe60b562be3609aa2eebe4d348b41.pdf.

Part Two

Christ in Theology and Church History

9

Christology in Africa En Route

Encounter between Biblical and Indigenous African Concepts

Daniel Mwailu
*Adjunct Professor in Theology and Biblical Studies,
Africa Nazarene University, Nairobi, Kenya
Currently serving as a church minister in Leeds, UK*

Abstract

This article examines the development of christological thinking in Africa. It briefly traces the route of such inquiry. It gives its raison d'être as emanating from the need to develop linguistic vehicles for communicating christological concepts using relevant indigenous perceptions capable of translating biblical truth using indigenous African concepts. It evaluates the factors that delayed the process of christological contextualization in Africa, and the laxity of the missionary and African church leadership and its scholars in rising to the task of contextualization. This article posits that if there must be blame apportioned for the delay, it lies with both the missionaries and the African church in general, with the more substantial liability carried by the latter. The paper argues that contextualization finds precedents in the early church in the formulation of doctrinal creeds. As Christianity traveled from its Judaic cradle to the Hellenistic culture, it formulated the Nicene and the Chalcedonian

Creeds in response to the encounter with Greek concepts. When the church traveled from the Roman papal scene, dominated by dogma, and encountered the Western scene, dominated by Enlightenment philosophical presuppositions, it formulated further contextualization. Similar contextualization needs to happen in Africa. The article concludes by presenting an evaluation of research on christological concepts carried out in two new religious movements in Kenya. The article appeals to young aspiring African theologians to continue the task of contextualizing Christology in Africa as they seek to answer Jesus Christ's question: "Who do you say I am?" This question needs an authentic biblical answer from authentic African voices.

Key words: African, biblical, Christology, contextualization, concepts, encounter, indigenous, theology

Introduction

The title of this paper deliberately mimics the title of a book edited by Kofi-Appiah-Kubi and Sergio Torres, *African Theology En Route*.[1] The purpose of the mimic is to signal a similar journey, a quest for contextual Christology in Africa. The papers in that book evaluated African theology and religious beliefs and practices, and also appraised the quest for African authenticity and the theology of liberation in Africa. Five years after that book was published, a group of African theological students of which I was part assembled at the University of Aberdeen in Scotland for the formation of the African Theological Students' Association in the UK, where it was stressed that

> any theological reflection that is to be identified as Christian must be Biblical and Christocentric while giving full attention to the milieu in which it is being worked out and practiced . . . This is the key to a true Biblical Christocentric theologizing in Africa and anywhere. To affirm Christ in the milieu of the realities of life is the theological attitude that can stand the test of time.[2]

The theological emphasis in African scholarship, up to the time of that book, emphasized African traditional religions that germinated from the German *Religionsgeschichtliche Schule* – "the history of religions school" – whose theological ripples persist to this day. The papers presented in the

---

1. Appiah-Kubi and Torres, *African Theology En Route*.
2. Bediako, "Consideration of Some Agenda Items," 3.

book drew attention to African reflection on contextual theology. At that time, studies and scholarly articles on contextual Christology in Africa were anecdotal, lacking depth of research. In the 1960s, Taylor posed the question, "If Christ was to appear as the answer to the question that Africans are asking what would he look like?"[3] In the 1970s, J. S. Mbiti asserted that theology stands or falls on understanding, translation and interpretation of Jesus Christ, suggesting that Christian theology ought to be Christology.[4] He pioneered the field of inquiry into African Christology, citing the concept of the Son of God as paralleled in the Ndebele and Shona of Zimbabwe, the Shilluk of Sudan, the concept of "Nommo" in the Dogon of Upper Volta, the Bemba of Zambia and the Sonjo of Tanzania, as well as the "assistant creator" in Fon of Dahomey cosmology and a similar idea in the Tiv of Nigeria.[5]

Looking at the global context in the West in the late 1950s through the 1970s, the standard christological approach was to examine the New Testament titles for Jesus as used in the Bible.[6] The quest for a Christology in Africa intensified in the 1980s, spearheaded by Kwame Bediako with his assertion, "The heart of the encounter of Good News is Christology."[7] John S. Pobee echoed this and said, "Christology is at the very heart of any theology of inculturation."[8] Most Africans are familiar with the concept of God from their traditional religions, but not with that of Christ.[9]

Turning back to our title, I started on this route at the height of the quest in 1984, with a dissertation on Christology in the Gospel of Mark and its relevance for the African messianic movement.[10] This was followed by a doctoral thesis on Christology in Africa.[11] Since that time there has been a resurgence of interest in Christology, with attention shifting from African theology to Christology, such that Oborji observed that the reverse is now the case; Christology in Africa is now receiving much more attention by African

---

3. Taylor, *Primal Vision*, 16.
4. Mbiti, *New Testament Eschatology*, 190.
5. Mbiti, "Some African Concepts of Christology," 5.
6. See Moule, *Origin of Christology*; Taylor, *Names of Jesus*; Marshall, *Origins of New Testament Christology*; Cullman, *Christology of the New Testament*; Vermes, *Jesus the Jew*.
7. Bediako, "Biblical Christologies," 110.
8. Pobee, "In Search of Christology in Africa," 15.
9. See Hood, *Must God Remain Greek?*, 143. See also Potgieter and Magezi, "Critical Assessment," https://doi.org/10.4102/ids.v50i1.2136.
10. Mwailu, "Messiahship in Mark's Gospel."
11. Mwailu, "Christology in Africa."

theologians.¹² In similar vein, Akper avers that Christology in Africa now occupies center stage in contemporary theologizing;¹³ in contrast, four decades ago De Jongh lamented that before 1970 there was minimal literature in the form of written Christology by African theologians.¹⁴

My Interest in Christology in Africa

What stimulated my interest in the study of Christology in Africa?

Communication Challenge

My two pieces of research stemmed from life experiences in an attempt to communicate the Christian faith. Three experiences were germane catalysts:

Χριστός versus *Kiliso*

Between 1967 and 1968, I desperately attempted to communicate the Christian faith to Mbeleete, an older woman from my extended family. I told her to accept Christ as her savior. As she could not understand English, I had to communicate this concept in the vernacular, Kikamba. The transliteration in Kikamba of the word "Christ" also happens to be a transliteration of the Greek word Χριστός, rendered in Kikamba as *Klisto*. When so transliterated, the term *Klisto* carries no meaning in the Kamba cultural thought-forms. The older woman was unable to conceptualize in Greco-Anglo-Saxon terms; hence she thought that I was referring to the nearest Kamba noun that sounded in pronunciation like *Klisto*, which is *Kiliso*, meaning a steep climb! So she kept laughing mockingly at me, saying, "You grandson of mine, you are a fool; can't you see I am old and that I cannot climb anything?" Every time I mentioned Christ (*Klisto*), she would retort, "What *Kiliso*? I cannot climb anything!" Therefore, the impasse continued. I had only recently become a Christian myself, and as a young Christian I could not see where I was going wrong; all I could see was that we were deadlocked and unable to communicate. The key point is that I could not adequately communicate the concept of Christ to this elderly uneducated woman because she could not form a mental image of the concept of Christ understood in a Judeo-Christian sense.

---

12. Oborji, "African Theology, Roman Catholic," 16.
13. Akper, "Person of Jesus Christ," 224–43.
14. De Jongh, "Critical Analysis of Contemporary Developments," 2.

Christ as Anathema

A similar incident occurred in 1974 when a small group of us went to the northern part of Kenya for a Christian evangelistic mission among the Turkana tribe. I was preaching in an open-air market at Lodwar with a Turkana bilinguist translating. As I went on preaching, the people were very attentive – up to the point when I made what now I can only describe as a typical verbal doctrinal blunder: that of associating faith in Christ with material blessings. I said to my audience that if they accepted the gospel of Christ, Christ would bless them and make their desert district blossom with greenery. Then I made it explicit that Christ would send them rains. Rains! That was anathema to them, but to me, rains were a much-needed blessing in that part of Kenya.

At that point, there was a tumult in the crowd, with the people turning to look at each other and muttering, reminiscent of the response to Paul's preaching in Athens when he mentioned the resurrection (Acts 17). I inquired from my translator, Isaya, what had gone wrong. He told me it was because I said "rains" and associated them with Christ. "What is wrong with that?" I asked. My translator explained that, in the arid desert area of Turkana, people associate rains with disaster, homelessness and death. Because the Turkana do not build permanent houses, when the rain pours, it destroys their feebly constructed mud huts thatched with straw, rendering them homeless. Besides, when it rains in the Kenyan mountains, the water collects in the rivers, drowning unawares many people who sleep on the riverbeds. In most parts of Africa, and indeed in most parts of the world, people associate rains with blessings as a source of life. For this nomadic tribe, however, the underlying nuance of the word "rains" is "disaster!" If Christ was going to bring rains that night, then accepting him would be implicitly welcoming disaster. In this incident, the novelty of the statement in my sermon is not in doubt. I should have known better or explained differently.

Black Messiah and the Black Jews

The third experience occurred in 1977 in the final year of my vocational training. My graduating class went for evangelistic outreach and field experience in Western Kenya. One morning a few of us encountered the followers of Legio Maria. As we tried to explain to them about the gospel of Jesus Christ, they heckled us, calling us "Black Jews!" They said a Jewish messiah was of no consequence to them. They had their messiah. He lived with them in *Got Kwer* (Jerusalem) near Migori. They ridiculed us for following a white Christ. Our enthusiastic evangelistic zeal had reached a Waterloo.

We were unable to communicate because we were operating in two different universes of discourse.

These three experiences set me en route in search of contextual Christology in Africa. They convinced me that regurgitating ready-made, Euro-American theological concepts would not do in the African context. Nor would a wholesale acceptance of the defensive theological attitude of some African theologians who, in reaction to Western imperialism and conceptual paternalism, seem to produce another type of reactionary negative theological reflection.[15] To achieve relevant christological reflection in Africa, we need to get alongside the African peoples and learn from them what they are learning from God's revelation in the Scriptures and in their encounter with the living Christ, and then enter into a dialogue in finding the right language to articulate this experience. There has been an excellent successful example of this among the Sukuma of Tanzania.[16] It requires the African theologian to be at the same time a learner and a catalyst.[17]

The christological quest in Africa is a colossal one; the vastness of the African continent and its diversity of cultures and subcultures rules out the premise that one size of Christology fits all. While a concept among one tribe or subtribe like the Bantu might mean one thing, it might mean something quite different among another tribe. For example, J. S. Mbiti studied over five hundred tribes and languages and discovered one thousand six hundred names and concepts for God.[18] Küster noted the magnitude of the task of defining African Christology.[19]

Contextualization has precedents in the architects of the Chalcedonian christological formulations, the leading bishops and churchmen who grappled with christological concepts familiar to their parishioners. When Christianity traveled from its Judaic cradle and encountered Hellenistic Greek

---

15. See Moila, "Christology in the Context of Oppression in South Africa," 223–31; Bujo, *African Theology*; Waliggo, "African Clan," 111; Banda, "Sufficiency of Christ in Africa"; Parratt, *Re-inventing Christianity*; Okure, *Inculturation of Christianity in Africa*; Mbogu, *Jesus in Post-Missionary Africa*; Kanu, *Towards an Igbo-African Christological Construct*; Gathogo, "Reconstructive Hermeneutics in African Christology," http://dx.doi.org/10.4102/hts.v71i3.2660; Mugambi and Magesa, *Jesus in African Christianity*; Nthamburi, "Christ as Seen by an African," 54–59. See also Njoroge, "Confessing Christ in Africa Today," 131–36.

16. See Healey, "Three Case Studies," 1.

17. See Mwailu, "Christology in Africa," 3. See also Cook, "African Experience of Jesus," 668–92.

18. See Mbiti, *Concepts of God in Africa*, 91–157.

19. Küster, *Many Faces of Jesus Christ*, 58–68.

philosophy, it necessitated christological formulations at the councils of Nicaea and Chalcedon. The Judaic concept of Messiah had to find new expression in dialogue with Greek concepts: λογος ενδιαθετος: "God having His word immanent in Himself, rational thought in the mind"; λογος προθορικος: "the thought uttered as a word"; or λογος σπεμαρτικος; or Origen's concepts of λογος and λογικοι.[20]

The christological approach that incorporates concepts and ideas prevalent in African communities is the safest method of producing a Christology that is authentically biblical, culturally African, and which lasts. Such an approach takes theological reflection in Africa a step further by moving from the peripheral observations and prophecies of African theology into the heart of the matter, Christology.[21]

Christological Theological Imperative

Two factors demonstrate the need to contextualize Chalcedonian Christology: first, the skeptical philosophical quest, which poses the difficulty of maintaining belief in the Christ of traditional theology; and, second, the desire to establish the relevance of Jesus Christ in new cultures. Bultmann's quest in existentialist philosophy expressed agnosticism regarding the "life and personality of Jesus,"[22] questioning whether "Jesus existed" and stating that "what counts is the work of Jesus."[23] Paul Tillich defined Christ as "New Being."[24] Oscar Cullman developed his Christology in a constant polemic with Bultmann. He concluded that "Jesus Christ is the central event of Heilsgeschichte,"[25] contrary to Schweitzer and Dodd, who described Christ as the end of history. Cullman argued for a strictly biblical Christology drawn from the Bible. He rejected existentialism, historical skepticism and other philosophical speculations in formulating the Christian message. He opted for a functional and descriptive Christology instead of one based on personal and metaphysical models; he approached the figure of Christ through the titles assigned to him by the

---

20. See Kelly, *Early Christian Doctrine*, 10, 18, 96, 99–100.

21. See Magezi and Magezi, "Healing and Coping with Life," a4333, https://doi.org/10.4102/hts.v73i3.4333. See also the erudite evaluation in Magezi and Igba, "African Theology and African Christology," a4590, https://doi.org/10.4102/hts.v74i1.4590.

22. Bultmann, *Jesus and the Word*, 8; McGrath, *Making of Modern Germany Christology*, 127.

23. Bultmann, 13.

24. Tillich, *Existence and the Christ*.

25. Cullmann, *Salvation in History*, 93–94; also Cullmann, *Christ and Time*.

New Testament.²⁶ He argued that Christology has to do with history and not mythology. He said that New Testament authors understood Christology as a redemptive history, which extends from creation to the eschatological new creation, the center of which is the earthly life of Jesus.²⁷ Other scholars²⁸ have attempted to contextualize Chalcedonian Christology. Contextualization paves the way for "a dynamic and functional Christology."²⁹

Hermeneutic Circle Imperative

The concept of the hermeneutic circle asserts that the interpretation of concepts is an ongoing process. The thought of Schleiermacher, Dilthey, Heidegger and Gadamer developed the term "hermeneutic circle." It states that the part and the whole are related circularly; to understand the part it is essential to understand the whole, and vice versa.³⁰ In this regard, contextualizing Christology in Africa requires understanding the biblical concepts in their original context, but also understanding the African cultural indigenous background, the currency of the new African concepts.

Traditional hermeneutics maintains that proper understanding of the *Sitz im Leben* of the ancient text is almost the *summum bonum* of hermeneutics. According to the hermeneutic circle, however, the context of the recipients also matters, through the process of "cultural distancing."³¹ There has to be a fusion of the two horizons, the interpreter's and the context's. Hasselgrave aptly points out: "a people's world view must be taken with uttermost seriousness by the missionary if he wants to communicate Christ in the respondent culture."³² His view mirrors the theory of the hermeneutic circle defined as "the continuing change in interpretation dictated by the inevitable dialectical changes in our present reality."³³

African Christians cannot reflect on the person of Christ in a mental vacuum. There has to be "mental imaging" whenever an attempt is made to

---

26. Cullmann, *Christology of the New Testament*.
27. Cullmann, 317.
28. Moltmann's christological views are contained in his *Theologie der Hoffnung* (English translation: *Theology of Hope*); see also Pannenberg, *Jesus, God and Man*; Robinson, *Names and Titles of Jesus*; Schoonenberg, *The Christ*; Schillebeeckx, *Jesus*.
29. Mondin, "New Trends in Christology," 47.
30. See Thiselton, *Two Horizons*, 194–204; also Gadamer, *Truth and Method*.
31. Thiselton, 115–39.
32. Hasselgrave, *Communicating Christ Cross-Culturally*, 124.
33. Goba, "Towards a 'Black' Ecclesiology," 48.

describe and communicate who Jesus Christ is. It is these mental images that we need to tease out, merge and analyze before we can conjecture which African concepts best describe Christ. The African church needs "a manifestation of a Christian faith consistent with their own unique historical experience, rooted more self-consciously in their own cultures and contributing to a richer worldwide interpretation of the gospel."[34]

In 1910, at the World Missionary Conference in Edinburgh, a survey was held on the peoples in the missionaries' fields of service; of the fourteen Western missionary correspondents who replied to the survey, a dozen were "virtually convinced that the African peoples among whom they were working had nothing in their individual and social lives which could be considered of religious significance as 'preparation of the gospel.'"[35] For most missionaries who worked in Africa, they "felt it right that the African must receive Western culture with his Christianity."[36] The understanding of most of the nineteenth- and early twentieth-century missionaries was that Africans needed to renounce their culture because it was satanic. My tutor the late Thomas Cope, himself a missionary with the Africa Inland Mission, looked at the questions submitted to the Mission baptism candidates in 1910. He deduced the missionaries' belief that "all local culture and customs were evil . . . [that they] considered African culture, religion, and customs to be of the devil and to be discarded as soon as possible."[37]

"Christianity never travels without a cultural cradle."[38] What seems to have gone wrong, however, was "to reject African culture, if not in toto at least large segments of it."[39] "Until the 1920s missionaries were often frankly antagonistic to African culture."[40] The consequences of this cultural degradation have never been doubted; besides stifling early contextual theological reflection, it paved the way for nominal and superficial Christianity in Africa, as observed in Ghana, where "the implanted Christian faith failed to meet the Akan in his personally experienced need but rather [he] became a Christian by cleaving

---

34. Dickinson, *To Set at Liberty the Oppressed*, 50.
35. Bediako, "Consideration of Some Agenda Items," 27.
36. Atieno-Odhiambo, "Portrait of the Missionaries in Kenya," 5; cf. Strayer, "Missions and African Culture."
37. Cope, "Africa Inland Mission," 118–51.
38. Dickson, "African Culture and Christianity"; also cited by Gration, "Relationship of the African Inland Mission," 110.
39. Dickson, 118.
40. Fortes and Dieterlen, *African Systems and Thought*, 31.

to the new order introduced by the missionary, rather than by working out his salvation within the traditional religious milieu."[41]

These negative attitudes and legacies implicitly contributed to a delay in integrating African concepts in Christianity; nevertheless, we need to note two positives: First, most Western missionaries had the best intentions for the tribal peoples. In their rejection of African culture, they aimed at developing a complete understanding of the "pure gospel," untainted by tribal thoughts. Second, the missionaries laid down the foundations of theological reflection in their promotion of education so that the tribal people could read the Scriptures. They reduced some complicated, only spoken languages into written languages, which is the most valuable tool for theological reflection. They also wrote Bible dictionaries and concordances in tribal languages. Their rejection of African customs, ideas and traditions became self-defeating to their enterprise. Most missionaries did not envisage, nor realize, the far-reaching implications of their rejection of African concepts and culture. They failed to realize that what they considered to be African "superstitions," customs and traditional practices had deep psychological, religious and social roots, which were impossible to suppress by Christian creed and moral code. Pope Paul VI suggests ignorance rather than malice as the cause of the missionaries' rejection of African culture: "Missionaries . . . lacked an understanding of the positive value of customs and ancient traditions . . . they were not always able . . . to understand the full significance of the customs and unwritten traditions of the people they evangelized."[42]

Africans cannot attribute all the blame and failure to Western missionaries; African scholars and church leaders have also contributed to the apparent delay in authentic African christological reflection. Theses produced by African scholars in American and European universities in the first half of the last century indicate a lack of interest in relating the Christian message to the various African cultural milieus. It reached a point where scholars scathingly accused African theologians of being "brainwashed, out of touch with their African people at the grassroots level, becoming black skins in white masks."[43] This negligence evoked concern and a response from Africans in the latter part

---

41. Williamson, *Akan Religion and the Christian Faith*.
42. Dirven, "Maria Legio," 69; cf. Pobee, *Towards an African Theology*, 53.
43. Fashole-Luke, "Footpaths and Signposts," 388–89; cf. Fanon, *Black Skin, White Masks*.

of the century,⁴⁴ as well as from other non-Africans who are conversant with the theological situation in Africa. The following observations from Oosthuizen sum up the case:

> The selfhood of the church in Africa is important. Africa needs its own *confessio Africana*, in which the young church takes notice of its existential situation. The independence of a church does not lie in its organization, but in the way it answers Christ's question, "who do you say that I am?"⁴⁵

Regurgitating Western concepts to an indigenous African is like fitting a square peg into a round whole. Western Christian tradition has tended to be apparently anti-supernatural, highly intellectual and, in most cases, limited in its philosophically generated concerns, which in most cases are out of touch with those of the ordinary members of the community.⁴⁶ This intellectual, purely academic christological expression cannot work in Africa. The majority of African Christians are not as academic and at least find no problems with the supernatural; Africa needs a more down-to-earth christological formulation interwoven with the texture of Christian worship and practice. The African context assumes the supernatural. Africans stay at the level of the encounter between transcendence and the human. The African Instituted Churches "are thriving because they do not dwell on catechism or creeds, but their whole life is one entire religious continuum."⁴⁷ Sigqibo exposes the inadequacy to the Majority World of a Christology that does not

> exploit the full meaning of the fact that Jesus of Nazareth is the son of God. The very fact that Jesus was a real man must be aggressively asserted in formulating Christology for Africa. Then will the poor, dehumanized and degraded, recognize in Him their Liberator, who does not divinize them but humanizes all men, that is setting all people free.⁴⁸

---

44. In January 1972, a consultation at Makerere University, Kampala, with thirty-five participants, mainly African theologians, concluded that "Christianity is a common commodity which belongs to all peoples, wherever they are living. But Christianity has been received in Africa on foreign terms, it must now be made relevant to Africa." See Fashole-Luke, "African Theologians Consultation," 202–5.

45. Oosthuizen, *Post Christianity in Africa*, 10.

46. Mondin, "New Trends in Christology," 55.

47. Simbo, "African Critique of Western Theology," 32; cf. Mbiti, *African Religions and Philosophy*, 5.

48. Sigqibo, "Christology in the Third World"; also reviewed by P. J. Robinson, "Abstract no. 296", 103.

My tutor the late Dick France stimulated my thinking on contextual christological concerns in Africa when he gave the challenge that "the African church has to do its theological homework, and unless it finds theologians who take revelation as their non-negotiable starting point, but who are prepared to ask radical questions about its interpretation and application to their intellectual scene, its future is murky."[49] France's warning was echoed by M'Passou, who stated that "African churches are running the risk of great theological bankruptcy and their future will be bleak if they continue to rely on Western theological concepts."[50]

Most of the communities founded by Western missionaries imbibed wholesale what the missionaries taught without recourse to contextualization.[51] Evangelical Christianity tends to be reactionary rather than proactive. This reminds me of my favorite philosophy teacher, the late Richard Scheer, who used to say that evangelicals are taught what to think rather than how to think. The third illustration, of the "black messiah – black Jews" confrontation of the theological students, illustrates this point. The students had not prepared for how to engage with indigenous concepts. One further challenge that led me to embark on the route of exploring contextual christological concepts in Africa was the assertion that, in the planting of Christianity in Africa, Africa had no Paul; it was "a church without theology and theological concerns."[52]

Africans cannot go on blaming the missionaries ad infinitum for lack of contextual Christology in Africa or for the scarcity of African theological reflection. To do so would be to emulate African politicians who blame colonialism for all Africa's woes. Before independence, the politicians blamed the white man for cruelty, yet African political leaders have shed more blood of fellow Africans than was shed in total during the colonial years. African leaders have turned Africa from the "dark continent" into a bleeding continent. Under African leadership, some of the once prosperous, productive countries have been transformed from the gardens of Africa to begging baskets. The missionaries translated the Bible into local tribal languages. African scholars from those tribes, with their better knowledge of the vernacular language, have not even attempted to revise those Bibles into better translations. African

---

49. France, "Questions concerning the future of African Christianity," 32.

50. Dennis M'Passou gave this caution on 30 October 1981 in the *British Weekly and Church Review*; cf. Cyril Okorocha (ed.), the editorial comments, in *African Theological Student Association Bulletin*, Vol. 1, Aberdeen, 1981, 3.

51. Teasdale, "Evaluation of the Ecclesiology of the Africa Inland Church."

52. Mbiti, "Some African Concepts of Christology," 51.

theologians and the African church leadership must end the blame game, and theologically and christologically engage constructively in contextualization. The last three decades have seen positive responses, as already mentioned. The fact that ASET arranged a conference to discuss Christology in Africa is a clear indication that African theologians are responding to the challenge issued by Kurewa some thirty years ago, when he said that Christ's question "Who do you say I am?" is posed to the African church and "it demands christological response with African authenticity."[53] The last three decades have shown evidence of such a response.[54]

Signposts toward African Christological Concepts

The earliest response in developing christological concepts in Africa was in South Africa, driven by the pressures and injustice of apartheid. Black and liberation theology came up with different christological reflections. The point of departure for black theology is to stress that the God of the Bible is a God of liberation and to present in its Christology Jesus as Liberator.[55] According to Tatkaso Mofokeng,

> Black Christological reflection occurs in an interplay between the present context of praxis for liberation that is a response to Jesus Christ, who is present and active among the oppressed, as spelled out above and in scripture. This interplay that has the present praxis as its starting point is expressed in the following dialectically related questions: "Who am I? How can I be liberated to my authentic self?" on the one side, and "Who do you say that I am?" (Mark 8:29; also Matt 16:15). We also described the black praxis for liberation as one that goes through a process that is beset with crises and qualitative growth.[56]

To present Christ as the Liberator chimes with most indigenous thought forms, unlike Chalcedonian Christology. For Athanasius, who was the chief

---

53. Kurewa, "Who Do You Say That I Am?," 182–88.

54. See Magesa, *African Theology Come of Age*; Olsen, "Contextualised Christology in Tropical Africa"; Potgieter and Magezi, "Critical Assessment," a2136, https://doi.org/10.4102/ids.v50i1.2136. See also Schreiter, *Faces of Jesus in Africa*; Ilo, *African Christology*.

55. Boesak, *Black Theology, Black Power*, 9–11; Boesak, "Use of Scriptures in Black Theology," 28–37; cf. Boesak, *Farewell to Innocence*; Moore, *Black Theology*; Cleage, *Black Messiah*; Miranda, *Being and the Messiah*; Becken, *Relevant Theology*.

56. Mofokeng, *Crucified among the Crossbearers*, 241–42.

architect of the Nicene teaching later endorsed at the Council of Chalcedon in AD 451, understood salvation in terms of divinization – θεοποιησις. God comes to human beings to enable them to participate in himself. Athanasius approached Christology from above. Human beings, by grace, participate in God's perfect humanity and are made sons (ὑιοποιησις), or divinized, by sharing in the λογος. Incarnation is the reverse of the fall. The central teaching of Athanasius was the affirmation that Christ was indeed true man as well as true God. The concept in itself raises no severe problems, but "the route by which Athanasius travels to this destination has some snags for African people whose cultural outlook is in many ways nearer to the Hebraic world than to the Greek ideas."[57] To an African whose traditional religious culture observes a radical distinction between God and human beings,[58] this becomes hard to conceptualize. For African culture

> would readily receive the Christ, who is the Godman, as a realization of its longings for a more perfect mediator. But what seems difficult is to accommodate that such a mediator divinizes his fellowman . . . they would favor the picture of the Christ as one who humanizes His brethren.[59]

The concept of corporate Christ or Christ as the phenotype of perfect humanity finds no real problem in traditional African thought forms; what seems to be most alarming is the idea of divinization. In Greek philosophy, the concept of divinization chimes with the Greek notion of the soul as a divine spark, an effusion to be reabsorbed into divinity. This is frightening to the African mind, just as is the idea of Ἰμανυελ (God with us). The concept of liberator, however, finds a dynamic equivalent in most African tribal heroes. It is, therefore, serviceable for communicating Christ to Africans.

Concept of Christ as Messiah

My doctoral dissertation explored indigenous concepts for the biblical concept of Christ as the Messiah in two Kenyan tribes, the Luo and the Meru. In trying to establish the etymological background, my research revealed that "it is easier to give an account of the historical development than to define the

---

57. Dwane, "Christology in the Third World," 5.
58. Mbiti, "Some African Concepts," 56; cf. Mbiti, *African Religions and Philosophy*, 75–91, 149–65.
59. Dwane, "Christology in the Third World," 5.

term messianism which seems to mean all things to all men ... or at least to all theologians."⁶⁰ Of all the attempted definitions surveyed, the one that seems best comes from Oesterley: "Messianism in its widest sense: redemption from present ills by supernatural means embodied in a personality is elemental, one of the common characteristics of man. It is deeply embedded in human nature and finds a responsive chord in almost every environment."⁶¹

The standard works⁶² trace the etymology of "messiah" back to Israelite religion and define the term as a "promised ... liberator of [an] oppressed people or country."⁶³ They state that it "derives from the Hebrew word (משׁה – Mashiach), it denotes the Jewish religious concept of a person with a special mission from God." By definition, messianic movements imply the imminence of some decisive event.⁶⁴ Evidence suggests that "early Christianity took Jewish ideas about the Messiah and applied them to Jesus. Ideas centered on the expectation of the advent of a messiah derived from the Hebrew word (משׁה – Mashiach), meaning "the anointed one."⁶⁵

Ringreen and Werblowsky⁶⁶ point out that such semantic development emanated from the Jewish belief that a descendant of David's royal house would realize the ultimate salvation of Israel. For background, my research explored whether messiah/messianism derives from Judaism or whether it is a universal term, and what precipitates it. The evidence is split. According to Werblowsky, messianism is "a characteristic feature of Judaism that [was] transmitted to other religions and civilizations."⁶⁷ There is evidence, however, that the messiah concept has roots elsewhere in other religions – for instance, in Assyrian religion, in Ashurnasirpal's prayer to Ishtar.⁶⁸

Cheyne believes that Jewish messianic hope may be the result of Babylonian influence.⁶⁹ There is also a view that the messiah concept derives from Chaldea.⁷⁰ In Egypt, Merneptah is praised as the divinely sent protector of Egypt's peace.

---

60. Werblowsky, "Messianism in Jewish History," 30–45.
61. Osterley, *Evolution of the Messianic Idea*; as cited in Wallis, *Messiahs*, 268.
62. "Messiah," in *Encyclopaedia Britannica*, 1021; "Messiah–Messianism," in Eliade, *Encyclopaedia of Religion*, 469–81.
63. "Messianism," in *Oxford English Dictionary*.
64. See "Messiah," in *Encyclopaedia Britannica*, 1021.
65. See "Messiah–Messianism," in Eliade, *Encyclopaedia of Religion*, 472.
66. Eliade, 472–81.
67. Werblowsky, "Messianism in Jewish History," 30.
68. Wallis, *Messiahs*, 268.
69. Cheyne and Black, "Messiah," 2849.
70. Blavatsky, *Isis Unveiled*, 256.

He is hailed as "the victorious ruler, magnified king among the gods, the commanding Lord."[71] Sigmund Mowinckel[72] holds the two views in tension and contends that the word "messiah" as a title and name originated in later Judaism and should be reserved only for such a figure.[73] He then points out that the custom of anointing the king to install him in his sacred office was an adaptation by the Israelites from the inhabitants of Canaan. Mowinckel defines "Messiah" as "an abbreviation of the fuller expression Yahweh's Anointed."[74] Biblical evidence[75] seems to suggest both.

From this background information, I turned my attention to an investigation of the concept of the messiah among the Luo and Meru tribes, where two new religious movements had split from the Catholic Church and elevated their founders into messiah figures: the Legio Maria in Western Kenya led by Simeo Ondeto,[76] and OFCAM (Organization for Christian Acts of Mercy) led by Baikiao. These two leaders are a contrast: one is without formal academic education, while the other is an academic with a PhD from Rome. They both believed themselves to be, and practiced, as messiahs among their people. I conducted fieldwork between 1984 and 1987 among the Luo and Meru communities and interviewed both leaders. Through my research I found that some indigenous concepts chimed with and germinated in these two leaders. The concepts had christological notions serviceable as dynamic cultural resemblances or equivalent to the christological notion of "messiah" to communicate with traditional indigenous Luo or Meru.

A literature review on Luo spiritual specialists identified two indigenous concepts of christological value consonant with the biblical concept of "messiah" among the Luo: *Jabilo* and *Ajuoga*. According to M. G. Whisson, *Ajuoga* discerned the will of the Luo Supreme Being (Nyasaye) for the community and settled quarrels, functioning like a judge. He describes *Jabilo* as a manipulator of the supernatural, and also as a prophet-diviner.[77] *Jabilo* uses supernatural powers and prevents sick people from dying. My research established that among the Luo, the concept of *Jabilo* had the following aspects: power from

---

71. Breasted, *Ancient Records of Egypt*, 263; cf. *Encyclopedia of Religion and Ethics* (1899), s.vv. "God," "Egyptian."
72. Mowinckel, *He That Cometh*, 21.
73. Mowinckel, 3.
74. Mowinckel, 7.
75. Gen 3:15; Deut 18:18.
76. Dirven, "Maria Legio," 122.
77. Whisson, "Will of God," 9–14.

the spirit world, diviner, doctor, magician, prophet, fasting, visions, soothsayer, treating unexplainable diseases, able to cause death by a curse, offers prayers against adversaries, not hindered by distance, had resurrection episodes. The concept of *Ajuoga* had the same qualities as *Jabilo*. Fieldwork established that followers attributed the powers of *Jabilo* and *Ajuoga* to their ultimate leader, Simeo Ondeto, and elevated him to the status of the Messiah, Jesus Christ himself. He patterned his leadership of Legio Maria on that of Christ. Evidence showed that Ondeto's claims to dreams and divine instructions, and his charismatic authority, were reminiscent of the powers of the *Jabilo*, the only singular Luo traditional concept that seems to sum up Ondeto's leadership, but expressed and dressed up in Christian language. Indeed, some of the members in earlier days referred to Ondeto as the *Jabilo*.[78] I designated him with the honorifics "D.D., M.P., J.P." as acronyms for *Jabilo* as Doctor, Diviner, Magician, Prophet, Judge and Priest, all of which Ondeto exhibited through his mystical, spiritual powers. The two concepts *Jabilo* and *Ajuoga* permeate the Luo community's traditional religious lexicon, such that they are useful linguistic tools to use as christological concepts for explaining to a traditional Luo who Jesus Christ is, rather than using Chalcedonian concepts.

Research among the Meru revealed that the concept of *Mugwe* is a serviceable linguistic word to communicate the Christian concept of Christ the Messiah. The Meru interwove christological concepts into their cultural belief in an exodus similar to the biblical exodus of the children of Israel. There are many varied stories regarding the ethnological origin of the Meru.[79] The Meru exodus myth lies in the context of various movements of East African coastal populations.[80] This Meru "exodus" story comes within what historically was a broader ethnological phenomenon affecting Bantu-speaking peoples from the East African coast.[81] H. E. Lambert[82] gives more details of the exodus myth. The migration was due, first, to hostile raiding from the Gala Coastal people and, second, to harassment from Arab traders in the expansion of their commercial center around that time.[83] Fadiman disagrees with the theory of

---

78. Wipper, "Legio Maria," 24.

79. The earliest on record is in a paper entitled "How the Meru Came to Their Present Country," five pages of typescript by E. B. Horne, who was a District Commissioner in the British colonial administration in Kenya; contained in Lambert, *Lambert Papers*. See also Fadiman, "Early History of the Meru of Mount Kenya," 10; Needham, "Left Hand of Mugwe," 20–33.

80. Were and Wilson, *East Africa through a Thousand Years*, 88.

81. Freeman-Grenville, "The Coast."

82. Lambert, *Systems of Land Tenure*, 34.

83. Lambert.

Bantu general ethnic migration, on the grounds of a lack of evidence.[84] The Meru are not as elaborate as the Luo in their beliefs in religious specialists. The three significant specialists among the Meru are *Muga* (medicine man), *Murogi* (sorcerer, witch doctor) and *Mugwe* (the chief religious specialist consultant in all spiritual matters). From my research, it became evident that among the Meru, the concept of *Mugwe* is a powerful indigenous African concept that could act as a dynamic cultural vehicle to communicate the concept of Christ as the Messiah to traditional indigenous Meru, instead of the abstract Western Chalcedonian concepts.

Conclusion

This paper has signposted the route toward indigenous concepts that could enter into dialogue with biblical christological concepts. Although there is evidence of some progress, more needs to be done for Africans to adequately answer Christ's question "Who do you say I am?" in authentic concepts that leave no room for nominal Christianity nor an open doorway for syncretism. A current review of literature on Christology in Africa shows an upsurge of interest in Christology with various concepts suggested. Diane B. Stinton has given the most detailed account of these titles,[85] which describe Jesus as an ancestor, elder brother,[86] Life-giver, healer,[87] revealer, mediator, leader,[88] friend, king,[89] chief and liberator.[90] From these titles, the concept of Christ as an ancestor is the most prominent, and the one written about most in the last three decades, with Charles Nyamiti as its chief exponent, followed by other scholars.[91] Kwame Bediako, who has also contributed widely to theological

---

84. Fadiman, *Oral History of Tribal Warfare*, 26.
85. Stinton, *Jesus of Africa*, 72–215.
86. Kabasele, "Christ as Ancestor and Elder Brother," 123–24.
87. See Waliggo, "African Christology in a Situation of Suffering," 40–53.
88. See Wachege, *Jesus Christ Our Muthamaki (Ideal Elder)*.
89. See also Ukachukwu, *Christ the African King*.
90. As noted above, the concept of liberator dominated most of the christological reflection in South Africa, especially during apartheid. See Boesak, *Farewell to Innocence*; Boesak, *Black Theology, Black Power*; Boff and Boff, *Introducing Liberation Theology*, 40–53.
91. See Nyamiti, *Christ as Our Ancestor*; Nyamiti, "African Christologies Today," in *Jesus in African Christianity*, 17, 29; Nyamiti, "African Christologies Today," in *Faces of Jesus in Africa*, 3–23; Nyamiti, *Jesus Christ, the Ancestor of Humankind* 1, 69; Nyamiti, *Jesus Christ, the Ancestor of Humankind* 2; Beyers and Mphahlele, "Jesus Christ as Ancestor," Art.#132, DOI: 10.4102/https. v65i1.132; Beyers, "Jesus as Ancestor," accessed 24 February 2014, http://www.bmsworldmission. org/engagecatalyst/mission-catalyst-how-far-is-too-far/jesus-ancestor-a-challenge-missionaries-africa; Mutiso-Mbinda, "Anthropology and the Paschal Mystery"; Mutiso-Mbinda, "Eucharist

contextualization in Africa, including Christology, also advocates ancestral Christology.[92]

Although the concept of the ancestor is prominent, it has flaws as a dynamic equivalent of the concept of Christ, for several reasons. The limitations of this paper do not allow for a detailed critique of ancestral Christology, so here I mention just a few issues. First, ancestors who performed a mediatorial role were close relatives, sometimes referred to as "the living dead,"[93] and not any ancestor, as proponents of ancestral Christology seem to suggest. Second, the mystery and the paradox of the cross are slighted if not overlooked in the ebullience of making Christ Africans' ancestor. Jesus died the death of a criminal, and most African societies do not revere criminals, let alone making them mediators. My research among the Luo revealed that only heroes and heroines are venerated, such as *Luanda Magere* and *Gor Mahia*. Third, Christian theology stands or falls on the veracity of the resurrection: Jesus Christ is not a dead ancestor, he is alive! Fourth, ancestral Christology as presented seems to undermine the uniqueness of Christ and his pre-existence.

Therefore, there is a need for further research on ancestral Christology that juxtaposes African concepts with Scripture. For an erudite contextualization critique, see the discussion by Reed and Mtukwa.[94] Although Stinton's research mentioned above is thorough, it still reflects an anecdotal reference to these titles, whereas what is required is an in-depth study birthed within cultural indigenous thought forms, to avoid the conceptual communication impasse that I experienced with my clan grandmother who perceived *Klisto*, Christ, as *Kiliso*, a climb. I appeal to African theologians to take Christian faith seriously and develop Pauls of Africa to enculturate Christianity in christological African concepts that will stand the test of time. Africa needs a Christology that is culturally consonant in its conceptual expression and biblically authentic in its interpretation of the hermeneutic circle.

I therefore plead with African theologians to utilize biblical scholarship and African culture to bring Christian biblical concepts into dialogue with African indigenous concepts: to use sound biblical exegesis, with a thorough

---

and the Family"; Nyende, "Jesus, the Greatest Ancestor"; Oladosu, "Ancestral Veneration," 159–71; Palmer, "Jesus Christ: Our Ancestor?"; Wanamaker, "Jesus the Ancestor."

92. Bediako, "In Search of Christology in Africa," 9–20; Bediako, "Jesus in African Culture," in *Emerging Voices* and in *Jesus and the Gospel in Africa*; Bediako, *Jesus in Africa*; R. Fotland, "Christology of Kwame Bediako," 36–49.

93. For further elucidation on the concept of "the living dead," see Mwailu, *To Be Like Jesus*, 61–64; see also endnote 105 for further references; and Gehman, *Who Are the Living Dead?*, 3.

94. Reed and Mtukwa, "Christ Our Ancestor," 144–63.

understanding of indigenous cultural concepts, to construct a Christology relevant in Africa in answer to Christ's question, "Who do you say I am in Africa?"

Bibliography

Akper, G. "The Person of Jesus Christ in Contemporary African Christological Discourse." *Religion & Theology* 14, no. 3–4 (2007): 224–43. https://doi.org/10.1163/102308012X13397496507388.

Appiah-Kubi, Kofi, and S. Torres, eds. *African Theology En Route: A Collection of Papers from the Pan-African Conference of Third World Theologians.* Maryknoll: Orbis, 1979.

Atieno-Odhiambo, E. S. "A Portrait of the Missionaries in Kenya before 1939." *Kenya Historical Review* 1, no. 1 (1973): 1–14.

Baikiao, J. M'N. N. "Towards Africanisation of Christianity: An Approach to the Evangelization of the Meru of Kenya in Light of Their Tribal Anthropology and Post-Vatican Council II Magisterium." PhD diss., Urbaniana Pontifical University, Rome, 1977.

Banda, C. "The Sufficiency of Christ in Africa: A Christological Challenge from African Traditional Religion." MA diss., Faculty of Theology, University of South Africa, Pretoria, 2005.

Becken, Hans-Jürgen, ed. *Relevant Theology for Africa.* Durban: Lutheran Publishing, 1973.

Bediako, Kwame. "A Consideration of Some Agenda Items for Christian Theology in the Eighties, with Particular Reference to Christology." *The African Theological Student Association UK Bulletin* 1 (1982): 1–5.

———. "Biblical Christologies in the Context of African Traditional Religions." In *Sharing Jesus in the Two-Thirds World: Evangelical Christologies from the Contexts of Poverty, Powerlessness, and Religious Pluralism. The Papers of the First Conference of Evangelical Mission Theologians from the Two-Thirds World, Bangkok, Thailand, March 22–25, 1982,* edited by V. Samuel and C. Sugden, 115–75. Grand Rapids: Eerdmans, 1983.

———. "In Search of Christology in Africa." In *Exploring Afro-Christology,* edited by J. S. Pobee, 9–20. Frankfurt: Peter Lang, 1992.

———. *Jesus in Africa: The Christian Gospel in African History and Experience.* Yaoundé: Editions Clé, 2000.

———. "Jesus in African Culture: A Ghanaian Perspective." In *Emerging Voices in Global Christian Theology,* edited by A. Dyrness, 93–121. Grand Rapids: Zondervan, 1994.

Bediako, Kwame, ed. *Jesus and the Gospel in Africa: History and Experience.* New York: Orbis, 2004.

Bernardi, B. *Mugwe: A Failing Prophet*. London: Oxford University Press, 1959.
Beyers, Jaco. "Jesus as Ancestor: A Challenge for Missionaries in Africa." Accessed 24 February 2014. http://www.bmsworldmission.org/engagecatalyst/mission-catalyst-how-far-is-too-far/jesus-ancestor-a-challenge-missionaries-africa.
Beyers, J., and Dora N. Mphahlele. "Jesus Christ as Ancestor: An African Christian Understanding." *HTS Teologiese Studies/Theological Studies* 6, no. 51 (2009): Art.#132, 5 pages. DOI: 10.4102/hts.v65i1.132.
Blavatsky, H. P. *Isis Unveiled*. Vol. 2. Madras: Quest Books, 1910.
Boesak, A. *Black Theology, Black Power*. London: Mowbrays, 1978.
———. *Farewell to Innocence: A Socio-Ethical Study on Black Theology and Power*. New York: Orbis, 1977 (previously Kampen: J. H. Kok, 1976).
———. "The Use of Scriptures in Black Theology." In *Scripture and Use of Scripture*, edited by W. S. Vorster, 28–37. Pretoria: UNISA, 1979.
Boff, L., and C. Boff. *Introducing Liberation Theology*. Maryknoll: Orbis, 1987.
Breasted, J. H. *Ancient Records of Egypt*. Vol. 3. Chicago: University of Chicago Press, 1906.
Bujo, B. *African Theology in Its Social Context*. Maryknoll: Orbis, 1992.
Bultman, R. *Jesus and the Word*. New York: Nicholson & Watson, 1958.
Cheyne, T. K., and J. Sutherland Black, eds. "Messiah." In *Encyclopaedia Biblica*, Vol. 3. London: Watts & Co., 1903.
Cleage, A. B., Jr. *The Black Messiah*. Kampen: J. H. Kok, 1976.
Cook, Michael L. "The African Experience of Jesus." *Theological Studies* 70 (2009): 668–92.
Cope, Thomas H. "The Africa Inland Mission: Aspects of Its History 1895–1971." MPhil diss., CNAA, London Bible College, 1979.
Cullman, Oscar. *Christ and Time*. Translated by W. S. Vorster. London: SCM, 1951.
———. *The Christology of the New Testament*. London: SCM, 1952.
———. *Salvation in History*. London: SCM, 1967.
De Jongh, C. "A Critical Analysis of Contemporary Developments in Christology in Africa." MA diss., Faculty of Theology, University of Stellenbosch, Cape Town, 1996.
Dickinson, Richard D. N. *To Set at Liberty the Oppressed*. Geneva: World Council of Churches, 1975.
Dickson, Kwesi A. "African Culture and Christianity." Chicago University mimeo, n.d.
Dirven, Peter J. "The Maria Legio: The Dynamics of a Breakaway Church among the Luo in East Africa." PhD diss., Pontifical Universitas Gregoriana, Rome, 1970.
Dwane, Sigqibo. "Christology in the Third World." *Journal of Theology for Southern Africa* 21 (1977): 3–12.
Dyrness, William A. *Emerging Voices in Global Christian Theology*. Grand Rapids, MI: Zondervan, 1994.
Eliade, Mircea, ed. *Encyclopedia of Religion*. Vol. 9. London: Macmillan, 1987.

Ezigbo, Victor I. *Re-Imagining African Christologies: Conversing with the Interpretations and Appropriations of Jesus in Contemporary African Christianity*. Eugene: Pickwick, 2010.
Fadiman, J. A. "Early History of the Meru of Mount Kenya." *Journal of African History* 14, no. 1 (1973): 9–27.
———. *An Oral History of Tribal Warfare: The Meru of Mount Kenya*. Athens: Ohio University Press, 1981.
Fanon, F. *Black Skin, White Masks*. New York: Grove Press, 1967.
Fashole-Luke, E. W. "African Theologians Consultation." *Journal of Religion in Africa* 11 (1969): 202–5.
———. "Footpaths and Signposts to African Christian Theologies." *Scottish Journal of Theology* (1981): 388–89.
Freeman-Grenville, G. S. P. "The Coast," in *History of East Africa (Vol. 1)* edited by Roland Oliver and Gervase Mathew Vol. 1, 129–168. Oxford: Clarendon Press, 1963.
Fortes, M., and G. Dieterlen, eds. *African Systems and Thought*. London: Oxford University Press, 1965.
Fotland, R. "The Christology of Kwame Bediako." *Journal of African Christian Thought* 8, no. 1 (2005): 36–49.
France, Richard T. "Questions Concerning the Future of African Christianity." *Evangelical Review of Theology* 3, no. 1 (1979): 27–36.
Gadamer, Hans-Georg. *Truth and Method*. London: Sheen & Ward, 1975.
Gathogo, J. "Reconstructive Hermeneutics in African Christology." *HTS Teologiese Studies/Theological Studies* 71, no. 3 (2015): Art. #2660, 8 pages. http://dx.doi.org/10.4102/hts.v71i3.2660. See also http://www.hts.org.za.
Gehman, Richard J. *Who Are the Living Dead? A Theology of Death, Life after Death and the Living Dead*. Nairobi: Evangel Publishing House, 1999.
Goba, Bonganjalo. "Towards a 'Black' Ecclesiology." *Missionalia: Southern African Journal of Mission Studies* 9, no. 2 (1981): 47–59.
Gration, J. A. "The Relationship of the African Inland Mission and Its National Church in Kenya between 1895 and 1971." PhD diss., New York University, 1974.
Hasselgrave, David. *Communicating Christ Cross-Culturally*. Grand Rapids: Zondervan, 1978.
Hasting, James, ed. *Encyclopedia of Religion and Ethics*, Vol. 6. Edinburgh: T&T Clark, 1908.
Healey, Joseph G. "Three Case Studies of African Christology among the Sukuma People in Tanzania." *Tangaza Journal of Theology and Mission* 1 (2011): 1–31.
Hood, R. E. *Must God Remain Greek? Afro Cultures and God-Talk*. Minneapolis: Fortress, 1990.
Ilo, Stanislaus Chukwudiebube. *African Christology: A Comparative Study of the Contextual Christologies of Charles Nyamiti and Benezet Bujo and Their Implications for African Theologies*. Ottawa: Library and Archives, 2007.

Kabasele, F. "Christ as Ancestor and Elder Brother." In *Faces of Jesus in Africa*, edited by R. Schreiter, 123–24. Maryknoll: Orbis, 1991.

Kanu, Ikechukwu Anthony. *Towards an Igbo-African Christological Construct in Post-Missionary Africa*. Mauritius: Beau Bassin, 2017.

Kelly, J. N. D. *Early Christian Doctrine*. London: A&C Black, 1977.

Kurewa, Zvomunondita J. W. "Who Do You Say That I Am?" *International Review of Missions* 69, no. 274 (April 1980): 182–88.

Küster, Volker. *The Many Faces of Jesus Christ: Intercultural Christology*. Maryknoll: Orbis, 2001.

Lambert, H. E. *Lambert Papers*. Nairobi: University of Nairobi Repository, 1943. Serial number 54 Ref. Lamb 1/5/3.

———. *The Systems of Land Tenure, Part I*. Nairobi: University of Nairobi Archives, 1939.

Magesa, Laurenti, ed. *African Theology Come of Age*. Nairobi: Pauline Publications Africa, 2010.

Magezi, C., and J. T. Igba. "African Theology and African Christology: Difficulty and Complexity in Contemporary Definitions and Methodological Frameworks." *HTS Teologiese Studies/Theological Studies* 74, no. 1 (2018): a4590. https://doi.org/10.4102/hts.v74i1.4590; http://www.hts.org.za.

Magezi, V., and C. Magezi. "Healing and Coping with Life within Challenges of Spiritual Insecurity: Juxtaposed Consideration of Christ's Sinlessness and African Ancestors in Pastoral Guidance." *HTS Teologiese Studies/Theological Studies* 73, no. 3 (2017): a4333. https://doi.org/10.4102/hts.v73i3.4333.

Marshall, I. H. *The Origins of New Testament Christology*. Leicester: Inter-Varsity Press, 1977.

Mbiti, J. S. *African Religions and Philosophy*. London: Heinemann, 1969.

———. *Concepts of God in Africa*. Nairobi: Acton Press, 2012.

———. *New Testament Eschatology in an African Background: A Study of the Encounter between New Testament Theology and Traditional African Concepts*. London: Oxford University Press, 1971.

———. "Some African Concepts of Christology." In *Christ and the Younger Churches*, edited by Georg F. Vicedom, 51–62. London: SPCK, 1972.

Mbogu, N. I. *Jesus in Post-Missionary Africa: Issues and Questions in African Contextual Christology*. Enugu: San Press, 2012.

McGrath, Alister. *The Making of Modern German Christology*. Oxford: Basil Blackwell, 1986.

"Messiah." *Encyclopaedia Britannica*. Vol. 11. Chicago: Encyclopedia Britannica Inc., 1991.

"Messianism." *Oxford English Dictionary*. Oxford University Press, 1984.

Miranda, J. *Being and the Messiah*. Maryknoll: Orbis, 1977.

Mofokeng, Takatso Alfred. *The Crucified among the Crossbearers: Towards a Black Christology*. Kampen: J. H. Kok, 1983.

Moila, M. P. "Christology in the Context of Oppression in South Africa." *Africa Theological Journal* (March 1990): 223–31.

Moltmann, J. *Theologie der Hoffnung*. Munich: Kaiser Verlag, 1964. [English translation: *Theology of Hope*. London: SCM, 1976.]

Mondin, Battista. "New Trends in Christology." *Biblical Theology Bulletin* 1 (1974): 33–74.

Moore, B., ed. *Black Theology: The South Africa Voice*. London: Hurst & Co., 1973.

Moule, C. F. D. *The Origin of Christology*. Cambridge: Cambridge University Press, 1977.

Mowinckel, Sigmund. *He That Cometh*. Oxford: Basil Blackwell, 1959.

M'Passou, Dennis. *British Weekly and Church Review Newspaper*, 30 October 1981.

Mugambi, J. N. K., and L. Magesa, eds. *Jesus in African Christianity: Experimentation and Diversity in African Christology*. Nairobi: Initiative Ltd., 1989.

Mutiso-Mbinda, J. "Anthropology and the Paschal Mystery." In *The Paschal Mystery of Christ and of All Humankind*, edited by Amecea Pastoral Institute, 25–45. Spearhead 59. Eldoret: Gaba Publications, 1979.

———. "The Eucharist and the Family – in an African Setting." AMECEA Documentation Service 282. April 1984.

Mwailu, Daniel M. "Christology in Africa: An Investigation of the Encounter between Biblical and Indigenous Concepts with Reference to Messianism in Two New Religious Movements in Kenya." PhD diss., Birmingham University, 1989.

———. "Messiahship in Mark's Gospel and Its Relevance for the African Messianic Movement." MA diss., London School of Theology, 1984.

———. *To Be Like Jesus: An Appraisal of Biblical Theology in Practice of Personal and Ministerial Formation*. Bloomington: Westbow Press, 2019.

Needham, Rodney. "The Left Hand of Mugwe." *Africa: Journal of the International African Institute* 30, no. 1 (1960): 20–33.

Njoroge, N. J. "Confessing Christ in Africa Today." In *Exploring Afro-Christology*, edited by J. S. Pobee, 131–36. Frankfurt: Peter Lang, 1992.

Nthamburi, Zablon. "Christ as Seen by an African: A Christological Quest." In *Jesus in African Christianity*, edited by J. N. K. Mugambi and L. Magesa, 54–59. Nairobi: Initiatives Ltd, 1989.

Nyamiti, C. "African Christologies Today." In *Faces of Jesus in Africa*, edited by Robert J. Schreiter, 3–23. London: SCM, 1992.

———. "African Christologies Today." In *Jesus in African Christianity: Experimentation and Diversity in African Christology*, edited by J. N. K. Mugambi and L. Magesa, 17–39. Nairobi: Initiatives Ltd, 1989.

———. *Christ as Our Ancestor: Christology from an African Perspective*. Gweru: Mambo Press, 1984.

———. *Jesus Christ, the Ancestor of Humankind: Methodological and Trinitarian Foundations*. Studies in African Christian Theology 1. Nairobi: CUEA, 2005.

———. *Jesus Christ, the Ancestor of Humankind: An Essay on African Christology.* Studies in African Christian Theology 2. Nairobi: CUEFA, 2006.
Nyende, P. "Jesus, the Greatest Ancestor: A Typology-Based Theological Interpretation of Hebrews' Christology in Africa." PhD diss., University of Edinburgh, 2005.
Oborji, F. A. "African Theology, Roman Catholic." In *Global Dictionary of Theology: A Resource for the Worldwide Church*, edited by W. A. Dyrness and V. M. Kärkkäinen, 155–20. Downers Grove: IVP Academic, 2008.
Oesterly, W. O. E. *The Evolution of the Messianic Idea: A Study in Comparative Religion.* London: Pitman & Son, 1908.
Okorocha, Cyril, ed. *African Theological Student Association Bulletin.* Vol. 1. Aberdeen, 1981.
Okure, T., et al., eds. *32 Articles Evaluating Inculturation of Christianity in Africa.* AMECEA Gaba Publications Spearhead, 112–14. Eldoret: Gaba, 1990.
Oladosu, O. A. "Ancestral Veneration in the Religious Expression of the Indigenous Aladura Churches." *Ogbomoso Journal of Theology* 17, no. 2 (2012): 159–71.
Olsen, J. H. "Contextualised Christology in Tropical Africa." *Svensk Missionstidskrift* 85, no. 3–4 (1997): 247–67.
Oosthuizen, G. C. *Post Christianity in Africa.* London: C. Hurst, 1968.
Palmer, T. "Jesus Christ: Our Ancestor?" *Africa Journal of Evangelical Theology* 27, no. 1 (2008): 65–76.
Pannenberg, W. *Jesus, God and Man.* London: SCM, 1968, 2013.
Parratt, John. *Re-inventing Christianity: African Theology Today.* Grand Rapids: Eerdmans, 1995.
Pobee, John S. "In Search of Christology in Africa." In *Exploring Afro-Christology*, edited by John S. Pobee, 9–20. Frankfurt: Peter Lang, 1992.
———. *Towards an African Theology.* Oxford: Abingdon Press, 1979.
Potgieter, R., and C. Magezi. "A Critical Assessment of Bediako's Incarnational Christological Model as a Response to the Foreignness of Christ in African Christianity." *In die Skriflig* 50, no. 1 (2016): a2136. https://doi.org/10.4102/ids.v50i1.2136.
Reed, R., and G. Mtukwa. "Christ Our Ancestor: African Christology and the Danger of Contextualization." *Wesleyan Theological Journal* 45, no. 1 (2010): 144–63.
Robinson, J. A. T. *The Names and Titles of Jesus.* New York: Macmillan, 1967.
Robinson, P. J. "Abstract no. 296" in *Missionalia* 8, no. 2 (August 1980): 103.
Schillebeeckx, E. *Jesus.* London: Collins, 1974.
Schoonenberg, Piet. *The Christ.* London: Sheed & Ward, 1972.
Schreiter, R. J. *Faces of Jesus in Africa.* New York: Orbis, 1991, 2002.
Sigqibo, Dwane. "Christology in the Third World." *Journal of Theology for Southern Africa* 21 (1977): 3–12.
Simbo, Billy K. "An African Critique of Western Theology." *Evangelical Review of Theology* 7, no. 1 (April 1983): 32.

Stinton, Diane B. "Africa's Contribution to Christology." In *African Theology Come of Age*, edited by Laurenti Magesa, 13–34. Nairobi: Paulines Publications Africa, 2010.

———. *Jesus of Africa: Voices of Contemporary African Christology*. Nairobi: Paulines Publications Africa, 2004.

Strayer, Robert W. "Missions and African Culture." In *The Making of Mission Communities in East Africa 1895–1935*, by Robert W. Strayer, 78–86. London: Heinemann, 1978.

Taylor, John V. *Primal Vision: Christian Presence amid African Religion*. London: SCM, 1963.

Taylor, Vincent. *The Names of Jesus*. London: Macmillan, 1953.

Teasdale, Charles William. "An Evaluation of the Ecclesiology of the Africa Inland Church." MA diss., Wheaton Graduate School, Illinois, 1956.

Thiselton, Anthony. *The Two Horizons*. Exeter: Paternoster, 1980.

Tillich, Paul. *Systematic Theology*. Vol. 2, Existence and the Christ. Chicago: University of Chicago Press, 1957.

Ukachukwu, C. M. *Christ the African King: A New Testament Christology*. Frankfurt: Peter Lang, 1993.

Vermes, G. *Jesus the Jew*. London: Collins, 1973.

Wachege, P. N. *Jesus Christ Our Muthamaki (Ideal Elder)*. Nairobi: Phoenix, 1992.

Waliggo, J. M. "African Christology in a Situation of Suffering." In *Jesus in African Christianity*, edited by J. N. K. Mugambi and L. Magesa, 40–53. Nairobi: Initiatives, 1989.

———. "The African Clan as the True Model of the African Church." In *The Church in African Christianity: Innovative Essays in Ecclesiology*, edited by J. N. K. Mugambi and Laurenti Magesa, 111–27. 2nd ed. Nairobi: Initiatives Ltd., 1990.

Wallis, W. D. *Messiahs: Christian and Pagan*. Boston: Gorham Press, 1918.

Wanamaker, C. A. "Jesus the Ancestor: Reading the Story of Jesus from an African Christian Perspective." *Scriptura* 62, no. 3 (1997): 281–98.

Werblowsky, R. J. Zwi. "Messianism in Jewish History." In *Jewish Society through the Ages*, edited by H. H. Ben-Sasson and Samuel Ettinger, 30–45. New York: Schocken Books, 1971.

Were, G. S., and D. A. Wilson. *East Africa through a Thousand Years*. Ibadan: Evans Bros, 1968.

Whisson, M. G. "The Will of God and the Wiles of Men." Unpublished conference paper, East African Institute of Sociological Research at Limuru, Kenya, Jan. 1962.

Williamson, G. *Akan Religion and the Christian Faith*. Accra: Universities Press, 1965.

Wipper, Audrey. "Legio Maria." Sociology Discussion Paper No. 9. Nairobi University, n.d.

10

Jewish Messianism of the Intertestamental Period and Christological Confessions of the Early Church and Their Implications for African Christology

Juliana Nzuki

Lecturer and the Head of Theology & Biblical Studies Department, Kabarak University, Nakuru, Kenya

Elkanah Kiprop Cheboi

Lecturer, Theology & Biblical Studies, Kabarak University, Nakuru, Kenya

Abstract

The concept of the expected messiah is explicit in many of the Old Testament Scriptures. Apart from the prophetic literature, many other scriptures in the Pentateuch and wisdom and poetic literature came to be interpreted as messianic. These scriptures reveal both the identity and the work of God's anointed one. The future Davidic messiah is described in terms of the Old Testament offices of king, priest and prophet. However, during the intertestamental period, when the prophetic voices were silent, Jewish expectations of the messiah began to be reimagined based on the prevailing socioeconomic and political circumstances. The messianic hopes during the intertestamental period projected a political and military messiah who would deliver Israel from its enemies. These thoughts, perpetuated to the first century AD, were influential among Jesus's audience and even disciples. On several occasions, Jesus confronted misconceptions about his identity and ministry, thus prompting the disciples to reconfigure their understanding of the messiah. Later, in the book of Acts, the apostles redefined the identity of Jesus in light of their experiences and Old Testament scriptures. As the gospel spread among the Hebraic Jews, the apostles authoritatively preached the name of Jesus, declaring that through this name, human beings are forgiven of their sins, healed and saved, the dead are resurrected, and miraculous signs are performed. Implicitly, the apostles addressed the existential misconception of the military and political messiah by projecting an image of a Davidic king who had come to save and inaugurate God's spiritual kingdom. This paper highlights the messianic hopes in the Old Testament, the intertestamental period, and the christological confessions of the early church. Further, in connection with the African ancestor motif as a title for Jesus suggested by some African scholars, this paper proposes that a formulation of African Christology and contextualization processes should take into consideration the Jewish pitfalls of redefining the person and work of Jesus based not on biblical foundations, but on prevailing nationalistic circumstances.

Key words: messiah, Davidic, intertestamental, early church, Christology, ancestor

Introduction

The presentation of Jesus Christ in the gospel accounts as the Messiah, and the early church's proclamation of this truth claim, arose from a context with general messianic expectations. In the first century, the apostles were arguably aware of the prevailing expectations of a coming "anointed one" who would restore the fortunes of Israel. Messianism remained a key theme in Judaism, Jewish thought and literature during the intertestamental period. However, during this period, interpretations of the Jewish writings on the identity and work of the coming messiah took a nationalistic dimension, as the messiah was expected to fulfill the hopes of Israel and restore its lost glory. With widespread speculation and "localizations" of the messiah figure, the Jewish people ended up incorporating false notions of the messiah into their belief system. The gospel accounts clarify the identity and ministry of the messiah according to the Old Testament scriptures and the disciples' experience of Jesus.

In the early church era, the apostles also reimagined the concept of the messiah based on the claims, work and teachings of Jesus Christ. Their presentation of Jesus's messiahship stood in contrast to the prevailing political and nationalistic aspects of the Jewish messiah. Thus, an investigation of the messianic hopes of the intertestamental period in relation to the christological confessions of the early church reveals some pitfalls that theologians should avoid in the formulation of Christology in the African context.

This paper demonstrates that the presentation of the identity and work of Jesus Christ by the apostles involved a redefinition of the identity of the messiah as understood in Jewish thought. The early church, in their confessions and writings, addressed misconceptions and clarified the messiahship of Jesus, which had been marred by distortions during the intertestamental period.

This paper is divided into four sections. The first section focuses on the messianic expectations in the Old Testament, while the second section examines messianism in Jewish thought during the intertestamental period. The third section looks at the christological confessions of the early church within the Hebraic context (in Acts 2:38 – 4:20), with the intention of identifying the early church's convictions regarding the identity and work of Jesus Christ. The fourth section looks at the pitfalls that African theologians should avoid when formulating Christology in Africa; the ancestor motif, which has been suggested by some African scholars, is evaluated to illustrate the nature of the pitfalls.

Messianic Expectations in the Old Testament

Jewish messianic expectations during the intertestamental period were primarily based on the Old Testament scriptures. These scriptures laid the foundation on which the concept of the messiah was further developed. Several passages in the Old Testament were traditionally treated and interpreted as messianic.

In the Pentateuch, the blessing of Jacob on his son Judah came to be interpreted as messianic:

> The scepter will not depart from Judah,
>   nor the ruler's staff from between his feet,
> until he to whom it belongs shall come
>   and the obedience of the nations shall be his. (Gen 49:10)

In this passage, the patriarch Jacob anticipates a king from the line of Judah, one who will subdue his enemies and bring prosperity. Further, there was a promise of a future prophet with the characteristics of Moses (Deut 18:18–19); this promise took a messianic dimension as Jewish people anticipated someone like Moses in the end times.

Also, in 2 Samuel 7:12–16, God made a covenant with David:

> When your days are over and you rest with your ancestors, I will raise up your offspring to succeed you, your own flesh and blood, and I will establish his kingdom. He is the one who will build a house for my Name, and I will establish the throne of his kingdom forever. I will be his father, and he will be my son. When he does wrong, I will punish him with a rod wielded by men, with floggings inflicted by human hands. But my love will never be taken away from him, as I took it away from Saul, whom I removed from before you. Your house and your kingdom will endure forever before me; your throne will be established forever.

In this covenant, God promises that he will raise up an offspring from the line of David who will build his house, God will establish the throne of his kingdom forever, he will be God's Son, and God will be his Father. Although Solomon was the immediate heir to David's throne, it was clear that the promise went beyond the biological son of David to a future figure in the genealogy of David.

Additionally, the royal psalms came to be interpreted in light of God's future promise; for example, Psalms 2, 18, 20–22, 89 and 101. Specifically, Psalm 2:7 describes Israel's (future) king as the Son of God. The royal psalms envisage a figure who, by the power of God, overcomes ungodly enemies and establishes his everlasting reign on earth, thereby bringing peace, prosperity and justice to the poor and oppressed.[1] These scriptures expected a messianic king who would come and reign in justice and righteousness; "until the time of Isaiah, Israel's hope was confined to the restoration of the splendor of David's kingdom, whose glory increased in proportion to the deterioration of Israel's political and social condition. Isaiah castigated these expectations as the wishful thinking of a people in search of happiness."[2]

According to the prophetic section of the Old Testament, the coming messianic king would rule in righteousness and justice (Isa 11:1–5). During the preexilic and postexilic periods, the hope for the Davidic dynasty continued

---

1. Alexander, "Messianic Ideology," 21.
2. Bromiley, *International Standard Bible Encyclopedia*, 331.

to be expressed. It is convincingly argued that the spiritual failures of the Davidic kings in Judah might have reinforced Isaiah's prophecies regarding the ideal Davidic Messiah.[3] In the book of Jeremiah, the messianic figure is also described:

> "In that day," declares the LORD Almighty,
>   "I will break the yoke off their necks
> and will tear off their bonds;
>   no longer will foreigners enslave them.
> Instead, they will serve the LORD their God
>   and David their king,
>   whom I will raise up for them." (Jer 30:8–9)

The prophet Jeremiah prophesies that God will raise up "David their king," who will free the people from foreign oppression to serve their Lord. In addition, the postexilic prophet Ezekiel prophesied, "I will place over them one shepherd, my servant David, and he will tend them; he will tend them and be their shepherd. I the LORD will be their God, and my servant David will be prince among them. I the LORD have spoken" (Ezek 34:23–24). The prophet talks of a new David, a "shepherd," "king" and "prince," who will faithfully lead God's people. These few selected texts demonstrate that the Old Testament made specific references to the identity and the work of the coming messiah. The Davidic king and prophet would establish an everlasting kingdom and faithfully shepherd God's people.

The Jewish Messianism of the Intertestamental Period

The Old Testament expectation of the Messiah was carried over into the intertestamental world, but with some transformations. It is noted that the messianism of this era involved "an interaction between biblically-rooted tradition and the external political situation."[4] Thus, the apocryphal literature and pseudepigraphic literature expanded and reinterpreted the Old Testament expectations of the Messiah to address Israel's contemporary situations.

---

    3. Strauss, *Davidic Messiah in Luke–Acts*, 37.
    4. Horbury, *Messianism among Jews and Christians*, 50.

The Davidic Messiah

During the intertestamental period, the Davidic ideology continued to influence the understanding of the anticipated messiah. The coming messiah would be Israel's king, taking after David. The king would lead the people in justice and righteousness. As Craig Evans notes, "the prophecies of the second Temple and exilic periods anticipated the coming of a king who would fulfil the Davidic ideal – a king who would obey Torah, reestablish and defend in Jerusalem true worship, and bring about an everlasting and unprecedented era of peace and prosperity."[5] It is worth noting that the qualities of the Davidic figure would surpass those of his great ancestor.[6] Jewish literature predominantly featured the expected messiah as a descendant of David;[7] later this idea occupies a central place in the gospel accounts when the genealogy of Jesus is traced back to King David.

In the late Hasmonean and early Roman periods, the expectation of the Davidic king was further renewed due to the increased failures of the priestly leadership:

> Growing disenchantment with the Hellenizing tendencies and abuse of royal power of the later Hasmoneans, and the subsequent subjugation by Rome, renewed hope for a new Davidic king who would act as God's agent to judge corrupt rulers and priests, to purge the nation of foreign influence and domination, and to bring an era of justice, peace and prosperity.[8]

Additionally, in the Psalms of Solomon 18:3–9, the expected messiah is the "anointed of the Lord" who comes to Israel's rescue; he is also the ideal judge and ruler who will bring about justice and righteousness. Further, this pseudepigraphic literature hopes that the Davidic king will "destroy Israel's oppressors, reestablish her independence, and reign forever on David's throne in justice and righteousness" (Psalms of Solomon 17).[9] According to the Apocalypse of Moses (ch. 10), the messiah is an angel of the Lord who will eventually overcome Satan; also, 1 Enoch argues that the messiah will live

---

5. Evans, "Messianic Hopes and Messianic Figures," https://arts.ucalgary.ca/sites/default/files/teams/2/CLARE/Chair_Christian_Thought/2004nov2_evansmessianichopes.pdf.

6. Evans, 5.

7. See Sirach 47:11, 22; 1 Maccabees 2:57; Psalms of Solomon 17:5; 2 Esdras 13; Baruch 29; 72.

8. Strauss, *Davidic Messiah in Luke–Acts*, 40.

9. Strauss, *Four Portraits, One Jesus*, 193.

forever.[10] Although it is not clear whether the messiah would establish God's kingdom or only prepare for its advent (2 Esdras 12:34; 2 Baruch 40:3), in 2 Esdras the "anointed one" is from David's lineage (12:32), he is mortal like Israel's past kings (7:28), yet he is also the "son of God" (13:32).[11] Distinctively, in 1 Enoch 37–71, the Messiah is identified with a heavenly transcendent figure.[12]

The following Aramaic inscription for David's dynasty, from the ninth century BC, anticipates someone from the "house of David" who would restore the glories of the dynasty of King David:

> See, Lord, and raise for them their king, the son of David, to rule over your servant Israel . . . Undergird him with the strength to destroy the unrighteous rulers; to purge Jerusalem from Gentiles who trample her to destruction; in wisdom and righteousness to drive out the sinners from the inheritance; to smash the arrogance of the sinners like a potter's jar; to shatter all their substance with an iron rod; to destroy unlawful nations with the word of his mouth; at his warning, the nations will flee from his presence; and he will condemn sinners by the thoughts of their hearts.[13]

Concerning the messianic theme of the suffering servant who suffers on behalf of Israel (Isa 52:13 – 53:12), Emslie observes that messianic expectations in the apocryphal literature do not focus on the death of the messiah but on his conquering Davidic role. However, he acknowledges an exception in 4 Ezra (2 Esdras) 7:28–29: "For my son the Messiah shall be revealed with those who are with him, and those who remain shall rejoice four hundred years. After those years my son the Messiah shall die, and all who draw human breath" (NRSV).[14] It can therefore be noted that the apocryphal books have a selective and subjective focus in relation to the messianic hopes of the Old Testament. For example, the apocryphal literature contends not with a "weak" messiah but with a strong one, who does not suffer or die. Emphatically, the modified characterization of the messiah during the intertestamental era contributed to the false notions of the first-century understanding of Christ.

---

10. Bromiley, *International Standard Bible Encyclopedia*, 333.
11. Bromiley, 332.
12. Emslie, "Jewish Messianic Expectations," 3.
13. Strauss, *Four Portraits, One Jesus*, 194.
14. Emslie, "Jewish Messianic Expectations," 3.

It is worth noting that apart from the dominant Davidic messianic expectation, there were other competing messianic views within Judaism during the intertestamental era. Straus observes that Judaic groups such as the Sadducees were not expecting a messiah at all but were content with the present rule by the priestly leadership; other groups, such as the Samaritans, did not expect a Davidic messiah but a Moses-like deliverer known as *Taheb* (the "restorer" or "returning one").[15]

Following the promise in Deuteronomy 18:18–19, the apocryphal literature entertained the hope of an eschatological mosaic prophet (1 Maccabees 4:46; 14:41) who would inaugurate the final age of salvation and become God's restorer.[16] Speculation was rife concerning the identity of this prophetic figure; some thought it could be Elijah or Enoch (both of whom were taken up alive); still others thought that Old Testament figures such as Ezra, Baruch and Jeremiah would accompany the messiah during the establishment of the end age (4 Ezra 6:26; 7:28).[17]

The Qumran Messiah

The Qumran texts' portrayal of a messiah can be looked at in two ways: first, a military-political messiah from David's lineage; and second, a priestly messiah from the line of Aaron.[18] Just like the eschatological expectation of a prophetic figure, the Qumran community anticipated a messiah who would emerge at the end time to inaugurate a new age. The development of the priestly messiah concept seems to have been the Essenes' way of showing the supremacy of the tribe of Levi over the tribe of Judah.[19] It is worth noting that the three offices of the Old Testament (prophet, priest and king) continued to influence the intertestamental understanding of the coming messiah.

The descriptions of the anticipated messiah differed within Jewish literature.

> In some texts, the Messiah seems little more than a powerful human king who accomplishes God's purpose (e.g. *Psalms of Solomon*); in others, he appears as a heavenly figure with supernatural powers (4 Ezra). In the pseudepigraphic apocalypse known as *1 Enoch*, a preexistent heavenly deliverer identified as the "Elect One" and the

---

15. Strauss, *Four Portraits, One Jesus*, 194.
16. Longenecker, *Christology of Early Jewish Christianity*, 32–33.
17. Longenecker, 33.
18. Bruce, *New Testament History*, 125.
19. Longenecker, *Christology of Early Jewish Christianity*, 114.

"Son of Man" (image is drawn from Daniel 7) provides deliverance for God's people.[20]

These examples illustrate that while Jewish hopes focused especially on the Davidic messiah, there was significant diversity among the various sects and movements. The discrepancies can be partly attributed to the speculative nature of this literature.

Jewish messianic expectations during the intertestamental period were shaped by the prevailing political circumstances of the time: "In the Jewish texts the expectations and speculations about messiah(s) are tied to and overshadowed by other aspirations, such as freedom of the Jewish people from Gentile domination, and/or the triumph of a particular religious vision of the divine will."[21] The Jewish people allowed their prevailing situations to subjectively influence their understanding of the future messiah.

In summary, Jewish literature attributed different titles, functions and identities to the messianic figure, including the Davidic connection, priestly identity, a political-military figure, and prophetic titles such as Son of Man. Although there were divergent views in their understanding of the messiah, there were also some points of consensus: "The whole Jewish literature agrees on only one feature of the Messiah; he will be a political ruler and national hero. His saving power requires that he deliver Israel from its oppressors and restore the authority of the law"[22] – not forgetting that the messianic figure would be a military messiah from the house of David who would break the yoke of oppressors such as the Roman rule. Bruce notes that only a minority of the Jewish people expected a spiritual messiah:[23] that is, a messianic identity based on the Old Testament scriptures and devoid of the Jewish political aspirations.

The Messiahship of Jesus in the Gospels

The writers of the four gospels acknowledge the messiahship of Jesus Christ, although with varied emphases. Each book carries a different portrait of Jesus. For instance, Matthew describes the work of Jesus in line with the kingship ideology of the Old Testament (Matt 1:1, 6, 17, 20; 9:27; 20:20; 21:9, 15). In Luke's account, Mary's song talks about the child (Jesus) being given the throne of his father David (Luke 1:32–33). In addition, Luke's birth account features

---

20. Strauss, *Four Portraits, One Jesus*, 194.
21. Green, McKnight and Marshall, *Dictionary of Jesus and the Gospels*, 107.
22. Bromiley, *International Standard Bible Encyclopedia*, 333.
23. Bruce, *New Testament History*, 133.

Zechariah's doxology in which he praises God for raising up a redeemer from the house of David who will conquer Israel's enemies (Luke 1:68–75).

It is apparent that many of Jesus's hearers struggled to comprehend the messiahship of Christ. Unsure of Jesus's identity, John the Baptist had to send a delegation of his disciples to inquire whether he was indeed the messiah:

> "Are you the one who is to come, or should we expect someone else?"
>
> Jesus replied, "Go back and report to John what you hear and see: The blind receive sight, the lame walk, those who have leprosy are cleansed, the deaf hear, the dead are raised, and the good news is proclaimed to the poor." (Matt 11:3–6)

Jesus's response to John the Baptist was implicit: he alluded to the prophetic utterances concerning the person and work of Christ, so that John the Baptist could draw an informed conclusion. The prophet Isaiah talks about the blind seeing (Isa 29:18; 35:5), the lame walking (35:6; 61:1), the cleansing of persons with leprosy (61:1), the deaf hearing (29:18; 35:5), and the proclamation of the good news to the poor (61:1–2). Further, regarding the kingly role, the Roman authorities executed him as "the king of the Jews" (Mark 15:26), after (mis)interpreting his mission as political.

Confronting People's Perceptions of the Messiah

The warped messianic hope from the intertestamental period continued to be witnessed even during Jesus's ministry. At some point in his ministry, the people wanted to make him a king by force (John 6:15), but Jesus slipped away from the crowd to a remote place. He was simply not a political leader as understood in the Jewish ideologies. Also, in order to redefine his identity, Jesus preferred using for himself prophetic titles such as the Son of Man when predicting his suffering (Mark 8:27 – 9:1), and Son of God (Matt 11:27; Mark 13:32; Luke 10:22). Only in a few instances did Jesus accept being referred to as the messiah (Matt 9:27; 16:16, 20; Mark 10:47; 15:18), partly because he wanted to avoid the political nuances that came with the title "messiah" in contemporary Judaism.[24] Several times Jesus clarified that the kingdom he had come to establish was not a political kingdom but a spiritual one. In no instance did he advocate for a political or military uprising. He demonstrated

---

24. Bromiley, *International Standard Bible Encyclopedia*, 333.

that the real enemy was not the Roman powers but Satan.²⁵ He sought to challenge the long-held establishments and misconceptions about the messiah.

On one occasion, after Jesus had spoken about his rejection, suffering, death and resurrection, Peter rebuked him strongly (Mark 8:31–33) since he did not believe in a suffering messiah. Peter's understanding of the messiah was a typical representation of his first-century contemporaries who used the title to refer to a future deliverer of Israel, a man of splendor and power who would usher in God's kingdom, whether as a warrior king or as a cosmic judge of the earth.²⁶ However, Jesus redefined his identity as the suffering Son of God.

Christological Confessions of the Early Church

One of the central tenets of the early church was the affirmation and proclamation of Jesus Christ as the messiah prophesied in the Old Testament. In the book of Acts, and in obedience to Christ's commission, the apostles set out from one geographical location to another proclaiming "the name" of Jesus Christ. Longenecker notes that "the name" was the early Jewish Christian designation for Jesus.²⁷ The apostles proclaimed what they had seen (miraculous signs) and heard (gospel message) during their firsthand experience of Jesus Christ.

In Acts 2:38 – 4:20, as the gospel spread among the Jewish audience, the messiahship of Jesus was redefined. The name of Jesus was presented as the name through which human beings are forgiven their sins, healed and saved, the dead are resurrected, and miraculous signs are performed. The apostles demonstrated power and authority through this name by ministering healing, forgiveness, salvation and life, and performing wonders. They proclaimed a holistic gospel, one which extended beyond the political aspirations of the Jewish people. Also, it was the early church's conviction that Jesus was the prophesied messiah who had lived among them, been crucified, died, been raised from the dead, and was now seated at the right hand of God the Father.

In a context in which the Jewish people predominantly expected a political and military messiah, the apostles portrayed the messiah as a spiritual king, from the line of David, who had come to inaugurate his kingdom. The disciples affirmed the messiahship of Christ while correcting the prevailing Jewish misconceptions. "On the basis of Jesus' understanding of His ministry, the

---

25. Strauss, *Four Portraits, One Jesus*, 283.
26. Ehrman, *The New Testament*, 68–69.
27. Longenecker, *Christology of Early Jewish Christianity*, 45.

early church could acclaim and proclaim Jesus as Messiah in an entirely new way, which transcended both the OT understanding and the intertestamental development of the title."[28] Significantly, they presented the messiah as a fulfillment of the Old Testament offices of king, prophet and priest.

The Implications for African Christology

The messianic expectations of the intertestamental period thus distorted or reimagined the Old Testament messianic images. Though their identity of Christ was founded on the Old Testament, their expectations for the messiah to establish justice and righteousness overrode their understanding of his person and ministry. Their expectations of a liberator who would overthrow the yoke of the Greeks and later of the Romans distorted their image of the messiah: they hoped for a physical and not a spiritual king. That distortion is demonstrated when Jesus asks his disciples, "Who do people say I am?" (Matt 16:13–20; Luke 9:18–21; Mark 8:27–30). The disciples' response indicates that Christ's identity was not explicit to the people but was based on their knowledge and beliefs.

As noted above, the intertestamental identity of the messiah was redefined by Christ in the gospels and clarified by the early church through the apostles. The apostles articulated that the messiah was not only a physical liberator but also a spiritual one who would first conquer the hearts of men and women, turning them to God; in contrast, his second coming would involve overthrowing the kingdoms of the world. The identity of the messiah, according to the early church, was made known during Christ's ministry, accomplished in his crucifixion, and inaugurated in his resurrection. They gave a clear image of the messiah as depicted in the Old Testament, something that the Jews of the intertestamental period had missed.

From this discussion, we see that it is possible that our expectations can override the full presentation of the messiah. Therefore, it is important to know the overriding expectation in African Christology. Essentially, African Christian theology seeks to make Christ less foreign to Africans, as demonstrated by the use of existing titles such as Ancestor, Chief, Healer, Elder Brother, Liberator and King. However, the important question is: Do these titles present the Christ of the Old Testament, the gospels and the apostolic confessions, or a different Christ? A scrutiny of most of these titles presents a Christ envisaged

---

28. Bromiley, *International Standard Bible Encyclopedia*, 334.

according to Africa's existential challenges. To address these challenges, African theologians tend to be selective and subjective, just like the Jewish messianisms in the intertestamental period.

It is therefore critical to reevaluate the titles, lest we tread the same path as the intertestamental Jews. Their anticipation of the messiah as a liberator distorted his image, for they were selective and subjective in relation to the messianic hopes of the Old Testament. Our focus here is on the most dominant of the titles mentioned above: the ancestor motif. The dominance of this title in African Christian theology can be attributed to the fact that the ancestor theme cuts across the diverse tribes and cultures of Africa. The key exponents of the title are John S. Pobee (1979), who refers to Christ as the "Great Ancestor"; Charles Nyamiti (1984), who refers to him as "Brother-Ancestor"; Benezet Bujo (1992), who calls him the "Proto-Ancestor"; and Kwame Bediako (2004), who sees him as the "Supreme Ancestor."

A reevaluation of this title as used in African Christian theology is necessary lest, in theologizing for Africa, we fall into the pitfall of redefining the person and the work of Christ based not on biblical foundations but on the prevailing African circumstances, just as was the case in the intertestamental period. The place of ancestors in traditional Africa must not be downplayed; they have a significant role in Africans' spirituality, hence the exponents' concern is legitimate. However, the same title devalues the person and ministry of Christ as presented in the Old Testament and the early church confessions. According to Mbiti, an ancestor is a deceased family member who either still lingers in the minds of the living (the living dead), or whom the living can hardly remember.[29] The attributes of an ancestor, according to Nyamiti, include a natural relationship (a kinsman), a sacred status (superior to people but inferior to God), a mediator, and an intermediary between God and human beings.[30]

Fortunately, exponents of the ancestor Christology are not oblivious to its pitfalls; for instance, Pobee admits that every image of Christ is bound to be partial and only half-truth.[31] Additionally, Bediako concedes that the ancestral function "is one aspect that Jesus rarely fits into [in] the African context and that ancestors are, in fact, the product of the myth-making imagination of the community."[32] If the exponents are aware of this, why tread the path of Jewish

---

29. Mbiti, *African Religions and Philosophy*, 107.
30. Nyamiti, "Models of the Church in Africa," 82.
31. Pobee, *Toward an African Theology*, 97.
32. Bediako, *Jesus and the Gospel in Africa*, 30.

messianism and mispresent the identity of Christ in the search for relevancy in the African context? The Jews' anticipation of a physical king made them reject Christ, for they never anticipated a king who would suffer. Similarly, ancestral Christology could lead us to the same pitfalls of demeaning and distorting the deity and humanity of Christ, as well as watering down his ministry as presented in the Old Testament and the early church confessions.

Ancestral Christology demeans and distorts the deity and humanity of Christ in several ways. Though Christ is our kinsman, his kinsmanship is not like that of any other person: he is God incarnate. He is fully man and fully God, a status that no ancestor possesses or can attain. Ancestors cannot ascend to God; humans can only ascend to ancestors and never to God. Hence, Christ is not just one among the ancestors; he is not Lord among many, as Bediako indicates; he is the Lord of all. He is not in Sheol waiting for judgment; instead, Christ is alive forever and cannot be equated with the deceased in Sheol. He is in heaven, seated at the right hand of God, and therefore his resurrection is fundamental: for without it, our faith is in vain (1 Cor 15).

Therefore, ancestor Christology will detract Africans from the fullness of Christ's deity, rather than exalting it. At the same time, it will distort his humanity, considering what qualifies one to be an ancestor. This is a similar pitfall to the one we found in the intertestamental period, when Jews overemphasized a human king at the expense of Christ's everlasting kingship. Peter, in his inaugural sermon in Acts 2, projects a figure of Christ who is not just a son of David but also the Son of God.

In addition, ancestral Christology waters down the ministry of Christ by equating it with the role of the ancestors as mediators. This negates Christ as the only mediator between human beings and God, instead affirming that ancestors are also intermediaries, leading to syncretism, veneration of ancestors, and ultimately idolatry. Christ's ministry qualified him as the only mediator between human beings and God. He laid down his life for humankind; he was the priest as well as the sacrifice that appeased the wrath of God; and therefore "there is no other name under heaven given to mankind by which we must be saved" (Acts 4:12). It is only Christ the mediator who can forgive, save and bring the dead back to life, including the ancestors. Above all, as the only mediator, he is seated at the right hand of God; his mediatorship is alive, not memorial, as articulated above with regard to the reimagining of Christ in the apostolic confessions and the suffering servant of Isaiah. Also, his role of healing and protection is not equivalent to that of the ancestors in African Traditional Religion; to equate it with theirs is tantamount to placing it on a par with it, which is a slow but sure path to syncretism. It promotes the fallback option whereby, in times of crisis, a believer resorts to ancestral intervention measures.

Therefore, no matter how the ancestor motif appeals to Africans, it empties the very identity of Christ and hence is misleading. It falls short of the full representation of the identity of Christ, and is no different from the Jewish messianism of the intertestamental period. It is therefore pointless to persist in using this title. The search for relevancy in African Christian theology should not override the full presentation of the Messiah; caution must be exercised as we seek to give Christ an African face. There is therefore a need for critical evaluation of this title.

Conclusion

Jewish literature and thought during the intertestamental period concerning the expected messiah reflected a modification of the Old Testament messianic passages. The key prophetic description of the coming messiah, who would fulfill the offices of priest, prophet and king, was reimagined in terms of Israel's political situation. As a result, the Jewish people of the intertestamental period expected a political and military messiah who would deliver them from their foreign aggressors and oppressors. This reflects a deviation from the Old Testament definition of the identity and work of the coming messiah. These false notions remained influential among the people, even during the time of Jesus. In his ministry, Jesus confronted some false expectations of the messiah, even among his disciples. The early church's christological convictions affirmed the messiahship of Jesus. In their proclamation, the apostles redefined the identity of Jesus based on the Old Testament scriptures and their experience of Christ. The christological confessions of the early church not only proclaimed Jesus as the messiah, but also sought to correct the pitfalls of the Jewish messianic hopes of the intertestamental period.

Today, African theologians have reimagined Jesus using categories within the African cosmology. While this is a significant step in contextualizing the gospel, we should beware of some potential pitfalls like those of the Jewish concepts of the intertestamental period. This study has evaluated the ancestor motif proposed by some African theologians, and observed that referring to Christ as an ancestor may blur his divine identity. While the portrayal of Jesus as an ancestor or great ancestor may sound appealing, it does not faithfully represent the identity and work of Jesus as described in the Bible. This and many other pitfalls have been highlighted by the study.

Bibliography

Alexander, T. Desmond. "Messianic Ideology in the Book of Genesis." In *The Lord's Anointed: Interpretation of Old Testament Messianic Texts*, edited by P. E. Satterthwaite et al., 19–39. Tyndale House Studies. Carlisle: Paternoster, 1995.

Bediako, Kwame. *Christianity in Africa: The Renewal of a Non-Western Religion*. Maryknoll: Orbis, 1995.

———. *Jesus and the Gospel in Africa: History and Experience*. Maryknoll: Orbis, 2004.

Bromiley, Geoffrey William, ed. *The International Standard Bible Encyclopedia*. Vol. 3, *K – P*. Fully revised ed. Grand Rapids: Eerdmans, 1999.

Bruce, F. F. *New Testament History*. New York: Galilee Book, 1991.

Ehrman, Bart D. *The New Testament: A Historical Introduction to the Early Christian Writings*. 2nd ed. New York: Oxford University Press, 2000.

Emslie, Robert Sean. "Jewish Messianic Expectations in Intertestamental Jewish Writings and the Messianic Revelation in the Person of Jesus of Nazareth." Diss., Grand Canyon University, 2014.

Evans, Craig A. "Messianic Hopes and Messianic Figures in Late Antiquity." https://arts.ucalgary.ca/sites/default/files/teams/2/CLARE/Chair_Christian_Thought/2004nov2_evansmessianichopes.pdf.

Green, Joel B., Scot McKnight, and I. Howard Marshall, eds. *Dictionary of Jesus and the Gospels*. Downers Grove: InterVarsity Press, 1992.

Horbury, William. *Messianism among Jews and Christians: Twelve Biblical and Historical Studies*. London: T&T Clark, 2003.

Kato, Byang H. *Theological Pitfalls in Africa*. Nairobi: Evangel, 1975.

Longenecker, Richard N. *The Christology of Early Jewish Christianity*. Studies in Biblical Theology, 2nd series, 17. Naperville: A. R. Allenson, 1970.

Mbiti, John S. *African Religions and Philosophy*. New York: Frederick A. Praeger, 1970.

Nyamiti, Charles. *Christ as Our Ancestor: Christology from an African Perspective*. Missio-Pastoral Series 11. Gweru: Mambo Press, 1984.

———. "Models of the Church in Africa." In *Faces of African Theology*, edited by Patrick Ryan, 73–133. Nairobi: CUEA Publishers, 2003.

Pobee, John S. *Toward an African Theology*. Nashville: Abingdon Press, 1979.

Satterthwaite, P. E., Richard S. Hess, Gordon J. Wenham, and Tyndale Fellowship for Biblical Research, eds. *The Lord's Anointed: Interpretation of Old Testament Messianic Texts*. Tyndale House Studies. Carlisle: Paternoster, 1995.

Strauss, Mark L. *The Davidic Messiah in Luke–Acts: The Promise and Its Fulfillment in Lukan Christology*. Journal for the Study of the New Testament Supplement Series 110. Sheffield: Sheffield Academic, 1995.

———. *Four Portraits, One Jesus: A Survey of Jesus and the Gospels*. Grand Rapids: Zondervan, 2007.

11

The Unitive Understanding of the Person of Christ in Cyril of Alexandria's Christology and Its Relevance for Contemporary African Christianity

Henry Marcus Garba

Lecturer, Africa International University, Nairobi, Kenya

Abstract

Cyril of Alexandria is ranked among the precocious voices regarding the identity and meaning of Christ. Cyril left many questions unanswered regarding the classical understanding of the portrait of Christ; nevertheless, his work was fundamental for the unitive understanding of who and what construe the identity of Christ. Cyril's Christology was based on the *Logos–sarx* (word/flesh) Christology that affirms the single subject of the incarnate Christ. Cyril's focus on the nature and person of Christ was rooted in the ontological structure, as he sought to understand the mystery of Christ's subsistence within created history. The thrust of his work available to us from antiquity was apologetically construed against Nestorius. In our age of strong opinions and suspicious dispositions toward the Christian narrative of the Christ/human event, there is a pragmatic need to turn back to classical Christology. This chapter calls for African theologians to get the wheels of theological scholarship in Africa turning again in an astute collaborative and dialogical theological reflection, reminiscent of that of Cyril in the classical epoch of Christian history. Such praxis gave Cyril a unique position, both in antiquity and for modern times. Cyril's christological conception could help the African theologian in the re-presentation of the revelatory significance of Jesus for self-understanding.

Key words: African Christianity, Christology, Cyril of Alexandria, Nestorius, unitive

Introduction

We are caught up in an age characterized by strong opinions about what is sure and factual. In addition, there is a realization of the historical exigency of human events, and a suspicious disposition toward religious narrative. This has occasioned reflection among theologians, clergy and laity regarding the reality, identity and meaning of the Christ event. These reflections cut across Christian traditions – Catholic, Orthodox and Protestant – causing vacillation and a questioning of our common orthodoxy regarding the person of Christ Jesus: his divinity and humanity. At their best, these reflections have produced abstract and dogmatic rationalism concerning the identity and meaning of Christ.

Consequently, historicism and the relativizing of the abiding worth of Christology for religious faith have resulted. For example, what is ethically imperative is determined through "critical idealism" or "reason" rather than self-consciousness, thus questioning the very nature of biblical truth.[1] Thus, we need to revert to the sources of classical Christology in the first century, which saw in Jesus the fullness of God's saving revelation of himself and our human destiny, to reassert our understanding of God in the mystery of Jesus.

This paper aims to give only a cursory overview. It does not intend to break new theological ground or solve age-old problems of understanding in the field. Furthermore, it is not interested in clarifying the phrases used to express the unitive[2] understanding of the person of Christ, such as "substance," "nature," *hypostasis* and *prosōpon*.[3] The paper does not give a lengthy narration of Cyril's Christology but restates his contribution to the unitive understanding of the

---

1. Baur, *History of Christian Dogma*, 34.

2. The word "unitive" was adopted by Ambrose in his christological discussion in the Council of Chalcedon to further affirm Cyril's christological argument, which describes the incarnation as a union of humanity and divinity, thereby justifying the practice of worshipping Christ as a member of the Trinity. Smith, *Christian Grace*, 178.

3. Saint Cyril, *Three Christological Treatises*, 28.

person of Christ in terms of the formulation of Christian faith and theology. In light of this, the paper concentrates on the unitive understanding of the person of Christ forged by Cyril of Alexandria in 443 AD, which was seen as the peak of the process of christological reflection. It is vital first to look closely at the whole of Cyril's Christology to realize its intent and real value. However, the paper dwells only on Cyril's unitive understanding of the person of Christ and its relevance for contemporary African Christianity. Finally, the paper pays attention to the dogmatic, rather than speculative, character of Cyril's Christology.[4]

Initial Christological Viewpoint of the Early Church Fathers

The early centuries AD gave power and dignity to literary activities. The canon of Scripture was steadily completed, biblical texts were expounded, Christian eloquence was developed, and theological concepts were formed. Indeed, the work of the early church fathers of the first five centuries AD in matters of Christian faith and doctrine has received praise because of their scholarship and unparalleled contributions in history, literacy and theology. Roberts comments: "It is delightful to trace the hand of God from generation to generation, as from father to son, interposing for the perpetuity of the faith."[5] The influence of these church fathers was God's provision for the spiritual generation of the church's teachers.

Christology did not start with Cyril, nor was it his idea. James Dunn says that "before Jesus, 'Christology' did not exist, or [it] existed, properly speaking, only in different forms of 'messianic expectations.'"[6] Christology is rooted deep in Christianity because it began with Jesus and is the true meaning of Jesus, entrenched in what he said and did and how the early Christians understood him. Hardy opines that 2 Corinthians 5:19 presents the central conviction of true Christian faith and theology because it brings the human and the divine into an active union, and that, ever since, Christian theology has labored to preserve and defend, and better understand, this fundamental truth.[7]

---

4. It is important to assert that when Cyril put forth his argument against Nestorius, he began by affirming the place of Mary as *Theotokos*. Yet the Greek word does not appear in the New Testament, and such conceptualization is highly contested within evangelical circles, being considered somewhat speculative. This paper affirms the position of evangelicals. Russell, *Cyril of Alexandria*, 134.

5. Roberts, *Ante-Nicene Fathers*, 3.
6. Dunn, *Christology in the Making*, xii.
7. Hardy, *Christology of the Later Fathers*, 15.

In line with the struggle to present a unified doctrine distinct from heresy, the early church fathers strived to maintain the union of Christ, especially his true humanity.

Christian theology in the first three centuries of the early church tended to subscribe to the view of the person of Christ as fully God and fully man without much debate. Nevertheless, in the fourth century AD, the most significant concern of the church shifted to the relationship between the full humanity of Christ and his full Godhead. The logic behind the conception of such thought as held and modified by Cyril of Alexandria and his supporters is shaped by an emphatic *unitive* Christology decisively centered on the Logos.[8]

One outstanding aspect of the early church fathers was that many of them emphasized both the deity and the humanity of Christ, albeit in different forms, as exemplified in the writings of Ignatius (ca. 35–ca. 108) in his strong emphasis on the oneness of Christ and the reality of his twofold mode of being.[9] Clement of Alexandria set down the rich principles "of the idea of *paidagogos* in our relationship with Christ," in which Christ is presented as our teacher, with us sitting at his feet.[10] Ignatius acknowledged the deity of Christ, referring to him as "Jesus Christ our Lord," and to the "blood of God." It is noteworthy that in these confessions of the early church fathers, with their good intentions to uphold and promote the unity of Christ's two natures, each had his own area of emphasis. While it must be said that most of their teachings about Christ lacked clarity and contained many problems, their theological contribution laid the foundation for the conceptualization of Christology.

The Hobson's Choice of Cyril of Alexandria

The person of Cyril of Alexandria, while silent and inconspicuous on the stage of history, is inescapable in classical christological study.[11] Cyril seems to be on the margins, especially among evangelicals, when it comes to enumerating theologians who have contributed to shaping the theological thought of the early church; he is known as "a forgotten father," as Mathison writes:

---

8. Grillmeier, *Christ in Christian Tradition*, 445.

9. Kashchuk, "Logos-Sarx Christology."

10. Overview of, Clement of Alexandria, "Christ the Educator," accessed July 10, 2021, https://www.logos.com/product/120406/christ-the-educator.

11. Wilken, "Exegesis and the History of Theology," 141. Weinandy and Keating assert that the reason "why Cyril has not been appreciated is perhaps because his life and work are so long that they are not read." In addition, they believe that "Cyril's work has been read passively in generations." Weinandy and Keating, *Theology of St. Cyril*, 1.

Many evangelical Christians have heard of Athanasius, Augustine, Irenaeus, and perhaps even Tertullian or John Chrysostom, but Cyril of Alexandria (AD 376–444) is not a name with which most evangelicals are familiar. However, he was arguably one of the three or four most theologically influential figures in the early church. Regarding Christology, he was perhaps the most influential figure.[12]

In recent decades, several historical and theological essays have brought Cyril's christological thought into the limelight.[13] This paper depicts him as the resurgence of an African theologian, a choice made given the current paradigm shift in the center of Christianity from the Global North to the Global South, and in order to get the wheels of theological scholarship in Africa turning again. This should be the driving force for an astute collaborative and dialogical theological reflection which is practical and relevant, reminiscent of that in the classical epoch within which Cyril wrote from the African continent to address the christological controversy.

Cyril's Christology was immersed in a theological agenda, namely the rediscovery of the relevance of the Scriptures and the apostolic tradition for understanding the identity of Christ and his meaning for the church's theology.[14] In Cyril's view, in the apostolic tradition the Scriptures were not merely proof texts and footnotes but authentic sources, witnesses to the faith and reasoned insight. This understanding provided a vibrant theological vision and biblical interpretation.[15]

Cyril's Christology, as expressed in his theological treatises, was constructed to convey the church's faith in Jesus Christ as held through the apostolic traditions. It was characterized by a theological structure of the Christian religion and his keen interest in exegesis, and was biblically foregrounded by the heart of the narratives of Christian faith.[16] His purpose was to give enlightenment in the place of the misconceptions which had crept into the church in respect of the person of Christ, whom the church had come to conceive of as "one person in two natures."[17] Cyril's insight was doubtless

---

12. Mathison, "Forgotten Father," https://tabletalkmagazine.com/posts/2017/12/a-forgotten-father-cyril-of-alexandria/.
13. Saint Cyril, *Unity of Christ*, 32; cf. Mathison.
14. Saint Cyril, 32; cf. Mathison.
15. Willis, *Teachings of the Church Fathers*, 82.
16. Weinandy and Keating, *Theology of St. Cyril*, 188.
17. Hardy, *Christology of the Later Fathers*, 15.

the culmination of developments before his era, exemplified in his adoption of Athanasius's understanding of Jesus as the divine Savior who was God's own Son. The dominance and influence of Cyril's thought in the history of the dogma regarding the person of Jesus Christ then set the stage for the final formulation of the church's faith at Chalcedon in 451 AD.[18]

Furthermore, Cyril's christological conception of the ontological structure of the person of Christ was not definitive or exhaustive, but it laid the foundation for continuing reflection and, in addition, raises questions that aim at furthering a consideration of the single, indefatigable Mystery of God's saving appearance in history. The question one must ask today is whether a thorough reading of Cyril's Christology is still relevant for our Christian witness, faith in Christ and church life?

The Early Life of Cyril of Alexandria

Cyril was born into a Christian family in about 378 AD at Theodosius in Lower Egypt. His mother is said to have come from Memphis, the ancient capital and the stronghold of polytheism. Almost nothing is known about Cyril's father. Still, history reveals that Cyril's maternal grandparents were Christians who died earlier, leaving their two children, the young Theophilus and his sister, Cyril's mother, who was barely out of infancy. Through hardship and much struggle, Theophilus at sixteen traveled with his sister to Alexandria in 362–363 AD, where he enrolled in the catechumenate. There he drew the attention of Bishop Athanasius, who took them, baptized them, and placed Cyril's mother under the care of the community of mothers until she was given in marriage.[19] Theophilus, who remained under the supervision of Athanasius, finished his studies, and his zeal and dedication opened the way for him to enter the service of the church in Alexandria. In Alexandria, Theophilus served as secretary to Athanasius and was subsequently ordained a deacon. After the deaths of Athanasius, Peter II and subsequently Timothy, the brother of Peter II, Theophilus was made a bishop to oversee the episcopate in 385 AD, becoming the archdeacon of Alexandria at around only forty years of age.[20]

When Theophilus became bishop of St. Mark on 20 July 385 AD, Cyril was about seven years old; his education was probably supervised by Theophilus because he was the only close child of the family. Details concerning Cyril's

---

18. "Fathers of the Church Series (127 Vols.)."
19. Hillis, "Natural Likeness of the Son," 3.
20. Russell, *Cyril of Alexandria*, 4.

education are unclear, but he may have studied reading, writing and arithmetic in his primary education, and grammar in his secondary education.[21] However, it is evident that Cyril was advanced in the field of scholarship; according to McGuckin, "he was evidently schooled in rhetoric, but the substance of his learning [was] built upon the twin pillars of biblical theology and the prior patristic tradition, mainly of the Alexandrian church."[22]

Cyril might not be considered a philosopher since there is no evidence that he pursued formal philosophical studies; yet he worked with images and metaphors, and had a good knowledge of Aristotle and Porphyry's *Isagoge*.[23] Cyril handled Aristotelian terms confidently, amplifying with confidence the connection between substance and accidence and making extensive use of syllogistic intellectualism. Cyril was familiar with the exegetical approaches of Platonism. Still, he kept himself from the philosophical culture of defending paganism, as supported by Russell: "at Ephesus in 431 AD when he found his orthodoxy under attack, it was the ecclesiastical side of his education that he chose to emphasize."[24] He was known as the father of *orthodox Christology* par excellence. McGukin describes Cyril as "a great exegete as well as a spiritual guide, a saint in the full range of his doctrine, and in his life's energy and focus, the two aspects being attached in the Orthodox understanding of the nature of theology and sanctity."[25] Russell asserts that Cyril deserves better treatment in modern theology, noting that he was a man of iron will and an excellent ecclesiastical politician, a theologian of the first rank, and a biblical commentator. His insights can still be illuminating today.[26]

---

21. Lunn, *St. Cyril of Alexandria*, 6.

22. McGuckin, *St. Cyril of Alexandria: The Christological Controversy*, 3.

23. The word *Isagoge* literally means "an Introduction." Porphyry was a third-century Greek Neoplatonist who arranged Plotinus's writings. In his *Isagoge* (introduction), he addressed a student, Roman senator Chrysaorius, on the introduction of Aristotle's categories. Spade, *Five Texts*, viii. Eco says that to discover the right method for extrapolating amenable definitions, Aristotle propounded the theory of *predicables*, modes of categories that can be applied to a subject. In *Topics*, Aristotle lists four *predicables*: genus, property, definition and accident. Eco, *Semiotics and the Philosophy of Language*, 58.

24. Russell, *Cyril of Alexandria*, 5.

25. McGuckin, *St. Cyril of Alexandria*, 1.

26. Russell, *Cyril of Alexandria*, vii. Cyril of Alexandria has been described as "the seal of the fathers." His theological influence was weighty and it affirmed and encapsulated all that had gone before him. He is well known among the optimum Christian theologians of his time and beyond. In addition, Cyril stands out among the ranks of the greatest patristic writers and perhaps as the most powerful exponent of Christology the church has ever known. Historical records assert that after Athanasius, Cyril is the writer who has had the greatest historical influence on the articulation of the most central and seminal aspects of Christian doctrine. Thus,

Background of Cyril of Alexandria's Christology

Christological arguments mostly concern abstract concepts authenticated by the established witnesses of the Christian faith. These arguments are meticulously developed but only in relation to an already established tradition.[27] Before the Council of Nicaea in 325 AD, new views had emerged on the person of Jesus which deviated from the apostolic tradition. Thus, the Council of Nicaea was convened as an effort to deal with the christological controversy. It resulted in the Nicene Creed, which took about fifty years to be widely accepted as a central norm of orthodoxy, perhaps because the dialectical complexities of "person" and "nature," "unconfused" and "inseparable" may not have been easy to comprehend.[28]

From 431 to 451 AD tensions arose between rival theological schools of thought – Antioch and Alexandria – driven by leading clerical figures: Nestorius on the one hand, and Cyril on the other. The tensions were both theological and political. Antioch rejected the allegorical approach to the text of Scripture, while Alexandria welcomed and promoted it. Thus, a more considerable disagreement broke out on a philosophical and rhetorical trajectory regarding how meaning is drawn from a biblical text.[29] The Antiochene school focused on Christ's humanity, while the Alexandrian school affirmed the divinity of Christ, a controversy that threatened the unity of the Eastern patriarchates.[30] Thus, both Cyril and Nestorius were motivated by their perception of the person of Christ.

Significantly, the weight of the disagreement between Antioch and Alexandria was on liturgically and synodically formulated tradition, rather than on Scripture – perhaps because scriptural texts were capable of so many conflicting interpretations. The root of this conflict, as suggested by Papandrea,[31] was that the apostles and their followers were the custodians of the Christian truth as their writings were considered inspired and formed the canon of the New Testament. However, after the era of the apostles and their successors, there were no direct eyewitnesses to provide answers to the profound questions of Christology. Papandrea observes that "by the late first century, any apostle

---

he is described as a saint, patriarch and theologian. Tim Dowley notes that he was a brilliant representative of Alexandrian theology. Dowley, *Eerdman's Handbook*, 174.

27. Daley, *God Visible*, 13.
28. Saint Cyril, *Unity of Christ*, 32.
29. Ondrey, *Minor Prophets*, 12.
30. Cleenewerck, *His Broken Body*, 176.
31. Papandrea, *Earliest Christologies*.

still alive functioned like a bishop."[32] Consequently, during the early church period up to the second century, there was no definite transition to the postapostolic age. Thus, the Nestorian christological perspective and that of his Antiochene supporters was humanistic and overly analytical, while Cyril emphasized the organic, dynamic unity of action and consciousness in the divine Savior of humanity.[33]

Meanwhile, the Nicene Creed was an important hermeneutical rule for interpreting both Cyril's language and his Christology. Van Loon asserts that two normative sources influenced Cyril: Scripture and the Nicene Creed.[34] The Council of Nicaea was an embodiment of diverse rhetorical strategies that gathered bishops together to re-enact and reaffirm the unchanging orthodoxy through careful textual arrangement and argumentation.[35] The whole concern of the Council was the unity of the church and the source of its strife. Davis contends that the problem that necessitated the Council of Nicaea was not merely whether Jesus was God but how within the monotheistic system,

---

32. Papandrea, 11.

33. Markham, *Student's Companion*, 52. While Cyril emphasized the incarnation, the eternal Word and Son, Nestorius, on the other hand, emphasized the *prosōpon of a union*. Accordingly, when Cyril discovered what Nestorius believed, he sent letters to the bishop of Rome, Celestine I, noting Nestorius's errors. In his letters, Cyril affirmed that Emmanuel is God, teaching the mechanics of Christ's incarnation, and said that anyone who did not believe that Christ was born in the flesh should be anathema. "Cyril's assumption formulates the idea that in the incarnation both the divine nature (*ousia*) of Christ and the human nature (*ousia*) of Christ coalesced into one person (hypostasis). The Greek word *ousia*, in its original, means 'being, existing,' which comes to mean 'nature.' The word implies 'that which is one's own.' *Ousia* stands for *essence* as well as *being*. Hence, the word *ousia* means 'subsistence.' This word *ousia* indicates the subsisting, concrete reality of a being or nature, which Cyril continued to emphasize. Cyril's argument holds to one 'hypostasis.' The hypostasis is an individual representation of nature but does not necessarily have a substantive existence, which is immaterial." Transcribed from audio recording by Sbeshonertor, "History of the Catholic Church," 4 May 2018, link from https://catholicunderthehood.com/2018/05/04/439-a-history-of-the-catholic-church-prosopon-of-union/.

Nestorius used the term *prosōpon* to refer to the concrete person or substantive existence. *Prosōpon* is a word from the ancient theatre that means "face" or "mask." This term connotes "only an appearance of a distinct existence and not the actual existing entity." LoLordo, *Persons*, 23. While Nestorius argued for the *prosōpon*, Cyril championed the term *ousia*, which emphasizes the incarnation on the following grounds: the hypostasis emphasized the unique distinction of the Trinitarian personality of Christ; *physis* that is used for *ousia* reflects the humanity and divinity of Christ, which implies the unity of Christ's hypostasis yet without a mixing of the divine and the human natures. This concern led to the Council of Nicea in 325, and it was there that the Son was declared to be same with the Father in individual reality, yet distinct in and perfect in his personality; cf. Hames, "Introduction to Cyril of Alexandria," https://www.uniontheology.org/resources/doctrine/jesus/an-introduction-to-cyril-of-alexandria; Saint Cyril, *Unity of Christ*, 33.

34. Van Loon, *Dyophysite Christology*, 503.

35. Smith, *Idea of Nicaea*, 2.

which the church inherited and preserved, it was possible to maintain the unity of God while insisting on the deity of one who was distinct from God the Father.[36] It was in line with such perceptions that Cyril intended to address the controversial view of Nestorius to express the theological traditions which had become associated with the person of Christ. Cyril also envisioned restoring the balance between the church of Antioch and the church of Alexandria, which were the major centers of influence in the classical epoch. The above was made possible by sketching the outlines of the traditional apostolic faith in the Savior in confessing an unconfused union of two natures by which he coexists with the Father and with us as humans.[37]

> Cyril had to labor hard, later in the 430s, to persuade his own sympathizers – bishops like the Armenian Acacius of Melitene and Successus of Diocaesaraea in southern Asia Minor, an old admirer of Athanasius – that in agreeing to the carefully balanced phrases in which the Antiochene draft of 433 had expressed its understanding of the person of Christ, specifically in confessing an "unconfused union" "of two natures," by which "the same one is coessential with the Father as to his deity and coessential with us as to his humanity.[38]

The Unitive Understanding of the Person of Christ in Cyril's Christology

Cyril conceived Christ from a metaphysical perspective with a focus on his "nature" and "person." Cyril's Christology was premised on the ontological structure of the person of Christ and sought to understand the "mystery" by which the single, divine person of the Son or Word of God now "subsists" within created history, in two complete natures yet an unconfused union. This was Cyril's organizing focus within Christology, one which occupied classical thinking in interpreting the mystery of Christ.[39]

---

36. Davis, *First Seven Ecumenical Councils.*
37. Saint Cyril, *Three Christological Treatises*, 14.
38. Daley adds: "The principal agents of the peace of AD 433, however, were dead by the mid 440s: John of Antioch in AD 442, Cyril himself in AD 444, Proclus of Constantinople in AD 446." The controversy that ensued was motivated by political ambition and religious traditionalism between Constantinople, Antioch and Alexandria. Daley, *God Visible*, 11.
39. The Word became tangible (physical) and visible by means of the body and shares in the glory of the incarnate word. This implies that the sufferings were incurred in the flesh. Christ's subjection to the union does not mean that he became man to remain subject to the

The emphasis on the classical christological interpretation is considered to have been rigid by some scholars, who believe that a careful historical study should loosen the church's understanding of Christ from a rigid metaphysical focus on "nature" and "person."[40] These scholars opine that such a view led to grave distortions in how both theology and popular devotion understood the person of the Savior, especially with respect to Jesus's humanity.[41] It is important to note that more was at stake than merely the historical detail of Cyril's christological understanding of the theology of Christ's person. This was evident in the controversies that arose after the death of the agents of peace, resulting in the convening of the Council of Chalcedon in 451 AD.[42]

Meanwhile, a proper understanding rested on "getting Cyril's Christology right." Two aspects stand out when discerning what constituted Cyril's Christology. Foremost was the indispensable service philosophical analysis and technical vocabulary offered in the preservation and clarification of the apostolic message that "Jesus is Lord" (1 Cor 12:3).[43] This seems to have been expressly articulated in Cyril's interpretation, which he mainstreamed through the orthodox use of secular philosophical language. It was, therefore, not a syncretistic compromise or an intellectualizing of gospel faith, but was "intended to preserve the Christ of the gospels and the apostolic age for the faith of posterity."[44] This displayed Cyril's ability to employ new, often "secular concepts" in the interpretation of the Scriptures and the apostolic tradition in service of the maintenance of the living tradition regarding Christ's identity and meaning. Second, Cyril was very much concerned to emphasize "balance" in understanding the person of Christ: between his complete divinity and his

---

rule of pain and suffering or death, but rather it was to overcome death, restore order and ennoble human nature according to God's original purpose. This activity was not to undo all that human nature had become, but to make it what it ought to be; see Torrance, *Christology after Chalcedon*, 77. In the *communitio idiomatum*, Cyril aimed at preserving the *Kerygma Christi* of the apostolic and postapostolic church dogma by maintaining the biblical *Kerygma* of Jesus against rationalistic and mystical solutions. What influenced this passion in Cyril was not just Apollonarian logic, sacred philosophy and the theology of Athanasius, but, above all, the Scripture. McKinion, *Words, Imagery*, 18–19.

40. It is important to note that the Chalcedonian formula was not merely the end of an ancient controversy, but a starting point for new and more profound questions about the identity and role of Christ, and could become the center of intense contemporary debate. Daley, *God Visible*, 6.

41. Pontificium Consilium de Iustitia et Pace, *Social Doctrine of the Church*, 19.

42. Saint Cyril, *Three Christological Treatises*, 33.

43. Daley, *God Visible*, 6.

44. Grillmeier, *Christ in Christian Tradition*, 555.

complete humanity, both of which are to Cyril as a single, unique subject, a single divine agent, or "person."[45]

Cyril's christological model for understanding the person of Jesus was premised on the literal understanding of *Logos–Anthropos*, the Word–Human Being, of the Johannine gospel. The Alexandrian school affirmed an incarnational *Logos–sarx*, "a word/flesh Christology."[46] The catechetical school at Alexandria was founded by Clement of Alexandria in 195 and became famous under Origen and Athanasius. The core reverence of the Alexandrian school was for the transcendent unity of God.[47] *Logos–sarx* was the pillar of Alexandrian Christology that had its roots in the Apollonarian tradition that promoted the view that "the union of the divine in Christ took the form of the union of the eternal Logos with human flesh."[48]

Meanwhile, Clement spoke about Christ having "clothed Himself with a man," thus being God in the form of a man. On the other hand, Origen taught that the Word became fused with the soul of Jesus.[49] Note that the Alexandrian *Logos–sarx* Christology peaked with Athanasius. Athanasius emphasized strongly that Christ's human mind demonstrated that the Logos was not merely the governing part of Christ's human body but also the real physical source of all the actions of the life of Christ. Hence, God in Christ died for us, and reconciliation was the divine action of the Logos.[50] By implication, if Christ's humanity is not the same as ours, how can we understand the full concept of redemption?

Cyril passionately embraced and promoted the Alexandrian theological conception. Without knowing it, he followed the Apollinarian model of the union of the two natures of Christ. Cyril went further to teach the two aspects of Christ's nature, emphasizing double consubstantiality: the consubstantiality with God according to divinity, and consubstantiality with humans according to humanity. For Cyril, the two natures are one (essence), that is, equal and unconfused. In his unitive Christology, Cyril affirmed that God the Son incarnate, perfect in his divinity and perfect in his humanity, was allied with the Father in his divinity and congruent with mortal beings according to his

---

45. Welch, *Christology and Eucharist*, 29.
46. Tortorelli, *Christology with Lonergan and Balthasar*, 45.
47. Hudale, *Matrix of Mysticism*, 148; Haas, *Alexandria in Late Antiquity*, 183.
48. Rausch, *Who Is Jesus?*, 45.
49. Rausch, *Systematic Theology*, 6.
50. Meyer, "Athanasius' Use of Paul," 146.

humanity.[51] Thus, Cyril's unitive Christology affirmed the union of Christ's divine and human natures, which are inseparably united, yet without mixture, loss of separate identity, or transfer of properties or attributes. Puett explains that the two natures of Christ, divine and human, belong to their corresponding realities, though the qualities of either of them belong to the one person, Christ, with which each nature has its attribute that adheres to that nature.[52] For Cyril, human nature benefits from the divine nature through appropriation, but the human enhanced the divine for God's philanthropic relationship with humanity.[53] The sole idea is that of a life-giver, such that, until the substance is real and grounded existentially, genuine redemption is not possible. The implication of Cyril's unitive perspective is that any reduction or mixture of the two natures in body or soul denies the decisive role of obedience, and the body cannot fulfill the act of redemption in human experience and suffering.

Furthermore, in the "Word–Human Being" understanding of the person of Jesus, which relates to his humanity, Christ is implicitly conceived as the physical, sensible, bodily human form in which God's Word has lived among us.[54] This christological model understands "form" as a fully developed human being with a soul. Thus, Jesus possessed all the interior faculties and qualities that characterize and make possible human knowledge, human freedom and human love. Cyril's portrait of Christ depicted Jesus as a human being like us in all things except sin – a theological factor that was later elaborated in the history of the development of early Christology.[55]

It must be acknowledged that Cyril's Christology makes it clear that it is not meant to offer a theoretical explanation of the mystery of the person of Jesus, but to establish agreed standards for remaining within the tradition of orthodoxy affirmed by the Nicene Creed. Cyril's Christology was neither an end nor a beginning, but a crucial pivot in a much longer process of staking out the course for orthodox Christology. The draft Union Agreement of 433 AD, which is embedded in Cyril's christological discourse, continued as the cornerstone upon which christological dialogues were later anchored. His work, rather than abating the controversies surrounding the understanding of the person of Christ, aroused its continuous engagement. Its value for the orthodoxy of the Christian faith is lasting and still relevant today.

---

51. Gros, Best and Fuchs, *Growth in Agreement III*, 36.
52. Puett, *Bible Study*, 390.
53. Williams, "Mystery of the Incarnation," 41.
54. Dunn and Mayer, *Christians Shaping Identity*, 409.
55. McKinion, *Words, Imagery*, 183.

The Accomplishment of Cyril's Christology

Cyril's unitive Christology stemmed from the touchstone of biblical orthodoxy, expressed in the Nicene Creed, which was reformulated and produced by subsequent councils in conciliar efforts to deal with christological controversies. According to Hall, the Nicene Creed was a symbol of unity in Christology because it concluded the debate about the Holy Trinity by reaffirming the relationship of the Son and Spirit to the Father. The Creed can be used to understand the doctrine of Jesus concerning his two natures, God and man.[56] Cyril's accomplishment was to clarify the union of natures in the incarnate Christ. Cyril's account of the singleness of person and fulfillment of both humanity and divinity stands out as he saw any separation or division of the person of Christ to have soteriological consequences. Cyril viewed the incarnation as a significant soteriological event through which the unitive understanding facilitates the restoration of humanity through Christ's humanity. Cyril's unitive christological framework offers a systematic explanation of the union (*henosis*) and the natures (*hypostases*) of Christ.[57]

As they were presented in his classic letters, Cyril's christological stands were considered normative biblical orthodoxy of the common faith in the church's central understanding of Christ's person. Though Cyril's christological conception and submission regarding the ontological structure of the person of Christ cannot be deemed conclusive or exhaustive, they are concretized on the foundation of the Scriptures and the apostolic tradition. Nevertheless, Cyril's christological viewpoint raised questions for further understanding the unitive, inexhaustible mystery of God's saving presence in history.

The Council of Chalcedon in 451 AD affirmed that Cyril's Christology, as contained in his synodical letters, agreed with the tenets of the faith endorsed by the Council of Nicaea in 325 AD.[58] Thus, Cyril's letters were appropriately included as support of the correct christological teachings, in contrast to the theological position held by Nestorius and the Orientals, who were people of the East and southern Asia. The question one must ask today, however, is whether a thorough reading of Cyril's unitive understanding of Christ's person as contained in his Christology is still relevant for our Christian witness to faith in Christ and church life?

---

56. Hall, *Jesus Christ Today*, 89.

57. McGuckin, *Saint Cyril of Alexandria and the Christological Controversy*, 194–96.

58. According to some classical scholars, this would seem to mean only Cyril's "second" letter to Nestorius, not his more challenging "third," and his affirmation of the formula of agreement from AD 433. Daley, *God Visible*, 14.

Reactions to Cyril's Unitive Christological Understanding

The reception of Cyril's Christology cannot be captured within the limits of this paper as it has undergone modifications in terminology and nuanced qualifications. However, some aspects of Cyril's unitive Christology that remain outstanding are his soteriology and theological anthropology, and his God-centered portrait of Christ. Nevertheless, certain aspects of Cyril's Christology may have met with strong opposition within the classical epoch because of their representation of the person of the Savior. For instance, Theodoret of Mopsuestia, from the fourth century, Theodoret of Cyrus, and the fifth-century Syrian bishop Ibas of Edessa are known for their resistance to the form of Christology laid out by Cyril.[59] Cyril's Christology of single-subject flesh incarnate was always open to accusations of docetic tendencies, and Cyril struggled to demonstrate the radical difference between his christological position and docetism.[60] Also, Cyril's third letter to Nestorius was considered more polemical and controversial, although it was deemed to contain normative expressions of the Christian faith.[61] Accordingly, Greer and Caferro opine that Gregory of Nyssa explores the incarnation in two ways, outlining two contradictory conclusions: that the word of God remains unchanged and impassible, yet lives a human life, suffered, and died. In Gregory's view, the Christian faith obliges us to insist on both hypotheses. Thus, how shall we say that the word remains impassible even in the incarnation?[62] Hence, Cyril's Christology has been described as ambiguous and mystical rather than practical and semantical.

Most sixth-century theologians affirmed that Cyril of Alexandria was the touchstone of orthodoxy with respect to understanding the person of Christ. Some scholars believe that Cyril's Christology, especially in respect of the phrases he used about the person of Christ, can be understood in both orthodox and unorthodox ways. There is no doubt that Cyril's Christology was esteemed within classical scholarship and beyond. Thus, it has continuing lasting value as a church document in the expression of normative faith in the church's understanding of the person of Christ. Some modern scholars have described Cyril's fundamental christological insight as thorough, erudite and full of theological depth.

---

59. Schor, "Theodoret on the 'School of Antioch,'" 517–61.
60. Saint Cyril, *Three Christological Treatises*, 11.
61. Daley, *God Visible*, 18.
62. Greer and Caferro, *Broken Lights and Mended Lives*, 57.

In contrast, others have criticized Cyril's model of Christology regarding the person of Christ in Christian traditions. There remains a degree of unevenness and volatility in coming to terms with particular aspects of Cyril's christological perceptions. In their own right, Cyril's christological interpretations and ideas built upon the set pace in the development of classical christological reflection. It is my opinion that Cyril's christological insights will be better appreciated when seen through the lenses with which he wrote; only then can his approach and relevance be articulated for contemporary times. Nevertheless, the questions remain: Which of Cyril's writings best represent his normative position? Is Cyril's approach to Christ, read from the figures and themes, fully compatible with the Christology evangelicals hold as orthodox?

Christology in Africa

In past centuries, Africa has been at the forefront in addressing the fundamental questions that have perplexed the church. For example, on the issue of Christology, Houlden opines, "Like believers from every church era and every continent, African Christians address the fundamental question of Jesus: 'Who do you say that I am?'"[63] This question requires a christological response with genuine African authenticity. How Africans respond to this fundamental christological question will form contemporary African Christology. Michael, citing Walls, notes that the way Africans view and define theology today will affect Christianity's history many centuries from now because Christianity is massively migrating to "the global South," and Africa is its main driving force.[64] This is related to the christological foundation laid by Cyril of Alexandria, and therefore necessary for our consideration.

According to Clarke, Mbiti noted that before modern theological discoveries, "African christological concepts [did] not exist."[65] This reality has, however, changed over time, because modern African theologians have struggled to reinterpret christological realities, and many have gone beyond the norm of using biblical images to define Christology by opting for images from African traditions. Stinton, who ranks among those championing the cause of African Christianity, outlines some of the christological images that could help Africans perceive and respond to Jesus in ways that are applicable

---

63. Houlden, *Jesus in History*, 3.

64. Michael, *Christian Theology*, 1.

65. The statement accredited to John Mbiti was made in 1967. Clarke, *African Christology*, 1.

and relevant to the social needs of Africans; for example, Jesus as a life-giver, Jesus as a mediator, Jesus as a loved one, and Jesus as a leader.[66] To some degree, these African images have helped shape and give fresh insight into identifying the person of Jesus Christ.

Baur's assertion is equally relevant here: "The birth of an authentic African Christianity has been intimately connected with the rebirth of African culture."[67] This rebirth process can be described as decolonizing Africa from every aspect, be it political or intellectual, to have a self-perception with literary and historical roots. This clarion call for Africans to understand and appreciate Christology in a way that best speaks to their needs and conscience is for "inculturation and liberation."[68] Inculturation and liberation theology are a call for a shift from the inherited theologies of the West to a theology of a world cultural church movement where African culture and religion are given a dominant place in the theological enterprise and sociopolitical and economic structures are considered the primary sources of oppression. It is a movement that is linked with postcolonial discourse. Evaluating Geertz, Orji observed that the theology of inculturation helps us realize a new way of thinking as to how responsive we can be toward the particularities of people.[69] This implies that theology must be able to meet the everyday needs of people.

---

66. Stinton, *Jesus of Africa*.

67. Baur, *2000 Years*, 290. Two things affect the growing concern for an "African Christianity." First, the assertion that missionaries considered African tradition and culture to be barbaric has led to a dichotomy in African personality. The second is related to the writings of African laypeople on the colonial past which challenge both the activities of missionaries and the colonial system, which gained global favor, especially after World War II. Conferences were organized and churches were encouraged to use African cultures to promote Christianity. Bediako notes that the clarion call to reconstruct the prescribed theology brought by European theologians came because critical Europe was impatient with Africa out of their misunderstanding of the continent's cultural diversity. Bediako, *Jesus in Africa*, 16.

68. Schreiter, *Faces of Jesus*, n.p. Inculturation theology is the search for authentic and prophetic theology that promotes the acceptance of African realities and worldviews in theological hermeneutics, and which emerged out of a cultural-political movement. It is rooted in francophone and anglophone Africa, while the black theology of liberation is rooted in the Black Consciousness Movement in South Africa. Martey, *African Theology*, 1. There was a Special Assembly that was gathered in Rome in April 1994. The assembly gathered African Bishops who are called "Synods of Hope" to deliberate on issues affecting the church in Africa. In supporting this theology of inculturation, "the synod fathers strongly recommended dialogue with African traditional religion and with African cultural values and guardians of those values." Stinton, *African Theology on the Way*, 40.

69. Orji, *Semiotic Approach*, xvi. The link between inculturation/liberation and the postcolonial era is because of the thematic concerns embedded in the theories of inculturation theology, which are described as oppositional, and are concerned with the impact of colonialism on African cultures, traditions and worldviews. Antonio, *Inculturation and Postcolonial Discourse*, 1.

The Relevance of Cyril's Christology for Contemporary African Christianity

In Africa today, there are tensions among Christian traditions with respect to how each conceives the person of Christ. For instance, African paradigmatic approaches such as occupation, culture, family, genealogy and ritual, or mystical, anthropocentric and juridical paradigms, offer a reflective approach to Jesus.[70] Nevertheless, these African images struggle to provide an appropriate and authentic christological interpretation of the Christ event, which has raised tensions. Accordingly, some Africans conceive a "symmetrical" portrait of Christ, while others subordinate Christ to God.

It must be noted that not all tensions among these Christian traditions are based on how the person of Christ is conceived. Some are due to political issues. Others are religiously motivated, and still others are a complex mixture of political and religious sentiments. Accusations of treachery and extremism are thrown at each other. This volatility is not confined to Africa, as beyond the shores of the continent there are also those who are unable to conceive and comprehend the unitive understanding of the person of Christ. Some Christian traditions find it challenging to grasp Christ as two abiding "natures," or substantial operative realities, forming the "person" of the Incarnate Word.

The will to set Christian traditions on the right track in understanding the person of Christ seems to be lacking among African theologians. This deficiency could be due to either limited knowledge of Christology or a lack of interest in clarifying and understanding the mystery of the unambiguous terms[71] that are used to describe Christ. It is imperative to reawaken and conscientize these African Christian traditions through collaborative and dialogical theological reflections on the "two unconfused natures" and "double consubstantiality," to use the language of Cyril's Christology, which is essential for responding to the Christian calling and faith. Such a shared theological reflection holds the potential to hinder discord in the church, build peace by removing falsehood, and reaffirm the Christian tradition regarding the person of Christ. It is only in promoting the unitive, God-centered portrait of Christ that the gospel is preached and Christian faith and life are consciously awakened in faith, worship and polity. This awakening understanding can ensure the unity of both the church and society.

---

70. Mugambi and Magesa, *Jesus in African Christianity*, 136–61.

71. Terms such as "substance," "nature," *hypostasis* and *prosōpon*, and what they meant when applied to the reality of Christ's person. Markham, *Student's Companion*, 52.

The Task before the African Church

The mystery of Christ, then, is vital to Christian biblical interpretation and the Christian understanding of God and creation, of grace and the human potential. Christology, in the strict sense of the term, is more than focusing on faith in Christ but is the unitive understanding of the person of Christ in his incarnation.[72] Christology also encompasses other aspects of human thought about God, such as soteriology, Trinitarian theology, theological anthropology and biblical interpretation.[73] This was the same for Cyril's Christology, which includes other themes and emphases as well as his unitive understanding of the person of Christ. These multiple strands in understanding are also true of most Africans and Western theologians and lay members. They assume that the continuous historical development in Christology from the classical epoch to the present has solved all controversies surrounding the identity of Christ and meaning, and thus there is no need to reevaluate or be critical of their views. Daley opines that such complacency has weakened Christology.[74]

It is true that only a few seek to understand the identity of Christ and its meaning (Christology) to engage the existential concerns of the present-day church and society, especially those of Africa. Today, Christology falls short of what we may classify as unruffled orthodoxy. We tend to seek by the most inadequate means to keep the discussion limited to scholars. The task before the African church is to reaffirm what was generally understood to be the mainstream tradition of Christian orthodoxy, and to collaboratively and dialogically rule out the kind of language and thinking about Christ that seems most likely to present a serious danger of veering away from that tradition. Kato writes:

> For biblical Christianity to subsist and flourish in Africa, we must grasp fast the truth that man's fundamental problem is the sin against God, and that salvation is only through Jesus Christ. We must hold to the uniqueness of Christian revelation through the written Word and the Living Word. To seek salvation elsewhere than through the shed blood of Christ is heretical. It is preaching another gospel.[75]

---

72. Johnson, *Christology*, 9–10.
73. Sobrino, *Christology at the Crossroads*, 388–89.
74. Daley, *God Visible*, 6.
75. Kato, *Biblical Christianity in Africa*, 22.

Thus, the ability to offer a positive delineation of Christ's person and a seamless conceptual whole might in time become the basis for real concord in faith, worship and polity. However, it is essential to note that dialogue on theological issues in our contemporary era will be challenging as, at present, positions of Christian traditions on the understanding of the person of Christ have hardened into immovable fronts. Nevertheless, we should not for this reason abate our efforts.

Conclusion

The study of Cyril's Christology inevitably embodies a continuous historical development in articulating the identity of Christ and its meaning for the church's theology and life. The theologian needs to appropriate this historical approach to offer possibilities for a renewed appreciation of these long-held truths and their sense of lasting validity in our age of opinionated perceptions of what is certain and true about the unitive person of Christ. This will provide the avenue to critically query and sketch perspectives that have found no place in our commonly held orthodoxy, and to strengthen our unity in him. Thus, it is imperative to base our articulation of the unitive understanding of the person of Christ in Cyril of Alexandria's Christology from a historical perspective. Given the above, it can be asserted that the time to demonstrate the importance of history has once again come.

Bibliography

Antonio, Edward P. *Inculturation and Postcolonial Discourse in African Theology*. New York: Peter Lang, 2006.

Baur, Ferdinand Christian. *History of Christian Dogma*. Oxford: Oxford University Press, 2014.

Baur, John. *2000 Years of Christianity in Africa: An African History, 62–1992*. Nairobi: Paulines Publications, 1994.

Bediako, Kwame. *Jesus in Africa: The Christian Gospel in History and Experience – Theological Reflections from the South*. Yaoundé: Editions Clé Regnum Africa, in association with Paternoster, 2000.

Clarke, Clifton R. *African Christology: Jesus in Post-Missionary African Christianity*. Eugene: Wipf & Stock, 2011.

Cleenewerck, Laurent. *His Broken Body: Understanding and Healing the Schism between the Roman Catholic and Eastern Orthodox Churches*. Washington, DC: Euclid University Press, 2007.

Daley, Brian E. *God Visible: Patristic Christology Reconsidered.* Oxford: Oxford University Press, 2018.
Davis, Leo D. *The First Seven Ecumenical Councils (325–787): Their History and Theology.* Collegeville: Liturgical, 2017.
Dowley, Tim, ed. *Eerdman's Handbook to the History of Christianity.* 1st American ed. Grand Rapids: Eerdmans, 1987.
Dunn, Geoffrey, and Wendy Mayer, eds. *Christians Shaping Identity from the Roman Empire to Byzantium: Studies Inspired by Pauline Allen.* Leiden: Brill, 2015.
Dunn, James D. G. *Christology in the Making: A New Testament Inquiry into the Origins of the Doctrine of the Incarnation.* London: SCM, 2003.
Eco, Umberto. *Semiotics and the Philosophy of Language.* Bloomington: Indiana University Press, 1986.
"Fathers of the Church Series (127 Vols.)." Verbum. Accessed 12 May 2019. https://verbum.com/products/33665/fathers-of-the-church-series.
Greer, Rowan A., and William Caferro. *Broken Lights and Mended Lives: Theology and Common Life in the Early Church.* Pennsylvania: Penn State University Press, 2008.
Grillmeier, Aloys. *Christ in Christian Tradition: From the Apostolic Age to Chalcedon (451).* London: Mowbray, 1975.
Gros, Jeffrey, Thomas F. Best, and Lorelei F. Fuchs SA, eds. *Growth in Agreement III: International Dialogue Texts and Agreed Statements, 1998–2005.* Grand Rapids: Eerdmans, 2008.
Haas, Christopher. *Alexandria in Late Antiquity: Topography and Social Conflict.* Baltimore: JHU Press, 2006.
Hall, Stuart G., ed. *Jesus Christ Today: Studies of Christology in Various Contexts.* Berlin: Walter de Gruyter, 2009.
Hames, Daniel. "An Introduction to Cyril of Alexandria." Union Theology. Accessed 21 March 2019. https://www.uniontheology.org/resources/doctrine/jesus/an-introduction-to-cyril-of-alexandria.
Hardy, Edward Rochie. *Christology of the Later Fathers.* London: Westminster John Knox, 1954.
Hillis, Gregory K. "The Natural Likeness of the Son: Cyril of Alexandria's Pneumatology." Diss., McMaster University, 2008.
Houlden, James Leslie. *Jesus in History, Thought, and Culture: An Encyclopedia.* Santa Barbara: ABC-CLIO, 2003.
Hudale, Martin. *The Matrix of Mysticism: A Call for a New Reformation.* [USA]: Xulon Press, 2008.
Johnson, Mini S. *Christology: Biblical and Historical.* New Delhi: Mittal, 2005.
Kashchuk, Oleksandr. "Logos-Sarx Christology and the Sixth-Century Miaenergism." Accessed 13 May 2019. https://www.academia.edu/37012111/LOGOS-SARX_CHRISTOLOGY_AND_THE_SIXTH-CENTURY_MIAENERGISM.
Kato, Byang Henry. *Biblical Christianity in Africa: A Collection of Papers and Addresses.* Achimota: Africa Christian Press, 1985.

LoLordo, Antonia. *Persons: A History*. New York: Oxford University Press, 2019.

Lunn, Nicholas P., trans. *St. Cyril of Alexandria: Glaphyra on the Pentateuch*. Vol. 1, *Genesis*. Washington, DC: CUA Press, 2018.

Markham, Ian S. *The Student's Companion to the Theologians*. Chichester: John Wiley & Sons, 2013.

Martey, Emmanuel. *African Theology: Inculturation and Liberation*. Eugene: Wipf & Stock, 2009.

Mathison, Keith A. "A Forgotten Father: Cyril of Alexandria." Tabletalk. Last modified 4 December 2017. Accessed 18 March 2019. https://tabletalkmagazine.com/posts/2017/12/a-forgotten-father-cyril-of-alexandria/.

McGuckin, John. *Saint Cyril of Alexandria and the Christological Controversy*. Crestwood: SVSP, 2004.

———. *St. Cyril of Alexandria: The Christological Controversy – Its History, Theology, and Texts*. Vigilae Christianae Supplements 23. Leiden: Brill, 1994.

McKinion, Steven Alan. *Words, Imagery, and the Mystery of Christ: A Reconstruction of Cyril of Alexandria's Christology*. Boston: Brill, 2000.

Meyer, John R. "Athanasius' Use of Paul in His Doctrine of Salvation." *Vigiliae Christianae* 52, no. 2 (1998): 146–71.

Michael, Matthew. *Christian Theology and African Traditions*. Eugene: Wipf & Stock, 2013.

Mugambi, Jesse Ndwiga Kanyua, and Laurenti Magesa, eds. *Jesus in African Christianity: Experimentation and Diversity in African Christology*. 3rd ed. Nairobi: Acton, 2003.

Ondrey, Hauna T. *The Minor Prophets as Christian Scripture in the Commentaries of Theodore of Mopsuestia and Cyril of Alexandria*. Oxford: Oxford University Press, 2018.

Orji, Cyril. *A Semiotic Approach to the Theology of Inculturation*. Eugene: Wipf & Stock, 2015.

Papandrea, James L. *The Earliest Christologies: Five Images of Christ in the Postapostolic Age*. Downers Grove: InterVarsity Press, 2016.

Pontificium Consilium de Iustitia et Pace (Pontifical Council of Justice and Peace). *Compendium of the Social Doctrine of the Church*. Dublin: Veritas, 2005.

Puett, Terry L. *A Categorical, Alphabetical Bible Study*. Vol. 2, *E to L*. Pueblo: T&L, 2014.

Rausch, Thomas P. *Systematic Theology: A Roman Catholic Approach*. Collegeville: Liturgical Press, 2016.

———. *Who Is Jesus? An Introduction to Christology*. Collegeville: Liturgical, 2016.

Roberts, Alexander. *The Ante-Nicene Fathers*. Boston: Christian Literature, 1888.

Russell, Norman. *Cyril of Alexandria*. London: Routledge, 2002.

Saint Cyril of Alexandria. *On the Unity of Christ*. New York: St. Vladimir's Seminary Press, 1995.

———. *Three Christological Treatises*. Washington, DC: CUA Press, 2014.

Sbeshonertor. "A History of the Catholic Church: Prosopon of Union." Catholic under the Hood, 4 May 2018. Accessed 13 May 2019. https://catholicunderthehood.com/2018/05/04/439-a-history-of-the-catholic-church-prosopon-of-union/.

Schor, Adam M. "Theodoret on the 'School of Antioch': A Network Approach." *Journal of Early Christian Studies* 15, no. 4 (24 Dec. 2007): 517–62.

Schreiter, Robert J. *Faces of Jesus in Africa*. Maryknoll: Orbis, 2015.

Smith, J. Warren. *Christian Grace and Pagan Virtue: The Theological Foundation of Ambrose's Ethics*. New York: Oxford University Press, 2011.

Smith, Mark S. *The Idea of Nicaea in the Early Church Councils, AD 431–451*. New York: Oxford University Press, 2019.

Sobrino, Jon. *Christology at the Crossroads: A Latin American Approach*. Eugene: Wipf & Stock, 2002.

Spade, Paul V. *Five Texts on the Mediaeval Problem of Universals: Porphyry, Boethius, Abelard, Duns Scotus, Ockham*. Cambridge: Hackett, 1994.

Stinton, Diane B., ed. *African Theology on the Way: Current Conversations*. International Study Guides 46. London: SPCK, 2010.

———. *Jesus of Africa: Voices of Contemporary African Christology*. Maryknoll: Orbis, 2004.

Torrance, Iain. *Christology after Chalcedon: Severus of Antioch and Sergius the Monophysite*. Eugene: Wipf & Stock, 1998.

Tortorelli, Kevin. *Christology with Lonergan and Balthasar*. Ely: Melrose Press, 2005.

van Loon, Hans. *The Dyophysite Christology of Cyril of Alexandria*. Boston: Brill, 2009.

Weinandy, Thomas, and Daniel A. Keating. *The Theology of St. Cyril of Alexandria: A Critical Appreciation*. New York: A&C Black, 2003.

Welch, Lawrence J. *Christology and Eucharist in the Early Thought of Cyril of Alexandria*. San Francisco: Catholic Scholars Press, 1994.

Wilken, Robert L. "Exegesis and the History of Theology: Reflections on the Adam-Christ Typology in Cyril of Alexandria." *Church History* 35, no. 2 (28 July 2009): 139–56.

Williams, Kyle. "The Mystery of the Incarnation: Towards a Reconciliation of Cyril and Nestorius." Master's diss., George Fox University, 2018.

Willis, John Randolph, ed. *The Teachings of the Church Fathers*. San Francisco: Ignatius Press, 2002.

12

Who Are You for Us, *Yesu Kristo?* Christological Confessions of the Early Church in Contemporary Africa

A Methodological Question

John Michael Kiboi
Senior Lecturer, St. Paul's University, Limuru, Kenya

Abstract

Since all theology is contextual, attempting to offer answers to contextual problems, this article places the christological confessions of the early church in the context of the Greek philosophy of the classical period (400 BC–AD 400). During this period, the Greeks were concerned with finding the basic principle (*the one*) behind existence (*the many*) and how the one related to the many. The debate can be summarized as (1) the many *versus* the one (Sophists and skeptics); (2) the one *behind* the many (Socrates); (3) the one *above* the many (Plato, the "hedonists" and the Neoplatonists); and (4) the one *in* the many (Aristotle). This Greek philosophical background influenced the early church to concentrate on the person of Christ as opposed to his work. Today, christological conversation revolves around the question of the relevance of ontological (the person) versus functional (the work) Christology. In Africa, the question raised by functionalists is the relevance of ontological Christologies in addressing African experiences and aspirations; on the other side, the ontologists are asking how one can appreciate the work of a Christ one does not know. Imperative questions arise: Is the African question exclusively functional? Aren't African people also concerned with spiritual and ontological issues? This article shows how both the ontological (the person) and the functional (the work) of Christ are important and relevant to all times, and thereby recommends the ontological approach as the starting point to arrive at correct imaging or to answer Christ's question "Who do people say I am?"

Key words: christological confessions, christological controversies, ontological, functional, the one and the many

Introduction

The sociopolitical, cultural and economic contexts shaped the theology of the Old Testament, the New Testament and the church. Each epoch articulated its Christology according to its needs. The church fathers during the classical period (100–400 AD), informed by Greco-Roman philosophical needs, articulated a Christology that was abstract and philosophical. This type of Christology was relevant to them then and addressed their concerns. Today, in regions previously colonized, the church has produced liberation theologians who have adopted a nonspeculative systematic theological approach to Christology. This school of thought has argued that the Christology of the early church[1] is abstract and irrelevant to contemporary experiences. Therefore, Christ's question "Who do you say I am?" needs new responses that address the needs of each generation. This is the debate between functional and ontological Christologies.

The argument is that an ontological approach produces an intellectual, abstract Christology that is irrelevant to functional realities. For its part, a functional approach produces a functional Christology that is not orthodox – that is, it does not uphold the apostolic Christology, Christology as articulated by the church councils. Therefore, we need an approach that will produce for us a Christology that is not only orthodox or apostolic, but also relevant to our realities.

---

1. More precisely, the classical period (between 1st and 5th centuries AD).

For the sake of the church's apostolicity, this article seeks to establish an appropriate approach whose end product upholds both the ontological and functional Christologies in balance. This article shows how the Greek debate over *the One* and *the many*[2] influenced the early church in articulating their Christology, so that they ended up with a pure, abstract ontological Christology, one which is accused of being irrelevant to human realities today. The article then goes further to illustrate how the functional nonspeculative systematic approach could easily lead to placing the many *above* the one – a form of heresy today.

Background to Early Church Christological Confessions
Judeo-Christian Background

The traditional Jewish perception of God was not that of pure transcendence; God was concrete and immanent. Later on, as the Jewish people interacted with the outside world, especially during the exile and postexilic period, their God became more hidden or was only partially revealed. It is suspected that the Greek perspective of God as purely transcendent and metaphysical may have infiltrated the Jewish traditional understanding, leading to transcendentalism. It is observed that "epithets for God, such as Heaven or Supreme . . . or the Master of all Creation [are] Hellenistic phrases which crept into Jewish literature, but never received, in the mouth of a Rabbi, the significance which they had with an Alexandrine philosopher."[3]

Tim Labron notes that "these conceptions of a transcendent and metaphysical foundation, in a theological context, yield an immutable and eternal God that is more of a Greek conception of God than a Judeo-Christian conception."[4] He goes further: "The Greek conception of God deals in abstractions, while the Judeo-Christian conception of God is more concrete . . . The Jewish conception of God is also concrete."[5] This then forms the background upon which Christology is interpreted variously by Judeo-Christians, especially in the early church.

---

2. The *one* or the *universal* being the Ultimate (God) and the *many* being creations of the universe.

3. Solomon Schechter, *Aspects of Rabbinic Theology* (Jewish Lights Publishing, 1993), 22, in Labron, *Wittgenstein and Theology*, 67.

4. Labron, *Wittgenstein and Theology*, 67.

5. Labron, 67.

Given this context, it is evident that the incarnation could not have made sense to Greco-Roman Christians who were influenced by Greek metaphysical abstraction and the transcendental perspective of God, but it did make sense to Judeo-Christians who were influenced by their traditional Judaistic view of God's immanence (see Isa 7 and 9; and the shekinah during the consecration of the temple, 2 Chr 7:1–3). Yet the conception of God of both Judeo-Christians and Greco-Roman Christians is that the Word is made flesh.[6]

Classical Greek Influence

Pre-Socratic philosophers in Greece were concerned with finding the basic principle behind existence. What would account for the existence of the universe? During this period (mainly 400 BC–AD 400), the debate mutated and concentrated on the relationship between *the one* and *the many* – that is, the *universal* and the *particulars*, the "one" being the Ultimate (God) and the "many," the creations of the universe. The debate could be summarized as the many *versus* the one (Sophists and skeptics); the one *behind* the many (Socrates); the one *above* the many (Plato, the "hedonists," and the Neoplatonists); and the one *in* the many (Aristotle).[7] Subsequent philosophers built their debate basically on this framework, and "the relationship between God and man dominated philosophy."[8] This is the context in which the Christology of the early church was developed. The church over the ages has articulated its Christology based on the early church confessions, especially as stated by the Councils of Nicaea (325), Constantinople (381), Ephesus (431) and Chalcedon (451).

Early Church Christological Controversies and Confessions
Christological Controversies

Debates over the relationship between *the one* and *the many* informed the Christology of the Bible and the first four ecumenical councils. During the patristic period (ca. AD 100–500), the debate led to christological controversies occasioned by some people trying to emphasize either Christ's divinity or his humanity. Four constructs of the incarnation vied for control of the doctrine of Christ: "the one *over* the many (Gnosticism, Apollinarianism, and Eutychianism); the many *over* the one (Ebionism and Arianism); the one

---

6. Labron, 67.
7. Pate, *From Plato to Jesus*, 23–33.
8. Pate, 99.

and the many (Nestorianism); and the one *in* the many (the four ecumenical councils' formulation of the hypostatic union employing Neoplatonic thought)."[9]

Depending on the different persuasions of the debate, there arose various distortions of the nature of Christ. Docetism, which elevated the one *over* the many, accepted Christ's deity but not his humanity.[10] A first-century proponent of this version of Christology was Cerinthus, whose teachings are rejected in the first letter of John. He denied the humanity of Jesus Christ (a heresy referred to as Cerinthian docetism). Cerinthian docetism claimed that the Christ (deity) came upon Jesus (humanity) at the latter's baptism but departed from him on the cross before Christ died. "Informing all of this is the Platonic notion that spirit is superior to flesh, that the soul is better than the body, and that the one is *above* the many."[11] Therefore, based on this understanding, Jesus Christ was a pure spirit who only appeared to be human.

Plato's dualism had taught that matter was evil and spirit was good. This teaching influenced the gnostic and Neoplatonic teaching that spirit is good and the one *above* the many. For this reason, the divine (spirit or logos) could not intermingle with matter, and therefore gnostic Christians rejected the divinity of Christ.

Thus, classical christological heresies emanated from these two strands: docetism (the one *over* the many) and Gnosticism (the many *against* or *versus* the one), with, however, varying emendations.

Arius, a deacon in Alexandria, following in the gnostic tradition, denied the deity of Christ. Arianism understood Jesus as God's creature, though created in eternity.[12] He is of like/similar essence (*homoiousios*) with the Father[13] and therefore could not be of the same essence (*homoousios*) as the Father. Arius argued that, in fact, Christ himself testified that "the Father is greater than I" (John 14:28), and 1 Timothy 6:16 teaches that God alone possesses immortality. Following this thought, Arius concluded that Christ was subordinate to the Father and did not possess eternal self-existence.

The second christological perspective was that of Apollinarius (bishop of Laodicea, Asia Minor, from 362). Appolinarianism appears to be a residual of

---

9. Pate, 106–7.

10. Pate, 100.

11. Pate, 105.

12. Prov 8:22–30: "The LORD created me at the beginning of his work, the first of his acts of old . . ." (RSV). He is "the first-born of all creation" (Col 1:15 RSV).

13. Anderson, *Journey through Christian Theology*, 442.

Plato's position of the one *over* the many. Neoplatonism held that since the soul was immaterial, eternal and governed by reason, it was good, unlike the body, which was material and temporal and subject to evil because of its appetites.

Following in this tradition, Apollinarius defended the deity of Christ but went to the extreme of denying that Jesus's mind/will was human. He claimed that the divine spirit of God, *nous* or *Logos*, had, at incarnation, replaced the human mind in Jesus. Thus, Jesus's humanity was a glorified and spiritualized one.

Another christological controversy was that advanced by Nestorius, bishop of Constantinople (428). Nestorianism held that "the human and divine natures of Christ were essentially distinct and separate . . . divine nature favoured Christ's human nature."[14] It taught that in Jesus, there were two separate persons: the human and the divine. He denied that the Virgin Mary was the God-bearer, *theotokos*, but instead maintained that Mary was *anthropotokos* (man-bearer).[15] His argument was as follows:

> It is not possible that the unmade (should become) made and the eternal temporary and the temporary eternal and that the created (should become) uncreated by nature; that that which is uncreated and which has not come into being and is eternal should thereby become made and temporary, as if it became part of a nature made and temporary; nor that there should come forth a nature unmade and eternal from nature made and temporary to become an *ousia* [substance] unmade and eternal; for such things are not possible nor conceivable.[16]

This perspective is very much in line with Platonic philosophy that understood God as unchanging, impassible, immutable and eternal. According to Platonic philosophy, it is only humans who are passable, mutable and mortal. Influenced by this Platonic view and the Greek philosophies of the one *outside* the many, Nestorius outrightly denied the divinity of Christ by emphasizing the separation between the two natures of Christ.

The Christology of Eutyches may have been influenced by Plato's argument of the one *above* the many. Eutychianism held that at conception, Christ's deity and humanity mixed to form one new nature: the human nature was absorbed

---

14. Diegue, "Christological Controversies," 3.
15. Pate, *From Plato to Jesus*, 109.
16. Nestorius, *The Bazaar of Heracleides*, trans. G. R. Driver and Leonard Hodgson (Oxford: Clarendon Press, 1925), 27, quoted in Labron, *Wittgenstein and Theology*, 71.

into the divine nature resulting in a third, new nature that was neither fully God nor fully man. This Christology was declared heretical.

The Church's Christological Confessions

The Ecumenical Council of Nicaea in AD 325, persuaded by Aristotelian philosophy of the one *in* the many, condemned Arianism[17] and taught, regarding Jesus, "We believe in one Lord Jesus Christ, the Only Son of God, eternally begotten of the Father, God from God, Light from Light, true God from true God, begotten not made, consubstantial [*homoousios*] with the Father. Through him all things were made."

At the Council of Constantinople (381), Gregory of Nazianzus (archbishop of Constantinople) disagreed with Apollinarius's teachings, arguing that Jesus's mind/will was human. He stated, "We do not separate the Man from the Deity, no, we assert the dogma of the unity and identity of the Person, who aforetime was not man but God, the only Son before all ages, who in these last days has assumed manhood also for our salvation."[18] Thus the council at Constantinople consolidated, confirmed and reaffirmed the Nicene Creed. The Council fathers believed that without Christ's true human experience there would be no genuine salvation.

Nestorianism was condemned as a heresy by the Council of Ephesus (431). The Council explained the nature of the union as a *hypostatic* union.[19] It went further to anathematize any teaching that went against the church's position on the following points: that the holy Virgin was *theotokos*; that the Word which is from God the Father was personally united with flesh, and with his own flesh is one Christ; that the separation of the union or even calling Christ a "God-bearing man" was wrong.

At the Council of Chalcedon (451), the creed that was developed explained the two natures of Christ. This creed became the standard document that defines the Christology of most of the Christian world: Eastern Orthodox, Roman Catholic and most Protestant churches subscribe to it.[20] Regarding Jesus Christ, this creed states that he is

> truly God and truly man, of a reasonable [rational] soul and body; consubstantial [coessential] with the Father according

---

17. Diegue, "Christological Controversies," 3.
18. Pate, *From Plato to Jesus*, 108.
19. Diegue, "Christological Controversies," 12.
20. Diegue, 15.

to the Godhead, and consubstantial with us according to the Manhood . . . begotten before all ages of the Father according to the Godhead, and in these latter days, for us and for our salvation, born of the Virgin Mary, the Mother of God, according to the Manhood; one and the same Christ, Son, Lord, Only begotten, to be acknowledged in two natures, inconfusedly, unchangeably, indivisibly, inseparably; the distinction of natures being by no means taken away by the union, but rather the property of each nature being preserved.[21]

It is worth noting that the four councils were influenced by Aristotle's position of the one *in* the many to develop the doctrine of Christology – especially the *hypostatic* union.

The Problem
The Problem of Pure Intellectualism

The question being raised by contemporary functional theologians in Africa today is the relevance and value of the type of Christology born in the classical period, that of abstract intellectualism, to a twenty-first-century Christian in Africa. Does such a Christology address African needs and aspirations?

These theologians have criticized Western philosophical speculative theologies (and, for that matter, ontological Christology) as irrelevant and nonsensitive to African issues; such a Christology does not address the African question. They claim it is a theology that has been "modified to suit the European mind or idiosyncrasies."[22]

The claim of liberation theologians that intellectual and abstract (ontological) Christology is irrelevant to African concerns is synonymous with the nineteenth-century European attitude that, since Africans were nonintellectual, all they needed was a functional (concrete) Christology that would make sense to them.

The Danger of the Nonspeculative Approach

Protestant theologians who did not approve of the use of philosophy in doing theology asked, "What has philosophy got to do with theology?" Many

---

21. Edited to retain only that which is relevant to our discussion. See Grudem, *Systematic Theology*, 557.
22. Bediako, *Christianity in Africa*, 11.

Protestant theologians today are against systematic speculative theology. They advocate for a systematic nonspeculative approach. Labron observes that because of their rejection of the use of philosophy in doing theology, the Reformers became victims of Platonic dualism. For instance, Zwingli and Calvin held that "there lurks in man a something separated from the body . . . an intellect by which we are able to conceive of the invisible God and angels – a thing of which the body is altogether incapable."[23] Labron concludes that it is for this reason that "Calvin thinks the soul is to be freed of the 'prison-house of the body,' since 'men cleaving too much to the earth are dull of apprehension' and the soul is the 'nobler part.'"[24] Based on this inference, Labron concludes, "The most important point is that Calvin clearly regards the body as less noble."[25] Therefore, according to Labron, the Reformed tradition separated the mind from the world, akin to the Platonic and gnostic worldview. This separation of the mind from the world led Calvin to separate the human nature from the divine nature in Christ: "The Reformed tradition not only separates the mind from the world, but also the human nature from the divine nature in Christ. For example, given the great divide between the divine and the human it follows that the human attributes of Jesus cannot be communicated to the divine."[26] To justify this claim, he cites the Reformers' opposition to the Roman Catholic understanding of transubstantiation of the Eucharist, averring that the same position of separation is

> central to the Reformed understanding of the sacrament of the Lord's Supper . . . where, in contrast to the Catholic tradition, there is a similar separation of the physical from the divine. Given the emphasis on reason, and the chasm between the human/physical and the spiritual/divine, it is thought to be clearly unreasonable to assume that the divine is physically present in mere bread – it is only a symbol of a heavenly reality.[27]

This discussion suffices to illustrate the claim that classical Greek philosophy in the debate of *the one* and *the many* had an impact on this particular epoch. While the Catholic Church followed in the tradition of Thomistic-Aristotelian monism of the one *in* the many, the Reformers followed

---

23. Calvin, *Institutes*, 1.15.2, quoted in Labron, *Wittgenstein and Theology*, 68.
24. Calvin, 1.15.2, quoted in Labron, 68.
25. Labron, 69.
26. Labron, 69.
27. Labron, 69.

in the tradition of Platonic dualism (of the one *over* or *against* the many), and unknowingly rejected the possibility of the divine (the risen Christ) *in* the elements of the Eucharist. Nonspeculative Christology stands in danger of emphasizing the many *over* or *against* the one and impoverishing the mystery. Such a Christology is also criticized for separating the person of Christ from his work. Many contemporary functionalist liberation theologians are emphasizing the work of Christ over his person, leading to separation of the person from the work of Christ, akin to gnostic tendencies.

John Macquarrie warns against the tendency of separating the work of Christ from the person of Christ. He states, "The doctrines of the person of Christ and of the work of Christ are really inseparable, and are simply aspects of the Church's single confession of Christ as Lord and Word."[28] He then goes further to link Christ's life and his death.

A clear explication of how through incarnation Christ's divinity (ontological) was conjoined to his humanity – the God-man – will achieve for us an understanding of Christ's work, that is, his death on the cross, as that of the God-man. Such understanding and clarity can be achieved only through a systematic ontological speculative approach.

Dangers of Scientific and Philosophical Approaches in Christology

During the modern period (nineteenth century, i.e. between the 1860s and the 1950s), people's perspectives were informed by philosophy and science (which demanded scientific proof). It was a period which held that

> people's knowledge is derived from scientific and rational thinking rather than religious faith, magic or superstition. During this period, people have looked to science and logical thinking to explain the world. Natural disasters such [as] earthquakes, for example, have tended to be explained scientifically rather than as an "act of God."[29]

This new perspective gave birth to empirical skepticism which influenced the way Christology was interpreted. Pate notes that "the breakup of philosophy and theology in the modern and contemporary periods was accompanied by a major shift in perspective toward Christology – the many (humanity)

---

28. Macquarrie, *Principles of Christian Theology*, 311.

29. Thompson, "From Modernity to Post-Modernity," https://revisesociology.com/2016/04/09/from-modernity-to-post-modernity.

took precedence over the one (deity)."[30] The new focus was on humanity, over against the medieval period's attention to God. For example, Humean empirical skepticism led to denying Jesus's deity and miracles. Followers of Humean empiricism offered a de-supernaturalized Jesus, such as David Strauss in his work *Life of Jesus* (1835), which inspired Thomas Jefferson to leave out all things miraculous in the gospel accounts of Jesus.[31] Pate notes that "this 'Christology from below' . . . was purely from a human perspective, leaving next to no supernatural components to the story of Jesus. This combination of Hume's philosophy and Strauss' theology replaced the *one* by the *many* relative to Christology. And it has been with us in some form ever since."[32]

This Christology from below deprives Christ of his essential divine being, thereby falling into some form of the gnostic heresies of the classical period. "The triumph of the many (humanity) over the one (deity) in discussions of the Incarnation has continued throughout the contemporary period."[33] An example of such a Christology from below is liberation Christology. Liberation theologians borrow their functional approach from Marxist ideology.[34] The approach in liberation theology is "see, judge and act."[35] The masses are conscientized and challenged to act against the oppressive structures to liberate themselves.[36] There is no place for the divine in the process of liberation; it is humanistic.

The modern period was followed by the postmodern period from the twentieth century to date. Being influenced by the triumph of the *many* over the *one* of the previous period, "Friedrich Schleiermacher and Albrecht Ritschl offered a Jesus devoid of the supernatural, but they tempered their German liberalism by focusing on the loving humanitarian acts of Jesus."[37] This functional approach to Christology, or humanistic perspective, led Albert Schweitzer to teach that "Jesus was a sincere man but not the Messiah."[38] It also led to the teaching that "we must abandon trust in miracles and in a resurrected

---

30. Pate, *From Plato to Jesus*, 122.
31. Pate, 122.
32. Pate, 122.
33. Pate, 122.
34. Ford, *Modern Theologians*, 175.
35. See Mueller, *What Are They Saying about Theological Method?*, 17.
36. Ford, *Modern Theologians*, 182.
37. Pate, *From Plato to Jesus*, 122.
38. Pate, 122.

Christ. That is to say, we must embrace the Jesus of history (humanity), not the Christ of faith (deity)."[39]

The Jesus Seminar (the American rendition of the radical Germanic school of Bultmann) combined Humean skepticism and Bultmannian existentialism and, as a result, denied Jesus his deity, instead portraying him as "a Cynic sage who went around Galilee uttering proverbial niceties."[40] Functional theologians' emphasis of Jesus's work over and against his being is akin to the Jesus Seminar and Germanic humanism.

A Critical Reflection on the Criticisms Raised

Before the nineteenth century, before Christianity was introduced in Africa, Europe understood Africa to be a dark continent, whose people were savages, ignorant, backward and superstitious, and who did not have the capacity to reason.[41] An African was conceived as one who never attempted to formulate any concept of the great Creator and hence had no theology, even though that person was a spiritual being.[42] Since Africans were irrational beings, they were not allowed to ask questions about what they were converting to. In this way, "the Gospel of Christ was travestied and diluted before it came to him [African person] to suit the peculiar institution by which millions of human beings were converted into 'chattels.'"[43] A keen analysis of the foregoing criticisms reveals that functional theologians' criticisms of the irrelevance of ontological abstract Christology are remnants of these nineteenth-century European attitudes toward African mental abilities to comprehend the deity. Unfortunately, many African theologians, especially advocates of functional theology, have fallen victim to these negative colonial attitudes.

Over twenty-six years ago, Kwame Bediako raised the question: "Will African Christianity be able to find viable *intellectual* grounds upon which to validate and secure its African credentials?"[44] This question appears to persist even today.

---

39. Pate, 122.
40. Pate, 122.
41. Hollis R. Lynch, ed., "Black Spokesman," quoted in Bediako, *Christianity in Africa*, 11.
42. Lynch, quoted in Bediako, *Christianity in Africa*, 11.
43. Edward Blyden, "Christianity and the Negro Race," in *Christianity, Islam and the Negro Race* (Edinburgh: Edinburgh University Press, 1967), 31ff., quoted in Bediako, *Christianity in Africa*, 7.
44. Bediako, 4.

From the foregoing criticisms, we note that the pure ontological approach may lead to intellectualism and abstraction of Christ from human realities and aspirations; pure functionalism, on the other hand, denies Christ of his ontological being and impoverishes the mystery, and the use of philosophy and science exclusively leads to humanism. Pate notes the necessity of having a balanced Christology, taking into account both Christ's deity and his humanity in equal measure:

> Just as the key philosophers maintained the right balance between *the one* and *the many* (Aristotle, Aquinas, Kant), so keeping the right balance between Jesus' Deity and humanity is the recipe for accurate Christian doctrine. Conversely, an imbalance between the one/Jesus' Deity and the many/Jesus' humanity distorts Christian theology, even as it does philosophy.[45]

Therefore, there is a need to uphold both the ontological and the functional approach in balance. This leads us to propose the ontological approach as a point of departure.

Methodology
Justification for the Search for a Methodology

According to Peter Gichure, theology seeks new ways of explaining and meaningfully presenting the church's teachings to the contemporary world so that it becomes relevant and useful for the questions that are asked daily. It aims at debunking theories that misrepresent the correct understanding of faith.[46] Gichure says, "If the objective is to make the faith to be understood in a coherent way, then the method must meet those standards."[47] He further explains, "A method ensures that an inquiry is conducted systematically. A method allows others to know how conclusions are arrived at."[48]

Gichure adds, "A method presupposes that the theologian knows his or her starting point and the route to take. So, a method or methodology may be defined as the means of arriving at an interpretation."[49] LaCugna states, "Methodology . . . as a means of arriving at an interpretation includes both the

---

45. Pate, *From Plato to Jesus*, 99.
46. Gichure, "Doing Theology," 29.
47. Gichure, 29.
48. Gichure, 29.
49. Gichure, 30.

point of origin (metaphysical assumptions) and a connecting link between the starting point and the end point; the link or route is the ordering of the sources germane to the discipline."[50] Therefore, as we seek the right methodology for imaging Christ and other Christian mysteries, it should be one that adheres to this principle: that its starting point is right. An argument whose premises contain falsehood will always be an invalid argument. In the same way, if our starting point in finding images of Christ in Africa is faulty, we will always end up with heretical images. It is for this reason that a top-down ontological approach is recommended.

Ontological Approach

Process

As has been observed, the early church's pure ontological approach gave birth to an abstract, intellectual Christology irrelevant to the human experience. In the top-down ontological approach proposed here, the point of departure is the process; we begin with the being before we move to human experiences, because a process that begins with the functionality of a mystery is like "putting the cart before the horse."

The first step is knowledge of God. This is a theological reflection on the being and explication of the divine mystery. The imperative for understanding the mystery first is premised on the argument that human beings cannot understand who they are and why there is suffering in the world in the face of a loving and powerful God until they understand who God is. As Calvin put it, "It is evident that man never attains to a true self-knowledge until he has previously contemplated the face of God, and come down after such contemplation to look into himself."[51] Thus to understand the human predicament, we have to begin with understanding who God is and, in this case, who Christ is. For example, understanding the doctrine of creation enables one to understand that sin is the root cause for all forms of oppression, and that "other forms of slavery find their deepest root in slavery to sin."[52]

The second step is knowledge of the human self. This is a research into and reflection on human experiences. At this stage, we ask questions such as: What is the cause of particular human suffering (experience)? Why do

---

50. C. M. LaCugna, *The Theological Methodology of Hans Küng* (New York: Scholars, 1982), 7, quoted by Gichure, 32.

51. Calvin, *Institutes*, 1.1.2.

52. Sacred Congregation for the Doctrine of the Faith, *Instruction*, IV:2.

we suffer? How can we come out of suffering? Such questions will lead us to understand the link between human experiences and nature or God's being. Calvin recommends that we begin our theology from the Being so that we can understand the reason behind human experiences. He states, "Though the knowledge of God and the knowledge of ourselves are bound together by a mutual tie, due arrangement requires that we treat of the former in the first place, and then descend to the latter."[53]

The third step is pastoral action. This is a reflection on human experiences in the light of the divine mystery. This is because "the Christian mysteries not only give adequate answers to all our human problems and legitimate aspirations, but they also immeasurably transcend them."[54] Every attempt should be aimed at liberating humankind from sin (because it is from sin that all forms of human oppression emanate), and all forms of oppression should be removed. This understanding then informs our pastoral action.

After understanding Christ's work (*mission ad extra*) in the light of his *mission ad intra* (Trinity), we can now image him appropriately. Thus, orthodoxy generates orthopraxis.

Justification of the Ontological Approach

The functional approach recommends the process of "see, judge and act." Its proponents believe that through conscientization, human beings can rise against oppressive structures and liberate themselves. Calvin seems to argue against such an attitude when he states: "We always seem to ourselves just, and upright, and wise, and holy, until we are convinced, by clear evidence, of our injustice, vileness, folly, and impurity. Convinced, however, we are not, if we look to ourselves only, and not to the Lord also."[55] He further states:

> So long as we do not look beyond the earth, we are quite pleased with our righteousness, wisdom, and virtue; we address ourselves in the most flattering terms and seem only less than demigods. But once we begin to raise our thoughts to God and reflect what kind of Being he is and to which, as a standard, we are bound to be conformed, what formerly delighted us by its false show of righteousness, will become polluted with the most splendid iniquity. What strangely imposed upon us under the name of

---

53. Calvin, *Institutes*, 1.1.3.
54. Nyamiti, *Jesus Christ*, 31.
55. Calvin, *Institutes*, 1.1.2.

wisdom will disgust by its extreme folly, and what presented the appearance of virtuous energy will be condemned as the most miserable impotence. So far are those qualities in us, which seem most perfect, from corresponding to the divine purity.[56]

To understand Christ's mission on earth becomes clearer if we begin from the Being. As observed by Neuner and Dupuis, "Christ has dominion over all creatures, a dominion not seized by violence nor usurped, but his by essence and by nature. His kingship is founded upon the ineffable hypostatic union . . . Christ has power over all creatures, meaning Christ is transcendental king of creation."[57]

Thus, human beings cannot understand Christ's work if they do not have knowledge of themselves. And they cannot understand who they are until they come to the true knowledge of God. True knowledge of God reveals to us that Christ is God, and thereby we can link his divinity to his humanity and his person to his work. Nwaigbo demonstrates this interconnectivity when he relates Christ's earthly priesthood (functional) to his heavenly (ontological or immanent) existence:

> The theology of the priesthood of Jesus Christ cannot be fully grasped apart from the doctrine of the Trinity. The priesthood of Jesus Christ, which has its effect in His passion and death on the Cross, has its anchor in the eternal Trinity. God the Father called His only begotten Son, Jesus Christ, to this mission, to this honor through the Holy Spirit, the communion of love of the Father and the Son.[58]

The functional approach makes it difficult to understand Christ's work at the cross as God's redeeming work. The ontological approach enables one to link Christ's *missio ad extra* (i.e. functional kenosis) to his *missio ad intra* (i.e. immanent kenosis).

Those who saw Jesus perform miracles wondered who this man was. Even at the cross, those who began from a functional point of view mocked him: "If you are the Christ, liberate yourself, and liberate us too" (cf. Matt 27:39–44; Mark 15:27–32; Luke 23:35–43). But those who contemplated the Being recognized him as the Son of God and understood the whole event as God dying for them (cf. Luke 23:42, 47). This means that if we begin by imaging

---

56. Calvin, 1.1.2.
57. Neuner and Dupuis, *Christian Faith*, no. 652.
58. Nwaigbo, "Priesthood of Jesus Christ," 38.

him from a functional point of view, we are likely to mistake him for a human being like any other, and not the God-man. For example, when Jesus asked his disciples, "Who do people say the Son of Man is?,"[59] Peter's confession was followed by Jesus's approval and assertion that such revelation came from above: "Blessed are you, Simon son of Jonah, for this was not revealed to you by flesh and blood, but by my Father in heaven" (Matt 16:17). Peter gave an accurate answer because he had contemplated the Being and had come to understand Jesus as the Son of the living God. This demonstrates that to understand the work of Christ (and, by extension, any other divine mystery), we need first to contemplate the Being or have divine intervention: a revelation from above – a top-down ontological approach.

Advocating for an ontological approach is premised on the fact that human beings created in the image of God can transcend the self to appropriate the Being *via a priori* i.e., without experience. Philosophers have argued that "God gave humans reason and therefore truths reached by reason are reconcilable with theology in a metaphysical system."[60] René Descartes maintained that "the mind alone can discover truth apart from empirical experiences."[61] Therefore, through reason or what theology may term meditation (*via a priori*), one can come to full knowledge of the Being.

Conclusion

In this paper, we have argued that when the ontological approach is used without functional considerations, the type of Christology produced is defective. We used the Christology of the early church to demonstrate how pure intellectualism produced an abstract Christology that does not address African experiences and aspirations. Similarly, we noted that the nonspeculative approach leads to Christology akin to any of the early church christological heresies. We also noted that contemporary advocacy for scientific and philosophical approaches could lead to depriving Christ of his essential divinity, leading to the triumph of the many *over* the one. All these shortcomings in each emphasis have demonstrated to us the need for an approach that produces an orthodox Christology that is also practical. To mitigate the problem, we have

---

59. See Matt 16:13–16; Mark 8:27–29; Luke 9:18–21.
60. Labron, *Wittgenstein and Theology*, 24. By *via a priori*, we mean the position that mind, through the power of reason, has the ability to know truths that are logically prior to experience.
61. Quoted in Labron, 25.

proposed a top-down ontological approach that begins from the Being before it reflects on human experiences and (pastoral) reflections.

Bibliography

Anderson, W. P. A. *Journey through Christian Theology*. Minneapolis: Fortress, 2010.

Bailey, Jon Nelson. "Paul's Political Paraenesis in Romans 13:1–7." *Restoration Quarterly* 46, no. 1 (2004): 11–28.

Bediako, Kwame. *Christianity in Africa: The Renewal of a Non-Western Religion*. Edinburgh: Edinburgh University Press, 1995.

Calvin, John. *Institutes of the Christian Religion*. Translated by Henry Beveridge. Grand Rapids: Eerdmans, 1998.

Diegue, R. "Christological Controversies of the First Four Ecumenical Councils." Master's diss., New Orleans Baptist Theological Seminary, 2014.

Ford, David F., ed. *The Modern Theologians: An Introduction to Christian Theology in the Twentieth Century*. Oxford: Blackwell, 1996.

Gichure, I. Peter. "Doing Theology: Methodological Issues." In *Challenges to Religion in Africa in Light of Vatican Council II: Essays in Honour of Charles Nyamiti*, edited by Charles Nyamiti, Peter I. Gichure, Frederick Wanjala, and Nicholaus Segeja, 29–48. Nairobi: CUEA Press, 2016.

Grudem, Wayne. *Systematic Theology: An Introduction to Biblical Doctrine*. Leicester: Inter-Varsity Press, 1994.

Labron, Tim. *Wittgenstein and Theology*. New York: T&T Clark, 2009.

Macquarrie, John. *Principles of Christian Theology*. London: SCM, 1977.

Mueller, J. J. *What Are They Saying about Theological Method?* New York: Paulist, 1984.

Neuner, J., and J. Dupuis. *The Christian Faith in the Doctrinal Documents of the Catholic Church*. New York: Alba House, 2001.

Nwaigbo, Ferdinand. "Priesthood of Jesus Christ in the Modern World." *Africa Ecclesial Review* 52, no. 2–3 (2010): 33–55.

Nyamiti, Charles. *Jesus Christ, the Ancestor of Humankind: Methodological and Trinitarian Foundations*. Nairobi: CUEA, 2005.

Pate, C. Marvin. *From Plato to Jesus: What Does Philosophy Have to Do with Theology?* Grand Rapids: Kregel, 2011.

Sacred Congregation for the Doctrine of the Faith. *Instruction on Certain Aspects of the "Theology of Liberation."* Vatican Polyglot Press, 1984.

Stead, C. *Philosophy in Christian Antiquity*. Cambridge: Cambridge University Press, 1994.

Thompson, Karl. "From Modernity to Post-Modernity." ReviseSociology, 9 April 2016. Accessed 6 May 2019. https://revisesociology.com/2016/04/09/from-modernity-to-post-modernity.

13

Jesus Christ as *Ker*

Toward an African High Priest Christology

E. Okelloh Ogera
Adjunct Lecturer, Faculty of Theology, St. Paul's University, Kenya

Abstract

As he walked toward Caesarea Philippi, Jesus turned to his disciples and asked them, "Who do you say I am?" (Matt 16:13–20). In the biblical text, Peter is recorded as answering that Jesus is the Messiah. However, this question has taken on new and significant dimensions for different people in different times and contexts. African Christians still grapple with this question. In response, this paper seeks to develop a christological motif from the concept of *Ker* (high priest) among the Luo community of Western Kenya. The paper begins by comparing the biblical concept of a high priest with the understanding of a high priest among the Luo community. The paper then argues that a *Ker* Christology is suitable for introducing Jesus Christ to African people, primarily for two main reasons. First, the high priest motif is present in the Bible and therefore its use is suitable among Christians of different theological persuasions. Second, since the concept of a high priest is also present among the Luo community, and indeed among many African communities, the concept becomes a suitable means of inculturating Jesus Christ in African Christianity. This ultimately ensures that Jesus Christ does not remain a stranger among African Christians. However, this manner of understanding Christ is anthropocentric: it highlights the functionality as well as the humanity of Christ over his ontological being. This motif also presents a challenge concerning the universality of Christ, because while the concept of high priest is present in many African and other communities around the world, it is absent from others. The paper concludes by proposing that a high priest Christology is suitable for bridging the gap between the "Jesus of faith" and the "historical Jesus."

Key words: Christology, high priest, inculturation, Luo traditional religion

Introduction

The question concerning the identity of Jesus is one of the most common questions that has been most asked ever since his appearance on the stage of human history some two thousand years ago. In an attempt to know what people thought of his identity during his time here on earth, he asked his disciples, "Who do people say I am?" (see Matt 16:13–20). Jesus received varied answers which were by no means exhaustive, for a plethora of Christologies has since emerged from the pages of the New Testament, borrowing images from Greco-Roman culture as well as Jewish ideas from the Old Testament, such as King, Messiah, Rabbi and Lord. In an attempt to answer the simple question "Who is Jesus Christ?" people have come up with diverse views and interpretations of his person.

Christianity is now universal. African people, having welcomed Western missionaries, have embraced the Christian faith. Douglas Waruta[1] says that ever since the early missionary era, African Christians have been more or less content to embrace the answers supplied to them by the "mother church" to theological questions, often with the excuse that these arguments are orthodox and faithful to the faith handed down by the apostles. This stifles any attempts by African Christians to find their own answers, particularly to the question "Who is Jesus Christ?" This paper looks at the Luo concept of *Ker*, meaning "high priest," and argues that this concept can be used for an inculturated Christology suitable for African people. As Molobi, quoting Okoye, argues,[2] "African Theology is meant to reflect on the gospel, Christian tradition, and the total reality in an African manner and from the perspectives of an African worldview." In essence, this means that theology premised on African cultural perspectives seeks to give an African expression to Christianity. Beginning by

---

1. Waruta "Who Is Jesus Christ for Africans Today?," 40.
2. Molobi, "African, Black and AIC Theologies," 494.

articulating the socioreligious system of the Luo people, this paper therefore builds a theology of the high priest as understood by this community. The paper also looks at the relevance of *Ker* Christology for African people, and concludes by presenting some limitations to the christological model.

The Socioreligious System of the Luo People

The history of how the Luo people came to settle in Western Kenya around Lake Victoria has been well documented.[3] The Luo have an intricate web of clans which are used to form semi-autonomous social and quasi-political units. This autonomy is facilitated by, and is therefore a factor in the cohesion created by common clanship traced to the great ancestor Ramogi Ajwang. In other words, membership of the clan is by right of birth and members trace their genealogy to their clan founder, a direct descendant of Ker Ramogi Ajwang.[4] In the past, a chief (*ruoth*) headed these clans. However, in the contemporary times the role of the traditional chief is largely obsolete; and has been taken over by governmental administration. In the traditional context, the position of a chief was normally inherited by the first son of the first wife (*mikayi*). The *ruoth* was neither a political nor a ritual leader in any official sense, but he always had a council of elders (*buch jo dongo*) to consult and guide him on political, social and religious issues. Note that this was at the clan level. Members of the *buch jo dongo* were recognized elders of the clan known for their wisdom, wealth, knowledge in religio-spiritual matters or prowess in battle. The clan eldership has largely remained intact where even today every clan has its council of elders. Every leader or chair of the clan eldership automatically becomes a member of the "national" council of elders, headed by the *Ker*. It needs to be noted that even though the Luo clans are semi-autonomous, they do have a unity of purpose, in that they help each other in times of calamity, such as drought, famine or war, and they intermarry. Their common ancestry binds them together. They look to their great ancestor Ker Ramogi Ajwang and the office of the *Ker*[5] as a unifying factor. The *Ker* sits as the chair of the powerful Luo council of elders (*buch jo dongo* / *buch adit*), which has the mandate to discuss matters affecting all the Luo people in East Africa and the diaspora.

---

3. See Ogot, *History of the Southern Luo*; Ochieng, "Transformation of a Bantu Settlement," 44–65.

4. Ker Ramogi Ajwang is believed to be the father of the Kenyan Luo; hence the Luo are often referred to as *Nyikwa Ramogi Ajwang* (grandchildren of Ramogi Ajwang).

5. According to Ogutu (*Ker in the 21st Century Luo Social Systems*, 23), the *Ker* is the custodian of the Luo religion, norms, values and culture, and his office is that of a *Ja-dolo* (priest).

Priesthood in Luo Traditional Religion and in the Bible

The concept of *dolo* (priesthood and priestly functions) in Luo cosmology is interesting in the sense that the *Ja-dolo* (priest) in Luo traditional religion is not a professional in the general sense of the word. It is only the *Ker* (high priest) who is considered a professional in his own right. The *Ja-dolo* could be any adult male in a family, extended family or clan. At the community level, the *Ker* performs the priestly duties. *Dolo*[6] depends on the nature and magnitude of the problem that calls for a *Ja-dolo* to act in a certain way. For *dolo* to be effective and relevant, it has to be situational: a reaction to certain situations that are about to happen or are in the process of happening and which could be detrimental to the well-being of the society. All aspects and elements of *dolo* fall on an individual. In addition, an array of other people such as wise men, diviners, medicine men and prophets are also involved, one way or another, and at different levels.

At the family and extended family level, the firstborn son of the main house (*ot maduong*[7]) acts as the *Ja-dolo*, while at the clan level an *Ajuoga* (diviner) would be called upon to *kiro gagi* (perform acts of divination)[8] to find the right person to act as the *Ja-dolo*. This person must be someone in whom there is *Juog-dolo* (a priestly spirit). *Dolo* could be done *ei od dhako* (at the household level) or at the homestead level, that is, the home of a family, polygamous or monogamous, where the sons of the head of that family (*wuon pacho* or *wuon dala*) are also married. If a calamity befalls such a family, the *wuon pacho* might then become the *Ja-dolo*. At the clan level, after divination, the *Ja-dolo* is identified and acts accordingly, whereas at the communal level, the *Ker* is automatically the *Ja-dolo*.[9] As has been said, *dolo* must be situational for it to be relevant and effective, and it also depends on the nature and magnitude of the problem causing disharmony. There are several things that the *Ja-dolo* can do to bring about religious harmony and the general welfare of society. Some are as simple as praying to the rising sun. At other times, the *Ja-dolo* is expected to perform certain religious practices, such as *kwayo* (supplication), *sayo* (petition), *lamo* (prayer), *timo liswa* (pouring libation) or *timo/chiwo misango* (offering sacrifices).

---

6. The concept of *dolo* encompasses all the ideologies and activities concerning the well-being of the people in the family, clan or community – that is, correcting any works by people or spirits that might negate this well-being.

7. "Main house" here refers to the genealogy of the firstborn sons of the family.

8. Also known in Luo as *gwa jawo* (performing acts of divination).

9. For a detailed historical analysis and contemporary explanation of the concept of *Ker* among the Luo people, see Ogutu, *Ker in the 21st Century Luo Social Systems*.

According to the *Theological Word Book of the Old Testament*,[10] men, in the beginning, served at sacrifices as the priests (Gen 4:3; Job 1:5), and by Noah's time, priestly ministration had become the responsibility of the patriarchal family head (Gen 8:20; 12:8; Job 1:5; Exod 19:22, 24). The first mention of a priest (Hebrew: *kohen*) in the Bible is in Genesis 14:18, where Melchizedek is called a priest of God Most High. The second mention is in Exodus 18:1, where Jethro, father-in-law to Moses, is identified as the priest of Midian. In Exodus 28, God chooses Aaron and his sons from among the Israelites to be his priests. It was only the sons of Aaron who were to serve as priests of Yahweh (Num 3:5; 4:33). All priests were Levites because Aaron was a grandson of Levi, but not all Levites were priests. The office of high priest[11] (Hebrew: *hakkohen haggadol*) was exercised by the eldest representative of Eleazer's family.

The New Testament presents two different pictures of the priesthood. On the one hand, it presents the priesthood as being in continuity with the Old Testament understanding of priesthood. References to priests and high priests in the gospels and Acts assume a historical and religious continuity with the Old Testament, as evidenced by the fact that Jesus recognized the lawful functions of the priest (Matt 8:4; Mark 1:44; Luke 5:14; 17:14). The other picture presented in the New Testament is of the priests and the high priest conflicting with the gospel and the mission of Jesus Christ.[12] The priests and the high priest were not alone in their opposition to Christ; they were joined by the Pharisees (John 12:1; 18:19–24) and the Sanhedrin (Luke 23:13; 24:20), as well as by the scribes (Matt 2:4; 20:18; 21:15). The high priest in the New Testament was also the president of the Sanhedrin, that is, the Jewish Supreme Council.

The functions of the priest were to teach the Israelites all the statutes that the Lord had spoken to them through Moses (Lev 10:11), and to offer sacrifices of purification on behalf of the people (Lev 12:6–7; 13:2–3, 9–10, 18–19, 24–25). They also offered sacrifices to the Lord on behalf of the people after performing the preliminary rites, such as hand cleaning and slaughtering and washing the offered animal (Lev 1:1–9). Then the priest continued and finished the sacrificial ritual at the altar, acting as the intermediary between the people and God (Lev 1:5–9). The priests also served as military chaplains, accompanying Israel's armies to the battlefields (Num 31:6). The high priest performed certain specific duties, such as representing the Israelites before God to offer sacrifices of atonement in the holy of holies of the tabernacle on

---

10. Harris, Archer and Waltke, *Theological Wordbook*, 431.
11. See Exod 31:10; Lev 4:3; 21:10.
12. See Matt 12:1–7; 26–27; 28:11; Mark 2:23–27; Luke 6:1–5; John 7:32, 45; 11:47.

the Day of Atonement. The high priest was also to ascertain the will of God by using the ephod (1 Sam 23:6–12) and the Urim and Thummim (Num 27:21; Deut 33:8; 1 Sam 14:41; 28:6; Ezra 2:63).

The New Testament, particularly the epistle to the Hebrews, is at pains to prove that the Christian faith is superior to and has replaced the Old Testament patterns of worship with its priestly rules. George Ladd[13] says that the author of the book of Hebrews seeks to demonstrate that the Old Testament priests were inadequate because they were mortal men (Heb 7:23–24) who had to offer sacrifices for their own sins as well as for those of other people. He says that Hebrews, on several occasions, describes the inadequacy of the Old Testament era in terms of failure to bring people to perfection.[14] The central theme in the Christology of Hebrews is the high priesthood of Christ, which is far superior to the Aaronic priesthood.[15]

As the followers of Jesus Christ, African Christians will want to view Jesus Christ from their religious consciousness. Waruta says that the Jesus who deals with Africans and their existential situation in a real and dynamic way will be comprehensible to the African people.[16] He goes on to say that "Africans are not interested in suffering through their problems now while waiting for the bliss of heaven." On the contrary, "Africans want a leader who shows them the way to liberation now: *liberation from diseases, oppression, hunger, fear and death.*"[17] Hence the high priesthood of Jesus Christ, which is the high priesthood par excellence, mediates and intercedes on behalf of the people of God, including Africans (Heb 7:25; 9:12, 24). Jesus Christ is the High Priest who offers the sacrifice as well as being himself the sacrifice that is offered. This brings about the forgiveness of sins and leads to the people being reconciled to their God.

It is therefore clear that one can draw parallels between the priesthood in the Bible and the traditional religion of the Luo people. The *Ker* of the Luo people can beseech the Supreme Being and offer sacrifices so that the entire community might be saved from an impending calamity. Through his sacrifice, Jesus Christ, as High Priest, destroys the one who has the power of death, that is, the devil. In so doing, he frees those held in slavery by the fear of death.

---

13. Ladd, *Theology of the New Testament*, 375.
14. See Heb 2:11; 9:9; 7:11–19; 10:1; 6:1.
15. The Aaronic priesthood is the priesthood that was initiated by God in Exod 28.
16. Waruta, "Who Is Jesus Christ for Africans Today?," 51.
17. Waruta, 51–52. Emphasis mine.

Toward an African Christology of *Ker* (High Priest)

It is important at this juncture to give a brief definition of the term "Christology." Justin Ukpong[18] says that Christology is a comprehensive term for the statement of the identity and significance of Jesus; it involves the interpretation of the person of Jesus, his fate, what he did and what he said, and the meaning of these for humanity, the cosmos, and God–humanity relations. In other words, Christology can be defined as the theology of the person, work and natures of Jesus Christ.

Since this paper deals with Christology from an African perspective, it is important to clarify that it is a Christology of inculturation.[19] Ukpong[20] gives three characteristics of this theological thinking: first, in expressing the Christian faith, using resources belonging to the culture being evangelized; second, that the good news of Jesus is pronounced to challenge and animate the culture; and finally, that it is done from the perspective of the culture and through the agency of an insider. Ukpong notes that in this approach of inculturation, the theological task consists of rethinking and re-expressing the original Christian message in an African cultural milieu. It is the task of confronting the Christian faith with African culture.[21] In the process, there is an interpenetration of both. Christian faith enlightens African culture, and the basic data of revelation contained in the Scriptures and traditions is critically re-examined for the purpose of giving them African cultural expressions. Thus there is an integration of faith and culture. And from it is born a new theological reflection that is African and Christian. In this approach, therefore, African theology means Christian faith attaining African cultural expressions. This is captured by Ojewole when he describes how Jesus Christ has to become all things to all people that he may save them: he springs forth from every culture and tradition to engrain himself in the hearts of the people; he seeks to make himself relevant to their experiences; he speaks human languages as they differ from culture to culture.[22]

---

18. Ukpong, "Current Theology," 34.

19. Although Jesse Mugambi in *From Liberation to Reconstruction*, 5, argues that those who do theology of inculturation are, in essence, doing a theology of liberation. This chapter does not share this view.

20. Ukpong, "Current Theology," 21.

21. See Stinton, *Jesus of Africa*.

22. Ojewole, "Christ, Our Ancestor," 1220.

Inculturation of the High Priesthood of Jesus Christ in the Context of the *Ker*

The point of departure for every Christology must be affirming the humanity and divinity of Jesus Christ. Any Christology that does not affirm, or downplays, either the humanity or the divinity of Christ is worthless. John Pobee says that diverse Christologies converge and agree on two issues: that Jesus is truly man and, at the same time, that he is truly divine.[23] It is these two points that any Christology is concerned to capture, and all christological titles come back to these two ideas. Pobee concludes by stating that the humanity and divinity of Jesus are the two nonnegotiable ideas of any authentic Christology.[24]

This christological study has chosen to explore the category of the high priesthood of Jesus Christ. As we have seen, the *Ker* principally plays the role of the high priest, whose supreme function and business is that of reconciling human beings to God through religious acts such as prayer, petition, supplication, pouring of libations or offering sacrifices; his work is thus more or less the same as the work of Jesus Christ. However, Jesus Christ is a better or perfect *Ker* (high priest) because he has accomplished the reconciliation of people to God. He not only prayed for people while he was here on earth, but he also keeps praying and interceding for them now in heaven. Jesus Christ is a better or perfect *Ker* because he has reconciled not only the Luo people to God, but all humanity throughout the whole world.

The way that the *Ker* reconciles people to God is chiefly through the sacrifice of animals at the designated shrines. The sacrifices offered need to be approved as acceptable by an *ajuoga* (diviner). The sacrifice that Jesus Christ offered was a once-and-for-all sacrifice that God accepted, for Christ offered himself as the sacrifice.[25] The *Ker* receives approval to perform his duties from both human beings and the Supreme Being. This approval and acceptance authenticates his work as a high priest. Similarly, Jesus Christ also receives acceptance and approval from those who believe in him (John 4:42; Heb 2:10–13; 6:19) as well as from God (Matt 3:16–17; Heb 7:20–21). The *Ker* is so chosen because the spirit of *Nyasaye* (God or the Supreme Being) is believed to be in him. This guides him to do the will of God. In addition to the spirit of God, he has *juog-Ker* (the spirit of the legendry *Ker*) upon him.

---

23. Pobee, *Toward an African Theology*, 46.
24. Pobee, 46.
25. There are some myths about the Luo offering human sacrifices to appease the ancestors as well as God. See Ogot's story "And the Rain Came." However, this practice cannot be ascertained.

This makes him a *Ker* in the manner of the legendry Ker Ramogi Ajwang. In a similar way, Jesus Christ was High Priest in the order of the legendary high priest Melchizedek (Heb 6:20; 7:17). But Jesus is not just a better or perfect *Ker*, he also has the Spirit of the living God (Matt 3:16), and his Spirit lives on forever, helping his people who believe in him (John 15:26; Acts 2:38–39).

The Luo people of Western Kenya see themselves as the grandchildren of the great Ker Ramogi Ajwang (*nyikwa Ramogi Ajwang*), without whom the Luo nation would not exist. This makes the legendary *Ker* the great ancestor of the Luo people. But Jesus Christ is the perfect *Ker* due to his human and divine nature.[26] He is thus also the great and perfect *Ker* of the Luo people. And to paraphrase John Pobee who described Jesus as the Great Ancestor (*Nana*, in the Akan language),[27] to say that Jesus is *Ker* is to let his standards reign supreme in personal orientation, in the structures of society, in economic processes and in politics. Therefore Jesus Christ, as the great and perfect *Ker*, is superior to all spiritual beings, ancestors and all living people, and hence has the power to judge, reward, punish and, above all, to forgive and purify, thus reconciling all people to Almighty God. Jesus Christ is also the great and perfect High Priest because, as a man, he was tempted in all things as all people are, yet he did not fall into any sin (Heb 4:15). The fact that Christ was sinless makes him the best possible mediator between people and God. This is also in line with the *Ker*, for the *Ker* should not be found in any *richo* (sin or bad habits). The *Ker* must be clean in all aspects of life, even though, humanly speaking, all people have their weaknesses. Thus Jesus Christ is the *Ker* par excellence, for in him there is no sin.

Therefore, because Jesus Christ has characteristics that are similar to those of the *Ker*, he can be incorporated into Luo cosmology and be introduced as the ideal *Ker*.

An Analysis of *Ker* Christology

In addition to his authority and powers, Jesus Christ, as the *Ker* par excellence,[28] has roles to perform. This includes the roles of liberation and reconciliation,

---

26. Even though the *Ker* of the Luo is believed to have the spirit of *Jok* (God) in him, this does not make him divine. He remains a human being until his death, when he lives on as a spirit.

27. Pobee, *Toward an African Theology*, 87.

28. Jesus Christ can assume the role of *Ker* either as God or as man. Even though for the Luo, God is detached from their daily lives, yet God is still *Kumu* (the one who helps mysteriously) and *Nyakalaga* (the omnipresent one). In this sense, Jesus Christ is the *Ker* par

being the guardian of religion, and offering leadership, in the sense that he led an exemplary and distinguished life that should be emulated by all people. We have discussed the fact that the concept of *dolo* (priesthood) is situational. The *Ja-dolo* (priest) or the *Ker* (high priest) performs his duties according to the situation in which the person being ministered to finds him- or herself. But the ultimate aim of *dolo* is that the person or people being ministered to may once again live in harmony with God, the spirit world, their fellow human beings and nature. *Dolo* needs to come in when this harmony is broken or has been interfered with. This harmony contributes a great deal to one's position in the afterlife. If a person is able to join the faithful ancestors and be among the benevolent spirits (*nyiseche*), then this shows that the person was already in salvation, according to the Luo concept of salvation. In this sense Jesus Christ, as the *Ker* par excellence, acts as the ultimate Savior of humanity. Jesus Christ did not only perform the sacrifice, he was also himself the perfect sacrifice that enabled all human beings to be reconciled to God and to each other, such that all those who come to him by faith can be in harmony with God, the spirit world, nature and other people. This is because, as God, Jesus Christ has the power and authority to bring about the salvation of humanity.

Traditionally, the people, by faith, would go to the *Ker* so that they might, in a sense, be "saved" from their problems and difficult situations. In the same manner, people can go to Jesus Christ, the perfect *Ker*, in order to receive, by faith, a better and long-lasting salvation, knowing that they are assured of eternal life with Jesus Christ himself and the saints who have gone before them. Jesus Christ, the perfect *Ker*, also has powers over evil spirits and evil forces. These evil spirits in Luo cosmology torment people by bringing about calamities such as disease, famine, drought, floods, storms and even death. They instill fear in people. Yet Jesus Christ has powers over them and thus protects people from them. In the Gospel of Luke 8:22–56, there are narratives of Jesus Christ exercising his power to calm the storm in the lake and to rebuke evil spirits and cast them away from the people. Jesus also has powers over sickness and even death. Jesus Christ, as the perfect *Ker*, also has power and authority to teach, lead, and to shepherd his people. That is to say, he is very much concerned with the welfare of his people. Jesus himself said that he is the good shepherd (John 10:11) who lays down his life for his sheep. This means that he values his people more than his position: it was for this reason that he left his throne in glory for the cross.

---

excellence in that he is omnipresent and transcendent at the same time.

Ker Christology, therefore, aims at the reconciliation of human beings to their creator God. This is mainly achieved through the sacrifice offered by Jesus Christ of himself on the cross. This blends and ultimately unites with the goal of salvation for humankind. This is a holistic salvation that begins when people are still here on earth and extends to the hereafter. Thus, while the image of *Ker* is culturally limited to the Luo people, the concept of a high priest is not. It transcends different people in different continents.

Comparison with Other African Christological Models

One way in which Christology has been studied and propounded by African theologians, notably John Mbiti,[29] is by reflecting on the traditional titles of Jesus Christ to see if they resonate with African traditions. These titles include Son of God, Lord, Servant of God, Savior and Redeemer. Reflecting on these categories, Elizabeth Johnson and Susan Rakoczy say that some African people have a tradition of understanding a father–son relationship in God.[30] For example, the Shona people of Zimbabwe have a father–mother–son triad, while the Dogon people of West Africa talk of "son of God" as a symbol of the ordered universe. This category to some extent fits with *Ker* Christology, because in Luo mythology, the first *Ker*, Ramogi Ajwang, was created by God and placed on *Got Ramogi* (Ramogi's hill), where he fathered the Luo nation. Thus, in this sense, he can be referred to as *Wuod Nyasaye* (son of God). The only difficulty is that the Luo people hardly ever use this terminology for their great ancestor. It is used only to refer to the historical Jesus in Christian circles.

Other models that have been used for Jesus Christ in Africa include our Ancestor, Master of Initiation, Elder Brother, Chief and Healer. Scholars such as Charles Nyamiti[31] use this thematic approach to examine the mystery of Christ from either the perspective of the African worldview or from the angle of some particular theme taken from the African worldview or culture. Such a model of African Christology can address theological and pastoral concerns in an African context, and also has an affinity to the African worldview.

The ancestor Christology blends very well with *Ker* Christology, for in Luo cosmology, the first *Ker* is the proto-ancestor and the parent ancestor. He is also the great ancestor and the ancestor par excellence. Another model or image used by African theologians as a christological construction

---

29. Mbiti, *African Concepts of Christology*.
30. Johnson and Rakoczy, *Who Do You Say That I Am?*, 89.
31. Nyamiti, "African Christologies Today," 17–39.

is that of the healer or the traditional doctor. Nyamiti writes that Shorter discovered similarities between the African traditional medicine men and the techniques Jesus employed to heal, saying that both practiced a holistic form of healing on the physical, psychological, emotional, moral-spiritual, social and environmental levels.[32] This category can, to a certain extent, be ascribed to the *Ker* Christology. This is because both Jesus Christ and the *Ker* of the Luo people work for the holistic well-being of all people. Jesus Christ used several means to heal people when he performed miracles. The traditional *Ker* would, however, need to employ other specialists, especially medicine men/women and diviners, in cases where his powers were limited. Looking at the above discussion, Jesus as *Ker* falls into the two categories of mediator identified by Robert Falconer: living and spiritual.[33] This is because the *Ker* can be envisioned both as a living mediator and a spiritual mediator, because Africans understand the Supreme Being to be supremely transcendent; thus, they feel a need to approach him via an intermediary such as the *Ker*.[34]

Another African christological model commonly used is that of Christ as Chief. This to some extent draws on a biblical equivalent, namely *Kyrios* (Lord). For African theologians such as Françoise Kabasele,[35] "chief" (*mukalenge* in the Luba language) is a title of power and authority. Jesus, as Son of God, is also Chief because God is the Chief of the universe. This is one category that does not fit the *Ker* Christology because, for the Luo people, a *Ker* cannot be a political leader, whereas the chief is above all a political and military leader. For the Luo people, the chief is supposed to bring peace whether through peaceful or violent means; Jesus Christ, however, advocates peace through peaceful means. He is the Prince of peace. It must be pointed out that Luo Christian literature, including the Bible, uses the term *Ruoth* (Luo for "chief") to refer to Jesus Christ as Lord and also for God as the Lord God (*Ruoth Nyasaye*). The meaning of "chief" (*ruoth*) in Luo is different from the English "Lord" or the Hebrew *Adonai* because *ruoth* was not ascribed to God in the same manner as "Lord" or *Adonai*. The practice of ascribing the term *ruoth* to God began with Christian missionary activity in Luo country, enabling Luo Christians to perceive Jesus Christ as the victorious Lord over the powers of darkness, sickness and death.

---

32. Nyamiti, 28.
33. Falconer, *Spectacular Atonement*, 87.
34. Falconer, 87.
35. François Kabasele, "Christ as Chief," 103–15.

The Relevance of *Ker* Christology to African People

The question of the relevance of *Ker* Christology is significant because of the conceptual novelty regarding the person and place of Christ in African religiosity. As Potgieter and Magezi argue, "Africans are familiar with God; however, Christ is an unfamiliar concept."[36] The unfamiliarity of Christ in African religiosity was worsened by the emergence of Christ with the early Western missionaries, who presented him as a Western savior interested in the worldviews and problems arising in the Western world.[37] From this perspective, *Ker* Christology is premised in accordance with Mbiti's observation that theology stands or falls according to how it understands, translates and interprets Jesus Christ in a given time, place or situation, and that therefore Christian theology ought to be Christology.[38]

Jesus Christ as *Ker* is perfectly relevant for African peoples today since in this way they can comprehend him. This is because the model or category of *Ker* (high priest) is not a traditional concept that is fast fading into oblivion. On the contrary, the *Ker* is still very much alive and meaningful for the Luo and for Christian peoples in all walks of life. For Christians, especially those who ascribe to episcopal models of church polity, Jesus Christ is the Head of the church. He is the Chief Shepherd and the High Priest, under whom are other priests, being led by bishops, archbishops or the Pope (for Roman Catholics); this category is therefore very relevant for African peoples.

Second, as has been said, people encounter Jesus Christ differently within their diverse contexts and experiences. The African context and experiences are unique, unlike those of any other people in the world. African experiences to this day have included different forms of oppression such as slavery and the slave trade, apartheid, colonization, neo-colonization, economic oppression, gender oppression, and so on. Africans also continue to experience poverty amid abundance, famine and hunger, diseases such as HIV/AIDS, and other calamities. Jesus Christ, as *Ker*, has come to be the liberator of the African peoples, despite their diverse situations. He breaks down all oppressive structures so that people can experience life in abundance. However, the experiences of Africans have not all been negative, but positive as well. African people have triumphed over slavery, colonialism and apartheid. Jesus Christ, as *Ker*, has always been there to rejoice with them and help them to chart new ways forward. For example, after many African nations became independent,

---

36. Potgieter and Magezi, "Critical Assessment," 2.
37. Potgieter and Magezi.
38. Mbiti, *African Concepts of Christology*, 190.

and the new leaders inherited systems of oppression and corruption, the voice of Jesus Christ as *Ker* was heard in the words of his prophets such as Bishops Henry Okullu and Alexander Muge, and David Gitari in Kenya, Bishop Janani Luwum of Uganda, Archbishop Desmond Tutu of South Africa and the Reverend Timothy Njoya of Kenya. Furthermore, African people have never discarded their cultural heritage, which remains potent in their lives. Jesse Mugambi describes Africans as follows:

> On the one hand, they accepted the missionaries' norms who saw nothing valuable in African culture. On the other hand, the converts could not deny their own cultural identity. They could not substitute their denominational belonging for their cultural and religious heritage. Yet they could not become Europeans or Americans merely by adopting some aspects of the missionaries' outward norms of conduct.[39]

That being so, cultural aspects such as the high priest are still useful to African people in interpreting and explaining religious concepts, including those offered by contemporary religions such as Christianity. This is because, in the incarnation, "God in Christ fully identified with all mankind as the new Adam, acting from the ontological depth of his divine-human existence to save African Christians from sin and all its consequences, including death and opposing spiritual forces."[40]

Limitations of *Ker* Christology

There are several limitations in the development of a *Ker* Christology. For example, the title *Ker* is reserved exclusively for the use of a Luo male. No other person from any other tribe can be accorded the title *Ker*. Hence for Jesus Christ to be *Ker*, he has to be a Luo. It is a known fact that the historical Jesus was a Jewish man born in Galilee about two thousand years ago. This makes it impossible for Jesus Christ to be a Luo, although, as God, he transcends cultures and tribes. Also, the *Ker* of the Luo has to be an elder of the Luo, and as an elder, he has to have at least a *Mikayi* (first wife). Being polygamous is an added advantage. As is known, the historical Jesus of Nazareth never married and died as a young bachelor. There is no relationship or kinship between the Jesus of history and the Luo people. This presents some difficulties for Luo

---

39. Mugambi, "Christianity and the African Cultural Heritage," 519–20.
40. Magezi and Magezi, "Adamic Incarnational Christological Framework," 152.

people comprehending Jesus Christ as *Ker*, for in the Luo cosmology, God cannot become a man. There is no idea of incarnation among the Luo people. God is God, the Creator, while people are the creatures. Even though spirits can possess different creatures, objects or people, God cannot.

In recent times, the *Ker* of the Luo has become increasingly a cultural figure; a majority of the Luo people now belong to the Christian faith. Luo traditional religion is also increasingly becoming dormant as fewer people practice it. Many of the ideologies of the Luo religio-cultural ethos and practices have been "modernized" and assimilated into Christianity and have become Christian practices. This has left the office of *Ker* as merely an advisory office that is desperately trying to renew the Luo cultural ethos and practices.

Ker Christology, being a functional Christology, also emphasizes the humanity of Jesus over his divinity, creating a Christology that is too immanent at the expense of the transcendent Christ. This then raises serious ontological questions concerning the omnipotence and the omnipresence of Jesus Christ.

Conclusion

This paper reveals that using *Ker* as a christological model is a robust means for communicating Christ to the Luo people in their context. It is a model that can be used to introduce Jesus Christ to the Luo people. When the Luo ask, "Who is Christ for us?" they can comfortably say that Christ is their perfect *Ker*, the *Ker* par excellence, because he has the authority, power and ability to reconcile us to God. He is also able to deliver us from the troubles of this world, physical, spiritual or otherwise, thus ensuring our salvation in this world and guaranteeing our existence in the world of the hereafter.

However, it is also important to note that the title *Ker* is compelling in communicating Christ in his human nature at the expense of his divine nature. This is because it dwells particularly on the functionality of Christ. The use of human titles such as *Ker* to refer to Christ leads to an anthropocentric rather than a Christocentric view of Jesus Christ. This then reduces Christ from being immortal to mortal, thereby failing to communicate his ontology. As God, Jesus Christ cannot be compared to or equated to the *Ker*, who is human. Jesus Christ is worshipped, but the *Ker* is not worshipped. In addition, Christ cannot be equated to the *Ker* because he offers mediation between human beings and God through divine grace, an act of God, and not through human activities, such as those performed by the human *Ker* in offering sacrifices.

However, *Ker* Christology does have strength in the fact that it is a Christology of the high priest, and thus enjoys biblical parallels. Hence it would be easily acceptable to mainstream Christianity. In addition, the concept of a high priest is familiar to many peoples around the world. For example, the Maasai had the *Laibon*; the Nandi, the *Orkoiyot*; the Mijikenda, the *Simba Wanje* and the *Kaya* (shrine) elders. The Incas of South America had priests and high priests for their religion of the sun. The concept of the priesthood was also found in the Greco-Roman world, Asiatic religions and many other animist religions. Thus, it is not challenging to introduce Jesus Christ as a high priest to many peoples. This is in line with Magezi and Igba's argument that African Christian theology should endeavor to develop theologies that go beyond the African continent:[41] that is to say, African theology should bear in mind an overall goal of making specifically African contributions to the theology of the universal church. The significance of the task of African Christian theology is heightened by the spread of Christianity in Africa, along with the attendant need to remain faithful to the essentials of the Christian faith. This thinking is in tandem with Victor Ezigbo's conclusion that for the "biblical representation of Jesus Christ to remain meaningful and relevant in Africa, [theologians] must be allowed to engage a mutual integration with the cultural, religious and socio-economic experiences of Africans."[42]

Bibliography

Ezigbo, Victor. "Rethinking the Sources of African Contextual Christology." *Journal of Theology for Southern Africa* 132, no. 1 (2008): 53–57.

Falconer, Robert. *Spectacular Atonement: Envisioning the Cross of Christ in an African Perspective*. Johannesburg: South African Theological Seminary Press, 2015.

Harris, R. Laird, Gleason L. Archer Jr. and Bruce K. Waltke. *Theological Wordbook of the Old Testament*. Chicago: Moody, 2003.

Johnson, Elizabeth A., and Susan Rakoczy. *Who Do You Say That I Am? Introducing Contemporary Christology*. Pietermaritzburg: Cluster, 1997.

Kabasele, François. "Christ as Chief." In *Faces of Jesus in Africa*, edited by Robert J. Schreiter, 103–15. Maryknoll: Orbis, 1991.

Ladd, George E. *A Theology of the New Testament*. Cambridge: Lutterworth, 1974.

Magezi, Christopher, and Jacob T. Igba. "African Theology and African Christology: Difficulty and Complexity in Contemporary Definitions and Methodological Frameworks." *HTS Teologiese Studies/Theological Studies* 74, no. 1 (2018). DOI: 10.4102/hts.v74i1.4590.

---

41. Magezi and Igba, "African Theology and African Christology."
42. Ezigbo, "Rethinking the Sources," 53.

Magezi, V., and C. Magezi. "An Adamic Incarnational Christological Framework as a Theological Approach for African Contextual Ministry." *Missionalia: South African Journal of Missiology* 44, no. 2 (2016): 152–74.

Mbiti, John S. *Some African Concepts of Christology*. London: SPCK, 1972.

Molobi, V. S. "African, Black and AIC Theologies as the Main Historical Sources of Construct for an African Church." *Scriptura* 105 (2010): 494–506.

Mugambi, J. N. Kanyua. *From Liberation to Reconstruction: African Christian Theology after the Cold War*. Nairobi: East African Educational Publishers, 1995.

———. "Christianity and the African Cultural Heritage." In *Christianity and African Culture*, edited by J. N. K. Mugambi, 516–42. Nairobi: Acton, 2002.

Nyamiti, Charles. "African Christologies Today." In *Jesus in African Christianity*, edited by J. N. K. Mugambi and Laurenti Magesa, 17–39. Nairobi: Acton, 1987.

Ochieng, William. "The Transformation of a Bantu Settlement into a Luo Ruothdom: A Case Study of the Yimbo Community in Nyanza Up to 1900." In *History and Social Change in East Africa*, edited by B. A. Ogot, 44–65. Nairobi: East African Literature Bureau, 1976.

Ogot, B. A. *A History of the Southern Luo*. Nairobi: EAPH, 1967.

Ogot, Grace. "And the Rain Came." In *Land without Thunder*. Nairobi: EAPH, 1974.

Ogutu, G. E. M. *Ker in the 21st Century Luo Social Systems*. Kisumu: Sundowner Institute Press, 2002.

Ojewole, Afolarin Olutunde. "Christ, Our Ancestor." *Scholars Journal of Arts, Humanities and Social Sciences* 5, no. 9B (2017): 1220–27.

Pobee, John S. *Toward an African Theology*. Nashville: Abingdon Press, 1979.

Potgieter, R., and C. Magezi. "A Critical Assessment of Bediako's Incarnational Christological Model as a Response to the Foreignness of Christ in African Christianity." *In Die Skriflig* 50, no. 1 (2016): 1–9.

Stinton, Diane B. *Jesus of Africa: Voices of Contemporary African Christology*. Nairobi: Paulines Publications Africa, 2004.

Ukpong, Justin. "Current Theology: The Emergence of African Theologies." *Theological Studies* 45, no. 1 (1984): 501–36.

Waruta, Douglas W. "Who Is Jesus Christ for Africans Today? Prophet, Priest, Potentate." In *Jesus in African Christianity*, edited by J. N. K. Mugambi and Laurenti Magesa, 40–53. Nairobi: Acton, 1998.

14

The Forgiven and Forgiving Body of Christ

Musekura's Communal Perspective on Forgiveness in Dialogue with African Wisdom

Stephanie A. Lowery
*Theology Lecturer and BTh Program Coordinator,
Africa International University, Karen, Kenya*

Abstract

Célestin Musekura argues for the necessity of a communal, not merely individualistic, or even interpersonal, view of forgiveness. Communal forgiveness focuses on forgiveness between social groups and the effects of forgiveness for communities, not just individuals. Musekura maintains that understanding Christ's forgiveness is crucial for Christians, as they are called to offer similar forgiveness to others. To develop a more profound, contextualized understanding of forgiveness, African wisdom related to giving and forgiving is explored, to understand Musekura's perspective compared with traditional ones. African wisdom tends to commend forgiveness, offering various reasons why it is beneficial to both the individual and the community. However, while similarities exist, Christian forgiveness is rooted in the nature of the Triune God and the work at the cross, giving it a revolutionary character that exceeds other perspectives on forgiveness. Furthermore, for the concept of communal forgiveness to spread, more work needs to be done to identify and study biblical bases that will illustrate and root the concept.

Key words: Célestin Musekura, *ubuntu*, communal forgiveness, forgiveness, reconciliation, Desmond Tutu, Miroslav Volf, L. Gregory Jones, restorative justice, punitive justice

Introduction

Jesus loved to ask questions of those around him. Indeed, he asked so many questions that one writer published a book on the subject of Jesus's inquiries, entitled simply *Jesus Asked*.[1] One famous question Jesus posed to his disciples was, "Who do you say I am?" (Matt 16:15). This question is relevant to each Christian and his or her Christian community: each Christian needs to wrestle with the question of how to explain Jesus in his or her context. For example, some christological models in Africa emphasize Christ as mediator or redeemer, who, by his death, makes available forgiveness and reconciliation with God. The goal of this paper is to ponder the orthodoxy (right belief) and orthopraxy (right practice) of Christlike forgiveness. The forgiveness Christ offers is the basis for the Christian life, and Christians are commanded to forgive others *as they have been forgiven* by Christ. Therefore, the goal of this work is to deepen understanding of the forgiveness offered by Christ and of how his disciples, in turn, are to forgive others.

I will first explore what forgiveness entails (as well as briefly mention some objections to forgiving), before turning to an analysis of Musekura's argument for communal forgiveness. From there, I will move to a survey of African wisdom concerning forgiveness, and next propose some biblical foundations for collective forgiveness.

Forgiveness

To begin with, what is meant by forgiveness? Following Miroslav Volf, L. Gregory Jones and Célestin Musekura, forgiveness is here defined as a choice to release a guilty party; the victim gives up his or her right to seek revenge, absorbing a great pain (or cost) in order to have the opportunity for reconciliation. The very fact that a person would feel the need to forgive

---

1. Gempf, *Jesus Asked*. He addresses the Matt 16:15 question in ch. 6.

an offense indicates that something is wrong. Forgiveness does not ignore wrongs; instead, it acknowledges them and their seriousness. If a wrong had not occurred, forgiveness would be unnecessary, so by this definition, forgiveness is not overlooking or downplaying the seriousness of the victim's hurt.

The common advice to "forgive and forget" suggests that along with forgiveness should come forgetting. The one who forgives should then act as if the wrongdoer had never committed that particular wrong that was forgiven. Yet can a person truly remove a hurt from his or her memory, somehow wiping it from recall? It seems both impossible and possibly even wrong to try to remove some things from memory.[2] Further, is it wise to try to forget a wrong in this broken, sin-wounded world?[3] Miroslav Volf's *The End of Memory* ("end" in the sense of *telos*) delves deep into this topic, exploring the "*memory of wrongdoing suffered by a person who desires neither to hate nor to disregard but to love the wrongdoer.*"[4] Indeed, Volf recommends that remembering should be part of forgiveness in this fallen world. He argues that we must seek to remember rightly, as speaking the truth about a wrong is one aspect of justice: it brings us to condemn the wrong committed. This condemnation is wrapped up in the process of seeking reconciliation with the one who wronged us.[5]

Tutu argues that we must neither deny that wrongs have occurred (by commission or omission) nor demonize the wrongdoers. Speaking of the South African Truth and Reconciliation Commission, he notes that

> so frequently we in the commission were quite appalled at the depth of depravity to which human beings could sink and we would, most of us, say that those who committed such dastardly deeds were monstrous because the deeds were monstrous. But theology prevents us from doing this. Theology reminded me

---

2. Tutu, *No Future without Forgiveness*, argues that we should not try to forget or ignore wrongs, because "the past, far from disappearing or lying down or being quiet, has an embarrassing and persistent way of returning and haunting us unless it has in fact been dealt with adequately. Unless we look the beast in the eye we find it has an uncanny habit of returning to hold us hostage" (28).

3. For a biblical instance where "forgetting" is used in a relative manner – more to mean "not dwelling excessively upon" than "total removal from memory" – see Phil 3:1–13, where Paul recounts his heritage, then says that he "forgets" what is behind and presses on toward the goal (v. 13). Paul had very clear memories of past negative experiences he had endured for the sake of the gospel (2 Cor 11:21–27), so "forgetting" must mean something other than the denial of past wrongs, or complete amnesia with regard to the same.

4. Volf, *End of Memory*, 9, emphasis original.

5. Volf, 15.

that, however diabolical the act, it did not turn the perpetrator into a demon.[6]

Instead, the wrongdoer must be seen as a human, because "if perpetrators were to be despaired of as monsters and demons, then we were thereby letting accountability go out the window because we were then declaring that they were not moral agents to be held responsible for the deeds they had committed."[7] Instead, Tutu insists wrongdoers must be treated as responsible agents. But what about those memories of being hurt? Volf argues that the key is what we do with our memories of hurts suffered, and how we allow those memories to shape our identities.[8] Once Christ returns and restores the world, freeing it from all sin, then perhaps we may truly and fully forget. As Volf puts it, "memories of sin can end only *after* the sins have been named and condemned and the sinners transformed."[9]

Another counter to the advice to "forgive and forget" is that seeking actually to forget a wrong can be shortsighted. If we forget, we are not seeking to mend the circumstances which first brought about that wrong. Indeed, it is as if we are denying the wrong happened, which would harm the victims all over again.[10] If we desire to resist repeating the offense, we must remember it.

What about the accusation of some that forgiveness negates justice? Célestin Musekura, L. Gregory Jones, Miroslav Volf and Tutu all reject this idea. They appeal to an important difference between punitive or retributive justice – which has the end goal of punishing the offender – and restorative justice, which has the end goal of reconciliation. Musekura notes that some thinkers oppose forgiveness because they think forgiveness undermines justice.[11] Musekura disagrees with this view; Tutu also addresses this objection: "One might go on to say that perhaps justice fails to be done only if the concept we entertain of justice is retributive justice, whose chief goal is to be punitive," but

> we contend that there is another kind of justice, restorative justice, which was characteristic of traditional African jurisprudence. Here the central concern is not retribution or punishment. In the

---

6. Tutu, *No Future without Forgiveness*, 83.
7. Tutu, 83.
8. Volf, *End of Memory*, 24–26.
9. Volf, 137.
10. Tutu, *No Future without Forgiveness*, 28–29.
11. Musekura, *Contemporary Models of Forgiveness*, 21–22.

spirit of *ubuntu*, the central concern is the healing of breaches, the redressing of imbalances, the restoration of broken relationships.[12]

Tutu's book describes the work and goals of the South African Truth and Reconciliation Commission, and assists in understanding how forgiveness (whether between communities or individuals) has effects on communities. In other words, punishment is not ignored in either view, but with restorative justice, the goal is to move beyond punishment and seek to restore relationships. Certainly, forgiveness can be rejected or abused, but ultimately forgiveness offers a chance for reconciliation.

The New Testament repeatedly reminds Christians of the necessity of forgiveness. For instance, Jesus's disciples are commanded to forgive if we desire God's forgiveness, to forgive seventy times seven, and to forgive as we have been forgiven (Matt 6:12–15; Luke 6:37–38; Matt 18:21–22; Col 3:13). Tutu points out that one reason why we offer forgiveness to wrongdoers is because Scripture makes it quite clear that God offers that costly forgiveness to humans.[13] The obvious question then is: *How* has God forgiven sinful humans?

Christian Communal Forgiveness

Christian theologians have long agreed on Christian forgiveness: Christians are to forgive because we have first received forgiveness from God, while we were still his enemies (Rom 5:10). It is this prior divine forgiveness that provides the foundation and motivation for Christians to offer forgiveness to others.[14] One could say that the divine forgiveness is the beginning of our story as adopted sons and daughters, and should indeed provide direction for how we continue to live out our new identity.

There has rightly been a great deal written about Christ's work on the cross; however, Rwandan Célestin Musekura emphasizes that until recent decades there has been much less research from a Christian perspective about forgiveness offered by humans.[15] Musekura's work addresses human forgiveness from a Christian perspective, bringing out an aspect that has been generally overlooked: namely, communal forgiveness. He argues that forgiveness between communities and the effects of forgiveness on communities must be addressed:

---

12. Tutu, *No Future without Forgiveness*, 54–55.
13. Tutu, 84.
14. For instance, see Tutu, 84–85; Volf, *End of Memory*, 114–26.
15. Musekura, *Contemporary Models of Forgiveness*, 4. For a popular-level work, see Jones and Musekura, *Forgiving as We've Been Forgiven*.

for example, in his setting, forgiveness between Hutu and Tutsi, as well as between the Rwandan church and the Western church, which did not take steps to intervene in the genocide.[16]

Thus far, there is generally agreement. However, Musekura's work identifies a blind spot in Christian writings on forgiveness: these works tend to view forgiveness as individualistic or interpersonal. In other words, many are overly focused on the individual from a therapeutic angle, meaning they explore the benefits of forgiving to the one who forgives, benefits such as freedom from the burden of bitterness, and so forth. The emphasis here is on how choosing to ignore sets an individual free from the burden of unhappy feelings. This may be called an atomistic view of the person, exploring how forgiving will benefit that individual. However, there are many cases where forgiveness is much more relational than this portrayal, situations where forgiveness affects the relationship between individuals. Interpersonal views of forgiveness explore forgiveness as a transaction of sorts between two individuals, studying how forgiveness affects both parties.

Musekura's contention is that both of these perspectives are insufficient. He argues that in our age, many conflicts are between groups, not just individuals.[17] Therefore, to restrict our study of forgiveness to individuals is shortsighted and dangerous; we also need to explore the effects of forgiveness on and within communities. Even when one person forgives another, the health of their relationship will have repercussions in the various communities to which those two belong. So he is urging a consideration of communal forgiveness, "a forgiveness that strengthens and maintains the unity of spiritual and social communities in which the church is called to bear witness."[18] Another way to say this is that we need to widen our perspectives on forgiveness and see how it applies to groups and has effects beyond the parties directly involved.

Thus, Musekura alleges that from an African perspective of *ubuntu*, where my humanity is bound up inextricably with other humans, we must think further about forgiveness in communal settings and between communities. Indeed, traditional African cultures do bear examples of such an approach. In some cultures in Africa, there was a means of establishing peace in a community. The elders of that community would gather to discuss a given issue and decide how to settle it. Once the elders agreed to forgive a particular party, there were binding rituals that would follow so that all in the community

---

16. Musekura, *Contemporary Models of Forgiveness*, 4.
17. Musekura, 17.
18. Musekura, 5.

could be united on the issue. To acknowledge and seek to redress the wrong, the offending party would be instructed about what form reparations would take. After this resolution, no one was permitted to raise this issue again or object that they had not forgiven.[19] In other words, there was indeed a culturally approved means of addressing forgiveness communally, implicitly recognizing that forgiveness was needed for the community's health. This same linkage of *ubuntu* and forgiveness is seen in Tutu's *No Future without Forgiveness*, where he argues that both the victim and the offender, by virtue of their shared humanity, were harmed by apartheid.[20]

According to L. Gregory Jones, baptism "provides the initiation into God's story of forgiving and reconciling love . . . In response, people are called to embody that forgiveness by unlearning patterns of sin and struggling for reconciliation." Christian forgiveness

> is at once an expression of a commitment to a way of life, the cruciform life of holiness in which people cast off their "old" selves and learn to live in communion with God and with one another, and a means of seeking reconciliation in the midst of particular sins, specific instances of brokenness.[21]

Another way we might say this is that the divine forgiveness offers us absolution as well as a new identity, and we are then called to manifest that new identity in offering "forgiving love" to others.[22]

For Jones, Volf and Musekura, the Christian identity is based on knowing ourselves as forgiven sinners. This is a call back to the gospel, which begins with God in Christ acting on behalf of those who oppose him. Indeed, it is because *we* have received grace that we are expected to *offer* that grace to others. Jones notes that non-Christians, too, can seek to be more forgiving, and he agrees that "there is a crying, urgent need for people . . . to become more forgiving in their relations with one another. But for Christians this can only happen when we simultaneously learn to embody what it means to be *forgiven* – by

---

19. Heartfelt thanks to Prof. James Nkansah-Obrempong and Adamson Nkandu, who informed me about this process in their respective cultures. This indicates that there are cultural bases on which the church in Africa could develop a contextually appropriate Christian forgiveness and reconciliation process.

20. For example, Tutu, *No Future without Forgiveness*, 103–4, 196.

21. Jones, *Embodying Forgiveness*, 5.

22. I am indebted to Festo Kivengere for this phrase (Kivengere with Smoker, *Revolutionary Love*). For a detailed study of Kivengere's message of reconciliation, see Olwa, *Missionary of Reconciliation*.

God and by one another."²³ When we acknowledge our sin and lack of merit and the immeasurable grace given by God, it is hoped we will then extend the grace of forgiveness to others.

In Matthew 18, Jesus tells the parable of the unforgiving servant, who has been forgiven an incredibly large debt by his master but then refuses to forgive a relatively small debt of a fellow servant. The parable concludes with the master berating the forgiven servant:

> Then his master summoned him and said to him, "You wicked servant! I forgave you all that debt because you pleaded with me. And should not you have had mercy on your fellow servant, as I had mercy on you?" And in anger, his master delivered him to the jailers, until he should pay all his debt. So also my heavenly Father will do to every one of you, if you do not forgive your brother from your heart. (Matt 18:32–35 ESV)

Most Christians, then, affirm that we are to forgive others, not just because it benefits me (what Jones and Musekura call "therapeutic forgiveness") or even brings healing in a relationship, but because, in doing so, we are imitating Christ. We forgive because – and as – we have been forgiven: freely, with costly love. We forgive to be ambassadors of reconciliation (2 Cor 5:18–20). Indeed, Christ's work at the cross is the embodiment of communal reconciliation: in his sacrificial purging of our sins, he modeled forgiveness and reconciliation that affects communities.

Contributions from African Wisdom

The African continent is full of wisdom passed along for centuries, so it will only be possible to sample some of the proverbs and sayings on this topic. Included are wisdom sayings related to forgiveness, as well as ones that touch on peace and reconciliation. The goal of this brief survey is to understand more about the context in which the Christian message of forgiveness is received, and also to identify points of continuity and discontinuity that may need to be addressed when discussing Christian forgiveness.

An article by John S. Mbiti provides a helpful bridge between Musekura's work and African wisdom.²⁴ Mbiti's presentation examines some prayers which address the topic of peace and reconciliation. A prayer of the Wapokomo

---

23. Jones, *Embodying Forgiveness*, 47.
24. Mbiti, "Never Break the Pot."

people of Kenya indicates their belief that peace comes from the divine, and that peace contains both personal and communal dimensions.[25] It can and should be personally appropriated. Further, peace "penetrates into the heart of the individual and does not vanish into thin air. Where there is no peace, there is suffering for the individual and the wider community suffers: children, husband, wife, family, village, neighbors, clan, society, and the environment (nature), even extending to peoples of the world."[26] When an individual has a peace-filled heart, it will shape that person's relationships with his or her community. There are three points here that will arise in the proverbs studied: God gives peace; peace must be internalized; and the individual's heart-state will affect the community in various ways.

What has just been said about peace can equally be said about its cousin, forgiveness. So just what do various proverbs have to say about forgiveness? A Cameroonian proverb states, "Those who refuse to forgive, break a bridge on which they must pass."[27] This can be taken from either a pragmatic angle (we forgive because we know we will later need to ask for forgiveness) or to advocate humility (acknowledging our own need for forgiveness ought to lead us to be forgiving toward others). Regardless, the basic advice is clear: forgiveness is the wise path to take!

While it is a wise way, it is not necessarily easy. For example, "the Bahema of Congo-Kinshasa calls a person 'noble' when he does not 'bear grudges,' or when he refuses to seek revenge and instead grants pardon even when his enemy does not ask this of him."[28] During initiation, young people learn several life skills, such as

> learning to yield in a conflict, even when one is in the right, in order not to endanger peace. Ultimately, this means forgiving, even where one's enemy cannot understand such a gesture and scorns it. Only one who is faithful in the face of all unfaithfulness is a truly "noble person" who takes thought for the growth of the vital force of the entire community.[29]

Again, questions may arise at this point: Does a person forgive to be seen as noble? Or does someone forgive because that person's character, his or her

---

25. I am not engaging with the argument of whether or not ATR god(s) are the same as the Christian God of the Bible. My desire is to highlight their belief in the origins of peace.
26. Mbiti, "Never Break the Pot."
27. Mbiti.
28. Bujo, *Foundations of an African Ethic*, 86.
29. Bujo, 86.

heart, truly is noble and desires to offer forgiveness? If it is the latter, then one can conclude that forgiveness is commended because it indicates a heart that is generous and (for)giving. Either way, forgiveness is held in high esteem.

Forgiveness is costly to the person offering it, yet forgiveness is critical for the community within which forgiver and forgiven live. Congolese Bénézet Bujo recounts a traditional myth that communicates the need for unconditional forgiveness. An uncle and nephew are each making unrealistic demands of the other. At the end of the story, the nephew's demand leads to the death of the uncle's daughter. Examining the unhappy cautionary tale, Bujo concludes that the "hardness of both [nephew's and uncle's] hearts, and the nephew's yearning for revenge, not only led to the death of the little daughter, but totally destroyed the entire existential community."[30] Bujo and Musekura agree in this regard: forgiveness affects interpersonal relationships as well as communal relationships.

Patrick Ibekwe records a pithy piece of wisdom from the Mongo in DRC: "War begets no good offspring."[31] This proverb reflects upon the consequences of war, noting that it simply results in more problems. Like sin, conflict grows by destroying others. A proverb exploring the opposite (forgiveness) might say something like, "Forgiveness multiplies joy and peace." While war leads to more harm, forgiveness can bring joy and peace that overflows beyond the original parties: forgiveness has communal effects.

Similarly, a Swahili proverb of East Africa recommends, "It is better to build bridges than walls."[32] This proverb, too, advises reconciliation and relationship instead of conflict and division. Bridges reduce the effects of "gaps" between sides, allowing them to be joined, while walls represent division. Another Swahili proverb claims that "forgiving is victory," while the Twi of Ghana suggest, "If you do not forgive a crime, you commit a crime."[33] Examples of proverbs and other forms of wisdom advocating forgiveness can quickly multiply. Generally, African wisdom agrees: to withhold forgiveness is to wrong another and to compound the problem. The communal effects of forgiveness are also noted.

A Kipsigis proverb provides this advice: "A calabash that is used to carry milk from dairy to a place of food crops is to be returned with posho to the dairy." Elijah K. Soi interprets this as "*a saying often quoted in advising people*

---

30. Bujo, 87.
31. Ibekwe, *Little Book of African Wisdom*, 72.
32. Ibekwe, 72.
33. Ibekwe, 129.

to remember to repay and reciprocate deeds of goodness and generosity done to them by others."[34] Besides enjoying the benefit of peaceful relationships, why would a person forgive? Two other proverbs Soi records expand on a key reason for offering forgiveness: *"A cow slips even though it has four legs. All men, even geniuses can make mistakes"*; and *"People have to be cleansed. People need to be purified of their sins."*[35] These proverbs advance the argument for forgiveness based not on its benefits, but as a result of remembering one's fallibility. In short, if all make mistakes and sin, and all need cleansing, then it behooves us to offer each other grace and forgiveness, just as others have offered us the same.

This Kipsigis wisdom perhaps comes closest to Musekura's argument that Christians need to begin by acknowledging themselves as forgiven by Christ, and on that basis to offer forgiveness to others. We do not forgive because it benefits us, or only because other (sinful) humans have forgiven us. We must begin by realizing our own need for the costly forgiveness that only God can give, as he is ultimately the one we have sinned against. The reality of the sinless Christ dying for sinful humanity illustrates clearly that Christlike forgiveness is motivated by grace: Christ prayed for his enemies who were crucifying him. The life and death of Christ, the perfectly obedient Son, and final sacrifice is the beginning of the Christian's story; it is the basis on which a person can enter the kingdom of God.

In short, from a biblical perspective, human forgiveness is based on its predecessor, divine forgiveness. God desires that the forgiveness of our debt will lead us likewise to be a people known for forgiving others, as this is one witness that we are indeed a new creation in Christ. So Christian forgiveness is distinct in terms of its basis (the work of Christ) and at least one of its motives (to forgive as we have been forgiven, thus demonstrating our gratitude for what our heavenly Father has done for us). Christian forgiveness is also radical because it tells of a God who has been offended by human sin but nevertheless takes the initiative to forgive and reconcile with the offenders, paying the ultimate cost for this divine peace.

John S. Mbiti's studies led him to conclude that though there are various tales in African Traditional Religions (ATRs) of how God and humans became estranged, they offer no hope of a future reconciliation and restoration.[36] Here, too, Christianity is unique in its message of hope, promising that the

---

34. Soi, *Kipsigis Words of Wisdom*, 2, emphasis original.
35. Soi, 9, 18, emphasis original.
36. Mbiti, *African Religions and Philosophy*, 98.

damage humans have done will one day be completely undone by God. Mbiti concluded that

> behind these fleeting glimpses of the original state and bliss of man, whether they are rich or shadowy, there lie the tantalizing and unattained gift of the resurrection, the loss of human immortality and the monster of death. Here African religions and philosophy must admit a defeat: they have supplied no solution.

Indeed, "these traditional religions cannot but remain tribal and nationalistic, since they do not offer for mankind at large a way of 'escape,' a message of 'redemption' (however that might be conceived)."[37] Whether they are compared with other world religions in general (as Mbiti does) or with Christianity specifically, ATRs fall short in this area.

The story of redemption through Christ is indeed radical, and this story is a key reason for Christians to forgive others. Musekura argues specifically for a communal view of forgiveness, a view that takes more consideration of forgiveness between communities and interpersonal forgiveness, which affects communities. African cultures have tended to emphasize community, so it is not surprising to see African wisdom affirming the *ubuntu* philosophy to which Musekura refers. Unfortunately, Musekura does not provide much exploration of communal forgiveness from a biblical perspective. Below I suggest a way forward by identifying and briefly commenting on some biblical examples of communal forgiveness and reconciliation, as begun by Christ and pursued by his body.

Biblical Foundations for Christian Communal Forgiveness

A critic may ask: Does the above definition of forgiveness overlook the demands of justice? Has God's righteousness or justice been "set aside" in some way, to offer forgiveness to sinners? Most importantly, do we see any biblical evidence to support adopting a communal perspective on forgiveness? Examining the biblical record can help bring clarity on what forgiveness is and how it functions.

The first Old Testament example of God's justice and forgiveness intertwined together, along with the promise of a redeemed future, is found in Genesis 3, after the fall. An immediate consequence of Adam and Eve's sin is alienation: they attempt to hide from God, they begin blaming each other,

---

37. Mbiti, 99.

and God predicts that even the ground itself will become hostile to them. God's righteousness and justice can be seen clearly in that address to Adam and Eve, as well as the serpent, as he declares the consequences of their sin. At the same time, God does not leave Adam and Eve without hope or a future. God addresses the demands of justice – the price of sin will be paid – but also promises to undo the effects of sin by providing a redeemer who will defeat and destroy Satan (Gen 3:15).

Another Old Testament example that can assist in understanding the communal effects of interpersonal forgiveness is Jacob's return to his homeland when he meets and asks forgiveness of his brother Esau, whom Jacob had wronged (Gen 32–33). Note that Jacob plans to appease – and partly repay – Esau, so that Jacob's past offense might be forgiven (32:13–20). Jacob realized that some gesture would be necessary to indicate that his repentance was sincere. The following chapter recounts the forgiveness and reconciliation between them; as imperfect and shaky as they were, the resulting agreement between Jacob and Esau meant peace for Jacob personally and for all those who were journeying with him. What began as interpersonal forgiveness affected the entire community with Jacob.

The best way to grasp how justice and forgiveness are related is to examine the cross. Indeed, we must study the cross if we are to fulfill the command to forgive as we have been forgiven. Like Musekura, Croatian Miroslav Volf studies forgiveness for personal reasons and with a communal emphasis. In *The End of Memory: Remembering Rightly in a Violent World*, Volf begins by recounting his own experiences in the former Yugoslavia in 1984, living under state surveillance and being interrogated. This topic is far from being abstract and theoretical for Volf; it is highly personal. He rejects retributive justice – the notion that the offender should receive due punishment, in equal measure to his or her offense – because, in his view, it violates a key command of Christ: "if I were to share this view [retributive justice], I would have to give up on a stance toward others that lies at the heart of the Christian faith – love of the enemy, love that does not exclude the concern for justice but goes beyond it."[38] What does Volf mean by suggesting that Christian love must include but go beyond justice?

At its heart, Volf's argument for love surpassing the demands of justice is based on the cross. The cross of Christ indicates the necessity for sins to be punished, for the price to be paid, for justice to be served. Naming wrongdoing

---

38. Volf, *End of Memory*, 10.

is one part of justice, Volf argues; wrongs must not be ignored or minimized.[39] However, at the cross, God's justice is satisfied, while wrongdoers are redeemed. Studying the exodus, Volf concludes that "the memory of wrong suffered becomes exemplary when God's command to do justice and love mercy directs it and God's liberation of the downtrodden undergirds it."[40] Another way to say this is that justice is one stage in that story, but not its end. The Israelites were commanded to focus not on the injustices done to them, but on God's deliverance. Indeed, God's justice and deliverance should be followed by his people showing mercy and compassion toward others. To seek only retributive justice would result in further destruction, Volf concludes.[41] Such justice can only bring more pain, not healing or hope for a better future. God's way includes justice but moves past it to offer restoration. The cross makes this clear: "Without disregarding justice, Christ's death pointed beyond the struggle for retributive justice for victims to the wonder of transforming grace for perpetrators and reconciliation of the two."[42] In Christ, God makes available the offer of forgiveness, which can be received by any sinner who repents. Volf concludes that "Christ's Passion embodies the core conviction that, under certain conditions, *the affirmed claims of justice should not count against the offender.*"[43]

Unsurprisingly, the forgiveness offered by Christ must be the foundation for Christian thoughts about and practice of forgiveness. What Volf and others highlight is that God's forgiveness in Christ includes but supersedes the demands of justice. The divine justice is accompanied by the offer of forgiveness and mercy; likewise, Christians are to offer restorative justice to those around them, regardless of the enormity of the offense. It will be costly and painful to the one forgiving, but we are commanded to do so nonetheless.

We may look at forgiveness from another angle, in terms of the results of being forgiven by God. The Pauline epistles portray the gospel as an offer of personal or individual peace with God, which leads to peace with others in God's family. God offers the costly gift of forgiveness to rebels – sinful humanity – thereby enabling humans who accept this gift to be restored to fellowship with the Triune God. The gracious self-giving of God means that the debt of sin has been paid, yet not in a way that requires humans to die for

---

39. Volf; see 18, 29, 55–56.
40. Volf, 106.
41. Volf, 110.
42. Volf, 111.
43. Volf, 111, emphasis original.

their sins. Instead, the Son robes himself in our flesh, atones for sins not his own, and ushers former rebels back into the divine communion. Upon entering that communion with God, the repentant person will find other repentant ones. The divine forgiveness, then, initiates and empowers forgiveness and reconciliation with other individuals and within and between communities. So what begins as interpersonal forgiveness – from God to an individual – has communal effects, just as Musekura emphasizes.

In the New Testament, one example of divine forgiveness leading to communal reconciliation is Acts 15. This passage presents an instance of two communities – Jewish Christians and gentile Christians – who had both received divine forgiveness and reconciliation.[44] As a result of the divine reconciliation, they are expected then to be reconciled to and fellowshipping with each other. The question was, how could they live together? Should gentile Christians conform to Jewish cultural practices? Peter and James, the brother of Jesus, argued against such an idea, and the council concluded that gentile Christians should refrain from four practices in order to be able to fellowship with their Jewish fellow believers without causing undue offense (Acts 15:22–29). An underlying assumption of the church leaders in that situation was that the two parties should be reconciled and indeed fellowshipping together; what united them – their "in Christ" identity, or new nature – was more important than their differences, and the gospel truth of this new identity needed to be seen in practice.

For Paul, reconciliation, and unity between Jewish and gentile believers, was a crucial demonstration of the gospel message. Paul describes the cross as accomplishing peace, a peace that reconciles individuals not just to God but also to each other. For this reason, Paul publicly confronted Peter when the latter withdrew from table fellowship with gentile Christians (Gal 2:11–14). Paul preaches that the gospel unites believers together in such a way that what formerly divided them is no longer important in light of their shared life in Christ (Gal 3:27–28). The work of Christ makes available divine forgiveness, which brings reconciliation with God (the vertical result of forgiveness, one might say); those who accept that forgiveness receive a new identity as well as the transformation of relationships with others who are "in Christ" (the horizontal extension of that forgiveness). As Schnelle puts it, "the change of status granted in baptism includes a real transformation of social relationships. The first pair of contrasts [Jew or Greek] is directed against the distinctions

---

44. I agree with the view that Acts 15 presents a different event from that described in Gal 2. For more on this, see Marshall, *Acts*, 242–48.

that divide all humanity into two classes: for Jews, the Jew/Gentile distinction; and for Greeks, the Greek/barbarian distinction."[45] Another way to frame this change Paul describes is to say that divine forgiveness is intended to have not just interpersonal effects (peace between God and the individual), but also communal effects: it overflows to and shapes a person's relationships with other forgiven people, regardless of the barriers that previously divided them. Because Jews and Gentiles (in the Gal 3 case) had been "clothed" in Christ by baptism, indicating their new birth, the act of baptism "counters and subverts ancient dichotomies exercised by humanity."[46] The divinely granted forgiveness was the impetus for the Jews and Greeks "in Christ" to reconcile, disregarding what previously had seemed important and even caused hostile attitudes toward each other. There is no mention in the text of Jews and Gentiles forgiving each other, but it is clear that the forgiveness of Christ changes social relationships (community). In Musekura's terms, forgiveness and reconciliation between Christ and the individual repentant sinner motivate Christians to begin acting differently in their human relationships. Thus, the implications of forgiveness move beyond the interpersonal and into the realm of the communal.

Again in Ephesians 2, Paul preaches this same point: what Christ has done on the cross offers forgiveness and reconciliation with God and bridges the previous divisions between fellow believers. First, Paul describes Gentile believers as having formerly been strangers and aliens of the covenant and promises of God (v. 12). Then he notes that in Christ, gentile believers are "brought near," not just to God but to Jewish Christians (vv. 13–14); in fact, these two groups of Christians are now one "new man," or a new type of humanity, the in-Christ, new-creation humanity (vv. 15–16). As a result, these two groups are now privileged to be described as members of God's household, built together into God's temple (vv. 19–22). Presumably, for these two, once-hostile groups to be reconciled to each other will take work on their parts, as they seek to view each other in a new light and to love each other with the love of Christ, unlearning old ways of relating to each other. Former grudges – and ongoing resentments or hurts – would need to be forgiven in order to maintain the Spirit-given unity (Eph 4:1–3).

From these brief examples, one can see that Scripture provides multiple instances of the effects of forgiveness on communities and that these examples warrant further study. As previously said, the New Testament contains definite commands that Christians are to forgive in ways similar to how God forgave us.

---

45. Schnelle, *Apostle Paul*, 291.
46. Niang, *Faith and Freedom*, 107.

While there is much benefit in further study of African wisdom, which affirms the value of community and often urges the benefits of forgiveness, both personally and communally, there is still a distinct and indeed crucial – in every sense of that word – difference between that and a biblically based view of forgiveness, due to the Trinitarian love and communion which led to Jesus going to the cross. Christian forgiveness begins with the Triune God, and is defined by Jesus and empowered by the Holy Spirit – and that makes all the difference.

Conclusion

The atonement is an ongoing area of interest in Christology; the work of Christ is indeed the foundation for Christian life. But have we done sufficient work in applying the doctrine in practice? Have we considered what it means to be forgiven by Christ, and then put into practice our knowledge about forgiveness?

My proposal is simple: if Musekura is right about a communal perspective on forgiveness being overlooked and yet urgent to address, and I believe he is, then more biblical work is needed to help communicate this concept to the average believer.[47] Similarly, I would hope that our institutions would teach the idea, and that our churches and Christian organizations would seek to practice it, so that we may truly be witnesses of an alternative way of living to a watching, and increasingly hostile, world. Christians are united with the Christ who forgives and reconciles, and so regardless of our different christological models, I hope we can agree that Christlike living – both individually and communally – means offering forgiveness and seeking reconciliation. And when we forgive as we have been forgiven, we are witnessing to God's kingdom and the work of Christ.

Bibliography

Bujo, Bénézet. *Foundations of an African Ethic: Beyond the Universal Claims of Western Morality*. Translated by Brian McNeil. Nairobi: Paulines Publications, 2003.

Gempf, Conrad. *Jesus Asked: What He Wanted to Know*. Grand Rapids: Zondervan, 2003.

Ibekwe, Patrick. *The Little Book of African Wisdom*. Oxford: New Internationalist, 2002.

---

47. As Samuel Bussey pointed out in his presentation at ASET in March 2020, pursuing communal forgiveness in church settings would mean more consideration of *how* the church can support this type of forgiveness (liturgically and otherwise).

Jones, L. Gregory. *Embodying Forgiveness: A Theological Analysis*. Grand Rapids: Eerdmans, 1995.

Jones, L. Gregory, and Célestin Musekura. *Forgiving as We've Been Forgiven: Community Practices for Making Peace. Resources for Reconciliation*. Downers Grove: InterVarsity Press, 2010.

Kivengere, Festo, with Dorothy Smoker. *Revolutionary Love*. 3rd ed. Moscow: Community Christian Ministries, 2016.

Marshall, I. Howard. *Acts*. Tyndale New Testament Commentaries 5. Leicester: InterVarsity Press, 1980.

Mbiti, John S. *African Religions and Philosophy*. London: Heinemann, 1969.

———. "'Never Break the Pot That Keeps You Together': Peace and Reconciliation in African Religion." *Dialogue and Alliance: Peacebuilding in Africa* 24, no. 1 (Spring/Summer 2010). http://www.upf.org/resources/speeches-and-articles/3226-js-mbiti-peace-and-reconciliation-in-african-religion.

Musekura, Célestin. *An Assessment of Contemporary Models of Forgiveness*. American University Studies Series 7, Theology and Religion 302. New York: Peter Lang, 2010.

Niang, Aliou Cissé. *Faith and Freedom in Galatia and Senegal: The Apostle Paul, Colonists and Sending Gods*. Bible Interpretation Series 97. Leiden: Brill, 2009.

Olwa, Alfred. *Missionary of Reconciliation: The Role of the Doctrine of Reconciliation in the Preaching of Bishop Festo Kivengere of Uganda between 1971–1988*. Carlisle: Langham Monographs, 2013.

Schnelle, Udo. *The Apostle Paul: His Life and Theology*. Translated by M. Eugene Boring. Grand Rapids: Baker Academic, 2005.

Soi, Elijah K. *Kipsigis Words of Wisdom*. Nairobi: Rift Valley Review Associates, 1984.

Tutu, Desmond Mpilo. *No Future without Forgiveness*. New York: Doubleday, 1999.

Volf, Miroslav. *The End of Memory: Remembering Rightly in a Violent World*. Grand Rapids: Eerdmans, 2006.

15

African Images of Christ

"Jesus as Healer": Narratives and Treatable but as Yet Incurable Illness

Thandi Soko-de Jong

PhD student, Protestant Theological University, Groningen, the Netherlands

Abstract

One important African image of Christ is "Jesus as Healer." There have been many studies on suffering and the prosperity gospel as they relate to faith and healing. Very little research, however, has been done concerning treatable but as yet incurable diseases. This paper focuses on narratives of "Jesus as Healer" from the perspective of faith communities responding to the question: "How do you understand 'Jesus as Healer' in situations of living with treatable but not yet curable illness?" I highlight some Pentecostal and Baptist insights that have so far emerged from my ongoing field research in Blantyre, Malawi. The empirical data reveals that images of Jesus as Healer in this liminal space (in which people whose conditions do not yet have a cure rely on biomedical treatment to sustain their health) are diverse even *within* communities of the same denomination. In this paper, I focus on three respondents whose experiences overlapped. They described God's sovereign will, how the Bible records stories of both healing and nonhealing, and how the healing goes beyond the physical to encompass the whole being. Their responses reflect their personal spiritual experiences, medical knowledge, exposure to chronic illness, and theologies that may not always necessarily fit (nor contradict) a denominational narrative, but add nuance and fresh perspectives. I will discuss the data using the *tcheni pa kalanka* (orthodoxy in context) ethos, which I am using in my ongoing research. Finally, the paper concludes with some ways the knowledge gained through this study contributes to ongoing theological conversations about "Jesus as Healer."

Key words: African images of Christ, Jesus as Healer, narratives of health, Malawi, liminality

Introduction

This paper discusses one of the most popular African images of Christ, "Jesus as Healer." On a broader scale, scholars such as Kofi Appiah-Kubi[1] and Diane Stinton[2] have highlighted some of the main contemporary African Christologies from which this image is derived. These Christologies include "Jesus the Great Physician,"[3] and "Jesus as Life-giver."[4] In this paper, the image of Jesus as Healer primarily falls within the Christologies of "Jesus the Great Physician" and "Jesus as Life-giver." This image has relevance as, according to some African theologians, it relates to Jesus's salvific power over all forms of oppression, including illness, particularly where it is caused or sustained by sociopolitical and socioeconomic injustice.[5]

The application of the image of Jesus as Healer is well known, not only among scholars but also in contexts where imagery based on healing passages in the gospels is used (such as in Christian hospitals) and where church teaching pays attention to this image. For example, I have heard many sermons on passages such as Matthew 9 (and Mark 5; Luke 8), which narrates the story of the woman who suffered from bleeding touching the hem of Jesus's garment; Mark 10:46–52, where we read that Jesus healed a blind man

---

1. Appiah-Kubi, "Christology," 76.
2. Stinton, *Jesus of Africa*. See also Dube, "Who Do You Say That I Am?," 346–67.
3. Appiah-Kubi, "Christology," 76.
4. According to Stinton, "Jesus as Life-giver" is a Christology that encompasses images of "Jesus as Healer" and "Jesus as Traditional Healer." See Stinton, *Jesus of Africa*, 54–108.
5. For further discussions on faith, well-being and social realities in the African context, see, for example, Ackerman, "From Mere Existence to Tenacious Endurance."

named Bartimaeus; and Mark 1:34a, in which Jesus healed many.[6] Based on passages like these, many pastors, church leaders and lay believers pray for the restoration of health for the sick. Thus, for many, Jesus's saving mission includes our holistic well-being.[7]

The image of Jesus as Healer is also visible in academic inquiries dealing with the topic of faith and illness, particularly in African countries that have been grappling with issues of health. Most notably, much research has gone into investigating the phenomenon of faith healing,[8] particularly in instances where the practice of beliefs clashes with that of biomedical agencies. For example, the World Council of Churches' publication *In the Name of Jesus! Healing in the Age of HIV*[9] brings together several African theologians, medical professionals and religious activists to interrogate the practice of faith healing in light of HIV/AIDS.

In this paper, I discuss some of the insights that show different ways in which evangelicals, particularly Pentecostals and Baptists, in Blantyre, Malawi, reflect on this image. The research is based on my ongoing doctoral research in Intercultural Theology, where I am exploring how faith communities understand "Jesus as Healer," particularly in situations of living with treatable but not yet curable or difficult to cure illnesses (e.g. hypertension, diabetes, asthma, HIV). The respondents in my research described their experiences of encountering situations of illness like those named above that defy the definite closure of certainty of a once-for-all cure. However, although their responses of faith adapted to their situations, they all referenced Bible narratives based on their faith responses. Thus, I find it helpful to (briefly) engage with their responses in this paper with reference to the ethos of *tcheni pa kalanka*. This term means "fixed to the core" (literally, "chain on the crank"), and the idea was developed by the Malawian Reformed community (Nkhoma Synod of the Church of Central Africa Presbyterian). The term recognizes that communities of faith constantly encounter changes in their social contexts and must find ways of responding to these changes using biblical hermeneutics that are

---

6. In the world of the gospels, sickness and ailments were often associated with evil and sin. Thus, while this paper focuses primarily on the physical aspects of illness, the author recognizes that the Bible passages cited bear significance beyond physical illness. See Kok, *New Perspectives*, xiii.

7. See, for example, Soko-de Jong, "Belief in a Liminal State of Health," 499–510.

8. In this paper, the term "faith healing" is understood in line with the *Cambridge Dictionary*'s definition: "the belief that sick people can be cured using the power of prayer and religious belief." Available online: https://dictionary.cambridge.org/dictionary/english/faith-healing.

9. Chitando and Klagba, *In the Name of Jesus!*

supported by their doctrines of faith. This means that believers observing *tcheni pa kalanka* constantly reflect on their social contexts using hermeneutics that are in line with their shared denominational beliefs. In other words, this method is about responding to all of life circumstances with one's (denominational) orthodox interpretation of the canon of Scripture. In this paper, *tcheni pa kalanka* means "hermeneutical orthodoxy in light of one's circumstances."

An Overview of African Images of Jesus as Healer

As noted above, there are several African images of "Jesus as Healer" that relate closely to this paper, and this paper responds primarily to those of "Jesus the Great Physician" and "Jesus the Life-giver." Considering Jesus as the Great Physician, the Ghanaian theologian Kofi Appiah-Kubi notes that many African Christians draw from biblical passages in which Jesus miraculously heals for an image of "the great physician, healer, and victor over worldly powers par excellence."[10] At the same time, passages such as John 10:10, in which Jesus declares that he came that "we might have life and have it more abundantly,"[11] overlaps with a traditional African concept of "life," "health" and "wellness."[12] For many, therefore, passages like John 10:10 depict Jesus as one who makes a "fuller" life possible for us. He is also, in turn, understood to make it possible to fulfill a fuller, holistic life according to an African traditional conceptualization of "life." According to Cameroonian theologian and sociologist Jean-Marc Ela, one's well-being is seen from a holistic perspective:

> Viewed as being more than biological, encompassing physical, mental, spiritual, social, and environmental wellbeing, illness signifies an unfortunate disruption of harmony in these factors. Organic causes may well be recognized, yet the overriding belief attributes sickness to spiritual or supernatural causes such as offending God or ancestral spirits, possession by evil spirits, witchcraft, breaking taboos, or curses from offended families or community members.[13]

---

10. Appiah-Kubi, "Christology," 76.

11. This is a paraphrasing of John 10:10 in the King James Version which states that, "The thief cometh not, but for to steal, and to kill, and to destroy: I am come that they might have life, and that they might have it more abundantly."

12. Stinton, *Jesus of Africa*, 62.

13. Ela, *My Faith as an African*, 44–50.

"Jesus as Healer" is an image that is also important in socioeconomic and sociopolitical discourses as they relate to issues of health. In his article "Jesus as Healer?," for instance, Cécé Kolié[14] argues that in light of the challenges that negatively impact health systems in many African nations, proclaiming Jesus as "the Great Healer" calls for a great deal of explaining to those suffering.[15] Appiah-Kubi puts it succinctly: "to many, Jesus came that we might have life and have it more abundantly. But the perturbing question is, where is this abundant life when all around us we see suffering, poverty, oppression, strife, envy, war and destruction?"[16]

It is beyond the scope of this paper to discuss the breadth of discourse relating to images of Jesus as Healer across Africa. Thus, we turn next to some of the study's respondents to discuss the images of Jesus as Healer that they bring into the discussion, based on their experiences and reflections on treatable but not yet curable illness.

Images of Jesus as Healer among Respondents in Blantyre, Malawi

As stated above, this paper forms part of an ongoing study that collected responses from interviewees in Blantyre, Malawi, from July to August 2019. It is important to note that the study targeted evangelical participants who self-identified as believers. Therefore, the respondents did not refer to faith beliefs outside of their particular evangelical traditions (i.e. African Traditional Religions and other faith systems were not reference points). It is beyond the scope of this paper to include the responses of all respondents. What follows is therefore based on a small sample of three respondents who were representative of the broader evangelical[17] study participants, specifically, Baptist and Pentecostal.[18]

The three respondents related to the topic of faith and health in ways that were both similar and different. One is a pastor (Baptist) living with bipolar disorder; another is a lay Christian (Pentecostal) living with lupus; and the third is a lay Christian (Pentecostal) and consultant physician. Their hermeneutical

---

14. Kolié, "Jesus as Healer," 128–50.

15. Kolié, 128.

16. Appiah-Kubi, "Christology," 76.

17. The three participants are understood to belong to churches that are part of the Evangelical Association of Malawi – a national association with expressed, shared evangelical beliefs.

18. In this paper, I refer to the respondents' church traditions (i.e. Pentecostal, Baptist) and not the specific names of their respective congregations.

approaches overlapped and can be said to confirm the two images discussed above, Jesus the Great Physician and Jesus the Life-giver. However, their responses held experiential particularities which added nuance, to the effect that even where the tradition and denomination were shared, there was a difference in perspective (influenced by personal spiritual experiences, medical knowledge, exposure to chronic illness, and theologies). I will refer to them as Participant 1, 2 and 3 respectively, due to the sensitive nature of issues of health.

Participant 1[19]

Participant 1 manages bipolar disorder. He is a Baptist pastor and church planter in the city of Blantyre. His image of Jesus as Healer is one that takes into account the fact that each biblical narrative of healing stands on its own, forming a mosaic of healing accounts. For him, Jesus's healing ministry is part of a broader biblical narrative *balanced* by not negating long illnesses or the absence of miraculous healing in some cases. To explain, he refers to Mark 5:25–34 (the narrative of the healing of the woman suffering from bleeding):

> The Bible narratives are honest and balanced when it comes to illness. In some cases, people got healed, such as the woman with the issue of blood. The Bible states that she was ill for twelve years (Mark 5:25–34) and that she was healed the moment she touched Jesus's garment. The Bible does not hide her [long] illness. We also read of illnesses that were not healed, such as in the case of Timothy. And in Galatians 4:14, Paul mentions his illness. So the Bible is frank about illness and presents both sides – both those who were healed and those who were not![20]

Participant 2[21]

Participant 2 is a consultant physician at Queen Elizabeth Hospital. She teaches undergraduate and postgraduate medical students at the University of Malawi's College of Medicine. She is also a lay member of a Pentecostal church in the city of Blantyre. Her image of Jesus as Healer is born out of paying careful attention to the healing narratives that help her uncover the more holistic nature of

---

19. Participant 1 is a Baptist minister and church planter.
20. Partcipant 1, in interview by author, Blantyre, 16 August 2019.
21. Participant 2 holds an MD and is a "Consultant Physician" in Blantyre, Malawi.

Jesus's ministry. She gave the following example of how she approaches the healing narratives of Jesus:

> The dramatic [healing] narratives of the Bible tend to focus on the cure. But when you look at the [less dramatic ones], like the story of the ten lepers, for instance, they weren't cured immediately upon meeting Jesus, but only after they had left. We don't know the time period; we assume it was the same day, but we don't know.[22]

Participant 3[23]

Participant 3 lives with lupus. She is also a lay Pentecostal Christian in Blantyre. She reflected on her personal experience with lupus to share how she understands Jesus as a Healer, particularly concerning the link some believe to exist between sin and illness. She believes that healing narratives found in the Bible point out that God's mysteries are never "black and white" regarding health and sin:[24]

> Ultimately, all glory goes back to God, regardless of the circumstances. For a long time, I struggled with this question because people would say I had a sin I had not repented of, or it was because of something I had done. But then you find those scriptures like John 9:3, where [Jesus] is saying, "It wasn't either the parents or the child. This was done so that the glory of God can be revealed." I began to realize that God might take this [lupus] away, or he might not. But for every day, I have the attitude that God still has me here, so there must be something that he wants me to do, whether it's to do with me being healed miraculously, or whether it's just for me to live my life, to the glory of who God is. As believers, where we tend to go wrong is when we allow illness to define who we are, rather than living outside of that and realizing that God has a far bigger purpose, regardless of our health conditions – and what we have to go through going to the hospital here and there, and having to buy expensive medications. So, as hard as it is, I just feel like God knows better than I do.[25]

---

22. Partcipant 2 in interview by author, Blantyre, 30 July 2019.
23. Participant 3 is a health activist and lives in Blantyre, Malawi.
24. This is not about beliefs concerning the fall; rather, it is about personal sin.
25. Participant 3, in interview by author, Blantyre, 30 July 2019.

The Respondents' Images of Jesus and Their Relevance for Catholicity

It is important to bring these personal experiences and the images of Jesus they present into conversation with other voices on healing in the worldwide church community. The importance of such a conversation can be drawn from the value of the notion of "catholicity." An Intercultural Theologian, Benno van den Toren defines catholicity in this context as follows:

> The catholicity of the church in the theological sense should not be reserved for the Roman Catholic Church. It refers to the reality that the church unites **Christ-believers** worldwide and in a great variety of cultural and social contexts. This notion moves beyond contextuality to interculturality in that it invites us to read the Scriptures with the church through the ages and worldwide. Only together will Christians be able to both discover the weaknesses of their particular readings and grow into the fullness of the knowledge of the love of God in Christ (cf. Ephesians 3:18).[26]

Respondents' Perspectives and Their Contextual Relevance

Thus, first, in terms of healing and catholicity, the respondents' images of Jesus as Healer above offer a fresh voice to ongoing discourses on faith and health in the evangelical church around the world. Specifically, a number of those interviewed in the wider group from which the three interviews here are drawn were Pentecostal or had some degree of Pentecostal/charismatic influence. Their views offered some divergence from the perspective many in the global church have of Pentecostals in Majority World countries such as Malawi. Additionally, the respondents did not adhere to the so-called prosperity gospel. Rather, they had what Participant 1 referred to as "balance" in their approach to narratives of illness and healing in the Bible. They paid attention to the range of narratives, not only to the ones Participant 2 described as the "dramatic" miracle stories.

Orthodoxy in a Broader Church Context

Second, much can be said about beliefs regarding healing and orthodoxy from

---

26. van den Toren, "Contextuality, Catholicity and Canonicity in Biblical Hermeneutics."

my ongoing research in the Malawian context.²⁷ The respondents seem to share in an ethos coined by the Nkhoma Presbyterian Synod of Malawi: *tcheni pa kalanka*. This ethos, which means literally "chain on the crank," simply means being Bible-centered in the face of new information, new perspectives on life or changing circumstances. Nkhoma Synod scholar Phoebe Chifungo describes it as an ethos that means the chain is fixed to its place or is fixed to its axis and is intact. Similarly, the faith community reflects on experiences by referring back to the Bible as it is the basis of their faith and "nothing or nobody can move them from this basis."²⁸ Put simply, it is about orthodoxy in the face of changing circumstances. This can be seen in, for example, Participant 1's comment describing how his interpretation of the Bible's narratives was influenced by his changing circumstances, while the essence of his interpretation of Jesus as the Healer has remained the same:

> God has a purpose for his will, and that is to humble us, as we see in the case of Paul (2 Cor 12:8–10). Looking at my own life, God healed my leg after years of not walking, but I suffer from bipolar disorder, and God has not healed me of that, to humble me and keep me dependent on him. So, it is safe to say that when God does not heal, it is not because he is cruel, but because he wants to keep us dependent on him and not on ourselves! That is the major reason why God chooses not to heal us.²⁹

Similarly, Participant 2 seems to echo the Reformed, Bible-centered approach of the *tcheni pa kalanka* ethos by emphasizing the importance of believers learning to read and understand the Bible. In regard to the topic of chronicity and Jesus's healing narratives, she pointed out that Jesus did, in fact, respond to illness on a case-by-case basis. Her example below of the ten persons with leprosy, and the Samaritan who returned to give thanks in particular (Luke 17:11–19), highlights the important point that Jesus responded to the whole person. That is, healing is ultimately about Jesus's relationship with us. In other words, Jesus's physical healing holds a spiritual dimension as well. Thus, in the case of the Samaritan with leprosy, he returned to thank Jesus for his physical healing, thereby showing his faith and in turn receiving salvation. This is the ultimate gift/miracle from God which provides validation for physical healing

---

27. This study includes Reformed, Pentecostal and liberation theology respondents' viewpoints.
28. For a fuller discussion, see Chifungo, "Women in the CCAP Nkhoma Synod."
29. Partcipant 1, in interview by author, Blantyre, 16 August 2019.

and gives glory to God. In terms of *tcheni pa kalanka*, this implies that there are multiple (orthodox) lessons that can be learned from Jesus's ministry as he dealt with people's diverse needs. Of the ten persons with leprosy, she relates:

> For me, the story of the lepers is fascinating because it focuses on more than physical healing. This implies that there are a lot of different ways Jesus answers prayer for healing that are so dependent on the individual and what his will is for that particular time. So, in the story of the lepers, ten people were healed, but only one came back to thank Jesus. And what did Jesus say? "Your faith has made you whole," which particularly means to me that he got much more of a whole package than the others. When you talk about chronic illnesses, they don't just affect you physically. They affect you emotionally, psychologically, as well as spiritually. So, to me, I feel like those are components that matter. We invest a lot in medicine to cure, but Jesus considers the individual and their circumstances.[30]

Influence from the Global Church

Finally, like many other Christians, the respondents draw from various global Christian voices in shaping elements of their faith, including images of Jesus as Healer. In that sense, we can safely say that images of Jesus as Healer are rarely only African. All three respondents constantly interacted with faith traditions from other parts of the world through travel, work, ministry, business, and so on. But they also participated in the theological formation of the worldwide evangelical faith community – through, for example, the influence of social media, music, literature and film. Perhaps this is best exemplified by Participant 3's reference to the 2019 American evangelical film *Breakthrough*:

> I was watching a film entitled *Breakthrough* yesterday. It's about a child who fell into frozen water and remained in it for a long time. He was not expected to survive. When he survived miraculously, a woman asked him: "Why you? My husband was sick and he did not survive." [Indeed] why does God choose some and not others? I feel like some of these things are God's mysteries, for him alone to know. If we knew everything, you know, there'd be no point in having a Creator God. But I just came to a place where I'm just

---

30. Participant 2, in interview by author, Blantyre, 16 August 2019.

at peace with: *maybe it will happen, maybe it will not happen*. But I'm going to choose to walk in a straight line.[31]

Conclusion

Many African Christians, in finding images of Jesus as the Great Physician and the Life-giver, draw from biblical passages in which Jesus intervenes miraculously and heals. In this paper, respondents gave the images of Jesus as a Healer that were important to them, based on their experiences and reflection on treatable but not yet curable illnesses. Their approach to Jesus as Healer can be said to confirm that, for them, Jesus is indeed the Great Physician and Life-giver, but, more than that, Jesus's response to human illnesses cannot be generalized. They read healing narratives critically and pointed out that these healing narratives were diverse.

Thus, in light of Jesus as Physician and Life-giver, Participant 1 displayed a theology that seemed to imply that the "abundant life" of John 10:10 was not contingent on whether a person's illness was cured. For him, Jesus's healing ministry was part of a broader, balanced biblical narrative, which was not a one-size-fits-all approach to illness but included cases of people like Timothy or Paul who lived with longer illnesses or health problems. Participant 2 further explored the process and meaning of healing, concluding that there are various ways of being healed (but not necessarily cured). She spoke of spiritual healing, pointing to the role salvation plays in the holistic well-being of an ill person. This also points to the realization that ultimately it is the gift of salvation that fulfills or validates physical healing. Jesus was interested in the *whole* person in his healing ministry. This is reflected in the social,[32] spiritual and physical aspects of the account of the ten persons with leprosy.[33] Participant 3 emphasized that whether physical healing came or not, she was committed to serving God so that her life would glorify God.

It is important to bring these personal experiences and the images of Jesus they present into conversation with other voices on the topic of healing in the worldwide church community that offer different perspectives but remain evangelical and orthodox: that is (1) they believe in Jesus as Healer, and

---

31. Participant 3, in interview by author, Blantyre, 30 July 2019.
32. Luke 17:14.
33. Luke 17:19.

(2) they have a Bible-based view that agrees with, for example, the Lausanne Movement's integrated approach to faith and healing:

> The church has historically been involved in healing the sick. For a good reason – the very heart of Jesus' ministry included the integration of preaching, teaching, and discipling, with works of deliverance and healing. Today this integrated approach has often been lost. Western models tend to show a strong emphasis solely on curative care, relying mainly on individuals coming to healthcare facilities to receive high-quality treatment for their disease. On the other extreme, some "faith healing" ministries rely only on prayer and ritual means such as anointing with oil, denying that healthcare resources are God-given and complementary to prayer and supplication.[34]

Thus, probing stories like those discussed in this paper reveals that there are more diverse, positive approaches to health and healing in African (evangelical) images of Jesus as Healer than those often focused upon in the prosperity gospel.

Bibliography

Ackerman, Denise M. "From Mere Existence to Tenacious Endurance: Stigma, HIV/AIDS and a Feminist Theology of Praxis." In *African Women, Religion and Health: Essays in Honor of Mercy Amba Ewudziwa Oduyoye*, edited by Isabel A. Phiri and Sarojini Nadar, 221–42. Eugene: Wipf & Stock, 2006.

Appiah-Kubi, Kofi. "Christology." In *A Reader in African Christian Theology*, edited by John Parratt, 68–81. London: SPCK, 1987.

Bussey, Sam, Elizabeth Mburu and Benno van den Toren. "Biblical Hermeneutics." In *Encyclopaedia of African Theology*. Forthcoming.

Chifungo, Phoebe Faith. "Women in the CCAP Nkhoma Synod: A Practical Theological Study of Their Leadership Roles." PhD diss., Stellenbosch University, 2014.

Chitando, Ezra, and Charles Klagba, eds. *In the Name of Jesus!: Healing in the Age of HIV*. Geneva: WCC, 2013.

Dube, Musa. "Who Do You Say That I Am?" *Feminist Theology* 15, no. 3 (2007): 346–67. DOI: 10.1177/0966735006076171.

Ela, Jean-Marc. *My Faith as an African*. Translated by John Pairman Brown and Susan Perry. Maryknoll: Orbis, 1988.

---

34. Lausanne Movement, "Lausanne Movement Launches 'Health in Mission' Issue Network," https://www.lausanne.org/news-releases/lausanne-movement-launches-health-in-mission-issue-network-to-connect-health-influencers-for-global-mission.

Kok, Jacobus. *New Perspectives on Healing, Restoration and Reconciliation in John's Gospel.* Leiden: Brill, 2016.

Kolié, Cécé. "Jesus as Healer." In *Faces of Jesus in Africa*, edited by Robert Schreiter, 128–50. Maryknoll: Orbis, 1992.

Lausanne Movement. "Lausanne Movement Launches 'Health in Mission' Issue Network to Connect Health Influencers for Global Mission." Lausanne Movement, 2020. https://www.lausanne.org/news-releases/lausanne-movement-launches-health-in-mission-issue-network-to-connect-health-influencers-for-global-mission.

Soko-de Jong, Thandi. "Belief in a Liminal State of Health: A Christological Review of *In the Name of Jesus! Healing in the Age of HIV*." *The Ecumenical Review* 70, no. 3 (Nov. 2018): 499–510. DO: 10.1111/erev.12378.

Stinton, Diane. *Jesus of Africa: Voices of Contemporary African Christology.* Maryknoll: Orbis, 2004.

van den Toren, Benno. "Contextuality, Catholicity and Canonicity in Biblical Hermeneutics." *African Theology Worldwide* (March 2021). https://african.theologyworldwide.com/blog/contextuality-catholicity-and-canonicity-in-biblical-hermeneutics?highlight=WyJjaHJpc3QtYmVsaWVWV2ZXJzIl0=.

Part Three

Christ in Praxis

16

Who Do You See and Say That I Am?

Responses of Thirty-Seven St. Paul's University Staff and Students after Viewing Drawings of Jesus from *African Posters to Teach the Bible* and *Vie de Jésus Mafa*

Rowland D. Van Es Jr.
Lecturer, St. Paul's University, Limuru, Kenya

Abstract

Eight drawings of Jesus, four from *African Posters to Teach the Bible* and four from *Vie de Jésus Mafa*, were shown to eleven small groups of twenty-six staff and eleven students at St. Paul's University in Limuru, Kenya. Each group responded to the drawings by answering six open-ended questions. From compiling all their responses, six Christological categories emerged: Jesus as Teacher; Jesus as Leader; Jesus as Comforter; Jesus as Parent/Loved One; Jesus as African/One of Us; and Jesus as a Countercultural African. Each category was checked against seven criteria and two tests to ensure it was both biblical and contextual. If this result is confirmed by field testing with other groups, then this "visual approach" to Christology can be recommended for the development of other African Christologies.

Key words: Biblical Christology, contextual Christology, visual Christology, Jesus as African, Jesus as a Countercultural African, African images of Jesus, Visual exegesis

Introduction to a Visual Approach to African Christology

If it is true that "a picture is worth a thousand words," then perhaps it may be useful for African Christians to view images of Jesus portrayed in African drawings in order to understand him. This hypothesis was tested by getting eleven groups of St. Paul's University staff and students to view eight drawings of Jesus depicted as an African in four gospel stories in two different sources: *African Posters to Teach the Bible* (Nairobi: Paulines Publications, 2002) and *Vie de Jésus Mafa* (Life of Jesus as interpreted artistically by the Mafa people of Cameroon in 1973). The results of these viewings are reported and summarized below. The various group responses to the drawings were clustered into six categories or typologies, which if replicated with other groups suggests that this visual approach could be used to develop other African Christologies that are both biblical and contextual.

Introduction to African Christology

There are many models of African Christology. The book *Jesus in African Christianity: Experimentation and Diversity in African Christology* (1998)[1] contains numerous African Christologies proposed by its ten contributors. Charles Nyamiti distinguished between those moving from the Bible to African reality and those moving from African reality to Christology.[2] He also discussed African Christologies of liberation. Douglas Waruta proposed Jesus as Prophet, Priest and Potentate as "the most perfect model for Africans today."[3] Zablon Nthamburi proposed that "the starting point must be the

---

1. Edited by Mugambi and Magesa.
2. Nyamiti, "African Christologies Today," 17–39. The top-down models of Mbiti and others are discussed on 17–18; the bottom-up models of Nyamiti, Sawyer, Pobee, Dickson, Shorter and others are discussed on 18–27. Christologies of liberation (both South African black theology and African) are discussed on 28. The chapters in the volume are actually based on papers presented in 1989.
3. Waruta, "Who Is Jesus Christ for Africans Today?," 52.

praxis of Jesus of Nazareth," and that "Christ must be seen to identify with humanity's suffering, weakness, and pain."[4] He also warned that "if Christ is not concerned about our social, political, economic, and spiritual realism of existence, He will not be relevant in Africa."[5] Laurenti Magesa agreed, saying, "No messiah, no liberator will deeply, sincerely, and lastingly be recognized and accepted as such in Africa today except as an enemy, in word and deed of these and similar inhumanities."[6] Other authors made similar pleas for starting from the local context and considering local realities.

Anne Nasimiyu-Wasike, in the same volume, made a strong plea for including African women's experiences in any African Christology, saying,

> For African women, Jesus Christ is the victorious conqueror of all evil spiritual forces; He is the nurturer of life and a totality of their being. Christ is the liberator of the sufferers, the restorer of life of all those who are broken, the giver of hope and the courage to be . . . He is the one who calls all people forth to mutually participate in the creation of a better world for all.[7]

In the concluding chapter, Jesse Mugambi offered twenty-seven different possible biblical paradigms for consideration, concluding that "there are unlimited perspectives which African Christian theologians can explore and cultivate."[8] To date, only a few of these twenty-seven possible paradigms have been used by African theologians to develop an African Christology.

In *Jesus of Africa* (2004), Diane Stinton proposed just four main models (some with subtypes): Jesus as *Life Giver* (including Jesus as Healer and/or Traditional Healer);[9] Jesus as *Mediator* (including Jesus as Ancestor);[10] Jesus as *Loved One* (including Jesus as Family Member [Elder Brother] and Jesus as Friend);[11] and Jesus as *Leader* (including Jesus as King/Chief and Jesus as Liberator).[12] Many similar models of African Christology have been proposed

---

4. Nthamburi, "Christ as Seen by an African," 57.
5. Nthamburi, 58.
6. Magesa, "Christ the Liberator," 89.
7. Nasimuyu-Waskie, "Christology and an African Woman's Experience," 134.
8. Mugambi, "Christological Paradigms," 161. His hope was that someone would select one theme from the twenty-seven and build a Christology to edify the church.
9. Stinton, *Jesus of Africa*, chapter 3, "Jesus as Life Giver," 54–108.
10. Stinton, chapter 4, "Jesus as Mediator," 109–42.
11. Stinton, chapter 5, "Jesus as Loved One," 143–76.
12. Stinton, chapter 6, "Jesus as Leader," 177–218.

since.[13] As Stinton concluded, "the multiplicity of christological images arising in Africa enhances the discovery of the fullness of Christ, which transcends all cultural constructs of the gospel."[14] All four give us a fuller Christology.

Seven Criteria and Two Tests for the Relevance of Any Proposed African Christology

In *Jesus of Africa* (2004), Stinton also proposed seven factors to consider for the contextual relevance of any proposed African Christology:[15]

1. *Historical relevance:* Is Jesus understood meaningfully in relation to Africa's history, particularly in relation to the suffering of Africa? [This fits with some of the concerns above.]

2. *Theological relevance:* How is Jesus understood in relation to ATR [African Traditional Religion], to the contemporary context, and to fundamental biblical affirmations regarding Jesus?

3. *Cultural relevance:* Is Jesus still perceived as a "foreigner" by African Christians, or has he found "a place to feel at home" in Africa?

4. *Contemporary relevance:* Do Africans view Jesus as being significant to the contemporary realities of life in their own context (politically, economically and socially)? Does [this African Christology] bear witness to the liberating dimensions of the gospel?

5. *Gender appropriateness:* Does [this Christology] adequately address the concerns [of women]? [See Nasimiyu-Wasike's concerns above about including African women's experiences.]

6. *Credibility of witness:* Does [this Christology] lend credible and appropriate witness to Jesus (in Africa) today?

---

13. See, for example, the four pillars for building an African Christology proposed by Tennent in *Theology in the Context of World Christianity*, chapter 5, "Christology: Christ as Healer and Ancestor in Africa." The first pillar is a biblical, exegetical standard. The second pillar is the Christology of the historic ecumenical confessions. The third pillar is the African worldview. The fourth is connecting to the lived experience of Africans, including the church in Africa. All four are found on 117.

14. Stinton, *Jesus of Africa*, 253.

15. Stinton, 46. She used all seven criteria to evaluate the four models she examined in part 2 of her book. They are also included in Figure II-1, "Models of Contemporary African Christologies," 52.

7. *Linguistic and conceptual relevance:* Does [this Christology] capture and incarnate the existential realities of life and African self-understanding? Does it reflect indigenous perceptions that "the gospel has now become our story" and not just a foreign story transliterated into local languages? [This counters the negative example below related to the *Jesus* film.]

More recently, Victor I. Ezigbo (2014) suggested that "an African Christology must pass both the test of 'African-ness' and the test of 'Christian-ness.'"[16] To pass the first test, it must "engage the experience, history, cultures, and religious aspirations of Africans." For the second test, it must "also demonstrate its faithfulness to the understandings of Jesus Christ that are present in the Christian scripture and the Christologies of the earliest ecumenical Christian councils," especially the Councils of Nicaea, Constantinople and Chalcedon. For Ezigbo, any African Christology that "fails to pass both these tests should not bear the name 'African Christian Christology.'"

Ezigbo's two-test criteria are very similar to an earlier proposal by Kevin Vanhoozer (2006) that "the task of theology involves both text and context,"[17] and so in contextualizing any theology we must use two principles: the "Canonic Principle" and the "Catholic Principle."[18] For the first, the story of Jesus is the church's authoritative script. For the second, in performing or representing the story of Jesus today, we sometimes need to use "improvisational wisdom"[19] to act biblically in new situations. In our global village, there is now a need for more vernacular performances in the different regional theaters, because "there is no one way of embodying the gospel."[20] The goal then is to enlarge our understanding by performing the gospel in terms of our own cultural contexts.

---

16. All the quotes are from Ezigbo, "Jesus as God's Communicative and Hermeneutical Act," 37. He uses the tests to critique African Christology from the 1980s to the present, looking first at what he calls "Neo-Missionary Christologies," 43–48, then "Ancestor Christologies," 49–52, and finally "Revealer Christology," 52–57, which is the one he prefers.

17. Vanhoozer, "One Rule to Rule Them All?," 105.

18. Vanhoozer, 105. His Canonic Principle is described on 108–15; the Catholic Principle is described on 115–22. He reminds us to "speak and do the truth of Jesus Christ in our respective contexts," 124.

19. Vanhoozer, 113. He describes this wisdom as "acting Biblically in New Situations," 113–15.

20. Vanhoozer, 117. He then elaborates, "No one performance of the biblical script serves as either a template or paradigm for all others." What we need instead now, he says, is a "Pentecostal plurality," 119.

It is a mistake to exaggerate either "the One" or "the Many."[21] That is why we must now have a variety of theologies, including a variety of Christologies. There must be both canonical unity and Catholic diversity for *any* Christian theology to fit in all our regional contexts.

Justification for Using African Drawings for African Christology Research

The words of Jesus have been translated into thousands of languages. The life of Jesus has been portrayed by actors in dozens of movies. But in Africa, Christianity is still often seen as a foreign religion, and even Christ is seen as "foreign" or "Western."[22] For example, in July 2019 a stir was caused in Kenya when a local pastor claimed to have found the real Jesus,[23] who was just a white man dressed up to look like Jesus (with blond hair and blue eyes as seen in the *Jesus* film etc.). No wonder Christian theology in Africa and elsewhere is still seen as "white theology." The films, paintings and drawings of a white, European-looking Jesus seem to have influenced people in Africa and Asia more than we realized.

Fortunately, in Kenya, there exists an alternative: *African Posters to Teach the Bible* (2002), with sixty-two color posters, all created by Samuel Bullen Ajak Alier, a South Sudanese artist, portraying all the biblical characters as Africans. All sixty-two images were later used in *The Illustrated African Bible* (2008). Also available at the Catholic bookstore in Nairobi is a set of sixty drawings of Jesus also portraying him as an African – *Vie de Jésus Mafa* (1973). According to the Vanderbilt Divinity Library, *Vie de Jésus Mafa* "is a response to the New Testament readings from the Lectionary by a Christian community in Cameroon, Africa. Each of the readings was selected and adapted to dramatic interpretation by the community members. Photographs of their interpretations were made, and these were then transcribed to paintings."[24] Set in Africa, everything in the drawings looks African.

---

21. Vanhoozer, 101, on exaggerating "the One" which leads to Religious Globalization; and on 104 on exaggerating "the Many" which leads to Theological Ethnification. We are often guilty of one or the other.

22. Potgieter and Magezi, "Critical Assessment," 1–4, discuss this, and on 4 they say, "This requires a deforeignisation of Christ in African Christianity" to prevent syncretism (http://dx.doi.org/10.4102/ids.v50i1.2136).

23. Chifamba, "In Case You Missed It," allafrica.com/stories/201907290430.html.

24. "Art in the Christian Tradition," Vanderbilt University, http://diglib.library.vanderbilt.edu/act-imagelink.pl?RC=57503.

For centuries, the Madonna and Child and Christ's nativity have been drawn to represent Jesus as incarnated into different nationalities to help people imagine Jesus as being born into their culture. In the same way, the drawings in *African Posters to Teach the Bible* and *Vie de Jésus Mafa* help Africans to see themselves in the story and to see Jesus as living in their own context. As Jones says, "Historical accuracy is *not* the point," as Jesus was actually neither black nor white; rather, "the point is to see Jesus as the Savior of your own people, as incarnated very close to you and relevant to your life today."[25]

My project of showing eight drawings of Jesus as an African from four gospel stories is a way of moving from the doctrine of the incarnation to an African Christology. As S. D. Gordon said, "Jesus was God spelling himself out in language humanity could understand."[26] The drawings help people see Jesus again (or maybe for the first time) as "God spelling himself out" again for Africa. According to Caroline Blyth and Nasili Vaka'uta, there is "a *slowly* developing recognition of the value of the visual arts within the wider academy of biblical scholarship, particularly within the sub-discipline of biblical reception studies."[27] They cite several volumes of *The Bible in the Modern World* (Sheffield Phoenix Press). As Blyth and Farrell then describe it, "visual exegesis refers to both the artist's process of putting a text into image form and the viewer's encounter with the text made possible through their exploration of this image . . . allowing each to inform the other."[28]

Methodology: Method of Selecting the Drawings and the Groups, and Getting the Responses
Method for Selecting the Eight Drawings

First, I made a list of all the drawings of Jesus found in both *African Posters to Teach the Bible* and *Vie de Jésus Mafa*. This gave me a list of thirteen drawings that overlapped. Next, I eliminated the more familiar images of Jesus's nativity and crucifixion, which people might have already seen and contemplated.[29]

---

25. Jones, "Nativity Paintings from around the World," thejesusquestion.org/2011/12/25/nativity-paintings-from-around-the-world/.

26. Quoted in Jones, "More Nativity Paintings from around the World," thejesusquestion.org/2015/12/25/more-nativity-paintings-from-around-the-world/.

27. Blyth and Vaka'uta, "Introduction," in *Bible and Art*, 2.

28. Blyth and Farrell, "Exploring Visual Exegesis," 144.

29. For images of the nativity, see Jones, "Nativity Paintings from around the World," and "More Nativity Paintings from around the World." For images of the crucifixion, see Jones, "Journey to the Cross, Part 1," www.imb.org/2017/04/07/journey-cross-artists-visualize-christs-

This left a list of seven overlapping drawings from each source. Looking at the list, I decided to pick one drawing from each gospel (Matthew, Mark, Luke, John) to provoke a variety of responses to both the Christology (the *person* of Jesus) and the soteriology (the *work* of Jesus) expressed in the eight drawings of four gospel scenes from the four gospels.

The final list of four drawings selected from each book was as follows: from Matthew 5:1–10, Jesus and the crowd; from Mark 10:13–16, Jesus and the children; from Luke 10:38–42, Jesus with the two sisters (Mary and Martha); and from John 13:1–9, Jesus washing the feet of his disciples. The drawings can be seen in appendix A, with those from *African Posters* drawings on the top, and the *Jésus Mafa* drawings on the bottom.

Notes on the Composition and Inspiration behind the Eight Drawings

In *Vie de Jésus Mafa*, based on sixty New Testament Lectionary passages, all the scenes were portrayed by the Mafa people of Cameroon. Jesus is often shown wearing a red robe, but otherwise he is indistinguishable from the other people, just as was the case in history (so Judas had to kiss Jesus to identify him to his captors in the garden of Gethsemane in the Synoptic Gospels).

In *African Posters to Teach the Bible*, there are sixty-two drawings from almost every book of the Bible, which were later used in *The Illustrated African Bible*. Each poster has one main color drawing surrounded by smaller, simpler line drawings of other scenes from the same Bible book. The artist, Samuel Bullen Ajak Alier, a Dinka from South Sudan, fled to Kenya in 1993 and drew all the posters in Kenya. The back of each poster notes his interpretation of the main drawing. In *The Illustrated African Bible*, his notes are put directly under the main drawing of each poster. The line drawings are now more colorful and used with shortened versions of the stories they are based on, to summarize each book of the Bible.

For his Matthew 5 drawing, Alier says, "Jesus as a young teacher. A small group listens to him. There is a huge crowd in the background representing people of all nations. Though young, Jesus is considered an 'elder' because of his wisdom."[30] In the *Jésus Mafa* drawing, Jesus is under a tree, with small

---

passion-part-1/; and "Journey to the Cross, Part 2," www.imb.org/2017/04/12/journey-cross-artists-visualize-christs-passion-part-2/. Jones includes several African artists in her four collections of global Christian art.

30. Alier, *African Posters*, 92. Also found on the back of poster #42, and in *Illustrated African Bible*, 172.

children closest to him while others listen in groups in various places. In the foreground is a blind beggar, with another group of women and children to the right.

For his Luke 10 drawing, Alier says,

> Jesus with Mary and Martha. Mary is content just to sit at his feet while Martha takes care of the material welfare. In Africa, both actions, listening to the visitor's stories and preparing food to share together, are equally important. Jesus breaks a taboo and allows Mary to sit at his feet as a disciple. Jesus puts a hand of assurance on Mary's shoulder.[31]

In the *Jésus Mafa* drawing, Jesus is sitting on a chair under a palm tree, with Mary seated directly opposite him. Martha is also nearby, pounding something with a mortar and pestle. There is another woman working in the background, and two children talking together on the right.

For his Mark 10 drawing, Alier says, "Jesus is seen as a man who loves children. The children are boys and girls and are dressed in various fashions representing all the children of the world."[32] This image was used on the front cover of *The Illustrated African Bible*. In the *Jésus Mafa* drawing, Jesus is sitting instead of standing. There are thirteen children of various ages close to him, as opposed to just five in Alier's drawing. In both drawings, Jesus's eyes are almost closed (from looking down), and his face has a slight smile.

For his John 13 drawing, Alier says,

> A knowing smile on the face of Jesus as he washes the feet of his questioning and rather puzzled disciples. Washing of the feet is an important service in Africa, where people are used to walking on murram roads. Jesus teaches us that we should wash each other's feet regardless of age or social position.[33]

In the *Jésus Mafa* drawing, there is only Jesus and one disciple (Peter), who has his hands raised (as if objecting) and appears to be having a conversation with Jesus (as Peter does in John).

---

31. Alier, 104. Also on the back of poster #38, and in *Illustrated African Bible*, 196.
32. Alier, 98. Also on the back of poster #45, and in *Illustrated African Bible*, 182.
33. Alier, 106. Also on the back of poster #49, and in *Illustrated African Bible*, 200.

Method for Selecting the Eleven Groups

I wanted to get responses to the drawings from both St. Paul's University (SPU) staff and students. I involved twenty-six staff members who gathered for staff fellowship on 13 February 2020. A few were lecturers, administrators or clergy, but most were mid-level or junior staff (on that particular day, several departments were holding faculty meetings). The twenty-six staff members were divided into eight groups, of three to four members each.

The groups were formed randomly as people came into the room, with eight circles of five chairs set up around each drawing. I made sure each group had gender balance (at least one member of each gender present), and I also made sure that no more than one clergy member was in any group. The twenty-six people were composed of fifteen women and eleven men (four clergy, or 15%).

For the students, I involved eleven theology students selected from two of my classes and from a denominational studies group that I met with weekly. One class had four, another three, and the last group had four students. All but one small group had gender balance. My sampling method for both staff and students was therefore convenience sampling.

Method of Getting Responses from the Group Members

For the SPU staff, I only had one thirty-minute session, so I divided them into eight groups, giving one drawing to each group. I used modified versions of the questions Middleton used in his "Jesus in Fiction and Film" class.[34] Each group was given the following six questions to consider, with one member of each group given the task of writing down all their responses. I then collected all these responses.

> Q1: What African images in this drawing would you want to *affirm* and why?
>
> Q2: What African images in this drawing would you want to *reject* and why?

---

34. Middleton, "On Teaching 'Jesus in Fiction and Film,'" 52. His questions were about reacting to Jesus in song and were the following: What images and symbols are used in the song? Which symbols would you want to affirm, and why? Which symbols would you want to reject, and why? And what, if anything, do you learn about Jesus from this song? I removed his first question and replaced it with two about the person and work of Jesus, and added Question 6 concerning any other comments or reactions they had. Middleton says his course goes beyond just a historical survey of Jesus in fiction and film: it is also "an exercise in imaginative theologizing," 56.

Q3: What (if anything) did you learn about Jesus from this African drawing of a gospel scene?

Q4: What can you say about the person of Christ (who Christ is to them and to us) in this drawing?

Q5: What can you say about the work of Christ (what Christ does for them and for us) in this drawing?

Q6: Any other comments/remarks/insights you want to make about this particular drawing?

After fifteen minutes, the small-group discussions were stopped and the whole room was shown projections of the two drawings of each scene side by side. Each group was also given a photocopy of the second drawing of their scene. I then asked for their reactions at seeing the two drawings together, and gave them an opportunity to make comments. I encouraged them to compare and contrast the two drawings and to give their reactions to seeing both drawings of each scene. I recorded these comments as additional responses from each group to Question 6. All their responses were transcribed for further analysis.

For the first group of students in the denominational studies class, I had one hour, so they all looked at all eight drawings, two at a time (of the same gospel scene). I asked them the following questions to elicit their reactions to each, while also encouraging them to make comparisons of the two drawings side by side. This group had four students: three women and one man (a clergy member).

Q1: What African images in *either* drawing would you want to *affirm* and why?

Q2: What African images in *either* drawing would you want to *reject* and why?

Q3: What (if anything) do you learn about Jesus from these *two* African drawings of a gospel scene?

Q4: What can you say about the *person* of Christ (who Christ is to them and to us) in these two drawings?

Q5: What can you say about the *work* of Christ (what Christ does for them and for us) in these two drawings?

Q6: Any other comments/remarks/insights you want to add after viewing these *two* African drawings?

For the other students, I had just twenty to thirty minutes before or after class, so I presented each group with just two scenes with both drawings side by side (for a total of four drawings each). One class saw Matthew 5 and Luke 10, while the other class saw Mark 10 and John 13. The first class had four students: three men and one woman. The second class had three students: all men. Both groups were prompted with the same six questions as those given to the denominational studies students above, giving me the reactions of two student groups to each scene. I recorded their answers to each question and transcribed them for further analysis.

Summary of Responses to Each Question and Each Set of Drawings

All the answers were typed and then printed out to look for common words and themes. The results for each set of drawings, and for each question, were also copied into an online word cloud generator to find the most common words that might have been missed by the researcher. The two lists of words generated were then searched for in various parts of the document, either by question or by drawing, to get common themes/categories for each. All the approximately seventy statements about Jesus were then put in a separate list to be sorted later by theme or category by the researcher.

Group Responses to Each Question

Responses to Q1 (What Was Affirmed)
Most groups liked the children, African clothing, houses, food, cooking, utensils, mat, and so on. Jesus, Mary and Martha also looked African to most groups. The most common words were dress/dressing (8x); children (7x); cook/s (6x); and people (4x).

Responses to Q2 (What Was Rejected)
In the *African Posters* drawing, Jesus's clothing or dress seemed "not African, too Western or too Jewish." Several did not like his sandals. Some did not like him carrying children ("An African man wouldn't carry a little one that close") or having children so close to him in Matthew 5 and Mark 10. Some thought Mary was not very African in the *Jésus Mafa* drawing of Luke 10: she was too close and should not sit at his level. One said of John 13, "Africans would reject an African leader washing the feet, since African leaders do not serve but are served." The most common words were dress/ing (6x); women (6x); children (4x); Mary (4x); and close (4x).

Responses to Q3 (What Was Learned about Jesus)
Jesus was seen as a teacher, a leader, as loving, humble, and so on. He identified with the people, was a man of the people, but also was seen as "breaking the cultural patterns of gender." He comes to people, he cares for people, he is concerned and compassionate, and so on. The most common words were humble and/or humility (8x); people (6x); and love/s/ing (5x).

Responses to Q4 (The Person of Christ)
Jesus was again seen as a teacher, leader, father, mother, friend, lover/loving and servant. He stands with them and identifies with them/his fellow Africans. The most common words were teach/ing (6x); people (5x); servant (5x); children (4x); and caring (3x).

Responses to Q5 (The Work of Christ)
Jesus is a teacher, leader, servant, and so on. He encourages them, and is teaching them about humility. In John 13 he is "introducing a new culture," he cares for them, and so on. The most common words were teach/er/ing (8x); people (5x); servant (5x); children (4x); and lead/er/ship (4x).

Responses to Q6 (Other Comments/Remarks/Insights)
From Matthew 5, women and children were mentioned; Jesus is not selective of gender. From Luke 10, Jesus was seen as a comforter, problem-solver. The most common words were children (7x); look/s/ing (7x); people (4x); women (4x); men (4x); Mary (4x); concerned (3x); different (3x); and close/er/est (3x).

Group Responses to Each Set of Drawings

Responses to the Two Drawings of Matthew 5
More women responding/listening than men. Many children. In *African Posters* his dress code/clothing is wrong. In *Jésus Mafa*, the beggar is separated from the others. People were mentioned (12x); African (10x); women (9x); men (7x); listen/ing (6x); dress/es/ing (6x); teacher (5x); and beggar (4x).

Responses to the Two Drawings of Luke 10
He is a man of the people. He is a comforter, friend. In *African Posters*, his hand on the lady (Mary) is not appropriate. In *Jésus Mafa*, Mary sitting at his same level is not proper. African mentioned (10x); Mary (10x); women (8x); people (7x); comfort/er (5x); dress/ing (5x); and gender (4x).

Responses to the Two Drawings of Mark 10

Jesus loved children. His love spreads to all/the whole community. He is caring, compassionate. He is a friend. In *African Posters*, his gender is not specific. He is like a mother or an African nanny. Children mentioned (14x); African (11x); kids (7x); caring (5x); good (5x); dress/ing (5x); and loving (4x).

Responses to the Two Drawings of John 13

Africans would reject a leader doing this. African leaders don't serve like that; they prefer to be served. He is humble, showing humility, servant leadership. Brings the picture home to Africa. His hair is not the normal European hair: it is easy to identify with this. Humble/humility mentioned (10x); African (9x); servant (9x); disciples (6x); and leadership (5x).

Most Common Words and Themes from All Responses

The most common words from all the responses of all the groups to all the questions about all the drawings were African (40x); children (25x); people (20x); women (19x); look/ing (19x); dress/ing (18x); love/ing (18x); teach/ing (16x); humble/humility (14x); close (10x); Mary (10x); come (9x); and listen (9x).

Responses Made Concerning Jesus in Particular (What Was Learned, His Person, His Work)

Looking through all the responses, about seventy statements were made about Jesus. These were mostly from Questions 3, 4 and 5, but not exclusively so. This list was looked at separately and grouped by theme into the following six categories or titles that attempt to capture them all.

Jesus as Teacher

Good teacher, speaker; he drew everyone to himself; calling us to come to him; he receives them all. Jesus as a liberator, a pioneer; deconstructing negative culture; Jesus as an encourager. Spreading the gospel. Teaching both women and children. Not all listened; the majority listening to him were women and children (men are missing). Empowering by teaching (in dialogue). He is paying attention, taking time to listen to them. Teaching on humility (John 13): servant leadership. He is showing humility to his students. He is teaching them what they should do to others. Jesus is convincing.

Note that most of these comments came in response to Matthew 5, which Alier described as "Jesus as a young teacher," but others came from John 13.

Jesus as Leader

Jesus is humble; the Master serving the servants; a servant; shepherd of his sheep. He cares for them; Jesus as health officer (washing feet). Practical leadership; servant leadership; role model. Jesus as protector. He is an influence, center of attention. He is selfless, leading by example (John 13); Jesus attained eldership in Africa.

Most of these comments came from John 13. As Alier said of Matthew 5, "Jesus is considered an elder because of his wisdom."

Jesus as Parent/Loved One

Jesus as loving children, accessible to children; Jesus connected to children; Jesus embraces all. Children run to Jesus. Jesus as their father or grandfather. Jesus as their mother or nanny (Ayah/Ya-Ya); Jesus as picking up and bringing up children (not very masculine). Jesus as a father figure; caring toward children. He is embracing them, caring for them, holding them. He lowers himself down to them, comes down to their level; he is accommodating of children of different status, equalizing their status. All ages accepted. Jesus is concerned with children, concerned with their needs. Jesus has no age boundaries. He connected.

Most of these comments came from Mark 10, but some also came from Matthew 5. As Alier said of Mark 10, "Jesus is seen as a man who loves children."

Jesus as Comforter

Jesus helps the weak and needy. Jesus is compassionate, comforting, accommodative, puts a comforting hand on Mary's shoulder. Jesus is patient, dependable, loving, humble, concerned. Jesus as a burden-carrier, someone I can bring my burdens to. Jesus as a counselor, encourager. He shows love and concern for them (and us). Jesus is concerned with all people. He came to people on the ground to seek and to find them. Even the ladies in the background are getting something. They all get his attention.

Most of these comments came from Luke 10. As Alier said, "Jesus puts a hand of assurance on Mary's shoulder."

Jesus as African/One of Us

Barefoot Jesus; Jesus sitting down. Jesus is close to the people; makes people come close to him. Jesus as African (skin color). Jesus went where people were.

Jesus identified with the people. Jesus as shoeless/barefoot; man of the people; one of us (way he sits and dresses). Jesus is communal, part of the homestead, part of the extended family. Jesus as close friend, good neighbor, easy to relate to, friendly, caring. Jesus identifies with his fellow Africans (their race, their friend). Jesus loves the whole community. Brings the picture home to Africa. Does not make us foreign. African hair is easy to identify with. Way of dressing and sitting also African.

These comments came from all the drawings, some from Question 1, others from Question 6. As Alier said of his Luke 10 drawing, "In Africa, both actions, listening to the visitor's stories and preparing food to share together, are equally important." For John 13 he said, "Washing of the feet is an important service in Africa, where people are used to walking on murram roads."

Jesus as a Countercultural African

Jesus breaks gender barriers; Jesus accepts and respects women, doesn't put them away as African men would. He puts his hand on Mary's shoulder, lets her sit at his level. He picks up and brings up kids. Africans would reject such a leader; too young to be an elder. A man for women. Jesus introduces a new/strange culture (John 13). Jesus doesn't lord it over other people. He is deconstructing negative cultural issues; all-inclusive (of gender); not selective of gender, health, age, and so on. Doing a strange thing, introducing a new culture (John 13). Jesus as Husband (of the two sisters). Jesus doesn't despise the one working (Martha and the one in the background).

These comments came from all drawings (but esp. Luke 10 and John 13). As Alier said of his Luke 10 drawing, "Jesus breaks a taboo and allows Mary to sit at his feet as a disciple." For John 13 he said, "Jesus teaches us that we should wash each other's feet regardless of age or social position."

Testing These Six Categories against Stinton's Seven Criteria and Ezigbo's Two Tests

First, Historical Relevance

Is Jesus understood meaningfully in relation to Africa's history, particularly in relation to the suffering of Africa? The results that best fit with these criteria are Jesus as Comforter and also Jesus as Leader, and perhaps Jesus as Teacher (if he teaches them a way out). Jesus as African/One of Us would also fit here, and even Jesus as a Countercultural African, if what he does counterculturally is to reduce Africans' suffering (such as being concerned with women and children). Jesus as Parent/Loved One works also in the sense that we need someone to love us when we suffer. Several people reacted strongly to the beggar being seemingly ignored in the *Jésus Mafa* drawing of Matthew 5.

Second, Theological Relevance
How is Jesus understood in relation to ATR, the contemporary context, and fundamental biblical affirmations regarding Jesus? None of the results above address ATR directly, but all of them fit the contemporary context, and they are all biblical since they are based on drawings of biblical scenes. The only comments related to ATR are perhaps those such as, "He is too young to be an African elder" and "African men wouldn't do . . ." (pick up children, take care of children, or touch another woman in public as in the *African Posters* scene of Luke 10). Jesus is countercultural.

Third, Cultural Relevance
Is Jesus still perceived as a "foreigner" by African Christians, or has he found "a place to feel at home" in Africa? Here all the drawings showed Jesus as African, and all the resulting categories have a home in Africa (Teacher, Leader, Helper, etc.). The most direct comments on this aspect were those in the category of Jesus as African/One of Us, especially comments like, "Brings the picture home to Africa. Does not make us foreign. African hair easy to identify with." This was a strength of using African drawings, particularly those of *Jésus Mafa*.

Fourth, Contemporary Relevance
Do Africans view Jesus as being significant to the contemporary realities of life in their own context (politically, economically, and socially)? Does this African Christology bear witness to the liberating dimensions of the gospel? Again, most of the results fit the contemporary context, especially perhaps those under the category of Jesus as Leader, where he was called a "protector," and also of Jesus as Teacher, where he was called a "liberator." Also, Jesus as Comforter was "someone I can bring my burdens to." Jesus as African/One of Us fits the contemporary reality, and even Jesus as a Countercultural African, where he is "deconstructing negative cultural issues" – but perhaps it is also true that "Africans would reject such a leader." After all, Jesus was rejected by those he came to and was crucified (as the Jewish crowd demanded in John's gospel).

Fifth, Gender Appropriateness
Does this Christology adequately address the concerns of women? Here again, most of the results were appropriate and addressed the concerns of women. Jesus as Teacher was "teaching both men and women," and in fact, "the majority

hearing him were women and children." Jesus as Leader is shepherd of all his sheep (including women). Jesus as Parent/Loved One seemed to some to look like a woman or a nanny in the *African Posters* drawing of Mark 10. Jesus as Comforter put a comforting hand on Mary, which was seen as both appropriate and inappropriate. Jesus as African/One of Us was a good friend, good neighbor, and cared for all people/the whole community. Jesus as a Countercultural African accepts and respects women, puts his hand on Mary's shoulder, and allows her to sit at his level. He is not selective of gender, doesn't despise the woman working. Most drawings are seen as African and appropriate.

Sixth, Credibility of Witness
Does this Christology lend credible and appropriate witness to Jesus in Africa today? Jesus as Teacher, Jesus as Leader, Jesus as Parent/Loved One, Jesus as Comforter and Jesus as African/One of Us were all seen by most respondents as credible. The only question was about Jesus as a Countercultural African, where there were mixed reactions – as indeed there were mixed reactions to the historical Jesus. To me, this adds to the credibility of the witness of these drawings: that they both affirm and challenge elements of African culture, just as the historical Jesus also both affirmed and challenged elements of his Jewish culture (especially the scribes and Sadducees).

Seventh, Linguistic and Conceptual Relevance
Does this Christology capture and incarnate the existential realities of life and African self-understanding? Does it reflect indigenous perceptions that "the gospel has now become our story" and not just a foreign story transliterated into local languages? Again, Jesus as Teacher, Jesus as Leader, Jesus as Parent/Loved One, Jesus as Comforter, Jesus as African/One of Us and even Jesus as a Countercultural African are all relevant. The titles teacher, leader, parent/loved one and comforter already exist in African languages. Thus, they are linguistically and conceptually relevant. As noted above, even being countercultural is relevant, in the sense that Jesus was also countercultural in his context. Being relevant to Africa must include views of women too.

Finally, the Two Tests of African-ness (Catholicity) and Christian-ness (Canonicity)
For the African-ness or "Catholicity" of Jesus as Teacher, Jesus as Leader, Jesus as Parent/Loved One, Jesus as Comforter, Jesus as African/One of Us and Jesus as a Countercultural African, as we have seen above, all of these models or titles are African. In all the drawings Jesus is seen as an African. This is just as

appropriate as any other drawings of Jesus as European or Asian, for example. They are part of our new global plurality.

For the Christian-ness or "canonicity" of Jesus as Teacher, Jesus as Leader, Jesus as Parent/Loved One, Jesus as Comforter, Jesus as African/One of Us and Jesus as Countercultural African, again, as we have seen above, all these models or titles are Christian, coming from the gospel stories or the historical Jesus, and the reaction to him by the Jews and Gentiles of the first century. He was both accepted and rejected by people.

As Teacher, Jesus brought "a new teaching – and with authority" (Mark 1:27). As a leader, they wanted to make Jesus a king by force (John 6:15), and he was crucified as "King of the Jews" (John 19:19). As a Parent/Loved One, he was "a friend of tax collectors and sinners" (Matt 11:19), close to women and children, and he called his disciples "friends" (John 15:15). As a Comforter, Jesus weeps with Mary and Martha over the death of Lazarus (John 11:35) and also weeps over Jerusalem (Luke 17:41). Of course, Jesus was not actually African, but this was just a historical necessity, not a theological necessity (the same goes for his maleness or his Jewishness). As God, Jesus could have been incarnated as either male or female, as either a Jew or Gentile. His coming as a Jewish male was merely "accidental" and necessary for his mission and work at that time, but not for all time. As noted above (and below) Jesus was also countercultural.

Summary, Conclusion and Recommendations

As E. F. Schumacher said, "an ounce of practice is generally worth more than a ton of theory."[35] There are many theoretical titles for an African Jesus, but from my own brief research, it appears that another fruitful way to get African answers to the question "Who do you say I am?" is to get African Christians to view some actual drawings of Jesus portrayed as an African. In just fifteen to twenty minutes, many insightful responses emerged. The visual approach to Christology or "visual exegesis" of drawings of Jesus was useful.

The findings of Jesus as Teacher, Leader, Comforter and Parent/Loved One were perhaps not too surprising, given the particular scenes selected. They also fit with Stinton's 2004 findings of Jesus as Leader, Life-giver and Loved

---

35. Schumacher, *Small Is Beautiful*. Others to whom this quote is attributed are Swami Vivekananda and Mahatma Gandhi, who reportedly said, "An ounce of practice is worth more than a ton of *preaching*," which I also agree with. We have too many scholarly discussions of Christology, and too few ideas coming directly from the laity, and/or directly from reading Scripture or from viewing drawings of Jesus.

One. The findings of Jesus as both African/One of Us and as a Countercultural African were more surprising, and perhaps prompted by Question 1, "What African images do you *affirm* and why?," as well as by Question 2, "What African images do you *reject* and why?" Those were two stimulating questions.

But the finding of Jesus as both African/One of Us and as a Countercultural African also fits with the historical truth that, while Jesus was born a Jew, looked Jewish and often behaved in a very Jewish way, he also broke some Jewish laws (such as those for the Sabbath) and associated with non-Jews (Gentiles, Samaritans, etc.), and was a radical (by having Mary sit at his feet). Jesus pushed the boundaries. The historical Jesus was both Jewish/one of them *and* countercultural. The mixed reactions to the drawings are a positive result.

Recommendations and Areas for Further Research

With more time and money, it would be good to confirm these findings with other wider groups, such as ordinary Christians of various ages in primary schools, secondary schools and technical schools. It would also be good to show the drawings to women's groups, men's groups, and even non-Christian groups, to hear all their different responses. If the initial findings are confirmed, they support using visual exegesis as a way to explore Christology that is both biblical and contextual. New responses to other drawings can be used to promote other African Christologies.

It may also be profitable to expose African Christians to other non-Western images of Jesus, such as more historically realistic Palestinian/Middle Eastern art, or to Asian Art and/or South American art, and other drawings of Jesus from the "one, holy, catholic and apostolic church," to see what additional themes about the *person* of Christ and/or the *work* of Christ emerge. We need more Christology that is non-Western in origin.

Another line of research might be to use these drawings (and others) in an exegesis class for the kind of "visual exegesis" that was done in Oceania.[36] After reading the story and examining the accompanying art, critical questions can be asked, such as the following:

- How does this artwork retell or represent the particular text it is based on?
- What meaning does this artwork suggest that the text conveys to the reader?

---

36. Blyth and Farrell, "Exploring Visual Exegesis," 143.

- What parts of the text are highlighted in the artwork?
- What parts of the text are altered and/or edited in the artwork?
- How does the artwork respond to the ambiguities, gaps and/or nuances in the text?

This technique of "visual exegesis" may be a good way to introduce skeptical students to the idea that every reader is also an interpreter, just as every artist must make his or her own interpretations. These African drawings and others like them would also make a very useful addition to projects such as Contextual Bible Study,[37] where people are encouraged to read and react to the Bible in their mother tongue. The drawings would draw out reactions different from those resulting from just hearing or reading the words. Each drawing, as a contextual interpretation, provokes a response and stimulates dialogue within the groups and between the groups present. Group members should also be encouraged to create their own local biblical art.[38] African images and drawings of Christ will promote African Christology.

Bibliography

Alier, Samuel B. A. *African Posters to Teach the Bible: Guide Book*. Nairobi: Paulines Publications Africa, 2002. [written to accompany 62 color posters of the Bible]

"Art in the Christian Tradition." Vanderbilt University. http://diglib.library.vanderbilt.edu/act-imagelink.pl?RC=57503.

Blyth, Caroline, and Alex Farrell, with Tony Brooking. "Exploring Visual Exegesis: A Conversation between Artist and Beholders." In Blyth and Vaka'uta, *The Bible and Art*, 143–61.

Blyth, Caroline, and Nasili Vaka'uta. *The Bible and Art: Perspectives from Oceania*. London: Bloomsbury T&T Clark, 2017.

Chifamba, Jerry. "Africa: In Case You Missed It, Jesus Christ Visited Africa This Weekend." AllAfrica.com. 29 July 2019. allafrica.com/stories/201907290430.html.

Ezigbo, Victor I. "Jesus as God's Communicative and Hermeneutical Act: African Christians on the Peron and Significance of Jesus Christ." In *Jesus without Borders:*

---

37. The "Contextual Bible Study Manual," produced by the Ujamaa Centre for Community Development and Research, can be found at various places, including anglicancommunion.org (https://www.anglicancommunion.org/media/253823/6-Ujamaa-Manual-doing-contextual-Bible-study-a-resource-manual.pdf) and http://ujamaa.ukzn.ac.za/Libraries/manuals/Ujamaa_CBS_bible_study_Manual_part_1_2.sflb.ashx. It consists of twenty-three Bible studies on themes such as HIV/AIDS, land, women, and rape. None of the four scenes I used are included, but several of the twenty-three texts are depicted in either *African Posters* or *Jésus Mafa*.

38. See Ladwig, *Psalm 23*, and the way it was illustrated for the African American context of Newark, NJ. This book could fairly easily be adapted by African artists to fit their own contexts.

Christology in the Majority Word, edited by Gene L. Green, Stephen T. Pardue and K. K. Yeo, 37–58. Grand Rapids: Eerdmans, 2014.

The Illustrated African Bible. Nairobi: Paulines Publications Africa, 2008.

Jones, Victoria E. "Journey to the Cross: Artists Visualize Christ's Passion, Part 1." International Mission Board, Arts and Culture. 7 April 2017. www.imb.org/2017/04/07/journey-cross-artists-visualize-christs-passion-part-1/.

———. "Journey to the Cross: Artists Visualize Christ's Passion, Part 2." International Mission Board, Arts and Culture. 12 April 2017. www.imb.org/2017/04/12/journey-cross-artists-visualize-christs-passion-part-2/.

———. "Nativity Paintings from around the World." The Jesus Question. 25 December 2011. thejesusquestion.org/2011/12/25/nativity-paintings-from-around-the-world/.

———. "More Nativity Paintings from around the World." The Jesus Question. 25 December 2015. thejesusquestion.org/2015/12/25/more-nativity-paintings-from-around-the-world/.

Ladwig, Tim. *Psalm Twenty-Three*. Grand Rapids: Eerdmans Books for Young Readers, 1997. Originally published in New York by African American Family Press, 1993.

Magesa, Laurenti. "Christ the Liberator and Africa Today." In Mugambi and Magesa, *Jesus in African Christianity*, 79–92.

Middleton, Darren J. N. "On Teaching 'Jesus in Fiction and Film.'" *Intégrité: A Faith and Learning Journal* 14, no. 1 (2015): 52–58.

Mugambi, Jesse N. K. "Conclusion: Christological Paradigms in African Christianity." In Mugambi and Magesa, *Jesus in African Christianity*, 136–61.

Mugambi, Jesse N. K., and Laurenti Magesa, eds. *Jesus in African Christianity: Experimentation and Diversity in African Christology*. Nairobi: Acton, 1998.

Nasimiyu-Wasike, Anne. "Christology and an African Woman's Experience." In Mugambi and Magesa, *Jesus in African Christianity*, 123–35.

Nthamburi, Zablon. "Christ as Seen by an African: A Christological Quest." In Mugambi and Magesa, *Jesus in African Christianity*, 54–59.

Nyamiti, Charles. "African Christologies Today." In Mugambi and Magesa, *Jesus in African Christianity*, 17–39.

Potgieter, Raymond, and Christopher Magezi. "A Critical Assessment of Bediako's Incarnational Christological Model as a Response to the Foreignness of Christ in African Christianity." *In die Skriflig/In Luce Verbi* [Online] 50, no. 1 (23 Sep. 2016). http://dx.doi.org/10.4102/ids.v50i1.2136.

Schumacher, Ernst F. *Small Is Beautiful: The Study of Economics as If People Mattered*. London: Abacus, 1978.

Sewell, Jacky. "'The Painting Is Suffering': Maori and Pasefika Boys Respond to Images of Christ and Peter." In Blyth and Vaka'uta, *Bible and Art*, 275–94.

Stinton, Diane B. *Jesus of Africa: Voices of Contemporary African Christology*. Maryknoll: Orbis, 2004.

Tennent, Timothy C. *Theology in the Context of World Christianity: How the Global Church Is Influencing the Way We Think about and Discuss Theology*. Grand Rapids: Zondervan, 2007.
Thomas, Eliza. "Seeing Incarnation: Christian Art Shows the Birth of Jesus Is for All Peoples." International Mission Board, Arts & Culture. 9 December 2016. www.imb.org/2016/12/09/seeing-incarnation-christian-art-shows-the-birth-of-jesus-is-for-all-peoples/.
The Ujamaa Centre for Community Development and Research. "Doing Contextual Bible Study: A Resource Manual." Rev. ed. 2014. http://ujamaa.ukzn.ac.za/Libraries/manuals/Ujamaa_CBS_bible_study_Manual_part_1_2.sflb.ashx; https://www.anglicancommunion.org/media/253823/6-Ujamaa-Manual-doing-contextual-Bible-study-a-resoruce-manual.pdf.
Vanhoozer, Kevin J. "One Rule to Rule Them All? Theological Method in an Era of World Christianity." In *Globalizing Theology: Belief and Practice in an Era of World Christianity*, edited by Craig Ott and Harold Netland, 85–126. Grand Rapids: Baker Academic, 2006.
Vie de Jésus Mafa (Life of Jesus Mafa). 1973. https://www.librairie-emmanuel.fr/recherche/Vie+de+Jesus+Mafa.
Waruta, Douglas W. "Who Is Jesus Christ for Africans Today? Prophet, Priest, Potentate." In Mugambi and Magesa, *Jesus in African Christianity*, 40–53.
Weber, Hans-Ruedi. *Immanuel: The Coming of Jesus in Art and the Bible*. Geneva: World Council of Churches, 1984.

314 Who Do You Say I Am?

Appendix A: Paired African Drawings Used in the Research[39]

Jesus and the people in Matthew 5
(*African Posters*, images; *Vie de Jésus Mafa*, web links provided below image)

https://diglib.library.vanderbilt.edu/act-imagelink.pl?RC=48284

---

39. Images by Samuel Alier in *African Posters to Teach the Bible*, used by permission.

Jesus and the two sisters in Luke 10
(African Posters, images; *Vie de Jésus Mafa,* web links provided below image)

https://diglib.library.vanderbilt.edu/act-imagelink.pl?RC=48311

316 Who Do You Say I Am?

Jesus and the children in Mark 10
(*African Posters*, images; *Vie de Jésus Mafa*, web links provided below image)

https://diglib.library.vanderbilt.edu/act-imagelink.pl?RC=4839

Jesus and the disciples in John 13
(African Posters, images; Vie de Jésus Mafa, web links provided below image)

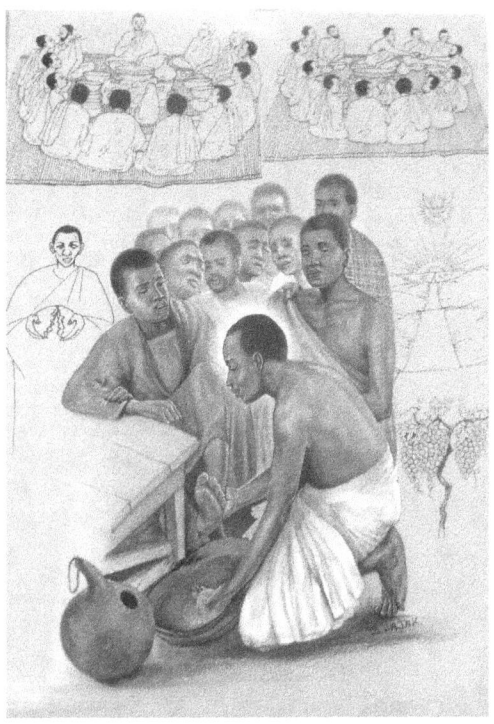

https://diglib.library.vanderbilt.edu/act-imagelink.pl?RC=48299

17

"Missionaries Did Not Bring Christ to Africa – Christ Brought Them" (Bediako/Mbiti)

Christ's Lordship in Mission in African Theology[1]

Alistair I. Wilson

Lecturer in Mission and New Testament, Edinburgh Theological Seminary, UK
Extraordinary Researcher, Unit for Reformed Theology and the Development of SA Society, North-West University, South Africa

Abstract

Kwame Bediako's striking christological modification of the original statement of John Mbiti, used as the title of a paper published in 2007, suggests a

---

1. I am grateful for helpful questions and comments from participants at the ASET conference, held 6–7 March 2020 at Africa International University, Nairobi, Kenya, where a summary of this paper was first presented. Thanks, also, to Joseph Mutei of St. Paul's University, and his postgraduate students, for thoughtful feedback following a presentation on 9 March 2020. Likewise, I appreciate the engagement with this paper by participants in the South African Theological Seminary Symposium (online) on 19 June 2020. Finally, I am grateful to Will Traub and Thomas Davis of Edinburgh Theological Seminary and Stephanie Lowery of AIU for written comments, and also for the comments of the two anonymous peer reviewers. All of the feedback from these colleagues has helped me to reflect on, and improve, my paper.

significant aspect of Christology: Jesus Christ is Lord of mission. I examine the statements of Mbiti and Bediako in context to ascertain whether their statements do indeed contribute to this christological theme, and I conclude that they do not provide what the short phrases promise. I go on to show how the Dutch missiologist J. H. Bavinck emphasizes the role of Jesus Christ as Lord of mission in a way that Mbiti, Bediako and other contributors to African theology have so far failed to do. I then highlight several relevant biblical texts that point to the importance of this christological idea in the New Testament. In conclusion, I argue that Bediako is correct to say that Christ brought the missionaries to Africa. I also argue that Bediako's reformulation of Mbiti's comment strengthens the original statement, in that it is no longer an ambiguous reference to an undefined supreme being, but it clearly ascribes the initiative in the expansion of the gospel to the risen Jesus.

Key words: Mbiti, Bediako, Kato, Bavinck, Christ, Africa, Lord, mission

Introduction

In the title of a paper published in 2007, Kwame Bediako echoed (apparently deliberately) the words of John Mbiti, written some twenty-seven years earlier. In an article published in *The Christian Century* in 1980, Mbiti had claimed, "The missionaries who introduced the gospel to Africa in the past 200 years did not bring God to our continent. Instead, God brought *them*."[2] Despite his clear dependence on Mbiti's words, Bediako altered them in a significant way. Bediako's title stated, "Missionaries did not bring Christ to Africa – Christ brought them."[3]

In this paper, I consider the theme of Jesus Christ as Lord of the mission of the church, prompted by the small, yet significant, change that Bediako made to Mbiti's words. The key theological claim I wish to make is not, as we shall see, based on the specific arguments of either Mbiti or Bediako, but that their memorable words highlight what I consider to be an important aspect of Christology, and they provide a useful launching point for further reflection. It is important to understand why Mbiti and Bediako wrote these particular words before I develop an argument based on these statements in a rather

---

2. Mbiti, "Encounter of Christian Faith and African Religion," 817–20, https://www.religion-online.org/article/the-encounter-of-christian-faith-and-african-religion/. I have not had access to the original printed publication and so am unable to provide page numbers. The emphasis in the quotation is the author's.

3. Bediako, "Missionaries Did Not Bring Christ to Africa," 18.

different direction. I will first examine Mbiti's claim in the context of his 1980 article and consider some implications of his view for a Christian theology of religions. I will then look at Bediako's engagement with Mbiti in his 2007 article. Having concluded that neither Mbiti nor Bediako develops a theology of Jesus Christ as Lord of mission in their articles, I draw attention to the work of one author who does develop this idea, namely the Dutch missiologist J. H. Bavinck. Finally, I briefly survey some relevant biblical texts and draw some conclusions concerning Jesus Christ as Lord of mission.

John Mbiti: God Brought the Missionaries

Is Mbiti correct to say that "the missionaries who introduced the gospel to Africa in the past 200 years did not bring God to our continent. Instead, God brought *them*"?

Before we can answer that question, we must ensure that we understand his claim correctly. Kenyan theologian John Mbiti (1931–2019) was one of Africa's most influential theologians.[4] Mbiti's words, quoted above, were written in the context of a reflective article he was invited to write for *The Christian Century*.

It is important to recognize that Mbiti's comment is an aphorism. He uses language creatively to make a point, but his words require explanation, and possibly further nuance. The point Mbiti appears to make is that, contrary to the perception that God (meaning the God of the Christian Scriptures) was introduced to the African continent by Western missionaries during the eighteenth and nineteenth centuries, God was present and active in Africa long before that time, and acted in providence in the lives of the Western missionaries to bring them to Africa where they would proclaim the Christian gospel. Mbiti expresses his fundamental claim as follows: "The God described in the Bible is none other than the God who is already known in the framework of our traditional African religiosity."[5]

In one sense, it is not controversial to claim, as Mbiti does, that missionaries of the past two hundred years "did not bring God to our continent." It is recognized by many that, as Elias Bongmba states, "Christianity is an African

---

4. Bediako comments, "John Mbiti is the modern African theologian with by far the weightiest bibliography." Bediako, *Theology and Identity*, 303. Many studies of African theology, including those by Bediako and Kato discussed in this paper, devote considerable attention to Mbiti's work.

5. Mbiti, "Encounter of Christian Faith and African Religion," https://www.religion-online.org/article/the-encounter-of-christian-faith-and-african-religion/.

religion because its roots in North Africa go back to apostolic times."[6] But Mbiti is going further than this. He is making a claim about the very nature of God.

While Mbiti touches on a number of issues in his paper, in the first section of the article Mbiti is particularly concerned to reflect on the relationship between the actions of God with respect to the biblical documents and his dealings with African peoples. He writes,

> At many points, I see intriguing parallels between the biblical record and African religiosity. In particular, the concepts about God provide one area of great commonality. There are also other parallels in social, political, and cultural areas, just as there are some significant differences. In one case the thinking and experience of the people produced a written record of God's dealings with the Jewish people in particular. In the other case, no such written record exists. But God's dealings with the African people are recorded, nevertheless, in living form – oral communication, rituals, symbols, ceremonies, community faith.[7]

Mbiti claims, then, based on his perception of "parallels" and "one area of great commonality," that there is some form of similar relationship between the revelation of God to the people of Israel as recorded in the Jewish and Christian Scriptures and the experience of the divine described in the religious traditions and rituals found in African Traditional Religions. Mbiti bases his view on a foundational biblical claim, from which he makes a deduction: "Since the Bible tells me that God is the Creator of all things, his activities in the world must clearly go beyond what is recorded in the Bible. He must have been active among African peoples as he was among the Jewish people."[8]

Mbiti's claim is theological so we may test it against Scripture. The Christian Scriptures affirm that there is only one true God (Deut 6:4–6). What is more, this God, who has revealed himself as YHWH, the covenant God of Israel, is the creator of all that exists. According to Scripture, the one true God created

---

6. Bongmba, "Christianity in North Africa," 25. For further discussion, see Oden, *How Africa Shaped the Christian Mind*; and Bantu, *Multitude of All Peoples*, chapter 2, "The First Christians of Africa."

7. Mbiti, "Encounter of Christian Faith and African Religion," https://www.religion-online.org/article/the-encounter-of-christian-faith-and-african-religion/.

8. Mbiti.

all things and rules over all the earth. That YHWH is Creator is expressed richly in the opening words of Psalm 24:[9]

> The earth is the LORD's, and everything in it,
>   the world, and all who live in it;
> for he founded it on the seas
>   and established it on the waters.

As Creator of all things, the God is Lord of all things, exercising sovereign control. Psalm 47 reads:

> Clap your hands, all you nations;
>   shout to God with cries of joy.
> For the LORD Most High is awesome,
>   the great King over all the earth.
> He subdued nations under us,
>   peoples under our feet.
> . . .
> For God is the King of all the earth;
>   sing to him a psalm of praise.
> God reigns over the nations;
>   God is seated on his holy throne.
> The nobles of the nations assemble
>   as the people of the God of Abraham,
> for the kings of the earth belong to God;
>   he is greatly exalted.

In this psalm, "all [the] nations" are called to "clap [their] hands" and "shout . . . with cries of joy" (v. 1) because YHWH is "the great King over all the earth" (v. 2; cf. v. 7). YHWH is not a local or national deity. His status as Creator gives him authority over all nations. So we may affirm Mbiti's claim that God has been "active among African peoples" in the sense that all peoples owe their lives to YHWH, the one creator God. It appears to be a significant leap, however, to argue that any religious tradition that affirms that God is Creator is necessarily speaking of the same God as the God revealed in the Christian Scriptures. In fact, such a view comes into conflict with a number of texts of Scripture. For example, Psalm 96:3–5 proclaims,

---

9. Quotations from Scripture are from the New International Version (Biblica, 2011) unless otherwise noted.

> Declare his glory among the nations,
>> his marvelous deeds among all peoples.
> For great is the LORD and most worthy of praise;
>> he is to be feared above all gods.
> For all the gods of the nations are idols,
>> but the LORD made the heavens.

"All the earth" is commanded to "sing to the LORD" (v. 1), and "all you families of nations" are called to "ascribe to the LORD glory and strength" (v. 7), but this does not imply that every religious expression of the nations is such an act of praise to the LORD. Rather, a sharp contrast is drawn between the LORD, the one creator of all things, and "the gods of the nations," which are idols.

In his book *Introduction to African Religion*, Mbiti states, "It is generally believed all over Africa that the universe was created. The Creator of the universe is God. There is no agreement, however, on how the creation of the universe took place."[10]

This immediately highlights significant disagreements in the worldviews of particular African peoples. Yet Mbiti does not see this as a problem for his argument. He states,

> [The missionaries] proclaimed the name of Jesus Christ. But they used the names of the God who was and is already known by African peoples – such as Mungu, Mulungu, Katonda, Ngai, Olodumare, Asis, Ruwa, Ruhanga, Jok, Modimo, Unkulunkulu and thousands more. These were not empty names. They were names of one and the same God, the creator of the world, the father of our Lord Jesus Christ.[11]

What are we to make of this claim? Samuel Kunhiyop asks, "Is the Supreme Being whom Africans acknowledge the same as the God of the Bible?," and notes "John Mbiti believes this to be the case."[12] Kunhiyop's own view, however, is that John Mbiti is incorrect: "At most, the beliefs and practices of African Traditional Religion convey only a faint and incomplete understanding of who God is."[13] We must explore this further.

---

10. Mbiti, *Introduction to African Religion*, 35.

11. Mbiti, "Encounter of Christian Faith and African Religion," https://www.religion-online.org/article/the-encounter-of-christian-faith-and-african-religion/.

12. Kunhiyop, *African Christian Theology*, 44.

13. Kunhiyop, 44.

John Mbiti and a Christian Theology of Religions

Mbiti's views raise the issue of a Christian theology of religions. This topic has been addressed by numerous scholars in recent years, though rarely with a focus on African Traditional Religion.[14]

One of the most forthright critics of Mbiti's views was the Nigerian theologian Dr Byang Kato (1936–75). Kato devotes much of his book *Theological Pitfalls in Africa*[15] to an analysis of Mbiti's views.[16]

One of Kato's criticisms of Mbiti's work lies at the level of methodology. He argues that Mbiti's work is flawed because he attempts to draw general conclusions based on limited knowledge of a large number of different traditions rather than engaging in detail with one or more specific traditions. Kato writes,

> John Mbiti's strength turns out to be the source of his weakness. He sets out to defend African Theology by taking African peoples as one in their thinking and reasoning, despite the fact that "there are about one thousand African peoples (tribes), and each has its own religious system."[17]

In contrast to Mbiti's approach, Kato devotes a chapter to one specific form of African Traditional Religion: that practiced by "the Jaba people of North Central State of Nigeria."[18] According to Kato's own assessment, he "will be able to deal with the Jaba religion with a greater understanding, having been born and brought up in it."[19]

Kato states that the Jaba have some conception of a Supreme Being, called "Nom."[20] As Kato describes the characteristics of Nom, as they are understood by the Jaba, he argues that they are markedly different from the characteristics of Yahweh, or the characteristics of the Father of the Lord Jesus Christ, as

---

14. For important recent treatments of this topic, see particularly McDermott and Netland, *Trinitarian Theology of Religions*; and Strange, *"Their Rock Is Not as Our Rock."* One recent book on world religions that aims to give more attention to African Religion is Hexham, *Understanding World Religions*. A recent discussion with a particular focus on Africa is Wijsen, "Mission Practice and Theory in Africa."

15. Kato, *Theological Pitfalls*.

16. For discussions of Mbiti and Kato, see Hesselgrave and Rommen, *Contextualization*, 96–112; and Bediako, *Theology and Identity*, 303–46, 386–425.

17. Kato, *Theological Pitfalls*, 59. The citation in the quotation from Kato is from Mbiti's own work: John S. Mbiti, *African Religions and Philosophy* (New York: Frederick A. Praeger, 1969), 18.

18. Kato, *Theological Pitfalls*, 27.

19. Kato, 27.

20. Kato, 29.

described in the Christian Scriptures. For example, Nom "is not said to be everywhere," and "the worship of [Nom] is conspicuously absent."[21]

Recent African scholarship recognizes the need for contextualization while being alert to the danger of syncretism, whereby African traditions are accepted without careful scrutiny. For example, Elizabeth Mburu recognizes that there are points of contact between an African worldview and the biblical worldview.[22] She is careful, however, to emphasize that "while African religious and traditional beliefs can and should be used in some measure to formulate an understanding of the Bible from an African context, they must not be allowed to displace biblical revelation."[23]

It appears to me that Mbiti does not sufficiently recognize that restriction. Mbiti claimed that "the missionaries who introduced the gospel to Africa in the past 200 years did not bring God to our continent. Instead, God brought *them*."[24] I submit that this statement is not sufficiently defined to be suitable as the foundation of a mission theology for Africa. What is more, Mbiti's claims regarding the identification of the divinities found in African Traditional Religion with the God and Father of the Lord Jesus Christ are theologically problematic, to the extent that Mbiti's original statement can no longer be regarded as simply insufficiently defined, but as fundamentally flawed theologically.

Kwame Bediako: Christ Brought the Missionaries

Ghanaian theologian Kwame Bediako (1945–2008) established himself as another formidable African theologian within the evangelical tradition. In his 2007 article, Bediako engages directly with Mbiti's thought, as he had done more extensively in the published version of his dissertation.[25] Although Bediako modified Mbiti's words to form his title, it is clear that Bediako regards Mbiti's approach as fundamentally valid. Bediako cites Mbiti's words as follows:

---

21. Kato, 29–35. The examples are found on 31 and 34.

22. Mburu, *African Hermeneutics*. Mburu recognizes that the notion of a single African worldview is contested, but argues that there are "certain underlying commonalities" that permit consideration of an "African worldview" (25).

23. Mburu, 8.

24. Mbiti, "Encounter of Christian Faith and African Religion," 817–20, https://www.religion-online.org/article/the-encounter-of-christian-faith-and-african-religion/. The emphasis is the author's.

25. Bediako, *Theology and Identity*. Bediako devotes a whole chapter to Mbiti's thought (303–46).

"God the Father of our Lord Jesus Christ is the same God who for thousands of years has been known and worshipped in various ways within the religious life of African peoples. [Therefore] He was not a stranger in Africa prior to the coming of missionaries."[26]

Bediako wishes to emphasize that Mbiti's "concentration is on the person of Christ."[27] He explains the significance of Mbiti's position as follows: "Jesus Christ is not a latecomer on the scene in African religious life, nor, therefore, is his gospel a subsequent arrival, that is, subsequent to our cultures. Rather, Jesus Christ and his gospel are prior and constitute the foundation of our cultures."[28]

While we may be able to understand the words here, the question of the meaning is less clear. What does Bediako mean by saying "Jesus Christ and his gospel are prior"? This does not seem to be a statement of historical record but rather a statement of theology. Something of what Bediako means can be gleaned from his reference to John 1:3-4 in the context of his rejection of the approach of Byang Kato. Bediako writes,

> The real problem with his outlook is that strange as it may sound, by throwing out the whole African cultural heritage as valueless and theologically useless, one is also throwing out Jesus Christ, for Jesus Christ too was in that African cultural heritage. For . . .
>
> Through him all things were made; without him nothing was made that has been made. In him was life, and that life was the light of men. (John 1:3-4)
>
> "All things" includes all humanity, and therefore African peoples, in their cultural heritage.[29]

Aside from the overstated charge that Kato is "throwing out the whole African cultural heritage as valueless and theologically useless" (which I will comment on shortly), Bediako is surely correct that "all things" includes "all humanity, and therefore African peoples, in their cultural heritage," as the same is true of all people everywhere, but that fact cannot be used to justify every cultural and religious expression. All human beings, including those who reject the true God and follow other gods, owe their existence to the creative Word. That does not justify every cultural and religious expression in all places, as

---

26. Bediako, "Missionaries Did Not Bring Christ to Africa," 18, citing John Mbiti, "On the Article by John W. Kinney," *Occasional Bulletin of Missionary Research* 3, no. 2 (April 1979): 65–67.
27. Bediako, "Missionaries Did Not Bring Christ to Africa," 19.
28. Bediako, 19.
29. Bediako, 19.

every human being has turned away from God in sinful rebellion (Ps 14:1–4; cf. Rom 3:9–18).

In his article, Bediako notes a significant difference in position between John Mbiti and himself on the one hand and Byang Kato on the other hand. His fundamental concern appears to be that the Christian faith of Africans should be expressed in appropriate linguistic and cultural forms. Bediako writes,

> All this means that we cannot speak of serious Christian engagement with our African cultural heritage and the meanings within it if we ignore hearing, understanding and reflecting theologically on the Scriptures through the categories provided for us in the Scriptures in our African languages. It is not an adequate response to claim that in the present climate of "globalization," our indigenous African languages are set to be superseded by so-called world or "global" languages, such as English. If the Scriptures give an insight into the purposes of God, then the Scriptural pattern of world community is not one in which all the other languages in which God speaks are eliminated in the interest of one or a few dominant languages.[30]

This call for appropriate cultural expression does not seem controversial. In fact, as Tite Tiénou has pointed out, there is evidence to suggest that Byang Kato would not have disagreed with this point. Tiénou cites two key statements made by Kato: "Let *African* Christians be *Christian* Africans"; and "Every effort should be made to make the gospel indigenous in the local culture where it has been introduced."[31]

According to Bediako, however, Kato's analysis is fundamentally problematic. In *Theology and Identity*, Bediako writes, "It becomes hard to avoid the conclusion that Kato's generally negative estimation of African pre-Christian religious tradition was not only the result of observation and previous participation, but also a necessary corollary of the kind of theological presuppositions with which he operated."[32] This may or may not be so, but such an appeal to the theological presuppositions of another is double-edged. If Kato's presuppositions shape his conclusions, then surely the same is true for Bediako and Mbiti. Earlier in the same chapter, Bediako identifies the specific presuppositions he has in mind:

---

30. Bediako, 23.
31. Tiénou, "Evangelical Theology," 219.
32. Bediako, *Theology and Identity*, 389.

Whilst it cannot be said that Kato was entirely lacking in critical discernment regarding the theological models and viewpoints he espoused, it is nonetheless the case that there is little which does not stem from his deep roots in the conservative evangelical tradition – particularly the North American variant – of Christianity.[33]

This is a rather strange comment, not least because both Kato and Bediako did their initial theological training at the same evangelical institution in the UK, namely London Bible College. It is true that Kato pursued his postgraduate studies in the USA, but Bediako's comments appear to suggest a problematic influence on Kato from the evangelical tradition even though he himself has been exposed to that same influence.

So, for Bediako, Christ is understood here primarily as the creator of the cultural heritage expressed in African religion. But what of Jesus Christ as the bringer of Christian missionaries? Despite the title of his article, Bediako does not engage in any detail with the concept that Jesus Christ is sovereign in the way in which the gospel is brought to people in Africa and elsewhere, as his article title might suggest. It is to that theological theme that we now turn.

Jesus: Lord of Mission

To recap, John Mbiti employed a phrase which suggests that the arrival of Christian missionaries in Africa was directed by God. We have seen, however, that Mbiti's understanding of God is problematic because he identifies the deities named and venerated in various African religious traditions with the God of Israel and the God and Father of the Lord Jesus Christ. As Kwame Bediako adopted Mbiti's phrase but modified it into a statement of Christology, we might have expected a modification of Mbiti's position and an emphasis on Jesus Christ as the initiator and director of mission. But, in fact, we have seen that Bediako affirms Mbiti's position on African Traditional Religion and does not develop the christological argument with respect to mission. So the words used by Mbiti and Bediako have pointed to a christological concept that is worthy of serious attention, but they have not themselves developed that concept. It is important to state that Mbiti and Bediako apparently did not *intend* to develop the topic of Christ as Lord of mission. I am not, therefore, criticizing them for failing to take their discussions in a direction they did

---

33. Bediako, 386.

not intend. Instead, I am claiming, first, that their views regarding how God was active in African Traditional Religion are problematic, and, second, that Bediako's striking rephrasing of Mbiti's original comment suggests a theological reality which Bediako does not explore directly but which deserves further attention.

In this section of the paper, I will discuss whether any other African theologians have developed this idea that Jesus is Lord of mission. I will then outline how one missiologist from outside Africa has begun that task. I will then highlight some biblical texts which deserve attention in this regard and, finally, draw some conclusions.

Jesus as Lord

The fundamental Christian confession is "Jesus Christ is Lord" (John 20:28; Rom 10:9; 1 Cor 8:5–6; 12:3; Phil 2:11). This remarkable use of the typical Greek term used to translate the Tetragrammaton (YHWH) with reference to Jesus demonstrates that Jesus was understood to have the highest conceivable status: "If Jesus Christ is portrayed as the *Kyrios* who was, and is, fully involved in God's creative work, then whenever the church speaks of God the Creator, it cannot do so without also bringing in Jesus Christ."[34]

This is a claim to supreme power and authority. The same holds true with respect to providence. Colossians 1:16–17 brings creation and providence together, declaring, concerning the Son, that "in him all things were created: things in heaven and on earth, visible and invisible, whether thrones or powers or rulers or authorities; all things have been created through him and for him. He is before all things, and in him all things hold together."

So, how does this relate to the mission of the church?

Jesus as Lord of Mission in Recent African Scholarship

Scripture does not call Jesus "the Lord of mission."[35] For this reason, it is perhaps not surprising that recent African scholarship does not address the relationship between Christology and mission directly. In a selection of recent

---

34. Van der Kooi and van den Brink, *Christian Dogmatics*, 428.

35. There is also no clear statement on Jesus as Lord of mission in the Cape Town Commitment (Lausanne Movement). The closest to such a statement is found in section IIF2: "Partnership in mission is not only about efficiency. It is the strategic and practical outworking of our shared submission to Jesus Christ as Lord" (https://www.lausanne.org/content/ctcommitment#p2-6).

books on African Christology, there was no explicit reference to Jesus as Lord of mission. Diane Stinton's important book, *Jesus of Africa: Voices of Contemporary African Christology* (2004), examines several "models" for Jesus employed in contemporary Christologies: "life-giver," "mediator," "loved one" and "leader." Of these, "leader" comes closest to "Lord," and particularly in the form which describes Jesus as "King/Chief."[36] At no point, however, does Stinton make a connection between Christology and mission. Victor Ezigbo, in *Re-Imaging African Christologies* (2010), uses the phrase "Missionary Christology,"[37] but the term is used to refer to the christological formulations of missionaries rather than as a constructive presentation of Jesus's role in mission. Bediako has an essay entitled "How Is Jesus Christ Lord?,"[38] but he does not address the issue of Jesus's lordship in mission in that article.

Jesus as Lord of Mission according to J. H. Bavinck

One (European) author who does highlight the link between mission and Christology, albeit relatively briefly, is J. H. Bavinck, in his *An Introduction to the Science of Missions*.[39] For example, in discussing the material in the gospels, Bavinck writes,

> The gospel of Matthew bases the command of missions strongly upon the power and authority given to Jesus because of his finished mediatorial work. This redemptive power must be proclaimed and all peoples must bow before it: "go ye therefore and make disciples of all nations." The gospel contains something of the glory of a king's commission. It must, therefore, end with a summons to proclaim the kingship of Christ over the whole world.[40]

Bavinck appears to recognize here a link between Jesus's own person and his command to make disciples of all nations.

Likewise, Bavinck recognizes the role of the risen Jesus in the mission activities of the early Christian community recorded in Acts. Noting that "the book of the Acts of the Apostles is a missions document par excellence," Bavinck comments,

---

36. Stinton, *Jesus of Africa*, 178–92.
37. Ezigbo, *Re-Imaging African Christologies*, 7–17.
38. Bediako, "How Is Jesus Christ Lord?," in *Jesus and the Gospel in Africa*, 34–45 (ch. 3).
39. Bavinck, *Introduction to the Science of Missions*.
40. Bavinck, 34.

> It is first of all striking that the work of missions in the book of Acts is portrayed as the work of the glorified Christ. In this respect its name is actually improper: it should be called the Acts of Christ through his Apostles rather than the Acts of the Apostles.[41]

Bavinck points to several passages that provide support for his claim. First, he points out the implicit claim in Acts 1:1 that Acts recounts "what Jesus continues both to do and to teach."[42] Bavinck then draws attention to several verses in which Jesus is identified as the agent who accomplishes certain acts that extend the kingdom in the narrative: Jesus pours out the Spirit (Acts 2:33); mighty acts are done in Jesus's "name" (Acts 3:16; 4:10, 30); Jesus commissions Saul "to proclaim my name to the Gentiles and their kings and to the people of Israel" (Acts 9:15); Christ directs Peter to go to Cornelius although, in fact, the biblical text states that "the Spirit" gave this direction, Acts 10:19–20; Bavinck appears to treat actions ascribed to the Spirit as acts of Jesus (Acts 10); Jesus (or, more precisely, "the Spirit of Jesus") forbids Paul to go into Bithynia (Acts 16:9–10).[43] Referring particularly to Paul's missionary activity, Bavinck states, "It is clear on every page that Paul experienced his entire activity as a work in which Christ held the initiative and is the sole author; he himself is only an instrument (Acts 18:9–10)."[44]

Later in his work, Bavinck cites words from Answer 54 of the Heidelberg Catechism: "The Son of God gathers himself a church out of the whole human race," and comments, "Missions is not the work of man. We are not to raise with our weak hands that mighty edifice, the temple, holy in the Lord, but that edifice grows as of itself through the irresistible working of Christ, who is alone the corner-stone (Ephesians 2:20–22)."[45]

Bavinck sums up his comments,

> If we were to define missions, there would be every reason to declare: Missions is the great work of Jesus Christ, through which after his completed work as mediator, he draws all peoples to his salvation and makes them to partake of the gifts which he has obtained for them.[46]

---

41. Bavinck, 36.
42. Bavinck, 36.
43. Bavinck, 37–38.
44. Bavinck, 38.
45. Bavinck, 57.
46. Bavinck, 57–58.

Bavinck appears to recognize, in a way that few if any other theologians have, that there is an essential connection between Christology and mission, not simply in terms of the *content* of the gospel that is proclaimed, but also with respect to the authorization, direction and success of mission.

Jesus as Lord of Mission in Scripture

I will now briefly discuss a selection of biblical texts that provide foundations for the theological claim that Jesus is Lord of mission. These texts would provide support for Bediako's claim that it was Christ who brought missionaries to Africa, but he does not discuss them.

John 20:21

Perhaps the most obvious place to begin consideration of this theme is John 20:21, where the risen Jesus appears to his disciples, pronounces peace upon them and declares, "Just as the Father has sent me, I also am sending you" (καθὼς ἀπέσταλκέν με ὁ πατήρ, κἀγὼ πέμπω ὑμᾶς).[47] This is one of the key texts underpinning the concept of the *missio Dei*.[48] There are strong affinities between this text and the famous "Great Commission" passage in Matthew 28, although the settings are quite different and they should not be conflated. In both cases, the risen Jesus gives a commission to his disciples. This commission is given in the context of a claim to have authority to issue such a commission. In Matthew 28, the claim is explicitly stated ("all authority has been given to me"); here in John, it is implicit in the wounds that Jesus displays (20:20), which demonstrate that he has overcome death.[49] Jesus draws a close analogy between the Father's action in sending him, the Son, and his action in sending the disciples ("just as . . . I also").

Matthew 9:35–38

While Scripture does not call Jesus "the Lord of mission" explicitly, it perhaps comes very close to this description in Matthew 9. The reason that I use the cautious expression "perhaps" is that there is a measure of ambiguity in the text. In this passage, Jesus has compassion on the crowds (v. 36), states that

---

47. Greek text is from Holmes, *Greek New Testament*. My translation highlights the "just as . . . I also" construction more clearly than the NIV.

48. Latin for "mission/sending of God." See Ott, Strauss and Tennent, *Encountering Theology of Mission*, 61–62.

49. Gorman, *Abide and Go*, 136.

"the harvest is plentiful but the workers are few" (v. 37), and then calls on his disciples to "ask the Lord of the harvest, therefore, to send out workers into his harvest field" (v. 38). Who is "the Lord of the harvest"? This enigmatic title is not found elsewhere. R. T. France regards this reference as simply part of the harvest image and understands it as a reference to God.[50] Likewise, Bitrus Sarma includes this text among those that speak of the Father's activity in Matthew's gospel.[51] Keener agrees that this would be a reasonable conclusion, but comments, "It is interesting, however, that it is Jesus who sends the workers forth."[52] Sarma, along with other commentators, notes that there are echoes of Ezekiel 34:5 and Zechariah 10:2 in this passage.[53] In this context, Jesus embodies the role of Yahweh in the Old Testament texts, acting as the true shepherd of the people (compare also John 10:11, 14). This is a strong contextual clue to suggest that Jesus may also be identified as "the Lord of the harvest," particularly since, in the verses that follow, Jesus is specifically described as the one who "sent out" the Twelve (10:5). Sarma also acknowledges similarities with God's act of sending the prophets (e.g. Jer 1:7),[54] which also, in my view, makes the identification of Jesus with "the Lord of the harvest" more likely.

Matthew 28:16–20

Matthew 28:16–20 is a crucial text for understanding the connection between Christology and mission. Jesus claims all authority and commands his disciples to make disciples. David Bosch devotes a significant portion of a chapter entitled "Matthew: Mission as Disciple-Making" to a discussion of "the Great Commission,"[55] yet, surprisingly, he does not dwell on Jesus's introductory words, which provide the foundation for the commission that he gives his disciples, instead focusing only on the instructions Jesus gives. Sarma, on the other hand, correctly recognizes that "in the final commission (28:16–20) Jesus sends the disciples with the authority ($\dot{\varepsilon}\xi o u \sigma i \alpha$) that has been given to him by the Father."[56] Similarly, Joe Kapolyo comments that, in his view, lack of engagement in mission on the part of the African church constitutes

---

50. France, *Gospel of Matthew*, 374.
51. Sarma, *Hermeneutics of Mission*, 30–31.
52. Keener, *Gospel of Matthew*, 309.
53. Sarma, *Hermeneutics of Mission*, 30.
54. Sarma, 45.
55. Bosch, *Transforming Mission*, 56–68.
56. Sarma, *Hermeneutics of Mission*, 45.

"disobedience to the words of the Lord of heaven and earth."[57] The Christology implied by the passage is that the risen Jesus has all authority to be the Lord of mission.

Acts 8

Among the numerous striking features of the narrative of the encounter between Philip and the Ethiopian eunuch is the emphasis on the divine choreography of the encounter. At this point, I must acknowledge that there is no explicit reference to the agency of Jesus in the passage. There is, on the other hand, reference to the "angel of the Lord" and to "the Spirit." It is certainly true, as Schnabel says, that "Luke repeatedly emphasizes God's initiative (Acts 8:26, 29, 39),"[58] but, in line with Bavinck's comments on the significance of Acts 1:1 cited above, I would go further and argue that the references to "the angel of the Lord" and "the Spirit" ultimately speak of the sovereign activity of the risen Jesus. Alan Thompson, in his book *The Acts of the Risen Lord Jesus*, makes the point effectively, arguing that "as important as the Holy Spirit is in Acts, it should be noted that even this designation does not quite capture the emphasis of Luke in Acts." In agreement with Bavinck, Thompson claims that "the 'Acts of the Risen Lord Jesus' would be a better title."[59] But that raises the question of why, in this passage, it is the angel of the Lord and the Holy Spirit who are identified as agents. Thompson suggests that this title "could be understood as a shorthand expression for something like 'the Acts of the Lord Jesus, through his people, by the Holy Spirit, for the accomplishment of God's purposes'!"[60] Although Philip is directed by the angel of the Lord and the Holy Spirit, Acts 1:1 reminds us that it is the risen Lord Jesus who continues to act. This association of the activity of the Spirit and the activity of Jesus is particularly evident in Acts 16:7, where Luke says that "the Spirit of Jesus [τὸ πνεῦμα Ἰησοῦ]" would not allow them to enter Bithynia.

It is not clear how Africans who became disciples of Jesus in the early period of the expansion of the church worked out his command in their experience, but the New Testament gives us every reason to assume that they did. Thus, while we are given no indication in Acts of the ongoing story of the Ethiopian official who met Philip (Acts 8:26–40), and "there are no Christian

---

57. Kapolyo, "Matthew," 1170.
58. Schnabel, *Jesus and the Twelve*, 685–86.
59. Thompson, *Acts of the Risen Lord Jesus*, 48–49.
60. Thompson, 49.

remains from that period,"[61] we have every reason to imagine that his conduct would have been similar to that of the disciples mentioned at the beginning of that same chapter, who, when scattered by persecution, "preached the word wherever they went" (Acts 8:4). Bayo Famonure's short article on "Indigenous Missions" in the *Africa Bible Commentary*[62] describes the activities of African Christians in the twentieth century, but we can be confident that Africans were living as Christian disciples and missionaries from the earliest days following Pentecost. Our brief consideration of several key texts demonstrates that there is a biblical foundation for the claim that Jesus is the Lord of mission and that it was his sovereign will that was being worked out as people from Africa encountered the gospel in various circumstances and then made it known in their own contexts.

Conclusion

John Mbiti's striking reference to the agency of God in bringing missionaries to Africa is, in my view, vulnerable to the charge that it blurs the distinction between the God revealed in the Christian Scriptures and the divinities worshipped in African Traditional Religions. Kwame Bediako's christological rephrasing of Mbiti's statement is a vast improvement theologically, but Bediako's article disappoints in two ways: first, he largely affirms Mbiti's problematic approach to African Traditional Religion; and second, he does not take the opportunity that his title offers to develop a constructive "mission Christology." In response to the words of these two distinguished African scholars, I have attempted to sketch the outline of a reading of selected New Testament passages so as to show that Jesus is indeed the Lord of mission in the sense that he is portrayed as the authorizer and initiator of mission both before and after his death and resurrection, and that, with due regard for the overstatement in the aphorism, there is justification for claiming that "Missionaries did not bring Christ to Africa – Christ brought them."

Bibliography

Anderson, William B., and Ogbu U. Kalu. "Christianity in Sudan and Ethiopia." In *African Christianity: An African Story*, edited by Ogbu U. Kalu, 67–101. Asmara: Africa World, 2007.

---

61. Anderson and Kalu, "Christianity in Sudan and Ethiopia," 68.
62. Famonure, "Indigenous Missions," 1348.

Bantu, Vince L. *A Multitude of All Peoples*. Downers Grove: IVP Academic, 2020.
Bavinck, Johan H. *An Introduction to the Science of Missions*. Philadelphia: P&R, 1960.
Bediako, Kwame. *Christianity in Africa: The Renewal of a Non-Western Religion*. Maryknoll: Orbis, 1995.
———. *Jesus and the Gospel in Africa: History and Experience*. Maryknoll: Orbis, 2004.
———. "Missionaries Did Not Bring Christ to Africa: Christ Brought Them; Why Africa Needs Jesus Christ." *AICMAR Bulletin* 6 (2007): 17–31.
———. *Theology and Identity: The Impact of Culture upon Christian Thought in the Second Century and in Modern Africa*. Oxford: Regnum, 1999 (originally 1992).
Bongmba, Elias Kifon. "Christianity in North Africa." In *The Routledge Companion to Christianity in Africa*, edited by Elias Kifon Bongmba, 25–44. Abingdon: Routledge, 2016.
Bosch, David J. *Transforming Mission*. Maryknoll: Orbis, 1991.
Dinkelaker, Bernhard. *How Is Jesus Christ Lord? Reading Kwame Bediako from a Postcolonial and Intercontextual Perspective*. New York: Peter Lang, 2016.
Ezigbo, Victor I. *Re-Imagining African Christologies: Conversing with the Interpretations and Appropriations of Jesus in Contemporary African Christianity*. Eugene: Pickwick, 2010.
Famonure, Bayo. "Indigenous Missions." In *Africa Bible Commentary*, edited by Tokunboh Adeyemo, 1348. Nairobi: WordAlive, 2006.
France, Richard T. *The Gospel of Matthew*. NICNT. Grand Rapids: Eerdmans, 2007.
Fretheim, Sara J. *Kwame Bediako and African Christian Scholarship*. Eugene: Pickwick, 2018.
Gorman, Michael J. *Abide and Go: Missional Theosis in the Gospel of John*. The Didsbury Lecture Series. Eugene: Cascade, 2018.
Hesselgrave, David J., and Edward Rommen. *Contextualization: Meanings, Methods, and Models*. Grand Rapids: Baker, 1989.
Hexham, Irving. *Understanding World Religions*. Grand Rapids: Zondervan, 2011.
Holmes, Michael W., ed. *The Greek New Testament: SBL Edition*. Bellingham: Logos Bible Software; Atlanta: Society of Biblical Literature, 2011–13.
Kalu, Ogbu U., ed. *African Christianity: An African Story*. Asmara: Africa World, 2007.
Kapolyo, Joe. "Matthew." In *Africa Bible Commentary*, edited by Tokunboh Adeyemo, 1105–70. Nairobi: Word Alive, 2006.
Kato, Byang H. *Theological Pitfalls in Africa*. Kisumu: Evangel, 1975.
Keener, Craig S. *A Commentary on the Gospel of Matthew*. Grand Rapids: Eerdmans, 1999.
Kunhiyop, Samuel Waje. *African Christian Theology*. 2nd ed. Nairobi: Hippo Books, 2012.
Lausanne Movement. Cape Town Commitment. 2010. https://www.lausanne.org/content/ctcommitment/.
Mbiti, John S. "The Encounter of Christian Faith and African Religion." *Christian Century*, 27 August–3 September 1980, 817–20. Reproduced at Religion Online.

Accessed 13 July 2020. https://www.religion-online.org/article/the-encounter-of-christian-faith-and-african-religion/.

———. *Introduction to African Religion*. Long Grove: Waveland, 1991 (originally 1975).

Mburu, Elizabeth. *African Hermeneutics*. Carlisle: HippoBooks, 2019.

McDermott, Gerald R., and Harold A. Netland. *A Trinitarian Theology of Religions: An Evangelical Proposal*. Oxford: Oxford University Press, 2014.

Oden, Thomas C. *How Africa Shaped the Christian Mind*. Downers Grove: IVP Academic, 2010.

Ott, Craig, Stephen J. Strauss, and Timothy C. Tennent. *Encountering Theology of Mission*. Grand Rapids: Baker Academic, 2010.

Sarma, Bitrus A. *Hermeneutics of Mission in Matthew*. Carlisle: Langham Monographs, 2015.

Schnabel, Eckhard J. *Early Christian Mission*. Vol. 1, *Jesus and the Twelve*. Downers Grove: InterVarsity Press, 2004.

Stinton, Diane B. *Jesus of Africa: Voices of Contemporary African Christology*. Maryknoll: Orbis, 2004.

Strange, Daniel. *"For Their Rock Is Not as Our Rock": An Evangelical Theology of Religions*. Nottingham: Apollos, 2014.

Thompson, Alan J. *The Acts of the Risen Lord Jesus: Luke's Account of God's Unfolding Plan*. Nottingham: Apollos, 2011.

Tiénou, Tite. "Evangelical Theology in African Contexts." In *The Cambridge Companion to Evangelical Theology*, edited by Timothy Larsen and Daniel J. Treier, 213–24. Cambridge: Cambridge University Press, 2007.

van der Kooi, Cornelis, and Gijsbert van den Brink. *Christian Dogmatics: An Introduction*. Grand Rapids: Eerdmans, 2017.

Wijsen, Frans. "Mission Practice and Theory in Africa." In *The Routledge Companion to Christianity in Africa*, edited by Elias Kifon Bongmba, 189–200. Abingdon: Routledge, 2016.

18

Jesus in Islam

A Theological Argument with a Missional Response

Lawrence Oseje
*Senior Lecturer, Department of Theology and Biblical Studies,
School of Education, Kabarak University, Nakuru, Kenya*

Abstract

Throughout history and in many places in the world, Christians and Muslims have coexisted. They have interacted in business, workplaces and communities everywhere. Both Christianity and Islam are missionary religions whose goal is to propagate their faith and win as many people as possible to their side. Their interactions and relationships have been marked by both conflict and also peaceful coexistence. In their encounters with Christians, Muslims have raised questions that center on the humanity and divinity of Christ. They also have reservations about the Trinity as understood by many Christians. In their conversations, Muslims often doubt and sometimes discredit Christian beliefs about the divinity of Jesus, terming it as inaccurate or misplaced. They refer to the Bible, Qur'an and Hadith to justify or support their arguments or queries. Such conversations elicit much debate and emotion, and sometimes end abruptly. The answers or reactions of Christians sometimes seem unconvincing to Muslims, a clear indication of the Christians' lack of preparedness in handling Muslim objections or queries about the attributes of Jesus. This question of the nature of Jesus Christ is so pivotal to the Christian faith and mission that it becomes almost impossible not to explore it. In this paper, the researcher has looked at the subject by examining Christian–Muslim relations. He explores Muslim perspectives on Jesus, and the defense Muslims make and the arguments they put forward. Finally, the researcher has examined Christian responses to Muslims' understanding of Jesus, from both theological and sociocultural perspectives. Even though giving total satisfaction to Muslims' queries might be hard to achieve, the researcher proposes approaches that the church can apply in its evangelism among Muslim communities. This includes building loving relationships and helpful support systems.

Key words: Jesus, Islam, theological, argument, responses, missional

Introduction

The theme that ASET has proposed is "Who Do People Say That I Am? Christology in Africa." It is based on the conversation between Jesus and his disciples (Matt 16:13–20 NIV). The disciples' response to his question was quite striking: "Some say John the Baptist; others say Elijah; and still others, Jeremiah or one of the prophets" (Matt 16:14). Even though the religion of Islam came several centuries after the death of Jesus Christ, Jesus could still ask the same question today to his disciples, the church, and get similar answers about who Muslims say he is.

The second part of this question, "Who do you say I am?," is specifically directed to his disciples, which is the church today. Jesus's response to Peter's assertion, "You are the Messiah, the Son of the living God," is that this truth is beyond human comprehension. From this scripture, three categories of people emerge. The first category is other people, which includes Muslims. The second category is represented by the disciples of Jesus and is Christians or the church. The last is the group that represents all people, everyone. This group represents the ultimate point Jesus Christ wants every human being to reach. Peter's confession represents a deep revelation about the identity of Christ. This conversation between Jesus and his disciples reflects the kind of interaction between Christians and Muslims in our society today. Christology is, therefore, a pivotal subject that the church needs to address to meet the felt needs of the Muslim community.

Christian–Muslim Relations

Goddard, among other scholars, records that Christians and Muslims have existed side by side for many centuries in many parts of the world.[1] Conflict as well as peaceful coexistence characterize their relationships. Both are missionary religions (*Dawwah* in Islam), and therefore possess missionary zeal. Husseini states: "In Christian–Muslim interactions or debates, many issues come up including matters of faith and morality."[2] Husseini goes on to say that in Christian–Muslim relations these issues of faith center on the nature of God, the Trinity, the person and divinity of Christ, and the Crusades. Questions such as "Is Jesus the Son of God? Did he die on the cross? Is Jesus God?" often come up as Christians witness to Muslims.

The Bible, Qur'an and Hadith share some similarities with regard to Christology. Yet Christology is the most pivotal area in Christian–Muslim dialogue and relationships, being perceived by some scholars as the "center for polemical, irenic conversations, [the] most disputed and intriguing area in Christian–Muslim debate."[3] The debate divides the two faiths[4] and strains their relationship.[5] Other scholars view Christianity and Islam as diametrically opposed to each other, with no or little possibility for adjudication on the matter.[6] Part of the dialogical learning process that Mahmoud discusses is to get to know what Muslims believe about Jesus and what informs their beliefs.[7] First, this understanding answers the question "Who do [Muslims] say I am?" Second, it is through such dialogue that Christians may have the opportunity to help Muslims clarify their beliefs and perspective on Jesus, thus enabling them to answer the question "But who do you say I am?" Finally, based on what they have learned, the church can then devise ways of clarifying and responding to Muslims' inquiries about Jesus in a way that will conform to its mandate of the Great Commission.[8]

---

1. Goddard, *Christians and Muslims*, 1–8.
2. Husseini, *Early Christian–Muslim Debate*, ii.
3. Siddiqui, *Christians, Muslims, and Jesus*, 149, 226.
4. Maqsood, *What Every Christian Should Know*, 122.
5. Travis, "Diversity and Change," 195. Cf. George, 2009, 20.
6. Geisler and Saleeb, *Answering Islam*, 233.
7. Ayoub, "Towards an Islamic Christology," 165.
8. Damon, "Christology and Trinity," 124.

Muslims' Perspectives of Jesus

The question "Who do people say I am?" (Matt 16:13 paraphrased) sounds familiar in our Christian engagement with Muslims today. Who do Muslims say Jesus is? Muslims have views about Jesus that are different from those of the majority of Christians. Muslim views on Jesus are based on Christian–Muslim encounters in the past, such as the Crusades, colonialism, and the current political policies of the "Christian" West.[9] Their views are also drawn from the Qur'an, what the prophet Muhammad says about Jesus in the Hadith, their interpretation of the biblical texts centered on Jesus, Christian lifestyle and the Christian way of worship, testimonies, and the experiences of Muslims themselves.

The Crusades bring a bitter memory that still lingers on, making evangelism difficult among Muslims.[10] This Crusades mentality has made some Muslims view Christians or the Jesus whom Christians proclaim as unreal or deceptive. In other places, Muslim converts to Christianity identify themselves as "followers of Jesus" rather than as Christians.

Muslims' Positive Views of Jesus

While Muslims view Jesus differently from Christians, there are numerous positive things that they attribute to Jesus. First, they claim that Jesus (*Isa*) is a Prophet (*nabi*) and an apostle (Messenger of Allah). Jesus is quoted in the Qur'an as acknowledging his prophethood and apostleship as a messenger from Allah (Q 19:30; 4:171; 2:253; 3:49; 5:78; 57:27; 61:6).[11] According to the Qur'an, the title of an apostle bestowed upon Jesus was very special: "Those Messengers we endowed with gifts, some above others . . . Jesus, the son of Mary . . . and strengthened him with the Holy Spirit" (Q 2:253 paraphrased). This, however, in no way translates into any "kind of divinity or self-revelation of God."[12] But the Qur'an makes him equal with the other prophets (Q 3:84),[13] as Ziafat notes.[14] Some Muslims believe that *Isa* is greater than Muhammad. Larson, for example, quotes a Pakistani Muslim villager saying to a Christian

---

9. Travis, "Diversity and Change," 195.
10. Tucker, *From Jerusalem to Irian Jaya*, 93.
11. Terry, *Missiology*, 342. Cf. Geisler and Saleeb, *Answering Islam*, 63.
12. Siddiqui, *Christians, Muslims, and Jesus*, 226.
13. Sookhdeo, *Understanding Islamic Theology*, 209.
14. Ziafat, "Sharing the Gospel," 157.

friend: "Your Prophet was a Prophet from birth, ours became one at age 40; Your Prophet did miracles, ours did none; Your Prophet is alive, ours is dead."[15]

Second, Jesus is viewed as the Messiah (Al-Masih), who was supernaturally born and is respected in Islam: "The account of Jesus' birth (Q 3:45–46; 19:16–40) suggests that he was supernaturally born, but still strongly refutes the title 'Son of God.'"[16] Larson also states that "'Messiah' is a very significant term for Jesus in the Qur'an, and he receives this title (Christ) eleven times (Q 3:45; 4:157; 4:169; 4:170; 5:17; 5:75; 9:31)."[17] Acceptance of Jesus runs beyond just acknowledging him as a Al-Masih: "Our love of Jesus (Peace be upon him) knows no bounds, and our feelings towards him run so deep that we give our children the names of Jesus and Mary."[18] Kaltner expresses a similar sentiment.[19] One of the imams is quoted as saying: "At the mention of Jesus, 'I [imam] was overcome with tears of joy and veneration. I love Jesus so very much!' Then he added, 'But Jesus was only an apostle of God. He was not the Son of God.'"[20] Regarding the end times, as Chatrath says, "Muslims believe that Jesus is a prophet who will return at the final resurrection."[21]

Third, Jesus is viewed as the *Kalima* (Word) and *Ruh* (Spirit) of Allah (Q 2:87; 3:39; 4:171; 19:35).[22] Parshall adds that the most exciting title given to Jesus in the Qur'an is "God's Word." He urges Christians to use this title to explain the title "Son of God" to Muslims.[23] "Jesus is mentioned more than ninety times in the Qur'an as the Word of God. Some Muslims believe that the Qur'an elevates Jesus but respects Muhammad."[24] This, however, may not reflect the reality on the ground.

> It is reported that when Muhammad realized his dream and occupied the city of Mecca in AD 630, he proceeded to cleanse the *Ka'aba* of idols. He gave the command that all icons be destroyed, but when he saw the Virgin Mary and her son, he covered them

---

15. Larson, "Jesus in Islam," 338.
16. Djaballah, "Jesus in Islam," 19.
17. Larson, "Jesus in Islam," 329.
18. Al-Madkhalee, *Status of Jesus*, 5.
19. Kaltner, *Islam*, 55–56.
20. Shenk, *Journeys of the Muslim Nation*, 88.
21. Chatrath, *Reaching Muslims*, 67.
22. Tanagho, *Glad News!*, 87.
23. Parshall, *New Paths*, 135.
24. Masri, *Connecting with Muslims*, 123.

with his coat. Another tradition relates that Jesus and his mother were the only people not touched by Satan at birth.²⁵

Fourth, Muslims believe that Jesus was born of a virgin and was sinless – his virgin, supernatural birth are declared in the Qur'an (Q 19:16–21; 3:37–45). "Mary, still a virgin, gives birth to Jesus beneath a palm tree, which miraculously provides fresh ripe dates for her to eat" (Q 19:20–27). Other prophets, such as Noah (Q 1:49) . . . Abraham (Q 26:80–82) . . . Moses (Q 28:15) [and] Muhammad (Q 40:57; 47:21; 48:1, 2) are said to have sinned and needed forgiveness, but not Jesus. Both the Christian and Muslim scriptures claim that Jesus was without sin (cf. Q 19:9; John 8:46; 14:30; Heb 4:15; 7:28).

Fifth, Jesus is also believed to have been a healer and a miracle-worker. He speaks as a newborn in the cradle.²⁶ He also proclaims his prophethood (Q 19:29–31; 5:113). He heals and raises people from the dead. He breathed into a bird made out of clay (Q 3:49; 5:110). Miller notes: "Even to this day, if a person wishes to compliment a doctor in Iran, he may say something like, 'Doctor, you perform miracles; you have the breath of Jesus.'"²⁷ In response to Jesus's request, God sends down a table from heaven that is meant to be "a festival for all generations for his disciples" (Q 5:112–114).

Sixth, many Muslims believe that Jesus was taken to heaven and will come back. They in fact, say that Allah raised him to himself (Q 3:54–55; cf. 4:155–59). Saleeb, for his part, states: "The words 'God raised him up unto Himself' have often been taken to mean that Jesus was taken up alive to heaven without dying."²⁸ Kathir quotes Ibn Abbas narrating how Mary watched and waved at her son until he was taken up unto heaven.²⁹ Jesus's return, as perceived by Muslims, will be very dramatic. For instance, it is believed that "He [Jesus] will descend on earth as a just judge, a righteous *imam*; he will break the cross, kill the pig, and impose the *jizya* [a special tax on unbelievers paid to Muslim rulers for their protection]."³⁰ On his return to earth, he will destroy the Antichrist (*Dajjal*). Doi further narrates what Muhammad said about Jesus:

> He will marry, have children, and live forty-five years, after which he will die and be buried along with me [Muhammad] in my

---

25. Larson, "Jesus in Islam," 327.
26. Abu Huraira, "Al-Bukhari," Hadith 6, no. 60, 236 (n.d.).
27. Miller, *Christian Response to Islam*, 77.
28. Geisler and Saleeb, *Answering Islam*, 67.
29. Kathir, *Islamic View of Jesus*, 92–93.
30. Ibn Taimiyah and Michel, *Muslim Theologian's Response*, 306.

grave. The Muslims will pray over him. Then "Jesus, son of Mary, and I [Muhammad] shall arise from the grave between Abu Bakr and Umar."

Other titles [given to Jesus] include "the Speech of Truth" (Q 19:34–35), "a sign (Ayah) unto men," and "Mercy from (God)" (Q 19:21).[31]

Muslims' Negative Views of Jesus

The following views are negative in the sense that they are contrary to what most Christians "believe about Jesus. First, Muslims claim that Jesus was just a Prophet not the Prophet. He was put lower than or inferior to Muhammad."[32] On the other hand, Muhammad is viewed to be the "seal" of the prophets. Qur'an attributes him not to be more than a prophet(Q 5:75), a sentiment that Geisler and Saleeb also express.[33] Some Muslims, however, consider Jesus to be on a par with Muhammad and other humans in this earthly life and the hereafter.[34] This low view of Jesus is also necessitated by Muslims' claim that Christians have refused to reciprocate or acknowledge Muhammad as the Prophet.[35] Muslims claim that Jesus foretold the coming of Muhammad ("another advocate," John 14:16) as they interpret it.[36]

Second, there is a claim that Jesus was a Muslim, and as such, his basic message was about the oneness of God (Q 3:51; 19:36; 43:64). The Qur'an states that Jesus warned the Children of Israel that Paradise would be denied to those who ascribe partners to God (Q 5:72), cursed those who rejected faith (Q 5:78), but those who worship in truth are compared in the gospel with seeds that grow up strong, to the delight and wonder of the sowers (48:29). Jesus is also said to have called disciples and summoned them to be "helpers" in God's cause (Q 3:52–55; 5:111; 61:14).

Third, many Muslims reject the "notion that Jesus is God or the Son of God." These claims are viewed as pure lies and fabrication (Q 19:89–95; 112:1–4; 18:4–5).[37] The Qur'an states that Allah has taken neither a wife nor a son (see Q 72:3; cf. 19:35); Jesus and Adam were created by God's command

---

31. Doi, "Status of Prophet Jesus in Islam," 23.
32. Kateregga and Shenk, *Islam and Christianity*, 47.
33. Geisler and Saleeb, *Answering Islam*, 63.
34. Leirvik, *Images of Jesus Christ*, 22.
35. Kerr, "Prophet Muhammad," 119.
36. George, *Is the Father of Jesus the God of Muhammad?*, 33–34.
37. Al-Madkhalee, *Status of Jesus*, 15.

(Q 3:59). Anis quotes Ahmad Deedat as saying "that if Jesus is God, and the very Son of God because He has no earthly father, then Adam is a greater God, because he had no father and no mother! Simple, basic common sense demands this deduction."[38] To call Jesus "begotten son of God raises red flags immediately in the Islamic mind."[39] Muslims claim that Jesus was not the son of God, not God in human flesh and not a partner of God (Q 5:17, 73, 116–17). This constitutes a denial of their (Muslim) confession of *Tawhid*, a sin, which is *shirk* (associating God with other things).[40]

Fourth, there is a vehement denial that Jesus suffered, died on the cross and was . . . crucified (Q 4:157–59). Cragg also quotes Seyyed Hossein Nasr as having alluded to this.[41] Larson states: "[Muslims] have said that theologically it need not happen; morally it should not happen; historically it did not happen."[42] This is an apparent contradiction since the Qur'an suggests that the prophets of Allah can be killed (3:21; 2:87; 4:155). It is clear from the aforementioned study that the death of Jesus is denied by some Muslims. In contrast, the Bible is very clear about the death and resurrection of Jesus (see Mark 15:39; John 19:18, 25; Rom 6:10). The claim is that he was taken up into heaven in bodily form (Q 3:55).

Defense of Their Views about Jesus

This section underlines what informs Muslim views about Jesus. There are both positive and negative elements. First, there is a claim that Christians refuse to acknowledge Muhammad as the Prophet. Muslims usually react against this.[43] Some have even expressed that they will no longer respect Christ when Christians dialogue with them about him.[44] This perceived disrespect for Muhammad is historical and includes Jews.[45]

Second, the confession of *Tawhid* (oneness of God) is believed to negate the Christian claim of the Trinity: "So believe in God and His Messengers, and say not, 'Three.' Refrain: better is it for you. God is only One God. Glory

---

38. Anis, *Islam Revealed*, 266.
39. Geisler and Saleeb, *Answering Islam*, 263.
40. Rhodes, *Reasoning from the Scriptures*, 49.
41. Cragg, *Jesus and the Muslim*, 74.
42. Larson, "Jesus in Islam," 332.
43. Aydin, "Contemporary Christian Evaluations," 105.
44. Leirvik, *Images of Jesus Christ*, 223.
45. Chapman, *Islam and the West*, 22.

be to Him – and that He should have a son!" (4:168–69). Quoting the Qur'an, Johnson states: "Jesus is a great man, a prophet, but he is only a man."[46]

Third, the Christian gospel is considered compromised. In contrast, Muslims are ready to defend God against anything that might detract from God's absolute sovereignty and transcendence.[47] According to George, "Muslims allege that it is against God's nature to die on the cross or allow his son to go through such a humiliating experience. This horrific experience also denies the sovereignty of God. The whole issue of crucifixion has been turned to mean 'cruci-fiction.'"[48] There is also the argument that a holy and righteous God could not allow his beloved prophet to be killed.[49] Another view is that "Jesus was crucified but did not die on the cross. He was lifted to heaven to escape his enemies, and someone else was crucified instead."[50] The claim that Jesus was a human being makes it hard for Muslims to believe that he could bear the burdens of others as an atoning sacrifice (Q 39:7). According to Muslims, there is no way the death of one person could save others.[51]

Belief in Jesus "as the son of God, his crucifixion and death on the cross are considered as Christians' and Jews' myths or misguided information."[52] Muslims view Christian claims of Christ's death on the cross as bringing shame and dishonor on Jesus, whom they respect. They therefore argue that they honor Jesus more than Christians do. As such, the Christian preoccupation with the need to bring all people to the love of Jesus seems to them unnecessary.[53] Muslims argue that prophets encountered resistance, unbelief, antagonism and persecution from their enemies, but God vindicated them and put their enemies to shame. God would have failed if he had allowed Jesus to die in such a cruel and shameful way.[54] This disbelief in Christ's crucifixion is also based on Muslims' theological concepts of God's sovereignty and their rejection of Christian teaching on human depravity.[55] The Christian insistence on "Jesus' death on the cross makes some Muslims conclude that the Jesus of Christian

---

46. Johnson, *Judging Jesus*, 57.
47. Shenk, *Journeys of the Muslim Nation*, 90.
48. George, *Is the Father of Jesus the God of Muhammad?*, 99.
49. Larson, "Jesus in Islam," 332.
50. Masri, *Connecting with Muslims*, 132.
51. McDowell and Zaka, *Muslims and Christians*, 126.
52. Al-Madkhalee, *Status of Jesus*, 5.
53. Woodberry, *Muslims and Christians*, 167.
54. Anderson, *Islam in the Modern World*, 219.
55. Geisler and Saleeb, *Answering Islam*, 282.

Gospels and the *Isa* of the Qur'an are absolutely distinct from each other,"[56] a fact that Azhar also attests.[57]

Fourth, the Christian concept of Trinity and Jesus's birth is another area where Muslim defense abounds. Muslims associate the Trinity with pagan worship of the kind that was very prominent in the pre-Islamic era. The three common gods during this period were Allat, Al-Uzza, and Manat. They were acclaimed by the pagans of Mecca to be the "daughters of Allah" (Q 53:19–20). According to George, "the idea that the Almighty God of Creation should cohabit with mortals and produce progeny was anathema to Muhammad. 'What! Shall you have sons, and Allah daughters?' he asked in derision (Q 53:21)." George further adds that "it was the mission of Muhammad to destroy this kind of idolatry root and branch."[58] Trinity is understood to be the worship of three gods (the father, the Virgin Mary, and Jesus). This in the mind of many Muslims is considered as idolatry hence unacceptable. "The interpretation of Jesus being the son is that God had a physical union with Mary."[59] This understanding is purely anthropomorphic, as Rhodes asserts.[60] Jesus as the "begotten Son of God" (see John 1:18; cf. 3:16) is understood by Muslims literally and as an animal act. The term "begotten," according to Muslims, carries the notion of creating, and God cannot create another God.[61] The Qur'an refutes claims of God begetting a son (Q 17:111; 19:36).

The idea of the Trinity is also understood by Muslims through the lenses of the prophet Muhammad. He understood it as "tritheism," that is, three different entities of the Father, Mary, and their son Jesus.[62] "Islamic misunderstanding of the Trinity is encouraged by the words of Muhammad who said, 'O Jesus, son of Mary! didst thou say unto mankind: Take me and my mother for two gods beside Allah?' (Q 5:119)."[63]

The church's symbols and Christian heretics have also been responsible for the Muslim perception that Christians worship three gods. This includes the "Mariology" (images or pictures of Mary) of the Byzantine church.[64] The

---

56. Durrani, *Qur'anic Facts about Jesus*, 6.
57. Azhar, *Christianity in History*, 23.
58. George, *Is the Father of Jesus the God of Muhammad?*, 57–58.
59. Saal, *Reaching Muslims for Christ*, 64.
60. Rhodes, *Reasoning from the Scriptures*, 49.
61. Saal, *Reaching Muslims for Christ*, 23.
62. Riddell and Cotterell, *Islam in Context*, 75–76.
63. Geisler and Saleeb, *Answering Islam*, 264.
64. Register, *Dialogue and Interfaith Witness*, 28.

idea of the worship of three gods emanated from the heretical sect of the Collyridians. This sect was "made up mostly of women and regarded the Virgin Mary as a goddess, and sacrificed little round cakes to her called collyris."[65]

Fifth, the basis of the Muslim argument about Jesus emanates from their misinterpretation of the biblical texts. For example, in John 14:16, "another advocate" (or "counselor") is considered to refer to the coming of Muhammad. "The Greek word for 'Counselor' ('Comforter' or 'Helper' in some translations) is *paracletos*. Muslim scholars suggest, however, that the original word in this text from John's gospel was *periclytos* ('praised one')."[66]

Christian Responses to Muslims' Understanding of Jesus

We have seen the different perceptions held by Muslims about Jesus. In this section, we look at approaches used by Christians in their interactions with Muslims. Different approaches, models or theoretical concepts have been used by different Christians in such interactions or encounters with Muslims.[67] This researcher adopts a missional model as his theoretical framework. The choice of missional model is informed by the fact that the perception of Muslims toward Jesus is not limited to theological reasons but is also sociocultural. This missional model or approach is holistic and addresses other Muslim felt needs that are nontheological[68] and yet are vitally important.

These nontheological issues that the missional framework covers include emotional, cognitive, cultural and social hindrances that must be overcome.[69] Elements emphasized in the missional approach are proximate witness; prayer and miracles; Jesus, not religion; allowing the Bible to speak for itself; and new expressions of following Jesus.[70] As the two critical sides to this missional approach are theology and culture,[71] this section therefore approaches Christian responses to Muslims' understandings under these two aspects.

---

65. George, *Is the Father of Jesus the God of Muhammad?*, 59.
66. George, 33–34.
67. Renard, *Islam and Christianity*, 224. The approaches include polemic, scholastic, Christian-inclusivist, dialogical and intertheological, pluralist and missional models.
68. Bijlefeld, "Christian–Muslim Relations," 123.
69. Masri, *Connecting with Muslims*, 178–80.
70. Travis, "Diversity and Change," 192–201.
71. Woodberry, *Muslims and Christians*, 212.

Theological Aspects

Our theological engagement with Muslims should focus on the Bible and the Qur'an as they relate to the issues Muslims raise about Christ, such as his Sonship, birth, death and resurrection. Neville describes the threefold task of the theologian: "The elements are, first, scholarly responsibility in describing one's own tradition, including those aspects with which one can only disagree; second, the need to represent a tradition so defined that one can actively support it; and third, identifying one's role in effecting change in one's own tradition."[72] From Neville's assertions, it is evident that the first task of a theologian is to explain his or her tradition, which, in this case, is our understanding of Christology from a biblical perspective. From this we can then move on to the next level of representing, interpreting and supporting our biblical position on Christ to Muslims. This is an area where a study of the Qur'an is necessary. It can then be hoped that the lives of the Muslims with whom we are interacting will be transformed.

The beginning point is to be certain of our position in Christ and have an in-depth understanding of the doctrines of Christ. Without this we cannot accurately explain the doctrines to Muslims, and we will be fruitless in our efforts to witness to them,[73] knowing that our message is crucial.[74] In addition to our identity and message, Christian leaders should also teach their congregations different worldviews.[75] Important passages to teach the church center on the unity of God (Deut 6:4; Mark 12:29, 32; 1 Tim 2:5). It is important "to clarify that Christians do not believe in three gods."[76]

Second, the church should embark on biblical and qur'anic readings and interpretation. From our understanding of the Bible, we should be able to help Muslims understand biblical passages about which they have misconceptions. Baron narrates a story of a missionary who used to read portions of the Bible with her Muslim tutor. This tutor then got converted to Christ.[77] Testimonies abound of people who were converted through reading the Bible[78] or the Qur'an.[79] The Bible has had an impact on the lives of Muslims through means

---

72. Neville, *Behind the Masks of God*, 166–67.
73. Whitfield, "Do Christians and Muslims Worship the Same God?," 62.
74. Masri, *Connecting with Muslims*, 38.
75. Whitfield, "Do Christians and Muslims Worship the Same God?," 67.
76. Larson, "Jesus in Islam," 332.
77. Baron, *Orphan Scandal*, 43–44.
78. Qureshi, *Seeking Allah*, 23.
79. Moucarry, *Prophet and the Messiah*, 32.

such as studying the life of Jesus in the gospels,[80] including the story of how Christ washed the feet of his disciples – and especially the feet of Judas Iscariot, knowing that he would betray Christ.[81]

Third, Christians should memorize and use Bible verses as appropriate in their conversations with Muslims. This is because Muslims are "religious" and respect "other people who memorize God's word."[82] Therefore, there is no doubt that Muslims will respect and obey the word spoken to them from memory. Speaking the gospel in a language in which Muslims are most comfortable may be best. This means that there is a need to utilize Bibles translated into Arabic when speaking to Muslims, allowing them to understand what Jesus means to them in the language they know best.[83] The study of the Arabic language is a necessary undertaking in this Bible-translation process, but the grasp and translation of the Bible into the Arabic language will also enable Christians to study texts about Jesus in the Qur'an and Hadith.[84]

Such a study will, in turn, enhance Christians' comprehension of the gospel so as to apply it accurately in their dialogue with Muslims. The knowledge of Arabic will also provide Christians with proper insight as they look at both Scriptures with their Muslim friends and neighbors. This study may be mainly of benefit to ordinary Muslims who, in most cases, "tend to make their own understanding of religion from hearsay or tradition. Over time, they tend to twist or distort truths about Jesus."[85] Examples include the view that Jesus never died, but rather somebody else did.

The fourth point is centered on explaining the facts about Jesus. Many Muslims have misconceptions about Jesus. The gospels have valuable insights to help us in our conversations with our Muslim friends (Matt 26:28; Acts 4:12; Rom 1:4; 10:9–10; Eph 2:8–9; Phil 3:10–11; 1 Pet 1:3).[86] These truths or insights include the Sonship, divinity, death and resurrection of Christ. Scriptures such as Isaiah 7:14 can be referred to when explaining the birth of Jesus. It should be explained that the word "Immanuel" means "God with us," not "Prophet with us."[87] Scriptures that point to the Sonship of Jesus include

---

80. Masri, *Connecting with Muslims*, 119.
81. Masri, 22.
82. Masri, 56.
83. Travis, "Diversity and Change," 197.
84. Cragg, *Jesus and the Muslim*, xiv.
85. Masri, *Connecting with Muslims*, 121.
86. Masri, 134.
87. Ziafat, "Sharing the Gospel," 157.

Matthew 1:18–24 and Luke 1:26–35. Jesus himself also lays claim to Sonship (Mark 14:61–64; John 5:18); and Thomas's own confession states that Jesus is "Lord" and "God" (John 20:28). According to Halverson, "there are two Arabic words for 'son' that must be distinguished." He states:

> The word *walad* denotes a son born of sexual relations. Jesus is not a son [*waladdu'llah* – "Son of God"] in this sense. However, there is another Arabic word for son, *ibn*, that can be used in a wider figurative or metaphorical sense. A traveler, for example, is spoken of as a "son of the road" (*ibnussabil*). It is in this wider sense that it makes sense to speak of Jesus as the "Son" (*ibn*) of God. This is a metaphorical way of describing the eternal relationship between the Father and Jesus.[88]

Rhodes also writes:

> Ancient Semitics and Orientals used the phrase "Son of . . ." to indicate likeness or sameness of nature and equality of being. Hence, when Jesus claimed to be the Son of God, His Jewish contemporaries fully understood: He was making a claim to be God in an unqualified sense. Indeed, the Jews insisted, "We have a law, and according to that law he [Christ] must die, because he claimed to be the Son of God" (John 19:7; see also 5:18). Recognizing that Jesus was identifying Himself as God, the Jews wanted to kill Him for committing blasphemy.[89]

Jesus as the "begotten Son" is usually controversial and misunderstood by Muslims. Geisler and Saleeb clarify this misconception:

> The phrase "only begotten" does not refer to *physical generation* but *a special relationship* with the Father. Like the biblical phrase "Firstborn" (Col 1:15), it means priority in *rank*, not *time* (cf. vs. 16–17). It could be translated, as the New International Version does, God's "One and Only" Son. It does not imply creation by the Father but unique relation to him. Just as an earthly father and son have a special filial relationship, even so, the eternal Father and his eternal Son are uniquely related. It does not refer to any physical generation but an eternal procession from the Father. Just as for Muslims, the Word of God (Qur'an) is not identical to God

---

88. Halverson, *Compact Guide*, 114.
89. Rhodes, *Reasoning from the Scriptures*, 52.

but eternally proceeds from him, even so for Christians, Christ, God's "Word" (4:171) eternally proceeds from him. Words like "generation" and "procession" are used by Christians of Christ in a filial and relational sense, not in a carnal and physical sense.[90]

In explaining the concept of Jesus as the Messiah, it is important to clarify that the "word 'Messiah' is a Hebrew word and means 'anointed one.' It is 'Christos' in Greek, 'Christ' in English, and the Qur'an uses 'al-Masih' (most Anointed) in Arabic. In fact, that title is used for Jesus 11 times in the Quran! Nobody else in the Quran is called 'al-Masih'" (cf. Q 3:45; 5:14, 75).[91] McAuliffe also emphasizes the fact that the title "Al-Masih" was a very distinguished and unique title that was exceptionally ascribed to Jesus by both Christians and Muslims.[92] It can also be emphasized that the Old Testament teaches that "the coming Messiah would be God himself. So, when Jesus claimed to be that Messiah, he was also claiming to be God" (Isa 9:6).[93]

As noted above, many Muslims do not agree that Jesus suffered, died and was resurrected. Their argument is usually based on Qur'an 4:157–58, which says that "it was only made to appear." Four common theories that dispute the Christian claim to the suffering and death of Jesus are that someone else, such as Judas Iscariot, died in his place; that the Jews wanted to kill him, but God rescued his prophet; that Jesus was indeed crucified but just fainted (swoop theory); and that God, being sovereign, could not allow his son to be crucified. To counteract these arguments, Christians can use the many scriptures that point to the passion of Christ as he foretold it or the testimonies of eyewitnesses (Isa 53:1–12; Dan 9:25–26; Matt 16:21; Luke 9:18–22; 22:37; 23:26–46; John 19:13–20).

In explaining Jesus as the divine Word of God, Rhodes writes:

> In John 1:1, Jesus is called "the Word." The Greek noun for "Word" in this verse is *Logos*. Its importance lies in the fact that Christ, the *Logos*, is portrayed as a preexistent, eternal Being. Indeed, John even says the Logos is God. The Logos is also said to be the Creator of the universe, for "through him all things were made; without him nothing was made that has been made" (John 1:3). The Jewish Targums (simplified paraphrases of the Old Testament

---

90. Geisler and Saleeb, *Answering Islam*, 264.
91. McDowell and Walker, *Understanding Islam and Christianity*, 11.
92. McAuliffe, *Encyclopaedia of the Qu'ran*, 12–13.
93. Geisler and Saleeb, *Answering Islam*, 251.

Scriptures) reveal that the ancient Jews, out of reverence for God, sometimes substituted the phrase "the Word of God" in place of the word "Yahweh." The Jews were fearful of breaking the third commandment: "You shall not misuse the name of the LORD your God, for the LORD will not hold anyone guiltless who misuses his name" (Exodus 20:7).[94]

Lastly, as Christians provide theological answers and correct misconceptions that Muslims may have regarding the nature of Christ as viewed from both Scriptures, they should do so with much patience. As Rhodes also affirms, there is a need to respond to our Muslim friends in a loving, biblical way and be prepared to answer their questions about Jesus and the cross. Asking strategic questions such as "'Have you read the Bible?' or 'What do you think of Christians?' would help build a relationship and strengthen the conversation. As people respond and connect and share their thoughts, they feel valued and respected."[95]

Sociocultural Aspects

This section focuses on the sociocultural issues that can contribute to meeting the felt needs of Muslims. Theology is important, but this alone is not enough in our engagement with Muslims if its intent is simply logical. "The doctrine of uniting the divinity and humanity of Christ and Trinity makes no sense in a rational debate."[96] Mere arguments will simply attract skepticism from Muslims.[97] In Christian witness, there is a need to go beyond theological responses or inquiries from Muslims. The underlying reason is that the majority of Muslims, unlike some Christians, are practice-oriented rather than belief-oriented; they value orthopraxy as opposed to orthodoxy: "In religions of orthopraxy like Islam, actions express and articulate faith, and this is an important facet of the faith that non-Muslims should keep in mind."[98] Islam is a religion of actions (Q 9:105). Muslims tend to highlight praxis and prioritize jurisprudence.[99] Proper action such as love "is often considered as

---

94. Rhodes, *Reasoning from the Scriptures*, 134.
95. Rhodes, 55.
96. Thomas, *Christian Doctrines*, 30.
97. Bijlefeld, "Christian–Muslim Relations," 128.
98. Kaltner, *Islam*, 28.
99. Zebiri, *Muslims and Christians*, 9.

the true mark of one's membership in the community. This, however, is not to underestimate the need for correction nor exaggerate orthopraxis."[100]

Different approaches are therefore required depending on the context. Common approaches, especially among ordinary (sometimes referred to as 'Folk') Muslims, are healing and praying for miracles rather than witnessing through theological debates.[101] Different approaches are required because, as Bennett puts it, "there is one Islam but many Muslim societies."[102] This diversity in Islam calls for contextualization, exploring new and relevant ways of engaging with Muslims.[103]

Since Islam is more action-oriented, the heinous deeds of the Crusades need to be revisited whenever the subject resurfaces. There is a need to acknowledge that the massacre of Muslims was evil. At the same time, Muslims should be assured that, although what happened in the past was not right, there are many good Christians with good intentions in our society. There is a need to hold a genuine and open dialogue with Muslim friends over areas of cooperation as well as conflict.[104] In some situations, Muslims have responded well to the ministry of prayer, performing of miracles such as healing and power-encounter ministries.[105] The Qur'an also supports the idea of prayer (Q 3:49).

There are many testimonies of Muslims seeking prayer or showing how such prayer has brought healing and restoration in their lives. The ministry of power encounters is also valid, especially among ordinary Muslims whose primary concerns are centered on the evil eye, and the fear of death, sickness, calamity and evil spirits. They seek answers to these felt needs from witchdoctors, shamans or traditional practitioners. In our contemporary society in which technology has thrived, the use of media can be helpful in engaging with Muslims at any available opportunity.[106]

Conclusion

Christ's questions "Who do they/you say I am?" has been reviewed in the context of how Islam and Muslims view Jesus. People's responses reflect

---

100. Kaltner, *Islam*, 27–28.
101. Musk, *Unseen Face of Islam*, 7–8.
102. Bennett, *Studying Islam*, 67.
103. Reisacher, "Defining Islam," 222.
104. Amjad-Ali, *Critical Issues*, 577, 579.
105. Travis, "Diversity and Change," 195.
106. Travis, 187–88.

the many diverse views of Christ. On the other hand, Peter's answer "You are the Messiah, the Son of the living God" (Matt 16:16) reflects the proper perspective and truth of Christ that the church ought to know, embrace and apply in its missionary engagement among Muslims. May the church be full of this revelation and commit itself to knowing Christ and making him known through a biblically and theologically sound response, strategic witness through sociocultural means and a Christian lifestyle. Christology is pivotal in Christian evangelism to Muslims. Christians will need to be patient in explaining Jesus Christ to Muslims. Above all, the church should fully trust in the enabling power of the Holy Spirit in its mission to Muslims and the world.

Bibliography

Al-Madkhalee, Rabee Ibn Haadee. *The Status of Jesus in Islam*. [USA]: Al-Ibaanah, 2004.

Amjad-Ali, Charles. *Some Critical Issues for Muslim–Christian Relations and Challenges for Christian Vocation and Witness*. Oxford: Blackwell, 2009.

Anderson, Norman. *Islam in the Modern World*. Leicester: Apollos, 1990.

Anis, A. Shorrosh. *Islam Revealed*. Nashville: Thomas Nelson, 1988.

Aydin, Mahmut. "Contemporary Christian Evaluations of the Prophethood of Muhammad." *Encounters* 6 Part 1 (2000): 105–6.

Ayoub, Mahmoud M. "Towards an Islamic Christology: An Image of Jesus in Early Shi'i Muslim Literature." *The Muslim World* 66, no. 3 (1976): 63–188.

Azhar, A. *Christianity in History*. Lahore: Sh. Muhammad Ashraf, 1991.

Baron, Beth. *The Orphan Scandal: Christian Missionaries and the Rise of the Muslim Brotherhood*. Stanford: Stanford University Press, 2014.

Bennett, Clinton. *Studying Islam: The Critical Issues*. London: Continuum, 2010.

Bijlefeld, A. Willem. "Christian–Muslim Relations: A Burdensome Past, a Challenging Future." *Word & World* 16, no. 2 (1996): 117–28.

Chapman, Colin. *Islam and the West: Conflict, Co-Existence or Conversion?* Carlisle: Paternoster, 1998.

Chatrath, Nick. *Reaching Muslims: A One-Stop Guide for Christians*. Oxford: Monarch, 2011.

Cragg, Kenneth. *Jesus and the Muslim*. Oxford: Oneworld, 1999.

Djaballah, Amar. "Jesus in Islam." *The Southern Baptist Journal of Theology* 8, no. 1 (2004): 14–30. https://equip.sbts.edu/publications/journals/journal-of-theology/sbjt-81-spring-2004/jesus-in-islam/.

Doi, A. R. I. "Status of Prophet Jesus in Islam." *Muslim World League Journal* (June 1982).

Durrani, M. H. *The Qur'anic Facts about Jesus*. Delhi: Noor Publishing, 1992.

Geisler, Norman L., and Abdul Saleeb. *Answering Islam: The Crescent in Light of the Cross*. Grand Rapids: Baker, 2002.

George, Timothy. *Is the Father of Jesus the God of Muhammad? Understanding the Differences between Christianity and Islam*. Grand Rapids: Zondervan, 2009.

Goddard, Hugh. *Christians and Muslims: From Double Standards to Mutual Understanding*. London: Taylor & Francis, 2006.

Halverson, Dean. *The Compact Guide to World Religions*. Minneapolis: Bethany House, 1996.

Huraira, Abu. "Al-Bukhari" (The Hadith) 6, no. 60. 236 (n.d.).

Husseini, Sara Leila. *Early Christian–Muslim Debate on the Unity of God*. Leiden: Brill, 2014.

Ibn Taimiyah, Taqi al-Din, and Thomas F. Michel. *A Muslim Theologian's Response to Christianity: Ibn Taymiyya's al-Jawab al-Sahih*. Delmar: Caravan Books, 1984.

Johnson, Wayne G. *Judging Jesus: World Religions' Answers to "Who Do People Say That I Am?"* Lanham: Hamilton, 2016.

Kaltner, John. *Islam: What Non-Muslims Should Know*. Minneapolis: Fortress, 2016.

Kateregga, Badru D., and David W. Shenk. *Islam and Christianity: A Muslim and a Christian in Dialogue*. Grand Rapids: Eerdmans, 1981.

Kathir, Ibn. *The Islamic View of Jesus: (Peace Be upon Him)*. El-Mansoura: Dar Al-Manarah, 2000.

Kerr, David. "The Prophet Muhammad in Christian Theological Perspective." In *Islam in a World of Diverse Faiths*, edited by Dan Cohn-Sherbok, 112–11. London: Macmillan, 1991.

Larson, Warren. "Jesus in Islam and Christianity: Discussing the Similarities and the Differences." *Missiology* 36, no. 3 (2008): 327–41.

Leirvik, Oddbjørn. *Images of Jesus Christ in Islam*. 2nd ed. New York: Continuum, 2010.

Maqsood, Ruqaiyyah Waris. *What Every Christian Should Know about Islam*. Nairobi: Islamic Foundation, 2009.

Masri, Fouad. *Connecting with Muslims: A Guide to Communicating Effectively*. Downers Grove: InterVarsity Press, 2014.

McAuliffe, Jane Dammen. *Encyclopaedia of the Qu'ran*. Leiden: Brill, 2006.

McDowell, Bruce A., and Anees Zaka. *Muslims and Christians at the Table: Promoting Biblical Understanding among North American Muslims*. Phillipsburg: P&R, 1999.

McDowell, Josh, and Jim Walker. *Understanding Islam and Christianity: Beliefs That Separate Us and How to Talk about Them*. Eugene: Harvest House, 2013.

Miller, William A. *Christian Response to Islam*. Phillipsburg: P&R, 1976.

Moucarry, Chawkat G. *The Prophet and the Messiah: An Arab Christian's Perspective on Islam and Christianity*. Downers Grove: InterVarsity Press, 2002.

Musk, Bill A. *The Unseen Face of Islam: Sharing the Gospel with Ordinary Muslims at Street Level*. [n.p.]: Monarch, 2004.

Neville, Robert C. *Behind the Masks of God: An Essay toward Comparative Theology*. Boulder: NetLibrary, 1999.

Parshall, Phil. *New Paths in Muslim Evangelism*. Grand Rapids: Baker, 1980.

Qureshi, Nabeel. *Seeking Allah, Finding Jesus: A Devout Muslim Encounters Christianity.* Grand Rapids: Zondervan, 2014.

Register, Ray G. *Dialogue and Interfaith Witness with Muslims.* Fort Washington: Distributed in the USA by WEC, 1979.

Reisacher, Evelyne A. "Defining Islam and Muslim Societies in Missiological Discourse." In *Dynamics of Muslim Worlds: Regional, Theological, and Missiological Perspectives,* edited by Evelyne A. Reisacher, 219–42. Downers Grove: IVP Academic, 2017.

Renard, John. *Islam and Christianity: Theological Themes in Comparative Perspective.* Berkeley: University of California Press, 2011.

Rhodes, Ron. *Reasoning from the Scriptures with the Muslims.* Eugene: Harvest House, 2002.

Riddell, Peter G., and Peter Cotterell. *Islam in Context: Past, Present, and Future.* Grand Rapids: Baker Academic, 2004.

Saal, William J. *Reaching Muslims for Christ.* Chicago: Moody, 1993.

Shenk, David W. *Journeys of the Muslim Nation and the Christian Church: Exploring the Mission of Two Communities.* Waterloo: Herald, 2003.

Siddiqui, Mona. *Christians, Muslims, and Jesus.* Yale: Yale University Press, 2013.

So, Damon W. K. "Christology and Trinity in Mission." In *Foundations for Mission,* edited by Emma Wild-Wood and Peniel Rajkumar, 123–37. Regnum Edinburgh Centenary Series. Oxford: Regnum Studies in Mission, 2013.

Sookhdeo, Patrick. *Understanding Islamic Theology.* McLean: Isaac Publishing, 2013.

Tanagho, Samy. *Glad News! God Loves You, My Muslim Friend.* Colorado Springs: Authentic, 2004.

Terry, John Mark. *Missiology: An Introduction to the Foundations, History, and Strategies of World Missions.* Nashville: B&H, 2015.

Thomas, David. *Christian Doctrines in Islamic Theology: History of Christian-Muslim Relations.* Leiden: Brill, 2008.

Travis, John Jay. "Diversity and Change in Contemporary Muslim Society: Missional Emphases and Implications." In *Dynamics of Muslim Worlds: Regional, Theological, and Missiological Perspectives,* edited by Evelyne A. Reisacher, 183–201. Downers Grove: IVP Academic, 2017.

Tucker, Ruth. *From Jerusalem to Irian Jaya: A Biographical History of Christian Missions.* Grand Rapids: Zondervan, 1993.

Whitfield, Keith S. "Do Christians and Muslims Worship the Same God?" In *Islam and North America: Loving Our Muslim Neighbors,* edited by Micah Fries and Keith Whitfield, 61–67. Nashville: B&H Academic, 2018.

Woodberry, J. Dudley, ed. *Muslims and Christians on the Emmaus Road: Crucial Issues in Witness among Muslims.* Monrovia: MARC, 1989.

Zebiri, Kate. *Muslims and Christians Face to Face.* New York: Oneworld, 2014.

Ziafat, Afshin. "Sharing the Gospel with a Muslim." In *Islam and North America: Loving Our Muslim Neighbors,* edited by Micah Fries and Keith Whitfield, 155–64. Nashville: B&H Academic, 2018.

19

Jesus in Islam

Meaning and Theological Implications for Christian–Muslim Engagement

Billy Chilongo Sichone
Lecturer and Deputy Vice-Chancellor,
Central Africa Baptist University (CABU), Kitwe, Zambia

Abstract

The study explores how Jesus (*Isa*)[1] is perceived and positioned in Islam. Many non-Muslims are pleasantly startled to discover that the Jesus of the Qur'an is highly esteemed in Islam.[2] This inquiry is for the sake of lay Christians, helping them appreciate the perceptions, lenses and grids through which Muslims interpret the world, particularly Jesus. The research methodology of this qualitative study is simple. It gives an overview of the study and then demonstrates the study's significance, in the process alluding to conversations around the nature of *Isa* in relation to Christology, and concluding with some basic applications. Accordingly, this inquiry explores the Muslim worldview

---

1. In this paper, we use the terms *Isa* and "Jesus" interchangeably.
2. See brochure by the Muslim Student Association of the University of Alberta, "What Does the Qur'an Say about Jesus?" The document cites both the Qur'an and the Hadith. Accessible at https://sites.ualberta.ca/~msa/pdf/quran_jesus.pdf. Also see Ghafur, Prasojo and bin Haji Masri, "Qur'anic Jesus," DOI: 10.21274/epis.2019.14.2.349-373, a good read from an Islamic perspective.

as it affects Muslim perceptions of *Isa*. Islam states that *Isa* was a prophet of Allah, but it rejects the Christian understanding of *Isa*'s eternal generation, hypostatic nature and redemptive incarnation. The doctrine also denies the Trinity, substitutionary atonement, the crucifixion, or *Isa* being at the mighty right hand of the Father. In Islam, a person must earn and work for his or her own salvation by observing certain prescribed rituals, hence there is no need for a redeemer. This paper discusses the theological implications of the positions internally arrived at by the Qur'an, in relation to Jesus, in connection with other external sources. The study concludes that the Jesus of the Christian Bible and of the Qur'an are two different individuals, despite some shared aspects.

Key words: Islam, Trinity, Qur'an, worldview, *Isa*, prophet, hypostatic nature, *Tawhid*

Introduction and Background to the Study

In recent times, there has been an increase in the study of and attempts to understand Islam.[3] Various factors account for this upsurge in interest from both Christians and Muslims alike. For some, Islam comes across as a perfect alternative to other religions they have grown dissatisfied with.[4] In that sense, Islam would be classified as a "religion," though one could distinguish between Islam and religion. Islam is life,[5] belief and practice, rather than merely thoughtlessly conforming to prescribed rituals. For others, Islam, akin to any other religion, is a cause of concern, for religion is perceived to be the root cause of some of the world's conflicts, ethnic cleansing, genocides, and so on. For still others, Islam comes across as an incredibly peaceful religion which, unfairly, has earned a bad name, surprisingly given Muhammad's apparent aversion to war.[6] For some Christians, Islam poses a challenge to world peace as it is perceived to hamper, if not oppose, the gospel enterprise. For one thing, a number of the perpetrators of some of the terrorist acts broadcast via global

---

3. Esposito, *Great World Religions*, 1; Esposito, *Ten Things*, 1; Steger, *Globalization*, 1–6; Hill, *International Business*, 96–118.
4. Strakosch, *Middle Eastern Monotheism*, 2.
5. Wrapped around a single-unit deity.
6. Shadid and van Koningsveld, "Negative Image of Islam," 175, express similar laments; Aydin, "Islam the Religion of Peace," 1, DOI: 10.2478/jriss-2013-0022; Akhter and Qadoos, "Islam Is the Religion of Peace," 1; Cox and Marks, *West, Islam and Islamism*, 1.

cable news networks claim to do what they do "in the Name of Allah,"⁷ the absolute Muslim deity. A good number of the religious trouble spots worldwide are attributed or connected to radical Islam, although this is not the only religion that is culpable. What is puzzling and troubling to the layperson is that Muslims at times kill other Muslims!⁸

Why the heightened interest? We suggest some possible reasons. For one thing, Muslims claim that Islam is the supreme and final religion.⁹ All other religions must be obliterated or brought into total subjection, if not progressively flushed out. For another thing, Muslims are now located at nearly all points on this terrestrial ball. They are often easily identified by their unique customary dress, outlook, piousness, and by what they do or don't do. Furthermore, Muslims carry their religion wherever they go and do not yield to the pressure of conforming to the surrounding culture of a contradicting faith. Perhaps another recent reason could be the media attention, uprisings,¹⁰ the rise of Islamist radicals,¹¹ or the perceived missionary nature of Islam¹² far beyond its traditional boundaries. Lastly, Muslims claim to have the lucid final revelation from Allah, completing whatever the prophets had revealed in the previous centuries. These and many other reasons may account for the interest in Islam. On all sides, Islam seems to be on the rise.

This research explores the place and understanding of the Jesus of Islam and how Christians could effectively engage Muslims in profitable discourse.¹³ For the sake of the less knowledgeable in Islam, the paper gives brief, relevant

---

7. "Allah" is the actual proper name of the Muslim monotheistic God (see Rahman, "Major Themes of the Qur'an," 1). Allah is his proper name, not a title. "God" is a generic title and can refer to any deity. For instance, in Christianity or Judaism, God's actual name is "Yahweh"/"Jehovah," *Elohim* or *Adonai*. This negative perception of Islam is further strengthened by random attacks by Muslims, which are especially visible when they occur on Western turf, such as the recent (16 October 2020) beheading of Samuel Paty (schoolteacher) in France, or the *Charlie Hebdo* affair of 2012, 2015 and 2020. Some attacks are triggered by what Muslims consider to be deliberate blasphemy by infidels, attracting fatwas. Muslims claim they are provoked to outrage by haters but are otherwise peaceful; Onishi and Méheut, "A Teacher, His Killer"; Esposito, *Great World Religions*, 1.

8. Most people are not aware that internal tensions within the widely diverse religion exist, triggering conflict, to the outside world's surprise. Often, Sunnis and Shi'a are at daggers drawn over some historical succession issue (Q 4:92). Ideally, Muslims should never slay each other.

9. Esposito, *Great World Religions*, 5; Chapman, "Christian Responses to Islam."

10. That is, the Arab Spring.

11. Or "religious terrorists."

12. Or *Da'wa*; Racious, "Multiple Nature of the Islamic Da'wa," 5.

13. Djaballah, "Jesus in Islam," 14.

background information about the religion, its development, theology,[14] and, ultimately, how Muslims perceive *Isa* in relation to the Christian faith.[15] Its scope is limited to Jesus in Islam, thus it does not attempt to deal with broader issues such as the culture, practices, imperatives or ultimate quest of Islam, although it does make brief allusions to those aspects.

Significance and Justification of This Consideration

A set of questions then arise that require answering, such as: Why the exploration of Jesus in Islam? Why extend Christology to Islam? Many reasons could be advanced, but suffice it to say that a consideration of the subject at hand has been made necessary for the following reasons:

First, the Qur'an mentions *Isa Ibn Maryam*[16] in an apparent reference to the Jesus and Mary of the Bible. This reference is often a shocking discovery for many Christians. At the same time, it is a point of glee for Muslims. In my interactions with Zambian Muslims, one of the first things Muslims point out is that they recognize a shared prophet in Jesus. In one case, one sheikh stated that Christianity, Judaism and Islam were cousin religions and thus could easily interrelate. When I challenged him to demonstrate his claim, he pointed to the shared temple at Jerusalem, where each of the three religions has a spot or space on the same temple site.[17]

Second, Muslims claim that the *Isa* of the Qur'an and the Jesus of the Bible are the same person.[18] They premise their claim on what the Qur'an asserts about *Isa Ibn Maryam*. No matter what others think, the Qur'an has declared it, and it ought to be so, regardless of the varying narratives of the religious canons.

Third, Muslim theology highly regards *Maryam* and *Isa*, and thus expects reciprocal allegiance, honor and veneration of the final prophet from Christians. The Qur'an, no doubt, has a high view of both *Isa* and his virgin

---

14. And theological implications from a Christian perspective.
15. Alphonse, "Jesus in the Bible," 14.
16. Literally translated "*Isa* son of Mary."
17. Research conducted in October 2019 in Lusaka and Copperbelt provinces of Zambia.
18. Alphonse, "Jesus in the Bible," 14; Ghafur, Prasojo and bin Haji Masri, "Qur'anic Jesus," 349; Ismail, *Hermeneutics*, 89; Moucarry, *Prophet and the Messiah*, 17; Muslim Student's Association n.d., 1. https://sites.ualberta.ca/~msa/pdf/quran_jesus.pdf.

mother, *Maryam*. Mary is said to be a special person because she bore one of Islam's most important prophets and the apostle of Allah.[19]

The natural spillover effect of the above assertions results in the following compelling reasons why the world should pay attention to Islam's global advance:

First, Islam and Muslims cannot be ignored anymore on the world stage. Esposito is correct when he states that "Islam has a significant impact on world affairs."[20]

Second, Muslims claim to revere or respect Jesus far more than many people care to know. As earlier alluded to, Muslims hold a high view of Jesus and thus find it surprising that Christians vilify or oppose Islam, which itself points to Allah, whose prophet Jesus was.[21]

Third, Christians need to know what or how Muslims think about God in relation to Jesus. Esposito claims that Christians know very little about Islam except the few outlier extremists portrayed in the public media.[22]

Fourth, Christians need to know how best to engage Muslims with the minimum offense and yet be effective in their evangelistic interactions. Gilchrist, Sookhdeo, Chapman, Sproul and Saleeb and Brown, among others, strongly recommend exposure to and knowledge of Islam for effective engagement.[23] Islam is not monolithic, though it does have one shared core.[24]

Fifth (and connected to the first point), we cannot avoid Muslims in our neighborhoods, regardless of where one resides.[25] At one time, Muslims were thought to be an exotic lot, hailing from the Middle East or from places such as Pakistan and Indonesia. Now, however, we live and work side by side with indigenous Muslims! Therefore, it is imperative to try to understand them in order to peaceably dwell with them, in keeping with the 1 Timothy 2:1–3 injunctions on prayer.

---

19. Ghafur, Prasojo and bin Haji Masri dub *Isa* "the apostle of *ulul Azmi*" or Liberator Prophet in their paper "Qur'anic Jesus" (DOI: 10.21274/epis.2019.14.2.349-373). This demonstrates deep veneration and honor toward *Isa*.

20. Esposito, *Great World Religions*, 5.

21. Q 3:45–50.

22. Esposito, *Great World Religions*, 1.

23. Gilchrist, *Muslim Challenge*, 5; Sookhdeo, *Understanding Muslim Theology*, 1; Chapman, "Christian Responses to Islam," 1; Sproul and Saleeb, *Dark Side of Islam*, 8, 11–12; Brown, "Muslim Worldviews," 5.

24. Michael Cook (*Koran*) and Malise Ruthven (*Islam*) advance the view; Esposito, *Great World Religions*, 1.

25. Gilchrist, *Muslim Challenge*, 14; Esposito, "Muslim–Christian Relations," 1; Esposito, *Great World Religions*, 3.

Sixth, Islam is currently the fastest-growing religion,[26] poised to take the number one slot by the middle of the twenty-first century.[27] Once Muslims become a majority in a given context, the social dynamics begin to alter. Islam often adapts[28] to its context but infuses a systemic metamorphosis, resulting in a syncretic culture. According to the Pew Research's 2015 report, Islam has more than 1.8 billion adherents, against Christianity's estimated 2.3 billion or more.[29]

Seventh, Islam has an inherent tendency to set the tone for what is perceived to be ethically right or wrong in a given context. Some dictates may be favorable to Christianity, while others may not be. Islam, like Christianity, is a religion on a mission: to change the world. Akin to its cousin missionary religion, Islam will not stop at anything to change the world; after all, this inclination is inherent, part of its very DNA.[30] This inclination is the quest of Christianity, too.

The Basic Standard Narrative and Tenets of Islam

Islam is a religion that commenced with the emergence of the prophet Muhammad[31] in the Arabian Peninsula. Up to the age of forty, Muhammad was mostly an ordinary man. He perceived himself as such until the day he had a life-changing experience while meditating at a cave in Hira. This landmark encounter would affect the rest of his life. From AD 610, the prophet continued to receive intermittent revelations until his demise in AD 632.[32]

His career as a prophet was far from being a peaceful ride: it was intermingled with affliction, action, opposition, conflict, lawmaking, empire establishment, and brokering peace treaties where possible.[33] The prophet is best known for his inflexible insistence on the worship of one God (*Tawhid*), Allah, to whom all were to submit (i.e. *Islam*). To Muhammad, Allah was the one strictly monotheistic being without associations, sons, daughters or a wife. Muhammad insisted that if anyone was to be in good standing with Allah, he or

---

26. Esposito, *Great World Religions*, 1; Chapman, "Christian Responses to Islam," 1; Pew Research Center, "Future of World Religions."
27. See the Pew Research Center report "Future of World Religions."
28. Hence the claim by some that Islam has no unique worldview per se.
29. Pew Research Center, "Changing Global Religious Landscape."
30. Q 2:193; 3:85.
31. AD 570–632.
32. Jeffery, "Historical Muhammad," 1; Moucarry, *Prophet and the Messiah*, 219; Netland, Sweeney, Cole and Carson, "Message of Islam," 3.
33. Shaw, *Kingdom of God in Africa*, 83; Smith, "Quran," 42–43.

she needed to observe the imperatives set by Allah. Good deeds expressed faith, counting toward an individual's final destiny.[34] Furthermore, the Qur'an states that Muhammad was the final prophet, sealing all those who had preceded him, prominent among whom were Adam (*Aadam*), Noah (*Nuh*), Abraham (*Ibrahim*), Moses (*Musa*), David (*Dawud*) and Jesus (*Isa*). Akhter and Qadoos claim that Muhammad was in fact the *Rehmatul-Lil-Aalamin*, or "Mercy into the world."[35] His advent was a blessing to the world. Thus, all religions found their fulfilment in him, and it is claimed that the Jewish Torah and Christian gospels originally pointed to his coming, unlike what their latter corrupted versions suggest.[36] Muhammad aggressively attacked polytheism in any form, doing all he could to eradicate it to the very end.[37]

But what do Muslims believe and practice? Some have written at length on the nature and practices of Islam, but we limit our comment here. All Muslims hold to the "five pillars" of Islam as listed below:

1. Declaration of faith or confession that Allah alone is God. This declaration is referred to as the *Shahadah*.
2. Prayer (*Salah* or *Salat*): Prayer five times a day at specified times in the Masjid or the quietness of a convenient, serene prayer room.
3. Almsgiving (*zakat*): The giving of some prescribed amount to help the disadvantaged. It is a form of social security.[38]
4. Fasting (*Saum* or *Sawm*): Total fasting in the ninth month of the Muslim calendar called Ramadan.
5. Pilgrimage (*Hajj*): At least once in his or her lifetime, a Muslim is required to make a pilgrimage to Mecca, resources permitting.

Shi'ite Muslims add a few more tenets that are uniquely theirs, including lesser or greater Jihad.[39]

---

34. Q 17:13.

35. Akhter and Qadoos, "Islam is the Religion of Peace: Analytical Review from the Life of Holy Prophet (PBUH)," 1.

36. Muslims often refer to Deut 18:18 to bolster their claim. See Shabbir Ahmed, "Thus Speaks the Bible," 25.

37. Holmberg, "Hagerism Revisited," 63; Crone and Cook, *Hagarism*, 3.

38. Esposito, *Great World Religions*, 10.

39. Internal struggle is dubbed "greater Jihad"; religious expansion or war is dubbed "lesser Jihad," to defend Islam and khums – the giving of 20 percent of one's earnings to support good causes concerning Islam as far as possible.

Muslims engage in other practices (such as ablutions, dress, etc.) as elaborated in the Sunna. A detailed treatment of these is beyond the scope of this paper, but suffice it to say that new converts need to be taught what practices they ought to engage in beyond the five pillars mentioned above.[40]

Muslims hold to the essential doctrines listed below, though the interest in this study is on prophethood (#3):

1. Strict monotheism (*Tawhid*)
2. Angels (*Malaikah*)
3. Prophets and their scriptures (*Risalah*)
4. Final judgment (*Akhirah*)
5. Predestination/divine decree (*Al-qadr*)[41]

The Islamic Worldview[42]

Although we shall later delve with some level of detail into how the Qur'an shapes Muslim thinking, it is important to briefly state that adherents think uniquely, contingent on their worldview. Muslim thought revolves around three aspects: *theism* (the existence of one supreme being as a single unit), *vicegerency* (i.e. authority structure by Allah assigned to human beings in the world, *umma*) and *justice* (i.e. equity, fairness).[43] Nadvi and Abdullah argue that there is a healthy though unequal[44] interplay among these three organic elements influencing the thinking of any authentic Muslim. According to Nadvi and Abdullah, the existence of one single transcendent deity dictates that one should live daily in humble submission to Allah's will, which includes ordering life according to the way he has prescribed, where fairness and equity reign.[45] All things radiate from Allah, the pivot of life. Thus, for the faithful adherent,

---

40. Ar-Radaddi, *Basic Lessons*, 9.

41. And free will.

42. The word "worldview" has German roots but simply refers to how one looks at and responds to reality or the world. Definitions vary, but Charles Kraft gives a helpful explanation: "Perceptions of reality are patterned by societies into conceptualizations of what reality can or should be, what is to be regarded as actual, probable, possible, and impossible. These conceptualizations form what is termed the world view of the culture" (*Intercultural Communication*, 1).

43. Abdullah and Nadvi, "Understanding the Principles," 271.

44. "Unequal" in the sense that theism is the fountain from which vicegerency and justice flow.

45. Abdullah and Nadvi, "Understanding the Principles," 271.

if these three are in disarray, ignored or not observed, discontentment and agitation begin to brew, eventually manifesting in behavioral or verbal ways.

To the Muslim, Allah is everything and must be obeyed without question. This worldview deeply pervades and colors the Muslim mindset in decision-making, choices, behavior, and actions taken in a given context.[46] Thus, to adequately understand Islam, we need to know several things concerning Islam. We need to understand what the Islamic religion is: its history, culture and politics. Muslims think "community" or *umma*, making decisions with the highest premium ascribed to the family and the honor thereof.[47] Unlike individualistic contexts, Islam fosters togetherness, a sense of family, cordial relations, tranquility, belonging, and a workable family structure. Islam has a distinct, peculiar worldview[48] which, if ignored, will affect further interactions. Djaballah, in a 2004 paper titled "Jesus in Islam," holds a similar view, though writing in a different context.[49] Youssef further advises that, in the quest to carry out evangelistic efforts among Muslims, one must be aware that Muslims rarely make solo decisions, including that of religious conversion. Effective avenues must be devised to enable group conversion, however that may look.[50] In short, the Muslim thinks "unity of God," and this affects all other parameters, including social structure and equity. In such a world, everything hinges on or revolves around *Tawhid*.[51]

Given the foregoing discussion, the Islamic worldview therefore affects the interpretation and perception of who *Isa* is and his mission.[52] Was he a mere human prophet, or divine? Was *Isa* unique in the sense that Muhammad is, or not? If not, why? Given the Islamic worldview as it relates to prophets, revelation and orthopraxy, it immediately raises concern for Muslims when they hear sentiments to the effect that Jesus is God, when in fact they view him as a prophet like all others, though with a unique ministry, having bequeathed

---

46. Greg Haleblian, in Parshall, "Muslim Worldview," 42.

47. In the event of jurisprudence or where the Qur'an is silent over a matter, *Ijma* or consensus is held as infallible.

48. "Distinct" and "unique/peculiar" in the sense that the Muslim worldview differs from all other ideas whether theistic or not. The Islamic worldview revolves around one solitary unitary deity, unlike competing views. The Christian worldview, for instance, is Trinitarian, according divinity to Jesus Christ. The Hindu view accepts over 330 million deities.

49. Djaballah, "Jesus in Islam," 15, asserts that "to understand the Islamic conception of Jesus adequately, one must begin with the Muslims' conception of the Qur'an."

50. As quoted in Parshall, "The Muslim Worldview," 4.

51. Hoover, "Islamic Monotheism," 57.

52. Parshall, "Muslim Worldview," 1.

the gospel. The troubling suggestion of *Isa*'s divinity smacks of *shirk*, triggering instant reactions from the faithful.

The Muslim's grids are therefore set and revolve around the three critical elements highlighted above. Anything outside these is foreign, demanding immediate exorcising. Such practice is proper and natural for the faithful adherent of Islam.

The Place of Prophets in Islam

Muslims place a high premium on all the prophets by highly respecting them. They do not allow any mortal to disrespect any prophet, although Muhammad claims a special place, being the seal of the prophets.[53] Muslims view prophets in a particular light and are therefore immensely offended if any prophet is insulted, ridiculed or sidelined. In the Muslim understanding, first, a prophet is a messenger of Allah who brought a word to a people group. In several cases, prophets brought a scripture or word from Allah.[54] Second, prophets are considered sinless in some way.[55] Although prophets had human weaknesses, they were forgiven by Allah and made fit for paradise. Third, prophets were never killed shamefully or cruelly, but instead were preserved and taken away by Allah, and thus were unharmed.[56] Fourth, Muslims believe that prophets' bodies did not suffer decay but have been miraculously preserved by Allah.[57] Fifth, the prophets are often those who brought warnings to their respective contexts. Although, according to Sookhdeo, not all are apostles (*Rasul*), they are none the less messengers (*anabiya* or *nabi*).[58] Apostles bequeath and disseminate a universal scripture for all humanity, while prophets may only be for a specific people grouping, say Arabs or Jews etc.[59] Few are therefore apostles like *Isa*[60] and Muhammad. *Isa*, and especially Muhammad, are prime role models, human instruments for receiving revelation for believers

---

53. See Coplestone, *Jesus Christ or Mohammed?*, 81–84, for further details on this matter; Q 33:40, 45.

54. Q 2:87; 3:144; 5:75; 57:27; 10:47.

55. That is, the "*Isma*" doctrine; Gilchrist, *Muslim Challenge*, 46.

56. Although people plotted against them in some instances, they succeeded only by Allah's will, to their loss; Q 3:21, 145, 156, 186; 2:61, 91.

57. Sookhdeo, *Understanding Islamic Theology*, 188.

58. That is, prophets; Sookhdeo, 187, 189, 190.

59. Sookhdeo, *Understanding Islamic Theology*, 192.

60. Q 19:27–33.

in either religion.⁶¹ Muslims believe that over 124,000 prophets have been sent to humanity since the beginning, and each brought a special message for that time.⁶² These messages were refined over time with each successive prophet. Unfortunately, all previous messages have been corrupted, hence the need for the final correct revelation delivered to the world through the prophet Muhammad's instrumentality. This pure, unadulterated, unchanged final message comes directly from Allah. Consequently, Muslims revere the word of Allah.

The Mention, Meaning and Narrative of *Isa* in the Qur'an

As alluded to earlier, to understand Muslim thought processes, it is essential to have an intelligent grasp of what their corpus teaches. For Muslims, the Qur'an is the final, pure, unadulterated and direct revelation from Allah, shaping their theological grids, as Djaballah has well articulated.⁶³ The Qur'an cannot be questioned, scrutinized or treated lightly. It inherently carries divine authority, and any dissent will result in excruciating hellfire for the infidel. Its authority is absolute because Muslims believe the *Mushaf/Wahi*⁶⁴ passed down to humans is a replica of the original template in paradise.⁶⁵ It is special, unique, and of an exceptionally high literary class, encasing sublime truth not sourced anywhere in the world.⁶⁶ Try as they might, humans cannot imitate the Qur'an because it stands alone. Some Muslims reverence the Qur'an to such an extent that they dare not imagine questioning its narratives or instruction.⁶⁷ Only bona fide Muslims should touch a copy of the Arabic Qur'an, let alone read it, lest they defile it. By that token, the corpus is to be treated meticulously as sacrosanct, placed in the highest location in the home, and never just shoved under or among other human materials, such as books. It is majestic, deserving our

---

61. Esposito, *Great World Religions*, 8.

62. Sookhdeo, *Understanding Islamic Theology*, 189. Sookhdeo states that of these 124,000, 315 were apostles, though only twenty-five are mentioned in the Qur'an: Q 10:48.

63. Djaballah gives helpful insights in "Jesus in Islam," 18. According to Djaballah, 93 *ayah*s refer to Jesus.

64. "*Wahi*" is the literal verbally inspired revealed word of Allah while the *Mushaf* is the same *Wahi* but in written form such as the physical written words in the Qur'an. Sookhdeo (192) makes a further distinction between inspired words from Allah in *Wahi* and *ilham*, where the latter refers to immediate personal inspired word meant exclusively for the individual while the former includes visions, manifestations and intended for the entire *umma*.

65. Q 13:39.

66. Muslims argue that it is so sublime that it defies all human genre classifications.

67. Q 4:80.

utter devotion and veneration, even though only Allah is worthy of absolute veneration, for his revelation must be treated as special. Those venerating the book further claim that the Qur'an is eternal and uncreated.[68] It is unalterable, divinely protected, complete, and without contradiction, error, mistake or blot.[69] Not a word or letter of it has been changed over time.[70] The Qur'an is the very *Tanzil*, the literal revelation (*Wahi*) from Allah.

As evidenced by all that has been said above, the Qur'an wields a central place in a Muslim's life. Thus, if anyone is to connect with a Muslim, he or she must read the Qur'an in its pure Arabic form, in order to understand it.[71] All other translations are but mere interpretations of the original.[72] In engaging Muslims, anyone who understands or knows Arabic, and is able to articulate, will command greater respect because such a person can rightly divide, exegete and interpret Allah's revelation. However, some English translations have commanded respect among Islamologists, such as the one by Yusuf Ali.[73] With the advent of globalization,[74] good translations are increasingly available.

We now proceed to the fact that the Qur'an does make several statements about *Isa*, and to how Muslims view him. We consider what the Qur'an says about *Isa*, his purpose, life and ministry, while alluding to select *ayah*s.

Jesus, called *Isa*, a supposedly Eastern term, is in the Arabic Qur'an said to have been born of a virgin named Mary, or *Maryam*, the alleged sister of

---

68. Djaballah, "Jesus in Islam," 15–17; Cook, *Koran*, 110.

69. Q 4:82; 85:21–22; Anthony and Bronson, "Did Hafsah Edit the Qur'an?," 93; Shabab Ahmed, *Before Orthodoxy*, 1; Brubaker, *Corrections in Early Qur'an Manuscripts*, 1; Anthony, "Two 'Lost' Suras," 67; Crone and Cook, *Hagarism*, vii; Holmberg, "Hagerism Revisited," 53; Yuksel, Schulte-Nafeh and al-Shaiban, *Qur'an*, 13.

70. Djaballah, "Jesus in Islam," 16; Cook, *Koran*, 114; Q 13:39; 85:21–22.

71. Djaballah, "Jesus in Islam," 17. The Arabic Qur'an could be interpreted in seven ways according to some *Muftis*, *Mujtahids* or *Mullahs*, which is considered an *ijma* among Muslim scholars.

72. "Interpretations" or translations are not considered Qur'ans at all – Q 43:3–4. See the helpful comments by Patel ("Choosing a Quran Translation") and Kidwai ("Survey of English Translations"). Key insights can also be gleaned from Ismail, *Hermeneutics*, 129, 145; Karimi-Nia, "New Document," 293; Saheeh International, *Qur'an*, i–ii; MacFarquhar, "New Translation"; IslamAwakened, "Qu'ran Translation List (English)."

73. Rahman, "Major Themes of the Quran," v, additionally recommends translations or works by A. J. Arberry and Muhammad Marmaduke Pickthall, among others.

74. And with the push of the Reformist movements within Islam by the likes of Edip Yuksel, Wadud, Rahman (revisionist?) and others, things are progressively changing. It is interesting to see how the Reformist movement is effecting changes to the understanding and interpretation of the Qur'an: Abu Zayd, *Reformation of Islamic Thought*, 53; MacFarquhar, "New Translation"; Kidwai, "Survey of English Translations"; Saheeh International, *Qur'an*, ii–iii; Patel, "Choosing a Quran Translation."

Aaron.[75] The virgin is said to have hailed from a priestly line and was told that she would have a son whom she would name *Isa*, and who was destined to be great, respected, and a prophet bringing a scripture from Allah. He was a word from Allah, *al-Masih*,[76] who grew up among the Jews and was to prepare the way for the praised one, *Ahmed*[77] or Muhammad.[78] Although *Isa* was connected to the prophet John the Baptist,[79] *Isa*'s ministry was more remarkable because he was to prepare the way for the one who would come after him, as John's gospel, the Old Testament and the Qur'an state.[80] Toward his ministry's epilogue, *Isa* said he had to go away, and only then would the promised one appear.[81] *Isa* is said to have been an outstanding prophet, who worked miracles, announced the gospel, was sinless and regarded the righteous one.[82] After a fruitful three-year ministry, the Jews plotted to kill him, but he eluded them. Another was punished in his stead, probably Judas or Simon of Cyrene.[83] According to the Qur'an and other sources, *Isa* was never crucified but was taken up by Allah to himself, and he will return a second time at the end of history. Some claim that he was probably severely beaten, was assumed dead, but somehow revived (i.e. the swoon theory), then escaped to some remote, obscure location where he married and had children before his demise. The Qur'an, though, never clearly mentions how *Isa* died, if in fact he did. Sūra 19:33, however, makes an interesting assertion that Allah made *Isa* "be," live, die and rise again. A detailed analysis of this *ayah* beyond the scope of this paper; suffice it to say that the Qur'an does acknowledge that *Isa* was a mighty

---

75. Sookhdeo, *Understanding Islamic Theology*, 213. Some recent works by Muslims attempt to make the distinction between the Aaron of the Old Testament and the Aaron mentioned here, realizing that differences arise between the Torah, *Injīl* and the Qur'an's narrative; Q 19:28.

76. Q 3:45–50.

77. Or "the praised one" or *Periklutos* rather than *Parakletos*; see Gilchrist, *Muslim Challenge*, 129.

78. Q 61:6; John 14–16.

79. Q 19:7–15.

80. John 14–16; Deut 18:18; Q 61:6.

81. Some 600+ years afterwards?

82. Ghafur, Prasojo and bin Haji Masri, "Qur'anic Jesus," 349; Geisler, "Jesus and Muhammad," 51.

83. Matt 27:32, i.e. the substitution theory; Al-Tabari gives insightful views around this theory. See Reynolds, "Muslim Jesus," for potent arguments for the possibility of *Isa* having died.

prophet,[84] second only to Muhammad, who bequeathed the gospel and went to paradise. He will return as the destroyer of Satan at a future date.

That is the storyline of *Isa* in the Qur'an. But next we highlight further aspects the Qur'an vividly asserts about *Isa*.

First, we observe that *Isa* is often called "Son of Mary" without naming a human father.[85] *Isa* is repeatedly called *Ibn Maryam*, meaning that he is the actual biological son of Mary born through miraculous intervention. This phrasing equally suggests the importance of Mary, who is highly esteemed in the Qur'an. Sons are often referenced with respect to the male parent, such as "Son of [father's name]," rather than the mother. However, in this case, Mary's name is prominent.

Second, *Isa* was apparently born in a far-flung place rather than according to the story of the manger narrated in the Christian Bible. The nativity account is absent from the Qur'an. When visited by the angel Gabriel, Mary wondered how this conception could possibly be, but, similar to the Christian gospel narratives, *Isa* is said to have been conceived and born without any human male intervention.[86]

Third, once Mary conceived, she hastened to secluded places, bore her son under or near a date palm tree with excruciating labor pains, and then returned to civilization.[87]

Fourth, the infant is said to have defended his mother when he asserted Mary's innocence,[88] which qualifies as a miracle in itself.

Fifth, the Qur'an mentions that *Isa* did many other miracles, including breathing into a clay bird,[89] giving it life.[90] The corpus affirms that *al-Masih* performed outstanding miracles from infancy[91] right up to his being taken away by Allah, only to reappear at the end of time. The Bible equally credits Jesus with miracles, signs and wonders, all pointing to his being the Christ. At the same time, the Qur'an is silent about any tangible miracle worked by

---

84. Djaballah, "Jesus in Islam," 18. Reynolds, "Muslim Jesus," has done the best exegetical work I have come across on Q 4:157–58 in relation to 19:33.

85. Q 19:22–27.

86. Q 3:47; 19:18–22.

87. Q 19:22–26.

88. Q 3:45–46; 5:110; 19:27–33.

89. Q 3:49.

90. Some suggest that Muhammad sourced these ideas from the gnostic gospels or Jewish sources such as the Talmud, Mishnah, etc.

91. Q 3:49; 17:90; 19:27–35; 61:6.

Muhammad, except for the claim that the Qur'an is itself "The miracle."[92] From ancient times, the early biographies (*Sīratu Rasūli l-Lāh*)[93] of the prophet never mentioned any tangible miracle by his hand. However, with time, and probably pressure, all sorts of miracles have been generated, all claiming to be authentic.[94] One wonders whether there is robust and authentic *isnād*[95] tied to them. Are the claims of these works strong, reliable or weak?

Sixth, it is worth mentioning that the Qur'an text comparatively scarcely mentions the final prophet[96] by name in comparison to *Isa* and his mother *Mary*.[97] Although the Qur'an refers to the prophet by name several times, relative to *Isa* and *Maryam* his name is used far less. The real reason is unclear or not discernible, but one suggestion by Muslim scholars is that the Qur'an is about Allah, not Muhammad. The Bible and other scriptures have substantially more human bio-data about their founders, but the Qur'an, being the final revelation, corrects that abnormality by primarily focusing on Allah and his will. This logic sounds piously plausible at face value, though it is not entirely convincing. For instance, we would argue, were not *Isa* and *Maryam* humans? How is it that their names are found in the Qur'an? The Muslim argument fails.

---

92. Q 6:109; 17:59, 102–8.

93. One early and adequate Sira is by Muhammad Ibn Ishaq (AD 704–67) and translated by Alfred Guillaume, 1955; and perhaps one by Ibn Hisham (d. 833), though derived from the former. A more contemporary one, *The Sealed Nector*, published by Maktaba Dar-us-Salaam in 1996, is worth reading, though not as venerable as Ibn Ishaq.

94. An example is one by Ibn Kathir (AD 1303–73), *Book of Evidences: The Miracles of the Prophet (PBUH)*. The work appears to be ancient, though this author could not determine the exact date it was authored.

95. An *isnad* is basically a direct link to the Prophet having actually said a claimed thing or belief. In short, a strong *isnad* is one that can be traced, through a transmission chain directly to the Prophet. If it breaks or not able to clearly be connected to the Prophet, the strength of that hadith correspondingly deteriorates. Typically establishing an *isnad* would include who said it, where did they get it from and does the chain directly lead to the Prophet? That is how Sahih Bukhari and others diligently pursued and established their hadiths, sifting through literally thousands of claims, not a simple task by all standards, but it needed to be done!

96. Only twenty-five times according to Geisler, "Jesus and Muhammad," 57.

97. Djaballah, "Jesus in Islam," 18, gives some helpful leads to texts directly mentioning or alluding to Jesus: Q 2:87, 136, 253; 3:33–55, 59; 4:156–59, 171–72; 5:46, 78, 110–17; 19:2–34; 32:50; 43:63; 57:27; 61:6; 66:12; 112:2–4; Geisler, "Jesus and Muhammad," 57, suggests ninety-five mentions.

Titles/names of Jesus in Qur'an: *Isa* (25 times); *Son of Mary*: Q 2:87, 253; 3:45; 4:171; 5:17, 72, 75, 78, 110, 112, 114, 116; 9:31; 19:16–33; 21:91; 23:50; 33:7; 43:57; 52:27; 61:6, 14; *Word of Allah*: Q 3:39, 45; 4:171; *Prophet (nabi)*: Q 2:136; 3:84; *Apostle (Rasul)*: Q 4:157, 171; 5:75; 57:27; *Messiah (al-Masih)*: Q 3:45; 4:75, 171–72; *Spirit from Allah*: Q 4:171; *Servant/Slave of Allah*: Q 4:172; 43:59.

Seventh, though one can scarcely construct a comprehensive, complete Sira or biography of the prophet from the Qur'an, given the unique nature and genre of this scripture, it none the less gives some ideas of who Muhammad was, his task or purpose in life.[98]

The Qur'an's Statements about *Isa* Similar to or Different from Those in the Christian Bible

There are certain things that the Qur'an positively or negatively affirms which Christians need to be aware of, some of which we have already hinted at.[99] The Qur'an affirms that *Isa* is "Christ." Several times *Isa* is referred to as *al-Masih*.[100] Although it is unclear whether Muslims fully appreciate the meaning, import or implications of this title, suffice it to say that the Qur'an positively affirms this fact, which some external sources, including gnostic gospels (i.e. later "gospels" outside the canonical four), flatly deny. For instance, the controversial spurious gospels of Barnabas and Thomas both reject the idea that Isa is *al-Masih*. The Qur'an further positively affirms that *Isa* was virgin-born, the "Son of Mary"[101] or *Ibn Maryam*, which is in line with the Christian gospel narratives, although some additional details in the Qur'an leave one at a loss.

The Qur'an affirms that *Maryam* was highly favored among women for the role she would play. In fact, Sūra 19 is named after *Maryam* (Mary), a rare phenomenon in Arabic thinking and culture according to some sources.[102] The unique naming demonstrates the high honor and esteem that the Qur'an accords *Isa* and *Maryam*. From the narratives, the Qur'an seems to have a relatively higher view of Mary than do even the authentic gospels,[103] as attested by *Sūra Maryam*.

In addition, the Qur'an states that *Isa* was an apostle and prophet of Allah, of the rank of Muhammad, although slightly lower. *Isa* is said to be a "word of Allah"[104] and sinless, akin to other prophets,[105] although he seems to stand in a

---

98. Jeffrey, "Historical Muhammad," 327.
99. See Geisler, "Jesus and Muhammad," 50–59.
100. For example, Q 3:45.
101. Q 3:45–47; 19:19–21.
102. Note also that Sūra 4 is called "The Women."
103. Q 3:45–47.
104. Q 3:45–50; 4:171.
105. Q 4:171; 5:46; 6:85.

class of his own.[106] Not even Muhammad can match him, it appears.[107] In the Qur'an, *Isa* is said to have ascended bodily into paradise without experiencing death,[108] and will return in the future. Thus, the Qur'an, in agreement with the Bible, does positively affirm that *Isa* shall return a second time to the world.[109] However, the reappearing motive is unclear[110] in the Qur'an, but in the Bible, Jesus will return as the Judge of the world, at the last trumpet call.[111]

Lastly, the Qur'an unequivocally states that, similar to Adam, *Isa* was created by Allah's decree when he said "Be," and he was.[112] This point differs from the biblical narrative in which Jesus is neither created nor in the same nature or rank as Adam, though the Lord Jesus is likened to Adam in relation to the fall and redemption.[113]

However, the Qur'an has a different narrative from that of the Bible in the following areas:

The first difference is that in the Qur'an, *Isa* was not crucified, and did not die or rise again.[114] Second, the Qur'an rejects the idea that *Isa* is seated at the Father's right hand, as though God were a human potentate. Third, the Qur'an rejects the atonement[115] and instead affirms human works to contribute to one's pleasing Allah.[116] In effect, the Muslim corpus rejects critical Christian doctrines such as original sin, the atonement, justification by faith, or the idea

---

106. Q 33:36–38; 47:19; 48:2.

107. Q 6:85; 33:36–38; 47:19; 48:2.

108. Q 3:55; 4:157; 19:33.

109. Muslims believe that Allah will reinstate *Isa* from heaven to fight the antichrist; *Isa* will later die and be raised – a sequence of events that, apparently, covers for his having died on the cross.

110. Apart from the fact that *Isa* shall return to defeat the anti-*Masih* and, after that, live preaching Islam for forty years and then die.

111. 1 Thess 4:16–17; 2 Thess 1:7–8.

112. Q 3:59.

113. Rom 5:12–21; 1 Cor 15:21–23.

114. Q 3:55; 4:157–59, 171; 5:116–17; 19:16–33; See also Coplestone, *Jesus Christ or Mohammed?*, 45; also see several papers and writings available at the https://theologicalstudies.org.uk/pdf/jisca/02-1_087.pdf and https://www.muslim.org/islam/deathofj.htm (an alternative view claiming that Jesus actually died, within Islamic school of thought).

115. Or expiatory/propitiatory death, redemption. In his comments relating to the possibility of Christ having died, Moucarry says the following, as cited in Djaballah, "Jesus in Islam," 24: "The Jews wanted to subject Jesus to such a shameful death (death by hanging; which falls under the curse of Dt 21:22–23 and Matt 27:20–23). Did they succeed? They certainly thought they did, but they were under an illusion, for God saved his servant, cleared his name of guilt, and justified him by raising him from the dead." Could it be that Q 2:48, 157; 3:156–58, 169; 4:158–59 applied to Jesus's death?

116. Djaballah, 23.

that someone can know that he or she is truly saved in this life.[117] The Qur'an, in the fourth place, denies that *Isa* is the Son of God[118] or that he is divine.[119] John of Damascus, an early apologist, took issue with the local Muslims over this. He viewed Islam as a heresy of Christianity from Arabia.[120] That said, in the Qur'an, the hypostatic nature of Christ is repeatedly assaulted and denounced in the scripture, which strictly upholds *Tawhid*, strict monotheism.[121] In the Muslim canon, the biblical Trinity[122] is clear polytheism, although the view advanced by the Qur'an itself is defective. While rejecting the divinity of *Isa*,[123] it equally rejects his being the only way to God. The Qur'an, by that token, rejects the idea that any mortal can have an organic relationship with the divine one, so allusions to God being "love" or the "father" of saints appear absurd to Muslims, if not blasphemous. In short, the Muslim corpus rejects the idea of *Isa* being included within the alleged polytheistic Trinitarian Godhead[124] and that *Isa* was crucified.

What Other Islamic (i.e. Hadith and Sunna) or Spurious Sources (i.e. Gospels of Thomas and Barnabas) Teach about *Isa*

Having highlighted what the Qur'an says or does not say, we must now mention that Muslims equally appeal to other external sources to strengthen or buttress their claims. Although these sources are said to be secondary and, by that token, not inspired in the same sense the Qur'an is, they give meaning and context to the Qur'an's assertions. Their importance is contingent on how closely connected the claims are to the prophet Muhammad through a chain

---

117. See Abdullah and Nadvi, "Understanding the Principles," 282; Jones, "Wilfred Cantwell Smith," 248, 250; Kevan, *Lord's Supper*, 25.

118. Q 2:116; 4:171; 5:17; 6:100–1; 9:30; 10:68; 16:57; 17:40; 37:149–53; 72:3. The Qur'an rejects the monogenic idea found in John's gospel.

119. As far as the Qur'an is concerned, Jesus is only a prophet, nothing more: Q 4:171; 5:72, 75; 9:30–31; Husseini, "Early Christian Explanations," 73.

120. Janosik, *John of Damascus*, 1.

121. Abdullah, "Tawhid and Trinity," 89, 102; Hoover, "Islamic Monotheism," 57.

122. Interestingly, Boyarin ("Gospel of the Memra," 281) argues that even the ancient Jews held a binitarian rather than unitarian view of God.

123. Q 5:17.

124. Consisting of Father, *Maryam* and *Isa*. Several Sūras attack the Trinity, directly or otherwise. The qur'anic formula for the Trinity composed of Mary, *Isa* and the Father is incorrect. We may argue that the Qur'an in fact never rejects the authentic Christian Trinity but the defective pagan, unbiblical one. That said, the following are included in the category of sūras referring to the Trinity either in passing or directly: Q 4:171; 5:73, 75, 116; 6:1, 56, 100, 101, 106, 161, 163; 10:28, 68; 21:26.

called the *isnād*.¹²⁵ Any claim must meticulously be traced back to the prophet or else be discounted or degraded. The Hadiths are said to be the sayings and pronouncements of the prophet while he traversed this terrestrial ball, in public or private conversation. These have come down to us, the most prominent being the Sahih Bukhari, Muslim, Abbas or Malik, among others.¹²⁶ The said Hadiths are held in very high regard, almost to the point of inspiration, because they throw some insight on qur'anic interpretation.¹²⁷ Then we have the *Sunna*,¹²⁸ which are the practices of the prophet which the *umma Muslima* must imitate, learn and practice (i.e. ablution, cleanliness, etc.); how the prophet ate, what he loved or allowed (*Halaal*), what he despised, forbade or rejected (*Haram*), are all to be followed without question. Muslims also make use of other external sources, such as the gnostic gospels of Barnabas and Thomas.¹²⁹ Muslims value these books because they seem to agree with the Qur'an's claims on some points, despite the said books occasionally contradicting orthodox Islamic doctrine.¹³⁰ Muslims love other sources from liberal theologians relating to biblical textual criticism, such as the *Jesus Seminar*.¹³¹ Whatever contradicts the Bible immediately attracts the thirsty attention of ferocious pundits.

Is the *Isa* of Islam the Same Person as the Biblical Jesus?

The critical question we cannot evade is: Is *Isa* of the Qur'an the same person as the Jesus of the Bible? The question is vital because the Qur'an and Muslims

---

125. A chain of transmission directly connected to the prophet himself, often generated by his companions who had direct contact with the prophet.

126. See the respective Hadiths for more details. Muslims consider the Hadiths as inspired, in some cases equal to the Qur'an: see Wadud, *Conspiracies against the Qur'an*, and Shabbir Ahmed, *Criminals of Islam*.

127. Wadud, *Conspiracies against the Qur'an*, refers to *Wahi Jali* (Qur'an) and *Khafi* (Hadith).

128. Ar-Radaddi, *Basic Lessons*, 9.

129. Inloes, "Gospel of Barnabas," 59; Pagels, *Gnostic Gospels*, xvi; Ragg and Ragg, *Gospel of Barnabas*, 1.

130. Although one Muslim scholar (Dr. Amina Inloes) has recently argued against the use of one of these books, believing it not to be definitely authentic and to in effect misrepresent, if not contradict, the Qur'an. One probable reason could be that she has noted the inherent inconsistencies and at times contradicting theology. Rejecting the idea that Muslims drafted a false document, she concludes as follows: "despite Muslim enthusiasm for this document, the Gospel of Barnabas clearly does not relate the Qur'anic message. Therefore, Muslims should desist from presenting it as proof of the truth of Islam. If they would like to continue presenting it as truth of the continuity of the message, they should explore alternative interpretations of the term 'Messiah' as used in the Gospel" ("Gospel of Barnabas," 60–61).

131. Djaballah, "Jesus in Islam," 14; see also Sproul and Saleeb, *Dark Side of Islam*, 19, 21–22, on this matter.

in general claim that all other earlier scriptures were confirmed and superseded by the final revelation encapsulated in the Qur'an.[132] The implication is that what the Muslim canon says is the authentic and final correct version. In recent research I carried out among Muslims in the Copperbelt and Lusaka, I found it challenging to help them see that the Jesus of the Bible and the Jesus of the Qur'an are different. As far as they were concerned, what was stated in the Qur'an was final. The Qur'an further claims that all prophets, from Adam to Muhammad, have been represented in the various scriptures, which therefore are precursors to the Qur'an. Any narrative that is contradictory to the authentic Qur'an is therefore a forgery, corrupted, and not worth listening to.[133] As expressed earlier, the puzzle is that the Qur'an itself seems to both affirm and reject the already existing Hebrew Bible *Tawrāt* (Torah) and Christian Bible *Injīl* (gospel) at the time (i.e. before and during the Qu'ran revelation period of twenty-three years). There is a contradiction setting up divergent routes, making it difficult to decipher which to follow.[134] That said, for the Muslim, the Qur'an is the corrected version of the previously corrupted scriptures, and no other.[135] It contains some components found in the Hebrew Bible and the Christian gospels, though expressed differently and, at times, at variance with the biblical narrative. For instance, Muslims have extracted "the qur'anic Ten Commandments" scattered across the Qur'an. Naguib is at pains to demonstrate that these commandments exist in the Qur'an and somehow approximate to the biblical Decalogue of Exodus 20.

On the other hand, for the Christian, the points of apparent departure inherent within the qur'anic codex are too grave to ignore. This divergence points in different directions, leaving one at a crossroads. Further, some additional qur'anic narratives at times seem too refined or superfluous to be true. As with Sproul and Saleeb,[136] we ask: Where did Muhammad source the extra narratives? Was it a revelation crossroads? If so, does Allah contradict his word?

---

132. See Sproul and Saleeb, 8–10, 13.

133. Saeed, "Charge of Distortion," 419.

134. ul Haqq, "Contradictions in the Qur'an," http://imi.org.au/wp-content/uploads/2012/08/17-Contradictions-in-the-Quran.pdf.

135. Though some Muslim scholars claim that the apparent contradictions result from the eventual abrogation of the *Tawrāt* and *Injīl*, which were superseded by the Qur'an; so says Gilchrist (*Muslim Challenge*, 52). Other Muslims, such as Wadud, reject the abrogation theory held as *Ijma* among Muslim scholars; see Schirrmacher and Baldwin, *Islamic View*, 13, 23.

136. Sproul and Saleeb, *The Dark Side of Islam*, 17.

That said, when we make the comparisons, we arrive at the firm conclusion that *Isa* of the Qur'an is different from the biblical Jesus. "Muslims believe that every nation received a messenger from God. Just like the prophets before him, Jesus' message lasted in its original purity for a period of time, but the scripture he received was slowly altered and his original call to absolute monotheism became corrupted. Six centuries after Jesus, God sent His last messenger, Muhammad p and revealed His final scripture, known as the Quran."[137] Alternatively, could it be that the prophet of Allah had access only to the spurious gnostic gospels? Muslims argue that the prophet was unlettered (i.e. *ummi*),[138] unschooled and could not possibly have read anything, let alone produced such an outstanding, lofty and poetic[139] piece of Arabic writing.[140] It therefore had to be of supernatural origin, so they argue. Muhammad merely uttered what was divinely and mechanically revealed to him. If it coincides with what already existed at the time, this is beside the point, because Allah willed it to be so. In the Muslim mind, the charge of plagiarism, as advanced by orientalists[141] such as Gilchrist[142] or Coplestone,[143] therefore does not arise.[144] Muslims further claim that what was revealed was directly from the original template in paradise: in other words, the truth was revealed.

On the other hand, the Jesus of the Bible was born in a manger, commenced public ministry at the age of thirty, was crucified, atoned for sinners, and rose again on the third day. He ascended to heaven, sat at the right hand of the

---

137. https://isdonline.org/discover-islam/jesus-in-islam.

138. Q 7:157–58. However, some thinkers within Islamic ranks reject this interpretation, claiming that Muhammad was indeed unschooled till he received the first *Wahi*. Wadud (*Conspiracies against the Qur'an*) and Shabbir Ahmed (*Criminals of Islam*) hold this view.

139. However, certain scholars argue that the Qur'an is in a class of its own, defying any of the classic genre categories of poetry, history, wisdom, etc.

140. Q 6:25; 7:31; 20:113.

141. This leads Muslim scholars to have a negative view of Western/exotic orientalists. Berke Khan's work "Was Hadith Written 200 Years after the Prophet?" takes pains to list the following orientalists perceived as contributing to defacing Islam: Robert Morey, Ignaz Goldziher, D. S. Margoliuth, Joseph Schacht, Henri Lammens, Louis Massignon, Reymond Alleyne Nicholson, Sir Hamilton Gibb, Aloys Sprenger, Sir William Muir, Julius Wellhausen, Leone Caetani, Richard Bell, Theodr Nöldeke, J. Wansbrough, Yehuda D. Nevo, Régis Blachère, George Sale, Claude-Étienne Savary, Patricia Crone and Michael Cook. I would also add Arthur Jeffrey, Jay Smith and Montgomery Watt.

142. Gilchrist, *Muslim Challenge*, 17.

143. Coplestone, *Jesus Christ or Mohammed?*, 93. This is an important section challenging the absolute originality of the Qur'an.

144. Q 6:25; 7:31; 20:113.

Father, and will return in glory to wrap up history.[145] That is the summative biblical storyline. The biblical metanarrative suggests that the Messiah was foretold,[146] proclaimed the kingdom,[147] and has kingdom citizens whose characteristics are encapsulated in the Beatitudes.[148] The Bible's Christology is different from that of the Qur'an. The Christian canon points to Christ from Genesis to Revelation. From the protevangelium in Genesis 3:15, where a Savior is promised, all the way through Deuteronomy 18:18, on to Isaiah 7, 9 and 53, to Malachi 4:5–6, and finally in the four authentic gospel narratives, Jesus is foretold and then his life story is narrated. At his first advent, Jesus institutes the new covenant[149] by dying a substitutionary atoning death on the cruel cross for a sinful world, thereby redeeming the elect.[150] He physically died and rose again[151] to restore what existed in the garden of Eden[152] with attendant blessings accruing to justified, adopted and sanctified sinners.[153] Pardoned sinners access these benefits by faith in Jesus, not by works.[154] Christ is not merely an example of how to live, but he atoned for sinners on the cross, laying down his life as a ransom for many, that they might walk in newness of life. Having actively and passively propitiated and expiated for the world, Jesus procured eternal life, resulting in reconciliation and peace with God. Jesus is both God and man, possessing a hypostatic nature, perfectly divine and yet fully human, such that he was a fitting sacrifice for sin. Paul's Christology in Romans, Ephesians and Colossians, and the writer to the Hebrews, highlight these aspects, demonstrating what a great salvation redeemed sinners enjoy in Christ. These christological concepts are foreign to Islam.

The qur'anic *Isa*, on the other hand, while also virgin-born, rises to be a prophet, and disappears only to return at some future point. The *Isa* of Islam is never the Son of God, never died on the cross and does not atone for sinners, but is a mere mortal with a message bequeathing the *Injīl*. As stated earlier, he escapes, is raptured or whisked away by Allah, and never suffers the violent,

---

145. As narrated in the four biblical gospels plus Acts, Romans, Hebrews, etc.
146. For example, Deut 18:18; Isa 7:14; 9:6–7; Dan 12:1–4; Mal 4:5; etc.
147. Mark 1:14–15.
148. Matt 5:3–12.
149. Kevan, *Lord's Supper*, 25; Luke 22:14–21.
150. Denney, *Death of Christ*, 156.
151. John 20:1–9.
152. Gen 1–2.
153. Rom 5:8; 8:1.
154. Rom 3:21–26; Eph 2:8; Titus 3:5; etc.

shameful death that the Bible portrays.[155] *Isa* is therefore not divine, nor did he claim to be so, suggesting that what the Bible claims is false because Muslims know better.

For the reasons given above, the two "Jesuses" cannot be the same person. One of the narratives must be wrong, but which one? Depending on one's leaning and worldview, one will logically take a side consistent with one's creed. Such a binary view is what makes it advantageous for Christians to have a working understanding of Islam because, without it, they risk either being misunderstood or losing out on constructive engagement with Muslims toward conversion. Although regeneration is solely God's work, human responsibility dictates that Christians should make it a priority to know what others believe, in order to be competently effective.

The Theological Implication(s) of the Qur'anic *Isa* for Christian–Muslim Discourse

From the preceding discussion, it is evident that *Isa* has an exceptional place in Islam. He is highly regarded, respected, and ranked second only to the seal of the prophets, Muhammad. However, Islam presents a different perspective of *Isa* from that of the Bible. The Christians' view and that of Muslims are evidently at odds.[156] Granted, there are several commonalities between the narratives in the respective scriptures, but each appears to slant in a different direction. The Qur'an inclines toward *Tawhid* and thus negates all insinuations of *Isa* being more than a mere prophet.[157] In fact, the Qur'an rejects the idea of *Isa* being the Son of God because God cannot have a son, and with whom could he have a son anyway?[158] The Qur'an asserts that Allah is wholly other, transcendent and separate from his creation, thus he cannot have a biological son. The Qur'an vehemently rejects the claim that *Isa* is God, for that amounts to *shirk*,[159] the unpardonable sin in Islam. Allah is a unity, akin to what the *Tawrāt* asserts.[160] He cannot have associates, nor should any mortal associate anything with him. He is the self-existent, solitary and uncreated one. He

---

155. Reynolds, "Muslim Jesus," 237.
156. Sproul and Saleeb, *Dark Side of Islam*, 8.
157. Q 3:59; 19:30.
158. Q 2:116; 6:100–1; 16:57; 17:40; 37:149–53; 72:3.
159. Q 4:48.
160. Q 2:255; 3:2; 6:56; Deut 5:7; 6:4. Some modern sources, however, claim that Judaism is binitarian rather than strictly monotheistic in the sense Islam claims. See Boyarin, "Gospel of the Memra," 284.

alone is eternal, unique, with the ninety-nine beautiful names.[161] Though his attributes and the Qur'an are perceived to be equally eternal and uncreated, they are not eternal and uncreated in the same sense that Allah is.[162] The Qur'an is Allah's eternal word, unalterable, unchanging,[163] timeless and holy,[164] but again, not in the same sense that Allah is. Muslims are often confused and strongly debate this matter because it poses challenges for them just as the Trinity does for some Christians. That said, Allah stands alone and, in a sense, impersonal.[165] Some Muslim scholars, however, claim that while Allah is transcendent and communicates through secondary agents such as angels, he is none the less "near to his creation."[166] The logical question is: In what sense is Allah "near" to his creation? Is it in geographical proximity, awareness (omniscience), relationship, or something else? The problem remains unresolved.

For Muslims, as stated earlier when looking at their worldview, the Qur'an forms Muslims' view and is always perceived to be right. By that token, anything contradicting the Qur'an is automatically viewed as corrupted, whether it is the Christian Bible or not, despite the latter preceding the Qur'an by over five hundred years! Muslims claim that the Jews and Christians corrupted[167] the Bible to give a conflicting narrative to the final revelation, the Qur'an![168] How this could be is not explained. If for argument's sake we accepted this view, what exactly is the nature of this "corruption"? The type of "corruption" remains unclear: is it the text itself that was altered, or its interpretation?[169] A close analysis of the Islamic text suggests that the prophet was concerned with the interpretation of *Tawrāt* and *Injīl* by Jews and Christians. There is less evidence of him being concerned about the altering of the text, for that would generate another problem for Muslims.[170] The Qur'an upholds the extant *Injīl*

---

161. Rahman, "Major Themes of the Quran," 1–2.

162. Cook, *Koran*, 110; Q 2:267; 3:29; 6:59.

163. Q 6:34.

164. Q 4:82.

165. Though Rahman asserts that Allah is in a sense personal (i.e. loving, merciful, etc.) in "Major Themes of the Quran," 3.

166. Q 50:16.

167. That is, *Tahrif*; Q 2:75–81; 4:46–47; 5:12–15, 41–47. *Tahrif* has to do with the corruption or changing (e.g. in interpretation) of something, such as a religious text.

168. Djaballah, "Jesus in Islam," 16. Djaballah and others argue that Christians should push back against such charges, especially at a scholarly level; Tarakci and Sayar, "Qur'anic View," 227–40; Saeed, "Charge of Distortion," 419–35.

169. Djaballah, "Jesus in Islam," 16; Saeed, "Charge of Distortion," 419; Tarakci and Sayar, "Qur'anic View," 229–30.

170. Q 4:46; 5:13–14, 41.

and *Tawrāt* as authentic;[171] how then can it, in the same breath, claim that these are corrupted?[172]

Could it be that the Jews and Christians were not correctly interpreting their texts to their Arab counterparts? Could it be that a small circle of Jews and Christians were not being faithful to the truth, or indeed altered localized specific texts, hence the strong reprimands?[173] We have no way of telling for sure. If there were indeed at all any alterations to the text, then the inspired page would be corrupted and the message distorted, but that cannot be.[174] Yahweh, or even Allah for that matter, would not allow that.

The 1947 discovery of the Dead Sea scrolls at Qumran was a defining moment: it proved that the Scripture texts dating nearly a hundred years prior to Jesus's birth were the same as the texts of ten centuries later![175] That is remarkable, and proves the authenticity of the biblical narrative. The Qur'an, therefore, must have meant something other than textual corruption. Saeed, Gilchrist and others believe that the alleged "corruption" had to do with the interpretation rather than the text itself.[176] If this argument holds, then the Qur'an could be viewed in a different light.

Another point worth noting is that the Qur'an rejects the idea of atonement and thus the death of *Isa* on the cross. It repeatedly states that *Isa* was not killed, but was merely made to appear so. If this is true, it has grave theological implications for the Christian body of truth. The whole Christian system breaks down, as there is no original sin, no resurrection, no atonement, no redemption and no justification, and it practically erases all claims Christians have derived from passages such as 1 Corinthians 15, Romans 5:8 or John 3:16. Christianity places great emphasis on orthodoxy. To believe correctly by faith opens the door to eternal life. For the Muslim, it is orthopraxy that enhances the probability of escaping hellfire. The two systems are different. In Islam, people work their way into paradise by observing *Deen*,[177] strict adherence

---

171. Q 10:94; 32:240; 40:70–72.

172. Djaballah, "Jesus in Islam," 16. Djaballah concludes: "The Muslim accusation then, that Christians have corrupted their scriptures, does not seem to have a Qur'anic warrant." Q 2:78.

173. Q 3:113.

174. Q 6:34, 115; 10:64–65. The Hebrew and Christian corpuses have been very stable as far as doctrine is concerned. One needs to be wary of what sources one consults, whether liberal or orthodox theologians/scholars.

175. See the following on the Dead Sea scrolls: Varner, "What Is the Importance?"; Wilson, "Dead Sea Scrolls," 26–27; Brantley, "Dead Sea Scrolls," 25–30.

176. Saeed, "The Charge of Distortion of Jewish and Christian Scriptures," 434; Gilchrist, *Facing the Muslim Challenge*, 52.

177. The Islamic way of life or social order.

to inflexible imperatives, and seeking ways to increase good over evil in their lives. The net effect may just possibly result in eternal life rather than hell. In effect, Islam is essentially anthropocentric rather than theocentric.[178] Although Muslims tend to be physically (and materially) helpful to one another, perhaps the motivation is often to enhance the probability of a good entry into paradise, rather than love for God or a transformed heart. Islam does not know anything about regeneration by the Holy Spirit in the sense that Christians do.

Another troubling matter is the view and attachments Muslims impute to the Bible. Instead of establishing the Christian corpus's authorial intent, they force a meaning into Holy Scripture[179] which has attendant repercussions and implications. For example, in Islam, the "Holy Spirit" means the angel Gabriel, while Muhammad is "forced" into the biblical narratives. Where the Christian gospel narratives agree with the Qur'an, Muslims will accept them as accurate, but anything contrary to the Qur'an is believed to have been corrupted.[180] One would expect the same consistency extended to the gnostic gospels. Like other erroneous approaches to interpretation, the Islamic hermeneutical approach to Bible interpretation is suspect.[181]

Many other vital issues cause concern to Christians when processing the theological implications. Be that as it may, there is a need to know what Muslims believe so that we can intelligently engage them on different issues, bearing in mind that they have a given unique worldview distinct from that of Christians.

Conclusion

From this discussion, it is evident that Christians and Muslims have common talking points.[182] They can engage constructively. At the same time, they have different views about Jesus, and may not agree for that reason. These differences

---

178. Rahman agrees with this conclusion in his great work "Major Themes of the Qur'an": "The Qur'an is a document that is squarely aimed at man . . . the Qur'an is no treatise about God and His nature; His existence, for the Qur'an, is strictly functional – He is creator and sustainer of the universe and man" (1).

179. With or without correct motives, using incorrect hermeneutical approaches or tools.

180. Ally, *Is Jesus God? The Bible Says No*, 12.

181. Carson, *Exegetical Fallacies*, 17; Klein, Blomberg and Hubbard, *Introduction to Biblical Interpretation*, 4.

182. Baagil, *Muslim-Christian Dialogue*, 4; Brown, "Muslim Worldviews," 5; Kraft, *Intercultural Communication*, 1; Youssef, "Theology and Methodology"; Azumah, "Christian Responses to Islam," 83; Green, *Islam and Christianity*; Chapman, "Christian Responses to Islam," 2; Carson, "SBJT Forum," 90; Esposito, "Muslim-Christian Relations," 1.

have profound theological implications. Christians need to take a keen interest in Islam so that they can effectively give a reason for the hope they possess.[183]

Bibliography

Abdullah, Ismail. "Tawhid and Trinity: A Study of Ibn Taymiyyah's al-Jawab al Sahih." *Intellectual Discourse* 14, no. 1 (2006): 89–106. https://www.academia.edu/28090964/Tawhid_and_Trinity_A_Study_of_Ibn_Taymiyyahs_al_Jawab_al_sahih_1.

Abdullah, Muhammad, and Muhammad Junaid Nadvi. "Understanding the Principles of Islamic World-View." *The Dialogue* 6, no. 3 (2011): 268–89. https://www.qurtuba.edu.pk/thedialogue/The%20Dialogue/6_3/Dialogue_July_September2011_268-289.pdf.

Abu Zayd, Nasr. *Reformation of Islamic Thought: A Critical Historical Analysis.* Scientific Council for Government Policy (WRR Rapporten). Amsterdam: Amsterdam University Press, 2006. https://www.jstor.org/stable/j.ctt46mt56.

Ahmed, Shabbir. *The Criminals of Islam.* 2007. http://drshabbir.com/library/criminals.pdf.

———. "Thus Speaks the Bible." 2013. https://www.yumpu.com/en/document/view/12427160/thus-speaks-the-bible-dr-shabbir-ahmed.

———. *Thus Speaks the Quran.* 2010. http://drshabbir.com/library/THUS%20SPEAKS%20THE%20QURAN-Rev%201.pdf.

Ahmed, Shahab. *Before Orthodoxy: The Satanic Verses in Early Islam.* Cambridge, MA: Harvard University Press, 2017. DOI: 10.4159/9780674977372.

Akhter, Naseem, and Abdul Qadoos. "Islam Is the Religion of Peace: Analytical Review from the Life of Holy Prophet (PBUH)." *Burjis* 4, no. 2 (Dec. 2017): 1–30. https://www.researchgate.net/publication/333034365_Islam_Is_The_Religion_of_Peace_Analytical_Review_from_the_Life_of_Holy_Prophet_PBUH.

Al-Mubarkpuri, Safiur-Rahman. *The Sealed Nectar (Ar-Raheequl Makhtum): Biography of the Nobel Prophet.* Riyadh: Darussalam, 1996.

Ally, Shabir. *Is Jesus God? The Bible Says No!* Riyadah: Al-Attique Publishers, 1998. https://www.academia.edu/36944243/Is_Jesus_God_The_bible_say_No_by_DR_Shabr_ally.

Alphonse, Ndongo Kamdem. "Jesus in the Bible and the Qur'an: A Comparative Study." *Journal of Humanities and Social Sciences* 12, no. 1 (May–June 2013): 14–19. http://www.iosrjournals.org/iosr-jhss/papers/Vol12-issue1/C01211419.pdf.

Anthony, Sean W. "Two 'Lost' Suras of the Qur'an: Surat al-Khal and Surat al-Hafd between Textual and Ritual Canon (1st–3rd/7th–9th Centuries)." *Jerusalem Studies in Arabic and Islam* 46 (2019): 67–112. https://www.academia.edu/40869286/

---

183. 1 Pet 3:15.

Two_Lost_Sūras_of_the_Qur'ān_Sūrat_al_Khal'_and_Sūrat_al_Ḥafd_between_ Textual_and_Ritual_Canon_1st_3rd_7th_9th_Centuries_Pre_Print_Version_.

Anthony, Sean W., and Catherine L. Bronson. "Did Hafsah Edit the Qur'an? A Response with Notes on the Codices of the Prophet's Wives." *Journal of the International Qur'anic Studies Association* 1 (2016): 93–125. DOI: 10.5913/jiqsa.1.2017. 006.

Ar-Radaddi, Abdullah Buraik. *Basic Lessons for New Muslims*. Jeddah: King Fahd National Library, 2012.

Aydin, Hayati. "Islam the Religion of Peace." *Journal of Rotterdam Islamic and Social Sciences* 2, no. 1 (June 2008). DOI: 10.2478/jriss-2013-0022.

Azumah, John. "Christian Responses to Islam: A Struggle for the Soul of Christianity." *Church & Society in Asia Today* 13, no. 2 (Aug. 2010): 83–94.

Baagil, Hasan M. *Muslim–Christian Dialogue*. Jeddah: Islamic Education Foundation, 1984.

Boyarin, Daniel. "The Gospel of the Memra: Jewish Binitarianism and the Prologue to John." *Harvard Theological Review* 94, no. 3 (July 2001): 243–84. https://www.researchgate.net/publication/231982610_The_Gospel_of_the_Memra_Jewish_Binitarianism_and_the_prologue_to_John.

Brantley, Garry K. "The Dead Sea Scrolls and Biblical Integrity." *Apologetic Press: Reason & Revelation* 15, no. 4 (April 1995): 25–30. http://static1.squarespace.com/static/51fbf1e5e4b0a9dce7926cdb/586a9a7214fd83f0a9f0c21b/586a9a9714fd83f0a9f0c398/1483381399805/the-dead-sea-scrolls-and-biblical-integrity.pdf?format=original.

Brown, Rick. "Muslim Worldviews and the Bible: Bridges and Barriers – Part I: God and Mankind." *International Journal of Frontier Missions* 23, no. 1 (Spring 2006): 5–11. https://www.ijfm.org/PDFs_IJFM/23_1_PDFs/5-12%20Rick%20Brown.pdf.

Brubaker, Daniel Alan. *Corrections in Early Qur'an Manuscripts: Twenty Examples*. Lovettsville: Think and Tell Press, 2019.

Carson, Don A. *Exegetical Fallacies*. Grand Rapids, MI: Baker Academic, 2007.

———. "The SBJT Forum: Key Issues for Understanding Islam and Muslims." *Southern Baptist Journal of Theology* 8, no. 1 (Spring 2004): 90–95.

Chapman, Colin. "Christian Responses to Islam, Islamism and 'Islamic Terrorism.'" *Cambridge Papers* 16, no. 2 (June 2007): 1–6. https://www.jubilee-centre.org/cambridge-papers/christian-responses-to-islam-islamism-and-islamic-terrorism-by-colin-chapman.

Cook, Michael. *The Koran: A Very Short Introduction*. Oxford: Oxford University Press, 2000. DOI: 10.1093/actrade/9780192853448.001.0001.

Coplestone, F. S. *Jesus Christ or Mohammed? A Guide to Islam and Christianity That Helps Explain the Differences*. Fearn: Christian Focus, 2006.

Cox, Caroline, and John Marks. *The West, Islam and Islamism: Is Ideological Islam Compatible with Liberal Democracy?* London: Civitas, Institute for the Study of Civil Society, 2003. https://www.civitas.org.uk/pdf/cs29.pdf.

Cragg, Kenneth. *The Call of the Minaret*. New York: Oxford University Press, 1964.

Crone, Patricia, and Michael Cook. *Hagarism: The Making of the Islamic World.* London: Cambridge University Press, 1977. https://www.almuslih.org/Library/Crone,%20P;%20Cook,%20M%20-%20Hagarism.pdf.

Deedat, Ahmed. *Desert Storm: Has It Ended? Christ in Islam.* 1991. https://ia800809.us.archive.org/21/items/ChristInIslam_20170826/Christ_in_Islam.pdf.

Denney, James. *The Death of Christ.* Carlisle: Paternoster, 1997.

Djaballah, Amar. "Jesus in Islam." *Southern Baptist Journal of Theology* 8, no. 1 (2004): 14–30. https://equip.sbts.edu/publications/journals/journal-of-theology/sbjt-81-spring-2004/jesus-in-islam/.

Esposito, John L. *Great World Religions: Islam.* Chantilly: Teaching Company, 2003.

———. "Muslim–Christian Relations in a Multi-Faith World." Paper presented at Georgetown University, 2018. https://www.comillas.edu/images/Noticias/Curso_2017_18/Abril_18/DHC/Lecci%C3%B3n_doctoral_Dr._D._John_L._Esposito.pdf.

———. *Ten Things Everyone Needs to Know about Islam.* Strathfield: Columbian Mission Institute, 2002.

Geisler, Norman L. "Jesus and Muhammad in the Qur'an: A Comparison and Contrast." *Southern Baptist Journal of Theology* 8, no. 1 (Spring 2004): 50–59. https://equip.sbts.edu/publications/journals/journal-of-theology/sbjt-81-spring-2004/jesus-and-muhammed-in-the-quran-a-comparison-and-contrast/.

Ghafur, W. A., A. H. Prasojo, and M. S. bin Haji Masri. "The Qur'anic Jesus: Isa al-Masih in the Qur'an." *Epistemé: Jurnal Pengembangan ilmu Keislaman* 14, no. 2 (Dec. 2019). DOI: 10.21274/epis.2019.14.2.349-373.

Gilchrist, John. *Facing the Muslim Challenge.* Cape Town: Life Challenge Africa, 1999.

Green, Bruce. *Islam and Christianity: Reaching Out to Muslims.* Torrance: Rose Publications, 2004.

Hill, Charles. *International Business: Competing in the Global Market Place.* Toronto: McGraw-Hill, 2003.

Holmberg, Bo. "Hagarism Revisited." *Studia Orientalia Electronica* 99 (2004): 53–64. https://journal.fi/store/article/view/41583.

Hoover, Jon. "Islamic Monotheism and the Trinity." *The Conrad Grebel Review* 27, no. 1 (Winter 2009): 57–82. https://uwaterloo.ca/grebel/publications/conrad-grebel-review/issues/winter-2009/islamic-monotheism-and-trinity.

Husseini, Sara Leila. "Early Christian Explanations of the Trinity in Arabic in the Context of Muslim Theology." PhD diss., University of Birmingham, 2011. https://core.ac.uk/download/pdf/1631631.pdf.

Ibn Kathir, Hafidh Abi Al-Fada'ah Ismail. *Book of Evidences: The Miracles of the Prophet (P.B.U.H.).* Al-Mansoura: Dar Al-Ghad, n.d. (ISBN: 977/6050/04/2)

Inloes, Amina. "The Gospel of Barnabas: A Muslim Forgery?" *Islamic Writings: The Student Journal of the Islamic College* 6, no.1 (2016): 49–65. https://www.academia.edu/22980858/The_Gospel_of_Barnabas_A_Muslim_Forgery.

Ishaq, Ibn Muhammad. *The Life of Muhammad.* Translated by Alfred Guillaume. London: Oxford University Press, 1955.

IslamAwakened. "Qur'an Translation List (English)." Accessed 23 October 2020. https://www.islamawakened.com/index.php/qur-an/translation-list/.

Ismail, Alsayed M. Aly. *Hermeneutics and the Problem of Translating Traditional Arabic Texts.* Newcastle upon Tyne: Cambridge Scholars, 2017.

Janosik, Daniel J. *John of Damascus, First Apologist to the Muslims: The Trinity and Christian Apologetics in the Early Islamic Period.* Eugene: Pickwick, 2016.

Jeffery, Arthur. "The Quest of the Historical Muhammad." *Muslim World* 16, no. 4 (1926): 327–48. DOI: 10.1111/j.1478-1913.1926.tb00634.x.

Jones, Richard J. "Wilfred Cantwell Smith and Kenneth Cragg on Islam as a Way of Salvation." *International Bulletin of Missionary Research* 16, no. 3 (July 1992): 105–10. DOI: 10.1177/239693939201600302.

Karimi-Nia, Morteza. "A New Document in the Early History of the Qur'an." *Journal of Islamic Manuscripts* 10, no. 3 (2019): 292–326. DOI: 10.1163/1878464X-01003002.

Kevan, Ernest F. *The Lord's Supper.* 3rd ed. Welwyn: Evangelical Press, 1982.

Khan, Berke. "Was Hadith Written 200 Years after the Prophet?" https://www.academia.edu/34869673/Was_Hadith_Written_200_years_after_the_Prophet.

Kidwai, Abdur Rahim. "A Survey of English Translations of the Quran." *The Muslim World Book Review* 7, no. 4 (Summer 1987). https://www.ilmgate.org/a-survey-of-english-translations-of-the-quran/.

Klein, William W., Craig L. Blomberg and Robert L. Hubbard Jr. *Introduction to Biblical Interpretation.* Nashville: Thomas Nelson, 2004.

Kraft, Charles H. "Culture, Worldview and Contextualization." *Perspectives on Missions*, n.d. 384–91. https://www.perspectivesonmission.com/resources/Session07_Kraft_CultureWorldviewContextualization.pdf.

———. *Intercultural Communication and Worldview Change.* Pasadena: Pasadena School of World Mission, 1976.

Licona, M. R. "Using the Death of Jesus to Refute Islam." *Journal of Society of Christian Apologetics* 2, no. 1 (2009): 87–110.

MacFarquhar, Neil. "New Translation Prompts Debate on Islamic Verse." *The New York Times*, 25 March 2007. https://www.nytimes.com/2007/03/25/us/25koran.html.

Mohammad, Sher Hafiz. *The Death of Jesus.* Dublin, Ohio: Ahmadiyya Anjuman Isha'at Islam Lahore, Inc, 2003. https://www.muslim.org/islam/deathofj.htm.

Morey, Robert A. *Introduction to Defending the Faith.* Southbridge: Crowne, 1989.

Moucarry, Chawkat G. *The Prophet and the Messiah: An Arab Christian's Perspective on Islam and Christianity.* Downers Grove: InterVarsity Press, 2002.

Muslim Student's Association. "What Does the Qur'an Say about Jesus?" Accessed on 2nd March 2020. https://sites.ualberta.ca/~msa/pdf/quran_jesus.pdf.

Naik, Zakir. *Answers to Non-Muslims' Common Questions about Islam.* Islamic Research Foundation, 2011. https://www.zakirnaik.com/img/content/books/Common_Question.pdf.

Netland, Harold, Doug Sweeney, Graham Cole, and Don Carson. "The Message of Islam and the Gospel of Jesus Christ." Trinity Evangelical Divinity School, 2019. https://www.tiu.edu/wp-content/uploads/2019/08/ChristianityAndIslam-1.pdf.

Onishi, Norimitsu, and Constant Méheut. "A Teacher, His Killer and the Failure of French Integration." *The New York Times*, 26 October 2020. https://www.nytimes.com/2020/10/26/world/europe/france-beheading-teacher.html.

Pagels, Elaine. *The Gnostic Gospels*. New York: Vintage, 1989. https://static1.squarespace.com/static/52cdf95ae4b0c18dd2d0316a/t/53e074cee4b0ea4fa48a5704/1407218894673/Pagels%2C+Elaine+-+The+Gnostic+Gospels.pdf%20Bart%20Erhman.

Parshall, Phil. "The Muslim Worldview." Caleb Project, 2004. https://static1.squarespace.com/static/530b8735e4b0c1a4a93d8896/t/561c0d56e4b0ff1a3acb9cf7/1444678998912/Muslim+Worldview.pdf.

Patel, Youshaa. "Choosing a Quran Translation for College Classroom." Wabash Center for Teaching and Learning in Theology and Religion. 23 March 2016. https://www.wabashcenter.wabash.edu/print-blog-as-pdf/?id=44022.

Pew Research Center. "The Changing Global Religious Landscape." 5 April 2017. https://www.pewforum.org/2017/04/05/the-changing-global-religious-landscape/.

———. "The Future of World Religions: Population Growth Projections, 2010–2050." 2 April 2015. https://www.pewforum.org/2015/04/02/religious-projections-2010-2050/.

Racious, Egdunas. "The Multiple Nature of the Islamic Da'wa." Academic diss., University of Helsinki, 2004.

Ragg, Lonsdale, and Laura Ragg. *The Gospel of Barnabas*. Oxford: Clarendon Press, 1907.

Rahman, Fazlur. "Major Themes of the Qur'an." 2009. https://moodle.swarthmore.edu/pluginfile.php/152815/mod_resource/content/1/Major-Themes-of-Quran-Fazlur-Rahman.pdf.

Reynolds, Gabriel Said. "The Muslim Jesus: Dead or Alive?" *Bulletin of the School of Oriental and African Studies* 72, no. 2 (2009): 237–58. https://doi.org/10.1017/S0041977X09000500.

Riches, John. *The Bible: A Very Short Introduction*. New York: Oxford University Press, 2000. DOI: 10.1093/actrade/9780192853431.001.0001.

Ruthven, Malise. *Islam: A Very Short Introduction*. New York: Oxford University Press, 2000. DOI: 10.1093/actrade/9780199642878.001.0001.

Saeed, Abdullah. "The Charge of Distortion of Jewish and Christian Scriptures." *The Muslim World* 92, no. 3–4 (2007): 419–36. DOI: 10.1111/j.1478-1913.2002.tb03751.x.

Saheeh International. *The Qur'an: English Meanings and Notes*. [London]: Al-Muntada Al-Islami Trust, 2012.

Schirrmacher, C., and R. Baldwin. *The Islamic View of Major Christian Teachings: The Role of Jesus Christ, Sin and Forgiveness*. Bonn: World Evangelical Alliance, 2008.

Shadid, W., and P. S. van Koningsveld. "The Negative Image of Islam and Muslims in the West: Causes and Solutions." In *Religious Freedom and the Neutrality of the State: The Position of Islam in the European Union*, edited by W. Shadid and P. S. van Koningsveld, 174–96. Leuven: Peeters, 2002. https://www.interculturelecommunicatie.com/download/image.pdf.

Shaw, Mark. *The Kingdom of God in Africa: A Short History of African Christianity*. Katunayake: New Life Literature, 1996.

Smith, Jay. "The Quran: A Christian Apologetic." 99 Truth Papers, Hyde Park Christian Fellowship, 2002. http://storage.cloversites.com/uplandbrethreninchristchurch/documents/QURAN.pdf.

Sookhdeo, Patrick. *Understanding Islamic Theology*. McLean: Isaac Publishing, 2013.

Sproul, R. C., and Abdul Saleeb. *The Dark Side of Islam*. Wheaton: Crossway, 2003.

Steger, Manfred B. *Globalization: A Very Short Introduction*. New York: Oxford University Press, 2003.

Strakosch, Chris. *Middle Eastern Monotheism: A History of The Middle Eastern Monotheistic Religions*. 3rd ed. University of Queensland, Department of Medicine, 2009. https://www.scribd.com/document/29686742/Middle-Eastern-Monotheism-Chris-Strakosch.

Tahir-ul-Qadri, Muhammad. *Islam: The Religion of Peace or Terror?* Lahore: Minhaj-ul-Quran Publications, 2016. https://www.researchgate.net/publication/325205838_Islam_The_Religion_of_Peace_or_Terror.

Tarakci, Muhammet, and Suleyman Sayar. "The Qur'anic View of the Corruption of the Torah and the Gospels." *The Islamic Quarterly* 49, no. 3 (2005): 227–45. https://www.academia.edu/6709722/The_Quranic_View_of_the_Corruption_of_the_Torah_and_the_Gospels_in_English_.

ul Haqq, Mizan. "Contradictions in the Qur'an." http://imi.org.au/wp-content/uploads/2012/08/17-Contradictions-in-the-Quran.pdf.

Varner, Will. "What Is the Importance of the Dead Seas Scrolls?" Associates for Biblical Research. ChristianAnswers.Net, 1997. https://christiananswers.net/q-abr/abr-a023.html.

Wadud, Syed Abdul. *Conspiracies against the Qur'an*. Lahore: Khalid Publishers, 1976.

Watt, William M. *Muhammad: Prophet and Statesman*. London: Oxford University Press, 1961.

Wilson, Alistair. "The Dead Sea Scrolls on the High Street, Part 1." *The Monthly Record* (1997): 26–31. http://www.affinity.org.uk/downloads/foundations/Foundations%20Archive/42_26.pdf.

Youssef, Michael A. "Theology and Methodology for Muslim Evangelism in Egypt." MA diss., Fuller Theological Seminary, 1978.

Yuksel, Edip, Martha Schulte-Nafeh, and Layth Saleh al-Shaiban. *Qur'an: A Reformist Translation*. [USA]: Brainbow Press, 2010.

Part Four

Tributes to the Late Professor John S. Mbiti

20

John Mbiti's Perspective on Theological and Missiological Issues with Respect to Christianity and African Traditional Religion

David K. Ngaruiya

Associate Professor, International Leadership University, Nairobi, Kenya

Abstract

In this paper we will examine John Mbiti's concept of *praeparatio evangelica* and some related issues. While many other arguments may be provided regarding the thriving of Christianity in different contexts, I advance the following argument in the context of African Traditional Religion as reflected in the theology of John Mbiti: African Traditional Religion has an affinity with the gospel. The failure of mission approaches to distinguish between missionary Christianity and the gospel has led to polemics that have hurt gospel witness. Nevertheless, in spite of this protracted conflict, which is reflected in cultural clashes, African Traditional Religion, because of its affinity with the gospel, has been fertile ground in which the gospel has been able to thrive. In the Kenyan context, for example, the colonial prohibition of pluralism did not inhibit the embrace of the gospel among adherents of African Traditional Religion.

Key words: *praeparatio evangelica*, African Traditional Religion, culture, church, mission

Introduction

Professor John Mbiti was a pastor, author, teacher and theologian; some refer to him as the "father of contemporary African theology."[1] In this chapter, I will examine Mbiti's idea of *praeparatio evangelica* that is found in some of his writings. This study will cover the theological climate of John Mbiti's writing, his definition of African Traditional Religion, his methodology, *praeparatio evangelica* in relation to salvation, and other related aspects. A response to Mbiti's concepts and two implications will be discussed before the conclusion. A brief background of John Mbiti is provided in appendix 1.

Theological Climate of John Mbiti's Writings

Mission theory of Christianity, the legacy of colonization and intellectual forces in the academy were among the key factors pertinent to the theological climate in which John Mbiti wrote. These areas sometimes overlapped. John Mbiti grew up in a theological environment in which the mission of Christianity was to replicate, with as much precision as possible, European models of a believer's life and conduct, creating what Andrew Walls terms "Black Europeans."[2] Christianity was the mighty lever by which this would be accomplished. This may have been one of the factors that led Mbiti to assert that "mission Christianity was not from the start prepared to face a serious encounter with the traditional religions and philosophy or the modern changes taking place . . . The church in Africa now finds itself in the situation of having to exist without a theology."[3] In his study of African religions, Mbiti's interpretive framework was greatly influenced by Niebuhr's classic *Christ and Culture*, whose thesis that "Christ is the fulfillment of human culture enables Mbiti to reinterpret African traditional religion in a way that makes him see it as part and parcel of God's plan."[4]

We should also note that, until recently, the "curse" of Ham has been used to rationalize injustice toward the African. Talbot, for example, believed that the "curse" of Ham was placed on the black race in God's plan, asserting: "It is not by chance that the Negro has been a servant of the servants. This fact is prophecy fulfilled."[5] Others have echoed this thinking, considering Africa

---

1. "Mbiti, John Samuel," *Dictionary of African Christian Biography*, https://dacb.org/stories/kenya/mbiti-johns/.
2. Walls, *Missionary Movement*, 104.
3. Mbiti, *African Religions and Philosophy*, 232.
4. Olupona and Nyang, "Issues and Perspectives," 38.
5. Talbot, Bible Questions Explained, 77, cited in Adeyemo, *Is Africa Cursed?*, 17.

to be a "heartland of animism" which "has no books and no temples, nor has it produced great leaders, thinkers or scholars. Of course, it has its medicine men, its witch doctors, and its devil dancers."[6] Mbiti endured criticism not only from the West but also from within. In Kenya, someone asserted that "if all they [African theologians] want to say is that we need to praise the Lord while jumping up and down and full of emotions, singing our own tunes, or praying in the name of Jesus while we sit under a mugumo (wild) tree . . . then I ask for permission to remain as I am."[7]

Mbiti critiqued the work of some outsiders who studied African religions. He termed their work "descriptive" and said that their terminology, such as the concept of animism, was "inadequate, derogatory and prejudicial."[8] He rejected the evolutionary theory of religions which located African religions at the bottom of religious evolution. He asserted that, contrary to the theory that monotheistic religions such as Christianity and Islam are at the top of the evolutionary ladder on account of being monotheistic, it can be argued in another equally valid theory that religious development started with monotheism and shifted toward polytheism and animism. Like Said, Mbiti recognized the power of ascription by others. According to Said, for example, neither the term "orientalism nor the concept of the West has any ontological stability," because these are human constructs that can be manipulated.[9]

Mbiti did not overlook good etic scholarship; in his view, one of the best approaches to the serious study of African religions by outsiders was done by E. E. Evans-Pritchard in *Nuer Religion* and G. Lienhardt in *Divinity and Experience: The Religion of the Dinka*. Mbiti acknowledged the immense contribution made by African scholars such as J. B. Danquah, J. H. Nketia, A. Kagame and E. B. Idowu. In identifying his religious position, Mbiti echoed the truth that "it is only from the other that we become aware of what we ourselves are, and sure of our identity."[10] Mbiti was, however, not merely reactionary. Rather, he called for serious engagement of mission approaches with culture within the realm of African Traditional Religion. His theological climate was thus one characterized by theological conflict, in a neocolonial arena both within and without.

---

6. Kane, *Understanding Christian Missions*, 220–21.
7. Cited in Mbiti, "African Indigenous Culture," 83.
8. Mbiti, *African Religions and Philosophy*, 232.
9. Said, *Orientalism*, xvii.
10. Moltmann, "Dialogue or Mission?," 174.

What Is African Traditional Religion according to John Mbiti?

Mbiti posed this question and then presented five aspects for understanding "African religion":[11] beliefs; practices, ceremonies and festivals; religious objects and places; values and morals; religious officials and leaders. Ninian Smart's seven dimensions are the practical and ritual; the experiential and emotional; the narrative or mythic; the doctrinal and philosophic; the ethical and legal; the social and institutional; and the material.[12] Note that the categories are different. Mbiti pointed out that religion was a product of African ancestors who "formed religious ideas, they formulated religious beliefs, they observed religious ceremonies and rituals, they told proverbs and myths which safeguarded the life of the individual and his community."[13] Unlike Christianity and Islam, which were founded by known pioneers, African Traditional Religion evolved as humanity sought answers to the questions of life. The ideas and practices in African Traditional Religion have been shaped through "human experience and reflection."[14]

Mbiti recognized that there are those who use the term "African traditional religions." He, however, used the singular, "religion," to embrace a fundamental religiosity with its "diversities and commonalities."[15] Mbiti likened African traditional "religion" to the baobab tree: a gigantic baobab tree has numerous branches but only one trunk, which is, at times, difficult to see when the tree has full foliage.[16]

African Traditional Religion is a religion without sacred scriptures, but instead is written in the "people's hearts, minds, oral history, rituals and religious personages like the priests, rainmakers, officiating elders and even kings."[17] In its pragmatic and realistic nature, African Traditional Religion may change its practices in order to meet the needs of its adherents in their contexts. Mbiti defended African religion against those who referred to it as ancestor worship, superstition, animism, paganism, magic or fetishism. He sought neither to elevate nor condemn African religion, but rather to present it in the way its adherents practice it. Among the Kambas, Mbiti's ethnic group, "a person does not have to say 'I believe' – his creed is within him, it is part of

---

11. Mbiti, *African Religions and Philosophy*, 11.
12. Smart, *World's Religions*, 13–21.
13. Mbiti, *African Religions and Philosophy*, 14.
14. Mbiti, 16.
15. Mbiti, "Man in African Religion," 55.
16. Mbiti, 55.
17. Mbiti, *African Religions and Philosophy*, 4–5.

him. He simply knows and acknowledges the existence of God, who is known as Mulungu, although in Christian circles the word Ngai is used for God."[18]

Mbiti reckoned that religion was a hard word to define, and that for Africans, religion pertains to the issue of being or existence. Human beings live within the realm of a religious drama since they exist in a religious universe. African religions can thus be understood only within "religious ontology."[19] This religious ontology is highly anthropocentric, with five tightly knit categories: God as Creator and Sustainer of human beings; the spirits, which account for the destiny of human beings; human beings as the core of religious ontology; plants and animals; and natural occurrences which make up the environment where human beings dwell and with which human beings create a mystical bond as the need may arise.[20] In addition, there is a force, energy or power whose source and ultimate controller is God. Spirits can access this force, and some human beings, such rainmakers, priests and witches, possess knowledge and capacity to manipulate and use this force for good or evil. These five aspects are not unknown in the biblical world. Some parallels will be drawn below when we look at Mbiti's concept of *praeparatio evangelica*.

Mbiti's Methodology in the Study of African Traditional Religions

In the study of religion, Mbiti's approach treated religion as an "ontological phenomenon, with the concept of time as the key to reaching some understanding of African religions and philosophy."[21] Mbiti argued that in many African societies, and in particular the Kamba, time has two dimensions: the past or *tene*, and the present, which he termed *mituki*. *Mituki* is the time period marked by the greatest intensity, nearness and immediacy, while *tene* is the past realm of time, which is "where" cosmological challenges and national experience are sought. According to Mbiti, death is a process which takes a person from the *mituki* of his or her being, and that of the person's contemporaries, until he or she disappears to the remote *tene* period.[22] The hereafter of the dead in the African context is thus not futuristic but rather in the past. Mbiti referred to this conception of the hereafter as a "concrete myth." The next world of the dead is a carbon copy of the present world.

---

18. Mbiti, *Akamba Stories*, 14.
19. Mbiti, 15.
20. Mbiti, 16.
21. Mbiti, *African Religions and Philosophy*, 14.
22. Mbiti, 25.

From his study of the New Testament, Mbiti was very critical of the misapplication of time to eschatology. He argued that "time is subject to eschatology and not vice versa," and that any reversal bore a "false eschatology as useless as the face of a clock without hands."[23] Time, according to Mbiti, helps human beings to grasp the horizontal aspect of eschatology, but eschatology has another "non-temporal," vertical aspect which "defies" all efforts to "horizontalize" it.[24] Thus, Mbiti argued that in cultures where there is no future time dimension, Christians might be led to a "false spirituality to escape into the Christian world of the hereafter at the expense of being a Christian here and now."[25] When the parousia is falsely held as imminent, according to Mbiti, the resultant disillusionment results in many sects where a "central figure or doctrine" is perceived to provide at least a partial hope. Mbiti, however, admitted that his idea of time was not definitive, and he invited further discussion and research on the idea.

African Traditional Religion as *Praeparatio Evangelica*

In this section we will interact with Mbiti's argument of *praeparatio evangelica* and consider some of the parallels he drew between African Traditional Religion and Christianity. Mbiti's perspective on salvation, Christology and the mission of the church will also be presented below. John Mbiti argued that all African Traditional Religions constitute a *praeparatio evangelica* (preparation for the gospel), and categorically stated that "God the Father of our Lord Jesus Christ is the same God who for thousands of years has been known and worshipped in various ways within the religious life of African peoples."[26] According to Mbiti, the good news has come to complete and fulfill the African religiosity.[27] In this regard, one needs to be aware of the many theologies in the African context, because, according to Mbiti's argument, Christianity supplies what traditional religions lack as long as Christianity does not oppose traditional religiosity.[28] According to Mbiti, African religion and Christianity have turned out to be allies, with the former preparing the ground for the latter. Mbiti also asserted that the key new element that biblical teaching brought to Africa was

---

23. Mbiti, *New Testament Eschatology*, 61.
24. Mbiti, 61.
25. Mbiti, 60–61.
26. Kinney, "Theology of John Mbiti," 65–67.
27. Mbiti, "Christianity and African Religion," 313.
28. Mbiti, *Introduction to African Religion*, 36.

Jesus Christ and the gospel, and that Western missionaries did not bring God to Africa: instead it was God who brought them to Africa as bearers of the gospel of Christ.[29] Biblical teaching has enabled Christians in Africa to name Christ joyfully, whereas in the past "we had groped after him in the twilight. Now we see him in the dawn of day."[30]

In one of his publications, Mbiti concluded that 90 percent of the prayers from his data were addressed to God and 10 percent to the living dead, divinities, spirits and the "personification of nature."[31] Such a claim is by no means limited to Mbiti. "To the modern African Christians, it is self-evident that the God they now worship is the same as that of the past. The Fipa say 'Where the elders pray, there is the God of the Door and the God of the Door is the Christian God also.'"[32] Mbiti's work *Concepts of God in Africa* was the fruit of analyzing data from over two hundred and seventy people groups as documented by about two hundred authors and students in Africa. Bediako notes that in this work, the difference between the Christian understanding and pre-Christian understanding was "almost negligible."[33] Mbiti's conclusion was drawn from his analysis of the data.

In *Concepts of God in Africa* Mbiti presented the nature of God as revealed by God's intrinsic, external and moral attributes. Intrinsic attributes include transcendence and omniscience; the eternal attributes include God as first and last cause; while mercy, righteousness and anger are among his moral attributes. God as Creator, Provider and Sustainer, his governance as King, Lord and Judge, and God as One who afflicts reveal some of what Mbiti terms "the active attributes of God."[34] Based on his data, Mbiti claimed that "a few people conceive of God's salvation in moral terms," and he cited the example of the Lunda, who "believe that God saves the innocent and punishes the guilty."[35] God as Father, Mother and Elder are some of the anthropomorphic attributes that Mbiti's data yielded. Although I agree with Bediako's statement above that there are "almost neglible" differences between Christian understanding and a pre-Christian understanding, in general, I find it interesting that Mbiti used Western categories in his analysis. While this is very helpful for many

---

29. Mbiti, *African Religions and Philosophy*, 11.
30. Mbiti, "Man in African Religion," 12.
31. Mbiti, *Prayers of African Religion*, 3–4.
32. Isichei, *From Antiquity to the Present*, 7.
33. Bediako, *Theology and Identity*, 238.
34. Mbiti, *Concepts of God*, xiii.
35. Mbiti, *New Testament Eschatology*, 70.

audiences, it would have been interesting to explore other ways of categorizing the same data. The concept of guilt is, however, helpful in the revelation of a holy and just God. Some have identified Mbiti with universalism,[36] but the limits of this paper and the voluminous writings of Mbiti do not allow for that claim to be examined. His high view of Christ is, however, evident, as already noted.

Mbiti pointed out some parallels between African religion and Christianity, examples being the church, the concept of God, life after death and salvation. The Christian church is also the Christian family in which believers are related to one another through trust and baptism in Jesus Christ. This is parallel to traditional African life where kinship and the extended family are highly valued. Mbiti did not, however, downplay conflict between traditional beliefs and Christianity. He pointed out traditional rituals, initiation rites, witchcraft, evil magic, methods of dealing with sickness, misfortunes and suffering as areas of conflict. Nevertheless, Mbiti asserted that for adherents of African religion only, this conflict "is more of a clash between Western or European culture and African culture, than a specifically religious conflict."[37] In our time, the same truth is being echoed as "culture and cultural identities . . . are shaping the patterns of cohesion, disintegration, and conflict" in our world.[38]

Mbiti therefore saw the need for the church in Africa to grow in maturity and become accountable not only locally but also globally. He commented that

> sometimes African Christians feel terribly foreign within the doors of the churches to which we belong. Lutheran Christians have made us more Lutheran than the Germans; Roman Catholic missionaries have made us feel and behave more Roman than Italians; Anglican missionaries have made us more Anglican than the English, and so on.[39]

Others have also noted this fact. It is, for example, asserted that theology must address itself to "culturally-rooted questions." In the post-missionary period, "African" theology is equally a response to undermining the value of African Traditional Religion as an African's theological response to how the gospel relates to African culture.[40] Mbiti contended that

---

36. Kato, *Theological Pitfalls*, 75.
37. Mbiti, *Introduction to African Religion*, 190.
38. Huntington, *Clash of Civilizations*, 20.
39. Mbiti, "Man in African Religion," 19.
40. Bediako, *Theology and Identity*, 17.

even though officially Christianity either disregarded African religion altogether, or treated it as an enemy, it was, in fact, African religion more than anything else which laid down the foundation and prepared the ground for the eventual rapid accommodation of Christianity in Africa, and for the present growth of the church in our continent. Without African religiosity, whatever its defects might be, Christianity would have taken much longer to be understood and accommodated by African peoples.[41]

In my assessment, although Mbiti was very critical about uncontextualized missionary activity, he was hardly critical about the local church. Mbiti's claim may, however, by backed by the undeniable religiosity of humankind according to Romans 1. This religiosity points to general revelation.

Mbiti asserted that, in Africa, all religions must coexist, cooperate and even compete for the survival of humankind as a whole and for their own sake. Though Mbiti anticipated that Christianity will finally triumph, the main issue is whether these religions serve human beings in the search for their identity, in their response to their environment and in shaping their expectations and a hopeful future. Mbiti, to a great degree, articulated the reality of pluralism in Africa.

Mbiti's position on African Traditional Religion is contested, particularly in regard to the authority of Scripture. Tiénou, for example, recognizes the danger of pre-understandings while upholding the authority of Scripture. He notes that people in the African context will readily identify similarities of "social structures" and "religious institutions" with those of ancient Israel and those that exist in African traditional societies. The goal, according to Tiénou, is not for more social and institutional knowledge about God, but rather to know him as the Lord Almighty.[42] Tiénou calls for a deprogramming of one's hermeneutics so as not to be limited by the findings of hermeneutical keys. He further calls for reading the Bible with the goal of acquiring a new understanding and to appreciate how this applies to our total context.

A key term originally coined by Mbiti is the "living dead."[43] The living dead are the human spirits of those who died four to five generations ago. Neglecting the spirits of the living dead is believed to lead to misfortune. Being remembered is so critical that if one is not remembered in the African context,

---

41. Mbiti, "African Indigenous Culture," 86.
42. Tiénou, "Biblical Foundations," 435–48.
43. Mbiti, *Prayers of African Religion*, 101.

he or she is a nobody, similar to a flame that has been extinguished forever.[44] The living dead may manifest themselves through dreams, visions, spirit possession, mental instability and illnesses among the living. The living dead may also reincarnate themselves partially through a newborn child. Mbiti's idea of the living dead challenges the church to address the question of ancestors seriously and not to dismiss the topic as merely demonic. A contextual theology of ancestors can help address the fear that leads the Luos of Kenya, for example, to chase away the spirits in their ritual of *tero buru matin*. After all, it is the gospel that is both a prisoner and a liberator of culture.[45] People need assurance of their well-being as they battle with their traditional beliefs regarding the ancestors, and this can be a helpful bridge to connect with biblical teaching pertaining to death and resurrection.

Mbiti on the Issue of Salvation and Christology

How is salvation to be understood from Mbiti's perspective? According to him,

> it is true that certain varieties of missionaries from Europe and America have proclaimed a restrictive understanding of salvation from sin and largely for the soul. But with the reading of the Bible, African Christians have increasingly broadened their interpretation and application of biblical salvation beyond the question of sin and soul, however important this is.[46]

He highlighted two important dimensions of life in the "African traditional world": the physical and spiritual. Furthermore, the biblical world is marked by an ongoing struggle of "both physical and spiritual dangers and threats."[47] He asserted that since the "two worlds" "readily meet," the Bible finds application to the people of Africa. According to Mbiti, "salvation is a very wide and open concept in the Bible."[48] Thus, for believers in Africa, Christianity "has come to legitimize their case and to bring an extended understanding, scope and applicability of salvation."[49] Mbiti was reminding Christians that they should

---

44. Mbiti, *African Religions and Philosophy*, 33.
45. Walls, *Missionary Movement*, 3.
46. Mbiti, "Man in African Religion," 156.
47. Mbiti, 156.
48. Mbiti, 157.
49. Mbiti, "Some Reflections," 115.

not use the gospel to declare freedom of the soul while justifying physical or other oppression of converts.

Mbiti called for attention to be given to language, since "missionary teaching and preaching which have stressed spiritual salvation have consequently given the impression that the gospel is for matters spiritual and not physical as well."[50] He pointed out that the cultural and social background should be kept in view in the proclamation of the gospel, otherwise there will be miscommunication between the proclaimer and the hearer. Based on the study of his language, the Kikamba, Mbiti asserted that *utangiio* (salvation) and *wovosyo* (redemption), both abstract nouns, in practice are rarely used outside Christian circles. Words such as *mwovosya* (redeemer) and *mutangii* (savior), both concrete nouns, are rarely utilized in Kikamba, and when they are used, it is in a nontechnical sense. Accordingly, the hearer can only understand these words in a practical way. We may say that a person has saved someone from danger, but once this saving is done, the one saving does not continue in the act of salvation. Saving, according to the usual understanding, is an emergency act and no one can earn the title "savior." Being "ritualistic and utilitarian," African Traditional Religion presents salvation through ritual.[51] With this in view, Mbiti asserted that "there are no (and never have been) traditional saviors or redeemers."[52] The use of such technical terms is, however, necessary, and Mbiti singled out the words "Savior," "salvation," "redeemer" and "redemption" as key in evangelization among the Kamba and other peoples of Africa. On the concept of salvation, Mbiti highlighted two areas of inadequacy in African religion: the religion does not address the question of original sin, nor does it address the "question of salvation from moral evil."[53] Mbiti also recognized that though a language might be limited in its vocabulary in the concept of salvation, the Bible can provide a "linguistic enrichment" to the language in question. The local language is an indispensable vehicle for planting the gospel in Africa. Mbiti reiterated this not only literally but also metaphorically. He maintained, "We cannot effectively carry out mission in a foreign language," and called Christians in Africa to communicate mission in a "language" that others will understand. Africans have to sing their gospel tunes, according to their music, and with their musical instruments. "We must drum it out with our great drums, on our tom-toms, on our waist-shaped drums, for only these

---

50. Mbiti, 161.
51. Adeyemo, *Salvation in African Tradition*, 84–85.
52. Mbiti, "Some Reflections," 109.
53. Mbiti, 113.

can vibrate and awaken entire villages: the violin is too feeble to awaken the sleeping pagans of our society."[54] Since music stirs our human emotions, how appropriate it is to have those emotions directed toward God, the creator of human language!

In calling our attention to language, Mbiti was reiterating the importance of contextualization. Regarding Christology, Mbiti asserted that the final test for the validity and usefulness of any theological contribution is Jesus Christ. Because of Christ's incarnation, Christian theology must be Christology, for theology stands or falls on how it understands, transmits and interprets Jesus Christ at a given time, place and human situation.[55]

Apart from the historical aspect of salvation, Mbiti urged Christians to also pay attention to the geography of salvation. Geography, according to Mbiti, helps us to see and feel in concrete ways the places of our salvation, whereas history is irretrievable. In African communities, according to Mbiti, a person or animal, hiding in a sacred place, be it a shrine, rock or cave, "may not be killed – the sacred places in effect save life from destruction even if paradoxically they are the places where sacrifices are made. The point is that the concept of salvation is thereby given a geographical concretization: it is not just an abstraction."[56] Mbiti therefore considered a visit to the Holy Land to see Jerusalem, Nazareth and the Jordan, among other places, an important part of the Christian pilgrimage. Mbiti pointed out areas where salvation needs to be applied as the church matures in Africa: the "redeeming and sanctifying" of the good in our cultural heritage, while "destroying the evil . . . outdated structures" in which racism has been condoned in mission work; and embracing the "cosmic consequences of the Christ event" in which "it may well become clear that in a limited way, the African traditional experiences of salvation belong ultimately within the walls of the cosmic work of Christ."[57]

What was the role and place of Christ in Mbiti's theology?

> The uniqueness of Christianity is in Jesus Christ. He is the stumbling block of all ideologies and religious systems; and even if some of his teaching may overlap with what they teach and proclaim, His own person is greater than can be contained in a religion and ideology. He is the man for others and yet beyond them . . . I consider traditional religions, Islam and other religious

---

54. Mbiti, *Crisis of Mission*, 5.
55. Mbiti, "New Testament Eschatology," 190.
56. Mbiti, "Some Reflections," 111.
57. Mbiti, 119.

systems to be preparatory and even essential ground in the search for the Ultimate. But only Christianity has the terrible responsibility of pointing the way to that ultimate Identity, Foundation and Source of security.[58]

Thus Mbiti maintained the supremacy of Christ.

Mbiti's Fulfillment Motif and the Mission of the Church

Mbiti's fulfillment motif and its relation to culture, church and evangelization will now be examined. This motif reflects a high view of culture, human dignity and God's grace toward human beings. The fulfillment motif has an appeal to many theologians both in the West and in the non-Western world. For Clement, the early church father, philosophy "was a preparation, paving the way for him who is perfected in Christ."[59] In this thinking, Greek philosophy was the "schoolmaster" to lead the Greeks, just as the law led the Hebrews, to Christ.[60] Farquhar, another example, asserts that "Christ is the Liberator," who, by the power of truth about "human birth," liberates the Hindu from the caste. Christ "does not degrade the Brahman to the level of the Outcaste, but reveals the high truth that the savage, the cannibal, and the Outcastes are all Brahmans and more."[61] Accordingly, "every human unit" has the highest dignity and capacity of a child of God. Farquhar asserts that religion was God's means of training Israel. Thus Jesus "came to crown it by transforming it into the religion for all men, and to crown its knowledge of God by revealing Him as the Father of men."[62] According to Farquhar, Christ did not totally destroy the religions of the world because they contained visible though broken spiritual light. Christ therefore preserves "old" art, civilization, literature and philosophy, and these will all the more blossom in Christianity.[63] Christ is thus the crown of Hinduism and fulfils the ideals of the family; he overrules the Karma, repudiates the caste system, and is the true object of worship in place of the Hindu gods.

---

58. Mbiti, *African Religions and Philosophy*, 277.
59. "Clement of Alexandria," 305.
60. "Clement of Alexandria," 305.
61. Farquhar, *Crown of Hinduism*, 204–5.
62. Farquhar, 51.
63. Farquhar, 53.

It was the work of Niebuhr, however, that influenced Mbiti's perspective on the fulfillment motif. Mbiti referred to Niebuhr's work as "penetrating."[64] In the fulfillment view, Mbiti saw a "possible harmony between Christianity and culture." Mbiti found this view plausible because it came from the words of Jesus who came to "fulfill" and not to "destroy" the Jewish eschatological expectation. While expressing the need to examine the elements of this fulfillment and the methodology for this fulfillment in Christianity, Mbiti raised the question, "Can we talk of fulfillment when we have largely foreign modes of Christianity [in Africa]?"[65] In response, he identified and isolated the gospel as an entity by itself, pointing out values and traditions which are capable of being fulfilled, and sought out how this process might be achieved and the meaning of this fulfillment.[66] Mbiti did not achieve this in one work, but, as one reviews his work, the answers to this question emerge. His contention was not so much the validity of the gospel but how the gospel is presented by the missionary. Mbiti was opposed to missionary methods that are inappropriate and inadequate to address the complexity of African Traditional Religion which has served as the means of dealing with the welfare of the community held together by this fabric of religion. In keeping with this, "evangelism should be less future oriented, less escapist, and more relationship and tradition centered."[67]

The fulfillment motif can be appealing to African Traditional Religion, for many reasons. For example, first, there is a kind of resonance between the Hebrew culture and cultures in Africa. Second, there are political parallels between the formerly colonized nations of Africa and Israel under Egyptian rule. According to John Mbiti, "missionary work or evangelization is an eschatological transaction in content (proclaiming an eschatological message), in obedience (to the eschatological Adam) . . . and in anticipation of the end."[68] In assessing the work of modern missionaries and their national workers, Mbiti commended their devoutness, sincerity and dedication to their cause. He, however, assessed that the missionaries were not "theologians," and this had led to the founding of churches without theology and therefore unable to bring the gospel to take deeper roots in the culture of Christians in Africa.

How, then, did Mbiti suggest the gospel should be proclaimed in Africa? First of all, Mbiti recognized the importance of community life in Africa and

---

64. Mbiti, "African Indigenous Culture," 89.
65. Mbiti, 89.
66. Mbiti, 90.
67. Moreau, "Africa and the Future," 316.
68. Mbiti, "Some Reflections," 2.

pointed out the important place of kinship in corporate life. The identity of the African is in the "family, household, the clan, and the tribe or nation," and the individual cannot be "saved" alone. If we desire that the individual be saved, then we must allow that person to "bring with him into the body of Christ, all his relatives. African traditional religions are not departmentalized areas of life: they are incorporated into the whole life of the people." The task of mission, then, must have as its goal the "mass inoculation," if allegiance is to be transposed from traditional religion to the Lord Jesus Christ.[69] Once again, Mbiti echoed the need to understand the context of the mission field for better stewardship of the gospel.

The conduct of the church is also a critical way of communicating the gospel. The church cannot be "severed from her message, and neither can that message become meaningful"[70] without the endorsement of the church. Thus the gospel is not merely for individuals, but rather such individuals are part of a community that has embraced the message as authoritative in its life. In this perspective, the church community in no way obliterates the traditions of the African community, but rather fulfils the deepest longings of the African in his or her cultural environment. This perspective of Mbiti is well summarized in this way: "the Christian Gospel, far from being opposed to African religious ideas, is, in fact, the crowning fulfillment of African religiosity."[71] The church as a community, according to Mbiti, is not the place to dash the aspirations of the African. The church is the community by which the "corporate aspirations" are "fulfilled and intensified, in which tribal foundations" are dislocated and not "replaced with a vacuum but . . . made more secure in Christ."[72] This community, with its shared values, and moving toward a known eternal destiny with one's society, readily receives the gospel.

In his analysis of "African" culture and church life, Mbiti established a great deal of correspondence between the two: worship, community, education and church nurture, Christian ethics and values, the believer and his or her culture, the Bible and African culture, and the gospel and culture as allies. Many forms of worship are culturally determined, and therefore traditional music and African architecture can contribute toward spirituality. In community living, salvation is more than individual; according to Mbiti, salvation is "also

---

69. Mbiti, "The Ways and Means of Communicating the Gospel," 337.
70. Mbiti, 339. Bediako, *Theology and Identity*, 309.
71. Bediako, *Theology and Identity*, 310.
72. Mbiti, "Ways and Means," 342.

communal, corporate and cosmic."[73] While recognizing the value of schools, seminaries and other institutions, Mbiti noted that churches can become impersonal, silencing people plagued with problems. This is why the home becomes an important place to nurture children. Justice, truth and freedom are aspects of ethics and values which have a home in African spirituality just as they have a home in biblical teaching. Mbiti gave a prominent place to Christian witness through service in social action. He hinted at this when he asserted that "the centre of a hungry man is not his heart but his stomach."[74] He reiterated that it is the responsibility of the church to guide human beings in how to relate to their culture. Mbiti cited the exodus motif, stating that "African peoples have identified their political struggles with, and received inspiration from, the enslavement, deliverance and exodus account of the children of Israel in Egypt."[75] Considering that God raises believers within their cultural frameworks, appreciation and knowledge of a hearer's culture is a step toward discerning how best to teach and equip believers in transforming their culture. Thus the church is a relational and reconciliatory vehicle, and in this mode is affinitive to African Traditional Religion.

One important aspect that Mbiti pointed out in relation to evangelism and church development is the celebratory aspect of Christian life. He asserted that "African religion is deeply celebrational of life and this keynote of celebration could have been incorporated into church development thus making it unnecessary, ultimately, for so many African Christians to revert to the traditional way of celebrating life."[76] Fusing the two would be an area of continuity, thus good contextualization could yield an indigenous orthodox faith. Jesus attended a wedding and paid social visits, bearing witness to God's desire to be involved in all human circumstances and concerns.

Mbiti asserted that

> some elements of African religion are demonic and should be pruned, but the best should be preserved and used for the enrichment of life. Indeed, though the understanding of God in other religions is "partial and often distorted," it is not justifiable to totally reject everything in them.[77] Many of these useful elements are educational aids in communication of the faith, others help

---

73. Mbiti, "Christianity and African Culture," 277.
74. Mbiti, 277.
75. Mbiti, 280.
76. Mbiti, "African Indigenous Culture," 86.
77. Netland, *Encountering Religious Pluralism*, 333.

us to understand the Bible in African background; and there are elements which help us to understand pastoral problems.[78]

In Jewish history, there was a time when the detestable practice of child sacrifice was rampant. Good contextualization and teaching would thus guide societies to recognize the sanctity of human life in Africa, where the birth of twins may sometimes be considered a bad omen. Where does continuity lie between African Traditional Religion and Christianity? Mbiti highlighted five areas where continuity may be established: in beliefs that relate to God, humanity, death and the hereafter; practices such as prayers, ceremonies and rituals; celebration of life in marriage, and new seasons within religious activities; numerous traditional prayers; and sacred places and objects.[79]

Mbiti recognized the power of culture in shaping humanity. According to him, "culture is man's crown."[80] In his definition, Mbiti asserted the "human pattern of life in response to man's environment."[81] This pattern may find expression in physical forms, "inter-human" relationships and the whole of life, including language and the mystery of birth. When the gospel encounters human culture, as long as faith is generated, the product of this encounter is Christianity. Mbiti thus argued that it is culture that "sustains, explains, articulates, communicates and celebrates faith."[82] Mbiti called for African Christians to be attuned to their culture in hearing the gospel, while at the same time striving to be alien to sin. This, in my view, is what leads to an authentic faith that generates meaningful and changing traditions in the local church. Mbiti defended culture in Africa and contributed to its rehabilitation by the power of the gospel.

While greatly welcoming the gospel, Mbiti was opposed to deplorable mission approaches in which "Africans were told by word and example, by those who brought them the Gospel, that they first had to become culturally circumcised before they could become Christians." Mbiti called for the termination of "cultural imperialism" so that the gospel might take root without coercion. Far from shutting the culture in Africa to the outside world, Mbiti called the African believer to borrow from other cultures with wisdom. He likened unindigenized Christianity to spiritual castration or spiritual crippling,

---

78. John Mbiti, "Christianity and African Religion," in *Facing New Challenges*, 311.
79. John Mbiti, 312.
80. Mbiti, "Christianity and Culture in Africa," 273.
81. Mbiti, 273.
82. Mbiti, 274.

and asserted that "imported Christianity will never, never quench the spiritual thirst of African peoples."[83]

A critical question that Mbiti posed to Christians in Africa was, based on Acts 8:26–40, "Do you understand what you are reading?" His answer was "yes," but he also pointed out that this understanding is not always orthodox, but it has helped shape what he termed "Oral Theology" in which believers in Africa are thriving. This is a "theology of grief and joy, dripping with people's tears and thundering in their laughter." Mbiti noted that though the Bible is understood at different levels, such as the personal, communal and national, it is popular because in it issues of health, success and protection, so crucial to Africans, are addressed.[84]

A Response to Mbiti's Work

Mbiti's observation regarding the incongruence of the gospel message and the lives of some missionaries cannot be dismissed. In this regard Andrew Walls asserts that

> missionaries had a double identity. They were representative Christians trying (and in the process demonstrating all the elements of human fallenness and all the limitations of human vision and foresight) to do Christian things . . . But they were also representative Westerners, shaped by Western history and conditions and values, and Western social networks and intellectual discourse.[85]

The Bible speaks to all cultures and all religions, though not all cultures or aspects of culture and religion submit themselves to the teaching of the Bible. Thus, Mbiti was rightly concerned about how Christ is presented.

Mbiti, among other theologians, has been accused of inventing "an African traditional religion that never existed, in salutary reaction against a hundred years of missionary Eurocentricity."[86] This is not entirely true because Mbiti defined his use of the term "African traditional religion." While we recognize that there are common aspects of culture in Africa, such as how "cause and effect" relate, Mbiti could be taken to task for implying unity in African

---

83. Mbiti, 276.
84. Mbiti, "Do You Understand What You Are Reading?," 8.
85. Walls, *Missionary Movement*, xviii.
86. Isichei, *From Antiquity to the Present*, 325.

culture where the reality is actually diversity.[87] As an example, some ethnic groups exercise levirate marriages, but others may allow a man to inherit his stepmother.[88]

Mbiti could also be taken to task for holding the view that procreation is the absolute means by which personal immortality is ensured. While I do not ignore the injunction for human beings to be fruitful and multiply, and in my view the family is the most important institution following the church, this mandate is not for all in a Christian community. Christ was not married, and neither were the Nazirites. Immortality is tied to the second birth of both the married and the unmarried. It is true, however, that the family in Africa, and in the Bible, is a core institution.

Mbiti, in a sense, looked back and assessed mission Christianity. I believe he was right to highlight the conflicts resulting from the undermining of the culture of people in Africa. However, Mbiti did not clearly point out that not all missionaries could be accused of this. There were some missionaries who not only spoke local languages but also adopted many customs of Kenya's ethnic people. While we may not accuse Mbiti of stereotyping, it would have been better for him to have included a few case studies of some missionaries who adapted well to the culture of missionized people without compromising the essentials of the gospel.

Mbiti was also sometimes far from being irenic. While some languages, such as English, French, Spanish, Portuguese and Arabic, were wrongly considered superior to local languages, to term them "ex-colonial languages," even though this is true, is far from irenic. The positive role that Bible translation has played must also be taken into account. As a fellow pilgrim with many who committed their entire lives to the cause of the gospel, Mbiti could have spoken this truth in love. It may, of course, be objected that Mbiti's John the Baptist overtones were needed as a prophetic voice, something with which I concur. Moreover, in one of his last works, Mbiti stated that these "formerly colonial languages have . . . now become Africanized."[89] Nevertheless, we can still speak the truth in love.

Mbiti recognized that indigenization of the Christian faith would not in any way remove problems from the church. He highlighted seven challenges that the church in Africa needed to address,[90] including ethics and morals; the

---

87. Tiénou, "Christianity and African Culture," 200–1.
88. Tiénou, 200–1.
89. Mbiti, "Do You Understand What You Are Reading?," 15.
90. Mbiti, "Future of Christianity," 18–38.

inner life of the church; pluralism; financial dependency; social changes; and mission-mindedness. He called the church to pay attention to these, and in our day, these issues are a reality. In my assessment, Mbiti was the prophetic voice of the theologian par excellence.

Implications

As the mission force from Africa to other continents grows, educational institutions on the African continent can help expedite the process by offering more language courses, such as in Chinese, Japanese and Portuguese, in addition to English and French. This will help African missionaries to communicate the gospel in the "tongue" of the hearers and in categories they can understand.

While I maintain that missionaries from Africa should seek to be competent in the use of modern technology as the need arises, they will benefit the world by maintaining either a simplicity of lifestyle or a sophisticated one, depending on the context of the mission field. At the same time, missionaries from Africa should not forget the value of hospitality and the importance of having accountability, by establishing one's identity within a community that has deep social ties. The missionaries can make use of African high spiritual sensitivity, to discern how to present the gospel appropriately.

Short-term missions have become a huge trend in our day. Nationals in Africa should play their role in the appropriate training of short-term missionaries. The gospel mandate is for all believers, and effective disciple-making will need to address itself to issues in local culture.

Conclusion

Mbiti's assertion that African Traditional Religion is a *preparatio evangelica* has a measure of validity. This is reflected in the many parallels between Christianity and African Traditional Religion. African Traditional Religion has an affinity with the gospel in areas such as the creator God, concern for both the spiritual and the physical aspects of humankind, life after death, and the building of harmonious communities, and these areas have served to advance the gospel. The clash between "Christianity" and African Traditional Religion is a cultural one and should not be misunderstood as a rejection of the gospel. This clash has often been caused by uncontextualized mission approaches. Nevertheless, African Traditional Religion does contain elements such as traditional rituals and evil magic that are clearly opposed to the gospel. The response to such elements is a contextualization that submits to the authority of Scripture and does not cause the missionary to stumble.

Appendix 1: Social Location, Background and Credentials of John Mbiti

Geertz asserts that symbols are a storehouse of culture,[91] and the name "Mbiti" is symbolic. The name "Mbiti," or "Hyena," means "We vow away this child to God. He does not belong to us, but to God. Let it be an animal, an offering to God."[92] Mbiti is the name given to a child who survives after parents lose a first and second child.

John Mbiti grew up in a Christian home in Kenya where he heard his parents on numerous occasions share the gospel. Mbiti recalls that, when people visited his home, sometimes the Bible was read and hymns were sung, and if they visited other people, Mbiti's family would pray even if they were guests in a non-Christian home. At the age of eight, John Mbiti was already involved in the evangelization of his community.[93]

Professor John Mbiti was a pastor, author, teacher and theologian, and some refer to him as the father of contemporary African theology. He was born in 1931, between the two world wars. As a child he tended the fields, took care of cattle, sheep and goats, and attended school. Mbiti was an exceptionally bright child and completed his elementary school in three years instead of the normal six, and then embarked on his primary school education. Mbiti would walk about eight to ten miles each day to attend primary school. In 1946–49 Mbiti attended Alliance High School, which was a joint venture of Protestant missions. It was at high school that Mbiti wrote a novel, *Mutunga na Ngewa Yake* (Mutunga and his stories), which was later published in 1954. In an interview conducted in 2002, Mbiti expressed deep disappointment that the missionaries responsible for the assessment and recommendation of publications in Mbiti's mother tongue lost the second and only manuscript of his next novel, and did not "even apologize" for this "irreparable loss."[94] He graduated with a BA in 1953 and then began his collection of proverbs and traditional stories. He then went to New England, where he graduated with a BA in 1956 and a ThB in 1957 from Barrington University College in Rhode

---

91. Geertz, *Interpretation of Cultures*, 145.
92. Kalu, "Preface," xiv.
93. Mbiti, "Man in African Religion," 11.
94. Mbiti, 11.

Island. Mbiti then went on to the University of Cambridge, where he obtained a PhD in New Testament studies in 1963. It was at Cambridge that he met his future wife, Verena Siegenthaler from Switzerland, and the two were married in 1965. Upon ordination as an Anglican priest Mbiti served for fifteen months in London. From 1964 to 1974 he lectured at Makerere University in Uganda in the areas of world religions, New Testament and African religion, and he was also involved in the chapel ministry. From 1974 to 1980 John Mbiti became the director and professor at the World Council of Churches' Ecumenical Institute at Bossey, situated near Geneva in Switzerland. From 1981 to 1996 Mbiti served in parish ministry in the Reformed Church of Bern. From 1983 to 2003 he also taught part time as professor of the science of mission and extra-European theology at the University of Bern. He published over 400 reviews, articles and books in the fields of theology, religion, literature and philosophy. He held three honorary doctorates from Barrington College, the University of Lausanne and General Theological Seminary, New York. A Festschrift, *Religious Plurality in Africa: Essays in Honour of John S. Mbiti*, was published in 1993. John Mbiti died in 2019.

Bibliography

Adeyemo, Tokunboh. *Is Africa Cursed?* Nairobi: Christian Materials Learning Centre, 1997.

———. *Salvation in African Tradition*. Nairobi: Evangel, 1997.

Bediako, Kwame. *Theology and Identity: The Impact of Culture upon Christian Thought in the Second Century and in Modern Africa*. Oxford: Regnum, 1992.

"Clement of Alexandria, AD 193–217." *Ante-Nicene Fathers*. Translated by Alexander Roberts and James Donaldson. Grand Rapids: Eerdmans, 1951.

Farquhar, J. N. *The Crown of Hinduism*. Reprint. New Delhi: Oriental Books, 1971 (original 1913).

Geertz, Clifford. *The Interpretation of Cultures*. New York: Basic Books, 1973.

Huntington, Samuel. *The Clash of Civilizations and the Remaking of World Order*. New York: Simon & Schuster, 1997.

Isichei, Elizabeth. *From Antiquity to the Present: A History of Christianity in Africa*. Grand Rapids: Eerdmans, 1995.

Kalu, Ogbu U. "Preface." In *Religious Plurality in Africa: Essays in Honour of John S. Mbiti*, edited by Sulayman S. Nyang and Jacob K. Olupona, xv–xvii. Religion and Society 32. Berlin: Walter de Gruyter, 1993.

Kane, Herbert. *Understanding Christian Missions*. 4th ed. Grand Rapids: Baker, 1986.

Kato, Byang. *Theological Pitfalls in Africa*. Kisumu: Evangel, 1975.

Kinney, John W. "The Theology of John Mbiti: His Sources, Norms and Method." *Occasional Bulletin of Missionary Research* 3 (1979): 65–67. DOI: 10.1177/239693937900300206.

Mbiti, John. "African Indigenous Culture in Relation to Evangelism and Church Development." In *The Gospel and Frontier Peoples: A Report of a Consultation, December 1972*, edited by R. Pierce Beaver, 79–95. Pasadena: William Carey Library, 1972.

———. *African Religions and Philosophy*. Nairobi: Heinemann Educational Books, 1969.

———. *African Religions and Philosophy*. New York: Praeger, 1970.

———. *Akamba Stories*. London: Oxford University Press, 1966.

———. "Christianity and African Religion." In *Facing the New Challenges: The Message of PACLA, December 9–19, 1976, Nairobi*, edited by Michael Cassidy and Luc Verlinden, 308–13. Kisumu: Evangel Publishing House, 1978.

———. *Concepts of God in Africa*. London: SPCK, 1970.

———. *The Crisis of Mission in Africa*. Mukono: Uganda Church Press, 1971.

———. "Do You Understand What You Are Reading? The Bible in African Homes, Schools and Churches." Paper presented at the annual congress of the South African Missiological Society, Pretoria, South Africa, 2005.

———. "Dreams as a Point of Theological Dialogue." *Missionalia* 25 (1997): 511–20.

———. "The Future of Christianity in Africa, 1970–2000." *Communio Viatorum* 13 (1970): 18–38.

———. *Introduction to African Religion*. New York: Praeger, 1970.

———. "Man in African Religion." In *Africa and the West: The Legacies of Empire*, edited by Isaac James Mowoe and Richard Bjornnson, 55–68. New York: Greenwood Press, 1986.

———. *New Testament Eschatology in an African Background: A Study of Encounter between New Testament Theology and African Traditional Concepts*. London: Oxford University Press, 1971.

———. *The Prayers of African Religion*. Maryknoll: Orbis, 1975.

———. "Some Reflections on African Experience of Salvation Today." In *Living Faiths and Ultimate Goals*, edited by S. J. Samartha, 108–19. Maryknoll: Orbis, 1974.

———. "The Ways and Means of Communicating the Gospel." In *Christianity in Tropical Africa*, edited by C. G. Baëta, 329–50. London: Oxford University Press, 1968.

"Mbiti, John Samuel." *Dictionary of African Christian Biography*. Accessed 28 November 2020. https://dacb.org/stories/kenya/mbiti-johns/.

Moltmann, Jürgen. "Dialogue or Mission? Christianity and the Religions in an Endangered World." In *Christianity and Other Religions: Selected Readings*, edited by John Hick and Brian Hebblethwaite, 172–87. Oxford: Oneworld, 2001.

Moreau, Scott. "Africa and the Future: An Analysis of John Mbiti's Concept of Time." In *Issues in African Christian Theology*, edited by Samuel Ngewa, Mark Shaw, and Tite Tiénou, 306–19. Nairobi: East African Educational, 1998.

Netland, Harold. *Encountering Religious Pluralism: The Challenge to Christian Faith and Mission*. Downers Grove: InterVarsity Press, 2001.

Olupona, Jacob K., and Sulayman S. Nyang. "Issues and Perspectives on Religious Plurality in Africa." In *Religious Plurality in Africa: Essays in Honour of John Mbiti*, edited by Sulayman S. Nyang and Jacob K. Olupona, 11–40. Religion and Society 32. Berlin: Walter de Gruyter, 1993.

Said, Edward. *Orientalism*. New York: Vintage, 1978.

Smart, Ninian. *The World's Religions*. Cambridge: Cambridge University Press, 1998.

Talbot, Louis T. *Bible Questions Explained*. Grand Rapids: Eerdmans, 1938.

Tiénou, Tite. "Biblical Foundations for African Theology." *Missiology* 10, no. 4 (1982): 435–48. DOI: 10.1177/009182968201000405.

———. "Christianity and African Culture: A Review." *Evangelical Review of Theology* 3, no. 2 (1979): 198–205.

Walls, Andrew. *The Missionary Movement in Christian History: Studies in the Transmission of Faith*. Maryknoll: Orbis, 1996.

21

Reflection on John S. Mbiti

Esther Mombo
Professor, Faculty of Theology, Saint Paul University, Limuru, Kenya

I am grateful to be asked to contribute a short piece on Prof. J. S. Mbiti. My last two encounters with Prof. Mbiti were in person. I shared a platform with him at Arusha mission conference in 2018 and heard him give a public lecture at St. Paul's University on the topic of the Christology of the African theologian Afua Kuma of Ghana. Christology was the theme of the 2020 ASET conference. Here I will say a few things about encountering Prof. Mbiti, first as a student of theology and then at conferences and sharing platforms with him. As a theologian, he had a sense of humor, and he was not imposing when you met or shared with him.

Meeting Prof. Mbiti as a Student of Theology

I was first introduced to Prof. Mbiti when I was a theological student at St. Paul's United Theological College (now St. Paul's University). The course on which I met him was "African Traditional Religion." His book *African Religions and Philosophy*, published in 1969, was one of the texts that we were recommended. The study of African Religion in this context was, at the time, perceived with suspicion, especially when training people for ministry. Meeting Mbiti in class was both challenging and informative.

The first noteworthy aspect from his book was about the religiosity of Africans: "Africans are notoriously religious, and each people have their religious system with a set of beliefs and practices. Religion permeates all the departments of life so fully that it is not easy or possible always to isolate it."[1] The second was about the African concept of time: "according to traditional concepts, time is a two-dimensional phenomenon, with a long past, a present and virtually no future."[2] The third aspect was about the communal nature of African life: "I am because we are; and since we are, therefore I am."[3] These topics were analyzed and evaluated critically. When writing these reflections, I looked at my copy of his book and saw written in it my questions and comments. For example, on the aspect of religiosity, I commented, "Africans are a unique species of humanity. There is no sacred and secular in their community." On the concept of time I wrote, "Do Africans count backwards; is history not time?" "Time must be a universal thing, only it is contextualized." On the aspect of the communal life, I wrote something which must have been a comment from the lecturer: "'I am because we are' is the opposite of 'I think therefore I am' by René Descartes."

The above three areas were the ones that were hotly contested in class by second- and third-generation Christians. The other sections of the book, especially on the rites of passage, challenged us to seek a better understanding of some of the practices in my community. For my research project, I chose to write a project on the rites of passage, entitled "The Persistence of Female Circumcision among the Gusii of Kenya." My interest in this topic was due not only to the African Religion unit, but also to my church history class in which we had covered the subject of the female circumcision controversy in Central Province. From my research I concluded, "The persistence of female circumcision among the Abagusii is not because people are ignorant of the practice's health hazards. Instead, it was because the institution's origin, development, and theology appear to be still important to the people."[4]

The works of Mbiti have continued to impact the academy, especially the idea that the African worldview is very religion-centric, with religion permeating all realms of life to the extent that life is perceived holistically without separation of the "sacred" from the "profane." Studies on secularism in Africa point to the work of Mbiti.[5] The unit on African Religion, through

---

1. Mbiti, *African Religions and Philosophy*, 1.
2. Mbiti, 17.
3. Mbiti, 108.
4. Mombo, "Persistence of Female Circumcision," 56. The topic of female circumcision has continued to engage scholars over the years. See, for example, Mose, *Thinking the Gusii Way*.
5. Shorter, "Secularism in Africa," 1, https://sedosmission.org/bulletin/sedos-bulletin-3001.pdf; Mombo, "Secularization: Whose Discourse?," 206–14; van den Toren, Bangura, and Seed, *Is Africa Incurably Religious?*

Mbiti's works, contributed to my later scholarship, especially enabling me to look at issues from a critical angle and seek to gain a perspective on the things about which I read or write.

Meeting Mbiti and Sharing a Platform

I met Mbiti in person at a conference entitled "Exploring Stepping-Stones: Sexual Identity and Gender Equality" organized by the Centre for Research and Innovation for Change in 2010. I chaired the session and responded to his paper. In the paper, he used an ethnographic approach, combined with a selection of three myths and thirty proverbs. The legends were from the Vugusu of Kenya, Malagasy of Madagascar and the Boloki of Central Africa. These were representative of at least Anglophone and Francophone components of Africa. He picked the proverbs from different parts of Africa.

In his presentation on the topic, Mbiti observed,

> Sexuality is like the chameleon. It has many colours. In every community, sexuality is encased in innumerable attitudes, assertions, and beliefs. Some assertions affirm sexuality, while others deny or denigrate it. Every generation and every community cherish some forms of myths about sexuality. These are largely fluid, and they change like the colours of the chameleon. Many factors impinge upon contemporary myths of sexuality, such as religion, art and literature, economics, politics, movement of people, climate, education, etc. Every young or adult person, under normal health conditions, will sooner or later be sucked into the vast ocean of sexuality and that ocean will not evaporate for the rest of the person's life. These myths can be compared to a dish of tropical fruit salad, with chunks of both fresh and canned fruits, ripe and unripe fruits, sweet and sour fruits.[6]

After offering an analysis of both the myths and the proverbs, Mbiti concluded,

> Elements of human sexuality have roots in both myths of the distant past, and in views of contemporary society. Some of the elements are beautiful and support the growth of healthy sexuality and the search for more gender equality, for all parties involved. A proverb from the Akan of Ghana says: "When love

---

6. Mbiti, *Myths of Sexuality*, 1.

passed by, nothing else passed." The proverb means that "Love is the greatest moral principle." In that case, if love was generously applied in matters of "Sexual Identity and Gender Equality," the deep concerns of our Conference will be more than adequately addressed.[7]

In my response to this paper, I noted that he offered two essential stepping stones in line with the theme of the conference. The first was the different myths, and the second was the proverbs. While these were essential stones, they are culture-specific. In the works of theologians such as Musimbi Kanyoro, culture is like a two-edged sword. It can be used to affirm but also to exclude. Culture does not embrace all people equally, and it does not always serve the needs and interests of all the people who belong to it. Culture has been used to sanction the suppression of certain members of society.[8] On the proverbs, I observed that while sayings form a significant part of the language and are a vehicle of the culture in its most concentrated and communicable form, they are not as inclusive as we would want to think. Proverbs demonstrate how a people speak, think, and what they believe, and they reflect the collective attitudes about women, which are often negative and subordinating.

In 2018 I shared a platform with Prof. Mbiti at the World Mission Conference in Arusha. We were asked to speak to the Global Ecumenical Theology Institute (GETI). The theme of our section was "African Theologies and Realities of Mission Practice." Mbiti's topic was entitled "A Pilgrim Expedition with African Theology: Oral and Written." Using his life story, Mbiti showed how African theology was founded on the life story of the church in Africa. The family was the foundation of the church:

> My pilgrim journey with African Theology started at home before I went to school. We prayed morning and evening, for meals, before undertaking hunting in a group, going to visit, or traveling. The prayers embraced personal and family situations like sickness, happy events, working in the fields, weather conditions, looking after cattle, sheep, and goats, and going to school.
>
> The home was the place where we read the Bible and discussed theology.
>
> We talked about many Christian topics ranging from reading the Kiikamba New Testament of 1920. My family was one of the

---

7. Mbiti, 4.
8. Kanyoro, "Engendered Communal Theology."

very few families to have a Bible. We talked about many things about Christianity that missionaries had brought and introduced to us. The topics on which we shared views and questions were: the Bible, Conversion, Death, Evangelism, the fire of Gehenna ("the Gorge of Hinnom" [Ge-Hinnom], where at the time of Hezekiah, animal and human sacrifices were made), Health, Heaven, Jesus, Prayer, Salvation, Sin and our concern over the not yet converted people.

Using his life story and discussing the themes in African theology, Mbiti concluded the paper by showing the tension between written and oral theology:

I have stuck to African Theology and put the Bible as its playmate. I imagine that without the Bible, there is no Christian Theology. How African Theology might develop in the future is not for me to postulate, since it is not my property as such. But one concern that simmers in my mind is: With all my several doctorate degrees in written Theology, what and how can I communicate that Theology, to the Church at the congregational level? How can it, in reverse, become the raw material for generating and supporting Oral Theology? And that is the Theology of the masses as they are, and not of the elite, the Theology of the books. Africa is now filled with theological schools, institutions, colleges, and universities. They are simmering with the book Theology. The congregations in African Christianity are bubbling with oral Theology.[9]

This is a question theologians continue to grapple with in any context and in connection with any topic of theology. The commitment of Mbiti to hold the tension between oral and written theology was an example of how a theologian should be concerned to ensure that all people get to hear and know God's Word. This was for him a way of making the gospel relevant to each context of history.

The Christology of Afua Kuma

At the beginning of this chapter, I mentioned Mbiti's public lecture at St. Paul's University on the Christology of Afua Kuma. This was my last meeting with Prof. Mbiti. In the works of Prof. Mbiti, there is little about women and theology. In the article entitled "Flowers in the Garden: The Role of Women

---

9. Mbiti, "Pilgrim Expedition," 6–13.

in African Religion"[10] he used myths, proverbs and prayers to determine the role of women. From myths, he noted that women share a creative process with God. However, when it comes to misfortune, most myths blame women for evil in the world. From proverbs, he also observed that sayings point to a woman's value in African society, making her a valuable member of society as wife and mother. On the other hand, proverbs also show the prejudices of society toward women. He also observed that women have played a significant role in society's religious activities as mediums, priests and doctors.

However, Mbiti did not engage with Circle Theology. The Circle of Concerned African Women Theologians was established in 1989. The founder of the Circle, Prof. Mercy Oduyoye, describing theology in Africa, observed that a one-winged bird cannot fly. As a result, Circle Theology came to birth. Circle Theology is an expression of the fact that African women theologies belong to a "wider family of feminist theology . . . which may further be categorized as a form of liberation theology."[11] The characteristics of Circle Theology include a commitment to women's liberation from all forms of oppression. Moreover, it aims at ending injustices, particularly patriarchy in culture, society and religion, and providing a critical analysis of the causes of oppression in Christianity and African culture. Topics such as the Bible, theology and the story of the church have been well covered in research and writing.

Among the themes that are discussed in Circle Theology is Christology from women's perspectives. There is considerable curiosity among theologians about what women say regarding Jesus and liberation. Since the theme of Christology has generated a great deal of interest among theologians, it is perhaps important to mention some of the Circle's writings on Jesus and liberation. The works of Oduyoye, Hinga, Nasimiyu-Wasike and Amoah are among the most significant contributions to this topic. In 1988, Oduyoye and Amoah wrote an article entitled "The Christ for African Women." They observed,

> Amidst the dehumanizing experiences for women, culturally, economically, socially, religiously, Jesus Christ is the liberator and a savior of women from all the oppressive contexts. He is the one who empowers them in the contexts of powerlessness, and he is their friend and ally in the context of alienation and pain that women may be confronted with.[12]

---

10. Mbiti, *Flowers in the Garden*.
11. Phiri, "Southern Africa," 151.
12. Amoah and Oduyoye, "Christ for African Women," 44.

Christ, therefore, becomes the voice of the voiceless, the power of the powerless.

Teresia Hinga continued with the theme of liberation in her article entitled "Jesus Christ and the Liberation of Women in Africa." She emphasized that the received theology where Christ is presented as a primordial scapegoat is not liberating but perpetuates women's oppression. Hinga contends that "his emulation would lead women to take on a role which they are already playing, for women, in any case, fulfill the role of victims and scapegoats in their various cultures."[13] Nasimiyu-Wasike's writing also observes that, "by suffering, Christ took on the conditions of the African woman and the conditions of humanity. In his resurrection, the African woman is called to participate in the restoration of harmony, equality and inclusiveness in all human relationships in the family, society, and Church."[14]

If, as stated above, Mbiti did not engage with Circle Theology, why did he engage with the Christology of Afua Kuma, with whom the Circle members had interacted from as early as 1988? Mbiti engaged with her theology only thirty years later. Several reasons could be noted. First, the Christology of Afua Kuma is within the inculturation model of theology that is key in African theology.

Circle theologians engage the inculturation model further, and on Christology, they link the model to liberation. Nasimiyu-Wasike, for instance, observes,

> The historical Jesus is manifested as the oppressed one whose earthly existence was tied up with the oppressed of the land. Jesus' sole reason for historical existence was binding the afflicted's wounds, setting the captives free, giving sight to the blind, preaching the good news to the poor, etc. (Luke 4:18–22). The historical Jesus is the life of the Trinity in words, actions, and attitudes.[15]

Similarly, on inculturation, Kanyoro notes, "While affirming the need for reclaiming culture through the theology of inculturation, we African women theologians claim that inculturation is not sufficient unless the cultures we recycle are analyzed and are deemed worthy in terms of promoting and support for life and the dignity of all women."[16]

---

13. Hinga, "Jesus Christ and the Liberation of Women," 185.
14. Nasimiyu-Wasike, "Christology and an African Woman's Experience," 131.
15. Nasimiyu-Wasike, "Imaging Jesus Christ in the African Context," 105.
16. Kanyoro, "Engendered Communal Theology," 26.

The second reason why Mbiti took the Christology of Afua on board could be because her Christology fell within his broader study of Christology and African Religion. He observed in his lecture that in African Christianity, Jesus Christ is the subject, African religiosity is the verb, and the gospel is the object. As part of his study, he had collected a list of 166 christological contextual titles in Africa, such as Advisor, Big Tree, Bulldozer, Friend, Liberator, Master of Initiation, Physician and Torch. These, he said, were found everywhere, including on buses, in homes, on the radio, in books and in songs.[17] So the Christology of Afua Kuma was a paradigm that fitted his study.

In this context, Mbiti discussed the Christology of Afua Kuma when he said,

> Afua Kuma is a Ghanaian woman, a Farmer, who never went to school. She prayed and sang in Twi. In her natural environment, she sets out to praise the name of Jesus Christ with many titles. This phenomenon happens because she found and noted that "The deeds of Jesus are marvelous and powerful." She likened the power of Jesus to the python's power, which is the strongest snake in the forest. Jesus, she said, is like a big boat that cannot be sunk.[18]

To the poor, Jesus is their savior because they rely on him, just as the tongue depends on the mouth. Jesus is the Big Tree that cares for and provides food for the traveler. According to Mbiti, Kuma is not an exception in how she describes Jesus, because people sing and proclaim Jesus in this way orally. Christology becomes the most intensely creative encounter between Christianity and African Religion, according to Mbiti.

The third reason why Mbiti engaged with the Christology of Afua Kuma was that in it, the oral theology which is the backbone of African theology is strengthened. In the study of this Christology, Mbiti continued to hold the tension between oral and written theology.

Conclusion

In this reflection on my experience of Mbiti, I have shown how Mbiti was presented to me in my classes and how that impacted me to do my first research project. My other experience was meeting and sharing platforms with him. Finally, I have looked at my experience with Prof. Mbiti through

---

17. Mbiti, "Pilgrim Expedition," 4.
18. Mbiti, 5.

the eyes of Circle Theology, which he did not engage with much. I have also shown that his engagement with Afua Kuma fell within his broader scheme of African Christianity.

Bibliography

Amoah, Elizabeth, and Mercy Amba Oduyoye. "The Christ for African Women." In *With Passion and Compassion: Third World Women Doing Theology*, edited by Virginia Fabella and Mercy Amba Oduyoye, 35–47. Maryknoll: Orbis, 1988.

Behera, Marina Ngursangzeli, Michael Biehl, and Knud Jørgensen. *Mission in Secularised Contexts of Europe: Contemporary Narratives and Experiences*. Oxford: Regnum, 2018.

Conradie, E. M. *African Christian Theologies in Transformation*. Stellenbosch: EFSA, 2004.

Hinga, Teresa. "Jesus Christ and the Liberation of Women in Africa." In *The Will to Arise: Women, Tradition, and the Church in Africa*, edited by Mercy Amba Oduyoye and Rachel Angogo Kanyoro, 183–94. Maryknoll: Orbis, 1992.

Kanyoro, Musimbi. "Engendered Communal Theology: African Women's Contribution to Theology in the Twenty-First Century." In *Hope Abundant: Third World and Indigenous Women's Theology*, edited by Pui-Ian Kwok, 19–35. Maryknoll: Orbis, 2010.

———. *Introducing Feminist Cultural Hermeneutics: An African Perspective*. Introductions in Feminist Theology 9. Sheffield: Sheffield Academic, 2002.

Kanyoro, Musimbi R. A., and Mercy Amba Oduyoye. *The Will to Arise: Women, Tradition, and the Church in Africa*. Maryknoll: Orbis, 1992.

Kuma, Afua. *Jesus of the Deep Forest*. Accra: Asempa, 1981.

Mbiti, John S. *African Religions and Philosophy*. London: Heinemann, 1969.

———. "Flowers in the Garden: Women in African Religion." In *African Traditional Religions in Contemporary Society*, edited by J. K. Olupoona, 69–82. St. Paul: Paragon House, 1991.

———. "Myths of Sexuality, Sexual Relations and identity in Africa." Unpublished Paper presented at the Conference on Exploring Stepping Stones: Sexuality Identity and Gender Equality. 27 April–1 May 2010.

———. "A Pilgrim Expedition with African Theology: Oral and Written." Lecture, World Mission Conference on "Mission and Evangelism." Arusha, Tanzania, 6–13 March 2018.

Mombo, Esther. "The Persistence of Female Circumcision in Kisii." Unpublished paper, St. Paul's Library, 1982.

———. "Secularization: Whose Discourse?" In *Mission in Secularized Contexts of Europe: Contemporary Narratives and Experiences*, edited by M. Ngursangzeli Behera, Michael Biehl, and Knud Jorgensen, 206–13. Oxford: Regnum, 2018.

Mose, Grace B. *Thinking the Gusii Way: Insider Perspectives on Female Genital Mutilation (FGM)/Cutting and Strategies for Change.* Saarbrücken: VDM Verlag, 2008.

Nasimiyu-Wasike, Anne. "Christology and an African Woman's Experience." In *Jesus in African Christianity: Experimentation and Diversity in African Christology*, edited by Jesse Mugambi and Laurenti Magesa, 123–135. Nairobi: Acton, 1998.

———. "Imaging Jesus Christ in the African Context at the Dawn of a New Millennium." In *Challenges and Prospects of the Church in Africa: Theological Reflections of the 21st Century*, edited by N. W. Ndung'u and P. N. Mwaura, 102–18. Nairobi: Paulines Publications, 2005.

Phiri, Isabel. "African Women's Theologies in the New Millennium." *Agenda: Empowering Women for Gender Equity* 61 (2004): 16–24. Accessed 10 October 2020. http://www.jstor.org/stable/4066593.

———. "Southern Africa." In *Introduction to Third World Theologies*, edited by John Parratt, 137–62. Cambridge: Cambridge University Press, 2004.

Shorter, Aylward. "Secularism in Africa." *African Christian Studies* 13, no. 1 (March 1997). Also at https://sedosmission.org/bulletin/sedos-bulletin-3001.pdf.

van den Toren, Benno, Joseph Bosco Bangura, and Richard E. Seed. *Is Africa Incurably Religious? Secularization and Discipleship in Africa.* Oxford: Regnum, 2018.

Wanyoike, E. N. *An African Pastor: [The Life and Work of the Rev. W. Kamawe, 1888–1970].* Nairobi: East African Publishing House, 1974.

22

The Life and Legacy of the Late John S. Mbiti

A Tribute

James Nkansah-Obrempong
Professor of Theology and Ethics, Africa International University, Nairobi, Kenya
Dean of Nairobi Evangelical Graduate School of Theology, Kenya

His Life

This tribute gives a short biography of Professor John Samuel Mbiti and highlights aspects of his legacy for the academy and the church of Jesus Christ.

Professor John Samuel Mbiti was born on 30 November 1931 in Mulango, Kitui County, Kenya. His parents, Mutuvi Ngaangi and Valesi Mbandi Kiimba, were farmers. The African Inland Church influenced his thinking about his African culture during his formative years. As one who grew up in the church, he saw African Traditional Religion as pagan.

Mbiti went to Alliance High School in Nairobi. After completing high school, he studied at the University College of Makerere in Kampala, Uganda. He later went to the University of London, where he graduated with a Bachelor of Arts degree in 1953. He earned a Bachelor of Theology degree from Barrington College, a Christian liberal arts school in Rhode Island. He was awarded a PhD in New Testament studies at Cambridge University in 1963.[1] He married Verena Siegenthaler. He was ordained as an Anglican priest by the Church of England and served as a parish priest in England for some time before returning to Makerere in 1964 as a lecturer to teach traditional African religions, a subject he had very little knowledge about. It was during this time that his interest in African religion began. He taught at Makerere until 1974.[2]

Mbiti served as director of the World Council of Churches' Bossey Ecumenical Institute in Bogis-Bossey, Switzerland, from 1974 to 1980. As an ecumenist, he organized three important global conferences on intercultural or contextual theology, which brought together theological scholars from Africa and Asia for an ecumenical encounter. The first conference, in June 1976, concentrated on African and Asian contributions to contemporary theology. The second conference, held in July 1977 in Bossey, addressed the issue "Confessing Christ in Different Cultures." The third conference was dedicated to "Indigenous Theology and the Universal Church."[3]

After leaving the Ecumenical Institute, he became the parish minister in Bergdorf, Switzerland, for fifteen years. He taught as a part-time lecturer at the University of Bern (1983–2003) as a professor of the science of mission and extra-European theology. He also lectured at various universities around the world, mainly in Africa, Australia, the United Kingdom and North America.[4] He retired as a parish priest of the Reformed Church of Bern, in Bergdorf, Switzerland. He was professor emeritus at the University of Bern. As an accomplished scholar, he received three honorary doctorate degrees: Doctor of Humane Letters (LHD) in 1973 from Barrington College, USA, Doctor of Theology (DTh) in 1991 from the University of Lausanne, Switzerland, and the Doctor of Divinity (DD) in 1997 by the General Theological Seminary, New York.[5] He died on 6 October 2019 in Bergdorf.

His Legacy and Contribution to the Academy

Prof. Mbiti's legacy is most prominent in ecclesial life, as he was a minister of the gospel for many years, and in the academy, where he was a distinguished

---

1. Richard Sandomir, "John Mbiti, 87, Dies," https://www.nytimes.com/2019/10/24/world/africa/john-mbiti-dead.html.
2. https://www.nytimes.com/2019/10/24/world/africa/john-mbiti-dead.html.
3. "John Mbiti," https://en.wikipedia.org/wiki/John_Mbiti.
4. FrankTalk, "Bio of the Week: John Mbiti," http://sbffranktalk.blogspot.com/2016/01/bio-of-week.html.
5. FrankTalk, "Bio of the Week: John Mbiti."

biblical and theological scholar of international repute. He influenced and mentored many prominent African theologians through his prolific writings. His vast knowledge of African cultures, religions and philosophy opened up new frontiers for biblical and theological studies in Africa and in the quest for an African Christian theology. He shaped African Christianity and theology from the 1970s. His passion for seeing Christianity entrenched in African cultures and his love for practical theology that spoke to African existential concerns through his theological writings made him one of Africa's most influential theologians.

Prof. Mbiti was a great thinker and was passionate about Africa's religious and cultural heritage, which he believed was critical for Christianity and Christian theology in Africa. At a time when Western missionaries demonized Africa's culture and religious heritage, perceiving them to have no value, Mbiti's courage in challenging that notion was commendable. Because of his unflinching stand on the importance of African Traditional Religion for African Christianity and theology, he was strongly criticized by both secular and Christian scholars. Secular scholars thought he misrepresented African Traditional Religion in Christian terms, while Christians believed he was romanticizing African Traditional Religion, and they accused him of syncretism.

Prof. Mbiti made "a distinction between Christianity and Christian faith" or the gospel. Christianity, he asserted, is the result of the gospel encountering any given culture; it "is always indigenous, and culture-bound."[6] The gospel, however, is "God-given," eternal, and does not change.[7] As an African Christian, he sought an authentic African Christianity based on "African heritage, culture, and religiosity." This move did not mean the "indigenization of Christianity" nor the "indigenization of theology." Instead, as Bediako observed, what Prof. Mbiti was "seeking to establish" in essence was the "principle of the freedom of the African Christian conscience to define and formulate its apprehension of the Christian faith, not only in terms of the positive content of the faith itself but also in relation to the religious needs and the aspirations of the African background and context."[8] Prof. Mbiti was concerned that, due to the failure of missionary Christianity to have a "serious

---

6. Bediako, *Theology and Identity*, 305.
7. Mbiti, "Christianity and Traditional Religions," 438.
8. Bediako, *Theology and Identity*, 306.

encounter with traditional religions and philosophy," "the Church in Africa finds itself in a situation of trying to exist without a theology."[9]

Prof. Mbiti's seminal contribution to the development of African Christianity and theology was thus his insistence on what he termed "spiritual freedom." He theorized that it would allow African Christians to discern their questions, formulate those questions, and seek appropriate answers – and to do all that in the freedom of the gospel. He viewed religion as central to the African ethos, popularly expressed in his maxim "Africans are notoriously religious." He argued that African religion is "lived religion": that it affects all areas of African life. His passion for studying African Traditional Religion helped him to "pioneer a systematic analysis and study of African traditional religions and religious concepts,"[10] which became critical for the development of African Christian theology. He insisted that Christianity needed to encounter African culture in order for the gospel of Jesus Christ to become relevant and grow deep roots in the African religious and cultural consciousness.

In this connection, Prof. Mbiti was concerned about how the gospel was communicated in Africa so that it might take deep roots in the African cultural conscience. The implication was that the gospel needed to be communicated in languages and idioms that were not foreign to Africans. He posited that the African religio-cultural heritage could provide such expressions for communicating the gospel and developing African theology.

In his judgment, "mission Christianity" had not "penetrated sufficiently deep into African religiosity."[11] Prof. Mbiti held the view that Christianity "historically" was "very much an African religion."[12] For this reason, he was not advocating for the indigenization of the faith, because the faith, he argued, would always take a local form. If we grant that all theologies are contextual theologies because they respond to the questions being asked by particular people, it is logical that we provide answers to those questions. This methodological framework is critical if African theology is to withstand scrutiny and be faithful to the Bible and Christianity's doctrinal traditions.

One critical element in Prof. Mbiti's argument for his complimentary appraisal of African Traditional Religion was to see the "African pre-Christian religious heritage" as a *praeparatio evangelica*.[13] By this he meant that the

---

9. Mbiti, *African Religions and Philosophy*, 232.
10. Agbeti, "African Theology," 8.
11. Mbiti, *African Religions and Philosophy*, 233.
12. Mbiti, *New Testament Eschatology*, 189.
13. Bediako, *Theology and Identity*, 319.

African religious heritage not only helped to prepare Africans to receive the gospel, but it also shaped African Christianity and the development of African Christian theology. That the African religio-cultural heritage has valuable insights for Christianity and the Christian faith was his seminal contribution to the development of African Christianity. In arguing that the pre-Christian religious heritage was important for theological development, Prof. Mbiti was able to appraise and move the African religious and cultural heritage into a field study and investigation. He believed that understanding the African religious and cultural heritage would provide the raw material for theological reflection, and also the idiom for expressing and communicating the gospel in African Christianity and theology in the African context.

Prof. Mbiti was concerned for the church in Africa to develop its theology, one that would speak to the aspirations, questions and needs of Africans, but at the same time have relevance and contribute to the theology of the universal church. In doing this, he proposed four sources for such theology.

The first source was the Bible and biblical theology. Prof. Mbiti emphasized that the "Bible is the primary and essential source for theological development," observing that "biblical theology must be the basis of any theological reflection; otherwise, we shall lose our perspectives and may not claim the outcome to be Christian."[14] The second source was "Christian theology from the major Christian traditions of Christendom," which, he thought, was essential for providing African theologians with the opportunity to enter into "the mainstream of ecumenical and apostolic heritage" and into "the catholicity of the Church."[15] He insisted that, while Christian theology and the traditions of Christendom as developed in the West were essential, they needed to be understood and translated into the African context. In this way they would become relevant to the African church.

The third source Mbiti suggested was a "serious and critical study of African religions and philosophy."[16] He saw in the African pre-Christian traditions "its religion and thought in dialogue with the Christian message as embodied in Christ Himself."[17] Fourth was "the theology of the living church,"[18] that is, the actual life and experience of the church, which included the African Independent Churches and other religious movements as critical sources from

---

14. Mbiti, *New Testament Eschatology*, 189. See Bediako, 313.
15. Mbiti, 189.
16. Bediako, *Theology and Identity*, 313.
17. Bediako, 313.
18. Bediako, 313.

which African theology could make its unique contribution to global theology.[19] For it to be authentic and relevant, Christian theology needed to engage with these four critical sources.

These four sources for theological reflection and development are no different from the accepted sources for Christian theology in theological studies. Historically, Christian theology has been developed from these four sources, namely, the Bible, tradition, reason and experience. John W. Kinney sums up well the goal of Prof. Mbiti's theological method: "to retain its African religious and cultural heritage, to give Christianity an African imprint and character, and to uphold the uniqueness and catholicity of Christianity."[20]

Prof. Mbiti later added two more sources to African theology, namely, African culture and African history. Regarding African history, Mbiti stressed the experiences that have shaped African societies and which still affect them today, namely suffering, exploitation and liberation.[21] He insisted that culture was significant in the quest for African theology. If Christianity is a social and cultural embodiment of the gospel or the Christian faith, as Bediako observes, it "means [that] the cultural embodiment of the Christian faith in the African context is a subject to study in its own right and not as a cultural reaction to missionary imposition of European forms of Christianity."[22] This brings the study of culture to the fore. Mbiti developed "a theology of culture" as it applied to African life. Mbiti showed how the gospel might "be interpreted as fulfillment of the African cultural values," which can be brought into fruitful contact with the Christian faith as an African expression of that faith, seeing Christ as the fulfiller of all human cultures.[23] The above is evident in the following statement by Mbiti:

> I contend that, even though officially Christianity either disregarded African religion altogether or treated it as an enemy, it was the religion that laid down the foundation for the eventual rapid accommodation of Christianity in Africa, and the present rapid growth of the Church. Without African religiosity, whatever its defects might be, Christianity would have taken longer to be understood and accommodated by African peoples.[24]

---

19. Mbiti, *New Testament Eschatology*, 189.
20. Kinney, "Theology of John Mbiti," 66.
21. Bediako, *Theology and Identity*, 314.
22. Bediako, 314.
23. Bediako, 314.
24. Mbiti, "African Indigenous Culture," 86.

One of the critical theological concerns in African theology is the place of Jesus Christ in the African religious experience. In Prof. Mbiti's schema, the gospel brought Jesus Christ to meet African religious aspirations. Christology was a central concern in Prof. Mbiti's theological agenda. He had an "elevated christological perspective," according to John W. Kinney.[25] The Christian faith falls or stands on Christology, as Prof. Mbiti observed:

> The final test for the validity and usefulness of any theological contribution is Jesus Christ. Since His Incarnation, Christian Theology ought properly to be Christology, for Theology falls or stands on how it understands, translates, and interprets Jesus Christ, at a given time, place, and human situation.[26]

Prof. Mbiti believed that Jesus Christ has universal significance. He "holds the greatest and the only potentialities of meeting the dilemmas and challenges of modern Africa and of reaching the full integration and humanhood of individuals and communities."[27] Mbiti strongly affirmed the place of Jesus Christ in African religious tradition and experience and Christian theology.

Prof. Mbiti's academic works and contributions covered many fields: philosophy, theology, biblical studies, literature, ethics, politics, translation, pre-Christian religious traditions and their encounter with Christianity, to mention just a few. As a result, his impact on the academy has been enormous.

Prof. Mbiti made an immense contribution to African theological thought. His theological influence was not limited to Africa: he was a global scholar whose theological works were received by scholars all over the world. His ecumenical posture endeared him to all. His influence in the academic world transcended Christian tradition. He worked closely with all the Christian communities and showed maturity and restraint toward those who did not share his views.

For the last five years of his life, Prof. Mbiti was involved with the PhD program at Africa International University, leading seminars and sharing his great wisdom and insights with our students. One personal quality that stood out was his humility. His simplicity and humility are two virtues that I admired in him. A person of such stature, influence and immense learning is often proud and unwilling to mingle with people who are not of the same class. Not so with Prof. Mbiti. He was generous, welcoming and very respectful to all.

---

25. Kinney, "Theology of John Mbiti," 66.
26. Mbiti, *New Testament Eschatology*, 190.
27. Bediako, *Theology and Identity*, 329.

Our students learned much from his wisdom, insights and great humility as a world-acclaimed scholar.

As a result of his[28] seminal contribution to the development of African Christian theology, African scholars have described him as "the father of modern African theology,"[29] "the father of contemporary African theology,"[30] "the most productive African scholar in our time,"[31] "the leading African theologian"[32] and the "man with the weightiest bibliography among modern African theologians."[33] Furthermore, McVeigh observes that Mbiti, along with others, exerted "a function for Africa equivalent to Barth, Tillich, Niebuhr, and Rahner in Europe and North America."[34] He truly deserves these accolades.

Prof. Mbiti's enduring legacy is the prominent place and role he accorded to African Traditional Religion as a *praeparatio evangelica* and his insights into and interpretation of the gospel. As Bediako observes, "his thesis that the African pre-Christian heritage in religion constituted a *praeparatio evangelica* [is] significant in his theological scheme; it is this thesis and its outworking that may perhaps be his most enduring contribution to the theology of the Church in twentieth-century Africa."[35] His writings on African Traditional Religion, Christianity and theological works brought African Christian theology into global ecumenical theology.

Prof. Mbiti bequeathed over 400 published works to the academic community: books, articles, poems, essays, book reviews on theology, religion, biblical studies, philosophy, and much more. We are grateful to God for him and for his dedication and servant spirit in serving Christ's body with the gifts Christ gave him.

Before he died, Prof. Mbiti translated the Greek New Testament into Kikamba, his mother tongue. This was the first time an African scholar translated the New Testament into a local language directly from the Greek rather than from a translated version. This outstanding achievement speaks of the scholar Prof. Samuel Mbiti was. This gift from him to the church will remain one of his greatest legacies for the African church and the Christian community.

---

28. See Tarus and Lowery, "African Theologies," 311.
29. Heaney, *Post-Colonial Theology*, 3.
30. Perkinson, "John S. Mbiti," 455.
31. Olupona, "Biographical Sketch," 7.
32. Hastings, *History of African Christianity*, 232.
33. Bediako, "John Mbiti's Contribution," 367.
34. McVeigh, "African Christian Theology," 4.
35. Bediako, *Theology and Identity*, 333.

In July 2015, Prof. Mbiti was the speaker at the Graduation Ceremony at Africa International University. The university was honored to have him open the Derek Nurse Africana Library Collection in the Tony Wilmot Library on our Karen Campus. Here he was acknowledged and honored as the "father of contemporary African theology."

The African Christian academy acknowledges his courage, dedication and service to the academic community in Africa and around the world. Specifically, we at Africa International University are grateful to have had him share in our ministry. The church of Christ around the world and the academy have lost a great minister, a biblical and theological scholar of our time. May the Lord keep him in perfect peace as we wait to inherit our inheritance in Christ. Indeed, a great son of Africa has fallen and has been gathered to the heroes of the faith!

Bibliography

Agbeti, John K. "African Theology: What It Is." *Presence* 5, no. 3 (1972): 5–8.
Bediako, Kwame. "John Mbiti's Contribution to African Theology." In *Religious Plurality in Africa: Essays in Honour of John S. Mbiti*, edited by Sulayman S. Nyang and Jacob Olupona, 366–90. Berlin: de Gruyter, 1993.
———. *Theology and Identity*. Oxford: Regnum, 1992.
FrankTalk. "Bio of the Week: John Mbiti." 2016. Accessed 8 May 2020. http://sbffranktalk.blogspot.com/2016/01/bio-of-week.html.
Hastings, Adrian. *A History of African Christianity 1950–1975*. Cambridge: Cambridge University Press, 1979.
Heaney, Robert S. *From Historical to Critical Post-Colonial Theology: The Contributions of John S. Mbiti and Jesse N. K. Mugambi*. Eugene: Pickwick, 2015.
"John Mbiti." *Wikipedia*. Accessed 5 May 2020. https://en.wikipedia.org/wiki/John_Mbiti.
Kinney, John W. "The Theology of John Mbiti: His Sources, Norms, and Method." *Occasional Bulletin of Missionary Research* 3, no. 2 (1 April 1979): 65–67.
Mbiti, John S. "African Indigenous Culture in Relation to Evangelism and Church Development." In *The Gospel and Frontier Peoples: A Report of a Consultation, December 1972*, edited by R. Pierce Beaver, 79–95. Pasadena: William Carey Library, 1973.
———. *African Religions and Philosophy*. London: Heinemann, 1969.
———. "Christianity and Traditional Religions in Africa." *International Review of Missions* 9, no. 236 (Oct. 1970): 430–40.

———. *New Testament Eschatology in an African Background: A Study of the Encounter between New Testament Theology and African Traditional Concepts*. London: Oxford University Press, 1978.

McVeigh, Malcolm J. "Sources for an African Christian Theology." *Presence* 5, no. 3 (1972): 2–4.

Olupona, J. K. "A Biographical Sketch." In *Religious Plurality in Africa*, edited by Sulayman S. Nyang and Jacob K. Olupona, 1–7. Berlin; Boston: de Gruyter, 1993.

Perkinson, James W. "John S. Mbiti." In *Empire and the Christian Tradition*, edited by Pui-Ian Kwok et al., 455–69. Minneapolis: Fortress, 2007.

Sandomir, Richard. "John Mbiti, 87, Dies; Punctured Myths about African Religions." *New York Times*, 24 October 2019. Accessed 5 May 2020. https://www.nytimes.com/2019/10/24/world/africa/john-mbiti-dead.html.

Tarus, David Kirwa, and Stephanie Lowery. "African Theologies of Identity and Community: The Contributions of John Mbiti, Jesse Mugambi, Vincent Mulago, and Kwame Bediako." *Open Theology* 3, no. 1 (2017): 311. Accessed 5 May 2020. https://www.degruyter.com/view/journals/opth/3/1/article-p305.xml.

23

A Tribute to John S. Mbiti

Jesse N. K. Mugambi
Professor of Philosophy and Religious Studies, University of Nairobi, Kenya (Retired)

This tribute is in honor of Professor John Samuel Mbiti (30 October 1931 – 5 October 2019). He was the most widely published and the most distinguished African scholar in the research fields of African expressions of Christianity and African religions and philosophy. For more than sixty years, he devoted his vocation to teaching, research, translation and publishing, and to his pastoral career as an ordained minister within the Anglican Church.

Throughout his academic and professional vocation, Professor John Samuel Mbiti was a pacesetter and record breaker in mentorship, research and publishing. He studied biblical Greek and Hebrew, and focused on New Testament eschatology, with a doctoral thesis on this theme published in 1971.[1] His concern was to explore how the eschatological orientation of Christian doctrine had been received in the African worldview, with particular reference to the Akamba of eastern Kenya. Most of Mbiti's published books and papers dealt with this theme.[2] His research findings were received in Europe and

---

1. John S. Mbiti, *New Testament Eschatology in an African Background* (Oxford University Press, 1971).

2. For Mbiti's publications see, for example, "Books by John S. Mbiti," Good Reads, https://www.goodreads.com/author/list/579948.John_S_Mbiti; "Mbiti, John S.," WorldCat Identities, http://worldcat.org/identities/lccn-n50010247/. For his critics see, for example Scott Moreau, "A Critique of John Mbiti's Understanding of the African Concept of Time," in *Africa Journal of Evangelical Theology* 5, no. 2 (1986): 55–66, https://biblicalstudies.org.uk/articles_ajet-01.php; Philosophy Professor Kwasi Wiredu concurred with John Mbiti that the African worldview presupposes the future as "potential" or unrealized duration, which cannot be considered as

North America paradoxically. From one perspective Mbiti was acclaimed as the most eminent researcher and author on African Religions and Philosophy, and as an expert on the New Testament. On the other hand some of his critics responded negatively to his remark that in African ontology, duration is conceptualized as having "a long past, a present and virtually no future." Mbiti remained consistent, reiterating that the African worldview is different from the European one, as clearly indicated in African languages that distinguish between *sasa* (Present) and *zamani* (Past). Criticism of Mbiti on this point came from some scholars both African and Western.

The first book Mbiti authored was a storybook in Kikamba, first published in 1954 by the East African Literature Bureau (EALB). It is still in print under the Kenya Literature Bureau (KLB) as a primary school reader. Interestingly, Mbiti's last book to be published was also in Kikamba. That book was his translation of the entire New Testament from the Koine Greek into Kikamba, which I discuss here below. Thus Professor Mbiti's vocation as an author stretched over more than sixty years, with audiences ranging from primary school to a postdoctoral readership. Throughout his career, he communicated lucidly, with neither vagueness nor ambiguity. In addition to hundreds of academic papers, the following is a sample of the books authored by Professor Mbiti. Some of them have been translated and published in languages other than English:

- 1954: *Mutunga na Ngewa Yake*
- 1958: *English–Kamba Vocabulary*
- 1966: *Akamba Stories* (OUP)
- 1969: *African Religions and Philosophy* (Heinemann)
- 1970: *Concepts of God in Africa*, 1st edition (SPCK); 2nd edition, 2012 (Acton)
- 1971: *New Testament Eschatology in an African Background* (OUP)
- 1973: *Love and Marriage in Africa* (Longman)
- 1975: *The Prayers of African Religion* (SPCK)
- 1986: *Bible and Theology in African Christianity* (OUP)
- 1988: *Prayer and Spirituality in African Religion* (Charles Strong Trust, Australia)
- 2010: *Ngaeka Waeka: Myali ya Kiikamba*. Anthology of Kikamba Poems (Akamba Cultural Trust)

"real" until it is experienced. See Parker English, "Kalumba, Mbiti and a Traditional African Concept of Time," in *Philosophia Africana* 9, no. 1 (2006), Penn State University Press.

- 2014: *Utianiyo wa Mwiyai Yesu Kilisto*. The New Testament in Kikamba (KLB)[3]

I first learned of Professor Mbiti in 1968, during my training course as a secondary school teacher at Kenyatta College, Nairobi. The first lecture I heard him deliver was in April 1969, at the All Saints Cathedral, Nairobi, where he announced the publication of his famous book *African Religions and Philosophy* (London: Heinemann, 1969). He was at that time Head of the Department of Religious Studies at Makerere University, Uganda. In that role, Mbiti trained a cohort of African scholars. I have met some of them, and they cherished his mentorship – even in their retirement. He encouraged African lecturers and students to research and write papers on African religions and philosophy, on the worldviews and customs of their African communities. He would have the best of these papers edited, printed and bound in the series titled "Occasional Research Papers" as part of his work at Makerere University. Mbiti published these excellent papers in the journal he launched, called *Dini na Mila*.

It is a great joy for me to remember that Professor Mbiti published my first research paper, written in 1968 on the Embu people of Kenya, in volume 5, no. 1 of that journal *Dini na Mila* (1971) before we had met and got acquainted. For all these decades, Mbiti has remained one of my mentors and torchbearers. In 1973 I met him again at Union Theological Seminary, New York, where he was on sabbatical before proceeding to Geneva, having taught at Makerere University, Uganda, for a decade.

Professor Mbiti served as Director of the Ecumenical Institute at Bossey, near Geneva, Switzerland, under the auspices of the World Council of Churches (WCC). During his tenure at the Bossey Institute, Mbiti facilitated research seminars on New Testament studies, one of which culminated in a volume titled *Christ and the Younger Churches*, edited by Georg F. Vicedom (London: SPCK, 1972). A German edition of this book was also published.

The purpose of *Christ and the Younger Churches* was to illustrate that the Christian faith is profoundly relevant in all cultures. All perspectives on Jesus, and all metaphors, from different cultural contexts help in showing the profundity and relevance of the Christian faith as a global religion. In 1981 Professor Mbiti joined the University of Bern, Switzerland, as Professor in the Faculty of Theology. He continued researching and presenting papers at the invitation of many institutions and conferences. In 2002, Professor Mbiti was

---

3. The list of books authored by Professor John S. Mbiti can be accessed at https://www.thriftbooks.com/a/john-s-mbiti/221171/.

invited to Nairobi for the launch of a new edition of the Bible in Kikamba. He was hesitant to accept the invitation because he found in the latest version some deviations from the earlier version that had been published in 1952. After some persuasion, he attended the launch. He briefly expressed his critique and concerns about the new version.

Since the new version had already been launched and was in circulation, the most appropriate response was for him to undertake his own translation, based on the original Greek text of the New Testament. His translation took three years, until 2005. The Kenya Literature Bureau (KLB), publishers of his first Kikamba book, agreed to publish Mbiti's translation of the New Testament, titled *Utianiyo Mweu wa Mwiyai Yesu Kilisto*, and it was launched in Nairobi on 19 December 2014.[4] This event made Mbiti a record breaker: the first African scholar to translate, as the sole author, the entire New Testament from the original Greek text into an African language.

The only other African who had accomplished a similar feat was Bishop Samuel Ajayi Crowther (ca. 1809–91), who translated the Bible into Yoruba in Nigeria in the mid nineteenth century. Samuel Ajayi Crowther's translation, however, was from another translation – the English King James Version. Thus Professor John Mbiti's record as the pioneer African Bible translator from the original text cannot be broken.

It was a great privilege for me to be mentored by such a great scholar as Professor Mbiti, who was so humble, so firm, and yet so accomplished and committed. Mbiti challenges African biblical scholars to undertake the translation and publication of the Bible from the original sources into their respective African languages, as sole authors. Only when the Bible is translated into every African language by their native speakers will African Christianity fully come of age.

To God be the glory;

Great things he has done!

---

4. John S. Mbiti, *Utianiyo Mweu wa Mwiyai Yesu Kilisto: The New Testament of the Lord Jesus Christ* (Nairobi: KLB, 2014).

24

A Tribute to John S. Mbiti

Samuel Ngewa
Professor of New Testament, Africa International University, Nairobi, Kenya

Professor John Mbiti, a great African scholar, was characterized by humility and love for Africa. The number of times he has been quoted by different scholars (including me in my dissertation) as an authority in matters regarding Africa Traditional Religions proves his excellent scholarship. His writings have achieved a very high standing both in Africa and overseas.

John Mbiti and I are from the same people group, and so I began reading his popular writings when I was still in primary school. The focus of his writings was, at the time, the African values we must promote, including good neighborliness and treating others well, not forgetting our faults. It was not surprising to me that when he advanced his studies, he had a great interest in African practices and beliefs, of which he became one of the first academic experts in the continent of Africa.

One of his most evident life qualities was how he did not allow his achievements to make him proud in any way. The story is told of how he once traveled back to Kenya and needed to see his area's chief. Since the chief had not yet arrived on this particular morning, Mbiti simply joined the crowd, which was sitting on a form (one long seat), and eventually joined in the conversation that was taking place. When after some time the chief had still not appeared, Mbiti decided to do another errand and then return. When he left, someone asked who he was, and when another person, who knew him, replied that it was "mwanaa Mbiti" (Mbiti's son), many held open their mouths in amazement at how he had just identified with everyone on the form. My wife and I witnessed this kind of humility when we had to take care of him (he was living in a guesthouse but taking meals with us) when he visited our institution to speak at a graduation ceremony and give a few talks in Kenya.

When Mbiti was sure of something, he held to it firmly. Those who wanted to push their views on him, including missionaries, did not find him easygoing. At times, this led to a misrepresentation of his position, but as a whole, Mbiti considered other people's opinions carefully. It was this same quality that enabled him to tirelessly translate the Greek New Testament into the "original" Kikamba language even when some of the words may have fallen out of use, since languages are dynamic.

The Lord be praised for giving such a person as John Mbiti to the African continent. His work has formed an essential and firm foundation for many generations of scholars.

List of Contributors

Elkanah Kiprop Cheboi holds a PhD in Theological Studies (New Testament) from Africa International University, Nairobi, Kenya. Currently, he is a lecturer in Theology and Biblical Studies at Kabarak University, Kenya. In the past, he served as a local church pastor and as a chaplain in a mission hospital and nursing college. He is also the Founder and Director of ShahidiHub Africa, a Christian organization that deals with news perspectives, Christian research and publications.

Lydia Chemei is an ordained minister in the Reformed Church of East Africa. She received her Master of Theology from the Protestant Theological University in the Netherlands. She is pursuing a PhD in New Testament at St. Paul's University, Kenya, where she is also an adjunct faculty member.

Henry Marcus Garba is a pastor with the Evangelical Church Winning All (ECWA), Nigeria. He attended Kagoro ECWA Theological College and ECWA Theological Seminary in Kwara State, Nigeria, and Africa International University, Nairobi, Kenya. He holds a master's degree in Church History.

John Michael Kiboi is an ordained priest in the Anglican Church of Kenya, serving as a Senior Lecturer in the Faculty of Theology at St. Paul's University, Limuru, Kenya. He holds a PhD in Dogmatic Theology from the Catholic University of Eastern Africa. Previously he served as a parish priest in the diocese of Bungoma and as Principal at Wycliffe Centre for Theology. Currently, he is the Leader of PhD programs in the Faculty of Theology at St. Paul's University.

Stephanie A. Lowery is a lecturer in theology and coordinator of the BTh and DTh programs at Africa International University. She also teaches at Kalamba School of Leadership, as well as serving part-time in the Kalamba church district. She grew up in Kenya and considers Ukambani home. Her research interests include African theologies, African ecclesiological models, missional theology and hermeneutics, and the Trinity.

Elizabeth Mburu is the Regional Coordinator of Langham Literature in Africa. She is an Associate Professor of New Testament and Greek and teaches part-time at Pan-Africa Christian University, Nairobi, Kenya. She received her PhD (New Testament) from Southeastern Baptist Theological Seminary, USA. Her research and publishing interests are primarily in the areas of New Testament, Bible translation, intercultural hermeneutics, and culture and worldview studies. She is on the board of the *Africa Bible Commentary*. She is also Extraordinary Researcher at the Unit for Reformational Theology and the Development of the SA Society, North-West University, South Africa.

Esther Mombo is a Professor at St. Paul's University in Limuru, Kenya. She teaches in the Faculty of Theology of St. Paul's University and her research interests span the fields of church history, and theology and gender in church and society. She is a founder member of the Tamar Campaign in Kenya, a mechanism that seeks to acknowledge the existence of gender-based violence in the society and empower and facilitate churches to address this concern. She is a member of the Circle of Concerned African Women Theologians. She is a graduate of St. Paul's University, University of Dublin, and University of Edinburgh.

Timothy J. Monger works with Amigos Charity which equips churches in northern Uganda for integral mission. Previously he was a missionary in Tanzania, serving from 2010 to 2020 with Emmanuel International, which equips churches in mission among the poor, and was the Country Director from 2018 to 2020. He was also a part-time lecturer at St. Paul College, Mwanza, Tanzania. He received his Master of Christian Studies from Regent College, Vancouver, Canada.

Gift Mtukwa is an ordained minister with the Church of the Nazarene, and the Chair of the Department of Religion and Lecturer in the School of Religion and Christian Ministry at Africa Nazarene University, Nairobi, Kenya. He holds a PhD in Biblical Studies. He is also the lead pastor at the University Church of the Nazarene.

Jesse N. K. Mugambi has a BA in Education, MA in Philosophy and Religious Studies, and a PhD in Philosophy of Religion (Nairobi University). He is a Fellow of the Kenya National Academy of Science (FKNAS), and an Elder of the Burning Spear (EBS). Dr Mugambi retired in February 2021 as Professor of Philosophy and Religious Studies at the University of Nairobi, Kenya, where he had taught since 1977. His academic specializations include Philosophy of Religion; Phenomenology of Religion; Applied Ethics; Communication Policy and Planning; Religion and Ecology; Comparative Study of Religions; African Religion and Culture; Ecumenical Studies; History of Christianity; and

Contemporary Christian Theology. His publication profile stretches across this range of specializations. His professional training and practice is in Education, Ecumenical Relations, and Communication Policy and Planning.

He has spent most of his life in his country, Kenya, where he was born, brought up and educated, with short stints in Canada, Denmark, Norway, South Africa, UK, and USA. In addition to academic duties he is a senior consultant in Higher Education; Ecumenical Relations; Interfaith Relations; Applied Ethics; Ecology and Multi-Media Communication.

Telesia Kathini Musili is a Lecturer in the Department of Philosophy and Religious Studies, University of Nairobi. She holds a master's in Religious Studies from Katholieke Universiteit, Leuven, Belgium; a PhD from the Department of Philosophy and Religious Studies, Kenyatta University (KU), Nairobi, Kenya; and a master's in Bioethics from Atlantic International University, Honolulu, Hawaii. Her research interests revolve around ethics and religious research on HIV/AIDS and sexuality, bioethics, sexuality studies and biomedical ethics. She is currently the Kenyan coordinator of the Circle of Concerned African Women Theologians.

Daniel M. Mwailu has been an Adjunct Professor in Theology and Biblical Studies at Africa Nazarene University, Nairobi, Kenya, since 2011. He received his BA (Hons.) in Theology and MA in Aspects of Biblical Interpretation from London School of Theology, UK. He was awarded a PhD in Theology by Birmingham University, UK, in 1989 with a dissertation on Christology in Africa. He is a minister in the Methodist Church of Great Britain where he has served for twenty-six years, thirteen of which as superintendent minister and eight years as local preachers' tutor. He has also served as associate chaplain at the University of Birmingham.

David Ngaruiya is an Associate Professor at International Leadership University, where he is currently the Director of PhD in Theological Studies at the International Leadership University. He holds a PhD in Intercultural Studies from Trinity Evangelical Divinity School, USA. He served as Chair of the Africa Society of Evangelical Theology in 2015–16. He also served as one of the directors of the *Africa Leadership Study*.

Samuel M. Ngewa is Dean of the Graduate School at Africa International University, Nairobi, Kenya. He holds a PhD in Biblical Interpretation from Westminster Theological Seminary, Philadelphia, USA, and has published numerous works on New Testament studies. He is on the pastoral team at Africa Inland Church Lang'ata in Nairobi.

James Nkansah is a Professor of Theology and Ethics at Africa International University, Nairobi, Kenya, where he has been serving since 2003. Since 2010 he has been the Dean of Nairobi Evangelical Graduate School of Theology (NEGST). Before that he was the Head of Theology Department for eight years. He holds a PhD in Theological Studies from Fuller Theological Seminary, USA. He is the Chair of the Theological Commission of the Association of Evangelicals in Africa and the Vice-Chair of the World Evangelical Alliance Theological Commission.

Juliana Nzuki is a pastor with the Africa Inland Church–Kenya. She holds a MDiv in Biblical and Theological Studies from International Leadership University. Currently she is a Lecturer and the Head of Theology and Biblical Studies at Kabarak University, Nakuru, Kenya. Prior to that, she served as a local church pastor and part-time lecturer at International Leadership University.

Okelloh Ogera holds a PhD in Religious Studies from the Catholic University of Eastern Africa. He has published several journal articles and book chapters on African Christianity and is an Adjunct Lecturer within the Faculty of Theology at St. Paul's University. He is currently engaged in researching "Mega Churches in the Global South" organized by the John Templeton Foundation. He is also an ordained priest in the Anglican Church.

Moses Iliya Ogidis is a minister with Evangelical Church Winning All (ECWA) in Nigeria. Currently he is a PhD candidate in Theology (New Testament) at St. Paul's University, Limuru, Kenya.

Enoch O. Okode has been serving as a lecturer at Scott Christian University (SCU) in Machakos, Kenya, since 2009. Currently, he is the Dean of the School of Theology, a position he has held since 2020. Prior to that, he served as the Head of Biblical and Theological Studies for three years. He holds a PhD in Biblical and Theological Studies (New Testament) from Trinity Evangelical Divinity School, USA.

Lawrence Oseje is a senior lecturer in the department of Theology and Biblical Studies under the School of Education at Kabarak University, Nakuru, Kenya.

Rodney L. Reed is a missionary educator who has been serving at Africa Nazarene University in Nairobi, Kenya, since 2001. Currently he is the Deputy

Vice-Chancellor of Academic Affairs, a position he has held since 2010. Prior to that, he served as the Chair of the Department of Religion for nine years. He holds a PhD in Theological Ethics from Drew University, Madison, New Jersey, USA, and is an ordained minister in the Church of the Nazarene.

Billy Chilongo Sichone is Deputy Vice Chancellor at Central Africa Baptist University, Kitwe, Zambia. Prior to his current appointment, Billy served in various capacities at the university including Vice President for Academic Affairs, Head of Research/Library and as a member of Senior Faculty in Theology and Business. He also served with World Vision International-Zambia for seventeen years.

Thandi Soko-de Jong is a PhD student at the Protestant Theological University in Groningen, the Netherlands. She is also a tutor at the Foundation Academy of Amsterdam, a position she has held since 2019. She holds an MTh in Theology and Development from the University of KwaZulu-Natal, Durban, South Africa, and a Research Master in African Studies from the African Studies Centre, Leiden University, the Netherlands.

Rowland Van Es is a mission partner of Reformed Church Global Mission who has been serving at St. Paul's University in Limuru, Kenya, since 2004. Currently, he is the Interim Head of Department for History, Missions, Religion and Practical Theology. Prior to 2004 he and his wife Jane also served in the Gambia, Malawi and Sierra Leone. He has an MDiv and a ThM from Western Theological Seminary, Holland, Michigan, and an MA from Michigan State University. He is an ordained minister in the Reformed Church of America.

Alistair Wilson is a lecturer in Mission and New Testament at Edinburgh Theological Seminary, Edinburgh, Scotland, in the United Kingdom. He is also Extraordinary Researcher, Unit for Reformed Theology and the Development of SA Society, North-West University, South Africa.

Subject and Author Index

A
Abbey, Rose T. 46
Abraham 79, 81
Achaia 129
Adkins, A. W. H. 101
African Instituted Churches 165
African Traditional Religion 194, 267, 279, 322, 329, 398, 394–396, 400, 403, 406, 408, 412, 429
Africa, traditional 71, 193
Ajwang, Ramogi 241, 247
Allah 344, 361
Ambrose of Milan 7
Amoah, Elizabeth 147
anaideia 36
analyses, christological 45
ancient Near East 28, 84
ANE. *See* ancient Near East
animism 395, 396
Apollinarianism 224
Appiah-Kubi, Kofi 276, 278
approach
    christological 157, 161
    eurocentric 44, 45
    functional 61, 235
    ontological 222, 236
    speculative 230
architecture, African 407
Aristotle 100, 104, 109, 119, 140
Arius 225
Athanasius 168
atonement 383
Augustine, Saint 7

B
Bailey, Kenneth 27
Barrett C. K 125
Bavinck, J. H. 331
Bediako, Kwame 193, 232, 320, 326
believer, African 66

benefaction, Greco-Roman 96, 98, 103, 108
Best, Ernest 128
Borland, James 6
Bosch, David 334
Bujo, Bénézet 266

C
Caiaphas 86
Cassius, Dio 107
Christianity
    African 70, 212, 431
    contemporary 132
    evangelical 166
Christians
    African 41, 44, 51, 73, 193, 309
    Greco-Roman 224
    Jewish 271
Christ, Jesus 13, 18, 46
christology 6, 14, 15, 18, 26, 58, 62, 66, 79, 85, 106, 118, 198, 244, 253, 308, 380, 404, 422
    African 13, 59, 60, 157, 192, 212, 249, 292, 293
    Alexandrian 208
    ancestor 249
    ancestral 194
    Asian 59
    biblical 161
    Chalcedonian 161, 167
    functional 61, 222
    intellectual 234
    Ker 241, 249, 250, 252
    missionary 331
    multidimensional 73
    nonspeculative 230
    ontological 223
    Pauline 144
    traditional 44
Chrysostom, Dio 98, 119

church
  African 27, 64, 163, 167
  Anglican 437
  Byzantine 348
  Christian 400
  Ephesian 138
  Galatian 64, 67
Cicero 104, 108
Circle of Concerned African Women
    Theologians 422
clanship 241
Clarke, Andrew 97, 125
Clement 200
codes, household 140
communities, African 143
community, Qumran 188
confession, christological 183
context
  cultural 139
  Greco-Roman 139
Cossman, Brenda 17
Council of Constantinople 227
Council of Nicaea 204, 205, 224, 295
creed, Christian 164
criticism, textual 377
Crowther, Samuel A. 440
crucified Christ 89
crucifixion 347
Cullman, Oscar 161
culture
  African 13, 14, 58, 168, 245, 308,
    400, 422
  European 400
  Greco-Roman 140
  Jewish 308
  patriarchal 142
  village 37
  Western 163
curses 85, 87, 90
  judicial 85, 88
  African 90
Cyril 199, 207

D
Dawkins, Farida 147

Day of Atonement 244
death, substitutionary 87, 97
De Boer, Willis P. 118
Decalogue, biblical 378
De Jongh, Charles 61
Descartes, René 237, 418
dimensions, communal 265
discourse, christological 44, 47, 98
divinity 354
docetism, Cerinthian 225
doctrine, Islamic 377
dualism, Platonic 229
Dube, Musa 45
Dube, Zorodzai 15
Dunn, James D. G. 105
dynasty, Davidic 184

E
early church 183
Ecclesiastical History 8
egalitarianism 51, 52
Ela, Jean-Marc 278
Empire, Roman 68, 140
empiricism, Humean 231
End of Memory, The 259
enrichment, linguistic 403
eschatology 398
eunuch, Ethiopian 335
evangelist, Johannine 12
Evans, Craig 186
Evans-Pritchard, E. E. 395
Ezigbo, Victor 254

F
Falconer, Robert 250
family, Christian 29
Famonure, Bayo 336
fetishism 396
Fiorenza, Schussler 9
forgiveness 92, 258, 261, 262, 270, 272
  Christian 267
  Christlike 267
  communal 261, 262, 268
foundation, biblical 92

G
Galilee 48
gender equity, biblical 53
gender inclusivity 49
Gethsemane 35
Gichure, Peter 233
Global Ecumenical Theology Institute 420
Godhead, Trinitarian 376
Gordon, S. D. 297
gospel
  holistic 191
  Johannine 208
  Christian 378
gospels, gnostic 377
Gospels, Synoptic 46
Green, Joel 27
guidelines, Aristotelian 109
Guthrie, Donald 47

H
Hadith 341, 351, 377
Hare, Paul 10
Harrington, Daniel 9
Hawthorne, Gerald F. 126
heresies, christological 225
hermeneutic, christological 6, 15
hermeneutics
  biblical 277
  intercultural 59
  traditional 162
Hinga, Teresia 423
history, Jewish 409
HIV/AIDS among women 5
HIV infections 16
Hodges, Zane 7, 10
hospitality, African 27, 29
household codes 143

I
Ibekwe, Patrick 266
identity, Christian 64, 67
ideologies, Marxist 60
ideology, Marxist 231
Illustrated African Bible, The 296, 299
imitatio Pauli 127
imperialism, Western 160
implications, theological 384
infidelity 17
Injīl 378, 382
intellectualism 233
interactions, Christian–Muslim 341
interpretation
  biblical 15
  christological 144, 207, 212
Introduction to African Religion 324
Iscariot, Judas 353
Islam 341, 360

J
Jerome 7, 8
Jerusalem 35
Jesus as Healer 277, 284
Jews, intertestamental 193
Johnson, Elizabeth 249
John the Baptist 33, 87, 371
Jones, L. G. 263
Judaism 10, 64, 87, 170, 182

K
Kabasele, Françoise 250
Kanyoro, Musimbi 420
Kapolyo, Joe 334
Kato, Byang 327
Kenya. The National AIDS and STI Control Programme 5
Ker 248
Kiambi, Julius K. 15
King David 86
king, Davidic 186
Kinney, John W. 432
kinship 252
Kolié, Cécé 279
Kuma, Afua 417, 421, 423
Küster, Volker 13

L
Labron, Tim 223
Lambert, H. E. 171
law

Old Testament 71
Judaic 18
Levitical 11
Mosaic 19, 78, 82
leader
　Christian 54
　egalitarian 48, 51
leadership 52
　Christian 52
　egalitarian 44, 54
Linebaugh, Jonathan A. 97
literature
　apocryphal 187
　canonical 6, 119
　Christian 250
　Greco-Roman 118
　Greek 36, 119
　Jewish 122, 123, 186, 188
　New Testament 117
　pseudepigraphical 121
Longenecker, Richard 106
love
　sacrificial 148
　Trinitarian 273
Lu, Shi-Min 139

M
Macedonia 128
Macquarrie, John 230
Magesa, Laurenti 293
manuscript, Greek 8
Mariology 348
marriage, Christian 138
Maryam 363, 370, 373
masculinity, cultural 19
Mbiti, John S. 264, 321, 329, 394, 437, 441
Mburu, Elizabeth 326
Messiah 14, 45, 50, 97, 101, 169, 182, 195, 231, 340, 353
　Davidic 185, 188, 189
messiahship 183
messianism 169
metanarrative, biblical 380
ministry, Galilean 31

missionaries, Western 321, 399
model, egalitarian 54
Moses 11
Mugambi, Jesse 61, 293
Muhammad 342, 346, 348, 364, 368, 384
Musekura, Célestin 258, 261
music, traditional 407
Muslim, authentic 366
Muslims 350
　Zambian 362

N
narrative, biblical 383
NASCOP. *See* Kenya. The National AIDS and STI Control Programme
Nasimiyu-Wasike, Anne 13
Nasr, Seyyed H. 346
Nazareth 35
Neoplatonism 226
Nestorianism 226, 227
New Politics of Adultery 17
Nicene Creed 58, 205, 209
Nthamburi, Zablon 51

O
Oduyoye, Mercy A. 13, 138
Okullu, Henry 252
Okure, Teresa 45, 46
ontology, religious 397
orthodoxy
　Christian 215
　hermeneutical 278

P
PA. *See* Pericope Adulterae
paganism 396
paternalism, conceptual 160
Paul 65, 67, 69, 71, 79, 80, 131
Peninsula, Arabian 364
people
　African 252
　Bantu-speaking 171
　Jewish 223

Luo 246
Shona 249
Pericope Adulterae 7
perspective, communal 268
perspectives, cultural 27
Pharisees and scribes 6
Philo 122
philosophers, pre-Socratic 224
philosophy
 Greek 161, 168, 405
 Platonic 226
pilgrimage, Christian 404
Plato 119, 140
Pobee, John 246
polygamy 17
polytheism 365
praeparatio evangelica 394, 397, 434
priesthood
 Old Testament 243
Principle, Canonic 295
principle
 Christian 123
 theological 70
prophet, mosaic 188

Q
Qur'an 341, 342, 345, 350, 366, 369, 383

R
reciprocity
 African 110
 egalitarian 110
reconciliation 247, 268, 271, 380
 communal 264
 divine 271
relations, God–humanity 245
relationship
 Father–child 40
 household 140
religion, African 418, 422, 424
religiosity
 African 251, 430
 fundamental 396
resurrection 351

Ritschl, Albrecht 231
ritual, Akkadian 88
River Jordan 31
Rodríguez, Rafael 103
Ruether, Rosemary 14
ruler, Greco-Roman 106
rule, Roman 189

S
Samaria 48
Schleiermacher, Friedrich 231
scholarship
 African 156, 326
 biblical 297
scholars, New Testament 6
school, Antiochene 204
Schumacher, E. F. 309
Scriptures
 biblical 18
 Christian 322
 Muslim 344
secularism 16, 418
sense, Judeo-Christian 158
setting, Greco-Roman 48
sex, extramarital 16
societies, traditional 401
society
 African 422
 Greco-Roman 104
 Greek 102
Soi, Elijah K. 266
Son of Man 190
sonship 31
Sophocles 100
Special Laws, The 122
spirituality, African 408
Stinton, Diane 293
Sultana, Abeda 143
Sūra Maryam 374
Swartley, Willard M. 119
syncretism 194
system, sacrificial 72

T
Tawhid 381

Taylor, Mark 125
teaching
　christological 138, 144, 149, 210
　Neoplatonic 225
terms, Aristotelian 203
terms, Greco-Anglo-Saxon 158
Theologian, Intercultural 282
theologians
　African 249, 250, 276, 395
　Christian 261, 293
　liberation 231
　Protestant 228
theology
　African 157, 240, 394, 420, 423
　theology, Christian 157
　Circle 422
　contextual 157, 402
　intercultural 277
　Oral 410
　Trinitarian 215
Theophilus 202
time, eschatological 108
tradition
　Christian 214
　doctrinal 430
　pre-Christian 431
　religious 328
training, theological 54
transcendentalism 223
tritheism 348
truth, theological 72
Tshilumba, Noel 12

U
unblemished sacrifice 91

V
values, cultural 432
van den Toren, Benno 282
Virgin Mary 349
Volf, Miroslav 259, 269

W
Wallace, Daniel B. 129
Walls, Andrew 394

Waruta, Douglas W. 48, 292
woman, Samaritan 9, 45, 53, 147
women, African 6, 12, 13
World Council of Churches 277
world
　Greco-Roman 84, 107, 138, 142, 254
　intertestamental 185
　Mediterranean 11, 141
World Missionary Conference 163
worldview
　African 63, 66, 249, 326
　Islamic 367

Scripture Index

OLD TESTAMENT

Genesis
1:1 46
1–2 .... 28, 380
3 .... 81, 82, 268
3:14–19 78
3:15 .... 269, 380
4:3 243
8:20 243
12 81
12:8 243
14:18 243
32:13–20 269
32–33 269
49:10 183

Exodus
3:14 47
4:22 31
16:4 35
17:1–7 28
18:1 243
19:22 243
19:24 243
20 378
20:7 354
23:9 28
23:20–23 28
28 .... 243, 244

Leviticus
1:1–9 243
1:5–9 243
10:11 243
12:6–7 243
13:2–3 243
13:9–10 243
13:18–19 243

13:24–25 243
18:21 87
20:10 11
25:23 28

Numbers
3:5 243
4:33 243
14:21–24 28
27:21 244
31:6 243

Deuteronomy
1:34–35 28
6:4 350
6:4–6 322
18:18 380
18:18–19 .... 184, 188
24:17–22 28
26:9 28
27:26 .... 72, 82
33:8 244

Joshua
6:26 78

1 Samuel
14:41 244
23:6–12 244
28:6 244

2 Samuel
7:12–16 184
21:1–10 86

2 Chronicles
7:1–3 224

Ezra
2:63 244

Job
1:5 243

Psalm
2 184
2:7 184
14:1–4 328
18 184
20–22 184
23:5–6 28
24 323
42:7 323
47 323
47:1 323
47:2 323
72:1 103
89 184
96:1 324
96:3–5 323
96:7 324
101 184
117:1 103

Proverbs
8:22–30 225

Isaiah 348, 362, 368, 373, 380
7 .... 224, 380
7:14 .... 351, 380
9 .... 224, 380
9:6 353
9:6–7 380
11:1–5 184

25:6–8 28
29:18 190
35:5 190
35:6 190
52:13–53:12 187
53 380
53:1–12 353
61:1 190
61:1–2 .... 31, 190

Jeremiah
1:7 334

30:8–9 185

Ezekiel
34:5 334
34:23–24 185
36 34
36:22–23 35
36:24–36 35

Daniel
7:13–14 31
9:25–26 353

12:1–4 380

Jonah
1:1–10 86

Zechariah
10:2 334

Malachi
4:5 380
4:5–6 380

NEW TESTAMENT

Matthew
1:1 189
1:6 189
1:17 189
1:18–24 352
1:20 189
2:4 243
3:16 247
3:16–17 246
5 .... 298, 302,
303, 305
5:1–10 298
5:3–12 380
5:27 18
6:9–13 32
7:7–11 32
8:4 243
9 .... 276, 333
9:22 147
9:27 .... 189, 190
9:35–38 333
9:36 333
9:37 334
9:38 334
10:5 334
11:3–6 190
11:19 309
11:27 190
16:13–16 237

16:13–20 .... 192, 239,
240, 340
16:14 340
16:15 .... xiii, 167, 258
16:16 .... 190, 356
16:17 237
16:20 190
16:21 353
18 264
18:32–35 264
20:18 243
20:20 189
21:9 189
21:15 243
26:28 351
27:39–44 236
28 333
28:16–20 334

Mark
1:14–15 380
1:27 309
1:34a 277
1:44 243
5 276
5:25–34 280
5:34 147
8:27–9:1 190
8:27–29 237
8:27–30 192

8:29 167
8:31–33 191
10 .... 299, 302, 304,
305, 308
10:13–16 298
10:46–52 276
10:47 190
11:20–21 78
12:29 350
12:32 350
13:32 190
14:61–64 352
15:18 190
15:26 190
15:27–32 236
15:39 346

Luke
1:1–4 30
1:5–2:52 30
1:26–35 352
1:31–37 30
1:32–33 .... 34, 189
1:68–75 190
2:1–32 31
2:7 28
2:41–52 31
3:1–4:13 31
3:21 31
3:21–22 31

Scripture Index

3:22 31	11:1 31	24:20 243
3:38 32	11:1–4 ....32, 40	24:28–35 28
4 35	11:1–13 .....25–27, 30, 32, 40	
4:1–13 31	11:2 ....38, 40	**John**
4:14–9:50 31	11:3 39	1:1 ....46, 353
4:14–30 31	11:5 39	1:3–4 327
4:18–19 ....34, 35	11:5–8 ....29, 33, 36, 38, 39	1:14 46
4:18–22 423	11:8 36	1:18 348
4:22b 31	11:9 38	1:29 ....87, 91
4:41 31	11:9–10 ....33, 38	3:16 .... 348, 383
5:14 243	11:9–13 ....38, 41	4:1–42 .... 43–48, 54
5:16 ....31, 33	11:11–12 ....33, 39	4:4 48
5:17–26 31	11:11–13 39	4:26 50
5:24 31	11:13 ....33, 40	4:27 50
5:27–32 28	11:14 40	4:34 50
6:5 31	11:14–54 ....32, 40	4:39 50
6:12 31	12:1–13:9 32	4:40 50
7:11–17 31	12:1–48 40	4:42 246
7:34 31	13:10–35 32	5:18 352
7:36–50 .... 28, 31, 147	13:22–30 28	6:15 309
8 276	14:1–6 40	7:53–8:2 18
8:22–25 31	14:1–24 28	7:53–8:11 .... 3, 5, 18, 147
8:22–56 248	15:11–32 28	8:3–9 18
8:26–48 31	17:11–19 ....40, 283	8:10–11 19
8:48 147	17:14 243	9:3 281
8:49–56 31	17: 41 309	10:10 .... 278, 285
9:10–17 .... 28, 31, 35	18:1–8 38	10:11 .... 248, 334
9:13 39	18:35–43 40	10:14 334
9:18 ....31, 33	19:1–10 28	11:35 309
9:18–21 .... 192, 237	19:28–21:38 40	11:50 86
9:18–22 353	22:1–23:56 40	12:1 243
9:18–27 32	22:14–20 28	13 302–306
9:22 31	22:14–21 380	13:1–9 298
9:28 31	22:32 31	14:16 349
9:35 32	22:37 353	14:28 225
9:51–19:27 32	22:41–44 31	15:13 148
9:57–11:13 32	23:13 243	15:15 309
10 .... 299, 302, 303, 305–307	23:26–46 353	15:26 247
10:1–16 32	23:34 31	18:19–24 243
10:21–24 31	23:35–43 236	19:7 352
10:22 .... 33, 40, 190	23:42 236	19:13–20 353
10:25–37 32	23:45 40	19:18 346
10:25–42 28	23:46 31	19:19 309
10:38–42 ....32, 298	23:50 101	19:25 346
	24:1–53 40	20:1–9 380

20:20 333	5:6 .... 101, 105, 106, 108	**2 Corinthians**
20:21 333		5:18–20............................264
20:28 .... 330, 352	5:6–8............. 95, 97, 98, 104	5:19 199
20:31 47	5:7 ....95–98, 101, 104, 111	8:14 108
		11:21–13:9.........................105
Acts	5:8 .... 105, 106, 112, 380, 383	11:21–27............................259
1:1 .... 332, 335		12:8–10..............................283
2 194	5:10 261	
2:33 332	6:10 346	**Galatians** 81
2:38–4:20............... 183, 191	7:7–14 82	1:7–9 72
2:38–39.............................247	8:1 380	1:4 ....65, 72
3:16 332	8:15–16 39	1:6 ....78, 79
4:10 332	8:26 105	1:7 78
4:12 .... 194, 351	9:9 108	1:11–12 71
4:30 332	10:9 330	1:12 71
8 335	10:9–10 351	2 271
8:4 336	11:5 108	2:5 71
8:26 335	12:13 29	2:11–14 ....67, 271
8:26–40 .... 335, 410	14 68	2:16 ....72, 80
8:29 335	15:7 111	2:19 69
8:39 335	16 53	2:20 ....69, 89
9:15 332		2:21 69
10 332	**1 Corinthians**	3 272
10:19–20 332	1:23 ....83, 125	3:1 69
13:11 78	2:2 125	3:1–5 ....79, 81
15 271	2:2–4 79	3:1–6 71
15:1 71	4:5 108	3:1–14 ....77, 78
15:22–29 271	4:16 .... 117, 118	3:5 80
16:7 335	7:5 108	3:6–9 81
16:9–10 332	8:5–6 330	3:7 65
17 ....62, 159	9 125	3:10 ....72, 86
18:9–10 332	10:31 125	3:10–12 82
	10:24 .... 123, 125	3:10–14 72
Romans	10:27 123	3:10a 82
1–3 105	10:31 123	3:13 .... 65, 77, 78, 83, 85, 89
1:4 351	10:32 124	
1–5 105	10:33–11:1 125	3:13–14 83
1:18 105	11:1 .... 117, 118, 123, 131	3:14 84
2:12 106		3:23–24 73
3:9 .... 106, 108	12:3 .... 207, 330	3:26–29 68
3:9–18 328	15 .... 194, 383	3:27–28 271
3:10 108	15:43 105	3:28 53
3:21–26 380	16:22 78	4:1 65
3:26 108		4:4–5 65
4:5 105		4:6 39

4:9–10 65
4:10 65
4:14 280
4:28–5:1 65
5:1 .... 65, 69
5:5 69
5:10 78
5:12 78
5:13 .... 65, 69
5:14–15 68
5:22 69
5:22–25 69
5:24 69

Ephesians
2 272
2:8 380
2:8–9 351
2:12 272
2:13–14 272
2:15–16 272
2:19–22 272
2:20–22 332
3:18 282
4:1–3 272
5:1 118
5:21 141
5:21–22 140
5:21–33 137–139,
                            141–146, 149
5:22 141
5:24 143
5:24–33 146
5:25–27 .... 145, 147
5:25–30 144
5:28 146
5:31 149
5:33 149
6:10–24 139

Philippians 126
2:5 127
2:5–11 127
2:6–11 127
2:11 330

3:1–13 259
3:9 126
3:10 126
3:10–11 351
3:13 259
3:17 .... 117, 118,
                             126, 127

Colossians
1:15 .... 225, 352
1:16–17 .... 330, 352

1 Thessalonians
1:6 .... 117, 118, 128
1:7 129
1:9–10 130
2:14 .... 117, 118
2:17 108
3:3 128
5:1 108

2 Thessalonians
2:6 108
3:7 .... 117, 118
3:9 .... 117, 118

1 Timothy
2:5 350
5:8 146
6:16 225

Titus
3:5 380

Hebrews
2:10–13 246
2:11 244
4:15 .... 88, 91, 247
6:1 244
6:12 118
6:19 246
6:20 247
7:11–19 244
7:17 247
7:20–21 246

7:23–24 244
7:25 244
9:9 244
9:12 244
9:24 244
10:1 244
13:1–2 29

1 Peter
1:3 351
3:7 145
4:9 29

3 John
11 118

Langham Literature and its imprints are a ministry of Langham Partnership.

Langham Partnership is a global fellowship working in pursuit of the vision God entrusted to its founder John Stott –

> *to facilitate the growth of the church in maturity and Christ-likeness through raising the standards of biblical preaching and teaching.*

Our vision is to see churches in the Majority World equipped for mission and growing to maturity in Christ through the ministry of pastors and leaders who believe, teach and live by the word of God.

Our mission is to strengthen the ministry of the word of God through:
- nurturing national movements for biblical preaching
- fostering the creation and distribution of evangelical literature
- enhancing evangelical theological education

especially in countries where churches are under-resourced.

Our ministry

Langham Preaching partners with national leaders to nurture indigenous biblical preaching movements for pastors and lay preachers all around the world. With the support of a team of trainers from many countries, a multi-level programme of seminars provides practical training, and is followed by a programme for training local facilitators. Local preachers' groups and national and regional networks ensure continuity and ongoing development, seeking to build vigorous movements committed to Bible exposition.

Langham Literature provides Majority World preachers, scholars and seminary libraries with evangelical books and electronic resources through publishing and distribution, grants and discounts. The programme also fosters the creation of indigenous evangelical books in many languages, through writer's grants, strengthening local evangelical publishing houses, and investment in major regional literature projects, such as one volume Bible commentaries like *The Africa Bible Commentary* and *The South Asia Bible Commentary*.

Langham Scholars provides financial support for evangelical doctoral students from the Majority World so that, when they return home, they may train pastors and other Christian leaders with sound, biblical and theological teaching. This programme equips those who equip others. Langham Scholars also works in partnership with Majority World seminaries in strengthening evangelical theological education. A growing number of Langham Scholars study in high quality doctoral programmes in the Majority World itself. As well as teaching the next generation of pastors, graduated Langham Scholars exercise significant influence through their writing and leadership.

To learn more about Langham Partnership and the work we do visit **langham.org**

www.ingramcontent.com/pod-product-compliance
Lightning Source LLC
Chambersburg PA
CBHW071222230426
43668CB00011B/1263